Research Methods and Statistics in PSYCHOLOGY

3rd edition

Hugh Coolican

Hodder & Stoughton
A MEMBER OF THE HODDER HEADLINE GROUP

ACKNOWLEDGEMENTS

All the psychology staff at University College Northampton for various snippets, bright ideas, feedback and general support. Nicky Hayes, Karen Henwood, Derek Edwards, Jonathan Potter, Paula Nicolson, David Howell, Kate Arnold, Shelley Gooding, Bob Potter, Bert Brummell and John Hunt for information supplied in the past, and anyone else whose contribution I've omitted and apologies to them if I have. Nicky Hayes too for encouragement and nice words over the years.

Special thanks to Richard Gross for continuing advice and to Tim Gregson-Williams, Greig Aitken and other staff at Hodder and Stoughton for invaluable editorial and general support.

Thanks also to the most important people – my students who show me what's needed (one benefit of long nights of marking!) and who tolerate my tricks, and all tutors and others who have made enquiries and brought clarification points and new ideas to my attention.

The author and publishers would also like to thank the following for permission to reproduce material in this book:

Cambridge University Press for Figure 8.2 on p.189 from Berry *et al.* (1992) *Cross-Cultural Psychology: Research and Applications*; Sage Publications for Figure 10.14 on p.248 from Ross *et al.* (1970) Determining the social effects of a legal reform: the British 'breathalyser' crackdown of 1967 in *American Behavioural Scientist*, 13 (4) and for extracts of 'Shame and guilt among first- and second-generation Asian Americans and European Americans' by Ramsay Liem in *Journal of Cross-Cultural Psychology* 28 (4), 1997; The American Psychological Association for extracts of 'Racial identity in bi-racial children: a qualitative investigation' by Kerwin *et al.* in *Journal of Counselling Psychology* 40 (2), 1993

Orders: please contact Bookpoint Ltd, 130 Milton Park, Abingdon, Oxon OX14 4SB. Telephone: (44) 01235 827720, Fax: (44) 01235 400454. Lines are open from 9.00 - 6.00, Monday to Saturday, with a 24 hour message answering service. You can also order through our website: www.hodderheadline.co.uk

A catalogue record for this title is available from The British Library

ISBN 0 340 74760 9

First published 1999
Impression number   10   9   8   7   6
Year   2005 2004 2003 2002

Copyright © 1999

Typeset by Wearset, Boldon, Tyne and Wear.
Printed in Great Britain for Hodder & Stoughton Educational, a division of Hodder Headline Plc, 338 Euston Road, London NW1 3BH by J.W. Arrowsmith Ltd.

Dedication

To Frances

Contents

Preface

The first edition of this book was probably the first general research methods and statistics textbook, in this country at least, to include a substantial account of qualitative methods. Indeed, the intention in that text was to integrate qualitative methods into the research methods sections as far as was possible. Since then the publication of texts on qualitative methods has grown considerably but sadly few have attempted to help the novice psychology student by first, explaining the approaches at a relatively simple level and second, incorporating the principles into a general methods textbook. One exception is Robson's (1993) *Real World Research* which doesn't however contain the statistical methods required in almost all first year undergraduate psychology courses.

This third edition, then, remains a 'standard' methods and statistics textbook for use at degree and A level, still presented in its popular 'friendly' and accessible style, but it has further consolidated its aim to bring qualitative methods to the ordinary student. In this edition, and in recognition of several exam boards' inclusion of qualitative methods as legitimate approaches in assessed coursework, there is further guidance towards 'hands-on' qualitative researching and report writing. More practical advice is included as are references to several computer programmes for the analysis of qualitative data. Probably most important, however, and in response to many pleas (including my own) for a concrete example of good qualitative research reporting, is the inclusion of two synopses, with commentary, of recently published qualitative articles. This unique section of the book should help to give tutors and students alike the confidence to incorporate qualitative research into their practical coursework, in line with its growing prominence in the real world of psychological research.

Along with these synopses are the second edition's 'average student report', with marker's comments and, after some resistance from me and with some trepidation, a 'good' version of the same report. Trepidation, because I was bothered (still am) that a 'good' version might be taken as a 'golden standard' by students or even some tutors. I hope readers will realise that report writing must be adjusted to the specific practical issues at hand and to the 'local' requirements of psychology course or examination board.

The statistical sections continue to recognise the anxieties of the mathematically weak but again the new student is reassured that first, statistics calculations in psychology involve no more than the 'sums' performed by the average 11 year old at school and second, that many of the statistical *and* methods concepts in psychological practical work have already been developed in an informal way through one's everyday experience of being in the world. This is true even of the apparently daunting issue of significance testing and new approaches to making this 'concrete' have been included.

In the mid-1990s some criticism of the statistical concepts taught and examined at A level emerged in the psychology press. I have been at pains to address these in this third edition but would stress that the alleged 'wrong' teaching is frequently found in HE methods workshops as well as in A level classrooms. These common difficulties are mostly associated with significance testing (the null hypothesis, 1- or 2-tailed tests, so-called 'parametric' tests). Even in statistics there is hot debate and I have tried to make it clear where issues are still under discussion.

The text engages the reader fairly often with exercise boxes intended to encourage reflection on and questioning of the points currently being explained. Each chapter ends with a glossary which can be used as a self-test by covering up the glossary term.

Students should realise however that not *all* the terms will be included on their syllabus, especially at A level. A further new feature is the inclusion of a system within the References which guides the reader to the place where each referenced publication has been mentioned in the book.

Though this book started life as an A level text it could not stay that way, partly because of the needs of Higher Education courses for a general text and partly because methods and statistics requirements at A level have been substantially reduced, particularly by the AEB board of late. Nevertheless, the first Appendix contains the kind of structured questions which will be encountered in that board's examinations, along with some outline answers.

Finally, the main aim is to clarify, not obscure, and in progression of that aim I welcome enquiries and questions. Many readers have contacted me over the years and I hope you continue to do so in a spirit of exchange and interested debate – do look out for the developing Web site! I do hope you can *enjoy* doing psychological research with an emphasis on the 'doing'. Reports have to be written however and my advice is just *never* to leave it. While you toil away just keep thinking that none of the truly fascinating ideas about human behaviour and experience, none of the wonderful insights about ourselves that can be gained on a short psychology course, would be possible without someone (many committed people in fact) doing exactly as you are doing!

Psychology and research

This introduction sets the scene for research in psychology. The key ideas are that:

- Psychological researchers generally follow a scientific approach, developed from the 'empirical method' into the 'hypothetico-deductive' method. This involves careful definition and measurement, and the logic of testing *hypotheses* produced from falsifiable *theories*.
- Hypotheses need to be precisely stated before testing.
- *Scientific research* is a continuous and social activity, involving promotion and checking of ideas amongst colleagues.
- Researchers use *probability statistics* to decide whether effects are *'significant'* or not.
- Research has to be carefully planned with attention to *design*, *variables*, *samples* and subsequent *data analysis*. If all these areas are not fully planned, results may be ambiguous or useless.
- Some researchers have strong objections to the use of traditional scientific methods in the study of persons. They support *qualitative* and *'new paradigm'* methods which may not involve rigid pre-planned testing of hypotheses, and deal with meaningful verbal data rather than exact measurement and statistical summaries.

WHAT? METHODS AND STATISTICS IN PSYCHOLOGY?

Student: I'd like to enrol for psychology please.

Lecturer: You do realise that it includes quite a bit of statistics, and you'll have to do some experimental work and write up practical reports?

Student: Oh . . .

When enrolling for a course in psychology, the prospective student is very often taken aback by the discovery that the syllabus includes a fair-sized dollop of statistics and that practical research, experiments and report-writing are all involved. Though the lay image of psychology persists as having to do with individual analysis and baring one's private thoughts to an expert, students in their first psychology class are often dismayed to find that this new and exciting subject is going to thrust them back into two areas that many of them most disliked in school. One is maths – but rest assured! Statistics, in fact, will involve you in little of the maths on a traditional syllabus and will be performed on real data, most of which you have gathered yourself. Calculators and computers do the 'number crunching' these days. The other area is science.

In the first and second editions of this book I wrote that schools rarely taught psychology and that this was a pity since it was a subject which directly tackles issues of ourselves as members of society and school is where we prepare young people for social life. I also argued that, contrary to what happens in psychology, study of the natural sciences rarely involves studying what a science really is, this concept being taken for granted.

Happily, I can no longer say this. Psychology has become one of the 'boom' subjects at A level. There has been rapid growth in the number of schools teaching the subject, possibly in competition with the further education sector. Also, with the advent of the National Curriculum and a few other developments, children are introduced to the general concepts of scientific 'finding out' and theory testing well before they can use the word 'science' appropriately in their everyday speech. Nevertheless, there remains a general dislike of maths and, to perhaps a lesser extent, science – first year undergraduates still groan when these are mentioned!

In an age when computers have moved from being complex, frightening machines to everyday household objects within ten years, perhaps attitudes are changing. Perhaps the psychology tutor need no longer apologise so profusely for mentioning the subject. Some of us may have even enjoyed maths and science at school. For those of you who did, you'll find the statistical chapters of this book fairly easy going. But can I state one of my most cherished beliefs right now, for the sake of those who hate numbers and think this is all going to be a struggle, or, worse still, boring. Many of the ideas and concepts introduced in this book will *already be in your head* in an informal way, even 'hard' topics like probability and significance. My job is partly to give names to some concepts you can easily think of for yourself. At other times it will be to formalise and tighten up ideas that you have gathered through experience. For instance, you already have a fairly good idea of how many cats out of ten ought to choose 'Poshpaws' cat food in preference to another brand, in order for us to be convinced that this is a real difference and not mere feline caprice. You can probably start discussing quite competently what would count as a representative sample of people for a survey on attitudes to the Euro or to genetically modified food.

Returning to the prospective student then, she or he often has little idea about what sort of research psychologists do. The notion of 'experiments' sometimes produces anxiety. 'Will we be conditioned or brainwashed?' If we ignore images from the black-and-white film industry, and think carefully about what psychological researchers might do, we might conjure up an image of the street survey. Think again, and we might suggest that psychologists observe people's behaviour. I agree with Gross (1996) who says that, at a party, if one admits to teaching, or even studying, psychology, a common reaction is 'Oh, I'd better be careful what I say from now on'. Another strong contender is 'I suppose you'll be analysing my behaviour' (said as the speaker takes one hesitant step backwards) in the mistaken assumption that psychologists go around making deep, mysterious interpretations of human actions as they occur. (If you meet someone who does do this, ask them something about the evidence they use, after you've finished with this book!) The notion of such analysis is loosely connected to Freud who, though popularly portrayed as a psychiatric Sherlock Holmes, used very few of the sorts of research methods outlined in this book – though he did use unstructured clinical interviews and the case-study method (Chapter 5).

SO WHAT IS THE NATURE OF PSYCHOLOGICAL RESEARCH?

Although there are endless and furious debates about what a science is and what sort of science, if any, psychology should be, a majority of psychologists would agree that research should be scientific, and at the very least that it should be objective, controlled and checkable. Its findings should be *reliable* and *valid* – see Chapter 4. There is no final agreement, however, about precisely how scientific method should operate within the very broad range of psychological research topics. There are many definitions of science but, for present purposes, Allport's (1947) is useful. Science, he claims, has the aims of:

> '. . . understanding, prediction and control above the levels achieved by unaided common sense.'

What does Allport, or anyone, mean by 'common sense'? Aren't some things blindly obvious? Isn't it indisputable that babies are born with different personalities, for instance? Let's have a look at some other popular 'common-sense' claims.

Before reading my comments on the right-hand side of Box 1.1, have a think about any challenge you might wish to make to the claims made. In particular, what evidence would you want to get hold of?

I have used these statements, including the controversial ones, because they are just the sort of things people claim confidently, yet with no hard evidence. They are 'hunches' masquerading as fact. I call them 'armchair certainties (or theories)' because this is from where they are often claimed. Figure 1.1 depicts the difference between someone who accepts 'evidence' as 'obvious' and the sort of thinker needed in psychological research – one who instinctively says 'Ah, but . . .'

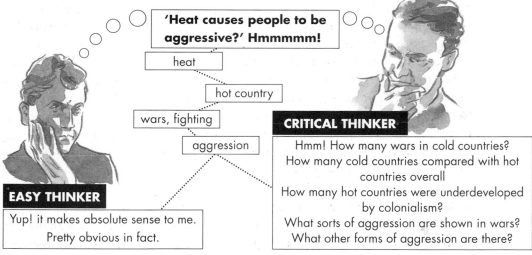

Figure 1.1 Obvious and not-so-obvious evidence for the hypothesis that heat makes people aggressive

I hope you see why we need evidence from research. One role for a scientific study is to challenge 'common-sense' notions by checking the facts. Another is to produce 'counter-intuitive' results like those in item three of Box 1.1. Let me say a little more about what scientific research is by dispelling a few myths about it.

Myth no. 1: 'scientific research is the collection of facts'

All research is about the collection of data but this is not the sole aim. First of all, facts are not data. Facts are *constructions* from perceived data organised by generous helpings of our expectancies, our assumptions and our learned prejudices. A good example is the

4

Box 1.1   'Common-sense' claims – do they really stand up to scrutiny?

1. Women obviously have a maternal instinct – look how strongly they want to stay with their baby and protect it.

How might men feel after several months alone with a baby? Does the term 'instinct' add to our understanding, or does it simply *describe* what mothers do? Do *all* mothers feel this way?

2. Michelle is so good at predicting people's star sign – there must be something in astrology.

Does Michelle do better than anyone would simply by guessing? Have we counted the times when she's wrong?

3. I wouldn't obey someone who told me to seriously hurt another person if I could possibly avoid it.

About 62% of people could have walked free from an experimenter who asked them to give electric shocks to a 'learner' who had fallen silent after screaming horribly.

4. Women are less logical, more intuitive, more suggestible and make worse drivers than men.

Women in general score the same as men in general on logical reasoning tests. As of 1994 in the UK, girls' performance equals boys' in GCSE Maths. Though far fewer girls take A level maths, those who do perform significantly better than boys (see SEG and AEB results, 1994). Women and men are equally suggestible but boys are *more* likely to agree with peer group views which they don't hold privately. Women are more likely to observe traffic rules and to have less expensive accidents. Why else would 'one lady owner' be a selling point?

5. The trouble with having so many black immigrants is that the country is too small.
[Quote from Call Nick Ross phone-in, BBC Radio 4, 3 November, 1992)

70% of immigrants to the UK are *white*. In 1991, the total black population of the UK (African Caribbean and Indian sub-continental Asian) was a little under 5%. Almost every year since the second world war, more people have left than have entered Britain to live. *Whose* country is it anyway?

easily used term 'race'. Most people find it easy to accept the 'fact' of distinct 'races' in the world. From perceptual differences there is an assumption of some fundamental underlying biological grouping. In fact, biologically and genetically speaking it is as impossible to distinguish 'races' as it would be to distinguish south from north Londoners – see page 168. Most people know little of biology anyway. We 'perceive' and understand 'race' *only* through our cultural training in the concept. If we are *told* there are significant differences, that is what we 'see'.

Facts do not speak for themselves. When people say they do, they are omitting to mention essential background theory or assumptions they are making.

A sudden crash brings us running to the kitchen. The accused is crouched in front of us, eyes wide and fearful. Her hands are red and sticky. A knife lies on the floor. So does a jam jar and its spilled contents. The accused was about to lick her tiny fingers.

I hope you made some false assumptions before the jam was mentioned. But, as it is, do the facts alone tell us that Jenny was stealing jam? Perhaps the cat knocked the jam over

Box 1.2   Fearing or clearing the bomb?

In psychology we constantly challenge the simplistic acceptance of facts 'in front of our eyes'. A famous bomb disposal officer, talking to Sue Lawley on Desert Island Discs, told of the time he was trying urgently to clear the public from the area of a live bomb. A newspaper published his picture, advancing with outstretched arms, with the caption, 'terrified member of public flees bomb', whereas another paper correctly identified him as the calm, but concerned expert he really was.

and Jenny was trying to pick it up. We constantly assume a lot beyond the present data in order to explain it (see Box 1.2). Data are what we get through EMPIRICAL observation, where 'empirical' refers to information obtained through our senses. It is difficult to get raw data. We almost always interpret it immediately. If we lie on the beach looking at the night sky and see a 'star' moving steadily we 'know' it's a satellite, but only because we have a lot of received astronomical knowledge, from our culture, in our heads. Asked to observe a three year-old in a nursery, child-care students will often report something like: 'She was nervous. She was insecure'. We don't actually *see* insecurity. We observe darting eyes, solo play and 'clinging' (itself a construction – we actually see long-term holding). We superimpose on this what psychologists would call a 'schema' – a developed notion of what insecurity is and enough 'evidence' for it.

Data are interpreted through what psychologists often call a 'schema' – our learned prejudices, stereotypes and general ideas about the world and even according to our current purposes and motivations. It is difficult to see, as developed adults, how we could ever avoid this process. However, rather than despair of ever getting at any psychological truth, most researchers share common ground in following some basic principles of contemporary science which date back to the revolutionary use of EMPIRICAL METHOD to start questioning the workings of the world in a consistent manner.

The empirical method

The original empirical method had two stages:
1. Gathering of data, directly, through our external senses, with no preconceptions as to how it is ordered or what explains it.
2. INDUCTION of patterns and relationships within the data.

'Induction' means to move from individual observations to statements of general patterns (sometimes called 'laws').

If a 30-metre-tall Martian made empirical observations on Earth, it (Martians have one sex) might focus its attention on the various metal tubes which hurtle around, some in the air, some on the ground, some under it, and stop every so often to take on little bugs and to shed others. The Martian might then conclude that the tubes were important life-forms and that the little bugs taken on were food ... and the ones discharged ...? Now we have gone beyond the original empirical method. The Martian is constructing *theory*. This is an attempt to explain *why* the patterns are produced, what forces or processes underlie them. If anything were a human 'instinct' it might be the unsuppressable need to ask 'why?'. Indeed, we often hardly need say it ('Look! There's *another* of those patches on the carpet!') In psychology we learn that individuals will give obviously wrong and apparently stupid answers to completely simple questions when in the company of several other people who do the same. It is impossible to hear of this without wanting to know *why* at the same instant. It is also naïve to assume we could ever gather data without *some* sort of background theory in our heads, as I tried to demonstrate above. Medawar (1963) has argued this point forcefully, as has Bruner, who points out that, when we perceive the world, we always and inevitably 'go beyond the information given'.

The hypothetico-deductive method – introducing theories and hypotheses

Mainstream psychological research tends to lean heavily on what has come to be known by the rather cumbersome term HYPOTHETICO-DEDUCTIVE method. Basically it means a method in which theories (general explanations of phenomena) are evaluated by generating and testing HYPOTHESES. These are predictions that follow from the theories. The Martian's theory, that the bugs are food for the tubes, can be tested. If the tubes get no bugs for a long time, they should die. This prediction is a HYPOTHESIS. A hypothesis is a statement of exactly what should be the case *if* a certain theory is true. Testing the hypothesis shows that the tubes can last indefinitely without bugs. Hence the hypothesis is not supported and the theory requires alteration or dismissal. We often try to get at the practical truth in everyday situations by testing out hypotheses following from theories. For instance, we find music coming from only one channel of the stereo and we suspect the CD player which the cat knocked off its shelf a while back. How to test our theory? Try a new CD player, known to be working. If it works we tend to assume the old CD player was at fault. If it doesn't we need to look elsewhere. Of course, this isn't conclusive. The new CD may have just broken in a similar way as we installed it; the fault may not be the old CD itself but its attaching leads; and so on.

A further example, more closely related to psychology, can be given using Natasha and her friends. You will re-encounter Natasha, who is eight years old, in the chapter on significance testing. Suppose, as we do there, that Natasha and her friends are fond of spinach. (There is a lot of 'supposing' in this book and this is one of the more fantastical occasions!) Researchers claim that spinach is packed with a newly discovered vitamin known as K5 which has a beneficial effect on reading ability. Children learn to read more easily and earlier if they have been given a lot of K5.

From the *theory* that K5 enhances reading we can generate the *hypothesis* that children fed on spinach will have better reading skills. This could form a RESEARCH HYPOTHESIS (see below) for a particular psychological study. We might set up a study, in this case, where the research hypothesis might be more precisely stated as: *'Children fed on spinach will have higher than average reading scores'*, going on to define what test of reading is to be used. This turns 'reading ability' into an OPERATIONAL DEFINITION and these will be covered in Chapter 2. For now, let's use Natasha's friends as an example of how the deductive logic of hypothesis testing works. Let's summarise the rationale of the spinach study:

- The *theory* investigated is that K5 enhances reading ability
- Spinach contains a lot of K5 and we have a group of high level spinach eaters
- The *hypothesis* to be tested is that Natasha's friends will have a higher reading score than average

- If the group *does* have a higher reading score than average, our hypothesis is confirmed and hence the theory is supported
- If the group does *not* have a higher reading score than average, our hypothesis is not confirmed and the theory it came from is challenged.

To put this in formal terms in order to draw out exactly the nature of the underlying deductive logic, and its implications, have a look at Table 1.1.

It didn't work – is that the end of our theory?

Line 3 of Table 1 appears damning. We say 'If theory X is true, Y should happen'. Then Y fails to happen. This implies that theory X is wrong. By contrast, line 5 is hesitant. 'If X is true then Y is true' is a purely logical rule. Logically, finding *true* examples of Y has no bearing on the truth or falsity of X. If X is false, Y can be either true or false (consider 'if the sun is made of custard, France won the 1998 World Cup'). This is important in scientific thinking too – Freud's theory might be quite false yet happens to predict a correct finding that males have more aggressive dream content. However, if Y is *false*, X cannot logically be *true*, because the rule states that if X were true Y would be true. This *does* work for simple universal claims like 'All swans are white' which carries the implication 'If this is a swan (X) it is white (Y)'. It would be tedious to point to each new white swan saying 'I told you so!' We only need find one black swan to destroy the claim. As we shall see in a moment, this is why Popper concentrated on *falsification*, rather than *verification*, of theories.

However, theories are not quite the same thing as universal claims. A *theory* is a speculative explanation. We might, for instance, speculate that all swans are white *because the sun bleaches their feathers*. Now, if we find a sun-loving black swan, we have a spectacular challenge to our theory. It is these kinds of challenges which lead to advancement. The strict logic (and the idealistic scientific line) here is that the feather bleaching theory would be dropped. In reality what happens is that the theory holders cast around for an explanation of this anomaly – perhaps the swan has a one-off genetic defect; perhaps it

Table 1.1 The logic of hypothesis testing

Logic	Applied to theory testing	Applied to spinach eaters
If X is true then Y must be true	If theory A is true, then hypothesis H will be confirmed	If K5 enhances reading then this group of spinach eaters will have higher than average reading scores
Y isn't true	H is disconfirmed	The group does not have higher than average reading scores
therefore X isn't true	Theory A is wrong/challenged	K5 does not appear to enhance reading
OR		
Y is true	H is confirmed	The group *does* have higher than average reading scores
X could still be true	Theory A could be true	Support for the K5 and reading theory

gets 'the wrong kind of sun' (haze may offset the sun's effect); perhaps it is the one swan that also eats oil!

For the vitamin theory too, failure to support the hypothesis is not necessarily the end of the road. Perhaps we picked a particularly slow-reading bunch of spinach eaters – something we'll refer to as 'sampling error' in Chapter 2. Perhaps they too eat the wrong type of spinach! . . . and so on.

It worked! – but we haven't proven anything!

It is best to avoid the terms 'proof' or 'prove' when discussing psychological research. It is always advisable to replace 'this proves . . .' with something like 'this provides support for . . .' As for all science, if things are 'proved true' they are no longer theories. The word 'proof' tends to derive partly from detective stories – where the victim's blood on the suspect's shoes is said to 'prove' their guilt. Of course it doesn't. There is always a perhaps stretched, but possible, innocent explanation of how the blood arrived there ('Oh, he borrowed those last week and I remember he cut himself shaving'). In psychology as for detective work, if theories are speculative explanations, then 'evidence' can only ever *support*, not 'prove' anything. The other source of 'prove' is probably mathematics where we *can* prove number theorems and the like, since we are working with formal, abstract logic which has clear but invented rules. Mathematical theorems are *not* speculations about the empirical world.

So, if the spinach eating group *does* have a higher reading score this does not *prove* our theory about K5 correct. It adds support for the theory and that is all. A critic could argue that some other content of spinach has caused the result (an example of a *confounding variable*, a concept to be met fully in Chapter 3). Alternatively they could argue again for *sampling error* (Chapter 2). Natasha's parents are teachers and so her friends are perhaps not an average bunch academically.

Theories in science don't get 'proven true' and they rarely rest on totally unambiguous evidence. There is often a balance in favour with several anomalies yet to explain. Theories tend to 'survive' or not against others depending on the quality, not just the quantity, of their supporting evidence. The conflict and tension between attempts to support one's own theory and challenge others is the driving force of research. It is what keeps the whole ball rolling. But for every single supportive piece of evidence in social science there is very often an alternative explanation. It might be claimed that similarity between parent and child in intelligence is evidence for the view that intelligence is genetically transmitted. However, this evidence supports *equally* the view that children *learn* their skills from their parents, and similarity between adoptive parent and child is a challenge to the theory.

Falsifiability

We saw above that a *challenge* to a theory is far more useful than repetitively mounting *confirmations* of it. Popper (1959) has argued that for any theory to count as a theory we must at least be able to see how it *could* be falsified – we don't have to be able to falsify it; after all, it might be true! Popper argues that what distinguishes scientific method is its:

'manner of exposing to falsification, in every conceivable way, the system to be tested. Its aim is not to save the lives of untenable systems but, on the contrary, to select the one which is by comparison the fittest, by exposing them all to the fiercest struggle for survival. (1959, p. 42)

We don't 'prove theories true'; we stay with the ones which have produced the best explanations of the data, and which have best survived attacks to date. As an example of a seemingly irrefutable (and therefore unscientific, useless) theory, consider the once popular notion that Sir Paul McCartney died in the 1960s (I don't know whether there is *still* a group who believes this; that he is bare footed on the cover of the Beatles' Abbey Road album is part of the 'evidence'). Suppose we produce Paul in the flesh. This won't do – he is, of course, a cunning replacement. Suppose we show that no death certificate was issued anywhere around the time of his expiry. Well, of course, there was a cover up; it was made out in a different name. Suppose we supply DNA evidence from the current Paul and it matches the original Paul's DNA. Another plot; the current sample was switched behind the scenes ... and so on. This theory is useless because there is only (rather stretched) supporting evidence and *no* accepted means of falsification. Freudian theory often comes under attack for this weakness. 'Reaction formation' can excuse many otherwise damaging pieces of contradictory evidence. A writer once explained the sexual symbolism of chess and claimed that the very hostility of chess players to these explanations was evidence of their validity! They were defending against the unacceptable motives for playing! Women who claim that they do *not* desire boy babies, a finding contrary to 'penis-envy' theory, are reacting 'unconsciously' against the fear that their unacceptable desire, originally for their father, might be exposed ... so the argument goes. With this sort of explanation *any* evidence, desiring boy babies or *not* desiring them, is taken as support for the theory. Hence, it is unfalsifiable and therefore untestable in Popper's view.

Conventional scientific method

Putting together the empirical method of induction, and the hypothetico-deductive method, we get what is traditionally taken to be the 'scientific method', accepted by many psychological researchers as the way to follow in the footsteps of the successful natural sciences. The steps in the method are shown in Box 1.3. Scientific research projects, then, may be concentrating on the early or later stages of this process. They may be exploratory

Box 1.3 Traditional scientific method

1. Observation, gathering and ordering of data
2. Induction of generalisations, laws
3. Development of explanatory theories
4. Deduction of hypotheses to test theories
5. Testing of the hypotheses
6. Support for or adjustment of theory

studies, looking for data from which to create theories which may be tested with further research; they may be studies which seek to set up psychological scales (measures) with which to measure psychological phenomena (a point we shall follow up in the next chapter). The majority of mainstream studies are hypothesis testing studies. A growing number, in the qualitative approaches to be discussed in Chapter 9, seek to analyse data and develop theory within the same study.

Contemporary alternatives to conventional scientific method

The approach presented here so far is very much the *'conventional scientific model'* which served the 'hard' natural sciences fairly well during the 19th century and through most of the 20th. However, there are many doubts about and criticisms of the applicability of this mainly laboratory based method to the study of human minds and behaviour, although the contemporary psychology mainstream cannot be understood by the student new to psychology without a solid grounding in the tradition, even if it is later rejected. The arguments are too detailed to enter into at this early point. We will encounter a brief outline of the objections at the end of Chapter 2, but Chapter 9 will concentrate entirely on alternative and 'New Paradigm', *qualitative* approaches. The reader wanting to read in greater depth might like to consult Gross (1996), Valentine (1992) or Bem and Looren de Jong (1997) and any of the literature cited at the end of Chapter 9.

Myth no. 2: 'scientific research involves dramatic discoveries and breakthroughs'

Classic discoveries and breakthroughs are what many lay people associate with scientific activity. In fact, research plods along all the time, largely according to Figure 1.2. Although, from *reading* about research, it is easy to think about a single project beginning and ending at specific points of time, there is, in the research world, a constant cycle occurring.

A project is developed from a combination of the current trends in research thinking (theory) and methods, other challenging past theories and, within psychology at least, from important events in the everyday social world. The investigator might wish to REPLI-CATE (repeat) a study by someone else in order to verify it. Or they might wish to extend it to other areas, or to modify it because it has weaknesses. Every now and again an investigation breaks completely new ground but the vast majority develop out of the current state of play.

Politics and economics enter at the stage of funding. Research staff, in universities, colleges or hospitals, have to justify their salaries and the expense of the project. Funds will usually come from one of the following: university, college or hospital research funds; central or local government; private companies; charitable institutions; and the odd private benefactor. These, and the investigator's direct employers, will need to be satisfied that the research is worthwhile to them, to society or to the general pool of scientific knowledge, and that it is ethically sound.

The actual testing or 'running' of the project may take very little time compared with all the planning and preparation along with the analysis of results and report-writing. Some procedures, such as an experiment or questionnaire, may be tried out on a small sample of

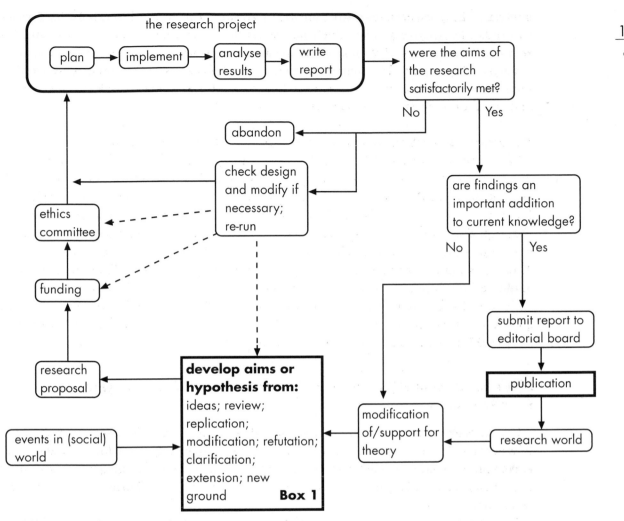

Figure 1.2 The research cycle – start at Box 1

people in order to highlight snags or ambiguities for which adjustments can be made before the actual data gathering process is begun. This would be known as PILOTING or the running of PILOT TRIALS.

The report will be published in a research journal if successful. This term 'successful' is difficult to define here. It doesn't always mean that original aims have been entirely met. Surprises occurring during the research may well make it important, though usually such surprises would lead the investigator to re-think, re-plan and run again on the basis of the new insights. As we saw above, failure to confirm one's hypothesis can be an important source of information. What matters overall, is that the research results are an important or useful contribution to current knowledge and theory development. This importance will be decided by the editorial board of an academic journal (such as *The British Journal of Psychology*) who will have the report reviewed, usually by experts 'blind' as to the identity of the investigator.

Theory will then be adjusted in the light of this research result. Some academics may argue that the design was so different from previous research that its challenge to their theory can be ignored. Others will wish to query the results and may ask the investigator to provide 'raw data' – the whole of the originally recorded data, unprocessed. Some will want to replicate the study, some to modify . . . and here we are, back where we started on the research cycle.

Myth no. 3: 'scientific research is all about experiments'

An experiment involves the researcher's control and manipulation of conditions or 'variables', as we shall see in Chapter 3. Astronomy, one of the oldest sciences, could not use very many experiments until relatively recently when technological advances have permitted direct tests of conditions in space. It has mainly relied upon *observation* to test its theories of planetary motion and stellar organisation.

It is perfectly possible to test hypotheses without an experiment. Much psychological testing is conducted by observing what children do, asking what people think and so on. The evidence about male and female drivers in Box 1.1, for instance, was obtained by observation of actual behaviour and insurance company statistics.

Myth no. 4: 'scientists have to be unbiased'

It is true that investigators try to remove bias from the way a project is run and from the way data are gathered and analysed. But they are biased about theory. They interpret ambiguous data to fit their particular theory as best they can. This happens whenever we're in a heated argument and say things like 'Ah, but that could be because . . .'. Investigators *believe* in their theory and attempt to produce evidence to support it. Mitroff (1974) interviewed a group of scientists and all agreed that the notion of the purely objective, uncommitted scientist was naïve. They argued that:

> . . . in order to be a good scientist, one had to have biases. The best scientist, they said, not only has points of view but also defends them with gusto. Their concept of a scientist did not imply that he would cheat by making up experimental data or falsifying it; rather he does everything in his power to defend his pet hypotheses against early and perhaps unwarranted death caused by the introduction of fluke data.

DO WE GET ON TO PSYCHOLOGICAL RESEARCH NOW?

Yes. We've looked at some common ideas in the language and logic of scientific research, since most, but not all, psychological investigators would claim to follow a scientific model. Now let's answer some 'wh' questions about the practicalities of psychological research.

What is the subject matter for psychological research?

The easy answer is 'humans'. The more controversial answer is 'human behaviour' since psychology is literally (in Greek) the study of mind. This isn't a book which will take you into the great debate on the relationship between mind and body or whether the study of mind is at all possible. This is available in other general textbooks (e.g. Gross 1992, Valentine 1992, Bem and Looren de Jong, 1997).

Whatever type of psychology you are studying, you should be introduced to the various major 'schools' of psychology (Psycho-analytic, Behaviourist, Cognitive, Humanist, . . .). It is important to point out here, however, that each school would see the focus for its subject matter differently – behaviour, the conscious mind, even the unconscious mind. Consequently, different investigatory methods have been developed by different schools.

Nevertheless, the initial raw data which psychologists gather directly from humans can *only* be observed behaviour (in the form of data from physiological responses, reaction times, computer decisions and so on) or language (verbal report).

Why do psychologists do research?

All research has the overall aim of collecting data to expand knowledge. To be specific, research will very often have one of two major aims: to gather purely descriptive data or to test hypotheses (though qualitative approaches – see below – are a growing third alternative).

Descriptive research

A research study may concentrate largely on the ages at which a large sample of children reach certain language development milestones or long term features of everyday memory. The work of Rubin, Wetzler and Nebes (1986) and Schuman and Reiger (1992), for instance, demonstrated that older people tend to recall a surprising number of both personal and public events occurring between the ages of 15 and 25 – the so-called 'reminiscence bump'. SURVEYS (see Chapter 6) might investigate current parental attitudes to physical punishment and general discipline techniques. Yet other studies concentrate on the establishment of a new psychological measure or on the validation of an existing one in a new format or across new cultures. For instance, McCrae, Costa, del Pilar, Rolland and Parker (1998) report studies showing that a popular personality measure (the 'NEO-PI-R' standing for Neuroticism, Extroversion and Openness Personality Inventory – Revised) could be translated from (US American) English to French and Filipino and produced apparently similar personality structures in countries speaking these languages.

Mainly QUALITATIVE DATA may be gathered through interview or case studies, or through certain types of observation study. Qualitative data are pieces of information in non-numerical form, such as words, speech, text, pictures and so on. As will be seen later on, some qualitative data gathering studies bridge the gap between descriptive study and hypothesis testing while others attempt to develop theory out of the data within the same investigation.

Hypothesis testing

A good majority of research in mainstream journals will contain one or more hypotheses, usually several. These can be crudely divided into EXPERIMENTAL (including so-called QUASI-EXPERIMENTAL designs – see Chapter 3) and *non-experimental* studies. Whatever the design of the study, our hypothesis will be predicting some well-defined and measurable outcome – very often that two groups will *differ* on some measure or that there will be some form of *relationship* between measures, such as a CORRELATION – see Chapter 15. For ease of explanation, a useful general term for such differences or correlation which we'll often use from now on is an EFFECT.

What is a research hypothesis?

Generally, a research article will explain its background theory and its rationale before stating explicitly what are the predictions for the current piece of research. For instance, suppose we were testing the 'old chesnut' that using mental imagery to learn a presented list of unconnected words will produce better recall than simple mental repetition of each item. Having explained why we expect imaging participants to do better we might make the specific prediction:

> 'Participants using imagery will recall more correct words than will participants using rehearsal'

For the vitamin study we predicted that:

> 'Children fed on spinach will have higher than average reading scores'

These are examples of DIRECTIONAL HYPOTHESES (see Chapter 11), because they predict in which direction the results are expected to run.

A NON-DIRECTIONAL version of the latter hypothesis would be:

> 'Children fed on spinach will have average reading scores different from the average for children not fed on spinach'

Let's look at two examples of hypothesis testing research, one laboratory based, the other from the 'field'.

Stay happy – turn off the news

Johnston and Davey (1997) showed participants three news bulletins edited to contain positive, neutral or negative content. Each group saw only one of the bulletins. The groups were measured before and after the viewing for *sadness* and *anxiety*. They were also tested, after the viewing only, for *'worried thought'*, using a special type of interview approach. Results showed that the group viewing the negative bulletin were, to a significant extent, sadder, more anxious and more worried than the other two groups.

They had tested the theory that negative content of news programmes has an adverse effect on people's own personal concerns. They tested this with the specific research hypothesis that the negative news group would differ from the positive news group on the measures taken. This *supported* the view that the negative mood created by the news had caused people to worry more about their own personal circumstances. Of course, it is also perfectly possible that the news had made them worry more and that this worrying had caused the lowering in mood.

The laboratory and studies in the field

Notice here that although this would be known as a 'laboratory experiment', there was nothing in the experimental rooms resembling the stereotype of a 'lab'. There were no retort stands and bubbling bottles. The psychological researcher's laboratory may consist only of interview rooms, group discussion rooms, or even a toddlers' nursery, though other psychological laboratories do contain technical equipment and computers. The term 'laboratory' is used where the research participants come to the premises of the psychologist, a controlled environment and often a university department, rather than the psychologist going 'into the field' to observe people in some form of their natural, everyday environment. Such studies are known as FIELD STUDIES or FIELD EXPERIMENTS, depending on whether the investigation is indeed a true experiment – see Chapter 4.

Does litter make you litter?

Cialdini, Reno, and Kallgren (1990) carried out a *quasi-experiment* (see Chapter 6) 'in the field'. They tested the general theory that, in performing acts contrary to social norms, people are influenced by other people's behaviour in similar circumstances. For instance, might you feel better leaving your litter in a public place if you knew that this was the way many other people behaved? The researchers tested precisely this notion by arranging for certain amounts of litter to be left on a path prior to distributing leaflets to people who had to walk down the path where the litter had been dropped. They predicted that the unwitting participants would be more likely to drop their leaflet on the ground if there were more pieces already there. They used six conditions varying only in the number of pieces of litter left on the ground: no pieces of litter, one piece, two pieces, four pieces, eight pieces and sixteen pieces. The researchers' hypothesis was supported. There was a very clear increase in number of leaflets dropped as the amount of litter already on the ground increased across conditions.

Theory or hypothesis?

It is easy to get confused about the notions of theory and hypothesis. This is partly because the literature itself often blurs the distinction. For instance, in discussing the issue of whether language precedes thought in our intellectual development, or vice versa, you will probably come across the 'linguistic relativity hypothesis' (see Gross, 1996, p. 317 for detail). This concerns the notion that the language we acquire determines how we will see the world, what categories we are aware of and what concepts we use to explain what we observe. Now this is far more a general *theory* than it is a specifically testable *hypothesis*. Similarly you may come across the 'carpentered world hypothesis' in the study of cross-cultural differences in perception, particularly of visual illusions.

We saw above that a hypothesis, for the purposes of research science, needs to be a highly specific, *testable* prediction emanating from a more general background theory. Several examples were given. K5 enhances reading ability. OK, let's test the hypothesis that spinach eaters will score higher than non-eaters on a reading test. People are affected by the anti-social behaviour of others? OK, let's set up a specific situation (dropping litter) and see whether more litter is dropped the more litter already exists.

Each of these predictions was a RESEARCH HYPOTHESIS. Here are a couple of examples from recent research journals (though most are more complex than these):

> 'Relative to a control group receiving no training, participants trained in the extension rule [will] commit fewer conjunction errors.' (Fisk and Pidgeon, 1997)

> '. . . inferred intellect of the warm-cold persons should be significantly higher than the normal neutral point of the intellect measure.' (Singh, 1997)

Notice that these researchers state specifically what they expect to happen in their study, what *effect* they hope to demonstrate. They also state specifically what they will be using as a measure of change or difference. In other words, they don't say 'participants will perform worse . . .' or 'participants will infer that the warm-cold persons are more clever.' In their research hypothesis they make carefully detailed RESEARCH PREDICTIONS so that another researcher, attempting to understand their work, to replicate it or to challenge it, has a clear opportunity to do so. The work is up front; cards are clearly on the table.

Replication

Replication of studies is extremely important in psychology as in any scientific research. Psychology in particular though depends on probabilistic statements about the world of people. Because people are so complicated and there are so many of them with widely diverging types, we can only make *estimates* from *samples* of people's behaviour as to how people behave in general. We see just this approach to prediction occurring before every major political election. It is also a big factor on the stock exchange or in marketing. For us to be able to be more certain that a demonstrated psychological effect is in fact a real one, we need several psychological researchers to be able to repeat or REPLICATE results of studies, just as you would expect me to be able to repeat a clever football trick if you're to be convinced it wasn't a fluke.

In order to replicate, researchers require full details of the original study and it is a strong professional ethic that psychologists communicate their data, procedures and results clearly to one another. People are considered charlatans in psychology, as else-where, if they claim to demonstrate effects (such as telepathy or exotic forms of psy-chotherapy) yet will not publish clearly (or at all) the predictions, the methods and the results of their research work so that the research public can *check* whether outcomes support declared aims. The US psychologist Arthur Jensen, for instance, has long been accused of evading scrutiny of his declared findings in the highly sensitive and controver-sial area of 'race' differences in intelligence, because he will not provide the raw data from his work on apparent reaction time differences between members of 'racial' groups (see Kamin 1977, 1981, 1995).

Experimental and research hypotheses (and the 'null' and 'alternative' hypotheses)

Although there is variation in the use of these terms, in psychological research writing, most uses of the term 'experimental hypothesis' are in place of the term 'research hypo-thesis' where the work referred to is indeed experimental. In this book we will use **'research hypothesis'** as the more general term and this will include studies which are both experimental and non-experimental. Chapters 11 and 23 distinguish between a typical research hypothesis, set out in a research journal report, and the strictly statisti-cal **'null'** and **'alternative'** hypotheses.

It is worth saying now that there is a multiplicity of terms within psychological research methods, and much duplication, mainly because psychology once thought of itself as an almost purely experimental science. Some would argue that it used to suffer (particularly in the middle part of the 20th century) from 'pure science envy' and that studies which did not conform to the experimental, laboratory based model were considered quite inferior. This is why, in fact, the term 'quasi-experiment' was promoted by Cooke and Campbell (1979) – see Chapter 3. Within different areas of psychology, this effort to emulate natural science can, even today, be either very strong (for instance, in cognitive or physiological psychology) or it can be only one influence among several others (e.g. in social or applied psychology). Hence, depending on the area you are consulting, you may be tapping into different traditions of scientific language.

When is a hypothesis test successful?

Suppose our research hypothesis concerning spinach eaters appears to be correct. We find that the reading scores for Natasha's friends are far higher than the normal average. Psychological researchers cannot simply claim to have 'definite proof' that spinach enhances reading, far less that K5 is responsible. We saw above that they can claim 'support'. However, they obviously can't claim even this if the difference found is only tiny. A tiny difference between samples may mean no difference at *all* between the populations they came from. What researchers need, in order to claim support, is a difference which will be counted, statistically, as SIGNIFICANT.

Again, the basic ideas used in social science statistical testing are not so far removed from the sort of thinking that occurs in everyday life. Imagine an England football fan in France for the 1998 World Cup. He orders a beer in a bar with some difficulty, given the usual English tendency for monolingualism. He notices that the top of his beer is a long way below the litre marker line on the glass and that most people's tops vary to just a small degree either above or below that line. He points this out to the barkeeper who replies 'C'est la chance'. The fan replies with 'Il faut que vous etes joking' or similar. He has made what we shall call in Chapter 11 a *'significance decision'*. He has decided that the barkeeper's measure is too unlikely to have occurred 'by chance' from among all the barkeeper's usual measures. He goes for the alternative view – this barkeeper, for some quite mystifying reason, is not fond of English football fans and has deliberately poured a very short measure. The difference, he believes, is significant.

When my children fall out because one packet of Smarties contains one more sweet than the other, one has the difficult task of explaining significance testing – 'Come on, that's just the way the cookie crumbles, kids!'. We mean, in effect, that this is not a *significant* difference. It is the sort of thing we'd expect to occur quite frequently if the Smartie packets came, as they should, from a batch of packets varying only a little and quite randomly around their average contents of, say, 40. If researchers are trying to demonstrate a psychological effect, for instance that bad news makes you worry, then they would want to achieve a *significant* difference in their results. How likely is it that you would be sold two packs of Smarties, one containing just 25 sweets and the other containing 50, if the average Smartie content is 40 sweets? Even young children get suspicious here! The children would undoubtedly claim that this just can't happen 'by chance'. This is also, very roughly, the thinking used in research decisions about results. If we obtain only a small difference, even if it is in the hypothesised direction, we will usually declare a 'non-significant' result (never be tempted to use the term 'insignificant' here). In Chapter 11 we will formalise these notions into the classic procedures of SIGNIFICANCE TESTING. The statistical tests used to decide whether differences or relationships between data are significant are known as INFERENTIAL (statistical) TESTS and these are the subject of Chapters 12 through to 20.

Students doing practical work often get quite despondent when what they predicted does not occur. It feels very much as though the project hasn't 'worked'. Some students I was once teaching failed to show, contrary to their expectations, that the 'older generation' were more negative about homosexuality than their own generation. I explained that it was surely important information that the 'older generation' were just as liberal as they were (or, perhaps, that their generation were just as hostile).

In a case like this the first priority is to review the design of the study, learning from errors made and speculating on why a reliable or large enough effect may not have emerged. Were sensible questions asked? In a sensible way? Were enough people questioned? Did we gather a 'fair' sample of the population intended? (almost certainly not) and so on.

HOW DO PSYCHOLOGISTS CONDUCT RESEARCH?

A huge question and basically an introduction to the rest of the book! A very large number of psychologists use the experimental method or some form of well controlled careful investigation, involving careful measurement in the data gathering process.

In Chapter 9, however, we shall consider why a growing number of psychologists reject the use of the experiment and purely numerical measurement. They also tend to favour methods which gather QUALITATIVE DATA – information from people which is in descriptive, non-numerical, form. Some of these psychologists also reject the scientific method as I have outlined it. They accept that this has been a successful way to study inert matter, but seek an alternative approach to understanding ourselves. Others reinterpret 'science' as it applies to psychology.

One thing we can say, though, is, whatever the outlook of the researcher, there are three major ways to get information about people. You either ask them, observe them or meddle. These approaches are covered in Chapters 6 and 7, Chapter 5 and Chapter 3 respectively.

Planning research

To get us started, and to allow me to introduce the rest of this book, let's look at the key decision areas facing anyone about to conduct some research. I have identified these in Figure 1.3. Basically, the four boxes are answers to the questions:

Variables: WHAT shall we study? (what human characteristics under what conditions?)
Samples: WHO shall we study?
Design: HOW shall we study these?
Analysis: WHAT sort of evidence will we get, in what form?

Before looking at these a little more closely, try planning a piece of research which tests the (loosely-worded) hypothesis that 'people are more irritable in hot weather' (and beware the 'easy thinking' depicted in Figure 1.1!).

Variables

Variables are tricky things. They are the things which alter so that we can make comparisons, such as 'Are you tidier than I am?' Heat is a variable in our study. How shall we

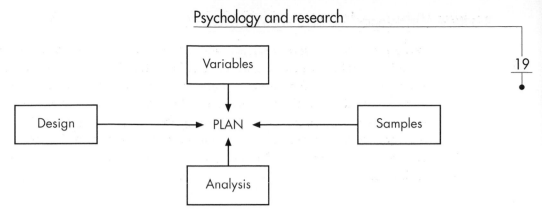

Figure 1.3 Key decision areas in a research project

define it? How shall we make sure that it isn't humidity, rather than temperature, that is responsible for any irritability?

The real problem is how to measure 'irritability'. We could, of course, devise some sort of questionnaire. The construction of these is dealt with in Chapter 7. We could observe people's behaviour at work on hot and cool days. Are there more arguments? Is there more swearing or shouting? We could observe these events in the street or in some families. Chapter 5 will deal with methods of observation.

We could even bring people into the 'laboratory' and see whether they tend to answer our questionnaire differently under a well-controlled change in temperature. We could observe their behaviour whilst carrying out a frustrating task (for instance, balancing pencils on a slightly moving surface) and we could ask them to assess this task under the two temperature conditions.

The difficulty of defining variables, stating exactly what it is we mean by a term and how, if at all, we intend to measure it, seemed to me to be so primary that it is included in the chapter immediately following this introduction.

Samples

These are the people we are going to study or work with. If we carry out our field observations on office workers (on hot and cool days) we might be showing only that these sort of people get more irritable in the heat. What about builders or nurses? If we select a sample for our laboratory experiment, what factors shall we take into account in trying to make the group representative of most people in general? Is this possible? These are issues of 'sampling' and are also dealt with in Chapter 2.

One word on terminology here. It used to be common to refer to the people studied in psychological research, especially in experiments, as 'subjects'. There are objections to this, particularly by psychologists who argue that a false model of the human being is generated by referring to (and possibly treating) research participants in this distant, coolly scientific manner. The British Psychological Society's 'Revised Ethical Principles for Conducting Research with Human Participants' were in provisional operation from February 1992. These include the principle that, on the grounds of courtesy and gratitude to participants, the terminology used about them should carry obvious respect (although traditional psychologists did not intend 'subjects' to be derogatory). The principles were formally adopted in October 1992. Although the term 'subjects' was commonly found in

The British Journal of Psychology up to and during 1995, by 1996 it had disappeared almost completely. However, this was not without some rearguard disgruntlement expressed by members of the psychological research establishment (see 'Letters' in *The Psychologist*, October, 1997), and the term is still common in several US journals and in those with a more traditionally hard, 'scientific' background (e.g. *Biopsychology*).

In the interest of clarity I have stuck with the term 'between-subjects' in the section on ANOVA calculations in Chapters 17–19 in order not to confuse readers checking my text with others on a difficult statistical topic. The term is used generically in the statistical world and would often refer to mice or even leaves!

Design

The decisions about variable measurement have taken us into decisions about the research design. The design is the overall structure and strategy of the research study. Decisions on measuring irritability may determine whether we conduct a laboratory study or field research. If we want realistic irritability we might wish to measure it in the field. If we take the laboratory option described above, we would be running an EXPERIMENT (see Chapter 3). However, experiments can be run using various designs. Shall we, for instance, have the same group of people perform the frustrating task under the two temperature conditions? If so, mightn't they be getting practice at the task which will make changes in their performance harder to interpret? The variety of experimental designs is covered in Chapter 3. There are several constraints on choice of design:

1 RESOURCES – The researcher may not have the funding, staff or time to carry out a long-term study. The most appropriate technical equipment may be just too expensive. Resources may not stretch to testing in different cultures. A study in the natural setting – say in a hospital – may be too time consuming or ruled out by lack of permission. The laboratory may just have to do.

2 NATURE OF RESEARCH AIM – If the researcher wishes to study the effects of maternal deprivation on the three-year-old, certain designs are ruled out. We can't experiment by artificially depriving children of their mothers (I hope you agree!) and we can't question a three-year-old in any great depth. We may be left with the best option of simply *observing* the child's behaviour, although some researchers have turned to experiments on animals in lieu of humans. The ethical issues involved in such decisions are discussed more fully in Chapter 22.

3 PREVIOUS RESEARCH – If we intend to *replicate* an earlier study we must use the same design and method. An *extension* of the study may require the same design, because an extra group is to be added, or it may require use of a different design which complements the first. We may wish to demonstrate that a laboratory discovered effect can be reproduced in a natural setting, for instance.

4 THE RESEARCHER'S ATTITUDE TO SCIENTIFIC INVESTIGATION – There can be hostile debates between psychologists from different research backgrounds. Some swear by the strictly controlled laboratory setting, seeking to emulate the 'hard' physical sciences in their isolation and precise measurement of variables. Others prefer the more

realistic field setting, while there is a growing body of researchers with a humanistic, 'action research' or 'new paradigm' approach who favour qualitative methods. We shall look more closely at this debate in the methods section.

Analysis

The design chosen, and method of measuring variables, will have a direct effect on the statistical or other analysis which is possible at the end of data collection. In a straight-forward hypothesis-testing study, it is pointless to steam ahead with a design and pro-cedure, only to find that the results can barely be analysed in order to support the hypothesis.

There is a principle relating to computer programming which goes: *'garbage in – garbage out'*. It applies here too. If the questionnaire contains items like 'How do you feel?', what is to be done with the largely unquantifiable results? There are other examples in Chapter 7 but see particularly item 11 on p. 163. Thoughts of the analysis should not stifle creativity but it is important to keep it central to the planning.

One last word on the nature of scientific research (for now)

Throughout the book, and in any practical work, can I suggest that the reader keep the following words from Rogers (1961) in mind? If taken seriously to heart and practised, whatever the arguments about various methods, I don't think the follower of this idea will be far away from 'doing science'.

> Scientific research needs to be seen for what it truly is; a way of preventing me from deceiving myself in regard to my creatively formed subjective hunches which have developed out of the relationship between me and my material. (cited in Reason and Rowan, 1981, p. 240)

Note: at the end of each chapter in this book there is a glossary of definitions for terms introduced (unless these are more fully defined in a subsequent chapter). If you want to use this as a self test, cover up the right hand column. You can then write in your guess as to the term being defined or simply check after you read each one. Sets of similar terms are grouped within the glossaries, as with the various types of hypotheses below.

Glossary

Relatively uninterpreted information received through human senses	_____	data
Logical argument where conclusions follow automatically from premises	_____	deduction
Methods for numerical summary of set of data	_____	descriptive statistics

Overall structure and strategy of a piece of research	_____	design
A demonstrated difference or correlation between sample measures which is used to support the theory of a *population* effect	_____	effect
Form of science which involves observation, recording and organisation of (sense) data, and the summarising of any consistent patterns in the data	_____ _____	empirical method
Research study where data are gathered outside the research centre, usually in an applied setting where the target participants usually work or live	_____ _____	field study
A field study (see above) which satisfies criteria for an experiment	_____ _____	field experiment
Precise prediction of relationship between data to be measured; usually made to support more general theoretical explanation	_____	**types of hypothesis**
Claim that populations vary in the way which will support the theory under investigation; very often the claim that population parameters (e.g. means) differ or that correlations exist between variables measured across a population	_____	alternative
Claim or prediction including the *direction* of proposed differences or correlations		directional
Research hypothesis tested in an experiment	_____	experimental
Claim that populations do not vary in the way which will support the theory under investigation; very often the prediction that population (mean) differences or correlations are zero	_____	null
Prediction tested in a particular piece of research	_____	research
Method of recording observations and regularities, developing theories to explain regularities and testing predictions from those theories, often by attempting to falsify alternative explanations	_____ – _____ _____	hypothetico-deductive method
Estimating form of a relationship between variables using a limited set of sample measures	_____	induction

Statistical test used to *infer* whether differences or relationships between samples of data are *'significant'* – whether they reflect real effects in the population. More specifically, these tests help us decide whether the difference or relationship between data could plausibly have occurred if there is no real effect in the population.

_____   inferential test
_____

Trying out prototype of a study or questionnaire on a small sample in order to discover snags or errors in design or to develop workable measuring instrument

_____;   piloting; pilot trials
_____
_____

Data gathered which are kept in non-numerical form

_____   qualitative data
_____

Data gathered which are in numerical form

_____   quantitative data
_____

Repetition of a study to check its validity; to check that other researchers, using the same procedures, obtain similar results or 'effects'

_____   replication

Precise predictions of expected data relationships expected to occur between measured variables in a research investigation and contained within the research hypothesis

_____   research predictions
_____

People or things taken as a small subset but assumed to be representative of the larger population

_____   sample

Method used to verify truth or falsity of theoretical explanations of why events occur

_____   scientific method
_____

Substantial difference occurring between sample measures in a research investigation and very unlikely to have occurred *if there is no real difference between the populations sampled*

_____   significant difference
_____

Proposed explanation of observable events

_____   theory

Phenomenon (thing in the world) which goes through observable and measurable changes

_____   variable

2

Measuring people: variables, samples and the qualitative critique

This chapter is an introduction to the language and concepts of measurement in social science.

- *Variables* are identified events which change in value.
- Many explanatory concepts in psychology are unobservable directly but are treated as *hypothetical constructs*, as in other sciences.
- Under the conventional research paradigm (the 'scientific' model), variables to be measured need precise *operational definition* (the steps taken to measure the phenomenon) so that researchers can communicate effectively about their findings.

The second part of this chapter looks at how people are selected for study in psychological research. Issues arising are:

- Samples should be *representative* of those to whom results may be generalised.
- *Random* selection provides representative samples only with large numbers.
- Various non-random selection techniques (*stratified, quota, cluster, snowball sampling, critical cases*) aim to provide representative, or at least useful *small* samples. *Opportunity* and *self-selecting samples* may well be biased.
- *Size* of samples for experiments is a subject of much debate; large is not always best.
- In strict experimental work, variance in participant performance should be kept to a minimum.

The qualitative-quantitative dimension is introduced as a fundamental division within the theory of methods in contemporary psychological research, with a general critique of *positivism*. The dimension will be referred to throughout as research varies in the extent to which it employs aspects of either approach. Some researchers see the two approaches as complementary rather than antagonistic.

VARIABLES

A variable is anything which varies. Rather a circular definition I know, but it gets us started. Let's list some things which vary:

1. Height – varies as you grow older; varies between individuals.
2. Time – to respond with 'yes' or 'no' to questions; to solve a set of anagrams.
3. The political party people vote for.

4. Your feelings towards your partner or parent.
5. Extroversion.
6. Attitude towards vandals.
7. Anxiety.

Notice that all of these can vary:
- within yourself from one time to another
- between different individuals in society.

The essence of studying anything (birds, geology, emotion) is the observation of changes in variables. If nothing changed there would be nothing to observe. The essence of science is to relate these changes in variables to changes in other variables.

MEASURING VARIABLES

A variable can take several or many values across a range. The value is often numerical but not necessarily so. In example 3 above, the different values are names. In example 4 we haven't yet decided how we could assess 'feelings'. Some of the variables are easy to measure and we are familiar with the type of measuring instrument required. Height is one of these and time another, though the equipment required to measure 'reaction times' (as in example 2) can be quite sophisticated, because of the very brief intervals involved.

Some variables are familiar in concept but measuring them numerically seems a very difficult, strange or impossible thing to do, as in the case of *attitude*, *anxiety* or *feelings*. However, we often make estimates of others' attitudes indirectly when we make such pronouncements as 'He is very strongly opposed to smoking' or 'She didn't seem particularly averse to the idea of living in Manchester'.

So far we have briefly looked at the problem of having a loose, familiar concept (like anxiety or attitude) and looking around for a way to measure it. In some areas of psychological research, however, rather than having a concept then casting round for a way to measure it, we start with a set of measures and use a statistical procedure, known as *factor analysis* to *generate* explanatory constructs (known as *'factors'*). This procedure is more fully explained in Chapter 7, but the situation is somewhat similar to physicists observing the behaviour of certain sub-atomic particles and speculating that a further, as yet undiscovered, particle must exist since this would explain most of the variations that have been observed. Various personality measures in psychology have been generated in this manner, famously including Eysenck's extroversion and neuroticism, but also several derived by Cattell and the various NEO-PI-R measures mentioned in Chapter 1.

If we are to work with variables such as *attitude* and *anxiety* we must be able to specify them precisely, partly because we want to be accurate in the measurement of their change, and partly because we wish to communicate with others about our findings. If we wish to be taken seriously in our work it must be possible for others to replicate our findings using the same measurement procedures. But what *are* 'attitude' and 'anxiety'?

Defining psychological variables

First, try to write down your own definition of:

a. intelligence
b. anxiety
c. superstition

Perhaps that was difficult. Now, give some examples of people displaying those characteristics.

You probably found the definitions quite hard, especially the first. Why is it we have such difficulty defining terms we use every day with good understanding? You must have used these terms very many times in your communications with others, saying, for instance:

I think Jenny has a lot of intelligence
Bob gets anxious whenever a dog comes near him
Are people today less superstitious than they were?

PSYCHOLOGICAL CONSTRUCTS

I hope you found it relatively easier, though, to give *examples* of people being intelligent, anxious or superstitious. Remember, I said in Chapter 1 that information about people must come, somehow, from what they say or do. When we are young we are little psychologists. We build up a concept of 'intelligence' or 'anxiety' from learning what are signs or manifestations of it; biting lips, shaking hand, tremulous voice in the latter case, for instance.

Notice that we learn that certain things are done 'intelligently'; getting sums right, doing them quickly, finishing a jigsaw. People who do these things consistently get called 'intelligent' (the adverb has become an adjective). It is one step now to statements like the one made about Jenny above where we have a noun instead of an adjective. It is easy to think of intelligence as having some thing-like quality, of existing independently, because we can use it as a noun. We can say 'What is X?'. The Greek philosopher Plato ran into this sort of trouble asking questions like 'What is justice?'. The tendency to treat an abstract concept as if it had independent existence is known as REIFICATION.

Some psychologists (especially the behaviourist Skinner, who took an extreme empiricist position) would argue that observable events (like biting lips), and, for anxiety, directly measurable internal ones (like increased heart rate or adrenalin secretion), are *all* we need to bother about. Anxiety just *is* all these events, no more. They would say that we don't need to assume *extra* concepts over and above these things which we can observe and measure. To assume the existence of internal structures or processes, such as 'attitude' or 'drive' is seen as 'mentalistic', unobjective and unscientific.

Other psychologists argue that there is more. That a person's attitude, for instance, is more than the sum of statements about, and action towards, the attitude object. They would argue that the concept is useful in theory development, even if they are unable to trap and measure it in accurate detail. They behave, in fact, like the 'hard' scientists in physics.

No physicist has ever directly seen an atom or a quark. This isn't physically possible. (It may be *logically* impossible ever to 'see' intelligence, but that's another matter.) What physicists do is *assume* that atoms and quarks exist and then work out how much of known physical evidence is explained by them. Quarks are HYPOTHETICAL CONSTRUCTS. They will survive as part of an overall theory so long as the amount they explain is a good deal more than the amount they contradict.

Taking a careful path, psychologists treat concepts like intelligence, anxiety or attitude as hypothetical constructs too. They are *assumed* to exist as factors which explain observable phenomena. If, after research which attempts both to support and refute the existence of the constructs, the explanations remain feasible, then the constructs can remain as theoretical entities. A state of anxiety is assumed from observation of a person's sweating, stuttering and shaking. But we don't see 'anxiety' as such. Anxiety is, then, a hypothetical construct.

Organisation of constructs

A construct can be linked to others in an explanatory framework from which further predictions are possible and testable. We might, for instance, infer low self-esteem in people who are very hostile to members of minority ethnic groups. The low self-esteem might, in turn, be related to authoritarian upbringing which could be checked up on. We might then look for a relationship between authoritarian rearing and discriminatory behaviour as shown in Figure 2.1.

If psychologists are to use such constructs in their research work and theorising, they must obviously be very careful indeed in explaining how these are to be treated as variables. Their definitions must be precise. Even for the more easily measurable variables, such as short-term memory capacity, definitions must be clear. One particular difficulty for psychologists is that a large number of terms for variables they might wish to research already exist in everyday English, with wide variation in possible meaning.

Discuss with a colleague, or think about, the terms shown below:

Identity	Attention	Reinforcement	Egocentric	Attitude
Neurotic	Instinct	Conformity	Unconscious	Conscience

How could any of these be measured or assessed?

Operational definitions

In search of objectivity, scientists conducting research attempt to 'operationalise' their variables. An OPERATIONAL DEFINITION of variable X gives us *the set of activities required to measure X*. It is like a set of instructions. For instance, in physics, pressure is precisely defined as weight or mass per unit area. To measure pressure we have to find out the weight impinging on an area and divide by that area.

Even in measuring a person's height, if we want to agree with others' measurements,

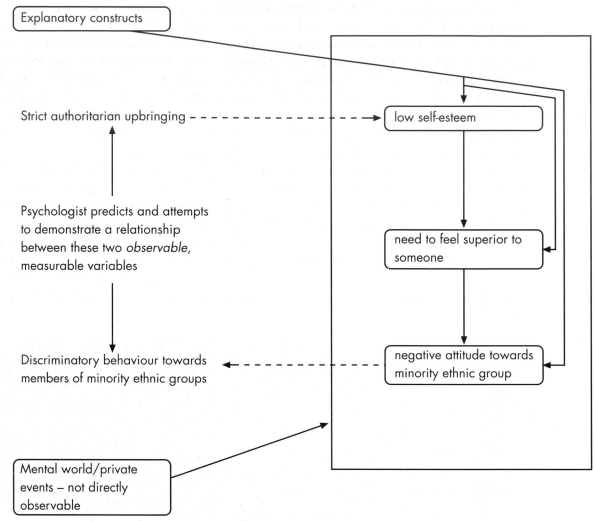

Explanatory constructs

Strict authoritarian upbringing

low self-esteem

Psychologist predicts and attempts to demonstrate a relationship between these two *observable*, measurable variables

need to feel superior to someone

Discriminatory behaviour towards members of minority ethnic groups

negative attitude towards minority ethnic group

Mental world/private events – not directly observable

Figure 2.1 Explanatory framework for hypothesised link between strict upbringing and discriminatory behaviour

we will need to specify conditions such as what to take as the top of the head and how the person should stand. In general, though, height and time present us with no deep problem since the units of measurement are already clearly and universally defined.

In a particular piece of memory research we might define short-term memory capacity as 'the longest list of digits on which the participant has perfect recall in more than 80% of trials'. Here, on each trial, the participant has to try to recall the digit string presented in the order it was given. Several trials would occur with strings from three to, say, 12 digits in length. At the end of this it is relatively simple to calculate our measure of short-term memory capacity according to our operational definition.

If a researcher had measured the 'controlling' behaviour of mothers with their children, he or she would have to provide the CODING SCHEME (see Chapter 5) given to assistants for making recordings during observation. This might include categories of 'physical restraint', 'verbal warning', 'verbal demand' and so on, with detailed examples given to observers during training.

The notorious example of an operational definition within psychological research is the definition of intelligence as 'that which is measured by the (particular) intelligence test used'. Since intelligence tests differ, we obviously do not have in psychology the universal agreement enjoyed by physicists. It might be argued that physicists have many ways to measure pressure but they know what pressure *is*. Likewise, can't psychologists have several ways to measure intelligence? But psychologists aren't in the same position. Physicists get almost exactly the same results with their various alternative measures. Psychologists, on the other hand, are still using the tests to try to establish agreement on the nature of intelligence itself. (See FACTOR ANALYSIS in Chapter 7.)

An operational definition gives us a more or less valid method for measuring some *part* of a hypothetical construct. It rarely covers the whole of what is usually understood by that construct. It is hard to imagine an operational definition which could express the rich and diverse meaning of human intelligence. But for any particular piece of research we must state exactly what we are counting as a measure of the construct we are interested in. As an example, consider a project carried out by some students who placed a ladder against a wall and observed men and women walking round or under it. For this research, 'superstitious behaviour' was (narrowly) operationalised as the avoidance of walking under the ladder.

Imagine you were about to start testing the hypotheses stated below. In each case, try to provide operationalised definitions for the variables involved. If it helps, ask yourself 'What will *count* as (aggression) in this study? How exactly will it be measured?' Think carefully, and then state the exact procedure you would use to carry out the measurement of the variables.

1. Physically punished children are more aggressive
2. Memory deterioration can be the result of stress at work
3. Language development is promoted in infants by parents who provide a lot of visual and auditory stimulation
4. People will be more likely to comply with a request from a person they trust
5. People told an infant is male will be more likely to describe the infant according to the popular male stereotype than will those told it is female

Here are some ideas:
1. *Physical punishment*: number of times parent reports striking per week; questionnaire to parents on attitudes to physical punishment. *Aggression*: number of times child initiates rough-and-tumble behaviour observed in playground at school; number of requests for violent toys in Santa Claus letters.
2. *Stress*: occupations defined as more stressful the more sickness, heart attacks etc. reported within them. *Memory*: could be defined as we did for short-term memory capacity, above, or participants could keep a diary of forgetful incidents.
3. *Language development*: length of child's utterances, size of vocabulary, etc. *Stimulation*: number of times parent initiates sensory play, among other things, during home observation.
4. *Compliance*: if target person agrees to researcher's request for change in street. *Trust*: might be defined in terms of dress, role and associated status; in one condition, researcher dresses smartly with doctor's bag; in the other, with scruffy

clothes. Alternatively, we could ask participants to assess trustworthiness *after* the request has been made.

5. *Stereotype response*: number of times participant, in describing the infant, uses terms coming from a list developed by asking a panel of the general public what infant features were typically masculine and typically feminine.

RELIABILITY AND VALIDITY

If measures are reliable and valid then other researchers will treat them with credibility. Without reliable and valid assessments the normal business of research cannot be conducted. If measures are unreliable or invalid then researchers are unable to communicate results and have them checked out by others. The problem is more acute for psychologists, however, since there is far less agreement among them than among other scientists about the measurement of constructs, or even on what constructs are at all relevant or meaningful to the subject area. A good example of the real dangers involved when researchers use concepts which are *not* objectively agreed by others is that of so-called 'slow schizophrenia' which was a condition only ever 'observed' by psychiatrists in the former Soviet Union. The only patients who displayed symptoms were dissidents opposed to the existing political system. In addition, the only psychiatrists who observed these symptoms were those trained by just one senior psychiatrist, and the only places of observation were certain clinics under the jurisdiction of the KGB (the government's then security service). (Joravsky, cited in Bem and Looren de Jong, 1997)

Not so long ago it became possible to buy from your pharmacist a plastic strip which could be placed on a baby's forehead and used to measure temperature. This was a great improvement on attempting to keep a glass thermometer under a wriggling armpit or in even more uncomfortable places! However, the first thing you'd want to check, before laying out money on this new measuring instrument, is whether it truly measured temperature as did your old thermometer. In addition, you would not be best pleased if, as you watched the colour of the strip, it kept changing between one shade and the next even though you knew that the baby's temperature could not be oscillating by so much in so little time.

In the first instance you would be querying the instrument's VALIDITY – does the instrument measure what it's *supposed* to? – and in the second, its RELIABILITY – is it *consistent*? Both reliability and validity will be discussed in some detail in chapter 7 where they are applied in particular to psychological tests and scales. However, the next few chapters are about overall methods in psychological research and, at times, we will need to refer to the general meaning of these terms, and a few others.

1. Reliability. Any measure we use in life should be reliable, otherwise it's useless. You wouldn't want your car speedometer to give you different readings for the same values on different occasions. This applies to psychological measures as much as any other. Hence, questionnaires should produce the same results when re-tested on the same people at different times (so long as nothing significant has happened to them); different observers measuring aggression in children should come up with similar ratings; ratings of the intensity of imagery should be similar for similar levels of image (though for internal *mental* images it remains a challenge as to how this can ever be ascertained).

2. Validity. In addition to being consistent we should also be able to have confidence that our measuring device is measuring what it's *supposed* to measure. You wouldn't want your speedometer to be recording oil pressure or your thermometer to be actually measuring humidity. In psychology this issue is of absolutely crucial importance since it is often difficult to agree on *what* a concept 'really is' and things in psychology are not as touchable or 'get-at-able' as things in physics or chemistry. Hence, validity is the issue of whether psychological measures really *do* make some assessment of the phenomenon under study. A psychological scale may measure an unintended variable or it may measure nothing much at all of interest. A questionnaire intended to measure assertiveness, for instance, may in fact measure something more akin to selfishness. A scale intended to measure 'animism' in dreams, and which counts the number of cats and dogs you report from your dreams, may simply count the number of cats and dogs in your dreams!

The special terms *internal* and *external validity* refer not to the validity of measures but to the validity of apparent *effects* demonstrated in experimental work and similar studies, e.g. did the research study *really* show that memory could be improved using a special type of training? These topics are covered in detail in Chapter 4.

SAMPLES

Suppose you had just come back from the airport with an Indian friend who is to stay with you for a few weeks and she switches on the television. To your horror, one of the worst imaginable game shows is on and you hasten to tell her that this is not typical of British TV fare. Suppose, again, that you are measuring attitudes to trade unions and you decide to use the college canteen to select people to answer your questionnaire. Unknown to you, the men and women you select are mainly people with union positions on a training course for negotiation skills. In both these cases an unrepresentative sample has been selected. In each case our view of reality can be distorted.

POPULATIONS AND SAMPLES

One of the main aims of scientific study is to be able to generalise from examples. A psychologist might be interested in establishing some quality of all human behaviour, or in the characteristics of a certain group, such as those with strong self-confidence or those who have experienced preschool education. In each case the POPULATION is all the existing members of that group. Since the population itself will normally be too large for each individual within it to be investigated, we would normally select a SAMPLE from it to work with. A population need not consist of people. A biologist might be interested in a population consisting of all the cabbages in one field. A psychologist might be measuring participants' reaction times, in which case the population is *not the people who could be tested* but all the times that could ever be produced.

The particular population we are interested in (managers, for instance), and from which we draw our samples, is known as the TARGET POPULATION.

SAMPLING BIAS

We need our sample to be representative of the population about which we wish to generalise results. If we studied male and female driving behaviour by observing drivers in a town at 11.45 a.m. or 3.30 p.m., our sample of women drivers is likely to contain a larger than usual number driving cars with small children in the back.

This weighting of a sample with an over-representation of one particular category is known as SAMPLING BIAS. The sample tested in the college canteen was a biased sample, if we assumed we were sampling from the general public's current attitude to trade unions.

According to Ora (1965), many experimental studies may be biased simply because the sample used are volunteers. Ora found that volunteers were significantly different from the norm on the following characteristics: dependence on others, insecurity, aggressiveness, introversion, neuroticism and being influenced by others.

A further common source of sampling bias is the student. It is estimated that some 75% of American and British psychological research studies are conducted on students (Valentine, 1992), well over half of the UK participants being volunteers. Sears (1986) showed that, in 1985, 74% of participants used in studies reported in all volumes of the four most significant US research journals were undergraduate students. To call many of the USA participants 'volunteers' is somewhat misleading. In many United States institutions (but also in some UK departments these days) the psychology student is required to participate in a certain number of research projects. The 'volunteering' only concerns which particular projects. Until the mid 1970s at least, it would also be the case that a vast majority of these US students would be white and male.

PARTICIPANT VARIABLES (OR 'SUBJECT VARIABLES')

In many laboratory experiments in psychology, the nature of the individuals being tested is not considered to be an important issue. The researcher is often specifically interested in an experimental effect, in a difference between *conditions* rather than between types of person. In this case the researcher needs, in a sense, 'an average bunch of people' in each condition. If the effect works on this group of people, arbitrarily selected from the target population, then later interest might be phrased as: 'On whom does this effect *not* work?'

An experimental group searches a word list for words rhyming with 'tree' whilst counting backwards in sevens. A control group does the same thing but does not have to count. The control group performance is superior. Could this difference be caused by anything other than the distraction of counting?

I hope that one of your possible explanations was that the control group might just happen to be better with the sound of words. There may be quite a few good poets or songwriters among them. This would have occurred by chance when the people were allocated to their respective groups. If so, the study would be said to be confounded by PARTICIPANT VARIABLES. These are variations between persons acting as participants, and which are relevant to the study at hand. In *some* studies these 'people differences' form the hypothesis of the study (see 'group difference studies' – p. 82). We might need one sample of men and one of women. Or we may require samples of eight-year-old and 12-year-old children, or a group of children who watch more than 20 hours of television a week and one watching less than five hours. Within each of these populations, however, how are we to ensure that the individuals we select will be representative of their category?

REPRESENTATIVE SAMPLES

If we are investigating for such group differences, we need samples representative of the population from which they are drawn. On the other hand, if we are investigating what is thought to be a general psychological effect, even if we can only test students, we want to ensure that our samples contain as little distracting bias as possible. For a task involving the recognition of unusual words on a computer we do not want too many poor readers or computer phobics.

Group A   Group B

Figure 2.2 Participant variables might affect a study on child care attitudes

How do we ensure that the individuals we select will not introduce sampling bias? The simple truth is that a truly representative sample is an abstract ideal unachievable in practice. The practical goal we can set ourselves is to remove as much SAMPLING BIAS as possible. We need to ensure that no members of the target population are more likely than others to get into our sample. What we want, in other words is a sample into which every member of the target population has an *equal probability* of being selected and this is the case with a SIMPLE RANDOM SAMPLE (or 'truly random sample').[1]

What is meant by random?

Random is not just haphazard. The strict meaning of random sequencing is that no event is ever predictable from *any* of the preceding sequence. Haphazard human choices

---

[1] Strictly speaking a simple random sample is one example of an 'equal probability selection method' (or 'epsem' for short). The definition given here defines all epsem samples and the simple random sample has a *stricter* definition which requires that any *combination* of target population members also has an equal probability of being selected, where this is not true for the other epsem methods described in this section (see Kalton, 1983). However, the sense of 'random sample' used here is generally accepted in normal research parlance and is adequate for studying research at this level.

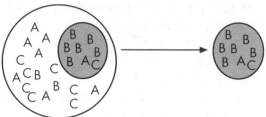

Figure 2.3   A biased sample containing too many Bs

may have some underlying pattern of which we are unaware. This is not true for the butterfly. Evolution has led it to make an endlessly random sequence of turns in flight (unless injured) which makes prediction impossible for any of its much more powerful predators.

SIMPLE RANDOM SAMPLES

Which of the following procedures do you think would produce a group of people who would form a random sample?

a. Picking anybody off the street to answer a questionnaire
    (Target population: the general public)
b. Selecting every fifth home in a street
    (Target population: the street)
c. Selecting every 10th name on the school register
    (Target population: the school)
d. Sticking a pin in a list of names
    (Target population: the names on the list)
e. Selecting slips from a hat containing the names of all Wobbly College students and asking those selected to answer your questionnaire on sexual behaviour
    (Target population: Wobbly College students)

The answer is that none of these methods would produce a simple random sample. In item (a) we may avoid people we don't like the look of, or they may avoid us. In (d) we are less likely to drop our pin at the top or bottom of the paper. In (e) the initial selection is random but our sample will end up not containing those who refuse to take part or who are absent on the day. In items (b) and (c), where SYSTEMATIC SAMPLING is being employed, the definition clearly isn't satisfied. However, suppose we *do* want a sample which is 1/10th of the population but instead of initially deciding to take every 10th person, we choose at *random* a number between one and ten, let's call it *n*, and then select every *n*th person on the list. This way, at the start, every individual *did* have an equal probability of being selected, though only ten rather than a very large number of possible samples can be drawn. This method of SYSTEMATIC RANDOM SAMPLING is another method for drawing a sample where every member has an equal chance of selection (and there are others), though it is not fully random – see footnote 1.

If no specific type of person (teachers, drug addicts, four to five-year-olds . . .) is the subject of research then, technically, a large random sample is the only sure way to acquire a fully representative sample of the population. Very few psychological research projects have ever drawn a truly random sample from a large population. A common method is to advertise in the local press; commoner still is to acquire people by personal contact, and most common of all is to use students. A very common line in student practical reports is 'a random sample was selected'. This has never been true in my experience unless the target population was the course year or college, perhaps.

What students can reasonably do is attempt to obtain as *unbiased* a sample as possible, or to make the sample fairly representative by selecting individuals from important sub-categories (some younger, some older and so on) as is described under 'stratified sampling' below. Either way, it is important to discuss this issue when interpreting results and evaluating one's research. The articles covered in the survey cited by Valentine did not exactly set a shining example. Probably 85% used inadequate sampling methods and, of these, only 5% discussed the consequent weaknesses and implications.

HOW TO SAMPLE RANDOMLY

Computer selection

The computer can generate an endless string of random numbers. These are numbers which have absolutely no relationship to each other as a sequence and which are selected with equal frequency. Given a set of names the computer would use these to select a random set.

Random number tables

Alternatively, we can use the computer to generate a set of random numbers which we record and use to do any selecting ourselves. Such a table appears as Table 1 in Appendix 2. Starting anywhere in the table and moving either vertically or horizontally a random sequence of numbers is produced. To select five people at random from a group of 50, give everyone a number from 1 to 50 and enter the table by moving through it vertically or horizontally. Select the people who hold the first five numbers which occur as you move through the table.

Manual selection

The numbered balls in a Bingo session or the numbers on a roulette wheel are selected almost randomly as are raffle tickets drawn from a barrel or hat, so long as they are all well shuffled, the selector can't see the papers and these are all folded so as not to feel any different from one another. You *can* select a sample of 20 from the college population this way, but you'd need a large box rather than the 'hat' so popular in answers to questions on random selection.

Other random procedures

Random allocation to experimental groups

In writing up reports it is possible to confuse the distinction between *random sampling* and *random allocation*. The former means having *all* your participants be representative of some target population and, as mentioned, this is very difficult to achieve, if it is possible at all. However, if you have obtained 40 participants it is a very easy task to RANDOMLY ALLOCATE these to the conditions of your experiment using tables as described previously. This can also be done by tossing a coin for the first participant, to decide in which condition they should participate, and alternating all successive allocations. Strictly speaking this would be an example of systematic random sampling. A slightly messier approach would be to toss a coin for each participant, leaving the possible problem that the last few participants will *have* to be allocated to one condition which represents the side of the coin which has turned up less frequently.

Random trial ordering and sequencing

We may wish to put 20 words in a memory list into random order. To do this give each word a random number as described before. Then put the random numbers into numerical order, keeping the word with it. The words will now be randomly ordered. If the words formed two sets, one of 10 animals and one of 10 plants, then this procedure would neatly RANDOMISE the individual trials in two conditions of an experiment designed to test difference in classification speed for the two categories of word. It would now be impossible to guess which trial was coming next, animal or plant.

ENSURING A REPRESENTATIVE SAMPLE

If a researcher, conducting a large survey (see Chapter 8), wanted to ensure that as many types of people from one town could be selected for the sample, which of the following methods of contacting people would provide the greatest access?

a. Using the telephone directory
b. Selecting from all houses
c. Using the electoral roll
d. Questioning people on the street

I hope you'll agree that the electoral roll will provide us with the widest, unbiased section of the population, though it won't include prisoners, the homeless, new residents and persons in long term psychiatric care. The telephone directory eliminates non-phone owners and the house selection eliminates those in residential institutions. The street will not contain people at work, people in hospital, and so on.

If we use near-perfect random sampling methods on the electoral roll then a representative sample should, theoretically, be the result. We should get numbers of men, women, over 60s, people with diabetes, young professionals, members of all cultural groups and so on, in proportion to their frequency of occurrence in the town as a whole.

This will only happen, though, if the sample is fairly large as I hope you'll agree, at least after reading the section on sample sizes below.

Stratified sampling

We may not be able to use the electoral roll or we may be taking too small a sample to expect representativeness by chance. In such cases we may depart from complete random sampling. We may pre-define those groups of people we want represented.

If you want a representative sample of students within your college you might decide to take business studies students, art students, catering students and so on, in proportion to their numbers. If 10% of the college population comprises art students, then 10% of your sample will be art students. If the sample is going to be 50 students then five will be chosen randomly from the art department.

The strata of the population we identify as relevant will vary according to the particular research we are conducting. If, for instance, we are researching the subject of attitudes to unemployment, we would want to ensure proportional representation of employed and unemployed, whilst on abortion we might wish to represent various religions. If the research has a local focus, then the local, not national, proportions would be relevant. In practice, with small scale research and limited samples, only a few relevant strata can be accommodated.

If we sample randomly from the various strata decided upon, and if our proportions are *entirely* accurate, then we have another method of equal probability sampling. This is because what we have done is merely ensure that, in the college example above, we do indeed select the 10% art students that we would have selected, by pure chance selection, with a large sample from a large population containing 10% art students.

Quota sampling

This method has been popular amongst market research companies and opinion poll-sters. It consists of obtaining people from strata, in proportion to their occurrence in the general population, but with the selection from each stratum being left entirely to the devices of the interviewer who would be unlikely to use pure random methods, but would just stop interviewing 18–21-year-old males, for instance, when the quota had been reached.

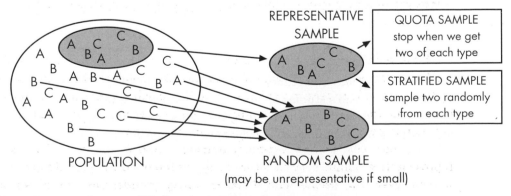

Figure 2.4 Random, stratified and quota samples

Cluster samples

It may be that, in a particular town, a certain geographical area can be fairly described as largely working class, another as largely middle class and another as largely Chinese. In this case 'clusters' (being housing blocks or whole streets) may be selected randomly from each such area and as many people as possible from within that cluster will be included in the sample. This, it is said, produces large numbers of interviewees economically because researcher travel is reduced, but of course it is open to the criticism that each cluster may not be as representative as intended.

Snowball sampling

This refers to a technique employed in the more qualitative techniques (see Chapter 11) where a lot of information is required just to get an overall view of an organisational system or to find out what is happening around a certain issue such as alcoholism. A researcher might select several key people for interview and these contacts may lead on to further important contacts to be interviewed. In the qualitative study described in Chapter 23, Kerwin *et al.* (1993) mention 'snowballing' as a method of finding more bi-racial children suiting their criteria for the study of identity.

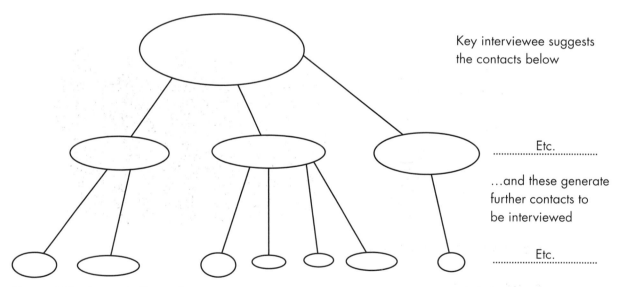

Figure 2.5 A snowball sample

Critical cases

A special case may sometimes highlight things which can be related back to most non-special cases. Freud's studies of people with neuroses led him to important insights about the unconscious workings possible in anybody's mind. Researchers interested in perceptual learning have studied people who have regained sight dramatically.

The self-selecting sample

You may recall some students who placed a ladder against a wall and observed how many men and women passed under or around it. In this investigation the sample could not be selected by the researchers. They had to rely on taking the persons who walked along the street at that time as their sample. Another example is a design in which people using a phone booth are asked if they have picked up a coin left in the booth purposely by the researchers. The *independent variable* is whether the person is touched while being asked or not. The *dependent variable* is whether people admit picking up the coin or not. *Volunteers* for experimental studies are, of course, a self-selecting sample.

The opportunity or convenience sample

Student practical work is very often carried out on other students. For that matter, so is a lot of research carried out in universities. If you use the other students in your class as a sample you are using them as an OPPORTUNITY SAMPLE. They just happen to be the people you can get hold of. The samples available in a *'natural experiment'* (see Chapter 5) are also opportunistic in nature. If there is a chance to study children about to undergo an educational innovation, the researcher who takes it has little control over the sample.

Hey you guys!

Figure 2.6 An opportunity sample?

SAMPLE SIZE

One of the most popular items in many students' armoury of prepared responses to 'Suggest modifications to this research' is 'The researcher should have tested more participants'. If a significant difference has been demonstrated between two groups this is not necessary unless (i) we have good reason to suspect sampling bias or (ii) we are replicating the study (see Chapter 4). If the research has failed to show a significant difference we may well suspect our samples of bias. But is it a good idea to simply add a lot more to our tested samples?

The argument FOR large samples

It is easier to produce a biased sample with small samples. I hope this example will make this clear. If you were to select five people from a group containing five Catholics, five Muslims, five Hindus and five Buddhists, you'd be more likely to get a religious bias in your sample than if you selected 10 people. For instance, if you select only five they could *all* be Catholics, but with 10 this isn't possible.

In general, the larger the sample the less likely it is that such sampling bias will occur.

When we turn to significance testing of differences between sets of scores we shall see that larger sample sizes increase the 'power' of statistical tests. They make it more likely that we will detect an effect if it exists. Small samples may lead us to conclude that there is no real difference between groups or conditions. Suppose there are somewhat more pro- than anti-abortionists in the country as a whole, the ratio being six to five. A small sampling strategy, producing 12 for and 10 against will not convince anyone that this difference represents reality, but a difference of 360 to 300 might. Although we haven't yet covered probability, I hope that your acquired sense of chance factors would agree with this.

Arguments AGAINST large samples

Large samples may obscure a weak design

As we shall see, experimental methods are about *control* of all variables except the ones under investigation. If we need a very large sample to demonstrate a difference between two experimental procedures then it could be that our measuring system or manipulation of conditions is faulty and we need to tighten that up, to tease out unwanted variables contributing to a lack of clear difference between scores. We need to investigate some of the 'threats to internal and external validity' described in Chapter 4.

Large samples may obscure participant variables

It may be that an effect works on some people but not others; it might work for good readers but not weak readers; taking a large sample will give us an eventual significant difference between groups (caused *only* by the good readers) but may cause us to ignore an important difference between people relevant to the effect and which would be worth further investigation.

Large samples are costly and time-consuming

Reasons such as cost should, ideally, never stand in the way of advancing science; however, realistically it is not always possible to test large samples and researchers (and psychology students) need to create good designs that don't always require this.

THE QUANTITATIVE QUALITATIVE DEBATE

Up to this point in the text, we have largely concentrated on the conventional approach to scientific study, in which the hypothetico-deductive method entails strict variable measurement and control, along with a fully structured approach to sampling. The approach, largely taken up by psychologists in the early part of the twentieth century, assumes that experimental study and data analysis always work towards the development of 'laws' which account for all relationships between variables and which can be validated by making consistently accurate predictions about further variables. A fundamental principle underlying the approach is to assert that the only meaningful phenomena which can be studied scientifically are those that can be *directly observed* and *measured quantitatively*. A term roughly covering this last principle is POSITIVISM. The approach, particularly the behaviourists' particular brand of positivism (e.g. Skinner, 1953), dominated psychological research in the middle of the twentieth century and through to the mid 1970s. Around that time, however, and partly triggered by changes in the philosophy of research in sociology, strong objections were raised against both the experimental method within psychological research and against the more generally pervasive emphasis on what is often seen as a pseudo-scientific over-emphasis on *quantification* of any psychological phenomenon in order to give it research respectability.

Not that voices had been entirely lacking in the past. There were many voices in the wilderness as it were. Lippmann (1922), universally credited with the coining of the term 'stereotype', had this to say:

> If . . . the impression takes root that these tests really measure intelligence, that they constitute some sort of last judgment on the child's capacity, that they reveal 'scientifically' his predestined ability, then it would be a thousand times better if all the intelligence testers and all their questionnaires were sunk without warning in the Sargasso Sea.

Here is a point from Bem and Looren de Jong (1997) concerning the hopes of nineteenth century European philosophers wishing to make *hermeneutics* (originally a method for making sense of classical texts in a cultural context) the fundamental method for human sciences:

> Wilhelm Dilthey (1833–1911) and others dreamt of making hermeneutics into a strong and central methodology of the human sciences. It was their intention to protect these studies against the obtrusive natural sciences and to guarantee their autonomy. The central idea is that human creations such as literary products, . . . and behaviour cannot be objectified as things disconnected from human subjects; instead they are laden with values and must be understood in the context of their time and cultural setting. (p. 23)

Quantification and qualitative experience

'Quantification' means to measure on some numerical basis, if only by frequency. Whenever we count we quantify and putting people into categories is a prelude to counting. Classifying people by astrological sign entails a crude form of quantification. So does giving a grade to an essay.

Qualitative research, by contrast, emphasises meanings, experiences (often verbally described), descriptions and so on. Raw data will be exactly what people have said (in interview or recorded conversations) or a description of what has been observed. Qualitative data can be later quantified to some extent but a 'qualitative approach' tends to value the data *as* qualitative.

It is rather like the difference between counting the shapes and colours of a pile of sweets as against feeling them, playing with them, eating them. Or counting sunsets rather than appreciating them. The difference between each one may be somehow quantifiable but such measurements will not convey the importance and the special impact of some over others.

By strict definition a variable can only be quantitative. As it changes, it takes different values. There may only be two values, for instance male and female. A positivist would argue that psychologists can only study variables because contrast and comparison can only be achieved where there is change; what changes is a variable and variables must be quantifiable.

The case against is eloquently put by Reason and Rowan (1981) in a statement on what they call 'quantophrenia':

> There is too much measurement going on. Some things which are numerically precise are not true; and some things which are not numerical are true. Orthodox research produces results which are statistically significant but humanly insignificant; in human inquiry it is much better to be deeply interesting than accurately boring. (page xv)

This is a sweeping statement, making it sound as though all research is 'humanly insignificant' if it does not used methods preferred by the authors. This is not so. Many possibly boring but accurate research exercises have told us a lot about perceptual processes, for instance, and about what prompts us to help others. However, the statement would not have been made without an excess of emphasis, within mainstream psychological research, on the objective measurement and direct observation of every concept, such that, important topics, not susceptible to this treatment, were devalued.

On the topic of 'emotion', for instance, in mainstream textbooks you will find little that relates to our everyday understanding of that term. You will find strange studies in which people are injected with drugs and put with either a happy or angry actor, and studies in which people are given false information about events they are normally oblivious of – such as their heart or breathing rate. These things are quantifiable, as are questionnaire responses, but they represent a very narrow window on the full concept of human emotion.

Varying research contexts and ideological positions

In reviewing the wide and increasing volume of relevant literature, and from informal discussion with a variety of researchers, it appears possible to identify something like a continuum of positions on the value and role of qualitative methods:

Pure quantitative position

This view rejects qualitative approaches as inherently lacking in objectivity, reliability and validity. It believes that measurement is fundamental to scientific activity and that without it, concepts and statements are meaningless.

Qualitative data may be quantified

Quantification of qualitative data is not a new procedure (see content analysis, Chapter 21). Even strict experiments must often start with a qualitative observation (e.g. 'the rat pressed the lever') and quantify it, e.g. by counting frequencies.

Quantitative findings can be augmented by or developed from qualitative data

In studies like those on bystander intervention/apathy, and especially those by Milgram (1963) on almost incredible patterns of obedience, post-experimental interviews serve to embellish the quantitative findings, adding explanatory meaning to people's otherwise sometimes incomprehensible behaviour. Data from such interviews can help direct *new* explanatory hypotheses and new research to test them. For instance, in bystander apathy studies, information from post-experimental interviews may prompt us to try new studies where we make the participant bystander more aware of the social value of helping others.

An early example of qualitative prompting of new quantitative research occurred when Jahoda-Lazarsfeld and Zeisl (1932) studied the effects of long-term unemployment in Austria in the 1930s. A small boy, in casual conversation with a research worker, expressed the wish to become an Indian tribal chief but added 'I'm afraid it will be hard to get the job'. The investigators developed and tested quantitatively the hypothesis that parental unemployment has a limiting effect on children's fantasies. Children of unemployed parents mentioned significantly less expensive items in their Christmas present wishes, compared with children of employed parents. (We assume, of course, that the parental groups were matched for social class!)

Qualitative and quantitative methods – different horses for different courses

If you're interested in the accuracy of human perception in detecting colour changes, or in our ability to process incoming sensory information at certain rates, then it seems reasonable to conduct highly controlled experimental investigations using a strong degree of accurate quantification. If your area is psychology applied to social work practice, awareness changes in ageing, or the experience of mourning, you are very likely to find that qualitative methods are appropriate to your work. In contrast to the position above, seeing qualitative work as important but always subsidiary to final quantitative research, the studies of Reicher and Emler (1986) used an initial quantitative survey to identify appropriate groups who were then taken through intensive qualitative interviews.

Pure qualitative position

There is no *one* qualitative position and this stance of using *only* qualitative methods, as a sort of new and radical dogma as well as a chosen procedure, is common to several 'splinter' movements in existence at the present time. Along with advocacy of qualitative methods alone, there tends to be an accompanying ideological position which absolutely rejects positivism and hypothetico-deductive approaches on theoretically argued grounds as being damaging to the proper understanding of human action. It can partly be held on the basis that resort to 'enemy weapons' leads to corruption. Feminist researchers, in particular, have argued that positivism and the hypothetico-deductive method are inherently sexist – 'masculinist' or 'masculine science' – promoting a power-subject relationship, unhealthy distancing from the object of study and a consequently distorted view of one version of reality (Ussher, 1992; Tavris, 1993). We shall investigate these arguments further in Chapter 9.

Relative values of quantitative and qualitative studies

In general, methods which are tighter and more rigorous give rise to more reliable and *internally valid* data (see Chapter 4), replicable effects and a claim to greater objectivity. However, results are open to the criticism of giving narrow, unrealistic information using measures which trap only a tiny portion of the concept originally under study. More qualitative enquiries, with looser controls and conducted in more natural, everyday circumstances give richer results and more realistic information. Advocates feel, therefore, that they are more likely to reflect human thought and action in a natural, cultural context. However, they have also had to defend a vigorous argument that qualitative data are usually less replicable and inevitably more subjectively organised than are quantitative data.

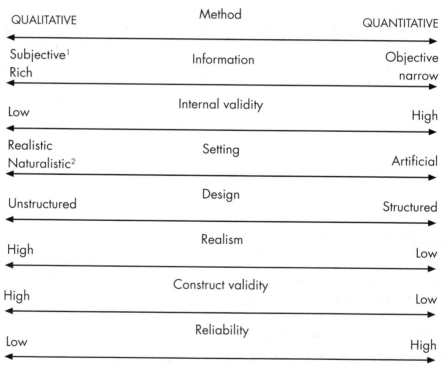

Figure 2.7 Variations in structure and control – qualitative and quantitative studies

1. Some qualitative proponents argue strongly that their methods do *not* necessarily invoke greater subjectivity at all. Numbers can be used subjectively, as when 'trained raters' use a rating scale to 'code' observed behaviour. A descriptive account of an abused person's experience can be written objectively and can be checked with them for accuracy and true reflection. A person's own, major reasons for objecting to abortion could be counted as more objective data than a number which places them at five on a zero to 30 abortion attitude scale.
2. Naturalistic studies (those carried out in natural surroundings) may use fully quantified data gathering procedures. Qualitative studies, however, will almost always tend to be naturalistic.

Loosely controlled methods will produce unpredictable amounts and types of information which the researcher has to sift, organise and select for importance but such methods leave more room for the researcher to manoeuvre in questioning the participants and in deciding what observations are more worthwhile, thus fostering more natural, less stilted human interaction with more realistic results. The price is a potential for greater individual bias (but this is not automatically excluded from the most 'scientific' studies) and less comparability across similar studies.

Studies can vary in their construction and control across all the dimensions shown in Figure 2.7. The qualitative-quantitative dimension tends to correlate with the other dimensions as shown, and it is worth bearing these in mind as we progress through the research methods commonly in use in psychological investigation today. Qualitative approaches are integrated into the chapters on observation and on asking questions. Others are covered in Chapter 9 and we shall return to this debate in some depth there. Now we are about to launch into the rigours of the experimental method, the quintessential method of the conventional paradigm. The reader should be aware however, that, although psychology's mainstream cannot be grasped and comprehended without a thorough knowledge of this conventional method, other approaches exist or are emerging and their principles will also need to be absorbed by the contemporary psychology student. For greater depth on these issues, the reader might like to consult Gross (1996), Valentine (1992) or Bem and Looren de Jong (1997).

Glossary

Phenomenon which is assumed to exist but is (as yet) unconfirmed; it is assumed to be responsible for effects or variations already observed; stays as a possible explanation of effects while evidence continues to support it	_____ _____	hypothetical construct
Definition of variable in terms of the exact steps taken in measurement of the variable	_____ _____	operational definition
All possible members of group from which a sample is taken	_____	population
Methodological belief that description of the world's phenomena, including human experience and social behaviour, is reducible to observable facts (at the most extreme, 'sense-data') and the mathematical relationships between them	_____	positivism

Description		Answer
Methodological stance gathering qualitative data and which usually holds that information about human events and experience, if reduced to numerical form, loses most of its important meaning and value for research and understanding	_____ _____	qualitative approach
Information gathered which is not in numerical form	_____ _____	qualitative data
Information about a phenomenon in numerical form which consists of measurement or frequency values	_____ ____	quantitative data
Number which has absolutely no relationship with the other numbers in its set	_____ _____	random number
Put people into different conditions of an experiment on a random basis	_____ _____	randomly allocate
Put various trials of an experiment into an unbiased sequence, where prediction is impossible	_____	randomise
Tendency to treat abstract concepts as real entities	_____	reification
Extent to which findings or measures can be repeated with similar results; consistency of measures	_____	reliability
Group selected from population for an investigation	_____	**Sample**
Sample in which members of a sub-group of the target population are over or under-represented	_____	biased
Sample selected from specific area as being representative of a population	_____	cluster
Sample selected because they are easily available for testing	_____	opportunity
Sample selected so that specified groups will appear in numbers proportional to their size in the target population; non-random because selection ceases when enough of specific sub-group has been found	_____	quota
Sample selected in which every member of the target population has an equal chance of being selected (and all possible samples can be drawn – see footnote 1)	_____	(simple) random

Sample selected so that specified groups will appear in numbers proportional to their size in the target population	_____	representative
Sampling selected for study on the basis of their own action in arriving at the sampling point	_____ – _____	self-selecting
Sample selected so that specified groups will appear in numbers proportional to their size in the target population; within each sub-group cases are selected on a random basis	_____	stratified
Sample selected by taking every nth case from a list of the target population; 'random' if starting point for n is selected at random	_____	systematic (random)
Systematic tendency towards over- or under-representation of some categories in a sample	_____ _____	sampling bias (or selection bias)
Extent to which instruments measure what they were intended to measure; also, extent to which a research effect can be trusted as real or is not 'contaminated' or confounded	_____	validity
Phenomenon which varies and can be given specific quantitative or categorical values	_____	variable

Exercises

1. What could be an operational definition of: 'noise', 'span of attention', 'smile', 'frustration' in the following loosely worded hypotheses?

   a. Noise affects efficiency of work
   b. Time of day affects span of attention
   c. Smiles given tend to produce smiles in return
   d. Aggression can be the result of frustration

2. A friend says 'My cat hates the Spice Girls' music. Every time I put on Spice World she rushes out of the house.' Would you say this measure of the cat's attitude to the Spice Girls' music was reliable, valid, both or neither?

3. The aim of a particular investigation is to compare the attitudes of working-class and middle-class mothers to discipline in child rearing. What factors should be taken into account in selecting two comparable samples (apart from social class)?

4   A psychologist advertises in the university bulletin for students willing to participate in an experiment concerning the effects of alcohol consumption on appetite. For what reasons might the sample gathered not be a random selection of students?

5   A simple random sample of business studies students in the county of Suffex could be drawn by which one of these methods?

   a. Selecting one college at random and using all the business studies students within it.
   b. Group all business studies students within each college by surname initial (A, B, . . . Z). Select one person at random from each initial group in each college.
   c. Put the names of all business studies students at all colleges into a very large hat, shake and draw out names without looking.

6   A researcher wishes to survey young people's attitudes to law and order. Interviewers complete questionnaires with sixth formers who volunteer from the schools which agree to be included in the study. Families are also selected at random from the local telephone directory. Young people are also questioned at the local youth club. Discuss several ways in which the sample for the complete study may be biased.

7   Give examples of human experiences which might be very difficult to quantify in any useful or meaningful way. Then suggest ways in which measurement *might* be attempted.

Answers

1   Examples:

   a. *Noise*: Use specific audio recording of mechanical noise or use tones measured at differing decibel levels.
   b. *Attention span*: Measured by number of 'blips' noticed on a radar-like screen.
   c. *Smile*: As recognised by rater who doesn't know research aim and lasting longer than one second.
   d. *Frustration:* Give participants very difficult puzzles to solve whilst rewarding them heavily for speed of solution

2   A reliable measure but does it assess the cat's liking of the Spice Girls' music rather than its attitude to pop in general or even to any kind of music or sudden sound?

3   E.g. area, number of children, age, etc.

4   Only volunteers; must read bulletin; no teetotallers.

5   Only *c.*

6   The sixth-formers are volunteers. Only schools which agreed to the study can be sampled from. Those without telephones cannot be included. Those who use the youth club are more likely to be selected.

7   E.g., love; but we could perhaps devise a questionnaire on non-romantic love using items which ask about efforts made to keep in touch, what would be sacrificed to see the other person and so on. E.g., experience of prejudice; but we could ask victims to keep a diary of incidents and to tick a checklist of feelings they had in response to incidents.

3

Experimental and non-experimental methods in psychology

This chapter introduces the general division of research into *experimental*, *quasi-experimental* and *non-experimental designs*.

- Simple experimental designs introduced and compared are: *independent samples, repeated measures, matched pairs* and *single participant*. Associated design problems include: *order effects, participant variables, allocation to conditions, problems with matching*.
- A *true experiment* attempts to isolate cause and effect and occurs when an independent variable is manipulated and all other salient variables are controlled, including the random allocation of participants to conditions.
- A major task in experiments is to avoid *confounding* which can occur through lack of control in: variables associated with the independent variable, *expectancies, participant reactivity, demand characteristics, procedures, sampling and selection, history effects*.
- *Quasi-experiments* occur when participants are not allocated by the experimenter into conditions of the manipulated independent variable (a non-equivalent groups design) or where the researcher does not control the independent variable. The latter is often termed a *natural experiment*. A further design described is that of the *time series*.
- Non-experiments investigate variables which exist among people irrespective of any researcher intervention, often by correlation of variables or by the investigation of *group differences*.
- Any of these studies may be used to eliminate hypotheses and therefore support theories.

WHAT IS A TRUE EXPERIMENT?

I was told just recently that if you put already yellow tomatoes into a box, with a banana that has brown spots on it (I kid you not!) the tomatoes will ripen up more quickly than if they are left alone. I do apologise to the reader who becomes weary of the horticultural and practical examples in this book but, in keeping with the philosophy outlined at the start, I do believe people new to psychology have nevertheless already picked up, from everyday events, the basic elements of research and statistics, including the logic of the 'true experiment'. It is also useful to give practical, physical examples because it is otherwise hard, sometimes, to see where the special language of experimental research in psychology is coming from. So, let's press ahead with a problem-solving exercise in order to tease out what are the fundamental features of a true experiment.

Suppose you wished to test out the tomato ripening hypothesis. How might you organise an experiment to show unambiguously that putting a brown-spotted banana into a boxful of yellow tomatoes speeds up their ripening?

I say 'unambiguously' because there are faulty approaches we could use. For instance, we might simply compare the ripening of the boxed tomatoes with those left on the tomato bush. The trouble here is that it could be the fact of bringing the tomatoes into the house which caused the ripening, rather than the variable of interest – the spotted banana. I hope you devised something like the following:

- take a group of yellow tomatoes
- divide them *randomly* into two identical boxes
- put a spotted banana in one of the boxes
- place and keep the boxes in identical conditions
- after a certain period count how many red tomatoes are in each box

In general, without wanting to treat people at the same level as tomatoes, this is also the logic of the psychology experiment.

THE REASON FOR EXPERIMENTS – ISOLATING CAUSE AND EFFECT

If we assume that the identification of *cause* and *effect* relationships is the fundamental aim of a science, then the experimental method is the strongest member of the researcher's toolbox. The logic of the experiment is really quite simple and is what we often follow in everyday life in order to isolate causes. For example, if your television starts to suffer from interference, it makes sense to turn off each electric appliance in the house, keeping all the others on, until the interference stops, in order to identify the offending item. Hence, the basis of a TRUE EXPERIMENT is that *one variable is manipulated while all others are held constant.*

If only one variable is altered then any *subsequent* changes in another variable under observation must be caused by the manipulated variable. For instance, we manipulate only the presence or absence of a spotted banana, keep everything else the same, and observe whether there is a subsequent change in the pace of ripening. Johnston and Davey (1997) (see Chapter 1) varied only the content of news stories (positive, neutral, negative) and observed the effect on worry. Cialdini *et al.* (also in Chapter 1) varied the number of pieces of litter on the ground and noted any change in rate of litter dropping.

INDEPENDENT VARIABLE AND DEPENDENT VARIABLE

In the example from Johnston and Davey, decide which of the two following statements makes sense and which does not:

1. The type of news stories seen depends upon the participants' amount of worry.
2. The participants' level of worry depends upon the type of news stories seen.

I hope you'll agree that the first makes no sense in this experiment, and the second is what the experiment aimed to demonstrate. Two variables are involved in this experiment and one is traditionally known as the INDEPENDENT VARIABLE while the other is known as the DEPENDENT VARIABLE.

> Could you decide now which variable (*amount of worry* or *type of news stories*) would be called the dependent variable?

I hope you agree that, since the amount of worry *depends* on the type of news stories, it makes sense to call the consequent worry change the *dependent variable*. Changes in this variable *depend on* changes in the *independent variable* (the news stories). The essential aim of an experiment is to demonstrate an unambiguous 'causal link' between these two variables. Suppose, through natural observation, we had merely noted a relationship between people's level of worry and the type of news stories they choose to view – a form of *correlational* design which we shall discuss later. Here, we would not be able to determine between two alternative explanations – news items might determine worry but so might worry determine type of news story tuned into. So, in an experiment we *control* the cause and *observe* the effect – see Figure 3.1.

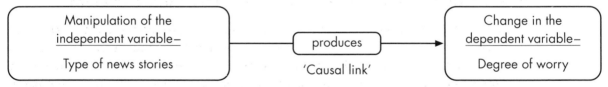

Figure 3.1   The causal link between independent and dependent variable in an experiment

> Try now to identify the independent variable and dependent variable in the Cialdini *et al.* example and in the research hypotheses given on p. 29. In each case ask 'What did the experimenter vary?' (often these are the conditions of the experiment) and 'What did they measure in each participant?' or 'What measure was expected to change as a result?'

Hopefully you came up with the following answers:

	Independent variable	**Dependent variable**
(Cialdini et al)	Amount of litter already on ground	Number of dropped leaflets
Ex. 1, page 29	Degree of physical punishment	Amount of aggression
Ex. 2, page 29	Degree of stress at work	Amount of memory deterioration
Ex. 3, page 29	Level of stimulation	Stage of language development
Ex. 4, page 29	Trustworthy or untrustworthy person	Comply or not
Ex. 5, page 29	Participants told baby is male or female	'Masculinity' of description

THE STRENGTH OF THE EXPERIMENT (1) – IMPROVING ON 'BAD' EXPERIMENTS

Just think of an alternative situation to the tomato experiment. Suppose you visit the friend who recommends the banana strategy and who shows you a wooden box 'she created earlier', lying near the central heating boiler. Sure enough, along with a brown spotted banana, the tomatoes inside are coming up nice and red. Of course, you ask for a comparison and she then shows you another, plastic box lying on the cool windowsill and containing mostly green tomatoes. 'These were picked at the same time. I haven't put a banana in and just look at the difference.' 'Were the [comparison] tomatoes picked from the same spot in the garden?', you ask. 'More or less', she says. Her children (whom you notice peering into the banana box to check the state of play) pipe up, 'No. These came from near the garage.' You tentatively suggest that the material from which the box is constructed, the place of growth, the children's interference with the banana box and the present position of the boxes might all be factors contributing to a different ripening pace. 'Ever since you started teaching psychology,' she says, 'you've become a bit of a bore! I just *know* this works.'

Hmm! Time for a change of subject and a secret resolution to conduct a truly scientific experiment at a later date (but not, perhaps, to let your friend know the results if they're unfavourable to the banana strategy).

Eliminating alternative explanations – confounding variables

What you were querying of course were *alternative explanations* for the apparent banana effect. One of the most valuable habits the psychology student can acquire is to *always* ask, when presented with a research finding (X causes Y) which supports a particular theory, 'Ah, but could some *other* variable have caused Y?' This is not being 'negative' or pedantic. It is a vital procedure for checking that we do not accept pseudo-scientific claims and theories and for stimulating further research leading to clearer knowledge about an area of interest. Simply put, it is the way we can *approach* truth out of speculation.

In the tomato example, the difference between the two boxes, the difference in position, the different attention and lid opening, and the fact that the tomatoes came from different areas of the garden might all make a difference to the rate of ripening. If you only had available your friend's 'experimental' evidence it would be hard to eliminate these possible alternative explanations. Each of these variables could CONFOUND results and lead you to conclude that the banana had caused ripening, whereas some other variable was in fact responsible.

The role of control in experiments

The true experiment gives us the opportunity to eliminate alternative explanations by *controlling* the action of possible CONFOUNDING VARIABLES – these are differences between conditions, other than the independent variable, that could account for observed differences. We should ensure that everything is as similar as possible for both groups of tomatoes.

Let's leave the horticulture behind for a while and apply the same form of reasoning to the psychology experiment. The experiment described below could be termed an 'old chestnut' of psychology practicals because it 'works'; that is, it produces a significant difference between conditions virtually every time it is run, with the 'imagery' group consistently doing better on recall.

Suppose we ask one group of participants to use mental imagery to learn a list of words which we present to them one at a time on a computer screen. This is done by instructing them to form a striking image of each item and to link it to the next item in some bizarre fashion – for instance 'wheel' is linked to 'plane' by imaging a candy striped plane flying through the wheel. A second group is simply asked to learn the list of words.

List the procedures you would use to ensure that a 'fair' experiment was run demonstrating unambiguously the effects of the imagery strategy on recall.

Let's hope you got the main elements of the following:

- find a group of willing volunteers (we *know* these can't be a truly random sample of 'the population' – see Chapter 2)
- divide the participants *randomly* into two equal sized groups
- give one group the instructions to use mental imagery on each item and the other group instructions simply to read the list and learn it
- make all testing conditions identical
- after presenting the list of words, ask each participant to attempt recall of as many words as possible under identical conditions. Investigate the difference between overall recall scores from both groups.

This procedure is very similar to that for the tomatoes and its general design is shown in Figure 3.2. Of course, it is very difficult to ensure, in most experiments, that truly *all* possible sources of influence on the dependent variable have been eliminated or held constant, apart from the manipulation of the independent variable. However, the point of the experiment is that we have hold of the reins. If someone comes up with a critical but uncontrolled variable in our design, we can attempt to build control of that variable into a new version of the experiment. Some practical examples of this are given further on, under the heading 'Tackling confounding'. The element of variable control then permits us to *refine* experimental studies and to consequently weaken alternative explanations of causes and effects.

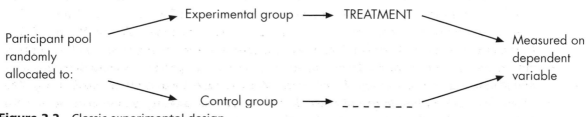

Figure 3.2 Classic experimental design

Control groups

One of the simplest forms of control to eliminate alternative explanations is the employ-ment of a CONTROL GROUP. These are participants who do not receive the 'treatment' thought to produce change in the dependent variable. This would be the group told only to read and learn the list in the imagery experiment just described. They serve the same purpose as did the box of tomatoes with no banana. They are our *baseline comparison measure* against which we can compare the performance of the experimental (or 'treat-ment') group in order to see whether, with the treatment, they have done much better than they would have done without.

Placebo groups

In medical trials of new drug treatments, one group of patients is often given an inert substance so that the patients *think* they have had new treatment (they initially *agree* to the possibility of being in this condition *and* to not knowing which group they are actually in). This is because the researchers want to eliminate an alternative explanation that patients might have improved because of the psychological *expectations* of improvement, or the hope given by the new approach. Since we are investigating psychological states it is even more important that psychological researchers rule out the possibility of unwanted psychological expectations being the causal variable responsible for any observed changes in experiments. Very often one group of participants is given a task to do during the same period as another group receives the experimental treatment, while a third acts as a control group and does nothing at all. The neutral news bulletin group in the Johnston and Davey (1997) experiment described in Chapter 1 served as a form of PLACEBO GROUP, whereas a control group in this study would have simply been measured before and after the video period but would have seen no bulletin at all.

THE STRENGTH OF THE EXPERIMENT (2) – ELIMINATING CAUSAL DIRECTIONS

Suppose experiments were outlawed and that we could only gather information from making *observations* about what people already do. Such designs are often called 'correla-tional' (see below) since we can mostly only demonstrate what *relates* to what rather than what *causes* what. For instance, we might ask people whether they use mental imagery when they attempt to memorise lists of words (e.g. shopping lists) and then find that those who say they do perform better than people who don't. I said above that you should always query, 'Ah but could something else have caused Y?'. On these occasions you should *also* ask, *if it makes sense*, 'Ah but, could Y have caused X?' For instance, in a study by Kraut *et al.* (1998) and described in the next chapter, a conclusion was that increased Internet use (X) caused increased levels of depression (Y). An alternative inter-pretation ('Y causes X') is that depressed people are more likely to use the Internet. For the non-experimental memory findings just described, we can't rule out the possibility that being good at memory is a factor causing people to start using imagery. The imagery may not actually help at all. Hence, along with looking for possible confounding variables one should also always query the *direction* of an apparent cause-effect relationship. *The experiment can eliminate one of these directions.* In the imagery experiment, it is plain daft to argue that the better recall of words could have *caused* people to use imagery. Use

Table 3.1 Strengths and weaknesses of experimental designs

The strength of experiments	Criticisms of experiments
Isolates cause and effect	Reactivity effects if participants *know* they are in an experiment; possible ethical problems if not
Can control many extraneous influences so that validity is high and alternative explanations of events are eliminated	Can produce quite artificial conditions and measures of variables
Alternative explanations of effects can be investigated/eliminated in extensions of the original paradigm because . . .	Participants' contribution completely pre-scribed. No unique view from participants is possible
Experiments should be very easy to replicate	Can invest results with false 'scientific' credibility. Limits the kind of phenomena that can be investigated

of imagery was the prior variable. However, we would need to make sure that our two groups were equivalent on memory ability before the experiment.

We can't always do experiments. Often they are quite inappropriate or they are simply unethical. Non-experimental methods, producing correlational or qualitative data, are an extremely important and common source of information in psychological research and we shall be looking at the appropriate methods in Chapters 5 to 8.

SIMPLE EXPERIMENTAL DESIGNS

Imagine this conversation between two psychology students with the need to start a psychology practical project at the back of their minds:

Emma: It really infuriates me. I drive really smoothly on my own, completely in control; then Susie gets in and I do stupid things like crash gears and stall.

Mel: Yeah?

Emma: Right! I'm sure people perform worse when someone important's watching them.

Mel: Well I'm not. I play pool better when Robert's around.

Emma: Perhaps it depends on what you're like. Perhaps extraverteds (or whatever you call 'em) do better and intrawhatsits do worse. I wonder if people in the middle aren't affected.

Let's suppose Emma decides to check out her first hypothesis. It predicts that people perform sensori-motor tasks worse in the presence of an (important) audience. She sets up a laboratory experiment. She needs to operationalise. She needs:

- a sensori-motor task
- an audience
- a measure of performance

For the performance measure, people could be asked to move a metal ring along one of those wiggly wire contraptions you see at village fêtes. If they touch the wire a buzzer sounds and an error is recorded. The dependent variable is operationally defined then, as the number of errors recorded, and this gives a neatly quantified measure of improvement in performance – fewer errors.

INDEPENDENT SAMPLES DESIGN

Emma sets up the equipment and gets five of her class colleagues to observe while, one at a time, 13 students, mainly in psychology, complete the task of moving the wire from 'start' to 'home'. Errors are recorded by an electronic counter attached to the wire and loop. She just about has time to test the students before she has to pack up quickly in order not to miss a class. When she sets the equipment up the following day in a quiet room, she finds and tests 12 students, mainly from a watch repair technician training course. Each student performs the task alone, the experimenter only re-entering the room when the participant calls out that they have finished. In fact, Emma observed her *control group* participants through a one-way mirror in order to ensure that no one cheated. She informed them of this later and no one objected. Emma finds that errors in the audience condition are much higher than in the alone condition. Emma here is conducting what is known as an INDEPENDENT SAMPLES design experiment. This title says just what it means. An entirely different group of people take each condition of the independent variable (there could be three conditions or even more), as in the 'classic' experimental design outlined in Figure 3.2.

> Just to check, what *is* the independent variable in the experiment described above?

Well, the recommendation early in this chapter was to look for the conditions which were varied. In this case then, the independent variable must be the presence or not of an audience.

Examples of independent samples designs would be:

1. Beltramini (1992) investigated the effect of randomly allocating a company's business customers into those who would receive a gift and those who would not (IV). The gift increased positive perception (one DV) of the company but not intention to contact it again (the other DV)!
2. The Johnston and Davey (1997) experiment described in Chapter 1 and returned to above.

This design also comes with the titles: INDEPENDENT GROUPS, INDEPENDENT SUBJECTS and BETWEEN GROUPS. This last title is commonly used when the statistical analysis is ANOVA (see Chapter 17).

We've proved it, Mel!

Suppose Emma reports the result to Mel. She is unimpressed. She says 'Well, the way you did it, I'm not really surprised you got higher errors in the audience condition.' What is she on about? What has she spotted? What might be responsible for poorer performances in front of an audience?

> What might be responsible for the difference between conditions? What might cause one group to do worse, other than the fact that they performed in front of an audience? Also list any other disadvantages you can see in this design.

Mel says, 'Who did the experiment?' Emma tells her. She smirks, 'Ah! So watch repairers — people well-trained in control of their fine movements — performed in the 'alone' condition, huh?' Could it not be this *sampling bias* that caused them to produce fewer errors, rather than the fact they didn't have an observing audience?

Participant variables

Mel is referring to the variations among people which may be unevenly spread across our two groups, especially the watch repair skill. *Confounding* (discussed more fully below) from PARTICIPANT VARIABLES can be a major weakness of independent samples designs. Differences found might *not* be caused by the independent variable at all, but may be the result of this unevenly spread skill difference. A *possible* effect of an audience may be *confounded by* these participant differences.

Dealing with participant variables

In an independent samples design it would always be difficult to rule out participant variables as a possible source of variation between the groups in our study, but there are certain steps we can take to reduce the likelihood that they were the cause of differences found.

Random allocation of participants to conditions

This follows the classic line of experimental design already discussed and is probably the best move. In biology, a researcher would randomly split a sample of beans and subject one sample to the treatment and use the rest as a 'control group'. In psychology, the same line is followed. When results are in, if the independent variable really has no effect, then differences between the two samples are simply the result of random variation among people and other non-systematic variables.

Here, of course, Mel has a point. Even student practicals should avoid obvious non-random differences between two samples of participants. Notice that in the Beltramini study mentioned above, customers were allocated at random to the receiving gifts or control group, as were the participants in Ganster's 1982 field experiment and Friedrich and Stein's 1973 study on children's learning of pro-social behaviour – see Chapter 4.

Pre-test of participants

In a more elaborate solution, we can show that both groups were similar in relevant performance *before* the experimental conditions were applied. For instance, Emma could PRE-TEST her two groups on the wiggly wire task. *Both* groups would be tested first in the quiet room. Here their scores should not differ. One group would then go on to the audience condition while the other would repeat the quiet room condition. The dependent variable then becomes, not the error score in the experimental trials, but the *difference* between the pre-test errors and those produced in the experimental trial. For the quiet room condition differences should be minimal, whereas for the audience group noticeable differences should be found.

Representative allocation

Pre-testing is time-consuming and will not cover all possibilities of confounding through participant variables. Both groups might score the same in the pre-test but the group given the audience condition may contain a greater number of people who are particularly inhibited with public performance. What appears to be a general effect may really only be an effect for certain sorts of people. If we knew this we could have *divided* these people between the two conditions, making our samples equally representative for this variable.

Hence we can make our two groups equally representative on several variables. However, we must decide intuitively, given the nature of the research topic and aims, which variables are going to be the most important to balance for. Mel thinks attention should have been paid to skills associated with watch repair. Within each category chosen as relevant (male, female, watch repairer etc.), allocation of *half* that category to one condition and half to the other would be performed on as random a basis as possible.

REPEATED MEASURES DESIGN

Emma has a bright idea. If differences between two samples, one in each condition, are such a problem why not have the *same* people do *both* conditions? That way, all differences between participants become irrelevant and we are really testing whether an audience has an effect on each *individual's* performance, compared with when they were alone. This is why the repeated measures design which we are about to investigate is sometimes called a WITHIN SUBJECTS design, since we are looking at differences *within* each participant (or 'subject'). The more usual term REPEATED MEASURES refers to the fact that the same measure[1] is repeated on people but under the various conditions of the independent variable. If the participants are the same for both conditions, and all other variables are controlled, any differences, we assume (though we could be wrong), must be the effect of the change in the independent variable.

It worked again Mel!

Suppose Emma runs the experiment as a repeated measures design and has people perform first in front of an audience, then alone. Again audience errors are far greater than errors made when alone. Doubting Mel again has a wry, patronising smile and says, 'Well, I'm not really surprised considering the way you did it this time. Of course performance was better in the second condition.'

> What might Mel have seen this time? What could explain these differences apart from the independent variable of being alone or having an audience? What has not been controlled?

Order effects

You probably realised that there is another possible *confounding* variable at work here. People might improve on the second condition simply because they've had some practice

[1] It is important to note that exactly the same measure is taken under two different conditions of the independent variable. In studies where, for instance, participants take a neuroticism and then an extroversion test we are *not* repeating measures and all we can do with the subsequent data is to *correlate* the pairs of scores (see Chapter 15). Such a study is in no way an 'experiment', nor even a quasi-experiment (see below).

(and they may be less anxious about learning a new task). If they had performed worse in the second condition, this might have been through becoming disheartened by failure, through boredom or through fatigue.

Effects from the *order* in which people participate in conditions are known as ORDER EFFECTS. Their existence is one of the major disadvantages of a repeated measures design.

> Can you make a list now of some solutions to the problem of order effects? How can a researcher design an experiment which avoids the contamination of order effects?

Dealing with order effects

1 Counterbalancing

If participants' performances in the alone condition might have been improved because of their prior experience in the audience condition, it makes sense to have half of them perform alone first. This is known as COUNTERBALANCING the conditions. Calling the conditions A and B, one group does the AB order while the other group does the BA order.

Would this in fact *eliminate* the order effect? Well, no it wouldn't. If practice *does* improve performance, and so long as it does not swamp any other effects, then it will produce improvements *for most participants*, but this would lead to a little improvement in the 'alone' condition for one group and a little improvement in the 'audience' condition for the other group. Thus, the improvements would cancel each other out, leaving only the effect we are interested in as a noticeable difference between the two groups.

Warning for tests and exams! It is easy to get fooled into thinking that, because the design involves splitting participants into two groups, we have an independent samples design. The splitting is *solely* for the purpose of counterbalancing. The question you need to ask yourself is, after the experiment is completed, did each participant serve in all conditions? If yes, we have a repeated measures design.

Asymmetrical (or 'non-symmetrical') order effects

This neat arrangement of counterbalancing may be upset though, if the practice effect occurring in the AB order is not equivalent to that produced in the BA order. For instance, suppose that in the alone condition it is possible to concentrate on improvement and that this transfers to the audience condition. However, when the audience is present in the first condition, perhaps people concentrate so much on coping with this distraction that no carry-over effect from learning the task is possible, even though performance is as good as in the alone condition. In this example, counter-balancing would lose its error balancing effect and we might wrongly conclude that an audience *facilitates* performance (because of the overall reduction in errors in the audience condition) when, in fact, it has no effect. If we did not inspect our results thoroughly we might only see the *overall* higher error rate in the alone condition, rather than change in one order group and not in the other.

2 Complex counterbalancing
a) ABBA

(Not an ageing Swedish pop group!) To balance even asymmetrical order effects (to some extent at least), all participants take conditions in the order ABBA. Their score in A is taken as the mean of the two A conditions and likewise for B.

b) Multi-condition designs

If an experiment has three conditions we might divide participants into six groups and have them take part in the following orders of condition:

ABC   ACB   BAC

BCA   CAB   CBA

3 Randomisation of condition order

Some experiments involve quite a number of conditions. For instance, a sensori-motor task may be performed under six different lighting conditions. Each participant would be given the conditions in a different random order. This should dissipate any order effects still further.

4 Randomisation of stimulus items

Suppose we want to see whether concrete words are easier to recall than abstract words. Instead of giving the same group of people a list of concrete words to learn and recall, then a list of abstract words, we can give them just one list with concrete and abstract words *randomly mixed together*. This approach *does* eliminate order effects since here participants do not complete one condition then the other. Note also that this could be a way to mix even three conditions together but either the list gets rather long or we have less of each item in the list. Typically this is done for experiments on 'levels of processing' where, on each trial, participants have to respond 'True' or 'False' to a statement and a word item, e.g.

i. has **four letters** or

ii. rhymes with **boat** or

iii. fits in the sentence **'John was butted by a _____'**

The word which then follows might be 'goat' which, in trial iii above, should produce the response 'True'. Later, participants are asked to attempt recognition of all the single words they have seen and the hypothesis is tested that they should recall more of the items which they have processed to a 'deeper' level, level iii being seen as deepest.

5 Elapsed time

We can leave enough time between conditions for any learning or fatigue effects to dissipate.

6 Using another design

We may have to give up the idea of using the same group for each condition. We could move to an 'independent samples design', but, since this design has important disadvantages, we might try to resist this more drastic solution to the problem of order effect.

Comparison of repeated measures and independent samples designs

Disadvantage of repeated measures – a strength of independent samples

- Repeated measures design has the problem of possible order effects, described above, which the independent samples design avoids
- We can lose participants between conditions of a repeated measures design whereas independent samples participants are just tested the one time
- The aim of the experimental research may become obvious to the participant who

takes both conditions and this makes 'pleasing the experimenter' (see below) or screwing up the results more possible

- In a repeated measures design we may have to wait until practice effects have worn off and the participant is ready for another test, whereas with independent samples we can run the two conditions simultaneously.

- If each participant experiences both conditions of, say, a memory experiment using word lists, we have to use a different list in each condition. This creates the problem of choosing words for each list which are equivalent. It is possible to obtain lists which give the frequency of occurrence of words in the written English language, obtained through literature surveys.

Disadvantage of independent samples – a strength of repeated measures

- The major problem is that of non-equivalence of samples, described above. Variation can occur because of *participant variables*.

- With repeated measures we obtain 10 scores in each condition using just 10 participants, whereas with independent samples we'd need double that number. Participants can be hard to find and individual testing takes time.

- If there is too great a difference between the statistical *variances* of two *independent* groups (dealt with in Chapter 10), we may *not* be able to proceed with a *t* test – a powerful statistical test appropriate to this design (see Chapter 14).

When not to use a repeated measures design

1. When order effects cannot be eliminated or are *asymmetrical*.

2. Often, people must be naïve for each condition. In VIGNETTE studies, for example, a person is shown one of two alternatives, with all other material the same. For instance, people may be asked to rate an article having been told that either a teacher or a student is the author. A baby is presented as either a boy or a girl and people are asked to describe it. Lewis *et al.* (1990) sent vignettes which varied the sex and race of a fictitious client to 139 psychiatrists. When the client was African-Caribbean the following differences in ratings occurred compared with when the client was supposedly white: the illness was of a shorter duration; fewer drugs were required; the client was potentially more violent; and criminal proceedings were more appropriate. In these sorts of study, obviously the same participants cannot be used in both conditions, since then the research aim would be transparent to participants. When discussing such studies, conducted as class practicals, people often think from the vantage point of the experimenter. But it is important to 'empathise' with participants in such cases in order to see how difficult it would be to work out what your experimenter is really after when you only take part in *one* of the conditions.

3. *Group difference* studies – see below – clearly *cannot* be repeated measures designs, i.e. where the 'independent variable' of interest is a category of persons, such as male/female, working class/middle class or extrovert/introvert.

4. Where an equivalent control group is essential. We might pre-test a group of children, apply a programme designed to increase their sensitivity to the needs of people with disabilities, then test again to measure improvement. To check that the children would not have changed anyway, irrespective of the 'treatment', we need to compare their changes with a control and/or placebo group.

MATCHED-PAIRS DESIGN

In the last example, we do not have to use an independent samples design and introduce the risk that participant variables will 'drown out' any difference from our independent variable. Suppose we suspect that any change in attitude to people with disabilities is likely to be slight. Differences between the children in the two groups might well be so great that any subtle attitude change would remain hidden. However, we are conducting a pre-test of attitudes. Why not compare each child in the 'treatment' group with a child in the control group who is similar to them in attitude to start with? We would hope that, for each such *pair* of children, the 'treated' one should change while the other should not. This compromise between the two designs so far discussed is known as a MATCHED-PAIRS design.

We would proceed by identifying the two highest scorers on our attitude pre-test. We would *randomly allocate* these, one to the control group and the other to the programme group. We would then identify the next two highest scorers and allocate in the same way and so on through the whole sample. This way we have most of the advantage of the repeated measures design (we can deal with *pairs* of scores) while avoiding the worst of the possible participant variables problem (our pairs of children are *similar*, not identical).

One of nature's most useful gifts to psychological researchers is, some believe, the existence of identical (monozygotic) twins. These represent the perfect matched pair – when they're just born at least – and create the perfect natural experiment – see footnote 3. Any differences between them later in life can fairly safely be attributed to differences in environmental experience. The converse is not true, however. Similarities cannot be easily attributed to common genetic make-up, since identical twins usually share fairly similar environments too. Even when they are reared in separate environments, they still share the same looks, metabolism, historical culture and so on.

SINGLE PARTICIPANT DESIGN

To hear of just one person being used for experimental research can make the scientifically minded recoil in horror. Surely this must produce quite unrepresentative results, impossible to generalise from? Quite rightly, they assume, one turns to objective psychological research in order to avoid the many generalisations which the lay person often makes from their own limited experience.

However, consider a physical scientist who obtains just one sample of weird moonrock from a returning space mission. The rock could be tested for amount of expansion at different temperatures, in a vacuum and in normal atmosphere, in order to detect significant changes in its behaviour. This would yield valuable scientific knowledge in itself. Further, from our general knowledge of the world of rocks, we could fairly safely assume that similar rock would exist on the moon. In the same way there are some sorts of things which people do which, we know for good reason, are likely to vary according to the same *pattern* (but not necessarily at the same level) for almost everyone. An example of this might be the experimental situation in which someone has to make decisions from an increasing number of alternatives – sorting cards according to colour, then suit and so on.

Ebbinghaus carried out an enormous number of memory experiments on himself using a wide variation of conditions and lists of nonsense syllables. Many modern studies of memory have used one participant over an extended series of experimental trials. Experiments can also be carried out on one or two people who suffer a particular condition or form of brain damage. Humphreys and Riddock (1993) experimented on two patients with Balint's syndrome – a difficulty in reaching under visual guidance caused by specific brain damage. The patient had to say whether 32 circles on a card were all the same colour or not. One patient performed much better when the circles were closer together, thus supporting a theory that the damage causes difficulty in switching attention although this is only true for *some* patients. Hence, single participant designs can be very useful in the investigation of cognitive deficits associated with specific medical conditions.

They can also be useful where very long term training is required which would not be financially or technically possible on a sample. For instance, Spelke, Hirst and Neisser (1976) gave five hours of training for many weeks to two students in order to demonstrate that they were eventually able to read text for comprehension at normal speed whilst writing down, again at normal speed, a separate list of words from dictation *and* recall these later having also written down the categories to which the heard words belonged!

RELATED AND UNRELATED DESIGNS

All the designs just covered can be divided into two major categories, RELATED DESIGNS and UNRELATED DESIGNS. In a related design, a score in one condition can be directly paired with a score in the other condition. This is clearly possible in a repeated measures design where each pair of scores comes from one person. It is also true for matched pairs designs. When we conduct an independent samples design, for instance comparing those trained on a memory task with a control group of untrained participants, it is very tempting to arrange data in two columns. This unfortunately can deceive us into thinking we have pairs of scores whereas in fact, consulting Table 3.3c, on the far right hand section, each score in 'Condition A' is in no way related to the score beside it in 'Condition B'. In the matched pairs and repeated measures examples, adjacent pairs of scores *are* related. This fact is important if you are entering data into a computer program such as *SPSS*. The correct way to enter the Table 3.3c data into the spreadsheet is to create a column for the dependent variable and a *separate* column for the independent variable. Both the independent variable and the dependent variable then have a value for each person. We then give each *value* of the independent variable a CODE, as shown in Table 3.4.

Where then do we place the *single participant* design? If the participant has completed two conditions of an experiment, it might be tempting at first to call this a related design since each score comes from the same person. However, contrary to this apparently obvious answer, if we think about it, looking at Table 3.3d, each score in condition 1 has no *particular* partner in condition 2. A particular score in 1 is related to *all* the scores in 2 to an equal degree, since the same person produced them all. But, in a related design, person H's score in condition 1 (see Table 3.3a) is *uniquely* related to their score in condition 2. In the matched pairs design (Table 3.3b), the score of child 1a is *uniquely* related to the score of child 1b. The single participant design *would* be related if we were

Table 3.2 Related and unrelated designs

Design	In each condition	
	Same people	**Different people**
Related	Repeated measures	Matched pairs
Unrelated	Single participant	Independent samples

Table 3.3 Arrangement of results in different experimental designs

A	Repeated Measures			B	Matched Pairs		
Person	**Condition**			**Child**	**Condition 1**	**Child**	**Condition 2**
	1		**2**				
H	7		13	1a	7	1b	13
I	4		8	2a	4	2b	8
J	13		9	3a	13	3b	9
K	12		7	4a	12	4b	7
L	13		16	5a	13	5b	16

C	Independent Samples			D	Single Participant		
!DO NOT ARRANGE DATA THIS WAY FOR COMPUTER ENTRY – see Table 3.4							
Person	**Condition 1**	**Person**	**Condition 2**	**Trial**	**Condition 1**	**Trial**	**Condition 2**
M	7	R	13	1	.579	1	.879
N	4	S	8	2	.621	2	.713
O	13	T	9	3	.543	3	.615
P	12	U	7	4	.567	4	.792
Q	13	V	16	. . .		. . .	

Table 3.4 Appropriate arrangement of data from an independent samples design (Table 3.3c)

Person	Condition	Score
M	1	7
N	1	4
O	1	13
P	1	12
Q	1	13
R	2	13
S	2	8
T	2	9
U	2	7
V	2	16

Box 3.1   Advantages and disadvantages of the various experimental designs

Design	Advantages	Disadvantages	Remedy (if any)
Repeated Measures	• Participant variables eliminated	• Order effects	• Counterbalance/randomise conditions
			• Leave long time gap between conditions
	• More economical on participants	• May not be able to conduct second condition immediately	• Do independent samples instead
	• Homogeneity of variance not a problem (see Chapter 14)	• Need different stimulus lists etc.	• Randomise stimulus materials
	• Need fewer participants	• Loss of participants between conditions	
		• Participants not naïve for second condition and may try to guess aim	• Deceive participants as to aim (or leave long time gap)
Independent samples	• No order effect	• Participant variables not controlled	• Random allocation of participants to conditions
	• Participants can't guess aim of experiment		
	• Can use exactly the same stimulus lists etc.	• Less economical on participants	
	• No need to wait for participants to 'forget' first condition	• Lack of 'homogeneity of variance' may prevent use of parametric test (Chapter 14)	• Ensure roughly equal numbers in each group (see p. 14)
Matched pairs	• No order effects	• Some participant variables still present	• Randomly allocate pairs to conditions
	• Participant variables partly controlled		
	• No wait for participants to forget	• Hard to find perfect matches and therefore time consuming	
	• Can use same stimulus lists, etc.	• Loss of one member of pair entails loss of whole pair	
	• Homogeneity of variance not a problem	• Can't generalise to other categories of people with confidence	
Single participant	• Useful where few participants available and/or a lot of time required for training participant	• Retraining required if original participant leaves project	• Treat participant very nicely!

somehow linking trial 1 in one condition to trial 1 in the other. This might happen if, say, we were correlating (see Chapter 15) equivalent trials under the two conditions to show that improvement takes a similar course under both. However, if we are simply looking for an overall difference between conditions 1 and 2, then *pairs* of scores are not at all related. Single participant scores are entered in the same way as the data in Table 3.4 except that the different persons in the left hand column are now different trials.

THE ESSENTIAL FEATURES OF A TRUE EXPERIMENT

Having looked at several popular forms of experimental design we need now to look more closely at the structure of experiments and several dangers that, if not checked, might be sources of confounding that lead us to false conclusions about the relationship between independent variable and dependent variable. It is important to keep in mind, throughout this section, just what it is that the true experiment is trying to achieve. As we have seen, the overall objective is to demonstrate an 'effect' – that is, a cause-effect relationship between an independent variable and a dependent variable – and we want this demonstration to be *unambiguous*. Ideally, we want no alternative explanation of the effect to be feasible. As we have seen, a central feature is that of *variable control*.

In particular, the main features of a true experiment are that we:

   a. Manipulate the independent variable in a controlled manner

   b. Maintain control over the effects of all other EXTRANEOUS VARIABLES so that they stay constant or are balanced

   c. Measure changes in the dependent variable

Extraneous variables

By 'extraneous variables' we mean the set of all variables which can interfere with the causal link in an experiment. Many of these variables, if not held constant, can exert a confounding effect on the interpretation of results, causing us to make errors in our assumption that manipulation of X has or has not affected Y. Other variables have a more general interfering effect and can be seen as a form of 'noise' getting in the way of clearer results.

CONFOUNDING IN EXPERIMENTS

If we do not control for confounding variables, we do not eliminate several alternative explanations of any apparent effect we might find – see Table 3.5. Suppose Sally was conducting the imagery experiment (p.54) and that, without realising it, she is more energised and dynamic when explaining the imagery system to the experimental group. For this reason the imagery group are more relaxed and they do better on the recall task. Sally will claim to have demonstrated that imagery improves recall when in fact a confounding variable – difference in motivation from the experimenter – is really responsible. This variable alters *with* the independent variable and *could* be responsible for any differences found. The research design would be confounded by a variable that varies *systematically* along with the independent variable.

Returning briefly to the tomato experiment, suppose the tomatoes in the banana box really do ripen more quickly. Can we be sure that the banana and its spots were the direct cause? Well, it could be that the tomatoes ripen more quickly just because there is less air in the banana box than in the other one. The difference between the two boxes in air volume is a confounding variable. *The aim of experimental designs is to reduce possible confounding to a minimum.* How could we control for this air displacement theory? We could place a wooden object, exactly the same shape and size as the banana in the other box and repeat the experiment. Much experimental work involves creativity and cunning in designing conditions to eliminate alternative explanations.

Why do those scores vary? – sources of influence in the experiment

A useful model for understanding what is going on in an experiment with confounding and other extraneous variables is depicted in Figure 3.3. In any experiment we hope to

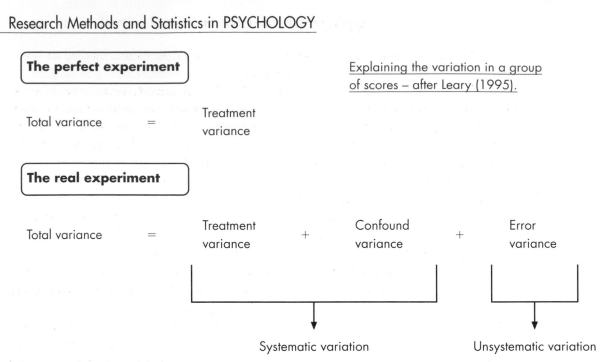

The perfect experiment

Explaining the variation in a group
of scores – after Leary (1995).

Total variance $=$ Treatment variance

The real experiment

Total variance $=$ Treatment variance $+$ Confound variance $+$ Error variance

Systematic variation   Unsystematic variation

Figure 3.3 Explaining variance in an experiment

show that the scores on the dependent variable vary because of the influence of the independent variable. We need to introduce the concept of score *variance* which we shall deal with more technically in Chapter 10. Imagine you plunge your hand into a barrel of six inch nails and pull out a sample. As you probably know, you could measure all these and find their average length (technically their 'mean'). This is a central point around which they all *vary*. The *amount* by which they all vary around their mean is known as their 'variance'. Though we shall calculate this statistic in later chapters, for now let's use variance to mean *variations in a set of measurements*. In the case of the nails, they will vary very slightly in length around the mean of six inches and all this variation should be the result of ERROR VARIANCE – tiny unsystematic effects, such as dust, cutting position, slight vibration, which cause slight differences in the length of each nail.

However, suppose instead that we were clutching two samples of nails, one from a six inch nail cutting machine and one from a four inch machine. In the perfect factory with perfect machines all the variation among the lengths of these nails would be caused *solely* by the different 'treatment' the two samples have received, one cut to six inches the other to four inches. However, in reality the variation among all the nails is actually explained by *two* sources, first the 'treatment variance' (being cut to 6 or 4 inches) and second the error variance as before. Finally, suppose the six inch nails pass over a very hot part of their machine but this is not so for the four inch nails. This would affect results in a *systematic* and unwanted direction. The 'six inch' nails would be slightly longer than the intended length overall because of the *confounding variable* of heat.

The 'treatment' and the 'confounding' here both have *systematic effects* – they produce a difference in one direction only. The errors (sometimes referred to as RANDOM ERRORS) are *unsystematic* – they affect both groups equally and in unpredictable directions in each instance.

I apologise for the rather 'heavy metal' feel to the last example but it helps explain why the language of psychology experimentation uses terminology like 'error'. This can be disconcerting for the new psychology researcher since to refer to variations among *people* or their responses as 'errors' seems a bit judgmental!

Let's apply this model to Johnston and Davey's (1997) experiment, described in Chapter 1 and just concentrate on the two extreme conditions – positive and negative news stories. In the perfect experiment we would want any variation in sadness scores to be entirely explained by the difference between these two news bulletins. However, suppose the negative news bulletin reader was more miserable than the other reader. This factor, rather than the content of the news stories, might be responsible for a change in sadness. The *confounding variation* in scores may cause us to declare an effect when there isn't any. On the other hand, if the positive news bulletin reader were the more miserable person, we may declare a failure when there really *is* an effect. For one group, the increase in sadness due to the negative news stories might be matched, in the other group, by an increase in sadness caused by the positive news bulletin reader. Notice here that the confounding variance would *subtract* from any treatment variance – the happier positive news group is brought back to the same level by their newsreader.

In addition to the possible confounding variables in this experiment, there will also be a myriad of sources of *error variance* – amount of physical movement in each story, personal excitement in each story, flicker on the television monitors, ambient temperature, small sounds in the room, fluctuations in light and so on. All these unsystematic errors are assumed to affect each condition equally so they do not produce a systematic bias in scores. However, if there are a lot of them we may find that any subtle treatment effect is buried under so much distorting 'noise'.

FORMS OF CONFOUNDING

The confounded explanation – focusing on the wrong variable

> Now think again about the imagery experiment and ignore any possible bias from the experimenter. If the imagery group does indeed recall far more items than the control group, can we be sure that the mental act of imaging-linking each item was responsible for the difference found?
>
> Can you think of reasons why the imagery group may have done better at recall, *other* than the fact that they used mental images?

When one has completed this experimental task it seems obvious that imagery is responsible for the far better performance. However, consider the possibility that the imagery is not at all responsible, rather it is the act of making up a meaningful link which causes the superior retention – see Figure 3.4.

> How could we devise a test of the alternative explanation that it is meaningful link-making, not the imaging itself, which is responsible for superior recall of words?

Well, we could find people who are very poor imagers and compare their performance, using imagery, with that of a group of average to good imagers. If imaging plays no part,

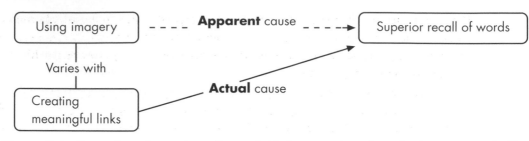

Figure 3.4 Operation of a confounding variable in an explanation of a demonstrated effect

but meaningful link-making does, we should find no difference in their recall ability, but we should still find that the poor imagers do better using 'imagery'.

Tackling confounds – the heart of science?

Attempts like this to eliminate possible confounding variables as alternative explanations are really the heart of scientific activity. It doesn't matter whether the proposed confounding variable really *does* have an effect. The name of the game is to produce a refined design which simply *rules out* the confounding variable as a competing explanation. If successful, the competing view has to find an even more subtle critique of the results. If a 'failure', then we have progress – we must take seriously the role of the confounding variable in our overall theory. Have a look, in Box 3.2, at the way in which Pepsi Cola's advertising was shown to exploit a confounding variable some years ago.

Box 3.2 The Coke-Pepsi wars

adapted from TIME, July 26, 1976

In the 1970s, Pepsi, concerned about Coca Cola's 3–1 lead in sales in the Dallas area of the United States, published a promotion supposedly showing that more than half the Coke drinkers tested preferred Pepsi's flavor when the two colas were served in anonymous cups. Coke was served in a glass marked 'Q' while Pepsi was served in a glass marked 'M'. A year later the Coke lead was down to 2–1. Coca Cola fought back by running their own consumer-preference test – not of the colas but of the letters. They showed that people apparently like the letter 'M' better than they do 'Q'. One Chicago marketing executive speculated that Q was disliked because of the number of unpleasant words that begin with 'Q'. (quack, quitter, quake, qualm, queer . . .).

Whether or not this perverse *explanation* is correct (what's wrong with 'quack'?), what would you do to check out Coca Cola's claim? What Coke actually did is printed at the foot of this page.[2]

[2] As a scientific test, Coca Cola put its own drink into *both* the 'M' and 'Q' glasses. Results showed that most people preferred the Coke in the 'M' glass. The consistent use of 'Q' associated with the competitor's drink had apparently confounded Pepsi's advertising 'research'.

Very many studies in research journals are designed to rule out possible confounding and creating these designs can be one of the most interesting and creative areas of scientific activity and, to some extent, is what drives discovery along. You might like to tackle the tasks in the following exercise box.

> Look back at the exercise on page 29. Assume that in each example research is carried out which supports the link between IV and DV (groups under greater stress *do* have poorer memory performance, for example). Can you think of a confounding variable in each example which might explain the link? Can you also think of a research design that might eliminate this variable as an explanation of the link?

Meanwhile, here are a couple of interesting examples of tackling possible confounding variables from the research literature.

Tackling confounding (1) – Did you really distort what I saw?

In a famous series of experiments by Elizabeth Loftus and her colleagues (e.g. Loftus and Palmer, 1974), participants were asked leading questions after seeing a film of a car accident. For example, 'How fast were the cars going when they *smashed into* each other?' was asked in one condition, whereas 'hit' was substituted for 'smashed into' in another condition. The people in the 'smashed into' condition tended to recall a greater speed and this was taken as evidence for the distortion of original memories by leading questions. The argument was later raised, however, that participants may have been simply responding to what they thought was required of them, and were not suffering permanent distorted memories. Loftus tackled this alleged confounding variable (immediate research demand) by re-doing the experiment but also asking participants to recall, *one week after the original test*, extra information about the film. They were asked, for instance, whether they recalled any broken glass in the incident. Those participants in the 'smashed into' condition one week earlier, tended to report glass more frequently (there wasn't any in fact) and this supported the view that original memories had been more or less permanently distorted by the questions asked immediately after viewing the incident. Lindsay (1990) even told participants that information given to them after viewing an office robbery was all wrong and to ignore it. Nevertheless, the information appeared to distort participants' recall of events in the film.

Tackling confounding (2) – Nice smell – good memory

A rich vein of research from the early 1980s has been the use of 'mood induction' to produce temporary up or down moods in participants and to measure several types of consequent effects (our newsreading example is a version). Typically, one group of participants is either given sad materials (written or filmed) or is instructed explicitly to get into a sad mood while a second group is induced or instructed into a 'happy' mood. They might then be asked to recall memories (e.g. of childhood) or to recall words from a set of both 'happy' and 'sad' words given earlier in a memory task. Erlichman and Halpern (1988) argued that induction or instruction techniques might not only create a temporary mood but also 'set' thought processes in the mood direction. In order to eliminate this possibly confounding variable, Erlichman and Halpern attempted to create a mood in participants simply by exposing them to pleasant or unpleasant smells. In support of their predictions, those exposed to a pleasant smell recalled happier memories than did those exposed to an unpleasant smell. This was important as it supports the theory that temporary mood affects mental processes, even when mental processes have not been used to induce the mood. However, this is also one of those findings which is intrinsically fascinating for the general public to hear about, irrespective of the theoretical position it was intended to bolster. It also looks good as a student practical exercise.

Avoidable confounding – improving validity

When we query the VALIDITY of an experimental result we question whether there really was an effect of the sort we are looking for. It has become popular to use the term THREATS TO VALIDITY to refer to *anything* that can interfere with the demonstration of a clear, universal cause-effect link in an experimental type of study. The thinking around validity is largely attributable to Campbell and Stanley (1963) and Cook and Campbell (1979), and we shall investigate their highly influential views on experimental control in the next chapter.

Earlier, in looking for an alternative explanation for the superior imagery group results, you may have suggested that perhaps the groups were treated slightly differently. Perhaps one group got slightly longer for recall, perhaps one group contained far better memorisers. These are all possible 'threats' to the validity of our *apparent* finding that imagery produced better recall. In these cases, the confounding variable is not usually of research interest. In the research examples above, however, we *would* be interested in the hidden, related variables since the alternative explanations they provide are still of fundamental interest to the theory behind our research project. By contrast, permitting the imagery group, by mistake, to recall for longer would generally be seen as a *nuisance* variable. It is not of interest to the theory we were trying to support with our hypothesis. If the imagery group were given longer then perhaps imagery itself (*or* the interesting alternative variable – making meaningful links) has no effect whatsoever on recall scores.

The confounding variables described below are usually seen as mere 'nuisance' variables, usually avoidable by more careful design, attention to procedures, materials and so on. Still, even confounding through design weakness can lead to dramatic research developments. When Pavlov was investigating digestive systems in dogs, it was their feeders' footsteps and the sight of their food buckets which acted as confounding variables causing the dogs to dribble *before* they were given food. These 'nuisance' variables, however, were instrumental in leading Pavlov to his monumental work on classical conditioning.

We should also sound a note of caution before starting out on a discussion of what can possible bias results and interfere with the optimum performance of participants in an experiment. Some of the proposed effects outlined below, if they exist, are very subtle indeed. However, consider an experiment by Hovey in 1928 where two groups of students were asked to complete an intelligence test, one group in a quiet room. The other group took the test in a room with 'seven bells, five buzzers, a 500-watt spotlight, a 90,000 volt rotary spark gap, a phonograph, two organ pipes of varying pitch, three metal whistles, a 55-pound circular saw . . . , a photographer taking pictures and four students doing acrobatics!' (Rosnow and Rosenthal, 1997, p.32). There was no difference in the performance of the two groups.

Confounding designs

In Fantz's (1961) well-known research, very young infants were exposed to simple and complex patterns in order to determine whether they could already tell the difference. This was done by measuring their 'preference' – defined operationally as the type of pattern (complex or simple) at which they spent a longer time gazing when one of each was presented simultaneously, side by side. Suppose the researchers had been thoughtless enough (they weren't) to always present the more complex pattern on the right hand side, with the simple pattern on the left. Here it might well be that the babies tested found it easier to look to the right. Perhaps the cot made it more comfortable to look to the right. Perhaps babies have a natural tendency to look to the right. We don't have to know whether any of these possibilities is the case. We simply need to eliminate these possibilities through our *research design* – in this case, present half the complex patterns to the right and half to the left in an unpredictable order – see randomised stimuli, p.61. We have already encountered this type of systematic bias in design with the example of the miserable newsreader and with Sally's differential enthusiasm.

Confounding measures

Suppose we wish to test for a difference between people's recall for concrete and abstract words. We create two lists, one for each type of word. However, it could well turn out, if we don't check thoroughly, that the abstract words we choose are *also* more uncommon – they occur less frequently in people's speech and in common reading. Any effect we find *may* be the result of *uncommon* words being harder to learn rather than *abstract* words being harder to learn. We can easily adjust for this by using commonly available surveys of word frequencies in the popular media.

Problems with measures also occur where there are 'floor' or 'ceiling' effects – see p. 257. If people improve in their ability to solve anagrams after training, it could be that a test measure is inadequate in showing this because participants who originally scored quite highly cannot show how much better they now are, since they have reached the top of the scale.

Confounding procedures – the role of a standardised procedure

Variations in the *procedure* of a research study can produce either random errors or a systematic confounding effect. The ideal is that, for each common aspect of an experimental procedure, every participant has *exactly* the same experience – the researchers operate a STANDARDISED PROCEDURE, identical for all participants in a specific condition. Very often, in the teaching of psychology, students are introduced to an interesting idea for testing (e.g. are smokers more anxious?). A procedure is explained and students set off to test their friends, family and/or whoever they can get hold of (the typical *opportunity sample*). This is very often all that can be done, given school or college resources. However, does anyone in these circumstances really believe that the procedure will be at all *standard*? Different testers are operating. Even for the same tester, with the best will in the world, it is difficult to run an identical procedure with your dad at tea time and with your boy/girl friend later that same evening. Paid researchers must do better but, nevertheless, it would be naïve to assume that features of the tester (accent, dress, looks, etc.), their behaviour, or the surrounding physical environment, do not produce unwanted variations.

Random errors produce higher levels of what is known as *variance* among the participants' scores (Chapter 10) and this makes it more difficult to demonstrate real statistical differences, as we shall see.

Even with standardised procedures, experimenters do not always follow them. Friedman (1967) argued that this is partly because experimenters may not recognise that social interaction and non-verbal communication play a crucial role in the procedure of an experiment. Male experimenters, when the participant is female, are more likely to use her name, smile and look directly at her (Rosenthal, 1966). Both males and females take longer to gather data from a participant of the opposite sex than a same-sex participant (Rosnow and Rosenthal, 1997, p. 26). Written procedures do not usually tell the experimenter *exactly* how to greet participants, engage in casual pleasantries, arrange seating and how much to smile. Where variations are *systematic*, as for the male experimenter bias, they may well produce a significant confounding effect and we move on now to discuss some of the more celebrated of these types of researcher and participant biases.

Confounding through expectations – the social psychology of the psychology experiment

Barber (1976) listed many sources of confounding through possible 'Pitfalls in human research' (his book title). Several of these are covered elsewhere in this section (for instance, 'loose procedures', experimenter personal attributes, data mis-recording, wrong design and so on). Two important sources were *fudging* and *expectancies*. 'Fudging' refers to a conscious or near-conscious 'massaging' of data to achieve desired results, a rather strong form of influence from expectancy (i.e. knowing what *should* happen). I would not like the reader to gain the impression that such conscious data manipulation is rife within psychological research but it certainly is not unknown. I have dealt elsewhere with non-disclosure of raw data by, for instance, Jensen according to Kamin (Chapter 1). Interestingly Kamin (1977) was also responsible for uncovering one of the biggest scientific frauds of all time, that concerning the almost certain data fudging by Sir Cyril Burt. The latter had gathered a large set of data apparently showing that identical twins, reared in different environments, had notably similar IQ levels – a very strong piece of evidence for the genetic transmission of intelligence, if valid. Kamin noted that there were too many amazing coincidences in the statistics over the years, given that Burt claimed to have added data at several points. One of Burt's 'assistants' almost certainly never existed. It is interesting that so many disreputable actions concerning data have surrounded the crucially important social issues of intelligence, genetic inheritance and race. Reticence in providing raw data continues to be associated with this controversial topic – see Kamin, 1995; Tucker, 1994 and further examples in the discussion of ethics in Chapter 22.

At a less dramatic level, experimenters may fudge results because they are hired for the job and wish to 'succeed', because they are PhD students supervised by the main researcher, assistants hoping to retain a temporary appointment, or because they simply fear comparison with other experimenters for the purposes of establishing EXPERIMENTER RELIABILITY – the extent to which two experimenters' results agree.

Experimenter/researcher expectancy

Most expectancies, thankfully, do not involve gross and conscious 'fiddling'. Since psychology experiments are carried out by humans on humans, it has been argued that the necessary social interaction which must occur between experimenter and participant makes the psychological experiment different in kind from any other. Is it possible that, completely beyond the level of conscious awareness, the experimenter's eagerness to 'get a result' could be a confounding variable? Experimenters rarely 'cheat' but they are human and might, without realising it, convey to participants what they are expecting to happen. Rosenthal and Fode (1963) showed that students given groups of 'bright' and 'dull' rats (actually possessing a random mixed of maze learning abilities) produced results consistent with the label of their rats. This was originally used to show that experimenter expectancies can even affect the behaviour of laboratory rats. In their infamous publication *Pygmalion in the classroom*, Rosenthal and Jacobsen (1968) reported that (randomly selected) children whose teachers 'overheard' that they were expected to make late gains in academic development, actually made significant gains compared with non-selected children. This suggested that teachers had responded to the 'dropped' information by somehow, unknowingly, giving them enriched attention.

Forty experiments between 1968 and 1976 *failed* to show evidence of experimenters passing on to participants influences which investigators (those *running* the research project) had 'planted'. However, Raffetto (1967) led one group of experimenters to believe that sensory deprivation produces many reports of hallucinations and another group to believe the opposite. The experimenters then interviewed people who had undergone sensory deprivation. The instructions for interviewing were purposely left vague. Experimenters reported results in accordance with what they had been led to believe. Eden (1990) demonstrated that where army leaders were told (incorrectly) that their subordinates were above average, platoon members performed significantly better than where this information was not given. Some studies have shown that experimenters *can* affect participants' responses through facial or verbal cues and that certain participants are more likely to pick up experimenter influence than others, particularly those high in need for approval. Finally, Rosenthal himself (Rosnow and Rosenthal, 1997), has conducted *meta-analyses* (see next chapter) of hundreds of expectancy studies in several quite different areas and claims to obtain overall effects far above chance levels. In fact the Rosnow and Rosenthal text is a little gem as a sourcebook for all manner of sometimes unbelievable experimenter and participant expectancy and bias effects, including many features of volunteers, the problems of student dominance in psychology experiments and so on.

Participant expectancy, Hawthorne effects and demand characteristics

If participants who need approval are affected by experimenter influence, as was just mentioned, then it suggests that they perhaps want to get the 'right' result and do well. *Participant expectancy* was proposed as the explanation of some now famous and peculiar effects demonstrated during a massive applied psychology project conducted in the 1920s at the Hawthorne electrical plant in the USA (Roethlisberger and Dickson, 1939). The productivity of five female workers was assessed over two years under a number of conditions of different variable manipulations, including for instance, changes of illumination and timing of rest breaks. The surprising result was that productivity increased *whatever the change* and even increased when conditions were returned to the worst set, those in operation at the outset. From that research, psychologists have derived the term HAWTHORNE EFFECT which is loosely defined as: *the effect on participants of simply being the focus of investigation*. It is not likely that the workers increased their rate simply because they thought this was expected of them. There was other evidence in the research to the contrary. What is intended by the term is simply that people are affected by being studied, a possible relative of the *social facilitation* and *inhibition* phenomena studied in social psychology.

If participants do wish to behave as expected they would need to know what was required of them in the first place. Orne (1962) argued that there are many cues in an experimental situation which give participants an idea of what the study is about, what behaviour is under study and perhaps what changes are expected or required of them. Those cues that may reveal the experimental hypothesis Orne named DEMAND CHARACTER-ISTICS and offered the following definition:

> The totality of cues that convey an experimental hypothesis to the subject become
> significant determinants of the subject's behaviour. We have labelled the sum total of such
> cues as the 'demand characteristics of the experimental situation'. Orne (1962), p. 779

Orne and Scheibe (1964) showed that participants asked to suffer 'sensory deprivation', who signed a liability release form and were shown a 'panic button' to use if they were desperate for an end to the stress (simply sitting alone in a room for four hours), reacted in a more extreme manner than did a control group. These cues that behaviour might be dramatically affected presumably had just that effect. An antidote to the confounding effects of demand characteristics was proposed by Aronson and Carlsmith (1968) who argued that 'experimental realism' – see Chapter 4 – should *lower* the potency of demand characteristics, because participants' attention is entirely grabbed by the interest of the procedure.

Participant reactions to demand characteristics and expectancy

Participants could react to demand characteristics in several ways. They may engage in what is termed PLEASING THE EXPERIMENTER. This was the force of the criticism of the Loftus experiment described above. In fact, Weber and Cook (1972) found little evidence that participants do try to respond as they think the experimenter might wish. Masling (1966) has even suggested that a 'screw you' effect might occur as participants attempt to alter their behaviour *away* from what is expected. Research suggests, however, that most participants try to appear normal and demonstrate that they *cannot* be influenced either way.

EVALUATION APPREHENSION is the term used for participants' anxiety that their performance is under scrutiny. Some may try to 'look good', to present particularly acceptable forms of behaviour – a phenomenon known as SOCIAL DESIRABILITY. Others may just not concentrate as well on the task at hand. A further problem, sometimes known as 'enlightenment', is the increasing awareness of psychology students (who are most often participants) and the general public about psychological research findings, even if these are often poorly understood.

Reactive and non-reactive studies

It must be emphasised that *any* research study, *experimental or not*, in so far as participants are aware of being a participant, can be affected by all the social and expectancy variables just described, perhaps social desirability in particular. Many studies use what has been called a REACTIVE design (or use a 'reactive measure') in that the participant is expected to react to being studied (rather than participate or collaborate – see Chapter 9). It could be argued that the closeness of the researcher, the awesome surroundings and formality of the procedures make reactive measures even more distorting in the traditional laboratory experiment. The general point however is that participants are people and people are active, social, enquiring human beings. They are not passive 'subjects' who are simply experimented *on*. Their social adjustments, thoughts and constructions of the world around them may seriously interact with research arrangements designed specifically to investigate the operation of those very thoughts, constructions and behaviour in psychological research.

Dealing with expectancies – blind and double blind procedures

In order to deal with participant expectancies it would make sense to keep participants unaware of the research aim. This is not always possible but where such a strategy is used the research is said to employ a SINGLE BLIND procedure. The term is borrowed from medical trials in which volunteer patients would not know whether they received a real drug or a placebo. In almost all psychology experiments participants are not told the aim of the study, and therefore the true nature of the condition they participate in, until after measures have been taken. This may at times involve a certain degree of deception and the moral and ethical implications of this are discussed in Chapter 22.

It has been argued above, however, that experimenters themselves may transmit cues or even 'nudge' events along to a desired conclusion, albeit without conscious awareness of the bias. In this case it makes sense to keep experimenters in the dark too. The employment of a DOUBLE BLIND procedure does just that – experimenters, observers, raters or other assistants who gather or assess data from participants, are not told the true experimental aims. Where a *placebo group* is used, for example, neither the participants, nor the data gatherers would know who has received which treatment.

Confounding through history

In field experiments, where a 'treatment' is to be applied that might last quite some time, such as an anti-racist training programme, it is particularly important to use a control group for comparison. Suppose, during the 'treatment' period, something occurs to which the entire populace is exposed. For instance, in July 1998, in connection with the Stephen Lawrence murder enquiry, a prominent chief of police admitted the existence of widespread and significant institutional racism within British police forces. This would be a 'history' event which might, in itself, be responsible for some weakening of racist attitudes among the general public. If we used only the training programme group, and not an additional control group, we would falsely attribute attitude change to the 'treatment' rather than to this confounding public event.

Some time ago, starting a Christmas vacation, a friend told me that switching to decaffeinated coffee might reduce some physical effects of tension which I'd been experiencing. To my surprise, after a couple of weeks, the feelings had subsided. The alert reader will have guessed that the possible confounding explanation here is the vacation period – a 'local' history effect because, in this period, *some* relaxation might occur anyway.

Confounding through selection (sampling)

If I may be permitted to return, just once more, to the tomato/banana experiment, you'll

Table 3.5 The role of confounding variables and random errors

CONFOUNDING VARIABLES can lead us to:	**example from the text**
• wrongly identify the causal component of an independent variable • assume the intended independent variable has an effect when it doesn't • assume an effect doesn't occur when it does	imaging seen as responsible for improved recall, rather than the making of meaningful links Sally's difference in enthusiasm is responsible for the better imagery group performance a miserable positive news reader might cause moods to stay the same that might otherwise have been 'lifted' by the news content

RANDOMLY ACTING VARIABLES can also help to muddy the water by 'smothering' a real difference with too much 'noise'. For instance a subtle difference in reaction time may not be detectable because the measuring equipment is too crude and people's performances generally too erratic for an actual difference between conditions to show through.

The hallmark of good experimental design then is to attempt to eliminate as much confounding and random variation as is possible.

recall that we separated the tomatoes into two groups on a *random* basis in order to avoid *sampling bias* – we don't want an existing difference between the groups of tomatoes to confound the effect of the banana. If, for the purposes of a demonstration, your teacher has the females in the class solve anagrams of animal words and the males solve anagrams of legal terms, and then claims that the animal task was clearly easier, you might just point out the possible confounding caused by having females do one task and males do the other. It doesn't matter whether females are, in fact, better at anagrams (they are often superior on verbal tasks as it happens). What matters is the *potential* for a sampling bias. As we saw in the independent samples design, it is essential to *randomly allocate* participants to conditions. Many student practical projects lack attention to this 'threat' where, very often, it is easily avoided with a simple allocation procedure. Other selection biases can occur where, for instance, certain types of people are more likely to volunteer for one condition than another, or where certain sorts of people are more likely to leave an experiment.

PROBLEMS IN THE VALIDITY OF FIELD STUDIES

Selection problems typically occur in FIELD STUDIES where the researcher studies naturally 'treated' groups in their everyday environment – studies sometimes described as NATURALISTIC. For instance, we may wish to study the effectiveness of new drivers displaying a green 'L' on their car for the first year after full qualification. Samples of those who do and do not choose to display a green 'L' would be termed self-selecting, since the researcher cannot randomly allocate them to their 'conditions'. If it turns out that green 'L' plate wearers have fewer accidents we cannot be sure that this is a result of their 'L' plate wearing, or of their general conscientiousness, an example of which is their decision to wear the plate. The issue of such non-equivalent groups is central to the concept of the QUASI-EXPERIMENT.

QUASI-EXPERIMENTS

It was design considerations such as the problem of comparing 'non-equivalent groups, that led Campbell, Stanley, Cook and others to promote, through their work in education field research, the concept of QUASI-EXPERIMENTS. Cook and Campbell (1979) is by far the best and most thorough place for a grounding in the issues of quasi-experimentation and in the concepts of *internal* and *external validity* to be discussed in the next chapter.

Social and applied psychologists (for instance, working in health, education, sport and so on) face the dilemma of wishing to research in realistic everyday settings but recognising the lack of control this can involve. This is not such a problem if we do not rely very heavily on the experiment as a research tool, but back in the 1950s and 1960s the psychology establishment suffered from an almost unswerving and extreme faith in the superiority of the experiment over all other research approaches. It was then sometimes hard to get non-experimental research taken seriously or published. The promotion of quasi-experimental designs was intended to boost the status of well-controlled field research

Experiment

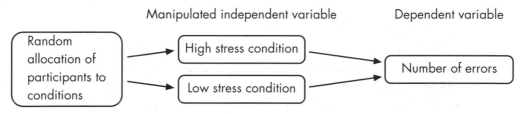

Quasi-experiment

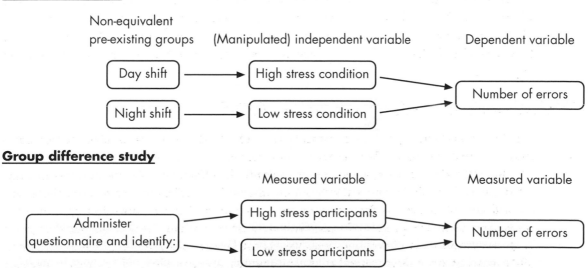

Group difference study

Figure 3.5 Relationship between variables in true, quasi- and non-experimental group difference studies

designs which were 'almost' experiments but lacked one or more of the essential features we have outlined above. Whilst admitting, via the general arguments about validity, that very many field designs are not truly experimental, they argued that, with sufficient attention paid to compensating controls, such work could nevertheless be presented as possessing a high degree of validity.

Some of the advantages and disadvantages of field experiments are outlined at the end of Chapter 4, along with a discussion of the strengths and weaknesses of laboratory studies. However, the issue here is not between field and laboratory (though problems with field studies triggered the debate); it is between the 'true' experiment and the 'quasi-experiment'. In a quasi-experiment one or more of the central features of a true experiment are missing. We shall consider in turn the most frequently missing features which are:

1. random allocation of participants to conditions   and/or
2. full experimenter control over the independent variable

Non-equivalent groups

The very nature of social or applied psychological research in the field often entails not being able to allocate participants to conditions of an experiment *at* random. Whenever we do not allocate at random we can usually imagine a way in which initial differences *between the groups* might be responsible for any difference found. In the Cialdini littering study, the participants were self-selecting. The researchers could not allocate passers-by to conditions at random. They could not select a participant then rush around strewing the appropriate amount of litter. For each set condition of the IV they simply had to use those who happened along to take their leaflet (itself another factor probably biasing the sample). The condition with a high amount of pre-existing litter might have been run early in the day. Perhaps people were rushing to work and were more likely to drop litter anyway; perhaps the pre-existing litter had nothing to do with the higher littering levels.

As another example, if health psychologists wish to study the effects of fitness training sessions on recuperation patterns they may have to compare those who attend the sessions with those who do not. Unfortunately, the comparison may well be between the more committed and the less committed. *This* variable may be responsible for later differences between groups. We can of course attempt to take representative samples and compare like with like, but there is always the possibility that some difference between attenders and non-attenders, not identified for matching, *could* be responsible for differences found in recuperation.

Applied researchers in the field might typically wish to assess the effects of:
- a stress reduction training programme on employees' sickness records and productivity
- a radical new rehabilitation programme for ex-drug addicts on readjustment
- an educational intervention programme (e.g. Headstart) on children's attainments.

In each case we often cannot allocate randomly and we may not be able to match up representative groups. We may have to use the ex-addicts attending a Thursday session for the new programme and compare these with the Tuesday group staying on the conventional programme. Here, we often cannot ensure that the two groups are roughly equivalent. If the programme is intended to improve self-esteem, among other things, then we *can* employ a pre-test and final test of participants on self esteem. The dependent variable would then become each participant's *change* in self-esteem over the period, not their final score. This way we control, to some extent, for pre-existing differences between the two groups.

Natural experiments – no control of the independent variable

Psychologists often have to exploit naturally occurring conditions rather than a programme that they have set up themselves. Again this is often the case in applied field research. In the examples given above it might well be the case that the researcher investigates the effects of 'compensatory' education programmes on children where the conditions and administration have all been set up by education professionals rather than the researcher. The trouble here is that conditions will not necessarily have been organised with research interests in mind but in a way that will be ethically acceptable and of greatest educational benefit to the children involved. Hence, the educational organisers will not always have been thinking about threats to validity and rigid adherence to a standardised procedure, closely comparable control groups and so on.

Nevertheless, these 'natural experiments' are sometimes the best conditions that a research psychologist can find when the topic of interest is some real practical programme that just could not be simulated in a laboratory setting. As we shall argue in Chapter 4, the laboratory may be excellent for some sorts of investigation in some areas of psychology but nowadays we do not hold the mid twentieth century view that all other settings are in some way lacking.

In one example of a natural experiment, Seaver (1973) showed elegantly that where the *same* school teacher had taught both an older and younger sibling, the two were closer together academically than were similarly aged and matched sibling pairs taught by *different* teachers. This was seen as providing support for the original 'Pygmalion' expectancy effects described earlier in the Rosenthal and Jacobson study (1968).

Time series designs

Some quasi-experiments do not study specific individuals but use data on large numbers of people – often referred to as ARCHIVAL DATA – in a TIME-SERIES design. A time-series design, which is also often used on single individuals or small samples, tracks performance over several measurements leading up to the introduction of a 'treatment' (the independent variable) and over several measurements *after* the intervention. An effect is then highlighted by a sudden change in the dependent variable of interest, and no change in variables *not* expected to be affected. Ross *et al* (1973) studied driver and accident behaviour before and after the introduction of the breathalyser to the UK. He wanted to show that drink-driving behaviour reduced as a result of the new measure. He showed that accidents dropped particularly during drinking hours (disputing the view that there was a *general* accident drop) and then, using further public data statistics, elegantly eliminated several alternative hypotheses. For instance, he showed that:

- the reduced accident rate was not simply a result of people generally driving less (he used British Road Research Laboratory data to show a reduction in *number of accidents per mile driven*)
- people were *not* drinking less after the measure (he showed no effect in alcohol sales)
- people were *not* just driving more carefully after drinking (his survey showed more people reporting walking home after drinking and post-mortem data to show that fewer post-breathalyser fatalities had alcohol in their blood).

Other typical 'natural experiments' include the following sorts of study:

- introduction of an anti-bullying programme into one school where another similar school can be used as a comparison group
- comparison of a new psychiatric ward regime (e.g. 'milieu therapy') in comparison to an adjacent and equivalent ward staying on the conventional regime
- comparison of numbers of people presenting for check-ups before and after a campaign on heart disease and preventive care.

Non-experimental research

Group difference studies

The dividing line between quasi-experiment and non-experiment is very hard to define. Many texts on experimental designs do not include, in their description of various experimental and quasi-experimental approaches, any mention of the design which is extremely common in practical work for the new learner in psychology. This is the design in which members of one group, defined by personality, biology or demographic characteristic, are compared with members of another group or with non-members. Very many studies, for instance, attempt to demonstrate some personality or behavioural difference between the sexes, an interesting example being the fairly regular finding that a sample of females will often rate their own IQ (in the absence of any specific knowledge about IQ tests and scores) lower than do a roughly equivalent sample of males. Other common studies are differences between samples of introverts and extroverts, between occupations (e.g. nurses vs. non-nurses), between economic classes and between members of different cultures or ethnic groups (see cross-cultural research in Chapter 8).

The trouble with fitting these sorts of studies into the quasi-experimental category is that they lack a central feature of experimental and quasi-experimental designs. Take a look back at Figure 3.2 on page 54. The classic experiment has some participants and then a 'treatment' which is applied to one of the groups. The treatment is almost always fairly time specific, although it can include, for instance, a therapy programme lasting a year or two.[3] In more sophisticated designs there are several different 'treatments'. In repeated measures designs participants are often tested with and without the treatment.

---

[3] An exception here (and there always *are* exceptions) are the sorts of study commonly conducted in researching the relative effects of genetic inheritance and rearing environment on characteristics such as intelligence or depression. Pairs of identical twins, separated early in life, are compared after several years. Here the independent variable is taken as the differing environments (rather a broad and diffuse 'treatment') and the measured dependent variable is, say, IQ level. Although this sort of work is quite often referred to in the literature as 'quasi-experimental', the researchers are very often looking for a *similarity* rather than a difference. However, there is a much stronger element of control than in typical sex-difference studies, in that the 'participants' are pretty well identical at separation into paired groups, rather than completely varied as is the case with two sets of males and females.

By contrast, in what I prefer to call GROUP DIFFERENCE[4] studies, it is difficult to see how we can talk of a treatment being applied to previously 'untreated' individuals. One can argue that foetuses had maleness and femaleness (plus the entire lifetime experience of being one sex or the other) 'applied' to them but this is a bit far-fetched and hardly 'controlled' in any way. The situation is even more blurred for characteristics like 'extroversion' and 'introversion'. When, exactly, is this 'treatment' applied? For occupations, over a relatively short period of time, it *is* possible to see the experience of being a nurse, say, as a 'treatment', especially if we can obtain before and after measures.

Correlational, observational and ex post facto studies

Some texts use the term 'correlational' for studies where we simply investigate whether there is a relationship between one variable and another 'out there'. The trouble with this term is that 'correlation', which we shall meet in Chapter 15, is a specific statistical technique and is *not* what we use to investigate a difference between two groups, for instance. Worse still, in true natural science experiments, correlation is precisely what *is* used to demonstrate, for instance, that the dependent variable of pressure increases as a direct result of the operation of a cause – the independent variable of heat.

Where 'correlational' is contrasted with experimental, what is meant is that we can only know there is some sort of relationship between two variables and that our evidence does *not* permit us to make inferences about *causal direction*. For instance, if we find that graduates have greater career motivation we may *not* conclude that the degree course experience *created* greater motivation. We may *only* say that the motivational difference is *related* to graduate status. University experience *might* cause increased motivation but, equally, having good motivation in the first place might influence the choice of a university course and success on it. We have lost that special strength of the experiment which is the opportunity to manipulate one variable and observe its effect on the other. We also cannot manipulate sex or gender to observe its effect on, say, IQ estimation. Certainly IQ estimation did not cause the sex difference (though it could just possibly contribute in some small way to an eventual *gender* difference!). From simply observing this difference there is no way we can begin to isolate the true causal variable. There will be a myriad of variables related to living as one sex/gender which are possible (and confounded) causal variables. There is a vast array of 'threats to validity' in this study if it is being asserted that 'being male causes people to rate themselves more highly on IQ'.

Some writers refer to this sort of non-experiment as an 'observational' study. The trouble with the term observational is that observation can be used as a technique for assessing the dependent variable in *true experiments* – see Bandura's (e.g. 1963) work and see Chapter 5. However, an 'observational study' again usually refers to one which is not an experiment and in which researchers record freely produced behaviour in a relatively natural setting. It will also cover 'observations' on existing groups, as in group difference studies, and Cooke and Campbell (1979) refer to such studies as being 'passive observational'.

Solso and Johnson (1989) use the term 'experimenter selected independent variable' for the variable measured in group difference studies (rather than 'experimenter *manipu-*

---

[4] 'Group difference study', though a more comfortable phrase, has the slight ambiguity that it could be taken to refer to a true experiment looking for a difference between experimental and control groups.

Table 3.6 Defining characteristics of experimental and non-experimental types of investigation and associated levels of variable control

Experiment	Quasi-experiment	Non-experiment
experimenter manipulation of independent variable	no control over independent variable	correlational[1]
		observational[3]
	and/or	interview
random allocation to groups	no random allocation to groups	survey
		case study
		group difference study[2]

High ← degree of investigator control over variables → Low

	Examples	
Independent Samples	Non-equivalent groups	See Chapters 5 to 9
Repeated Measures	'Natural' experiment	
Matched Pairs	Interrupted time series	
Single Participant		

1. *As explained in the text, 'correlational' is used in a general, not a statistical, way to refer to studies where we will only show that two variables are associated. Where one variable is categorical (see Chapter 10) such as gender or vegetarian/meat-eater, the statistical analysis will be a test of difference not a correlation, so the term can be misleading.*
2. *As explained in the text, there is some ambiguity about the status of group difference studies (e.g. male vs. female; extrovert vs. introvert) in terms of quasi-experimentation. They are certainly not true experiments. In effect, it is the extent to which particular research designs control for 'threats to validity' that determines the extent to which the study partakes of quasi-experimental design features.*
3. *As is explained in Chapter 5, observation can be used as a technique for data recording within a true experiment. The meaning here however, when contrasted with an experiment, is that pre-existing variables are only observed and measured, not manipulated.*

lated independent variable' for the true experiment). Robson (1993) talks of 'retrospective experimentation'. As he points out, if we are *not* interested in cause, but simply in, say, prediction for applied personnel purposes, then, with a clearly demonstrated group difference between, say, extroverts and introverts we have a valid selection technique and are not bothered about *experimental* validity.

So-called 'ex post facto' studies, also called 'retrospective', include any design where the events studied have already occurred (i.e. 'after the fact'). This can include natural experiments where a 'treatment' was applied to specific groups, but also includes group difference studies, since any differences found were already in existence, not created by the research design.

At present there is no clear agreement on the status and naming of group difference or 'person variable' type studies, yet they are extremely common in student practical work and in research journals where a variety of terms is used to describe them. The situation is trickier in the more complex experimental designs which some students will encounter in Chapter 18. Here, a person variable is very often used as one independent variable (or factor) when a second independent variable is a more typical 'treatment'. For instance, sex can be one 'independent variable' while the other independent variable is the presence or absence of feedback on a problem-solving task. Here, Leary (1995) wants to use the term 'experricor' designs – since one variable is experimental and the other correlational – but the term has not caught on so far!

I think the safest thing the student can do is to just *not* treat group difference designs as true experiments and to be aware of just how little a sex difference study (or extrovert/introvert comparison) tells us if it is not related to predictions from a general theory and, even then, just how ambiguous any result will be in terms of leading us to any cause-effect relationship. Sex-difference studies are certainly not true experiments. Some examination boards require the inclusion of an 'experiment' and a 'non-experimental design'. If *quasi-* experiments are permitted under the 'experiment' heading, then probably no examiner would reject a group difference study submitted under this heading, especially as some texts do clearly include sex-difference studies under their 'quasi-experiment' heading. However, a demonstration that males give themselves higher IQs than females could be incorporated into a *non-experimental* survey or questionnaire design, including *other* relevant questions. The most important thing of all, however, is to demonstrate awareness of the features of true experiments, to understand what definitely *would* be termed a quasi-experiment, and always to discuss possible 'threats' and weaknesses when interpreting the results of any type of study at all.

Glossary

Data obtained from existing, often public, records	_____ _____	archival data
Order effect which has greater strength in one particular order and where, therefore, counterbalancing would be ineffective	_____ _____ _____	asymmetrical order effect
'Dummy' number given to categorical levels of an independent variable in an unrelated design in order to proceed with computer analysis	_____ _____	variable code
Variable which is uncontrolled and obscures any effect sought, usually in a systematic manner	_____ _____	confounding variable
Group used as baseline measure against which, performance of experimental, treatment or criterion group is assessed	_____	control group
Study of the extent to which one variable is related to another, often referring to non-manipulated variables measured outside the laboratory	_____ _____	correlational study
Half participants do conditions in a particular order and the other half take the conditions in the opposite order – this is done to balance (not eliminate) any order effects	_____	counterbalancing

Cues in a study which help the participant to work out what is expected of him/her	_____ _____	demand characteristics
Variable which is assumed to be directly affected by changes in the IV	_____ _____	dependent variable
Procedure in an experiment where neither participants <u>nor</u> data gatherer (experimenter or assistants) know which treatment participants have received (i.e. which conditions they were in)	_____ _____	double blind
Variance among scores caused by the operation of randomly acting variables	_____ _____	error variance
Participants' concern about being tested, which may affect results	_____ _____	evaluation apprehension
Study in which an independent variable is manipulated	_____	**experiment**
Experiment which exploits the occurrence of a naturally occurring independent variable	_____ _____	natural experiment
Experiment in which experimenter does not have control over the allocation of participants to conditions and/or over the IV	____ – _____	quasi-experiment
Experiment in which the experimenter has complete control over the manipulation of the independent variable, over all extraneous variables, and in which, if the design uses unrelated groups, participants are allocated at random to conditions	_____ _____	true experiment
		Experimental Designs
Each condition of the independent variable is experienced by only one group of participants	_____	independent samples (between groups; independent/ unrelated groups/subjects)
Each participant in one group/condition is paired on specific variable(s) with a participant in another group/condition	_____	matched pairs
Each participant takes part in all conditions of the independent variable	_____	repeated measures (within subjects/ groups)
Design in which individual scores in one condition can be paired with individual scores in other conditions	_____	related
Design in which only one participant is tested	_____	single participant

Design in which individual scores in one condition cannot be paired (or linked) in any way with individual scores in any other condition	_____	unrelated
Research where pre-existing and non-manipulated variables among people are measured for difference or correlation	__ _____ ____ _____	ex post facto research
Tendency for experimenter's knowledge of what is being tested to influence the outcome of research	_____ _____	experimenter expectancy
The extent to which the results produced by two or more experimenters are related	_____ _____	experimenter reliability
Anything other than the IV which could affect the dependent variable; it may or may not have been allowed for and/or controlled	_____ _____	extraneous variables
An ex post facto study which compares the measurement of an existing variable in two contrasting groups e.g. male/female or introvert/extrovert	_____ _____ _____	group difference study
Effect on human performance caused solely by the knowledge that one is being observed	_____ _____	Hawthorne effect
Occurs when participants in an experiment have experiences, unconnected to the independent variable treatment, which confounds measures on the dependent variable of interest	_____ _____	history effects
Variable which experimenter manipulates in an experiment and which is assumed to have a direct affect on the dependent variable	_____ _____	independent variable
Design in which experimenters investigate participants in their everyday environment	_____ _____	naturalistic design
Study in which people are not aware that they are part of the study in any way	_____ _____	non-reactive study
Research which simply measures characteristics of how people are or behave but doesn't intervene OR (more narrowly) research in which the main data gathering technique involves looking directly at behaviour as it occurs and categorising or measuring it	_____ _____	observational study
A confounding effect caused by experiencing one condition, then another, such as practice or fatigue	_____	order effects

Person variables differing in proportion across different experimental groups and possibly confounding results

_____
_____

participant variables

Group who don't receive the critical 'treatment' but everything else the experimental group receive and who are (sometimes) led to believe that their treatment will have an effect; used to check expectancy effects

_____
_____

placebo group

Tendency of participants to act in accordance with what they think the experimenter would like

_____ ___
_____

pleasing the experimenter

Measure of participants before an experiment in order to balance or compare groups, or to assess change by comparison with scores *after* the experiment

___-_____

pre-test

Any error possible in measuring a variable, excluding error which is systematic

_____ _____

random error

Putting stimulus items or trial types into random order for the purpose of elimination of order effects

_____

randomisation

Study in which participants are required to respond in some way; they are therefore aware of being the subject of assessment

_____ _____

reactive study/design

Procedure in an experiment where participants do not know which treatment they received (i.e. which condition they were in)

_____ _____

single blind

Tendency of participants in research to want to 'look good' and provide socially acceptable answers

_____
_____

social desirability

Way of testing or acquiring measures from participants which is repeated in exactly the same way each time for all common parts of the method

_____
_____

standardised procedure

Design in which behaviour is recorded for a certain period before and after a treatment point in order to look for relatively sudden change

_____-____ _____

time-series design

Study in which participants are given a short account of a person or event and where just one aspect of the person or event is varied across conditions

_____
_____

vignette study

Exercises

1. For each of the following studies, select any of the following terms to describe them appropriately:

true experiment	natural experiment
quasi-experiment	field experiment
group difference	field investigation
ex post facto	laboratory experiment
correlational	laboratory investigation

More than one term might be chosen for any particular study.

a. A ladder is placed against a street wall to see whether more males or females will avoid it.

b. Randomly allocated students are asked to write essays in silence or listening to loud music.

c. Boys with no brother and boys with two brothers are observed under laboratory conditions to see which group exhibits greater aggression.

d. A researcher, dressed either casually or smart, approaches passengers at a station to ask for directions. The aim is to see whether smart dress elicits greater help.

e. Under laboratory conditions, people are asked to make a speech, contrary to their own view, first alone and then in front of others.

f. Drug addicts are compared with a control group on their tolerance of pain, measured in the laboratory.

g. Researchers visit various grades of worker at their place of employment and take them through a questionnaire on their attitude to authority. It is thought that salary level will be related to degree of respect for authority.

h. One of two very similar homes for the elderly passes from local government to private control. Workers in each are compared on job satisfaction over the following year, using informal interviews.

i. Children in one class at a school are given a six-month trial of an experimental new reading programme using a multi-media approach. A second class of children receive special attention in reading but not the new programme. Improvements are compared.

j. The number of days off sick for workers in a large factory is measured monthly for one year before and one year after the national introduction of new regulations under which people may 'self-certificate' sicknesses lasting under four days.

2. Of the designs outlined in 1:

a. Which are not likely to be affected by demand characteristics?

b. Which might involve rather loose procedures?

c. Which are subject to researcher bias?

d. In which could 'blind' data gathering procedures be employed?

3. In Fantz's famous 'looking-chamber' experiment, a baby is shown two patterns and the researcher records how much time is spent looking at either pattern. The idea is to see whether the baby prefers complex patterns to simpler ones. What is the independent variable, what is the dependent variable and what sort of experimental design is this?

4 In one version of the 'visual cliff' experiment, infants are observed while their mothers try to entice them to come to them across a glass sheet with a large drop beneath it. The babies are seated in the middle of the table and there is a 'safe' looking surface to the other side of the apparently deep drop. What condition can be added to make this a true experiment, and what sort of design would the experiment then be?

5 In Milgram's main demonstration of obedience (as it is described by most textbooks), it was shown that, if the experimenter insisted, participants would continue to shock a 'victim' who had screamed, given up screaming and not responded for several trials. This is not a true experiment as it stands. What condition(s) could be added to turn it into one?

6 Your tutor conducts an experiment on your class. Each student is given a set of anagrams to solve and the time to solve each one is taken. You find that some of the anagrams were of concrete words and the others were of abstract words, in no particular order. This was the IV. What design was this, and what special precaution, associated with this design, has your tutor wisely taken and why?

7 Again your tutor conducts an experiment. Students are in pairs. You time your partner while she learns a finger maze, first with the left hand, then with the right. She then times you while you learn first with the right, then the left. What sort of experimental design is this? What special precaution is taken and why?

8 A researcher looks for families in which there are two brothers or two sisters born within a year of each other and where one sibling has suffered a certain illness before four years old. They are tested at eight years old to see whether the illness child is poorer than the other on number and reading skills. What sort of research design is being employed here?

Answers

1 a. Group difference; field investigation.
b. Laboratory (true) experiment.
c. Group difference; laboratory investigation; ex post facto.
d. Field quasi-experiment.
e. Laboratory (true) experiment.
f. Laboratory investigation; group difference; ex post facto; if the experience of being an addict is counted as a 'treatment', then this is arguably a natural quasi-experiment.
g. Correlational; field investigation.
h. Natural quasi-experiment.
i. Field quasi-experiment.
j. Natural quasi-experiment.

2 a. a, d, j
b. g, h, i
c. all
d. all; in each case data gatherers need not know the true or full purpose of the research.

3   IV – complexity of pattern. DV – time spent gazing. Design – repeated measures (with randomisation and simultaneous presentation of IV).

4   Add condition with same babies enticed over the shallow side – this gives repeated measures; or, have control group enticed over shallow side – independent samples; or match control group with experimental group on stage of crawling – matched pairs.

5   Vary distance of victim, distance of experimenter. As a control group, have people give shocks but experimenter gives *no* orders to continue (this *was* done and almost all participants gave up at the first victim complaint – though few textbooks describe this).

6   Repeated measures. Randomisation of IV stimuli. Avoid order effects.

7   Repeated measures. Counterbalancing. Avoid order effects.

8   Matched pairs (but not a true experiment); form of natural quasi-experiment; ex post facto.

4

Internal and external validity in the field and laboratory experiment

- Experimental *validity* concerns the issue of whether an experimental procedure has isolated a genuine cause-effect relationship. *Threats to validity* are the many ways in which it is possible for an apparent but false effect to appear, or for a real effect to be obscured.
- *Threats to internal and external validity* have been emphasised in the literature promoting the value and pitfalls of quasi-experimental work in field research.
- *Internal validity* refers to the issue of whether an apparent effect would have occurred anyway, without the application of the experimental 'treatment'. This can occur through incorrectly applied statistics, sampling biases, history effects and other extraneous variables unconnected with manipulation of the IV.
- *Construct validity* concerns generalisation to other, perhaps fuller, measures of the variables tested. It includes most examples of *confounding*, and is intimately connected with the *operationalisation* of variables.
- *External validity* concerns whether an effect generalises from the specific people, place and measures of variables tested to the population, other populations, other times, other settings (*ecological validity*)
- One check on validity is *replication*, but particularly the relatively recent development of *meta-analysis*.
- The **laboratory experiment** is compared for validity with **field experiments** and studies.

The main message of the chapter is not that students need not get embroiled in hair-splitting debate about what exactly is a case of this or that type of validity. The point is to study the various 'threats' and try to avoid them in practical work, or at least discuss them in writing about practical studies.

AN INTRODUCTION TO INTERNAL AND EXTERNAL VALIDITY

The following description of various so-called 'threats to validity' might help in the process referred to at the very end of the last chapter, of analysing the possible weaknesses in any type of hypothesis testing study. No study is perfect and all will entail various possible 'threats' – that is, uncontrolled variables which might interfere with the interpretation of a clear cause-effect link in an experiment. It might be a good idea to refer to this chapter when you're stuck on the 'discussion' section of your practical report write-up in order to generate ideas about possible weaknesses in your study. Before we go further, would you like to anticipate some of the basic ideas by having a go at the exercise below?

Consider the following project carried out by a student at Rip-off College where staff have responsibility for 60 students per class, one hour a week and therefore have very little time to monitor what students set out to test. Tabatha feels she can train people to draw better. To do this she asks student friends to be participants in her study which involves training one group and having the other as a control. She tells friends that the training will take quite some time so those who are rather busy are placed in the control group, who need only turn up for the test sessions. Both groups of participants are tested for artistic ability at the beginning and end of the training period and improvement is measured as the difference between these two scores. The test is to copy a drawing of Mickey Mouse. A slight problem occurs in that Tabatha lost the original pre-test cartoon, but she was fairly confident that her post-test one was much the same. She also found the training was too much for her to conduct on her own so she had to get an artist acquaintance to help, after giving him a rough idea of how her training method worked.

The trained group have ten sessions of one hour and at the end of this period Tabatha feels she has got on very well with them, even though rather a lot have dropped out because of the time needed. One of the control group participants even remarks on how matey they all seem to be and that some members of the control group had noted that the training group seemed to have a good time in the bar each week after the sessions. Some of her trainees sign up for a night class in drawing because they want to do well in the final test. Quite a few others are on a BTEC Health Studies course and started a module on creative art during the training which they thought was quite fortunate. The final difference between groups was quite small but the trained group did better. Tabatha loathes statistics so she decides to present the raw data just as they were recorded. She hasn't yet reached the recommended reading on significance tests in her Rip-off College self-study pack.

Now, please list all the things you think Tabatha might have got a bit wrong in this study. *In particular*, list all the reasons why she might have got a difference but *not* because of the specific training plan she used.

'THREATS' TO VALIDITY

I hope that, even if you're new to the idea of scientific or experimental research, Tabatha's project offended your sense of balanced, fair, objective investigation. There are obviously many ways in which Tabatha might have got some differences but *not* because of her particular training programme. In the accepted language of experimental issues we need to distinguish between INTERNAL and EXTERNAL THREATS TO VALIDITY.

Threats to internal validity

These are ways in which the difference might have occurred (or appear to have occurred) which have nothing at all to do with the manipulation of the independent variable. The 'effect' would have occurred even if the 'treatment' had not been given.

Threats to external validity

If the difference did occur as a result of manipulation of the independent variable, to what extent is it legitimate to generalise from the manipulated variable and the measured dependent variable to a more general cause-effect relationship?

Table 4.1 Threats to internal, construct and external validity of research studies (based on Cooke and Campbell, 1979)

Threats to internal validity	Description	Comments
Using a low power statistical test	Different tests have varying sensitivity to detect difference	Dealt with in the statistics Chapters 10–20
Violating assumptions of statistical test used	Tests should not be used if the data don't fit the assumptions	Dealt with in the statistics Chapters 10–20
'Fishing'/capitalising on chance	Multiple testing of the same data gives a higher chance of getting a fluke 'significant' result – see p. 379	For all these three statistical points note that Tabatha didn't bother with testing her data, and that differences were small
Reliability of measures	Reliability as described in Chapters 2 and 7	Unreliable measures increase variance
Reliability of procedures	Standardisation of procedures – described in Chapter 3	Tabatha doesn't seem to have given *precise* instructions to her extra trainer
Random errors in the research setting	Described in Chapter 3	
Participant variance	Problem described in Chapter 3	
History	Events which happen to participants during the research which affect results but are not linked to the IV	Some of Tabatha's trainees started an art module
Maturation	Participants may mature during the study	A problem in child development studies, especially where there is not an adequate control group
Testing	Participants may get 'wise' to the tests if they're repeated	Tabatha's trainees might have practised on Mickey Mouse or at least recalled their original mistakes
Instrumentation	Measures may change in effect between first and second testing. Includes ceiling and floor effects.	Tabatha changed her measure because she lost the first version

Table 4.1 Continued

Threats to internal validity	Description	Comments
Selection bias	Occurs when more of one type of person gets into one group for the study – a big problem in field research where many unwanted factors may differ between, say, two groups of children under study	Those who were more busy selected themselves into the control group in Tabatha's study. Also, since the students knew what it was about, keener ones may have joined the training group
Drop-out	More of one type of person may drop out of one of the groups	More students dropped out of Tabatha's trainee group because of the time taken
Imitation of treatment	Control participants may get to know what treatment groups are doing	If mothers are being helped to stimulate their children, the techniques may pass to control group mothers simply by meeting in the community
Rivalry or demoralisation of control group	'Control' participants may try to do as well as the 'treatment' group or they may resent the 'treatment'	Some of Tabatha's control students seem to resent not being in the trainee group

Threats to construct validity		
Construct measures	To what extent do the measures employed actually tap the concept under study?	Discussed in this Chapter. How accurately or fully is Tabatha measuring 'artistic ability'? Suppose synchro-swimming ability were judged simply by the time swimmers could remain underwater?
Inadequate variable definition	To what extent are the measures used adequately defined?	Tabatha's 'rough idea' of her training, given to her extra trainer, suggests it isn't well defined
Mono-method bias	Construct validity is improved by taking a variety of measures of the same concept	For instance, better to have people give their 'sentence' of a fictitious criminal in writing *and* in public, and perhaps to get them to rate for guilt or 'criminality' also

Table 4.1 Continued

Threats to construct validity	Description	Comments
Hypothesis guessing	'Treatment' participants may well guess what is required of them in the study	Tabatha's trainees certainly knew what they were expected to do
Evaluation apprehension ('pleasing the experimenter' or 'looking good')	Hypothesis guessing may lead to trying to please the experimenter or looking good	See 'demand characteristics' p. 76. Note that Tabatha's trainees tried to do well
Experimenter expectancy	Dealt with in this Chapter	See also p. 74
Level of the independent variable (IV)	The levels of the IV used may not be far enough apart. Better to use several levels (in more advanced work)	One and three cups of coffee may make no difference but one and 10 might! Better to try one, four, seven and 10, perhaps
Threats to external validity		
Generalisation to the population	Dealt with in this Chapter	See also Chapter 2
Generalisation to other populations	Dealt with in this chapter	See also Chapter 2
Generalisation to other settings; 'ecological validity'	Dealt with in this Chapter	Will Tabatha's training work out of college?

INTERNAL VALIDITY

In 1979, Campbell and Cook, in an excellent resource text on validity issues, divided their attention between two areas:

1. Is there a real *statistical* effect here?
2. If so, what incidental events might have caused it?

1. This question mainly concerns statistical significance and will be dealt with in Chapter 11. It's the sort of question we raise when we say 'Sure there was a difference but it was so small – it could have just been a coincidence' – the sort of question we ask about those lines of plates in washing-up liquid commercials. For now, note, from Table 4.1 that if we use the wrong statistical test, use a test without satisfying its assumptions, do too many tests on the same data, or introduce too many random errors (which smother actual differences with 'noise'), we may be unable to state confidently that any difference found reflects a true difference in the population sampled which could therefore be repeated.

2. From Table 4.1 note that the other, non-statistical threats to internal validity concern reasons why the differences might have occurred even though manipulation of the IV didn't cause them. Most of these were covered in the sections on confound-

ing (selection, history, measures, designs, procedure). Note that rivalry or resentment by the control group, and so on, are seen as a threat to *internal* validity because the treatment isn't causing any effect on the treatment group. The control group is creating the difference. Tabatha's control group might draw half-heartedly since at least some appear to feel a bit left out. This factor, then, has nothing to do with the programme as such; manipulation of the independent variable is not causing any consequent difference that might occur from this factor.

EXTERNAL VALIDITY AND CONSTRUCT VALIDITY

Construct validity

Suppose manipulation of the independent variable *is* responsible for the change. This does not mean that the identified independent variable *itself* is the causal variable. As we saw above, a related variable can be responsible, for instance, making meaningful links rather than forming images. This is why it is so important to *operationalise* our variables in psychological research.

A scientific approach looks at a claimed cause-effect demonstration and asks the questions 'What exactly did you do?' (i.e. what *operations* did you perform?). In the mental imagery experiment we can't say that we directly observed an effect of imagery on improved memory. We can only say we observed a relationship between asking participants to form image links and higher correct recall of items. We don't *know* that people formed images – we know what our *operations* were. We don't *know* that all aspects of memory were 'better' – only that more items were recalled correctly, the latter being our *operational definition* of 'memory' in this study. Suppose we investigate the effects of hunger on illusory perception by asking people to eat dinner at 8 p.m. and testing them at 8 a.m. the next morning before they have eaten again. We ask them what they see in abstract ink-blots (see p. 165) and count only the 'edible items' reported. Our operational definition of 'hunger' is *restraint from eating for 12 hours* (we can't observe hunger) and our operationalised dependent variable is *number of reported food items*, not 'illusions of food'.

By emphasising construct validity, Campbell and his colleagues were requiring researchers to focus on just exactly what they might have demonstrated when they appear to have shown that X causes Y. As we have seen, it could be that A (related to or varying with X) causes Y, that X causes B (related to Y), or even that A causes B. In non-experimental research or in the loosely controlled quasi-experiment, it could be that X and Y are both caused by a third variable C (denoted X-C-Y). In some studies, especially those that are ex post facto and/or study group differences, we need to ask whether Y caused X instead. In Chapter 1 we saw that if we find that a group of vitamin K5 eaters are better readers than a group of non-K5 eaters, there is something about our schemas of what causes what in the world that leads us far more directly, and pretty instantaneously, to the 'X causes Y' explanation (vitamin causes reading improvement). However, we need to entertain the third variable X-C-Y possibility. Perhaps those parents who tend to have superior reading ability (Y) *also* tend to be more informed about health matters (C) and therefore tend to eat a more healthy diet *including* greater use of K5 rich spinach (X). It is even possible (but exceedingly far-fetched) to imagine a Y causes X possibility – that excessive reading (Y) causes a vitamin deficiency which children tend to make up by seeking out (without conscious recognition) more K5 rich foods (X)! Less far fetched is the possibility that increased reading by parents leads to a higher educational level which, in turn, creates the type of contact with people, literature and media that includes promotion of healthier eating. Parents, of course, pass on their reading habits to their children.

Although issues of construct validity can be a heady debate, at the very heart of what psychology tries to do, the practical point, which I cannot emphasise too strongly here for new psychology students, is the threat from *weak definition of variables*. We have already seen, in Chapter 2, the importance of careful definitions of variables. The worst crimes usually concern the dependent variable. Tutors often despair of writing 'how was this measured?' by the side of hypotheses or statements of aims in practical reports! Some examples are 'aggression will be greater . . .', '. . . will have better memory', '. . . are sexist in their attitudes'. What usually is to be assessed is whether one group of children will hit peers more, whether more words are recalled, whether more 'feminine' than 'masculine' terms have been used to describe a baby or a particular occupation. These are only a (small) part of the whole concept mentioned in the definitions. It may sound as though we're being pretty finicky here, like Stephen Fry and Hugh Laurie telling the waitress off because she brought them a glass of water and they didn't ask for the glass! But in psychology it is of crucial importance not to claim you've discovered or demonstrated something which you haven't. Consider a typical psychology class practical where we devise a questionnaire concerning, say, homosexuality. This is discussed as the measurement of an 'attitude'. However, almost all definitions of 'attitude' include something about an *enduring* belief – yet we've only measured a person's view at *one* moment. Will they think this next week? What *have* we measured exactly? In any case, does our questionnaire tap anything like the full range and depth of an 'attitude to homosexuality'?

Notice from Table 4.1 that hypothesis guessing, 'pleasing the experimenter' and experimenter expectancy are seen as construct threats by Cook and Campbell. This is because they vary *with* the independent variable and *because of it*. This is a rather subtle point and many writers treat these as internal threats. One should not lose sleep over these distinctions so long as the main idea is absorbed, of checking for threats from various perspectives and approaching research design with a view to elimination of as many of these as is feasible.

External validity

In their 1979 work Campbell and Cooke argued that construct validity was, for them, very similar to external validity. In questioning the external validity of apparent effects they were focusing on the extent to which the effect demonstrated could be generalised beyond the exact experimental context. As we have seen, construct validity is a rather subtle aspect of this concerning how far, exactly, we can generalise from the measures and operations used in the experiment to more abstract or broader constructs and to the direction of the relationships between constructs (i.e. causes and effects). In addition (and these are often seen as the only or main forms of external validity), they queried the extent to which the effect demonstrated could be generalised from:

1. the specific sample tested to other people
2. the research setting to other settings
3. the period of testing to other periods

Bracht and Glass (1968) labelled 1 as 'population validity' and 2 as ECOLOGICAL VALIDITY. I have treated this second term as a key term because, unlike the first, it is a very popular term, although its original use (Brunswik, 1947) was limited to the problem of generalising from perceptual 'cues' used in the laboratory investigation of perception to the use of such cues in one's culturally learned perceptual environment outside the laboratory.

Population validity

Think how often you've been frustrated by a media article which, on the basis of some single study, goes on to make claims such as '... so we see that women (do such and such) whilst men (do so and so) ...'. Obviously a class experiment can't be generalised to *all* students nor can it be generalised to all other groups of people. The matter of how important this issue is varies with the type of study. Work in cross-cultural psychology (see Chapter 8) has shown us that many effects published in US American student texts as apparently *universal* – e.g. the 'fundamental attribution error' and the 'self-serving attributional bias' – are limited, in fact, to *individualistic* (mainly 'Western') societies. Note the use of the term 'fundamental' as evidence of the belief that this effect is universal. Some psychologists extrapolate to whole continents with terms like 'the African mind' – see Jung's quotation on p. 185 and Lynn's (1991a) estimate of the 'Black African IQ', p. 185. We have already seen that a vast number of psychology experiments have been carried out on students (mainly male and mainly white until, at least, the mid 1970s, and certainly mainly Western).

Ecological validity

A big problem with psychological laboratory research is that it is often very difficult to see how results could be generalised to real-life circumstances, to naturally occurring behaviour in an everyday setting. A study's 'ecological validity', according to Bracht and Glass, has to do with the extent to which it generalises to other settings or places. A study has higher ecological validity if it generalises beyond the laboratory to field settings but a field study, in a naturalistic setting, is *not* automatically 'ecologically valid'. This depends on whether it too will generalise to other (natural) settings (see Hammersley and Atkinson, 1983, p. 11). Unfortunately this is one of those terms that has recently been 'popularised' beyond its original application and is often wrongly used to refer to and elevate the status of *any* naturalistic study. In fact, a study of a particular group 'in the field' may well be rich in *realism* but may not generalise at all to other settings and may therefore have *low* ecological validity.

A good example of the comparison between naturalistic study and ecological validity is to compare Milgram's famous laboratory studies of obedience (see p. 478) with the fairly famous obedience study by Hofling *et al.* (1966) in which it was shown that nurses working in a hospital, unaware of any experimental procedure, were telephoned by an unknown doctor and broke several hospital regulations by starting to administer, at the doctor's request, a potentially lethal dose of medicine. Many would be tempted to call Hofling's study 'ecologically valid' because it was carried out in a naturalistic hospital setting on real nurses at work. In fact, this would be quite wrong in the terms used by Cooke and Campbell and others. An attempted replication of Hofling's effect in fact failed to produce the original obedience effect (Rank and Jacobson, 1977), whereas Milgram's study has been successfully replicated in several different countries (population validity) using a variety of settings and materials (ecological and construct validity). In one well known variation by Milgram himself, ecological validity was demonstrated when it was shown that shifting the entire experiment away from the university laboratory and into a 'seedy' downtown office, apparently run by independent commercial researchers, did not reduce obedience levels to any significant degree. Here obedience levels were lower but the difference was not significant (several texts, failing to deal with significance, tend to give the opposite impression). This shows that the effect *will* generalise to other settings and thus confers ecological validity on the study, whereas Hofling's study would appear to still require some form of ecological validation.

However, if you claimed that many experiments in psychology are criticised because they lack ecological validity, this being because their results would not be replicated in real-life settings, you'd be correct. As an example of laboratory limitation, Asch's famous demonstrations of conformity (e.g. 1956) were conducted among total strangers, who had to judge the length of lines with no discussion. Real-life conformity almost always concerns familiarity and social interaction with one's peers. Asch's study would demonstrate more ecological validity if we could reproduce the effect, say, among friends in a school classroom setting. Several replications of Asch's work do indeed use student colleagues *and* a variety of cultures – see Smith and Bond (1993). Milgram (1961) increased conformity simply by having participants hear tape-recorded criticisms of their non-conforming judgements.

DOWN TO THE LAB OR INTO THE FIELD? STRENGTHS AND WEAKNESSES OF LABORATORY AND FIELD STUDIES

THE LABORATORY SETTING

The laboratory tends to be the preferred home of the experiment though many are carried out in the field and some studies carried out in laboratories are not experiments. The control over variables offered by the laboratory setting is very useful in pure observation studies, for instance, but it is the experiment per se that *demands* strong control over variables. A laboratory is ideal for highly accurate recordings of human cognitive functions, such as memory and selective attention, and for careful observations of rapid behaviour patterns. Whereas Bandura (1965) could strictly control the conditions of children seeing a film of rewarded, non-rewarded or punished adults, and could carefully assess consequent play behaviour with a (now notorious) Bobo doll, an equivalent attempt in the playground would involve such lack of control as children moving off, being obscured by others or simply lacking energy in cold weather. They may also wish to play with the observer if he or she isn't hidden.

Criticisms of the laboratory as research location

Many psychologists were rather taken aback in 1978 when Ulric Neisser, a leading cognitive psychologist who had been very much associated with the laboratory investigation of human cognitive processes, said publicly:

> The results of a hundred years of the psychological study of memory are somewhat discouraging. We have established firm empirical generalisations but most of them are so obvious that every ten-year old knows them anyway . . . If X is an interesting or socially significant aspect of memory, then psychologists have hardly ever studied X. (pp. 4–5)

This was pretty strong stuff and came from within the ranks! Neisser was calling for memory researchers to move towards studying 'real' memory in normal life. Mainstream memory research now includes a great number of 'everyday memory' studies and a whole new approach has developed around this theme, including the use of qualitative data recording (for instance, the diary method of Wagenaar, 1986 – see Chapter 5).

Psychologists were already used to the criticism of experimental laboratory procedures made by those who did not use them. Some of these were:

Narrowness of the independent and dependent variable

The aggression measured in Bandura's experiments is a very narrow range of what children are capable of in the way of destructive or hostile behaviour. Bandura might argue that at least this fraction of aggressive behaviour, we are now aware, could be modelled. However, Heather (1976) argued persuasively:

> Psychologists have attempted to squeeze the study of human life into a laboratory situation where it becomes unrecognisably different from its naturally occurring form. (p. 31)

Inability to generalise

A reliable effect in the laboratory may have little relevance to life outside it – a question of 'ecological validity'. For instance, demonstrations of effects concerning 'iconic memory' or very short-term 'visual information store', holding 'raw' sensory data from which we rapidly process information, have been considered by some psychologists to be just an artefact of the particular experiments which produced them.

Artificiality

The defence of artificial conditions in natural science is that one needs to isolate the variables of interest in an environment that permits control or nullification of all possible confounding variables and removal of as much random error as possible. Without this sort of control we would not know that feathers obey gravity in exactly the same way as lead, by falling with the same acceleration. Critics of the laboratory method in psychology, however, argue that behaviour studied out of a social context in an artificial setting can be meaningless. A laboratory is an intimidating, possibly even frightening place. People may well be unduly meek and in awe of their surroundings and the 'expert' technicians. If the experimenter compounds this feeling by sticking rigidly to a standardised procedure, reciting a formal set of instructions without normal interactive gestures such as smiles and helpful comments, people are hardly likely to feel 'at home' and behave in a manner representative of normal everyday behaviour.

In defence of the laboratory

In the study of brain processes, or of skilled human performance, stimulus detection and so on, not only does the artificiality of the laboratory hardly matter, it is the only place where highly technical and accurate measurements can be made, with random error reduced to a minimum. If we study human vigilance in detecting targets, for instance, does it matter whether this is done in the technical and artificial surroundings of a laboratory or the equally technical and artificial environment of a radar monitoring centre where research results will be usefully applied? If we wish to discover how fine new-born babies' perceptual discriminations are, this can be done with special equipment and the control of a laboratory. The infant, at two weeks, is hardly likely to know or care whether it is at home or not.

Without a laboratory, physicists would not have been able to split atoms. Psychologists have discovered effects in the laboratory which, as well as being interesting in themselves, have produced practical applications. Without the laboratory we would be unaware of differences in hemispheric function, the phenomena of perceptual defence or the extreme levels of obedience to authority which are possible. In each case, the appropriate interpretation of results has been much debated, but the phenomena themselves have been valuable in terms of human insight and further research. Stanovich (1992) states:

> . . . contrary to common belief, the artificiality of scientific experiments is not an accidental oversight. Scientists *deliberately* set up conditions that are unlike those that occur naturally because this is the only way to separate the many inherently correlated variables that determine events in the world . . .

In other words, artificiality is a direct consequence of the attempt to eliminate explanations. In this context it can be argued that we should not want to generalise results of laboratory studies to 'real life' at all, nor even demonstrated effects. In the laboratory we test out specific hypotheses which follow from the theory under investigation. If these are successful it is the *theory* which we might then attempt to generalise to more realistic contexts (Leary, 1995, p. 202). In medical research, the results and effects of laboratory trials are not generalised directly to human patients. They are fed into reports on theory and applications are made in quite a different sort of practical context.

The attempt to mimic real life inside the laboratory is often termed MUNDANE REALISM (Carlsmith *et al.*, 1976), whereas researchers are more likely to be interested in EXPERIMENTAL REALISM. This refers to a compelling context, perhaps quite unlike real life, but one in which participants fully engage because they are *caught up in the reality* of the experiment. In these circumstances we can be more confident that demand characteristics and expectancies are *less* likely to operate. The participant does not have the opportunity or inclination to work out 'what *should* happen here?'.

Research conducted under laboratory conditions is generally far easier to *replicate*, a feature valued very highly by advocates of the experimental method and an important factor in determining the generalisability of our theory.

Some effects created in a laboratory must surely be *stronger* outside the laboratory, rather than weaker without the artificiality. For instance, in Milgram's famous obedience study (p 478) participants were free to stop obeying at any time yet, in real life, there are often immense social pressures and possibly painful sanctions to suffer if one disobeys on principle. So Milgram's obedience effects could be expected to operate even *more* strongly in real life than he dramatically illustrated (with *experimental realism*) in his laboratory.

What counts as a 'naturalistic environment' is also sometimes hard to gauge. Much human behaviour occurs in what is not, to the individuals concerned, a natural environment, for example, the doctor's surgery, a visit to the police station, or the inside of an aeroplane. For some participants the laboratory can be no less natural than many other places. In Ainsworth's (1971) study of infant attachments, behaviour was observed when the mother was present, when she was absent, when a stranger was present and when the mother returned. From the infant's point of view it probably wasn't of great consequence where this study was carried out – the local nursery, a park or the laboratory (which looked something like a nursery anyway!). The infant is very often in situations just as strange, and what mattered overwhelmingly was whether the mother was there or not. If the infant behaves at the doctor's as she did in the laboratory, then the laboratory study has high ecological validity.

STUDIES IN THE FIELD

Having defended the use of the laboratory, it must also be admitted that if we wish to broaden the effects that psychology can study to more than just what can be 'trapped' in a laboratory, we must accept and deal with the problems of studying human behaviour in a natural context. Referring back to the Cialdini littering study described in Chapter 1, it would be difficult to invent within a laboratory setting a situation in which people might genuinely drop or not drop litter as they would in a public street. The organisational, clinical or health psychologist simply must work in the everyday world for much, if not all, of the time. The price paid, however, for studying behaviour in real-life settings with real and complex variables is, according to the conventional scientific model, a certain loss of precision because critical variables have not been and cannot be controlled. This in turn leads to a certain loss of confidence in the validity of any effect we might hope we are demonstrating.

For instance, Bowlby (1953) claimed (infamously) that institutionalised children displayed a significant amount of psychological distress because they lacked a single maternal bond. This explanation, based on field observations of children's behaviour in orphanages and the like, compared with the behaviour of two-parent children, was seriously confounded by the parallel presence of several other variables – regimented care, lack of social and sensory stimulation, reduced educational opportunity, rapid staff turnover and so on, all of which could potentially contribute towards an explanation of the children's behaviour. Lacking a single maternal bond might be a contributing factor to the children's psychological problems, or it might not contribute at all – it might simply co-exist with the real causes, some of which might be those just listed. The research and explanation are flawed because there are too many uncontrolled, possibly confounding variables. This research approximates to a 'natural ex post facto quasi-experiment'.

Many confounding problems could be associated with a recent field study by Kraut *et al.* (1998) (and ironically, you can read this report at the Internet site: homenet.hcii.cs.

cmu.edu/progress/research.html). This produced evidence of an association between increased use of the Internet and increased depression and loneliness, along with a loss of immediate social contacts. This is a good example of the media mis-representing the generalisations possible from exploratory psychological field research. In an article in which this work was reported, *The Guardian* (31 Aug 1998) states that 'One hour a week on the Internet *led to* an average increase of 1% on the depression scale . . .' [italics added]. The words 'led to' make the claim that Internet use *caused* the increased depression. There is of course the possibility that those participants who use the Internet more often were those who had reached that stage of adolescence where introverted activities, social withdrawal and experience of greater 'angst' often seem to coincide. There again, people who are depressed, or who are only going through a 'rough patch', might be more likely to turn to home interests such as the Internet.

In this case however, it would be feasible to run a true experiment which could eliminate all these typical interpretive problems from a correlational study. Student volunteers could have been randomly allocated to groups and either asked to use the Internet for certain periods (at the University's expense of course) or to refrain from doing so, over a certain period of time. In the Bowlby example, it would of course be totally unethical to have children randomly allocated to parent-rearing and institution-rearing experimental groups! To do useful realistic research psychologists cannot rely solely on the true, well-controlled experiment. They must use alternative methods which have both advantages and disadvantages over the true experiment – see Table 4.2.

Field experiments

This is not to say that well designed true experiments cannot be run in the field. Here are two examples where, it can be noted, participants were allocated to conditions on a random basis, making them true experiments since the independent variable was also experimenter controlled.

In an elegant design, Friedrich and Stein (1973) observed nursery school children to obtain a baseline for co-operative, helpful and friendly behaviour for each child. Children were then randomly assigned to two groups. Over a month, at regular intervals, one group watched 'pro-social' television programmes whilst the other (control) group watched neutral films of circuses and farm activity. The children were observed again at the end of the period and there was a significant rise in co-operativeness and peer-directed affection for the experimental group.

Ganster *et al.* (1982) randomly allocated 79 public service employees to a treatment group and a control group. The 'treatment' involved stress management training sessions and, at the end, this group showed relatively lower levels of adrenaline secretion, depression and anxiety. The effects, though small, were still present some four months later. The control group later received the same training.

One major advantage of some field experiments is the extent to which participants may not be aware of being involved in an experiment until effects have been recorded. The extent to which they are aware of being studied, or are aware of the experimental aims, determines the extent to which there may be threats from expectancy and demand

Table 4.2 Comparison of laboratory and field experiments

Field experiment	Comparison point	Laboratory experiment
Natural	**Environment**	Artificial
Controlled	**Independent variable**	Controlled
Random	**Allocation of participants to conditions**	Random
Participants *may* be unaware of study (if so, can't guess design, try to look good, etc.)	**Awareness of aims by participants**	Participants (except very young children) must be aware of being in experiment (though *not* what the design really is)
Weaker	**Control of extraneous variables**	Tighter
Higher	**Mundane realism**	Lower
Harder	**Replication**	Easier
Usually higher	**Expense & time**	Usually lower
To real-life field setting – good	**Generalisation (ecological validity)**	To real life – often very weak
To *other* real-life settings – probably weaker		
Perhaps can't be brought to field situation	**Equipment**	Can be complex and only usable in the laboratory
OTHER DISADVANTAGES More confounding possible because of researcher's need to negotiate with field setting personnel and managers		Narrow IV and DV can lead to low construct validity
		Setting more likely to create apprehension, wariness of strange surroundings, etc.

characteristics. Still, even with some distortion through this awareness, it may not involve the apprehension and artificiality of the laboratory.

The field experiment may be more expensive and time consuming. The researcher may require skills of tact and persuasion, not needed in the laboratory, in dealing with those who need convincing that the research is necessary, and in arranging details of the design which will ensure valid results whilst retaining co-operation with personnel such as the teacher or hospital worker.

The major disadvantage, however, is in the lack of control which the investigator can exert over extraneous variables, over strict manipulation of the independent variable and over careful, accurate measurement of the dependent variable. All these are vulnerable to far more fluctuation in the field setting than might occur in the laboratory.

META-ANALYSIS

Unfortunately for the scientific model of psychology which many psychologists adhere to, it is the exception, rather than the rule, to find a procedure which 'works' reliably every time it is tested. The world of psychological research is littered with conflicting results and areas of theoretical controversy, often bitterly disputed. A lot of the dispute is caused because researchers use different constructs, in different research settings, on different populations and at different historical moments. Here are some areas in which literally hundreds of studies have been carried out and yet without bringing us much closer to a definitive conclusion about the relationships they explore:

- sex differences and origin of differences in sex role
- the origins of intelligence – nature or nurture
- socio-economic position and educational or occupational achievement
- conformity and its relation to other personality variables
- cognitive dissonance (and alternative explanations)
- language development and parental stimulation
- deprivation of parental attachment and emotional disturbance

Periodically, it has been the tradition to conduct a LITERATURE REVIEW of a certain research topic area such as those above. Several examples of these will be found in the *Annual Review of Psychology*. The problem here is that reviewers can be highly selective and subjectively weight certain of the studies. They can interpret results with their own theoretical focus and fail to take account of common characteristics of some of the studies which might explain consistencies or oddities. In other words, the traditional review of scientific studies in psychology can be pretty unscientific.

META-ANALYSIS is a relatively recent approach to this problem, employing a set of statistical techniques in order to use the results of possibly hundreds of studies of the same or similar hypotheses as a new 'data set'. Studies are thoroughly reviewed and sorted as to the suitability of their hypotheses and methods in testing the theory in question. The result of each study is treated rather like an individual participant's result in a single study. The statistical procedures are beyond the scope of this book but here are some examples of meta-analytic research.

In one of the most famous and early meta-analytic studies, Smith and Glass (1977) included about 400 studies of the efficacy of psychotherapy (i.e. does it work?). The main findings were that the average therapy patient showed improvement superior to 75% of non-therapy patients and that behavioural and non-behavioural therapies were not significantly different in their effects.

Born (1987) meta-analysed 189 studies of sex differences in Thurstone-type intelligence measures across several cultures. In general, traditional sex differences were found but these were small and there were also some significant differences between clusters of cultures.

Rosnow and Rosenthal (1997) report meta-analytic studies on hundreds of studies of experimenter expectancy following doubts about their classic original work described in the last chapter.

Meta-analysis takes account of sample size and various statistical features of the data from each study. There are many arguments about features which merge in the analysis, such as Presby's (1978) argument that some non-behavioural therapies covered by Smith and Glass were better than others. The general point, however, is that meta-analysis seems to be a way of gathering together and refining knowledge (a general goal of science) in a subject area where one cannot expect the commonly accepted and standardised techniques of the natural sciences. It also brings into focus the various external threats to validity producing variation in a measured effect.

Glossary

Effect of attention grabbing, interesting experiment in compensating for artificiality or 'demand characteristics'	_____ _____	experimental realism
Review of all studies in a topic area with a view to highlighting overall trends and effects	_____ _____	literature review
Statistical analysis of multiple studies of the same, or very similar, hypotheses; an allegedly more objective version of the traditional literature review of all studies in a topic area	_____ – _____	meta-analysis
Research design which resembles everyday life but which is not necessarily engaging to participants	_____ _____	mundane realism
Extent to which a real effect has been isolated	_____	**validity**
Extent to which operational measures of variables match or encompass the intended theoretical construct	_____	construct
Extent to which investigation results can be generalised to other places and conditions, in particular, from the artificial and/or controlled (e.g. laboratory) to the natural environment	_____	ecological
Extent to which results of research can be generalised across people, places and times	_____	external
Extent to which effect found in a study can be taken to be real and caused by manipulation of the identified independent variable	_____	internal
Any aspect of the design or method of a study which weakens the likelihood that a real effect has been demonstrated or which might obscure the existence of a real effect	_____ __	threats to

Exercises

1 Which of the measures below might produce the best construct validity of a person's attitude to the elderly?

   a. answers to a questionnaire
   b. what they say to a close friend in conversation
   c. what they say in an informal interview
   d. the number of elderly people they count as close friends

2 You are discussing with a colleague two methods of measuring 'conformity'. One involves recording how often people will answer a simple question wrongly when several other people in the room have already answered wrongly (laboratory study). The other involves stopping people in the street who have infringed a traffic light or litter regulation and taking those who agree to do so through a short questionnaire (field study). Find arguments for and against each proposal, concentrating on the suggested location of the study. I hope you can think of at least three for and three against each one.

3 Each of the following statements from students discussing their practical work contains a reference to a form of internal or external validity issue. Pick 'internal', 'construct' or 'external', for each one and, where possible, name the threat:

   a. I mucked up the stats!
   b. Didn't you use the test we were given in class then?
   c. Useless questionnaire; didn't cover aggression – it was more to do with etiquette.
   d. 'course they knew what was going on; they know how to hide their prejudices.
   e. I bet you egged them on in the imagery condition!
   f. Bet it wouldn't work on the geography students.
   g. It was noisy in the student refectory; would they dislike that music so much in their own rooms?
   h. I got them to practise for 30 seconds in one condition and for one minute in the second condition. That second practice should have been for far longer; they didn't get any chance to improve in the second condition.

Answers

1 b. Most likely to avoid distortion through knowledge of testing, for instance.
   d. Is probably the most reliable; can get honest answers without divulging research aim.

3 a. internal (statistical error); b. internal (changed instrument); c. construct; d. construct (social desirability/'looking good'); e. construct (experimenter expectancy); f. external (population validity); g. external (ecological validity); h. construct validity; levels of independent variable too narrow.

5

Observational methods – watching and being with people

The chapter covers most methods which are generally classed as observation. In a sense, all data from people are gathered through some form of observation but the techniques described here mostly involve direct records of participant behaviour as it occurs, rather than methods of requesting information (interview, questionnaire) or of manipulation (experiment).

Distinctions are made between:

- observation as a *technique* and as an overall *research design*; observations can be the measurement mode of the dependent variable in an experiment; observation *studies* rely primarily on records of relatively unconstrained behaviour
- *participant observation* (where the observer acts in the observed group) and *non-participant observation*; so-called 'participant observation' studies often use interview techniques more than they use pure observation
- *disclosed* (people know what the observer is doing) and *undisclosed* observations
- *structured* and *non-structured* observations
- *controlled* observation (often in the laboratory) and *naturalistic* observation (observed person's own environment)
- Issues raised are the relative strengths and weaknesses of the various techniques and approaches, the objections of some qualitative researchers to structure and control in observational studies, reliability of observations, degrees of participation and specific ethical issues of undisclosed participant observation
- Advantages and disadvantages of the individual or group *case-study* are considered along with some research examples; the case-study provides unique information, unavailable by any other method, which may trigger more general and structured research.
- Further topics covered are: *role-play* and *simulation*, *diary studies*, *indirect observation* via

INTRODUCTION

We have seen that there can be fairly serious problems with the use of the experimental method in psychology, particularly in the laboratory where a very narrow, and perhaps artificial, selection of behaviour may be studied, where 'demand characteristics' may distort the procedure and where persons studied are 'dehumanised'. A set of methods which can avoid some, but not always all, of these criticisms is the set known generally as 'observational methods'.

In a sense, behaviour is observed in every psychological study. A researcher makes observations on the participants' reaction times, answers to a questionnaire, memory performance and so on. The emphasis, in using the term 'observational' however, is on the researcher observing a *relatively unconstrained* segment of a person's freely chosen behaviour.

'Observational' carries broad meaning in research literature. In a narrow sense it can refer simply to the *technique* of making observations and this can be conducted within an experimental design as a measure of a dependent variable, as well as being used in a variety of other settings. Used as a *general* description it can refer to all non-experimental studies where researchers simply take data from naturally occurring situations (also known as 'correlational' – see the last part of Chapter 3). If the basic *design* of a study is referred to as 'observational', however, then the emphasis is on observation as the main form of the study, a non-experiment in which records are made of relatively unconstrained behaviour as it occurs. This will be the main focus of the present chapter, though it should be noted that a quite common form of applied and often qualitative study – 'participant observation' – very often consists largely of interviews and notes on forms of social organisation.

OBSERVATION AS A TECHNIQUE OR AS AN OVERALL DESIGN

AS TECHNIQUE

Observation may be used as a technique within a traditional experimental design, as in Milgram's (1963) work on obedience where, in addition to mechanical recordings of participants' responses, film record was made in order to observe changes in emotional reactions. We have previously described Bandura's (1965) studies on children's imitations of models for aggression. Using observation as a technique for measuring the dependent variable of aggression, Bandura was able to manipulate a variety of independent variables, including the status or role of the model, the consequences of the model's behaviour and the degree of frustration experienced by the child just prior to observing the aggressive model.

The two examples above employ observational techniques in a laboratory setting. Field experiments very often use observation as a technique in the central role of measuring the dependent variable. Friedrich and Stein's (1973) study, described earlier, is a good example. Observation may also be employed within a role play or simulation study, described later.

AS OVERALL DESIGN

If an investigation is given the title 'observational', this is usually in order to contrast it with other designs, particularly the experimental. In this case, the researcher has chosen to observe naturally occurring behaviour and not to experiment with it, i.e. no independent variable is manipulated.

WEAKNESSES OF PURE OBSERVATIONAL STUDIES

Where the overall design is purely observational we encounter the major interpretative weakness, outlined in Chapter 3, of non-experimental studies.

> Suppose we observe higher levels of aggression among children who choose and watch more violent television programmes. What firm conclusion can be drawn from this study?

Newspaper readers, informed of this relationship, may well be drawn uncritically towards the conclusion that watching violent television is a cause of aggression. But of course, a moment's thought tells us that we have equal evidence for the conclusion that their aggression (arising from some other cause) directs their choice of viewing. If we discover a relationship between measures of different variables we are not usually in a position to establish the validity of a cause-effect relationship with any confidence. A manipulated independent variable has not led to changes in a measured dependent variable. A controlled experiment might provide enlightenment.

In an earlier chapter we saw that Friedrich and Stein (1973) assigned children to three experimental conditions – violent, pro-social and neutral television viewing programmes. After a month's viewing it was observed that the violent programme group were more aggressive in nursery-school play. Interestingly, the effect was greatest on those children who were initially highest in aggression. An experiment, then, can back up a hypothesis formed from observation, by showing a fairly clear-cut causal effect.

PARTICIPANT AND NON-PARTICIPANT OBSERVATION

A participant observer is to some extent a part of the group of individuals being observed, whereas a non-participant observer observes from a distance and should have no effect on the behaviour being observed. This is a 'dimension', since there are varying degrees of participation and these are described later on. There is also a dimension of DISCLOSURE in that researchers may or may not inform the people studied that they are being observed and the information given can be partial or can involve a certain amount of deception in order to obtain more genuine behaviour or at least behaviour which is not affected by knowledge of the research hypothesis.

The discussion of indirect, structured and controlled observation which follows is related entirely to non-participant studies. Participant observation is largely a qualitative approach and will be discussed later in the chapter.

STRUCTURED (OR 'SYSTEMATIC') OBSERVATIONS

The main features of a structured or systematic approach to observation are:
- the definition of behaviour categories to be recorded *prior* to commencing the main observational sessions*
- sampling of behaviour in a consistent manner using one of the sampling devices described below

● training of observers in the use of a *coding system* and to a good level of agreement prior to main data gathering sessions (INTER-OBSERVER RELIABILITY)

*In fact, Bakeman and Gottman (1986) argue that the early stages of an observational study need not be highly structured nor be certain of hypotheses. In this sense, the approach sounds much like many of the qualitative approaches (see Chapter 21) but their text is a good guide to what they would expect in the latter stages of the study – a structured and reliable system of gathering data to test hypotheses made specific if not prior to the study, at least prior to final data gathering sessions.

Data gathering devices

Records of behaviour can be made using any or a mixture of the following devices:
● film or video recording
● still camera
● audio tape (to record spoken observations)
● hand-written notes, ratings or coding 'on the spot'.

Visual recording has the advantage that behaviour can be analysed ('rated' or 'coded') after the event at the researcher's own pace and repeated viewing is possible. Any of the methods above might be used discreetly such that the participant is either completely unaware of the recording process (in which case ethical issues arise) or at least unable to see or hear the equipment during the observation session. This can be achieved with the use of screens or 'one-way' mirrors, which act as a mirror for the participant but a window for observers or camera.

Data gathering systems

Observers may often work to a specific 'grid' of behavioural categories. On the chart in Table 5.1, observers of children's behaviour during a free-play nursery session might record the amount of time or frequency that each child spent in each of the particular activities categorised (in columns).

In addition to simply recording what behaviour occurs, and how often, observers may be required to:

RATE behaviour according to a structured scale – for instance 1 to 10 on 'showing interest';

CODE behaviour according to a set of coding categories – for instance, graphic symbols which represent the positions of parts of the body.

Table 5.1 Grid for recording observations on children's play

Child	Inactive	Reading	Playing alone	Looking on	Playing with others		
					Different activity	Same activity	Cooperative activity
A							
B							
C etc.							

Table 5.2 Complete list of codes with short definitions for child observations (from Halliday *et al.*, 1986)

Verbal categories				Non-verbal categories			
				a)	**Vocal**	**b)**	**Non-vocal**
A	Demands attention	ON	Orders not to	B	Babbles (with intonation)	GO	Gives object
D	Describes, gives information	PR	Praises	G	Laughs, giggles	H	Holds, takes hold of
ET	Gives detailed label	PT	Prompts	QN	Makes questioning noise	L	Looks around
F	Corrects	Q	Questions	V	Makes monosyllabic	LO	Looks at object
I	Imitates completely	QT	Questions about a label		vocalisation	LP	Looks at mother
IP	Imitates partially	S	Tells story or recites	V2	Makes two-syllable	LI	Lifts child
IQ	Imitates as question		rhyme		vocalisation	OB	Obeys
IS	Imitates as sentence	T	Labels, names	VE	Makes an emotional noise	P	Points
N	Says 'no'	TH	Says 'thank you' or 'ta'	VN	Makes an object-specific	PL	Plays
NU	Count	Y	Says 'yes'		noise	R	Reaches
O	Orders, gives positive	Z	Adds tag	VS	Vocalises one-syllable	TO	Touches
	commands				continuously		
				W	Cries		
				YN	Makes affirmative noise		

In each case, some degree of standardisation would normally be sought by giving observers intensive training prior to commencement of observation sessions.

To exemplify some of these points we can look at a study by Halliday and Leslie (1986) in which acts of communication between mother and child (both ways) were coded from video recordings made over a period of six months' data gathering. The researchers sought to extend Bruner's ideas and show that children do more than just make requests or references in their interactions. They were interested in how these other actions might contribute to language acquisition as the child increasingly finds non-verbal methods inadequate. The researchers identified a set of 42 different actions, shown in Table 5.2, during pilot sessions with a couple of mother–child pairs. In the main study, an average of 12 half-hour sessions were recorded with 12 mother–child pairs. Each of these video sessions was coded using the 42 categories. There could be as many as five actions from the mother, and five from the child, in any five-second interval. I quote the detail here to give you some idea of the mountain of coding and analysis which goes on in such a study. The success of standardisation was estimated by finding the number of occasions upon which two observers agreed on 15% of the tapes. The figure was 76.7% and this is a form of INTER-OBSERVER RELIABILITY check (see below).

Time, point and event sampling

It may not always be possible or appropriate to record complete sequences of behaviour and interaction using video. If a session must be observed 'live', several observers might be required, one or two for each person observed. Where only one or a few observers are available, TIME SAMPLING techniques can be employed, in which observations of each individual are made for several short periods in, say, a two-hour session. In some cases, the short periods of, say, 15 seconds, are consecutive, so that a picture of the frequency of behaviour is built up.

In POINT SAMPLING, an observer concentrates on each individual in a group just long enough to record the category of their current behaviour before going on to observe the next person.

In EVENT SAMPLING, observations are made of a specific event each time it occurs, for instance, each example of a 'fight'. The event 'fight' would need to be *operationally defined* for the specific research project.

Reliability of observational techniques

Observers need to produce reliable observational records. The RELIABILITY of observers can be established by *correlating* (Chapter 15) their records with those of another observer or team. Such comparison will produce a measure of INTER-RATER RELIABILITY, 'rater' being another term for an observer who 'rates' behaviour.

An observer may remain consistent in their own ratings, even though they have a bias away from the desired rating scale. In this case of OBSERVER BIAS, correlations between their ratings and a more faithful rater should produce low inter-rater reliability. From the psychology of social perception we know that each person's view of a situation is unique and that our perceptions can be biased by innumerable factors. An untrained observer might readily evaluate behaviour which the researcher wants reported as objectively as possible. Where the trained observer reports a hard blow, the novice might describe this as 'vicious'.

There may be human error in failing to observe some bits of behaviour at all. One is reminded of the 'blind' soccer referee or ice-skating judge. In the study of animals it is easy to 'see' human characteristics in animal behaviour. This is known as 'anthropomorphism' and occurs, for instance, when birds are said to be 'talking' or a cat to be 'smiling'. In human studies, it could be falsely assumed that Jason 'follows' an adult (and is perhaps insecure) when he happens to be walking in the same direction. Or Jenny might be mistakenly described as 'copying' when she looks into a box to see what it was Sarah was looking at.

The problem may not lie with the human observers, however, but with the rating scale they are given which could be too vague or ambiguous. Reliability is enhanced by specifying in advance precisely what behavioural acts are to count in particular categories. Observers have to decide, for instance, when a push counts as 'aggressive' or when a child is being 'demanding'. Observers are usually trained to a standard of reliability and accuracy before the observational study proper begins.

CONTROLLED OBSERVATION

Observations can be controlled through structure as outlined above. Control can also be exercised over the environment in which observations take place. A high degree of environmental control can be exercised in the laboratory, though the participant need not be acutely aware that the environment *is* a 'laboratory'. Discussion groups may be observed in a comfortable 'seminar room', for instance. Ainsworth *et al* (1971) conducted a programme of research into infants' stranger and separation anxiety, mentioned in Chapter 4. In this study, the floor of a carefully organised playroom was marked into squares and trained observers recorded on film (and by speaking onto audio-tape) the movements of a child when its mother left and a stranger entered the room. The infants' behaviour was also filmed and the results were related to events of sensitivity in mothers' interactions with their children.

Problems with control – Naturalistic Observation

Studies in the laboratory do not escape many of the criticisms of laboratory experiments made in Chapter 4, in the sense that the laboratory can provide a highly artificial, possibly inhibiting atmosphere. Behaviour in the normal social context cannot be observed here. Some researchers, in search of realism, go out into the field and engage in NATURAL-ISTIC OBSERVATION in, say, the home, the nursery or the workplace. The method was inherited by psychology largely from the ethologists (Lorenz, Tinbergen) who studied animals in their natural habitat but nevertheless made very detailed and accurate recordings of what they showed to be instinctive patterns of behaviour.

The early 'baby biographers', whom we shall encounter below, were carrying out naturalistic observations, as did Piaget on his own children. Perhaps these studies also incorporated a certain amount of participative involvement on the part of the observers, however!

Because much of the behaviour observed in these studies, so long as the observer is discreet, would have occurred anyway, realism is high and behaviour observed is entirely genuine. In some studies, however, people are aware that they are being observed. This can mean a video camera following them around the house. In this case we still have the problem of possibly distorted behaviour, 'Hawthorne effects' and so on. As Shaffer (1985) records:

> Consider the experiences of one graduate student who attempted to take pictures of children's playground antics. What he recorded in many of his photos was somewhat less than spontaneous play. For example, one child who was playing alone with a doll jumped up when the student approached with the camera and informed him that he should take a picture of her 'new trick' on the monkey bars. Another child . . . said 'Get this' as he broke away from the kickball game and laid a blindside tackle on an unsuspecting onlooker. (p. 16)

Reactions to knowledge of observation can be more subtle. Zegoib et al. (1975) showed mothers under observation interacting more with their children, becoming more engaged in their activities and being more warm and patient. In Brody et al.'s (1984) work, it was shown that siblings tended to reduce teasing, to quarrel less and to use less threatening behaviour under observation. However, Jacob, Tennenbaum, Seilhamer and Bargiel (1994) conducted both high and low obtrusive observations at family meal-times and found very few reactivity effects in either condition.

Reactive effects could, of course, be eliminated by the use of hidden cameras but this introduces ethical problems and is anyway impossible where the researcher wants to investigate behaviour within the home setting, unless, say, parents collude and only children's behaviour is observed.

One way to reduce reactivity effects is to become a predictable and familiar part of the environment. For instance, Charlesworth and Hartup (1967) made several visits to a nursery school, interacted with the children, learnt their names and so on. This also gave them the opportunity to test out and improve the reliability of the observation scheme they were going to employ.

An example of non-participant naturalistic observation from the general literature would be Brown, Fraser and Bellugi's (1964) study of Adam, Eve and Sarah's speech productions in the home with parents every one or two weeks for several years. More recently, Sussman, Hahn, Dent and Stacy (1993) used naturalistic observation to study tobacco use among older school students and to attempt corroboration of previous questionnaire and interview studies. Unexpectedly, they found tobacco was offered infrequently, non-users associated with smokers and smoking alone was more common than expected. The authors concluded that, contrary to popular views, normative social pressure to smoke was perhaps not so strong as more subtle social effects.

Without consulting Box 5.1 below, try to list the advantages and disadvantages of naturalistic observation as you understand it so far.

Box 5.1   Advantages and disadvantages of naturalistic observation

Advantages	**Disadvantages**
Behaviour observed is unaffected by reactive variables (social desirability, Hawthorne effects, etc.) *if target is unaware of being observed*, and is therefore entirely genuine.	Extraneous variables poorly controlled and pose a much greater threat to validity than in the laboratory.
Even if target is aware of being observed, natural setting ensures that behaviour observed is more realistic than it could be in the laboratory.	Greater ambiguity from extraneous variables and unpredictable behaviour gives greater potential for observer bias than in more structured/laboratory studies.
An important and useful approach where: • intervention is unethical (e.g. unacceptable experimentation on children or animals) • co-operation from targets is unlikely • the full social context for behaviour is required	Difficulty of remaining undiscovered by targets. Replication often more difficult than in structured approaches. Cannot transport and use sophisticated equipment used for quality recordings in the laboratory (though new technology has greatly improved, e.g. digital video recordings)

Problems with structured observation

Because systematic observation can be so structured and rigid, it would be considered inadequate by groups of (usually social) psychologists who argue against the reduction of behaviour to artificially isolated units. What is the smallest unit we can work with? To describe a person as 'lifting an arm' may be objective physically but is stripped of social meaning compared with 'she waved', 'he made a bid' or 'she threatened the child'. Reduction to the simplest units of behaviour (the 'molecular' level) can create observations which are numerous, separated and meaningless.

The attempt to categorise interactions or assess responses by number can produce data at the 'reliable but not rich' end of the data-gathering spectrum. This positivist approach would be criticised by, for instance, humanists and phenomenologists, who promote a 'holistic' view of the person in psychology.

Diesing (1972) states that the holist (psychologist) studies a 'whole human system in its natural setting', and says:

> The holist standpoint includes the belief that human systems tend to develop a characteristic wholeness or integrity. They are not simply a loose collection of traits or wants or reflexes or variables of any sort . . . they have a unity that manifests itself in nearly every part . . . This means that the characteristics of a part are largely determined by the whole to which it belongs and by its particular location in the whole system.

Something is lost, it would be argued, by categorising responses and simply counting them, or by giving them a rating-scale value. It is more important to record events observed such that the social meaning of actions is preserved for analysis. This may mean recording as much as possible of the social context in which actions occurred. It may also mean making a comprehensive record of an individual's behaviour, such that specific actions are understood and perceived within the pattern of that person's unique experiences and motivation. It is not possible to do this using a highly constraining 'grid' or other pre-constructed framework for observation. We now turn to methods which attempt to generate a richer account of human behaviour in initially unquantified, descriptive form; that is, qualitative data (also see Chapters 9 and 21).

QUALITATIVE NON-PARTICIPANT OBSERVATION

In Ainsworth's study, described above, some of the observers produced a running commentary on each child's behaviour by speaking into a tape recorder as they watched. The same technique has been used by observers following the interactions of mothers and children in their own home. This generates a lot of raw data in qualitative form. These studies, however, are not usually conducted under the holistic banner. Rigid structure may be imposed on the data, during analysis, by independent raters trained in the ways already mentioned.

Some studies of this sort, though, do go further along the qualitative route. The unquantified, descriptive data may not be simply categorised or coded. The data may also be analysed for illuminative insights leading to fresh research topics, as occurred in Milgram's obedience studies. Or they may be presented alongside quantitative analysis in order to illustrate qualitative differences and issues which numerical reports cannot portray. Such is the cross-cultural psychological work of Edgerton (cited in Lonner and Berry, 1986), who compared eight communities in East Africa. He produced a broad 'portrait' of the personality type in each community prior to analysis of psychometric test data. The impressionistic descriptions were apparently in good accord with the subsequent test findings.

It is also possible, in GROUNDED THEORY approaches for example (see Chapter 21), that the sorts of observation made might change as the study progresses as a result of FORM-ATIVE revision of method, where feedback from early observations informs the researcher on optimum ways to proceed. The more the aim of the study tends away from purely positivist analysis, the more the data gathered become susceptible to the qualitative methods outlined in Chapters 9 and 21.

ROLE-PLAY AND SIMULATION

Discussion of these methods is situated here because, although some observations of role-play have been relatively pre-structured, the tendency has been to develop categories and models from fairly free-flowing, unrestricted participant behaviour and speech. In some cases, participants observe role-plays (non-active role), but, by and large, it is participants' role-playing which is observed (active role).

The techniques have been used for a long time in psychological research, particularly in the area of social psychology, but their use became highlighted when they were advocated as an alternative to the use of gross experimental deception during the 1970s.

Active role

The study might require active role-playing within a simulated social setting, such as being asked to get to know a stranger. Participants may take on a specific role – being chairperson of a group making risky decisions. Participants have been asked to role-play in juries of various sizes, under varying pressures, whilst dynamics of the situation are recorded. The focus of attention might then be, for instance, the informal rules which are developed within the group (Davis *et al.*, 1975). People have been asked to simulate various emotional feelings and accompanying behavioural expressions. In all these cases observations may be made at the time or behaviour might be filmed for subsequent detailed analysis.

Non-active role

Participants may be asked to watch a role-play or simulated performance and then be asked to report feelings, reactions or suggestions as to how the depicted scene might continue. They may be asked how they would behave in the continuing situation. In this case, the simulation simply serves as material for what is basically a question-asking method belonging in the next chapter. An example of a closely related research style is worth mentioning here, partly because it figured strongly in the controversy over experimental deception. Mixon (1979) was analysing Milgram's famous studies on 'destructive obedience' (for an account of this experimental paradigm, see Chapter 22). Mixon's objection was partly moral but also that the true social situation, for the participant in Milgram's experiment, had not been thoroughly understood.

Milgram described the experiment to a group of psychiatrists who predicted that less than one in a thousand people would continue obeying the experimenter in giving electric shocks to an obviously suffering 'learner'. Mixon argued that Milgram made it obvious to these people that the experiment was really about 'destructive obedience'. Mixon gave his participants scripts of the experiment to read with no clue given to the real experimental aims. He asked them to describe how they thought the experiment would continue. He then altered the scripts with different groups. Only when the script included the experimenter seeming a little concerned for the victim did all participants say that they expected Milgram's participants to discontinue obedience. Mixon argues that the social context of Milgram's experiment gives strong messages that the norms of scientific professionalism are in place and that no harm can come to the victim (though, obviously, pain is occurring).

In a few cases the participant can be actor and audience. Storms (1973) had people engage in a two-person interaction which was filmed. They then viewed the film, either seeing only their partner or only themselves. This had significant effects upon their attributions of causes to the observed behaviour.

Purposes of role-play and simulation

Ginsberg (1979) argues that these methods can be used for discovery and verification. In discovery, general observations might be made which lead to more specifically testable hypotheses or models. In verification, hypotheses such as Mixon's can be tested.

Ginsberg thinks that the most valuable use is for illuminating what he calls the 'role/rule framework' under which actions occur. They will not tell us a lot about individuals but perhaps a lot about the rules people assume or invent, and follow, given certain social situations. They may show us how people go about negotiating such rules. They may tell us about sequences and hierarchies of social action.

Weaknesses of role-play and simulation

Critics, early on, argued that role-play was non-spontaneous and passive; that people would act in socially desirable and superficial ways; and that what people said they would do and what they would do were very different matters.

Proponents argued back that experiments, too, can produce artificial, superficial behaviour and that deception itself, of the Milgram variety, introduced unreal conflict, for participants, between what seemed to be happening and what could be expected to happen in a humane, scientific establishment.

On the issue of spontaneity, several studies are cited as producing very great personal commitment and lack of pretence (a form of *experimental realism*), perhaps the most dramatic being that of Zimbardo (1972), described briefly in Chapter 22, which had to be ended after five of its planned 14 days because students acting as 'prison guards' were being too ruthless and callous, whilst 'prisoners' were becoming too submissive and dejected.

THE DIARY METHOD

Towards the end of the nineteenth century, some academics began to realise that they could not argue endlessly about whether children were born with innate tendencies – 'inherently good' as Rousseau would have claimed – or with a mind more similar to

Locke's empty-headed 'tabula rasa'. They realised that a scientific approach was necessary. The first steps towards this were taken by the 'baby biographers', of whom Charles Darwin (1877) is probably the most notable. Data were in the form of a diary of daily observations on the growth and development of his own son. Most diaries were developmental records of the observers' own children. The studies were therefore 'longitudinal' (see Chapter 8).

A problem with these diary accounts was that each biographer had their own particular perspective to support and tended to concentrate on quite different aspects of their child's behaviour from other diarists. They also tended not to standardise the intervals between their recordings.

Later, as child development study became a well-established discipline, Piaget kept diaries of the development of his children. He had a thorough model of cognitive development and his observations were used to exemplify aspects of the theory (not to serve as hypothesis tests). He developed procedures to demonstrate certain characteristics of children's thought at various ages – such as egocentricity – which he then used with other children, employing the clinical method (see Chapter 6).

Diaries are also kept during most *participant observation* studies. Where observation is covert these will be constructed, where possible, at the end of each day, either completely from memory or from any discreetly jotted notes recorded where opportunities have arisen.

In both these uses, the diary method has the great advantage that the observed persons are acting quite naturally, particularly so in the case of babies, since they are at home with their own parents. This must be a source of some of the richest, most genuine and intimate data in the business!

Jones and Fletcher (1992) asked couples to keep a daily diary of mood, stress and sleep variation over a period of three weeks. Comparing one partner with the other on these three variables, they found significant correlations overall, supporting the view that occupational stress is transmitted from one partner to the other, although individual couples varied very much in the extent to which their stress levels were comparable.

A further, unusual use of diaries has occurred in participative research (see Chapter 9) where participants themselves keep diaries of their activities and perceptions throughout a study. The researcher then subjects the diary content to some form of *content analysis* – see Chapter 21. Rajesh Tandon (1981) did this in a study aimed at improving peer group organisation and initiative taking in a rural agricultural training and modernisation programme. He found that questionnaire data gathered were often at odds with the diary records, the latter being far more congruent with the researcher's own field notes.

Diary studies can occur in that heartland of quantitative research, cognitive psychology. Two studies (Linton, 1975; Wagenaar, 1986) are described in Eysenck and Keane (1995). In the latter, Wagenaar recorded some 2000 events over a period of six years. The study involved investigation of which cues and prompts were more powerful in jogging 'lost' event memories and an overall conclusion was that not many of the events of our lives are actually lost but are usually stored away in long term memory requiring various levels of 'nudge' to retrieve them.

Box 5.2   Advantages and disadvantages of the diary method

Advantages	Disadvantages
Rich, genuine, realistic information	Observer bias can be high and unchecked
General advantages of naturalistic studies	Comparison with other studies difficult since emphasis usually unique
Simple to conduct if in observer's own home	Commitment to long term study and regular data gathering sessions
For babies at least, target is relaxed	

PARTICIPANT OBSERVATION

Where researchers are involved in taking notes on people's behaviour in their natural surroundings on a day to day basis, it is difficult to see how they can remain clinically detached from the context, apart from the odd shared cup of tea. Many researchers decide that more authentic observation of people can be made by being involved in their day-to-day interactions within their normal network of human group relationships. By coming round from behind the camera, into the social setting as an interacting person, the observer can experience life from the perspective of the individual, group or organisation of interest. The meaning of their behaviour should then be more accessible than with the passive approach and there should be less scope for the gross misrepresentations that can occur with 'snapshot' observations. Whether these objectives can be achieved in a manner which would still count as 'scientific' is a matter of heated debate and one which will be evaluated later on. What should be noted is that in many so-called 'participant observation' studies the methods used are not observation at all in the strict sense, but a combination of semi-structured interviews, open questionnaires and perhaps some data on roles and interactions within an organisation.

Degrees of participation

The degree to which an observer can participate in the group being studied is a continuum according to Patton (1980). He distinguishes between the following:

Full participant

The true research role is hidden ('undisclosed') and the observer is taken as an authentic member of the group. Hence, otherwise private information may well be disclosed. However, Douglas (1972) argues that a respected and trusted, *known* researcher may be handed secrets that a 'real' member might not receive for fear that the real member could use these against the divulger.

Participant as observer

The participant's observational role is not hidden but 'kept under wraps'. It is not seen to be the main reason for the participant's presence. Members relate to the participant mainly through roles and activities central to the group. An example here might be that of a researcher who effectively becomes a temporary member of a school's teaching staff in order to conduct research of which other staff are aware in general terms. Alternatively, a teacher might conduct research for a further qualification and use her work setting as the subject of her study.

Observer as participant

Here the observer role is uppermost and members of the group accept the observer in their midst as researcher. If valued, the researcher may be given quite intimate information but they may be constrained in reporting it if such information is offered in confidence.

Full observer

The role of uninvolved observer which we've already discussed as 'non-participant observation'.

Box 5.3 Undisclosed participant observation

Classic examples of undisclosed participant observation are:

Festinger *et al.* **(1956)**
Joined a religious sect which believed the world would end on a certain date. He and his colleagues followed developments up to and just past the fateful moment, observing reactions during the last moments of life and the subsequent 'reprieve', explained by the leader as caused by the members' great faith in their God.

Whyte (1943)
Studied an Italian street gang in Chicago by joining it. It was obvious Whyte was not a normal gang member. His 'cover' was that he was writing a book about the area. Most famous for his statement that

> I began as a non-participating observer. As I became accepted into the community, I found myself becoming almost a non-observing participant.

He also took on the role of secretary to the Italian Community Club in order to be able to take field notes unobtrusively.

Rosenhan (1973)
A still controversial study which promoted criticism of the (US) medical establishment's handling, labelling and diagnosis of psychiatric manifestations. Researchers presented themselves at hospital out-patients' departments complaining of hearing voices making certain noises in their heads. During their subsequent voluntary stays in a psychiatric ward they made observations on staff and patient behaviour and attitudes towards them. Patients often detected the 'normality' of the researchers well before the staff. An excellent example of seeing behaviour as pathological because of its producer's 'label' was the fact that a nurse recorded a researcher's note-taking as 'excessive writing behaviour'. To be fair, the nurse was dutifully carrying out strict instructions to observe and record anything unusual in patients' behaviour.

Ethical issues in undisclosed participant observation

One of the reasons humanists, for instance, object to many psychological experiments is that they involve deception of participants. Participant observation which is undisclosed obviously suffers from this criticism too. The researcher has also to decide what, if anything, can be published without the group's or any individual's consent. A particular hazard is that, when the observer 'comes clean' and declares the research role, any one individual studied may not be able to recall what they have divulged, or how they have behaved, since the research began. The individual should be allowed to view material for publication and to veto material which they object to where anonymity does not protect against the nature of the material identifying them.

Lack of consent-seeking leads to a greater mistrust of the distant and elite research body. An answer to the problem of deception is, of course, to disclose one's research role and objectives. These ethical issues are more fully discussed in Chapter 22.

Disclosed participant observation

An example would be the study of Becker (1958), whose observers joined a group of medical students in lectures and laboratory sessions and engaged in casual conversations both in work time and in the social atmosphere of their dormitories. They also joined in ward rounds and discussion groups and spent some time simply watching the students' various activities.

Contemporary participant observation studies are found very frequently in various areas of *applied* psychological research in a practitioner field such as health or sport and, in particular, disability research. Many are also conducted in organisations, such as Rachel (1996) who tracked radical organisational change in a computer systems design office partly by concentrating on the relationships between two groups – the 'Systems' and the 'Change Management' teams. Rachel's study, like many in the field, employed an ETHNOGRAPHIC APPROACH which descends from a long history in anthropological research, such as the work of Malinowski (1929) in the Trobriand islands. For a relatively contemporary summary see Hammersley and Atkinson (1983). Rachel made the point that worries the advocates of detached experimental, 'positivist' approaches, when she argued for the use of a conscious strategy *not* to impose a structure on the likely outcomes of the study before gathering any data, stating:

> The skill then becomes that of finding a way to . . . maintain oneself as a member of an academic community while opening oneself up to the possibilities that would follow from belonging to the community that one wants to study. (p. 115)

> With that radical difference from the laboratory experiment in mind, can you describe the strengths and weaknesses of participant observation? Also try to list the advantages and disadvantages of disclosure to participants.

Strengths of participant observation

Flexibility

A pre-set structure for observation, interview or survey questionnaire imposes the researcher's framework, assumptions and priorities on those who are to be studied. What is relevant in the target group's social world has already been decided. Participant observation is flexible. What is to be included as data in the study is not set in concrete at the outset. Indeed, the extent to which the observer will participate may not be the same throughout the study, as Whyte's famous statement above makes clear. Whyte also found that through participant observation, 'I learned the answers to questions I would not have had the sense to ask had I been getting my information solely on an interviewing basis.'

Relationship with observed group

Specific groups in the local environment, such as gangs or strongly-identifying cultural groups, are likely to see an establishment researcher as an authority figure and to be consequently suspicious. Methods for research, other than participant observation, such as interviewing or survey by questionnaire, do not give the researcher long enough to establish trust and to dissipate such suspicions. The research encounter is too brief to ensure genuine co-operation. Participant observation may sometimes be the only way to discover what truly makes such groups 'tick' and to find out which expressed attitudes stem from prior and perhaps deeper values and beliefs.

Kidder (1981a) argues that the longer the participant observer spends in a research setting, where their aims and purpose are disclosed to group members, the less likely it is that their presence will influence or distort the behaviour of the observed persons. This seeming paradox is explained by pointing out that, although group members may wish to appear in a certain light to the observer, if this behaviour is unnatural for them they will not be able to sustain it for long among friends and relatives. Even if the observer does not recognise artificiality, friends and co-workers will, and the observer is likely to hear about it. Kidder adds that it is much easier for experimental, one-day participants, whose identities remain anonymous, to distort reality by behaving quite uncharacteristically.

Difficulties with participant observation

The presence of a participant observer must change group behaviour to some degree, if only marginally, since, unless the researcher remains mute and passive (and therefore doesn't participate), interactions must occur which wouldn't have occurred otherwise. Here is a statement from one of the members of Whyte's gang:

> You've slowed me down plenty since you've been down here. Now, when I do something, I have to think what Bill Whyte would want me to know about it and how I can explain it. Before I used to do these things by instinct.

Pretty damning for the researcher who claims their presence to be unobtrusive and non-influential. However, researchers like Whyte argue that they blended into and became a part of the activities of the group, rather than changing what happened substantially, supporting Kidder's view above.

As Whyte's earlier statement testifies, the researcher obviously becomes socially and emotionally involved in the group and this must cast doubt on their eventual objectivity in reporting. The participant observation supporter would argue, however, that the attempt to be totally 'objective' leads to the artificiality and rigidity we discussed earlier.

The participant researcher can't usually make notes at the time of observation. Most have to rely on diary-keeping after the day's events (or by taking on a role which permits unobtrusive note-taking). Necessarily then, most participant observers are prey to the psychological factors of memory loss and distortion.

Since the researcher is the only observer present, and since events observed are unique, there is no opportunity to verify results with a second observer. Conclusions can only be loosely generalised to similar situations and groups.

Box 5.4   Advantages and disadvantages of types of observational study

	Advantages	**Disadvantages**
NON-PARTICIPANT		
Laboratory	Can study more continuous and flexible behaviour than that in other experiments.	Behaviour still in an artificial context.
	Data can be used to test cause–effect predictions.	Strong reactive effects possible such as participants guessing research aim.
Naturalistic	Greater realism of behaviour likely.	Rarely useful as strong cause–effect evidence.
	Can be used where: unethical to experiment, verbal reports unavailable, direct questioning would be rejected.	Higher potential for observer bias.
		Difficulty of hiding equipment.
	Possible to keep participants unaware of study and obtain natural behaviour.	Replication harder.
PARTICIPANT		
	Behaviour is generally natural.	Researcher may rely on memory.
	Richer data from lengthy and intense interaction.	Emotional involvement is a threat to objectivity.
	Meanings of actors' behaviour more readily available.	Problem of 'blowing cover'.
	Trust and informality give insights unavailable in other methods.	Researcher's behaviour alters that of group members.
		Replication hard and data accuracy can't be checked.
		Results are specific to context and may not generalise.

CASE STUDIES

A case-study involves gathering detailed information about one individual or group. Participant observation studies, such as Rachel's, above, are often better termed case studies on organisations. Festinger's study (1956), described above, would count as a case study of a group. Typically *individual* case studies would include a comprehensive CASE HISTORY, usually, but not exclusively, gathered by interview. This would be the person's record to date in employment, education, family details, socio-economic status, relationships and so on, and might include a detailed account of experiences relevant to the issue which makes the person of particular research interest. The interest might be in a rare medical condition which has psychological implications, in cases of severe deprivation, in an extraordinary ability (e.g. astonishing memory) or in a person's particular social position – single parent, manager, psychiatric patient, criminal.

The person would be regularly interviewed, mostly in an unstructured manner, and may be asked to take psychological tests. A case-study may not only use interviews. In some cases, particularly where the person is a young child, observation may play a large part in the collection of information, as when, for instance, the severely deprived child's play activities and developing social interactions are monitored for change.

In some instances the individual is selected for a forward-looking case-study because they are about to undergo a particularly interesting and possibly unique experience. Gregory and Wallace (1963), for instance, studied the case of SB, blind almost from birth, who received sight through surgical operation at the age of 52. The researchers were able not only to study in depth his visual abilities and development, but also gathered qualitative data on his emotional reactions to his new experiences and progress. This included his initial euphoria and his later depressions, caused partly by loss of daylight and his disillusionment with impure surfaces (flaky paint, old chalk marks on blackboards). A case-study, such as this one, though intrinsically valuable, can also shed light on general psychological issues such as the nature–nurture debate in perception. However, since SB had spent a lifetime specialising senses other than vision, his perceptual learning experiences cannot be directly compared with those of a young infant.

Freud developed his comprehensive psychoanalytic theory of human development using, as fuel and illustration, his records from dozens of patients' case histories. Much work in clinical psychology, by its nature, is based on case study work. In the area of developmental psychology, the research of Koluchová (1976) studied the effects of severe deprivation on two identical twins, discovered in dreadful conditions at the age of 5. They made impressive gains over the next two years. The value of such studies is to demonstrate not only just what the human organism can survive, but the extent to which it can still develop relatively normally.

The value of case-studies

Being a somewhat unstructured, probably unreplicable study on just one individual or group, the case-study design would seem to be of the rich but not generalisable type. Bromley (1986) has argued, however, that case-studies are the 'bedrock of scientific investigation'. Many psychological studies, he argues, are difficult to replicate in principle and it is the interesting, unpredictable case which has traditionally spurred scientists towards changes in paradigm or theoretical innovation. Bromley feels that a preoccupation with the experiment and psychometrics has led to a serious neglect of the case-study approach by most psychologists. He points out that psychological evidence can be valid and effective, yet remain unquantifiable. The case-study has a variety of specific advantages and useful points which follow.

1 Outstanding cases

A phenomenon may occur which is unique or so dramatic it could not have been predicted or studied in any pre-planned way. Thigpen and Cleckley (1954) reported on 'Eve White', a patient exhibiting three distinct personalities emerging through psychotherapy. Rather stern and 'prim' she was unaware of her other self, 'Eve Black', a gregarious life-lover who rejected Eve White. Finally, stable, contemplative 'Jane' emerged, aware of both the others. The Eves underwent the usual therapeutic interviews but were also given psychological tests and had EEG measures taken on their brain wave patterns. These distinguished Eve Black from the other two.

Luria (1969) studied a Russian journalist, Sherishevski, who had amazed his boss by not taking notes at briefing meetings, and who amazed Luria by being able to recall long word lists accurately over periods of 20 years or more.

Such cases may bring to attention possibilities in the human condition which were not previously considered realistic and may prompt investigation into quite new, challenging areas.

2 Contradicting a theory

One contrary case is enough to seriously challenge an assumed trend or theory of cause–effect relationship. It has been assumed that humans go through a 'critical period' where language must be heard to be learned, or where attachments must be formed and maintained in order to avoid later psychological problems. One case of an isolated child learning language, or of a maternally deprived child developing normal adult social skills, after deprivation during much of the critical period, is enough to undermine the critical period hypothesis quite seriously and to promote vigorous research seeking the crucial variables. The Koluchová (1976) study above served this purpose well.

3 Data pool

In an effort to identify common factors or experiences, a mass of information from many case-studies may be pooled, sorted and analysed. The focus may be, for instance, psychiatric patients or children with a particular reading disability. As a result, quantitative studies may be carried out, once linking variables appear or are suspected. Yin (1994) points out, however, and in the spirit of 'negative case analysis' to be covered in Chapter 21, that multiple case studies can be seen as similar to a series of experiments (*not* the gathering of a 'sample'). Multiple case studies serve as replications or as extensions of a prior study in order to refine an initially broad hypothesis or to check up on anomalies.

4 Insight

Whether or not case-studies of special circumstances lead to later, more formal, structured and quantitative studies, the *richness* they provide is their unique strength. Very often we could not possibly imagine the special experiences of the person studied, and we could not possibly draw up the appropriate questions to find out.

These experiences may cause us to quite restructure our thoughts on a particular condition, allowing us to empathise more fully, for example, with the AIDS sufferer or to understand the full impact of unemployment on a family. This adds to our overall knowledge pool and comprehension of human psychology, though it may not test any specific hypothesis.

Disadvantages of the case-study

1 Reliability and validity

There is an obviously high degree of unreliability involved. No two cases are the same. Many studies are quite unreplicable, indeed their uniqueness is usually the reason for their being carried out in the first place. Their strength is in richness, their weakness in lack of generalisability.

Some check on reliability can sometimes be made, however, by comparing information gained from different sources: for instance, the person themselves in interview, close relatives' accounts, documentary sources, such as diaries and court reports. This is similar to the notion of 'triangulation' described in Chapter 21.

Realism is high. The experiences recorded by the researcher are usually genuine and complex. Historical material, however, often depends on just the person's own memory. Memory is notoriously error-prone and subject to distortion. Experiences which we claim to recall from childhood are often our original reconstruction from relatives' stories told to us about our life before detailed memory was possible.

2 Observer interaction

Information collection is prone to the interpersonal variables discussed in the following chapter. The case-study necessitates a very close relationship between researcher and participant over an extended period and many intimate observation or interview sessions. Though the very depth of this relationship may promote an extremely rich information source, it may also seriously interfere with the researcher's objectivity.

3 Subjective selection

There is another possible element of subjectivity. Rather than present everything recorded during a case-study, which might take as long as the study itself, the researcher must be *selective* in what information enters the final report. This may well depend upon the points of background theory or issues which the researcher wishes to raise or emphasise. Further, for every illustrative case-study, we do not know how many cases did not deliver the kind of information the researcher wished to present.

But doesn't science contain 'case-studies'?

In Chapter 9 we shall meet the argument that psychologists probably worry about the rigidity of scientific method more so than do conventional scientists in physics, chemistry and the like. Case studies have been viewed with extreme suspicion or hostility by many psychologists because they are a 'sample of only one', often qualitative and subject to criticism, conventionally, of subjectivity and lack of reliability. However, 'real' science contains very many case studies and Robson (1993) argues that, anyway, experiments, surveys and the like should *themselves* be seen as types of case study in each instance. Nicky Hayes (1997) points out that studies such as those of Penfield and Rasmussen (who stimulated the cortex and recorded patients' consequent vivid memories) have *not* been queried as unscientific, probably because they are safely within the 'hard' science of medical research – 'scientific by association, and [were] therefore beyond suspicion.' (p. 2) The notorious study of Little Albert by Watson and Rayner (1920) (Watson being the founder of behaviourism and archetypal experimentalist) is written up very much as a diary-cum-case-study with qualitative observation throughout – see extracts in Gross (1994).

INDIRECT OBSERVATION

Archives

Some events have already occurred but can serve as empirical evidence for social science theories. Durkheim, a sociologist, made ground-breaking studies of relative rates of suicide, comparing these with varying social conditions.

Many events, like suicide, are of interest to psychologists and are either unpredictable or do not occur often enough for thorough scientific research. Governmental elections are relatively infrequent and make the study of voting behaviour somewhat inconvenient. Behaviour cannot be observed directly in events such as earthquakes and suicide.

Psychological researchers might, instead, use observed social statistics as data. These can be drawn from historical sources (ARCHIVAL DATA), government information or the media. Television programmes might, for example, be observed for examples of gender stereotyping. Records might show that young black people obtain fewer interviews and fewer jobs compared with white youngsters. This might be attributed to black youngsters having lower qualifications. A researcher can eliminate this hypothesis with an observation of employment statistics which show that this discrepancy occurs among black and white youngsters with *equal* qualifications. This could also be called a survey of labour statistics. The common use of 'survey' is discussed in Chapter 6.

Note that, although indirect, these studies do make observations on the behaviour of people and, through some interpretation, prevailing attitudes. Notice that this is a perfectly legitimate way to test and eliminate hypotheses about causal factors in social phenomena. The observation of electronic or printed media coverage could be subjected to *content analysis* which we shall look at when discussing qualitative data analysis in Chapter 21.

Verbal protocols

A further way to gather observations indirectly is through the use of VERBAL PROTOCOLS. These are the recorded product of asking participants to talk or think aloud during an activity. They may report on the thoughts they have whilst trying to solve a mental arithmetic problem, or 'talk through' the reasons for their decisions whilst operating a complex piece of machinery, such as the control-room instruments in a nuclear power installation. The method is closely linked with the practice of *knowledge elicitation*.

The interesting development has been this generation of basically qualitative data, as with diary studies above, within the overwhelmingly experiment based area of cognitive psychology. Ericsson and Simon (1984) made a strong case for the use of verbal reports as data. Good theories of problem-solving should produce rules from which problem-solving by humans can be stimulated. Verbal protocols can then be compared with the simulation in order to verify the theory. Ericsson and Simon argued that asking participants to talk while they work does not necessarily impair their performance. It depends on what the verbalising instructions are. These could be:

1. Verbalise your silent speech – what you would say to yourself anyway whilst solving this problem (doing this task) – known as a 'talk aloud' instruction.
2. Verbalise whatever thoughts occur to you whilst doing this task – a 'think aloud' instruction.
3. Verbalise your thoughts and decisions and give reasons for these.

In analysing the results of many studies they found that only type 3 instructions seriously affected performance – not surprising really, since the participant is being asked to do so much in addition to the task. Type 2 instructions did not seriously affect accuracy but did slow down solution times. Type 1 instructions had little effect on time or accuracy. In addition, they found that concurrent verbal reports (produced as a task is performed) were more accurate than retrospective ones.

Knowledge elicitation work has generated 'expert systems' – bodies of knowledge about procedures, for instance in medical diagnosis, derived from the verbal protocols of experts. In addition, the difference between experts and novices has been the subject of research, either for practical uses, in the reduction of life-threatening work errors for instance, or as pure academic research on expertise in problem-solving. A further academic use is in the investigation of people's 'mental models' of everyday systems (e.g. your central heating system) or laboratory produced simulations (e.g. launching a space ship).

Corcoran (1986) used verbal protocols with six expert and five novice nurses to investigate their approach to three cases of differing complexity. Novices were less systematic with the low complexity case, compared with experts.

Martin and Klimowski (1990) attempted to investigate the mental processes employed by managers as they evaluated their own and their subordinates' performance. It was found that they used more *internal attributions* when evaluating others than when evaluating themselves. An internal attribution occurs when we see behaviour as largely caused by a person's enduring characteristics, rather than blaming the surrounding situation.

Glossary

System used to categorise observations	_____	code (coding)
Data gathering method where participant makes regular (often daily) record of relevant events	_____ _____	diary method
Letting people know that they are the object of observation	_____	disclosure
Methodological approach deriving from social anthropology; involves 'immersion' in a setting and an attempt to reflect that context from the perspective of group/culture members	_____ _____	ethnographic approach
Observational sampling method focussing on specific events defined for the study	_____ _____	event sampling
Approach to observation in which the focus of observation may change as the study progresses and early data are analysed	_____ _____	formative revision
Extent to which observers agree in their rating or coding	_____ – _____ _____	inter-observer (or inter-rater) reliability
		Observation types
Observation in which many variables are kept constant	_____	controlled
Observations not made on people directly but using available records	_____	indirect/archival

Observation without intervention in observed peoples' own environment	_____	naturalistic
Observation in which observer does not take part or play a role in the group observed	_____	non-participant
Observation in which observer takes part or plays a role in the group observed	_____	participant
Observation which uses an explicitly defined coding framework for data recording	_____	structured/systematic
Study which is solely observational and does not include any experimentation	_____	observational design
Procedure using observation in some way and which may or may not be part of an experiment	_____	observation technique
Effect causing unwanted variations in data recorded which is related to characteristics of the observer	_____	observer bias
Observational sampling method where one person is observed long enough to record one category of behaviour before moving on to next target	_____	point sampling
Assessment of behaviour using a scale	_____	rate (rating)
Study in which participants act out parts	____ – ____	role-play
Study in which participants re-create and play through, to some extent, a social interaction	_____	simulation
Observational sampling method involving observations at set lengths of time at set intervals	_____	time sampling
Recording of participants' speech when they have been asked to talk aloud during a task	_____	verbal protocols

Exercises

1 Outline a research study which would use observation to investigate the following hypotheses:

a. During exploratory play, mothers allow their sons to venture a further distance away from them than they permit for their daughters.

b. When asked personal, or slightly embarrassing questions, people are likely to avert their gaze.

c. Women are safer drivers than men.

d. In groups asked to produce volunteers for an unpopular task it is possible to observe common patterns of behaviour among the group members.

Ensure that: variables are *operationalised* and that the *exact* method of data gathering is described, including the *location*, *sample selection*, *data collection method* and *equipment* used.

2   A student decides to carry out participant observation on her own student group. She is interested in the different ways her classmates cope with study demands and social commitments. Discuss the ways she might go about this work, the problems she might face and the ways in which she might surmount difficulties.

3   Describe ways in which Bandura's hypotheses, including those which investigate the influence of different types of child and adult model, could have been investigated using naturalistic observation rather than the laboratory.

4   A researcher is concerned that a rating scale is not producing good inter-rater reliability. The observations of two observers are as follows:

Observation for child X: altruistic acts in 5 minutes intervals									
	0–5	6–10	11–15	16–20	21–25	26–30	31–35	36–40	41–45
Observer A	1	3	4	2	5	12	9	4	8
Observer B	2	10	8	7	1	3	5	5	6

Would you say this represents good reliability or not? What statistical procedure could tell us the degree of reliability (see Chapters 7 and 15)?

5   Work with a colleague and decide on a variable to observe in children or adults. Make the variable something which is likely to occur quite frequently in a short observation period (10 minutes), such as one person smiling in a two-person conversation in the college refectory. Decide on a structure for data gathering including people, intervals, behaviour codes. Compare your results to see whether you tend to agree fairly well or not.

Answers

4   There is poor agreement between the two raters, especially in the 2nd and 6th intervals. Correlation could be used (Chapter 15). The result would be −0.25 (Spearman). A strong *positive* correlation is required for good reliability.

6

Interview methods – asking people direct questions

This chapter introduces general principles concerning the asking of questions. Methods can be *structured* or not, and they can be more or less *disguised*.

- Advantages and disadvantages of structure are discussed as the dimension of interview techniques across the structured–unstructured dimension are introduced, from *non-directive*, through *semi-structured* to *fully structured* (*survey* type) interviews. The *clinical method* is included in these. In general, less structured studies generate more rich and genuine, but more local and less generalisable data.
- The general possible effects of *interpersonal variables* (gender, ethnicity, roles, personality, cues to interviewer's aims) in the face-to-face questioning situation are discussed.
- Techniques to *achieve and maintain rapport* are introduced, with the underlying assumption that good rapport produces more useful and valid data from interviewees. Other aspects of *good interview practice* and *recording methods* are discussed.
- Types and sequencing of questions are covered along with a short discussion of recording techniques.
- Finally, *surveys* are introduced as fully structured interviews. Surveys can be used purely to gather descriptive data and/or to test hypotheses. Surveys can be conducted *face to face*, by *post, telephone* or *e-mail*. *Panels* and *focus groups* are briefly described as methods of assessing opinion on an issue.

INTRODUCTION

So far we have seen that the psychologist who needs information can set up experiments to see what people do under different conditions or use observation techniques to record segments of behaviour in more or less natural circumstances. Perhaps the reader has asked by now, 'Why don't psychologists just go and ask people directly about themselves?' We have only encountered this technique as part of the overall participant observation method. There are in fact many ways in which psychological researchers ask questions about individuals. This can occur as part of an experiment or observational study, of course. The interviews conducted by Asch and Milgram after their celebrated demonstrations of seemingly bizarre human behaviour give some of the most fascinating and rich data one can imagine and certainly formed the springboard for a huge volume of further illuminating and productive research. Here, however, we are concentrating on studies where the gathering of information through direct questioning, usually FACE-TO-FACE (but often by telephone or e-mail), is the primary research mode. Until we reach the 'Interviews' heading below, this section does not distinguish between the personal 'interview' and the situation where the 'interview' consists of the administration of a questionnaire in the presence of a researcher or assistant.

STRUCTURE

Questioning methods range across two major dimensions. They can be formally STRUC-TURED, in which case every RESPONDENT (person who answers questions) receives exactly the same questions, probably in the same order. Alternatively, the method can tend towards the UNSTRUCTURED, in which case responses are rich and perhaps more genuine, though reliability suffers, according to the positivist perspective. (This is similar to the observational dimension of structure covered in the last chapter.) In the unstructured study, technical comparison of cases and generalisability are weak but the researcher has the advantage of flexibility towards the respondent and of asking questions in a more formal, relaxed atmosphere in which complete and meaningful answers, *kept in context*, may be more forthcoming. However, the more unstructured the interview, the greater the skill required by interviewers and the more the success of the research depends on implementation of these skills. Also greater are the potential effects of researcher influence and selectivity.

This issue of structured vs. loose designs really takes us to the heart of the quantitative–qualitative debate again. A *positivist* view of interviews is that they are used to get the facts from respondents and that, using various technical guards against sampling and procedural bias, interview data should provide a close match with an objective reality waiting to be discovered and described. The interviewer is simply a utility to generate questions methodically. An alternative view, fairly common to qualitative approaches, is that interviewees *construct* their *unique* reality in the interview session which is a *social interaction* in which the interviewer is a human participant. Hence, interviewers should provide the most flexible and natural humanlike circumstances in which interviewees can express themselves fully and can uniquely define their world. De Waele and Harré (1979) say:

> By taking the participants' interpretations seriously we avoid the falsification of reality which occurs when self-reports are confined to the replies to questionnaires etc. which have been designed in advance by the investigator. (p. 182)

PROBLEMS WITH CLOSED QUESTIONS – THE KALAMAZOO STUDY

Questionnaires may be more or less structured. The importance of giving respondents the freedom to say what they really think is demonstrated by the results of a piece of applied psychological research conducted by Peronne *et al.* (1976) who were evaluating a new accountability system set up by the Kalamazoo Education Association in its schools.

The system had been heavily criticised. Teachers were asked to complete a questionnaire with fixed-choice questions – 'agree' or 'disagree'. The researchers also set a couple of open-ended questions to which staff could respond in their own words at any length.

School board members were prepared to dismiss the quantitative results from the fixed-choice questions as somehow biased but, on publication of the qualitative results they could hardly ignore the clear statements of fear, concern and frustration which dominated replies to the open-ended questions and they were influenced strongly enough to make substantial changes (Patton, 1980).

DISGUISE

A factor which might further enhance production of honest answers will be that of DIS-GUISE. The ethical principles involved in deceiving persons will be dealt with later. However, disguising the researcher's true aim may help to obtain valid information where issues are highly sensitive, potentially embarrassing or otherwise felt as a threat to the respondent if disclosed. Respondents may also try to 'look good' if they know what exactly is the focus of the study. On occasion though, people might be *more* inclined to co-operate when they know exactly what the researcher is after and why.

A matrix of assessment techniques which fall into four categories formed by these two variables, structure and disguise, is shown in Box 6.1. However, it must be remembered that each variable represents a dimension, not a pair of exclusive opposites. Some methods are only partially disguised and/or only relatively structured. In Hammond's technique, respondents were asked factual questions about days lost through strikes, for instance, and had to tick an answer from two, one of which was far too high and one far too low. Without it being obvious to the respondent, attitude to trades unions was said to be measured. Levin (1978) used psychoanalytic techniques to assess women's degree of the Freudian construct of 'penis envy'. The women she studied reported anything they thought they saw in Rorschach ink blots (see Chapter 7). Notice that in these two examples respondents are not aware of the information they apparently provide about themselves. Completion of Eysenck's questionnaire assessing extroversion and neuroticism makes it clear to respondents that they are offering information about themselves. Methods where this is so are known as SELF-REPORT techniques.

Box 6.1 Combinations of structure and disguise in questioning techniques

	Structured	**Loose**
Disguised	Hammond's (1948) 'error choice technique' Eysenck and Eysenck's (1975) EPQ questionnaire	Use of projective tests as in Levin (1978) Roethlisberger and Dickson (1939 Hawthorne studies)
Undisguised	Peronne *et al.* (1976) Most attitude questionnaires	Kalamazoo study Most qualitative studies

For the rest of Box 6.1, we have mentioned the Kalamazoo study and we shall mention the Hawthorne studies in a short while. These approaches used relatively undisguised methods. A further fairly common way to disguise research aims is to ask questions about the topic of interest and simultaneously record a physiological response, such as the respondent's galvanic skin response (GSR) to indicate level of anxiety.

The bogus pipeline disguise

In a cunning but deceitful exploitation of the GSR indicator, and as a way of dealing with interviewees who hide their true attitudes and wish to 'look good', Jones and Sigall (1971) introduced the 'bogus pipeline' technique. Participants are hooked up to a machine which, they are assured, can detect signs of anxiety – a form of 'lie detector'. The researcher already has some attitude information about each participant obtained by clandestine means. The participant is asked to lie unpredictably to some of a set of personal questions for which the researcher already has the correct answers. The machine therefore seems to work when the researcher 'detects' the false answers. Apparently, people tend to be more embarrassed at being found to be a liar than they do about revealing unpopular attitudes. This does seem to work but, as you'd imagine, the technique has come in for some ethical criticism (see Chapter 22).

EFFECTS OF INTERPERSONAL VARIABLES

This section is about asking people questions mostly to gather information and we continue to include questionnaire administration for now. We have seen that some research designs, particularly the laboratory experiment, have been criticised for their artificiality and for producing *demand characteristics*. But when we ask people questions, however informally, so long as they are aware that there is a research aim, there may also be an element of artificiality, distortion and reaction to the research context. There is an interaction of roles – interviewer and interviewee. Characteristics of the interviewer's style and presentation will affect the quality of information obtained. Demand characteristics may well operate in that the interviewee may use cues from the interviewer, or from the questionnaire, to try to behave according to perceived research aims. Researcher expectancies may also bias proceedings where the interviewer is aware of expected or desired results.

> The relationship and interaction between interviewer and interviewee will affect the quality and amount of information obtained in an interview. Make a list of various factors which you think might affect an interview situation and perhaps limit or distort the information obtained.

My list would include all the following points:
in particular, the class, sex, culture or 'race', and age of either person in the interview may make a lot of difference to proceedings. Cultural difference, here, doesn't have to be great – it could be the difference between Londoner and Scot or northerner and southerner.

Gender

That gender is an important variable is demonstrated in a study by Finch (1984) where young mothers gave her access to views which a man would have been highly unlikely to obtain. A woman interviewee can assume common understanding with a woman interviewer, as when one of Finch's mothers said '. . . fellas don't see it like that do they?'

Ethnicity

That race or ethnic group creates differential interviewing behaviour was shown by Word *et al.* (1974). They observed the behaviour of white interviewers with white and black interviewees. With white interviewees, the interviewers showed significantly higher 'immediacy' – which includes closer interpersonal distance, more eye contact, more forward lean and so on. They followed this up with a demonstration that 'job applicants' in the study reciprocated the low-immediacy behaviour of the interviewers and received significantly poorer ratings for their interview performance.

Formal roles

Sex and ethnic difference may have greater effect if the interviewee also views the researcher as an authority figure. This perception will partly depend upon the style the researcher adopts but even a highly informal style may not deter the interviewee from seeing her or him as very important. Interviewees' answers, then, may lack fluency because they are constrained by a search for 'correct' language or content. On the other hand, some respondents may feel quite superior to, or cynical about, the interviewer and consequently their answers may be somewhat superficial and cursory.

Personal qualities

Interacting with these major differences will be other personal qualities and characteristics of both people. The interviewer, instructed to be informal, may find this quite difficult with some people and may therefore behave rather artificially, this being detected by the interviewee. There may be something else about the interviewer that the interviewee just doesn't like.

Social desirability

A common problem in asking questions is that of *social desirability* – see Chapter 3. Faced with an esteemed researcher, people may well 'manage' their attitudes and behaviour to a misleading extent. It is notoriously difficult, for instance, to measure prejudice openly. When asked, many people will make statements like 'I believe we're all equal' and 'Everybody should be treated the same', whereas, in their everyday life, and in conversations with friends, other, more negative attitudes and behaviour towards some groups may well emerge. (Treating 'the same' is anyway often incompatible with granting equal rights.) On issues like child-rearing practice or safe driving, people usually know what they *ought* to say to an interviewer and may keep real views well hidden.

Randomised response – a way round social desirability and confidentiality

An extremely cunning technique, which increases validity and deals with the issue of privacy for respondents on sensitive issues, is the 'randomised response' technique, discussed by Shotland and Yankowski (1982). The participant is asked two questions simultaneously as, say, item 8 on a questionnaire. Only the participant knows which of the two is being answered and this is decided on the toss of a coin. One question is the sensitive issue on which information is sought. Let's say the question is 'Have you ever experienced sexual feelings towards a member of your own sex?' The second question is innocuous, say 'Do you drive a car to work?' The researchers already know the expected 'yes' response, from large samples, to the second question. Let's say this proportion is 70%. From 200 people then, about 100 will answer the driving question and about 70 of these should answer 'yes'. For all 200 people, the number answering 'yes' to item 8, above 70, is an estimate of the number answering 'yes' to the sensitive question. This way, the participant retains privacy, yet a fair estimate of attitude or behaviour on an otherwise unusable item may be obtained.

Evaluative cues

It is unusual to be asked for one's opinion, in a situation where no criticism or argument can be expected. The interviewer has to be careful not to inadvertently display behaviour, however subtle, which might get interpreted as either disagreement or encouragement since the interviewee may well be searching for an acceptable or desired position. Not all researchers agree with this passive role – see Box 6.2.

INTERVIEWS

Face-to-face interviews range in style across the range of structure from fixed to open-ended questions. Answers to open-ended questions will often be coded by placing them into categories, such as 'left wing' or 'right wing' for political questions, or by rating them

Box 6.2 The discourse analytic view of interview bias

Conventional research 'law' holds that interviewers should not engage or lead the respondent as one would in normal conversation. However, there is a contemporary research view quite the reverse of this. It is bound up with the discourse analysis approach which is discussed in more detail in Chapter 9. Potter and Wetherell (1987) explain that the entire focus of discourse analysis is on the ways in which people use language, in conversation, to construct and 'negotiate' a view of the world. They argue that we cannot assume some 'pure' truth in people's heads which we can get at if only we remove all possible bias and distorting influences. Their interest is in the ways people use discourse to promote certain versions of events, often those which serve their interests best or put them in the best light. Hence, for the discourse analytic interviewer, the interview should be naturalistic to the extent of promoting this everyday discursive use of language. The diversity which traditionally structured interviews try to minimise, in order to get 'consistent' responses from interviewees, is positively encouraged by the discourse approach. Consistency, for Potter and Wetherell, is a sign that respondents are producing only limited, probably compatible interpretations. They see the interview as 'an active site where the respondent's interpretive resources are explored and engaged to the full . . .' and as a 'conversational encounter' (Potter and Wetherell, 1987). The interview is therefore conducted on an 'interventionist and confrontative' basis – not as a dispute but as a situation in which the interviewer is prepared to come back to areas obviously difficult or ambiguous for the interviewee in order, perhaps, to elicit some alternative construction. The interviewer will also be prepared to use probes and follow-up questions in fruitful areas. This makes the interview something similar to the 'informal but guided' type below with elements, also, of the 'clinical method', discussed later.

on a scale of perhaps one to ten for, say, computer anxiety. In some surveys, interviewers code answers on the spot as they are received. In the less structured type of interview, response analysis is a long, complicated and relatively interpretive process. In qualitative research studies there may be no interest in quantifying responses at all beyond basic categorising. The emphasis will be on collating, prioritising and summarising all information acquired (see Chapter 21), analysing for themes, and perhaps suggesting areas and strategies for action. The setting and procedure for interviewing may also be more or less structured and we will consider five categories of interview, starting at the relatively unstructured end of the continuum.

Types of interview

1 Non-directive

Some psychology practitioners use interviews in which the interviewee can talk about anything they like and in which the psychologist gives no directing influence to the topics but provides reflective support throughout the session. The main aim would be to help the 'client' increase self-awareness and deal with personal problems. This method would be used by psychotherapists and counsellors and the main aim would not be academic research data gathering. However, clients do, in a sense, research their own perhaps troubled experiences and the psychologist may need the information in order to proceed with helping the client. The approach may be used in collecting data which form part of a case-study – as discussed in Chapter 5.

The insights derived from such studies often get drawn together into an overall psychological theory, model or approach which adds, in time, to the pool of knowledge and ideas. These may become a stimulus for further research by other means. Freud's insights, for instance, influenced Bandura in his development of social learning theory which he supported mainly by controlled observation experiments.

2 Informal

An informal interview has an overall research data gathering aim. At the non-structured extreme the session is similar to the non-directive approach just described. Though the fact is obscured by the more celebrated aspects of the Hawthorne studies described in Chapter 3, the researchers here were also responsible for an early use of the almost non-directive interview in industrial relations research work. Early structured interviews were not successful, not least because many were conducted by the worker's supervisor and the relationship was necessarily lop-sided in power. Employees were loathe to get marked out as complainers. The 'indirect approach' which the researchers then developed involved non-judgemental, neutral interviewers listening patiently, making intelligent comments, displaying no authority, giving no advice or argument and only asking questions when necessary, e.g. to prompt further talking, to relieve anxiety, to praise, to cover an omitted topic and to discuss implicit assumptions if thought helpful. 'Rules of orientation' for the interviewer took into account many of the points made strongly today by discourse analysts (Box 6.2 and Chapter 9). They found employees became far more articulate and, as an overall outcome of the study, management realised that seemingly trivial complaints were only the external symptoms of much deeper personal and social problems, requiring more than the superficial response to employee complaints they had originally envisaged. One man, for instance, exclaimed 'I tell you, it does a fellow good to get rid of that stuff'. (Roethlisberger and Dickson, 1970, p. 258, and see Hollway, 1991).

In the relaxed atmosphere of the informal, non-directive interview, interviewees can talk in their own terms. They don't have to answer pre-set questions which they might find confusing or which they just don't wish to answer. They are not constrained by fixed-answer questions which produce rather narrow information. The approach has been used in social science research for some time and has more recently become popular in areas of applied research, particularly by the proponents of qualitative approaches. Qualitative workers would argue that the attempt at objectivity, through being a cool, distant, impersonal and anonymous interviewer is only likely to instil anxiety. Interviewees grasp at clues to what is really expected from them and how their information will promote or hinder 'success'. I have been interviewed for research and remember feeling anxious to know what the context was so I could manage my answers more effectively, and perhaps recall more relevant ideas and experiences. I also remember the interviewer's '. . . well, I shouldn't strictly say this now but . . .' and similar straying from the structure at several points. Realistically, most of the more structured interviews run like this. Dropped comments and asides may well form some of the most memorable and insight-producing information.

3 The semi-structured interview (informal but guided)

One way to retain the advantage of the informal approach is to keep the procedure informal, not to ask pre-set questions in exactly the same order each time, but to provide interviewers with a guide which is an outline of topics to be covered and questions to be asked. The guide leaves the interviewer to decide, on the spot, how to work in and phrase questions on the various topics. Questions need not be put where respondents produce the required answers spontaneously in discussion. In other words, with specific data requirements and areas to be covered, the interviewer 'plays it by ear'. The semi-structured interview is exceedingly common and tends to be the interview style of choice in much qualitative work, although interview contents are also commonly subjected to *content analysis* (Chapter 21) and therefore partially quantified. Advantages are a natural conversation flow, freedom for the respondent to explore unpredicted avenues of thought, and flexibility of the interviewer in selecting aspects of the discourse to follow up. These are finely balanced against disadvantages, from the positivist point of view, of weak reliability or comparison across respondents. However, this begs the question of what kind of scientific research model proponents are following and is the starting point for Chapter 9. For an account of the semi-structured interview, and how to analyse associated data, see Smith (1995), Chapter 2.

4 Structured but open-ended

To avoid the looseness and inconsistency which accompany informally gathered interview data, the interview session can use a *standardised procedure*. The interviewer gives pre-set questions in a predetermined order to every interviewee. This keeps the multiplicity of interpersonal variables involved in a two-way conversation to a minimum and ensures greater consistency in the data gathered. The respondent is still free to answer, however, in any way chosen. Questions are open ended. For instance, 'Tell me how you feel about the company's sales policy' might be asked, rather than 'Do you approve of the company's sales policy?'

5 Fully structured

In this type of interview, as with the last, questions are pre-set and ordered, but here they are also fixed answer items of the types which can be found on p. 156. In fact, this approach is hardly an interview worth the name at all. It is a face-to-face data-gathering technique, but could be conducted by telephone or by post (which might reduce bias from interpersonal variables still further). The structured method is usually in use when you're stopped on the street as part of a SURVEY by someone with a clipboard. Responses can be counted and analysed numerically but can often be difficult to make because the respondent wants to say 'yes' (for this reason) but 'no' (for that reason) or 'I think so' or 'sometimes'. A sensitive structured system has a list for choosing responses including alternatives such as 'sometimes', 'hardly ever', or, 'certain', 'fairly confident' and so on – to be outlined in the next chapter.

Both the last two methods would be rejected by many researchers who would argue that structured approaches leave no room for an important aspect of normal conversation, that of constantly checking that the other has understood what you mean and that they are on the same wavelength with their answers. Semi-structured and looser approaches permit this doubling back and alteration of wording in order to permit the respondent the fullest opportunity to express what they might have to say. As Smith (1996) reminds us:

> . . . you may need to ask yourself how engaged the respondent is. Are you really entering the personal/social life world of the participant or are you forcing him or her, perhaps reluctantly, to enter yours?' Smith (p. 15)

The clinical method (or 'clinical interview')

This method uses a form of semi-structured interview method in a particular manner. It is usually aimed at testing fairly specific hypotheses or at demonstrating a clear and limited phenomenon. However, it also recognises the unique experience of each interviewee. Initially, each person questioned will be asked the same questions, but further questions are tailored to the nature of initial replies. The method was extensively used by Piaget. Anyone who has tried to test a child on one of Piaget's conservation tasks will know that the specific language chosen, and the quality of the adult's interaction with the child, are all-important factors in determining the progress of such a test. It is easy to get a four-year-old child to give the 'wrong' (i.e. non-conserving) answer with an injudicious choice of question wording or with 'clumsy' conversation.

'Is there more liquid in this glass?' is a leading question which may well prompt the child into saying 'yes' in order to please. Anyway, after all, after the typical conservation change, the column of liquid *is* 'more' – it's taller (though narrower). The question 'Is there more in this glass, more in this other one, or are they both the same?' is rather demanding on the child's short-term memory!

The clinical method, then, uses a non-standardised procedure but heads for a definite goal. Standardised questions, rigidly adhered to by the interviewer, can seem rather artificial to the adult respondent. The problem with children is greater. If they don't

Table 6.1 Advantages and disadvantages of loose and structured interview techniques

	Advantages	Disadvantages
Loose [Non-directive, informal, semi-structured]	Relatively natural conversation produces richer, fuller more genuine, more realistic information on interviewee's own terms; enables capture of respondent's construction or unique perspective. Interview questions can be adapted to context, interviewee's style and thoughts, and the general flow of answers. Relaxed, more informed and involved respondent.	Differences in procedure could make data comparison less fair and reliable. Difficulties in analysis of wide variety of qualitative information. Important topics could be missed. Length and depth of process may limit numbers it is possible to interview and some people may not want to commit the time and energy. Requires thoroughly trained interviewers.
Structured	Ease of data comparison and analysis. Can be replicated and data reviewed by other researchers. Reduction of interpersonal bias factors. High reliability from 'positivistic' view. Results more generalisable. Interviewers need not have all the skills and experience required for loosely structured procedures. Speedy administration; respondents may feel more ready to participate given low time/effort commitment.	Data obtained can be trivial. Narrow range and quality of information gathered. Respondent constrained and cannot express complexities and subtleties of an issue or experience. Question wordings cannot be adapted to levels of understanding of the respondent. Suffers general questionnaire weaknesses.

Box 6.3 Advantages and disadvantages of the clinical interview/method

Advantages
Leads to accurate assessment of person's thinking and memory
Interviewer can vary questions in order to check person's understanding
Information gained fairly rich
Interviewee relaxed
Disadvantages
Non-standardised method
Researcher's theoretical beliefs can influence questions asked and interpretations made of what person understands
Difficulty in comparing one interview protocol with another

understand the particular form of words they may well 'fail' when an alteration in question form might have revealed that the child does, after all, have the concept which is sought. Piaget believed, therefore, that he could get the most accurate information about a child's thinking by varying the questioning in what seemed to the child a fairly natural conversation with an adult. Of course, we end up with the alleged weaknesses of unstandardised procedures. Freud's methods too have been said to involve the clinical method, since the aim of some sessions was to test a specific hypothesis about the client's unconscious network of fears and ideas.

SEMI-STRUCTURED INTERVIEW TECHNIQUES – (USING OPEN QUESTIONS)

If the interview is completely structured, the interviewer will be using a questionnaire and the construction of these is outlined in the next chapter. The techniques and procedures described in the following pages apply to any other form of interview, particularly the semi-structured and those in which open-ended, qualitative data are sought.

Achieving and maintaining rapport

In an unstructured interview, the quality and characteristics of the interviewer's behaviour are of utmost importance and not just the interesting 'extraneous variables' they are often considered to be in the structured interview or survey study. People provide a lot more information about themselves when they are feeling comfortable and 'chatty' than in a strained, formal atmosphere where suspicions are not allayed. An awkward, 'stiff' or aggressive interviewer may produce little co-operation and even hostility from the interviewee. How may rapport be established?

Language
It is valuable to spend some time discovering terminology used by the group under study. They may have nicknames and use their own jargon, including sets of initials (such as 'SUDs' – standing for 'seriously underdeprived', i.e. upper-class children). Interviewees will be most comfortable and fluent using their normal language mode (dialect, accent, normal conversational style) and must be made to feel that its use is not only legitimate but welcome and valued.

Neutrality
Accepting the language style and any non-verbal behaviour of the interviewee will help to assure her/him that the interview is entirely non-judgemental. The interviewee must feel that no moral assessment of what they say is, or will be, involved.

Giving information
The interviewer can give full information at the start of an interview about the purpose of the research, who it is conducted for, what sorts of topics will be covered and how confidentiality will be maintained. Unlike the case with formal questionnaires, the interviewer can explain the purpose of any particular question. A natural questioning environment should encourage the interviewee to ask what the interviewer has in mind but *offering* this information is courteous and keeps the participant involved.

Confidentiality

If interviewees are to be quoted verbatim (one of the principles of most qualitative research) there is the problem that individuals can be identified from particular statements. In the 1950s, the people of Springdale village, in the USA, vilified researchers (Vidich and Bensman, 1958) who, though using pseudonyms, made identification of individuals possible because their problems were analysed in the research report. The villagers held an effigy of 'the author' over a manure spreader in their 4th of July parade! Participants should be reminded of their right to veto comments made throughout the project and should be aware of the final format in order to exercise discretion over information divulged.

Training

In order to establish and maintain rapport, interviewers can undergo some degree of training which might include the following.

Listening skills

The interviewer needs to learn when *not* to speak, particularly if he or she is normally quite 'speedy' and talkative. There are various skills in listening, too numerous to detail here, which include:

- not trivialising statements by saying 'How interesting, but we must get on.'
- hearing that a 'yes' is qualified and asking whether the interviewee wants to add anything – what follows may well amount to a 'no'
- not being too quick or dominant in offering an interpretation of what the interviewee was trying to say.

Non-verbal communication

The interviewer needs to be sensitive to non-verbal cues, though not to the point of awkwardness. In what position will an interviewee talk most comfortably? What interviewer postures are interpreted as dominating? What is a pleasant tone and manner for questioning? . . . and so on.

Natural questioning

This is really the biggest factor of all. How can the interviewer make the discussion feel natural, and therefore productive, whilst getting through a set of major questions? If the interviewer has only four or five target questions then it should not be too difficult to insert these into a freely flowing conversation. With a larger list it may be necessary to use prompt notes but some formality can be avoided by listing these on paper used for note taking.

Interest

It is essential that the interviewer remains interested and *believes* that the interviewee's information, as well as sacrificed time, are valuable. The interviewee needs to feel this is the case. Patton (1980) urges that the concept of the bad interviewee should be ignored, arguing that it is easy to summon up stereotypes (of the hostile or paranoid interviewee, for instance). He suggests that it is the sensitive interviewer's task to unlock the internal perspective of each interviewee by being adaptable in finding the style and format which will work in each case.

One overall necessity here is *practice*. Interviews can be made more effective with thoughtful preparation and by practising with colleagues as dummy interviewees until stumbling points and awkwardness have been reduced or ironed out.

Types of question

It is deceptively simple to ask poor or problematic questions. Some of the common mistakes to avoid are outlined in the principles of questionnaire design described in Chapter 7. Items to avoid are *double-barrelled*, *complex*, *ambiguous*, *leading* and *emotive* questions. In addition, the following points might be noted:

1. It is easy to ask two or more questions at once if the interviewer gets enthusiastic. For instance, the sequence: 'So tell me about it. What was it like? How did you feel? Did you regret it?' would put a memory strain, at least, on the interviewee.

2. Questions like 'Are you enjoying the course?' may well receive a monosyllabic answer. Open-ended questions like 'Please can you tell me what you are enjoying about the course?' will be more likely to produce rich information.

3. 'Why?' questions can be wasteful in time. Asking a student 'Why did you join the course?' will produce a variety of replies in quite different categories. For instance:
   'It'll get me a decent qualification'
   'To meet new people'
   'It was nearer than London'
   'My mother thought it was a good idea'
   are all possible answers. We can decide, during the planning stage, what *category* of reply we would like and design questions accordingly. What should certainly be avoided is an implication that the answer given is unwanted by saying, for instance, 'No, I didn't mean that . . .'.

4. Interest may not be maintained if too many personal background details are asked. This point is valid for surveys too, as mentioned below.

The sequence and progress of questions

Feelings and reactions

As with more formal questioning methods, the interviewee will feel more comfortable if the session does not kick off with emotionally charged or controversial items. Likewise, it will be hard to discuss feelings about or reactions towards an issue or event until the interviewee has had a chance to acclimatise by describing it. Early questions can be aimed at eliciting a description, and later questions can prompt feelings about or reactions towards events described.

Probes and prompts

PROMPTS are supplementary questions given to *each* interviewee unless they make these redundant by offering the exact information the interviewer was looking for. For instance, asked about reasons for joining a course, a respondent's answer of 'because it interested me' might be followed by 'in what ways did the course interest you?', which would have been asked whatever the interviewee's responses unless they happened to state sponta-neously what interested them about the course. PROBES are more general requests for further information, such as 'Could you tell me a little more about that', which interview-ers use according to circumstance.

Helpful feedback

An interview will run more smoothly if the interviewee is aware of the position reached and the future direction of questioning. In particular it might be useful to let the inter-viewee know:

1. When the interviewer is about to change topic. For instance, 'Now let's talk about the students on the course'.
2. That the next question is particularly important, complex, controversial or sensitive. For instance, 'You've been telling me what you like about the course. Now I'd like to find out about what you don't like. Can you tell me . . .'.
3. About what the interviewer thinks the interviewee has just said, or said earlier, without, of course, reinterpretations which depart far from the actual words used.

This feedback and summary of what the interviewee is understood to have said is central to semi-structured interviewing and most qualitative approaches. It permits the interviewee to realise they are making sense and being productive; also, that they are not being misrepresented. They can alter or qualify what they've said. The process also keeps the interviewee actively involved and confident.

However, it is important, of course, *not* to summarise interviewees' statements in a lan-guage form which makes them feel that their own statements were somehow inferior and in need of substantial rephrasing.

Recording data

Interviewers have three common choices for saving data: note taking, audio-tape or video-tape recordings.

Note taking

Taking hand-written notes will obviously slow down the procedure. It could be useful to develop some form of personal shorthand – at least short forms of commonly used terms and phrases. The note book does have the handy advantage of being a place to store dis-creetly the interview questions or outline. If used, the interviewer needs to be careful not to give the impression that what the interviewee is saying at any particular moment is not important because it is not being recorded.

Audio recording

Many people feel inhibited in the presence of a tape recorder's microphone. The inter-viewer needs to justify its use in terms of catching the exact terms and richness of the interviewee's experiences, and in terms of confidentiality. The interviewee has to be free to have the recording switched off at any time. The tape recorder has the advantage of leaving the interviewer free to converse naturally and encourage the greatest flow of information.

Video recording

A 'live' video camera in the room may dominate and can hardly help retain the informal, 'chatty' atmosphere which a loosely structured, open-ended interview is supposed to create. It is possible to acclimatise interviewees to its presence over quite a number of sessions, but this is costly in time. The great value, of course, is in the recording of non-verbal communication at a detailed level and the chance to analyse this at a comfortable pace. If this information is not required, however, then video is an unnecessary, intrusive gimmick.

Both video and audio recordings could be conducted unobtrusively by simply not revealing their presence to the interviewee, but, in this case, serious ethical issues must be addressed. Two answers to possible dilemmas here are:

1. Inform the interviewee of the recording process but keep equipment completely hidden.
2. Give information about the recording only after the interview has taken place, but emphasise that recordings can be heard or viewed, sections omitted or the whole recording destroyed at the interviewee's request.

Option 2 is of course potentially wasteful and time consuming.

The danger of both audio and video recording is of taking too much information if the intention is to TRANSCRIBE from spoken into written word. Pidgeon and Henwood (1997) estimate that it takes eight to ten times the duration of recorded speech to transcribe it into written form, and Potter (1996) puts this ratio at 20 to 1. For an example of transcription style see page 460.

SURVEYS

A survey consists of asking a relatively large number of people for information. In the informal, loosely structured interview, each respondent's answers form a small case-study. A survey can consist of a set of such small case-studies. Much more often, though, it would involve the use of a structured questionnaire, with answers open or closed, as described in interview types 4 and 5 above. Each set of responses forms an equivalent unit in a large sample. Interviewers usually work as a team and procedures are therefore fully standardised. Each will be briefed on the exact introductory statement and steps to be followed with each respondent. A survey may be used for two major research purposes: *descriptive* or *analytical*.

Descriptive

Here the researcher wants accurate description of what people, in some target population, do and think, and perhaps with what frequency. Bryant *et al.* (1980), for instance, studied child-minding in Oxfordshire and focused on the minders' behaviour and attitude towards their clients, as well as on the children's development. A more notorious and wide-ranging survey was that of Kinsey (1948, 1953) on American sexual behaviour. An extremely comprehensive survey (Jowell and Topf, 1988) gathered information on current British social attitudes. The issues covered included: AIDS, the countryside, industry's and unions' influences on political parties, the government's current economic policies, education, the North–South divide and which household jobs should be shared – according to married and single persons' opinions.

Analytic use

Survey data can be used to test hypotheses. Hatfield and Walster (1981) interviewed 537 college men and women who had a regular partner. Those who felt their relationship was equitable were far more likely to predict its continuation over one to five years than were those who felt one partner received or gave too much. This tested hypothesis supported a theory of human interaction based on calculated gains and losses.

In Sears *et al.*'s (1957) wide-ranging study of child-rearing practices, using mothers from two suburbs of Boston, USA, many hypotheses were tested by *correlating* (Chapter 15) rearing techniques with children's characteristic behaviour. Data were gathered by rating open-ended answers to structured questions given to the mothers. The raters assessed only from the interview recording and didn't meet the mother. The researchers found positive relationships between the use of physical punishment and a child's higher level of aggressive behaviour. Mothers who were rated as warm and used 'withdrawal of love' as a major disciplinary technique had children with stronger consciences. Both these variables, withdrawal of love and strength of conscience, were assessed indirectly from the interview data and are examples of constructs, operationally defined by the coding system.

Often, from a large descriptive survey, hypotheses can be formulated or checked against further information from the *same* survey. For instance, in the second report of the (UK) National Child Development Study (Davie *et al.* 1972), a survey of a large sample of children born in 1958, it was found that children from social class V (unskilled manual) were at a particular disadvantage on reading tests, compared with other manual and non-manual classes. Why might this be? Well, from the same survey data it was found that overcrowded homes and homes lacking basic amenities were related to serious reading retardation irrespective of a child's social class, sex, area of the UK or accommodation type. Children from social class V were more likely to live in such homes. So, reading deficiency could be related to factors only indirectly related to, but more prevalent within, one section of society.

Survey design

In survey work there are three major areas of decision-making necessary before initiating the contact with respondents. These are the sample, mode of questioning, and the questions themselves. The first two areas will be dealt with now. I shall leave dealing with the actual content of questions until the next chapter on questionnaires and tests in general.

The sample

Of all methods, the survey throws particular emphasis on the sample, since the aim, very often, is to make generalisations about a relatively large section of the population, if not all of it. If the sample *is* the whole population then the survey is known as a CENSUS.

Box 6.4 Advantages and disadvantages of the survey compared with the in-depth interview

Advantages	Disadvantages
Many respondents can be questioned fairly quickly	Structured questions miss more informative data
Can be a lot less expensive than in-depth interviews (which have a lot of information to be transcribed)	Large-scale surveys can be expensive in assistants
Less influence from dynamics of interpersonal variables	More influenced by superficial interpersonal variables; respondent has no time to trust and confide in interviewer
Less bias in analysing answers, since questions are structured	More likely to produce 'public responses', not respondent's genuine ideas
	Possibility of social desirability effect is higher

We have dealt with the main methods and issues of sampling in an earlier chapter. Survey work has produced two other forms of sample not used elsewhere. These are the PANEL and the FOCUS GROUP.

The panel

This is a specially selected group of people who can be asked for information on a repetitive basis. They are much used by market research companies, government survey units and audience research in broadcasting. It is easier and more efficient to rely on the same, well-stratified group to provide information each time it is required.

One problem can be that panel members become too sophisticated in their reviewing and can become unrepresentative in, say, their viewing habits since they feel they must watch all the programmes mentioned in their questionnaire.

Focus groups

The idea here is to bring together a group of individuals with a common interest and to conduct a form of collective interview. Discussion among members may provoke an exchange of views and revelations providing information and insights less likely to surface during a one-to-one interview. Though not providing much in the way of reliable, quantifiable data, such groups can be a starting point for research into a specific area, as an aid to exposing and clarifying concepts. The term 'focus group' has crept into news reporting in recent years as they have become a popular tool of modern political parties.

The mode of questioning

There are several ways to communicate with respondents: face-to-face, telephone, post and, in recent years, e-mail. Telephones are used rarely and produce a lower rate of agreement to be interviewed than does a face to face request. Since the boom in tele-sales, it is probably hard to convince people that there is not ultimately a selling motive.

The privacy of the postal method is likely to produce fewer but more honest answers. Interpersonal variables, discussed above, are reduced to a minimum in postal surveys though the respondent may make assumptions about the researcher from the style of the covering letter. The method is also less time consuming.

The disadvantages of postal surveys are first, that the questionnaire must be exceptionally clear, and unambiguous instructions for its completion must be carefully written. Even so, respondents may answer in an inappropriate way that a 'live' interviewer could have corrected. Second, the proportion of non-returners is likely to be higher than the number of refusals by other approaches. This matters a lot when, for instance, it is reported that 75% of respondents (300) agreed that government should continue to finance higher education substantially, if it is also true that only 400 out of 1000 persons contacted bothered to complete and return the form. Do we count the missing 600 as neutral or not bothered, or do we assume that $\frac{3}{4}$ of them also agree?

Glossary

Survey of whole population	_____	census
Interview method using structured questions to be asked but permitting tailoring of later questions to the individual's responses; also seeks to test specific hypothesis or effect	_____ _____	clinical method/ interview
Dimension of design which is the extent to which interviewees are kept ignorant of the aims of the questioning	_____	disguise
Interview in which researcher and interviewee talk together in each others' presence	_____-_-_____	face-to-face
Group with common interest who meet to discuss an issue in a collective interview in order for researchers to assess opinion	_____ _____	focus group
Interview in which interviewer does not direct discussion and remains non-judgemental	___-_____ _____	non-directive interview
Interview item to which interviewees can respond in any way they please and at any length	___-_____ _____	open-ended question
Stratified group who are consulted in order for opinion to be assessed	_____	panel
General request for further information used in semi-structured interview	_____	probe
Pre-set request for further information used in semi-structured interview if the information is not offered spontaneously by interviewee on an item	_____	prompt
Person who is questioned in interview or survey	_____	respondent
A general term for methods in which people knowingly provide information about themselves	_____-_____	self-report method

Interview with pre-set list of topics to cover but in which 'natural' conversation is attempted and the interviewer 'plays it by ear' as to whether sufficient information has been provided by the interviewee	_____-_____ _____	semi-structured interview
Dimension of design which is the extent to which questions and procedure are identical for everyone	_____	structure (to unstructured/loose)
Relatively structured questioning of large sample	_____	survey
Written recording of directly recorded speech, as exactly as possible, but depending upon approach; usually often includes pauses, intonation etc	_____	transcription (to transcribe)

Exercises

1   Without looking back at the text, try to think of several advantages and disadvantages the survey has compared with the informal interview.

2   Suppose you decide to conduct a survey on attitudes towards the environment in your area. Outline the steps you would take in planning and conducting the survey, paying particular attention to:
   • the sample and means of obtaining it
   • the exact approach to respondents you would use
   • the types of question you would ask
   To answer this last point in detail you will need to read pages 154 to 163 in the next chapter on questionnaires, at least briefly.

3   A researcher wishes to investigate specific instances of racism (abuse, physical harassment, discrimination) that members of minority ethnic groups have experienced. Four assistants are employed to conduct informal, guided interviews starting with individuals recommended by local community leaders.

   a. What kind of sample is drawn?
   b. One interviewer records far fewer instances than the other three. Can you give at least five reasons why this might be?
   c. Another interviewer argues that the study should follow up with a structured questionnaire over a far wider sample. Why might this be?

4   You are about to conduct an interview with the manager of a local, large supermarket. He is 43 years old, quite active in local politics and is known to be fairly friendly. Make a list of all the variables, especially those concerning your own personality and characteristics, which might influence the production of information in the interview.

5   Construct (and, if you have time, administer) a semi-structured interview schedule which would investigate people's reactions to the death of Princess Diana in August, 1997. Try to include questions which would elicit evidence of 'flashbulb' memory phenomena (where people tend to recall vividly and visually exactly what they were doing, down to trivial specifics, when they first heard the news). If you do interview several people as part of this exercise, try to adapt your schedule in the light of this experience, re-phrasing, adding and deleting items.

Answers

1   See page 149

3   a. Non-random. Opportunity sample. Start of snowball sample.
b. Initial interviewee unwilling to admit problem; initial interviewee gives fewer further contacts; interviewer doesn't see some incidents as 'serious'; interviewer doesn't want to record the incidents for personal, political reasons; interviewer is a poor questioner, is aggressive, shows prejudice etc.
c. Structured questionnaire more reliable; results more comparable; larger sample more representative.

Questionnaires – asking people using psychological scales and tests

This chapter looks at a variety of procedures for gathering data using some form of *questionnaire*, *scale* or *test*. There is some overlap with the last chapter since some interviews consist of going through a structured questionnaire with the respondent.

The first important matter is to consider carefully how people will, in reality, respond to certain types of question which are, for instance, difficult, embarrassing or controversial.

- Questions can be *fixed* or *open-ended* (in the latter the respondent has freedom in type and length of response).

- Features of good questionnaires are outlined: they should *discriminate*, be *reliable*, be *valid* and be *standardised*.

- The attitude scales of *Thurstone, Likert, Bogardus, Guttman* and *Osgood's semantic differential* are covered. Likert's is probably the most popular and with this, decisions must be made about how many points to use (often five) and how the 'neutral' mid-point will be interpreted or dealt with. Items should vary in direction to avoid *response bias* and *acquiescence*, dealt with below.

- Specific points about the pitfalls of question/item construction are described as are issues in item organisation such as *response bias, demand characteristics* and *social desirability*.

- *Projective* tests assume that unconscious mental processes can be assessed from the way people respond to ambiguous stimuli such as the *Rorschach* and *Thematic Apperception Tests (TAT)*.

- *Psychometric tests* are intended to be standardised measurement instruments for human personality and ability characteristics. They can suffer from cultural content bias and have been extremely controversial in the area of intelligence or mental ability testing. Tests are validated and made meaningful to some extent using *factor analysis* which investigates correlation 'clusters' and provides statistical support for theories about which underlying 'factors' cause results to be so arranged on tests or sections of tests.

- Methods for checking a test's reliability, and validity are detailed. *Reliability* is consistency within a test or between repeated uses of it. *Validity* concerns whether a test measures what it was created to measure. *Standardisation* involves adjusting raw scores to fit a normal distribution which makes comparison to norms possible but the assumption of a normal distribution underlying human characteristics can be controversial.

QUESTIONNAIRES AND ATTITUDE SCALES

Questionnaires, attitude scales and tests are tools for gathering structured information from people. Where they openly ask for information about the tested person, they are *self report* measures. Questionnaires used in surveys are usually constructed for the specific research topic and tend to test for current opinion or patterns of behaviour. Attitude scales and ability tests are usually intended to have a longer life span. They are seen by the PSYCHOMETRICIAN or PSYCHOMETRIST (a psychologist who practices PSYCHOMETRY) as scientific and technical measuring 'instruments', equivalent to the pressure gauge or voltmeter of 'hard' science. Such PSYCHOMETRIC TESTS (the science is in the term 'metric') require a lot of development work in the form of STANDARDISATION and demonstrations of high *reliability* and *validity*, terms to be properly defined at the end of this chapter but roughly equivalent, respectively, to the *consistency* of a measure, and its capacity to measure what the test was *intended* to measure. Such tests are created to tap a relatively permanent aspect of the individual's cognition and behaviour, such as attitude towards religion or authority, or their verbal and mathematical ability.

Although psychometric scales take a great deal of professional expertise and effort to develop, many of the features of attitude scale construction can be employed by the student wishing to measure people's views on a current issue, such as child discipline, preservation of the environment or treatment of animals. A thorough assessment of attitude would involve at least two measurements, at differing times, since a defining feature of an attitude is relatively *enduring* nature, but students can learn a lot about the difficulties of attitude scale construction by attempting to create a one-shot test.

Questionnaires, scales psychometric and projective tests can all be used as measures of the dependent variable in experimental work as well as in correlational or group difference studies. In an experiment, for instance, one group of participants might be assessed for 'self-esteem' before and after a 'treatment' in which they are made to feel successful. This can be compared with a control group's assessments.

QUESTIONNAIRES

Some general principles

The following principles are part of the common 'lore' of survey questionnaires. They apply particularly to the situation in which strangers, or people little known to the interviewer, are being asked a big favour in stopping to answer a few questions – see Chapter 6.

1 Ask for the minimum of information required for the research purpose

A respondent's time is precious so why ask for information which you are probably not going to use or which is obtainable elsewhere? A 'shotgun' approach is often taken in devising a questionnaire – we must know their age, subjects taken, area lived in and so on. But *must* we? Too much information may not be useful. Some questions may have been included only because they 'seemed interesting', which is too vague a basis for inclusion. In addition, personal (but not private) details may be available from company or school records. The respondent's time spent answering questions has a bearing on mood, and mood may well be altered if the interviewer asks what sex the respondent is! Other details, such as whether married and number of children may well be drawn from an introductory relaxing chat and, if not, during final checking.

2 Make sure questions can be answered

'How many times have you been to a supermarket this year?' may be quite difficult for most people to answer at all accurately.

3 Make sure questions will be answered truthfully

The question in point 2 is unlikely to be answered truthfully because of its difficulty. Other difficult or wide-ranging questions are likely to receive an answer based more on well-known public opinion than on the individual's real beliefs. Questions on child rearing, for instance, if not phrased very explicitly, are well known for producing, where wide error is possible, answers more in accord with prevailing 'expert' views on good practice than with the parent's *actual* practice.

4 Make sure questions will be answered and not refused

Some sensitive topics will obviously produce more refusals. Most respondents will continue on a sensitive topic, one started, but may balk at a sensitive question turning up suddenly in an otherwise innocuous context, for instance a sex-life question among items about shopping habits. The interviewer has to provide a context in order to justify sensitive points, or else avoid them.

Fixed and open-ended questions

At the least structured extreme, survey questionnaires have open-ended questions. Most questionnaire items are fixed choice, however, where respondents are asked to select an answer from two or more alternatives. Open-ended questions have several advantages, some of which we alluded to in the interview chapter.

- They deliver richer, fuller information
- The respondent does not feel frustrated by the constraint imposed with a fixed choice answer
- There is less chance of ambiguity, since the respondent says what he or she thinks and doesn't have to interpret a statement and then agree or disagree with it
- The questioning is more realistic. We rarely have to simply agree or disagree, or say how strongly, without giving our reasons
- Open ended interview questions can be used to generate information which is later organised into a structured questionnaire. This was done, for instance, by Niles (1998), who obtained from Australian and Sri Lankan interviewees open lists of achievement goals (what people most wanted in life) and means of satisfying these. She then organised these into a structured questionnaire which was administered to many more participants.

However, open-ended questions are also difficult to code or quantify, whereas fixed-choice items make numerical comparison relatively easy. Chapter 21 on qualitative data, discusses methods of dealing with open-ended answers.

Here are a few examples of fixed-choice items:

1. I voted in the last election   YES/NO
2. I would describe my present dwelling as:
   a) fully owned by me
   b) owned by me with a mortgage
   c) owned by me as part of a housing association
   d) rented from the local council
   e) rented from a private landlord
   f) provided by employer
   g) other (please state)
3. My age is: a) under 16   b) 16–21   c) 22–35   d) over 35
4. At what age did your baby start crawling? .... months

Some questions will permit the respondent to tick or check more than one item but if a single response is required then possible overlap must be carefully avoided.

> Is it possible to check more than one answer in any of the items given above? If so, which one(s) and why?

I would think there might be confusion if I were just 35 and answering item 3. In item 2, e) and f) might overlap. Although the fault is very obvious in item 3, it is very common for draft versions of student project questionnaires to contain this kind of overlap.

Note that Questions 1 and 2 above are not actually 'questions' as such but items with which the respondent has to agree – much like the items in attitude scales which we are going to investigate in a moment. We can see here that there is a world of difference between fixed choice 'questions' of the form 'Which of the following do you agree with/do every day etc.', or 'Are you nervous at meetings? (Yes/No), and normal conversational questions of the 'Why' and 'What do you think....' variety, which produce *qualitative* answers.

Features of good questionnaires and measurement scales

Where survey questionnaires are requesting purely factual information (such as occupation, number of children at school, hours of television watched, and so on) the following principles are not so crucial, though all measures should be reliable and valid ones. (Factual questionnaires usually have 'face' validity – see p. 173). Where scales and tests attempt to measure psychological characteristics, the following are extremely important:

1. They should DISCRIMINATE as widely as possible across the variety of human response. They shouldn't identify a few extreme individuals whilst showing no difference between individuals clustered at the centre of the scale. This is referred to as DISCRIMINATORY POWER and it is dependent on the sensitivity of items and the response system (e.g., 'yes/no' vs. 'strongly agree, agree,... etc.').
2. They should be highly RELIABLE (they should measure *consistently*).
3. They should be supported by tests of VALIDITY (they should measure what was *intended*).

4. They should be STANDARDISED if they are to be used as general, practical measures of human characteristics. (Similar measures should mean similar things within the same population.)

A questionnaire, scale or test will normally be piloted, perhaps several times, before the researcher is satisfied that it meets these criteria. Even a limited questionnaire, constructed by students as part of course practical work, should be piloted at least once to highlight pitfalls and possible misinterpretations. Tests for the criteria above are dealt with later in this chapter.

ATTITUDE SCALES

Attitude scales are quite like questionnaires but do not usually use questions. Most use statements with which the respondent has to agree or disagree to some extent. Questionnaires can vary along the dimension of *disguise*. Hammond's technique, mentioned in the last chapter, hides its purpose by appearing to assess knowledge of factual issues rather than prejudice. Some attitude scales give clues to their purpose while others are transparent, as in the case where a limited topic, such as dental hygiene, is involved. We will look at the techniques of five types of attitude scale, along with their advantages and disadvantages.

Equal appearing intervals (Thurstone, 1931)

The central idea of a Thurstone scale is that, for each statement on the scale, if a person agrees with it, they are given a score equivalent to the *strength* of that statement (or 'item'). For instance, part of an attitude to equal opportunities scale might appear like this:

Please tick any of the following statements with which you agree:

Companies should pay full salary for maternity leave (9.8)

Companies should provide more toilets for women (6.2)

Women are less reliable employees because they are likely to leave through pregnancy (2.1)

The scores in brackets would not appear to the respondent. They indicate the strength of the item (its SCALE VALUE), derived through the following scale construction process.

1. Produce a large set of statements, like the examples above, both positive and negative towards the attitude object.

2. Ask a panel of judges to rate each statement on a scale of 1 (highly negative on the issue) to 11 (highly positive on the issue). They are urged to use all of the scale and not to bunch items into a few categories.

3. Take the mean value, for each statement, of all the judges' ratings. Our first item above has been given an average rating of 9.8 for instance, while the second one scores only just positive at 6.2. These are the items' *scale values*.

4. In the interests of reliability, reject statements where the judges' individual values have a high *variance* (see Chapter 10), indicating general lack of agreement.

5. In the finished scale, a respondent now scores the scale value of each item agreed with. Hence, people favourable to equal opportunities measures will tend to score only on items *above* the average value and thus end up with a high overall score.

Box 7.1 Difficulties with the Thurstone Method

1. The judges themselves cannot be completely neutral, although they are asked to be objective. In an early debate on this issue, Hinckley (1932) was severely criticised for rejecting judges as 'careless' because they sorted a majority of items into a few extreme categories, against the exhortation mentioned in item 2 of the construction process above. It turned out that most of these judges were black (or pro-black whites) who rated as fairly hostile certain statements seen as relatively neutral by white judges unaware of, or unconcerned by, black issues
2. There is a difficulty in choosing the most discriminating items from among those with the same scale value

Summated ratings (Likert, 1932)

To construct a Likert-type scale

1. As for the Thurstone scale, produce an equal number of *favourable* and *unfavourable* statements about the attitude object (see 'response set or bias', below). These are the *scale items*.
2. Ask respondents to indicate, for each item, their response to the statement according to the following scale:

5	4	3	2	1
Strongly agree	Agree	Undecided	Disagree	Strongly disagree

3. Use the values on this scale as a score for each respondent on each item, so that the respondent scores *five* for strong agreement with an item *favourable* to the attitude object, but *one* for strong agreement with an *unfavourable* item.
4. Add up the scores on each item to give the respondent's overall score.
5. Carry out an *item analysis test* – see below – reject items which lower overall reliability and replace with new items. Repeat analysis until reliability is satisfactory.

Step 5 here is the Likert scale's greatest strength, relative to other scales. It means that, unlike in a Thurstone scale, an item does not need to relate obviously to the attitude issue or object. It can be counted as DIAGNOSTIC if responses to it correlate well with responses overall. For instance, we might find that respondents fairly hostile to equal

Box 7.2 Difficulties with the Likert method

1. For each respondent, scores on the scale only have meaning relative to the scores in the distribution obtained from other respondents. Data produced is therefore best treated as ORDINAL (see Chapter 12) whereas Thurstone considered intervals on his scale to be truly equal.
2. The 'undecided' score, 3, is ambiguous. Does it imply a neutral position (no opinion) or an on-the-fence position with the respondent torn between feelings in both directions?
3. Partly as a consequence of 2, overall scores, central to the distribution (say 30 out of 60) are quite ambiguous. Central scores could reflect a lot of 'undecided' answers, or they could comprise a collection of 'strongly for' and 'strongly against' answers, in which case, perhaps the scale measured two different attitudes.

opportunities issues also tend to agree with 'Women have an instinctive need to be near their child for the first two to three years of its life'. This could stay in our attitude scale since it might predict fairly well a negative attitude to equal opportunities.

The social distance scale (Bogardus, 1925)

Bogardus' scale was originally intended to measure attitudes towards members of different cultures or nationalities. Respondents had to follow this instruction:

> According to my first feeling reactions, I would willingly admit members of each race [respondents were given several 'races' or nationalities] (as a class, and not the best I have known, nor the worst members) to one or more of the classifications under which I have placed a cross.

They were then given this list to tick, for each race:
1. To close kinship by marriage
2. To my club as personal chums
3. To my street as neighbours
4. To employment in my occupation
5. To citizenship in my country
6. As visitors only in my country
7. Would exclude from my country

It is claimed that, in practice, it is unusual for respondents to accept the 'race' or nationality at a higher level than one at which rejection has occurred, for instance, accepting in one's street, but not to one's occupation. When this does occur it is known as a *reversal*.

It is possible to adapt this technique to test attitudes towards any category of people. On the equal opportunities theme, for instance, it would be possible to grade types of occupation into which respondents felt female workers should be encouraged.

Box 7.3 Difficulties with the Bogardus method

1. Reversals cannot be entirely eliminated. Some people are more protective about their employment than their streets, particularly in cities, I would suspect
2. The overall scale for scoring is narrow, leaving less room for sensitive statistical analysis

Cumulative scaling (Guttman, 1950)

Roughly speaking, the principle of the Bogardus scale is here extended to any attitude object, not just categories of people. On a Bogardus scale, if we know a person's score we know just how far up the scale they went, assuming no reversals. Hence, we can exactly reproduce their scoring pattern. This last achievement is the ideal criterion of a Guttman scale. A clear (but not particularly useful) example would be a scale checking height, where you would tick all those items below which are true for you:

Box 7.4   Cumulatively scaled items

1. I am taller than 1 m 20
2. I am taller than 1 m 30
3. I am taller than 1 m 40
4. I am taller than 1 m 50
5. I am taller than 1 m 60
6. I am taller than 1 m 70

A positive response to item 4 logically entails a positive response to items 1, 2 and 3 also. In the same way as this scale measures a unitary dimension (height), so a true Guttman scale is supposed to only measure one finite attitude and is known as a 'uni-dimensional scale'. The most likely attribute that such a scale *might* be developed for is some kind of ability or skill where achieving level 3 difficulty involves prior achievement of levels 1 and 2.

In practice, when measuring attitudes rather than height or skill, it is never possible to reproduce perfectly a respondent's exact answering pattern from their overall score. As we shall see below, items can very often be interpreted differently by respondents and it is rarely if ever possible to arrange attitude statements such that they reflect an increasingly positive attitude to an object for all people. For instance, one respondent, who is a member of a particular minority ethnic group, might disagree with 'members of all ethnic groups should be treated equally' since, in his or her view, the group has been treated pretty unequally in the past and requires compensatory action. Hence, from the tester's point of view this person's answers may seem inconsistent, since they are otherwise strongly favourable to minority ethnic groups, yet a negative response on this item is taken as hostility. Kline (1993) argues that Guttman scales are not in accord with most psychological theory and are probably not appropriate for psychological measurement.

Box 7.5   Difficulties with the Guttman method

1. Reversals cannot be eliminated
2. Guttman himself was criticised for not dealing with the problem of representativeness in selecting items. He claimed this could be achieved through intuitive thinking and experience

The semantic differential (Osgood et al., 1957)

The original intention behind this scale was to use it for measuring the *connotative* meaning of an object for an individual; roughly speaking, the term's associations for us. Thus, we can all give a denotative meaning for 'nurse' — we have to define what a nurse is, as in a dictionary. The *connotation* of a nurse may, however, differ for each of us.

For me, a nurse is associated with caring, strength and independence. For others, by popular stereotype, he or she may be seen as deferential and practical.

On a semantic differential test the respondent is invited to mark a scale between bipolar adjectives according to the position they feel the object holds on that scale for them. For 'nurse' on the following bipolar opposites, I might mark as shown:

good   <u>x</u>   —   —   —   —   —   —   bad

weak   —   —   —   —   —   <u>x</u>   —   strong

active   —   <u>x</u>   —   —   —   —   —   passive

Osgood claimed that *factor analysis* (see later in this chapter) of all scales gave rise to three general meaning factors, to one of which all bipolar pairs could be attached. 'Active (along with 'slow–fast', 'hot–cold') is an example of the **activity** factor. 'Strong' (along with 'rugged–delicate', 'thick–thin') is an example of the **potency** factor. 'Good' (along with 'clean–dirty', 'pleasant–unpleasant') is an example of the **evaluative** factor.

Adapted to attitude measurement, the semantic differential apparently produces good reliability values and correlates well with other attitude scales, thus producing high CON-CURRENT VALIDITY (see later this chapter).

Box 7.6 Difficulties with the semantic differential

1. Respondents may have a tendency towards a 'position response bias' where they habitually mark at the extreme end of the scale (or won't use the extreme at all) without considering possible weaker or stronger responses. This can occur with a Likert scale too, but is more likely here since the scale points lack the Likert verbal designations (of 'strongly agree' etc.)
2. Here, too, we have the problem of interpretation of the middle point on the scale

QUESTIONNAIRE OR SCALE ITEMS

What to avoid in statement construction

The questionnaire constructor has to be careful to phrase questions clearly and unambiguously, such that the respondent is in no doubt which answer to give. The supreme ideal is that all respondents will interpret an item in the same way. However, this is another of those unrealistic ideals, possible to *approach* in simple arithmetic tests perhaps, but completely contrary to what we know about how people vary in their interpretation of the world, including the interpretation of language. What we can aspire to is clear construction, avoiding most obvious ambiguities and biasing factors for *most* of the population the test or scale is intended for.

What do you think is unsatisfactory about the following statements, intended for an attitude scale?
1. 'We should begin to take compensatory action in areas of employment and training where, in the past, members of one ethnic group, sex or disability type have suffered discrimination or experienced disadvantages as a direct result of being a member of that category.'
2. 'Society should attempt to undo the effects of institutional racism wherever possible.'
3. 'Immigrants should not be allowed to settle in areas of high unemployment.'
4. 'Abortion is purely a woman's choice and should be made freely available.'

> 5. 'It should not be possible to ask a woman about her spouse's support, when husbands are not asked the same questions.'
> 6. 'The Labour government has deceived and betrayed its traditional voters.'
> 7. 'Don't you agree that student grants should be increased?'
> 8. 'Do you have a criminal record?'
>   And what can you see as problems with the following sorts of item and scale?
> 9. State to what degree you enjoyed the lecture course:
>   Very much indeed   quite a lot   a lot   a little   not much   didn't like it
> 10. I found the   I found the   I am undecided about   I did not enjoy the
>   sessions very   sessions quite   the helpfulness of the   sessions at all
>   helpful   helpful   sessions
> 11. Who did you think was most responsible for the attack?   man ☐   woman ☐ (referring to a sex attack by the man on the woman where the woman wore 'provocative' clothing)

1 Complexity

Not many respondents will take this in, all in one go. The statement is far too complex. It could possibly be broken up into logical components.

2 Technical terms

Many respondents will not have a clear idea of what 'institutional racism' is. Either find another term or include a preamble to the item which explains the special term.

3 Ambiguity

Some students I taught used this item and found almost everyone in general agreement, whether they were generally hostile to immigrants or not. Hence, it was not at all *discriminating*. This was probably because those positive towards immigrants considered their plight if new to the country *and* unemployed. Those who were hostile to immigrants may well have been making wildly inaccurate but popular racist assumptions about immigrant numbers – see Box 1.1, Chapter 1.

4 Double-barrelled items

This quite simple item is asking two questions at once. A person might well agree with free availability – to avoid the dangers of the back-street abortionist – yet may not feel that only the woman concerned should choose.

5 Negatives

In the interests of avoiding *response set* (see below), about half the items in a scale should be positive towards the object and about half negative. However, it is not a good idea to produce negative statements simply by negating a positive one. It can be confusing to answer a question with a double negative, even where one of the negatives is camouflaged, as in: '*It should not be possible to reject a candidate's application on the grounds of disability.*' This could be rephrased as: '*A candidate's disability should be completely ignored when considering an application.*'
The item in the exercise has two overt negatives in it and this can easily be confusing.

6 Emotive language

A statement such as this may not get an attitude test off to a good start, particularly in

'New Labour' constituencies. If there are emotive items at all it might be best to leave these until the respondent is feeling more relaxed with the interviewer or with the test itself.

7 Leading questions

As I said, most attitude tests don't have actual questions in them. Should this sort of question occur, however, it carries with it an implication that the respondent should say 'yes'. If you don't feel this is so, just try to imagine a friend or colleague opening the day's conversation with such a question. To the respondent it can seem hard to disagree, something which people would usually rather not do anyway. One might begin with 'Weeell...'. Respondents may well say 'Yes, but...' with the 'but' amounting to disagreement, even though the response is recorded as agreement.

8 Invasion of privacy

This is private information, along with sex life and other obvious areas. The student conducting a practical exercise should avoid any such intrusion.

9 Balance of scaled items

Here the student respondent cannot state just how *much* they disliked the lectures and the data can be 'massaged' with the claim that X% of students 'enjoyed' the lectures if the first four categories are collated together.

10 Balance again

The last category is not on the same issue as the first three and it is possible to agree with any one of these *and* the last one together.

11 Sensitivity of scaled items

This item was presented recently by a student who wanted to assess the degree to which people felt a female victim was *partly* responsible for an attack by wearing revealing clothes on a street late at night. Of course no participant blamed the woman *most*. The student had unfortunately chosen a *dichotomous variable* for the response – only two bipolar opposites. The item was too insensitive to capture the increased victim responsibility some men may have assumed in the 'provocative' condition (a hypothesis in the experiment). The student needed to use a *scale* instead, such as:

On a scale from   1 = not at all responsible   to   10 = entirely responsible
how responsible for the attack were: a. the man □   b. the woman □?

Organisation of items

1 Response set or bias

An effect called RESPONSE ACQUIESCENCE SET often occurs when responding to questionnaires. This is the tendency to agree rather than disagree ('Yeah saying') – see Figure 7.1. To avoid a constant error from this effect, items need to be an unpredictable mixture of positive and negative statements about the attitude object. This has the effect either of keeping the respondent thinking about each item or of giving the inveterate yeah sayer a central score, rather than an extreme one. There is also some evidence of a smaller bias towards *disagreeing* with items.

Figure 7.1 'Yeah saying' – the possible effects of response acquiescence set

2 Respondent's interpretation

With any questionnaire or scale, it is a good idea to make it clear that both positive and negative items will appear. There are several reasons for this. Respondents are likely to view the interviewer as believing the statements made. A set of statements all contrary to what the respondent thinks may well set up strong emotional defences. We have said already that for the same reason it would be best to start with less extreme statements.

There are also *demand characteristics* (see Chapter 3) associated with responding to a questionnaire. The respondent may well try to interpret the aim of the research or questions. Again, if all initial items are in the same direction the respondent may form an impression of the interviewer's aims or personality which can distort the respondent's later answers.

3 Social desirability

Defined in Chapter 3, this factor involves respondents guessing at what is counted as a socially acceptable or favourable answer and giving it in order to 'look good'. A further reason for guessing might be to 'please the researcher' by giving the results it is assumed are required. Some questionnaires attempt to deal with this problem by including items which only an angel would agree or disagree with. If too many such items are answered in the 'saintly' manner, the respondent's results are excluded from the research. Eysenck (1975) calls his set of items a 'lie scale', though an excluded respondent is not necessarily lying. They may be angelic or they may be distorting the truth just a bit.

Reliability and number of items

The number of items used in a questionnaire needs to be kept manageable in terms of time and the respondent's patience, but a larger number of items creates higher *reliability*. With a larger number of items, random errors, from respondent's individual interpretations and misunderstandings, should cancel each other out.

PROJECTIVE TESTS

These tests have been developed out of the psychoanalytic tradition of research and therapy. They are based on the Freudian notion that when we are confronted by an

Box 7.7   Steps in the construction of an attitude scale

1. Produce twice the number of items finally required, balanced for:
   a. Strength (some 'weak' statements, some 'hard').
   b. Breadth (is the whole attitude area covered?).
   c. Direction (in a Likert type scale, some items should be 'pro' the issue and as many should be 'anti'; half of each set should be weak and the other half strong).
2. Pilot these items on a few people for ambiguity, misunderstanding etc.
3. Replace deleted items by new ones, still keeping a balance.
4. Repeat 2 and 3 until all items are unproblematic.
5. Arrange items in a random or alternating order (to discourage response bias).
6. Pilot this arrangement on a good-sized sample (at least 30).
7. Tests for *reliability* by conducting a form of *item analysis* – see later – until reliability is at least about 0.75, preferably higher.
8. Inspect or test final version for *validity*. Do items still cover main issues? Do some topics now dominate? Some form of *criterion validity* procedure can be performed by, for instance, testing whether a 'sociability' scale discriminates between extroverts and introverts – see later. If validity is unsatisfactory, go through all steps again!

abstract or ambiguous picture, some of our inner thoughts, protected because they produce anxiety, are partially revealed by the way we *project* our interpretations onto the display.

The Rorschach ink blot tests is a set of abstract designs rather like children produce with 'butterfly' paintings (see Figure 7.2). The respondent reports what he or she feels they can see in the picture.

Similarly, the *Thematic apperception test* (TAT) is a picture, often of people with their emotional expressions ambiguous or hidden, about which, the test-taker is asked, 'What is happening?'

Figure 7.2   A Rorschach-type ink blot as part of a 'projective test'

Reliability of projective test ratings

Very often, in research applications, independent ratings of respondents' verbal Rorschach or TAT responses are made by 'blind' assessors. Brender and Kramer (1967) assessed participants' needs via TAT and through dreams. They found some significant correlations for some sorts of need (e.g. affiliation, dominance). They compared their ratings with those made by an undergraduate student. They state that the resulting reliability estimates were 'rather conservative' because the student 'had no previous experience with TAT [...] material'. There is of course the possibility that the system in use was rather subjective and/or that 'experienced' raters come closer together simply because they share the same (not necessarily correct) assumptions about the meaning of dreams and TAT associations.

Projective tests belong in the unstructured, disguised section of the quadrant formed by the structure and disguise dimensions. It is claimed that their open-endedness produces richer information and that their disguised nature provides genuine data, unbiased by people guessing the researcher's (or therapist's) intent.

It is argued that the tests can be used to measure such factors as the affective, usually hidden, component of attitudes. They have very often been used to assess concealed aggression, hostility, anxiety, sexual fantasy and so on in hypothesis testing work. Levin's study, mentioned early in Chapter 6, used Rorschach tests.

Box 7.8 Difficulties with projective tests

1. Being open-ended and initially qualitative, the tests are suspect for their reliability. Some users take great care in checking agreement between raters who code and categorise responses, ignorant of the research hypothesis. The researcher provides a comprehensive and subtle coding scheme. In Levin's study, agreement between Rorschach coders, ignorant of the research aim, was between 84% and 91%

2. It is quite possible for coders to be highly consistent, compared with one another, yet for the measures to be quite unrelated to any theoretical psychoanalytic principle. A person in Levin's study who said of people seen in the Rorschach blot 'I can't quite tell if they're male or female' may not actually be confused about their sexual body-image, for instance. Since the tests are also disguised measures of hypothetical concepts, the problem of validity is serious.

PSYCHOMETRIC TESTS

Psychologists have developed many *psychometric tests* which were intended to be *standardised* instruments (see below) of measurement for human psychological characteristics. The tradition goes back to Galton who began the measurement of mental abilities in the 1890s by testing thousands of people on many sensory and cognitive tasks (many of the people tested paid Galton a fee for the privilege!). Although some attitude scales have become highly refined, and even projective tests are sometimes called 'psychometric', if well standardised, it is intelligence and personality tests which have undergone a high degree of standardisation and scrutiny for validity. This is partly because such tests are used in professional practice where people's life chances can be affected.

These tests have also undergone much periodic revision, since they are highly sensitive to bias from cultural, class and other social factors. It is on these grounds that their validity has been most seriously challenged and thoroughly investigated. For instance, to the question 'What should you do if you find a stamped addressed envelope in the street?', it might be 'intelligent', in a very poor area, where petty crime is unremarkable, to steam off the stamp – a response which gained no mark in one famous test. A picture depicting a boy holding an umbrella at the wrong angle to falling rain was said by Puerto Ricans to be incorrect, not because of the angle but because the boy was holding the umbrella *at all*. This is apparently considered highly effeminate in Puerto Rican society!

It is beyond the scope of this book to cover intelligence and personality testing in depth, along with all the weaknesses and criticisms of the tests. This is covered very well in other available texts, in particular Gross (1996)[1]. The examples given above simply demonstrate the need for standardisation and constant revision from a research methods point of view. They also exemplify, I hope, what is meant by class and cultural bias in tests.

As with interviews and questionnaires, data from psychometric tests can be used as the dependent variable in experimental work, though it is more common to find them being used in correlational and group difference type studies, and in practical applications of psychology in the professional field.

Most tests will be beyond the scope of student use, since they are closely guarded as technical instruments of the psychological profession. Many come with user restrictions and all are subject to copyright laws. Most may not be copied or adapted without the supplier's permission. They also usually have quite complex scoring manuals which are even more closely monitored. People wishing to use tests in research or practice would be advised to contact the British Psychological Society in Leicester. The BPS also validates certificates of competence in occupational testing.

Factor analysis

Researchers often support the development and use of psychometric tests by employing a form of *construct validity* (explained later in this chapter), which involves a complex statistical procedure known as FACTOR ANALYSIS. The aim is to find 'factors' (hidden or 'intervening' variables) which might explain the observed relationships between people's scores on several tests or subtests. The steps involved are these.

1. A large sample of people are measured on several tests or subtests.
2. Correlations (see Chapter 15) are calculated between every possible pair of tests or subtests and arranged in a matrix as shown in Table 7.1 below.
3. The matrix of correlations is fed into the factor analysis programme which looks for 'clusters' – groups of tests or subtests which all correlate well together.
4. The researcher sets the programme to solve the matrix for a particular number of 'factors'. Factors, at this point, are nothing real, just mathematical concepts which will

---

[1] More specialist texts include:
Anastasi, A. (1988) *Psychological Testing* Macmillian
Cronbach, L.J. (1984) *Essentials of Psychological Testing* Harper & Row
Kline, P. (1993) *Handbook of Test Construction* Routledge
Loewenthal, K.M. (1996) *An Introduction to Psychological Tests and Scales* UCL Press
Murphy, R.M. & Davidshofer, C.O. (1991) *Psychological Testing: Principles and Applications* Prentice-Hall

'account for' as much as possible of the correlation found. The programme then gives the best configuration of this number of factors to account for all the correlations.

5. Alternatively, the programme will offer a solution in the best possible number of factors, with the least amount of variation unaccounted for. The whole 'explanation' is purely statistical, accounting for the numerical relationships.

6. The researcher might ask the programme to solve for a higher number of factors if the amount 'unexplained' is too high.

To make the concept of factor analysis a little clearer, I hope, imagine the following. We select a few hundred people of average fitness and subject them to various athletic events. We correlate the results of every event with every other, producing a table, part of which might look like Table 7.1:

As we'll see in Chapter 15, if people tend to score similarly on two variables, these variables are said to 'correlate positively' and we'd expect a value close to +1. If there is a tendency to be high on one variable whilst being low on the other, and vice versa, we'd expect a value approaching −1. No relationship at all is signified by a value close to zero.

As we'd expect from common-sense prediction, there is a strong correlation between 100 and 200 metres, and between 3 000 and 5 000 metres. There is a moderate correlation between discus and shot put and between 100 metres and long jump, whereas that between 100 metres and shot put is moderately negative.

Intuition might suggest that the underlying factors responsible for these relationships are *sprinting ability*, *stamina* and *strength*. If we asked the factor analysis programme to solve for just two factors it would probably tell us that, no matter which way the matrix was solved, a lot of relationship between variables was left unaccounted for. For three variables it might well give us a good solution with little variation unexplained. But it is important to note that it would be up to us to name the factors and to debate what real processes might be indicated by them. The model for this kind of attempt to explain inter-test correlations and to look for deeper psychological constructs is shown in Figure 7.3.

Roughly speaking, this is what factor analysts do with the scores of large samples on personality and intelligence tests and subtests. The factors emerging are recognised and named intuitively. They are also validated against existing tests and known factor arrangements. The factors are said to be responsible for the participants' variations in performance across the tests.

It is important to recognise that factor analysis does not 'prove' that a real psychological

Table 7.1 Correlation matrix for various athletic events

	200 Metres	3000 Metres	5000 Metres	Shot	Discus	Long Jump
100 Metres	0.87	0.24	0.31	−0.65	−0.32	0.47
200 Metres		0.19	0.28	−0.61	−0.29	0.39
3 000 Metres			0.91	−0.16	0.03	0.13
5 000 Metres				−0.08	0.11	0.09
Shot					0.65	0.14
Discus						−0.02

Matrix of correlations

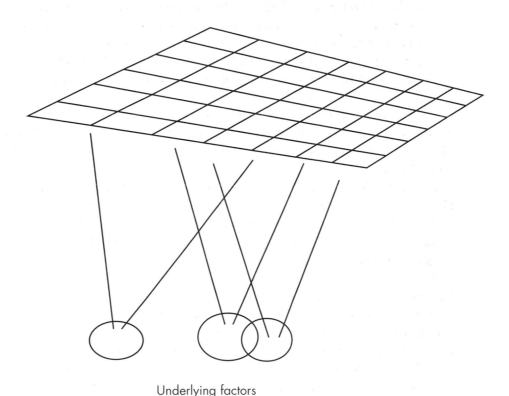

Underlying factors

Figure 7.3 Model of factor analysis – underlying factors 'explain' observed relationships between performance on tests

process exists corresponding to each factor. It simply provides supporting evidence which allows the researcher to claim that intelligence or personality *could* be organised in a particular way and that the factor analysis results don't refute this. As an example, Niles (1998), mentioned earlier, was able to identify four major achievement goal factors – family and social responsibility, material prosperity, personal fulfilment and personal development – where Sri Lankans scored more heavily on the first social and duty oriented factor, whereas Australians were more oriented towards the individualist goals of the last three factors. Factor analysis is a purely statistical process. As with all statistical results, researchers, with particular views and theories to defend, interpret and present statistics in a way which gives them the best support. There is a more extensive discussion of factor analysis and its limitations in Gross (1996). An extensive and severe criticism of the use of factor analysis to support models of intellectual structure is provided by Block and Dworkin (1974).

RELIABILITY, VALIDITY AND STANDARDISATION

It is common in psychological research to attempt the measurement of variables for which there is no universally agreed measure. Examples are 'attitude', 'motivation', 'intelligence'. Some variables appear as constructs invented within psychology, examples being:

'extroversion' and 'introversion' or 'ego-strength'. The tests which psychologists construct in order to measure such variables often serve as *operational definitions* of the concept under research. That is, our *measure* of, say, anxiety, is also our definition of it for the purposes of a study designed to show anxiety reduction. Here, our only evidence would be a reduction in anxiety test scores. That being so, we would expect to have confidence in such a measure by seeing that it produces consistent measures where we expect them (RELIABILITY) and that it somehow measures *real* anxiety, rather than mere nail-biting (VALIDITY). We would also expect such a measure to be applicable to a population of people and not just the few students participating in our study (STANDARDISATION). We will discuss each of these checks in turn.

RELIABILITY

We introduced the idea of reliability of measures back in Chapter 2. Here we look more closely and technically at how psychological researchers establish reliability and validity for their measuring instruments.

External reliability – stability across time

Any measure, but especially one we have just invented, must be queried as to the *stability* of its results on different occasions. A reliable measuring instrument is one which consistently produces the same reading for the same amount. Consider a practical example. If you have kitchen scales which stick, you won't get the same reading for the same amount of flour each time you weigh it. The measure given by your scales is unreliable. We can also say that your scales have poor reliability.

Internal reliability – internal consistency of the test

A difference between kitchen scales and instruments used for human characteristic measurement is that psychologists often use tests with many items whereas weight is measured by just one indicator – the dial reading. Psychological tests of, for instance, political attitude can be queried as to their INTERNAL RELIABILITY, meaning 'is the test consistent within itself?' High internal consistency generally implies that respondents answer related items in similar ways – a person high on 'conservatism' on the test *overall* tends to score in the conservative direction on each item. If internal consistency is not high, the argument goes, then the test must be measuring more than one variable – but see Kline (1993) for the dissenting argument of Cattell, who says that a test with high internal consistency will be an extremely narrow measure of anything. Despite Cattel's technical arguments, however, it is generally agreed by test constructors that internal consistency should be high for a test to be of any practical use.

The difference between INTERNAL CONSISTENCY and STABILITY might be pictured as follows. Imagine you were giving a statement to the police. Your statement might be found to be unreliable in two distinct ways:

1 Internal consistency – you may contradict yourself within the statement
2 Stability – you may alter important details when asked to remake the statement some time later.

Methods for checking internal reliability

Split half method

A psychological test which consists of several items or questions can be split so that items are divided randomly, or by odds and evens, into two sets comprising half the complete test each. If the test is reliable then people's scores on each half should be similar and the extent of similarity is assessed using correlation (Chapter 15). Positive correlations of 0.8 to 0.9, from the possible positive range of zero to one, would be expected. An alternative version of the split-half approach is to develop two *parallel forms* of the same test by selecting two sets of items from what is known as the same 'item universe' (which sounds rather metaphysical). Some writers (e.g. Rust and Golombok, 1989) see the use of parallel forms as a way of speeding up the *test-retest* procedure used to check for *external reliability* – see below.

Methods depending on item analysis

Cronbach's alpha

CRONBACH'S ALPHA is probably the most commonly used statistic for estimating a test's reliability. It depends largely on how people vary on individual items. If they tend to vary a lot on the individual items, relative to how much they vary overall on the test, then the test is assessed as unreliable and a low value for Alpha is achieved. High values are, like correlation coefficients (see Chapter 15), around .75 up to 1. If the items in the scale are *dichotomous* (answers are bi-polar, e.g. 'yes' or 'no' only), then a simpler version is used known as the KUDER-RICHARDSON measure.

Increasing the reliability of a test through item analysis

1. This method depends on removing those items in which there is low *discrimination*; that is, for each item, people scoring *high* on the test as a whole do not score very differently from people scoring *low* on the test overall. Even if we are not sure that our test is yet a good measure of say, attitude to economic union in Europe, we would not expect those scoring very high (pro-Europe) overall on the draft set of items to score the same as a group scoring very low overall on any particular item. The procedure here is to calculate individuals' scores overall on the draft test and identify the highest 10% and the lowest 10% of scores (this 10% is not fixed and could be 15% or 20% if desired). The scores of these two groups of people are then totalled on each item in the test. If these two extreme groups scored *very differently* then the item is discriminative. If not, it fails to distinguish between our two extreme groups; it is therefore contributing to low reliability and is best discarded.

2. Another way to check the discrimination of items is to *correlate* participants' scores on each item with scores overall. If people tend to score low or even average on an individual item, whilst scoring high overall (and vice versa), the item has low discriminatory power and the correlation will not be high. It is inconsistent with the general trend and it is best to discard items with the lowest 'item-whole correlations' as far as possible. For computer calculation with *SPSS* see the next method.

3. This method requires calculation of Cronbach's Alpha for all the items except the one under investigation. This means calculating Alpha once for every item in the test

and would be rather laborious by hand. However, using a computer program like *SPSS* the procedure can be performed in a flash. In *SPSS* choose: 'statistics'/'scale'/'reliability analysis', then enter the items which comprise your scale. The subtly hidden secret (with *SPSS* version 6 at least) is to click on the 'statistics' button and check 'scale if item deleted'. This is a very powerful move since *SPSS* will now calculate, amongst other things, the Alpha value that would occur as each individual item is singly deleted from the scale. All you need do now is find the item which, if deleted, would produce the *highest* value of Alpha and delete it from your set. Then run the analysis again. Repeat until alpha is satisfactorily high. The method in 2 above can also be performed this way, since *SPSS* will also give you your item-total correlations for each item.

All these methods may be accused of *circularity* since we are using overall *draft* totals to decide for each item, *contributing to that total*, how much it affects overall reliability. The totals themselves will change as each poor item is removed. That is, the test for reliability uses scores on an as yet probably unreliable test! At the end of all this item removal we may well have a highly reliable test which now contains nothing like the range of content that was originally envisaged. High *reliability* may well come at the cost of severe reduction in *validity*.

Checking external reliability

Test-retest reliability

To check that a psychological test produces similar results each time it is used, we would have to use it on the same people on each occasion, otherwise we have no comparison. 'Test-retest' means that a group of people are tested once, then again some time later. The two sets of scores are *correlated*, to see whether people tend to get the same sort of score on the second occasion. If they do, the test has high external reliability. Correlations achieved here would be expected to be at least around 0.75–0.8. Rather than testing at two different times it is also possible to test the same group of people on two *parallel forms* of the same test, though these are rare and expensive to create as well as raising doubts as to whether two 'versions' of the same test really can be entirely equivalent.

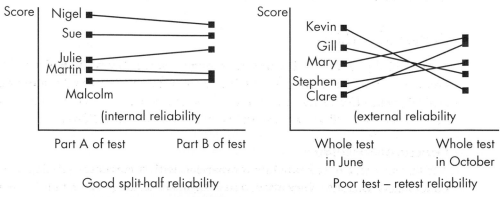

Figure 7.4   Split-half and test-retest reliability

VALIDITY

As we saw above, a test may well be rated as excellent on reliability but may not be measuring what was originally intended – it may lack validity. This criticism is often levelled at tests of intelligence which, though quite reliable, measure only a narrow range of intellectual ability, missing out, for instance, the whole range of creative thought which the public language definition would include. Raters can be highly reliable on projective tests but the validity of what they are claimed to assess is very much in dispute. There are various recognised means by which the validity of tests can be assessed.

Face validity

The crudest method for checking a test's validity is simply to inspect the contents to see whether it does indeed measure what it is supposed to. This is possible when devising a mathematics test, for example, for clearly the test should contain problems at the intended level and with sufficient breadth. It should not, inadvertently, involve use of higher level mathematics procedures in some of the problems. Even with more subtle attitude tests however, having conducted reliability trials, the remaining set of items can be inspected to see whether the original range intended is still sampled. Kline (1993) argues that a strength of face validity is its potential for motivating test-takers who can clearly see that the test is worthwhile, but its weakness is that the test also becomes quite easy to fake.

Content validity

A researcher may ask colleagues to evaluate the content of a test to ensure that it is representative of the area which it is intended to cover. They will carry out this task using their expertise in the topic area to judge whether the collection of items has failed to test certain skills or is unduly weighted towards some aspects of knowledge compared with others. In some ways this is a more sophisticated version of face validity, though for specific attainment or ability tests we can be fairly certain of real validity because our experts know what it takes to be good in a specific skill, whereas for personality measures (e.g. a depression test item such as 'Do you often just feel down?'), no expert can tell us that this *is* a valid item, even though it appears to have face validity.

Criterion validity

The validity of a test of neuroticism might reasonably be established by using it on a group of people who have suffered from a neurotic condition and comparing scores with a control group. Use of the neurotic group would be an example of what is called a KNOWN GROUPS CRITERION. There are several versions of criterion validity:

Concurrent validity

If the new test is validated by comparison with a currently existing criterion, we have CONCURRENT VALIDITY. Very often, a new IQ or personality test might be compared with an older but similar test known to have good validity already.

Predictive validity

A prediction may be made, on the basis of a new intelligence test for instance, that high scorers at age 12 will be more likely to obtain university degrees or enter the professions several years later. If the prediction is born out then the test has PREDICTIVE VALIDITY. *Both* these methods are in fact predictive since, in science, the term 'predict' does not mean 'forecast'. A social scientist may well predict a relationship between *past* events. Used in this sense, then, there is virtually no difference between these two concepts except for the point of time involved in the prediction. However, 'concurrent validity' tends to be reserved in the literature for those occasions where performance on a new test is compared with performance on a similar test or older version of the same test.

Construct validity

This takes us back to our discussion of variables which are not directly observable and the psychologist's tendency to propose hypothetical constructs (Chapter 2), and the discussion of construct validity in Chapter 4. Constructs require some form of validation, otherwise why should we continue to take them seriously? Typical of such constructs would be: 'achievement motivation', 'extroversion', 'dogmatism', 'dependency', 'ego-strength'.

In each case there is no *direct* evidence for such constructs having any kind of real existence. Construct validity entails demonstrating the power of such a construct to explain a network of research findings and to predict further relationships. Rokeach (1960) showed that his test for dogmatism predictably distinguished between different religious and political groups, as well as having relationships with approaches to entirely new problems and acceptance of new artistic ideas. Eysenck (1970) argued that extroversion was related to the activity of the cerebral cortex and produced several testable hypotheses from his theory.

Intelligence factors and personality variables are supported as valid by the use of *factor analysis*, as explained earlier, which is an elaborate part of construct validation. If a construct is sound then it should be possible to support the argument for its existence with a variety of measures of its effects on, or relationships with, other variables. If cognitive dissonance, for instance, is a genuine, common psychological process, then we should be able to predict effects from a variety of different sorts of experiment in the laboratory and field, with a variety of different groups of people performing a variety of qualitatively different tasks.

This might all sound a bit magical. Why can't we just observe nice concrete events and objects like physicists do? Well, this is a misconception of the way physicists work with theory. No physicist has ever seen an atom directly. What are observed are the effects of what is *assumed* to be an atom. Although the theory of atomic elements is beyond dispute, the construct of an atom is defined mathematically, is difficult for the lay person to understand and keeps changing in exact definition. Its validity as a construct is supported by a plethora of experimental support. Many psychological variables have a similar status. The use of factor analysis is an example of researchers' search for supportive evidence for their elusive psychological constructs, and replications in wider areas tend to increase that support. For instance, the McCrae study, mentioned in Chapter 1, provided support for the five factor personality construct by apparently replicating findings in several cultures.

STANDARDISATION

The process of standardising a test involves adjusting it, using reliability and validity tests to eliminate items, until it is useful as a measure of the population it is targeted at, and will enable us to compare individuals fairly and with confidence. To make such comparisons the test must be used on a large sample of the target population, from whom standard scores and means (see Chapter 10) are established. This will tell us what percentage of people tend to score between certain scores and what is the value which most of the population centre around.

Psychometric tests are used in research but also on an applied basis in decisions about people's life chances and opportunities. These may be related to education, psychotherapeutic treatment or job selection. Therefore, it is of the utmost importance that these tests do not discriminate, in a particular way, against some groups of people, a property which anyway would reduce their scientific value. Standardisation has, therefore, both ethical and scientific importance.

Standardisation to a normal distribution

Many tests are adjusted until testing of a large sample produces a score distribution which approximates very closely to the *normal distribution* (see Chapter 10). One reason for doing this is that the properties of the normal distribution allow us to perform some extremely powerful statistical estimates. The fact that IQ tests do produce normal distributions of scores for large groups has been used as 'evidence' by some researchers (e.g. Eysenck, 1970) that the test therefore measures a largely innate quality, since many biological characteristics are indeed normally distributed through the working of many random genetic processes together.

Critics (e.g. Kamin, 1977) have argued that the adjustment of the test to a normal distribution is an artificial procedure – which it most certainly is – and that far from showing that intelligence *is* normally distributed through the population, it merely shows that a measure can be constructed which *produces* a normal distribution. Furthermore, many biological characteristics are *not* normal in distribution. Certainly, some psychological phenomena need not be normally distributed. Attitudes to some issues on which people are somewhat polarised in position (for instance, on switching to the Euro as a currency or the morality of abortion) will be spread, as measured by questionnaire, in a *bi-modal* (two-hump) fashion (see Chapter 10).

An extremely important point here is that a test standardised on a particular population can obviously not be used with confidence on a different population. This criticism has been levelled at those who claimed a difference existed between white and black populations in the USA on intelligence. There *was* a difference in IQ score but, until 1973, the Stanford-Binet test had not included black persons in its sample for standardisation. Hence, the test was only applicable, with any confidence, to the white population. In addition, this is a particular issue for cross-cultural psychology researchers who attempt to transport 'Western'-based measures to 'non-Western' cultures and societies. Ben-Porath *et al* (1995) discuss three major reasons why a researcher might wish to use a personality measure, developed in one culture, for use with respondents of a different culture, while Paunonen and Ashton (1998) ask what criteria would establish that a personality measure is applicable to a culture other than that in which it was devised and standardised.

Glossary

		Attitude scales
'Social distance' scale on which, theoretically, the range of items the respondent would agree with is identifiable from their score	_____	Bogardus
Similar to the scale just described but items can concern any attitude object, not just categories of people	_____	Guttman
Scale on which respondent can react to a statement from a dimension of responses, often from 'strongly disagree' to 'strongly agree'	_____	Likert
Scale measuring meaning of an object for the respondent by having them place it between the extremes of several bi-polar adjectives	_____ _____	Semantic differential
Scale in which raters assess the relative 'strength' of each item and respondents agreeing with that item receive the average 'scale value' for it	_____	Thurstone
Item not obviously or directly connected to the attitude object yet which correlates well with overall scores and therefore has *discriminatory power*	_____ _____	diagnostic item
Extent to which item, or the test as a whole, separates people along the scoring dimension	_____ _____	discriminatory power
Statistical technique, using patterns of test or sub-test correlations, which provides support for theoretical constructs by locating 'clusters'	_____ _____	factor analysis
Test which attempts to quantify psychological variables: skills, abilities, character etc	_____ _____	psychometric test
Person who creates and works with psychometric tests	_____	psychometrist/ psychometrician
Procedures in the creation of tests to quantify psychological variables	_____	psychometry
Consistency of a measure		**Reliability**
A measure of test reliability using variation of respondents on non-dichotomous items	_____ _____	Cronbach's alpha
Stability of a test; its tendency to produce the same results when repeated on the same people	_____	external

Consistency of a test within itself	_____	internal
Checking each item in a scale by comparing its relationship with, e.g. the total scores on the scale	_____	item analysis
A special form of Cronbach's alpha performed on a test with dichotomous items (e.g. 'yes'/'no')	_____-_____	Kuder-Richardson
External validity of a test – tendency to produce similar scores on similar testing occasions	_____	stability
Comparing scores on two equal parts of a test	_____	split half
Tendency for people to agree with test items as a habitual response	_____	response acquiescence
On a Thurstone scale, the average rated value of an item; respondent is given this score if they agree with it	_____	scale value
Setting up of measurement norms for the population for whom a psychometric test is intended	_____	standardisation
Extent to which a test measures what was intended		**Validity**
Extent to which test results conform with those on some other valid measure, taken at the same time	_____	concurrent
Extent to which test results support a network of research hypotheses based on the assumed characteristics of a theoretical psychological variable	_____	construct
Extent to which test covers the whole of the relevant topic area, as assessed by experts	_____	content
Extent to which test scores can be used to make a specific prediction on some other variable	_____	criterion
Extent to which the validity of a test is self-evident	_____	face
Test of criterion validity involving groups between whom scores on the test should differentiate	_____	known groups
Extent to which test scores can predict scores on future behaviour or attitude	_____	predictive

Exercises

1   A scale measuring attitude towards nuclear energy is given a test-retest reliability check. It is found that correlation is 0.85. However, it is also found that scores for the sample as a whole have risen significantly.

　　a. Should the test be used as it is?
　　b. What might explain the rise in sample scores?

2   A student friend has devised a test of 'Attitude towards the British' which she wants to administer to a group of international students just about to leave the country.

　　a. How could the test be validated?
　　b. How could the test be checked for reliability?

3   Comment on any flaws in the following potential attitude scale or questionnaire items:

　　a. Don't you think that the government has moved too far towards Europe?
　　b. What do you think is the best way to punish children?
　　c. How many times were you late for work in the last two years?
　　d. People from other countries are the same as us and should be treated with respect.
　　e. It should not be possible to avoid taxation and not to be punished for it.
　　f. Women are taking a lot of management posts in traditionally male occupational areas (in a scale to measure attitude to women's rights).
　　g. Tomorrow's sex role models should be more androgynous.

4   A researcher administers a Rorschach test to a control and experimental group of psychiatric patients. She then rates each response according to a very well-standardised scale for detecting anxiety. How can she avoid the criticism that her ratings are biased and subjective?

Answers

1   a. It has been found reliable since the correlation is high, hence should be all right to use.
　　b. Recent nuclear accident?

2   a. Compare results with interview data?
　　b. Can't test the students again under similar circumstances so reliability will have to be checked only *internally*.

3   a. Question invites agreement i.e. 'leading'.
　　b. Assumes children *should* be punished.
　　c. Is this easy to answer?
　　d. Double barrelled – 'people *aren't* the same, but should be treated with respect' is a possible response.

e. Double negative.

f. Ambiguous responding. Extreme sexist *and* feminist might well agree. Question may not discriminate.

g. Technical term; will this be understood?

 4 Use blind assessment using a different naïve researcher to rate the test and analyse results.

8

Comparison studies – looking across, looking ahead and looking abroad

The chapter looks at studies which are comparisons, either of the same people as they mature over longish periods, or of several sub-group samples (e.g. ages, class, sex, occupation) studied at the same time. It also includes studies which compare samples from more than one culture.

- *Longitudinal studies* follow a group ('cohort', if a large group) through a longish period of time, possibly comparing with a control group if the first group is receiving some 'treatment'.
- *Cross-sectional studies* capture several groups, usually of different ages, at one specific point. The general goals are to map developmental stages or to compare differences across groups on a psychological variable.
- There is a very serious and strong issue of *ethnocentrism* involved in *cross-cultural study* and recognition of this has mostly replaced older studies which had a highly Euro/American-centred and/or colonial flavour, sometimes bearing clear signs of racism. More recent studies take on the political issues and attempt to avoid ethnocentrism. There is some development of *'indigenous psychologies'* – psychology originated by and geared to the socio-political needs of people within several cultures (e.g. India, Philippines).
- The *emic-etic* distinction is discussed in terms of attempts to merge findings from two or more cultures into *'derived etics'* (general dimensions of behaviour) rather than work, as in the past, with *'imposed etics'*.
- The student reader is warned of the need to clarify concepts of 'race', ethnicity and discrimination, through discussion and reading, before embarking on a possibly sensitive practical project which includes ethnicity issues. Attention to one's own stereotypes, received views and language is important.

WHAT ARE COMPARISON STUDIES?

In the design of many of the studies we have considered so far, the objective has not been to compare people but to search for some general feature of behaviour or mental life. The exception has been our glance at 'group difference' studies where comparison of groups *was* the aim. In a sense, a gender difference study is CROSS-SECTIONAL. That is, if the aim were to come up with some conclusion about a fairly common difference between males and females, we had better take a good, representative *cross-section* across genders. On the other hand, we may be interested in the way a group of girls develops in their social play, in which case we can conduct a LONGITUDINAL STUDY by studying the group over a relatively extended period of time, perhaps several years. Even then, we will not be able to say what is unique, if anything, to girls' development without a comparison group of boys. Stronger research in this area indeed consists of a mix of the cross-sectional and longitudinal designs – see Kohlberg below.

CROSS-SECTIONAL STUDIES

A cross-sectional study compares samples drawn from separate distinguishable subgroups within a population, very often, different age groups. Both cross-sectional and longitudinal studies can give information on changes in a psychological variable over time. A cross-sectional study can do this by taking groups of children or adults from different age bands and comparing them at the same moment in time. Comparisons may well highlight age-related changes and developmental trends. Cross-sectional data are often used to support developmental theories such as those of Piaget or Freud. Two specific examples of cross-sectional studies are:

1. Williams *et al.* (1975) interviewed five-, seven- and nine-year-old children. She asked the children to guess the sex of heavily stereotyped story characters. Five-year-olds showed some stereotyping but seven- and nine-year-olds showed far more.

2. Kohlberg (1981) developed his theory of changes in the style of children's moral reasoning from a study of ten-, 13- and 16-year-olds' attempts to solve several moral dilemmas. Kohlberg and his colleagues also extended this to a cross-cultural comparison in later work.

A cross-sectional study can also compare groups defined other than by age. A cross-section of classes might be studied, or of occupational or ethnic groups but always comparing the samples at the same chronological moment.

A recent example of an age cross-sectional design is that of Csapo (1997), who investigated the development of inductive reasoning in 2,424 Hungarian schoolchildren through the 3rd, 5th, 7th, 9th, and 11th grades (roughly 9 to 17 years old). Tests were of number and verbal analogies ('cat is to kitten as . . .' type questions), number and verbal series completion, and similar. The greatest development took place between 11 and 15 years old. Interestingly, results on the inductive reasoning tests predicted performance on applied science tests twice as well as did the children's general school grades.

LONGITUDINAL STUDIES

The big disadvantage of cross-sectional studies is that of comparability, a problem encountered in any study using independent samples. We can't ever be sure that our two or more groups are similar enough for fair comparison. The longitudinal approach surmounts this difficulty since it employs repeated measures on the same group of people over a substantial period, often a number of years. In this way genuine changes and the stability of some characteristics may be observed. If intervals between observations are not too long, major points of change can be identified.

In some longitudinal studies a control group is used for comparison where the 'treatment' group is receiving some form of intervention programme. This happened in several ways during the 1970s when there was a strong programme of *intervention research* in 'Educational Priority Areas'. Smith (1975) followed children through pre-school nursery projects, where children given special language training experiences tended to gain in mental age over a control group. Such gains were monitored into school in a further programme where carefully matched samples acted as controls or as experimental participants, the latter receiving language tuition each school day.

Kagan *et al.* (1980) showed that infants in day care during the working week were no different from home-reared children, on several developmental variables, so long as care facilities were good. This study used a naturally occurring independent variable.

Eron *et al.* (1972) demonstrated that longer viewing of television violence at age nine was related to greater aggressiveness at age 19, by following through a study using hundreds of boys. Colby *et al.* (1983) followed up on 7–13-year-old children originally tested by Kohlberg, The groups were tested at three yearly intervals right into their 30s and used to support Kohlberg's model of gradually more sophisticated cognitive processes in moral judgements.

Occasionally, huge longitudinal studies are carried out on a large section of the population, often children, in order to give some idea of national trends. In such cases the large sample of children is known as a COHORT. An example would be Davie *et al.* (1972) who followed almost 16 000 children from birth (one week in 1958) to the age of 11.

EVALUATION OF LONGITUDINAL AND CROSS-SECTIONAL STUDIES

Clearly there are strengths and weaknesses of purely cross-sectional or purely longitudinal designs. Perhaps you would like to make a list of these, as you see it, before checking against the contrasts made in Table 8.1.

Time lag studies

Cohort effects – see Table 8.1 – can be made the object of research by selecting a group of 16-year-olds, for instance, in the years 1995, 2000 and 2005. This is known as a TIME LAG study. Here we obviously can't make longitudinal comparisons (different people) or cross-sectional comparisons (same age, different time) but we can see whether attitudes have altered, or abilities improved, in the culture studied, so long as we have confidence that the samples are all representative enough of 16-year-olds in that year.

Cross-sectional, short-term longitudinal study

This is a compromise design for the study of age comparison. Three groups, say of 13-, 15- and 17-year-olds may be studied over two years on the effects of a programme designed to reduce drug addiction. Each group might be compared with a control group, as in a longitudinal study using one age group. But here we can determine the age at which the programme has maximum effect whilst investigating the range 13 to 19 in just two years. An example is Halliday and Leslie (1986) who studied mother–child communications with

Table 8.1 Advantages and disadvantages of cross-sectional and longitudinal studies

Cross sectional	Longitudinal
ADVANTAGES	
Few people lost during study (low 'attrition')	Can follow changes in same individuals, therefore stage type theories are better supported. We know the differences between seven- and nine-year-olds, for instance, are not the result of non-equivalent samples.
Relatively inexpensive and less time consuming. Support for theories achieved more quickly.	
Can't observe or detect maturational changes which confound results. For instance, difficult questions will be more easily answered by nine-year-olds than by seven-year-olds. We might falsely conclude that the younger children don't have the knowledge or concept which certain questions ask about. Older children might just be more capable of guessing what a researcher is after.	No *cohort effect* – see below and opposite.
	Useful where following through the effect of a 'treatment' (e.g. educational intervention) and comparing with a control group.
	Usually better knowledge of individuals and only way to observe changes over time within one individual.
Cross generational problem avoided (see below and opposite).	
DISADVANTAGES	
Non-equivalent groups may confound the differences observed e.g. a sample of seven-year-olds may have weaker verbal abilities than did a group of nine-year-olds when they were seven, thus making reading differences look greater than they might actually be.	ATTRITION – i.e. loss of participants through the course of the study. Decisions made at the start often cannot be reversed. Modification mid-way might ruin the potential for objective comparison.
COHORT EFFECT – if age difference between the groups studied is large then any difference found might be the result of different experiences by one group and not of, e.g. maturation or stage development.	Time consuming and expensive. A long wait for results. Replication very difficult.
Cannot observe changes in same individuals.	CROSS-GENERATIONAL PROBLEM – comparison of one developmental study with another may be confounded by different general conditions (e.g. war) for one of the generations

children ranging from 9–29 months at the start of the study, to 15–36 months at the end, so the age range of 9 to 36 months was covered in six months' recording. The design is similar to what Fife-Schaw (1995) terms a *'Longitudinal cohort sequential design'*. Breakwell and Fife-Schaw (1992), for instance, studied attitudes to AIDS/HIV and sexual activity preferences among 16- to 21-year-olds. They drew a sample of each age group (16, 17, 18, 19) in 1989, following these through to 1991 but adding an *extra* sample of 16-year-olds each year to 1991 (on the model in Figure 8.1(d) they would have added an extra 6 year old group in 2001 and another in 2002). Here they could compare longitudinal effects for the same samples but also they could check whether changes in one group of

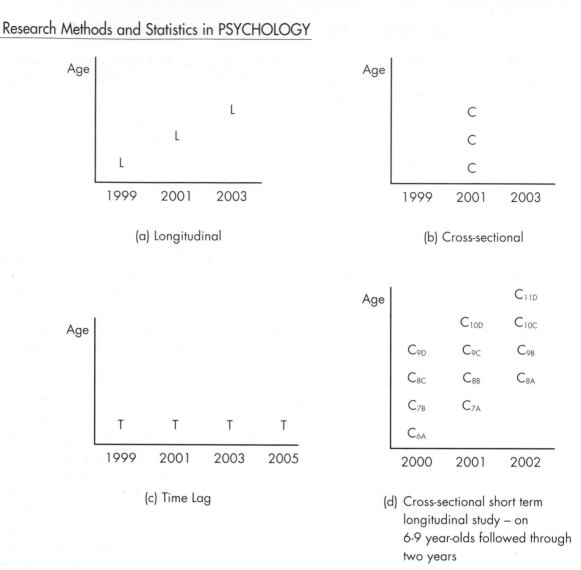

Figure 8.1   Different kinds of comparison study

16-year-olds would also occur for a later group of 16-year-olds. Yet again they could see whether an external event (say, a hard-hitting AIDS warning publicity campaign) had an effect on 19-year-olds similar to the effect it had on 17-year-olds.

CROSS-CULTURAL STUDIES

Problems with generalisation

Psychologists who discover reliable effects or who demonstrate strong developmental trends within one culture may well be interested in whether these may be found in cultures other than that of the original study. If the trends appear elsewhere, the case for *universal psychological factors* is strengthened. Aspects of grammar development, for instance, seem to occur in stages recognisable in all cultures so far studied, though debates arise about more specific details.

There are massive academic and political problems in attempting to generalise findings and theories from one culture to another. Fortunately, not many psychologists have been as overtly racist as C.G. Jung (1930) who claimed:

> The inferior (African) man exercises a tremendous pull upon civilised beings who are forced to live with him, because he fascinates the inferior layers of our psyche, which has lived through untold ages of similar conditions (1930)

and

> the famous American naïveté . . . invites comparison with the childlikeness of the Negro (1921)

It is staggering to me that anyone can, as people very often do, discuss, in one sweep, the 'African mind' or the 'Indian character', given the size and huge variety of the areas. Even talk of the 'Irish temperament' seems, to me, to be spoken from the wrong end of some very powerful binoculars. Researchers must be aware that their unquestioned preconceptions about 'races' and cultures *must* influence, if not dominate, any attempts to objectify the study of cultural differences. Jung's comments above demonstrate the frightening effect of having no objective method for comparison at all.

However, also dangerous is the *impression* of objectivity lent by the scientific aura of psychological instruments and methods when these are exported unquestioningly to cultures they were not developed with or standardised upon. In an astonishing example which is worth explaining at length in order to outline the serious dangers, beyond academic psychology, which some researchers can create, Lynn (1991a) estimated the black African IQ to be around 75 points. Africa is rather a large place so this would be a truly outstanding feat! In fact the data come from 11 studies ranging from 1929 to 1991 and conducted in just half a dozen countries, using a variety of non-equivalent samples (sometimes children, sometimes adults) and a number of non-equivalent assessments which were not IQ tests. Lynn 'converts' non-IQ scores into 'potential scores' using a dubious and unpublished formula (Kamin 1995). It is interesting that two thirds of the tests were carried out in South Africa under apartheid, since Herrnstein and Murray, in their controversial 1994 text *The Bell Curve*, use these very data as evidence that black people, other than in the US, *also* get low IQ scores. This in turn is intended to explain why the US phenomenon then can't be the result of general discrimination and racism! There is a noticeable silence over what apartheid meant in South Africa up to the 1990s. This kind of pseudo-science with a purpose really must be actively resisted and this has a bearing on the ethical issues concerning professional scientific publication described in Chapter 22 (and see the debate over the British Psychological Society's publication of virulently racist 'research' by Rushton in the May and July issues of *The Psychologist*, 1990).

The aims of cross-cultural studies

Cross-cultural studies usually compare samples from two or more cultures on some psychological variable(s). Differences found are attributed either to broad cultural socialising processes or to genetic factors. By far the greater number of recent studies emphasise the social environment as cause. Studies conducted earlier in the twentieth century often had a distinctive colonial or Euro-centred flavour. The 'natives' were interesting to study, whole societies were described as 'primitive' and the term 'negro' was commonplace, though this latter term occurred uncritically as late as the 1980s in some psychology texts.

'Race' – not a useful scientific concept

An emphasis on biological 'race' differences has diminished (except in the work of a few researchers such as Lynn) as biologists have impressed upon us, for much of this century, the scientific worthlessness of the concept of 'race'. The idea of large-scale, isolated breeding pools, with clear, genetically based behavioural or psychological differences is contrary to contemporary biological knowledge. There is vastly more genetic variation *within* 'races' than there is *between* them. The clear visual distinction between people of Afro-Caribbean origin and North Europeans leads some people to believe, superstitiously it turns out, that there must be some distinct genetic separation between them. One may as well distinguish between people with blonde and brown hair. There is, on average, about the same amount of genetic variation between any two members of neighbouring populations (e.g. England and Scotland) as there is between any two members of different so-called 'races' (Montagu, 1975; Jones, 1981; Gould, 1997; Richards, 1997). In any case, the lay person often confuses 'race' with appearance, ethnicity, culture, country of origin or even religion. People from India, Pakistan and England are all members of the same traditionally categorised 'race'. The term 'Aryan', much used by the Nazis and ironically misused even today, in fact refers to a nomadic group originally occupying Persia and Northern India.

Ethnocentrism in early cross-cultural studies

In early cross-cultural studies, psychologists often tested members of a tribal community on, say, visual illusions or counting tasks. The emphasis was often on what tribes 'lacked', and the studies tended to be ETHNOCENTRIC. An example of ethnocentrism is to describe eating with fingers as 'dirty' or rubbing noses in greeting as 'funny'. North Europeans, who generally greet with a firm handshake and full eye contact, tend to describe many Asian cultures' greetings, which involve a bowed head and no eye contact, as 'deferential' or as exhibiting a 'shy' cultural personality. This is an ethnocentric description filtered through a cultural perspective but it carries the unspoken implication that the interpretations are somehow true, and that North European greetings are the neutral basis from which to assess others. Such value judgements are culturally bound and have no universal validity.

Ethnocentrism very easily leads to false interpretations of behaviour. In Mozambique, I was told of an educational psychologist who got children to do the 'draw a man' test, a projective test (see Chapter 7) where the drawn man is interpreted psychodynamically. The children's' very tiny drawings were interpreted as demonstrating the poor self-image of Mozambican children resulting from centuries of Portuguese colonialism. It was pointed out to her that Mozambican school children were under strict instructions not to waste paper in times of great shortage and weak economy!

Working against ethnocentrism

Campbell (1970) argued that some protection against ethnocentrism could be gained by carrying out a design in which a researcher from culture A studies cultures A and B (a common cross-cultural design) whilst a second researcher from culture B also studies cultures A and B. A technique used by researchers to attempt to make questionnaires appropriate for a second culture is known as BACK TRANSLATION. Here a scale in language A is translated into language B then back again into language A. If the meaning is still as intended then the scale is said to have 'translation equivalence'. This procedure was followed in research by Niles (1998) on Sri Lankans and Australians.

Some lessons in non-ethnocentric work have been taken from social anthropologists, who tend to conduct intense participant observation studies as a member of a village community for many months if not years. These researchers have studied the community in its own right, not as a comparison with the West. They would attempt to record the interrelationship of local customs, norms, taboos and social interactions such as marriage and trade. Ruth Benedict (1934) used the term CULTURAL RELATIVITY to underline her view that an individual's behaviour and thinking must be viewed through, and can only be understood using, that person's own cultural environment.

Confounding in cross-cultural explanations

Where psychologists attempt to compare two cultures we return to the argument on group difference studies in Chapter 3. The independent and dependent variables of controlled studies are difficult or impossible to compare across wide cultural gaps. Lonner and Berry (1986) argue that even the quasi-experiment is not available to the cross-cultural researcher. Serious confounding is inevitable and sampling is crucial. A classic example of confounded explanation occurred with research on the 'carpentered world hypothesis' (see Segal, 1966). This explained cross-cultural differences in the effects of visual illusions by arguing that people in industrialised societies experience a multi-cornered environment and so are more susceptible to perspective cues in geometric designs. However, Gregor and McPherson (1965) found *no* differences between rural, outdoor living aborigines and urban aborigines in illusion susceptibility whereas they *did* find a difference between schooled and unschooled aboriginal people. They suggested the carpentered world effects could mostly be explained, *not* by the carpentered/non-carpentered variable, but by the confounding variable of general exposure to Western-style education and culture, which includes an emphasis on the interpretation of printed, two-dimensional graphic materials as representing three-dimensional scenes.

Research examples

Cross-cultural studies in psychology have increased markedly since the late 1960s. There is in fact a recognisable cross-cultural psychology research movement, led particularly by Triandis, Berry, Poortinga, Dasen, Segall, Brislin, Herskovits and Campbell, (whom we also encountered leading the debate on quasi-experimentation and internal/external validity). Texts by these authors are listed below. Research examples, along with discussion of many methods issues, can be found in the *Journal of Cross-Cultural Psychology*. Ironically, the movement is led by mainly US psychologists but the studies now conducted have lost a lot of their early ethnocentrism. Nevertheless, Nisbet (1971) has argued that the cross-cultural method is just another way, seemingly scientific and respectable, of placing European cultures at the top of a graded hierarchy.

Miller *et al.* (1990) have suggested that Kohlberg's theory of stages, originally tested in Taiwan, Turkey, Mexico, India and Kenya, was culture bound. Initially they found that (Asian) Indians tended to give moral priority to *social duties* whereas Americans were more individualistic, concentrating on a person's *rights*. In 1990, they found that Indians and Americans were similar in serious, say life-threatening, examples but Indians had a broader view of moral responsibilities and obligations, emphasising personal need more than the American sample. The distinction between *individualistic* (person-centred) and *collectivist* (social rule and relationship oriented) societies and thinking tends to pervade cross-cultural research findings. The lesson is that, if the researcher blissfully ignores the distinction, they will run into great difficulties when trying to 'transport' 'Western' based tests or to replicate Western findings in other societies. For instance, reading a US 'glossy' social psychology textbook section, one might conclude that certain attribution effects, such as the 'fundamental attribution error' or the 'self-serving bias', were *universal* aspects of human behaviour. This is far from the case. In fact, in several so-called 'non-Western' societies, people tend to perform in the opposite direction. In Miller *et al*'s study, mentioned above, the Indian participants made less than half the proportion of individualistic attributions (i.e. internal) that US participants made. Shikanai (1978) found that Japanese college students who succeeded on a task tended to make *external* attributions ('it was an easy task') whereas they blamed lack of ability and effort (an *internal* attribution) to explain failures. US students tend to do the opposite – using a 'self-serving bias'. Hess *et al.* (1986) found the reverse of the self-serving bias when Japanese mothers often explained their own children's poor performance as due to lack of effort (internal attribution – it was the children's 'fault'). US mothers were more likely to include external factors, such as quality of school training, in their explanations.

Stipek (1998), in a comparison of US and Chinese (People's Republic) college students, found Chinese students preferring to express pride in *others'* achievements (e.g. their child, a good friend or colleague) rather than the US preference for expressing pride in one's own achievements. Here is a good example of the dangers for the inexperienced researcher. It would be easy for the naïve British researcher to assume that people everywhere 'naturally' express pride in their achievements and see no harm in that. For many cultures, including Japan and not just China, this just is not the done thing.

The emic-etic distinction and psychological constructs

Pike's (1967) notion of emic and etic constructs was elaborated by Berry (1989) and is now generally associated with his work. An EMIC psychological construct is one which is peculiar to one culture, whereas an ETIC construct is thought to apply to all human behaviour or thought.

Berry argues that, because researchers so often cannot shake off the influence of their own culture in their usage and understanding of relevant psychological constructs (perhaps it is impossible ever to transcend one's original culture in this respect), they generally work with IMPOSED ETICS – they assume a construct is universal and impose it

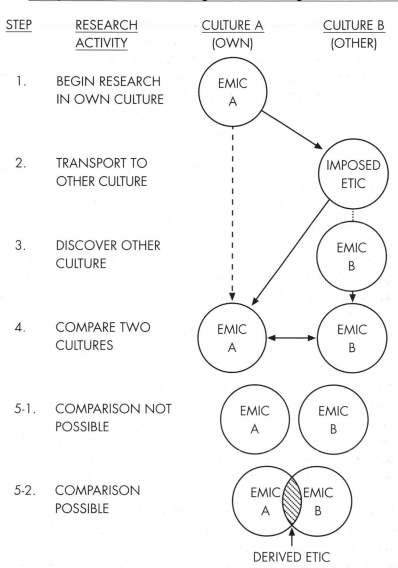

STEP | RESEARCH ACTIVITY | CULTURE A (OWN) | CULTURE B (OTHER)

1. BEGIN RESEARCH IN OWN CULTURE

2. TRANSPORT TO OTHER CULTURE

3. DISCOVER OTHER CULTURE

4. COMPARE TWO CULTURES

5-1. COMPARISON NOT POSSIBLE

5-2. COMPARISON POSSIBLE

DERIVED ETIC

Figure 8.2 Operationalisation of emics and etics

on new cultures. For instance, they might assume the self-serving bias occurs everywhere. A major goal for cross-cultural psychological researchers, according to Berry, is to change these imposed etics progressively, by becoming submerged *within* a new culture and working from an emic viewpoint, eventually modifying imposed etics to produce DERIVED ETICS – universal psychological dimensions which are valid cross-culturally, or at least can be used to compare several cultures.

For instance, the self-serving bias construct turns into a more *general dimension* where we discover to what degree people attribute successes to themselves or to others. The ('Western') construct of self-monitoring becomes something like 'person monitoring' when we discover that people in collectivist cultures spend more time monitoring *other* people's behaviour than their own. The Western *emic* of 'mental quickness' assessed by the use of strictly timed testing, may not be universally valid. For the Baganda people of

Uganda, intelligence is associated with slow, careful, deliberate thought – i.e. only fools rush in! (Gross, 1995).

Indigenous psychologies

As a contrast to this mode of thought, some psychologists in cultures outside of the 'Western' arena, and to some extent feeling dominated by it, feel that etics will always be imposed upon them to some extent by the 'Western' psychological mainstream. Members of cultures outside of the major industrialised nations have seen the imposition or model of 'Western' psychology as inappropriate to their needs and understanding of themselves. Sinha (1986) characterised the early stages of the development of Indian psychology as very much 'tied to the apron strings of . . . Western principles' and an almost reverent repetition of 'Western' studies. The 'final' stage, 'indigenisation', meant the transformation of methods to suit Indian economic and political realities and needs. Enriquez (1990) is even more radical and promotes the development of an entirely separate Filipino psychology from its own fundamental roots. This movement has three primary objections:

> . . . it is against a psychology that perpetuates the colonial status of the Filipino mind; it is against the imposition on a Third World country of psychologies developed in, and appropriate to, industrialised countries; and it is against a psychology used for the exploitation of the masses. (Berry et al. 1992, p. 383)

As with feminist psychology, these movements, have, to some extent, identified strict quantitative methods and positivism with a 'Western' approach and, without complete rejection, have generally favoured a more *qualitative* approach, more closely integrated with general socio-economic development and policy. Quantitative methods have moved towards development of 'home-grown', rather than imported Western assessment methods and scales. According to Ho (1998):

> . . . the wholesale importation of Western psychology into Asia represents a form of cultural imperialism that perpetuates the colonization of the mind. To an alarming degree, Asians are now confronted by stereotypes about themselves generated not only by Western researchers but also by Asian researchers relying on imported, mainly American, psychology. (p. 89)

Berry *et al.*'s (1992) view is:

> The ethnocentrism of Western psychology makes it necessary to take other viewpoints on human behaviour into account. One of the goals of cross-cultural psychology is the eventual development of a *universal* psychology that incorporates all indigenous (including Western) psychologies. We will never know whether all diverse data and cultural points of view have been incorporated into the eventual universal psychology unless we cast our net as widely as possible in order to gather all the relevant information. (p. 384)

For a recent and interesting summary of the debate, and some depth on the issue within Filipino and 'Confucian heritage' cultures (e.g. China, Japan), see Ho (1998). For a thorough review of 'indigenization' of psychology in many cultures, see Sinha (1997).

Ethnicity and culture within one society – doing a 'race' project

Research projects on differing cultures within one society are referred to as 'intra-cultural' studies. Students very often choose to do such a project on 'prejudice' or 'race', mostly for the best of possible reasons – they are concerned about racism and injustice or, more positively, fascinated by a different social perspective from their own. Such studies, however, are fraught with the dangers of ethnocentrism, stereotyping and misunderstanding. I feel it is not possible to be reared in the UK (white or black) without subtly absorbing the 'race' images and themes which existed in our past. Up to the 1960s, most people in this country would not have thought twice about Jung's statements.

I would recommend that students *do* concern themselves with race issues but, in choosing to do what might seem a simple project, there would need to be a lot of preparation and groundwork on cultural perspectives and the language of racism. For instance, I am very concerned when a student says, quite innocently, that she wishes to get the attitudes of 'coloured' people in her study. Will she use this term with the participants and possibly alienate the majority, giving psychology a worse name than it sometimes has anyway? The researcher needs to investigate his or her *own* sense of ethnicity first – white people often don't think of themselves as 'ethnic' in any way, the term having become a euphemism for the earlier euphemism of 'coloured', meaning 'not naturally uncoloured like us'! ('ethnic' often stands in for 'exotic' – but fish and chips and ballroom dancing are 'ethnic'!). The issue of language is crucial, since it is the conveyor of subtle, historically interwoven and politically tangled concepts. The student/ researcher should seek advice on all the terms to be used in, say, a questionnaire or vignette. Deeper still, students/researchers should study thoroughly their own politics on the relationship between their own ethnic group and another.

It is important that the researcher conveys an attitude of valuing difference whilst validating equal rights. British culture is not homogenous and never was (see bottom of Box 8.1). If the researcher's approach is open and receptive, ready to listen and appreciate the richness of cultural diversity, then participants will sense a positive approach and will forgive innocent 'gaffs', such as assuming that English is a 'second language' for most Indians. If they are, however, 'colour blind', assuming that 'we are all the same really' (i.e. white and English) then this too will be sensed and the research relationship will be strained.

Reading on 'race'

In 1994, the academic world of the USA was shocked and bitterly divided by the publication of Herrnstein and Murray's *The Bell Curve*. The book was apparently intended to focus on inequality in the USA and social scientists' 'refusal' to consider low intelligence (for which 'IQ' is quickly substituted) as the major underlying cause of poverty, unemployment, crime, child neglect and many other ills of modern industrial societies. Though the authors expressed innocent amazement at the massive academic adverse reaction, they almost certainly intended to re-generate the 1970s battle over 'race' and intelligence, where lower black average IQ scores were linked with the argument that IQ is largely innate, hence the gap is presented as somehow biological in origin. We return to the 'scientific' explanation of 'race' differences.

Box 8.1 Advantages and disadvantages of cross-cultural studies

Advantages	**Disadvantages**
Can demonstrate universal development trends and effects	Can support disguised ethnocentric assumptions
Can show that a psychological effect is limited to the culture it was first demonstrated in, or that the effect occurs in different directions in different cultures	Extremely costly and time consuming
	Variables may not be culturally comparable
Gives insight into quite different cultural systems, beliefs and practices	Difficulties of communication. Subtle differences between 'equivalent' terms may make large difference
Can provide reassessment of 'home' society's norms in culturally relative terms	Can ignore the fact that the 'home' culture is not homogeneous. British society comprises many identifiable cultures which include Afro-Caribbean, Indian (several separable cultures), Pakistani, Scots (highland and lowland), Irish, Welsh (north and south), Geordie, Liverpudlian, and Cornish, to name a few
Rich data	

Apart from pessimistically offering no solution to this supposed explanation, the authors mostly ignored the huge weight of criticism of the original evidence and introduced more highly suspect 'support' such as that from Lynn already cited. The good news from this sorry saga is that the reader may now get hold of another contemporary and fiery set of essays on the race issue in psychology and may appreciate the huge methodological flaws inherent in the easy 'explanation' of whole group differences (Fraser, 1995; Jacoby and Glauberman, 1995; Fischer *et al.*, 1996). Also highly entertaining, if the underlying motives of race difference proponents were not so sinister and frightening, is Gould's (1996) account of nineteenth century methods of 'proving' that members of non-White 'races' had smaller brains; the rest of his work on the weaknesses of race difference methodology through this century is absorbing and he includes in the 1996 edition a critique of *The Bell Curve*. A more recent and very welcome addition to the literature is Richards' (1997) work which is the most thorough review yet of racist methodology in psychological research and practice, filling in periods of the century which are not so popularly known about and also including a strong critique of the work and motives of Rushton, Lynn and *The Bell Curve*.

Readings on 'race', culture and psychology
*Recommended for cross-cultural psychological research
**Recommended on the psychology and race methodology debate

Berry, J.W., Poortinga, Y.H., Segall, M.H. and Dasen, P.R. (1992) *Cross-Cultural Psychology: Research and applications*. Cambridge: CUP.*

Brislin, R. (1993) *Understanding Culture's Influence on Behavior*. Orlando, Fla.: Harcourt Brace Johanovich.*

Fischer, C.S., Hout, M., Jankowski, M.S., Lucas, S.R., Swidler, A. and Voss, K. (1996) *Cracking the Bell Curve Myth*. Princeton, N.J.: Princeton University Press.**

Fraser, S. (Ed) (1995) *The Bell Curve Wars: Race, Intelligence, and the Future of America.* New York: Basic Books.**

Goldberger, N.R. and Veroff, J.B. (Eds) (1995) *The Culture and Psychology Reader.* New York: New York University Press.

Gould, S.J. (1997) *The Mismeasure of Man.* London: Penguin.**

Howitt, D. and Owusu-Bempah, J. (1994) *The Racism of Psychology.* Hemel Hempstead: Harvester Wheatsheaf.**

Jacoby, R. and Glauberman. N. (Eds) (1995) *The Bell Curve Debate.* New York: Times Books, **including especially** Kamin, L.J. (1995) Lies, damned lies and statistics.**

Littlewood, R. and Lipsedge, M. (1997) *Aliens and Alienists: Ethnic Minorities and Psychiatry* (3rd edition). London: Routledge.**

Richards, G. (1997) *"Race", Racism and Psychology.* London: Routledge.**

Segall, M.H., Dasen, P.R., Berry, J.W. and Poortinga, Y.H. (1990) *Human Behavior in Global Perspective: An introduction to cross-cultural psychology.* New York: Pergamon.*

Smith, P.B. and Bond, M.H. (1993) *Social Psychology Across Cultures: Analysis and Perspectives.* London: Harvester Wheatsheaf.*

Triandis, H.C. (1994) *Culture and Social Behavior.* New York: McGraw-Hill.*

Tucker, W.H. (1994) *The Science and Politics of Racial Research.* Chicago: University of Illinois Press.**

Glossary

Loss of participants from a research study	_____	attrition
Large sample of people, often children, identified for longitudinal or cross-sectional study	_____	cohort
Confounding in cross-sectional study when two different age groups have had quite different experiences	_____	cohort effect
Confounding occurring when one longitudinally studied group is compared with another who have generally had quite different social experiences	_____	cross-generational problem
View that a person's behaviour and characteristics can only be understood through that person's own cultural environment	_____	cultural relativity
General/universal psychological construct modified from its origin in one culture after researcher's immersion in one or more new cultures	_____	derived etic
Psychological construct applicable within one or only a few cultures	_____	emic
Bias of viewing and valuing another's culture from one's own cultural perspective	_____	ethnocentrism

Univeral psychological construct, applicable to all cultures	_____	etic
Psychological construct from researcher's own culture, applied to a new culture without modification	_____ _____	imposed etic
Psychological methodology developed by and within one culture, not imported from another	_____ _____	indigenous psychology

		Types of study
Comparative study of two or more different societies, or social/ethnic sub-groups	_____ _____	cross-cultural study
Comparative study of several sub-groups captured for measurement at a single time point	_____ _____	cross-sectional study
Comparative study of cross-sectional groups, followed through over a relatively short period (say two or three years)	_____ _____ _____ _____	cross-sectional, short term, longitudinal study
Comparative study of one individual or group over a relatively long period (possibly including a control group)	_____ _____	longitudinal study
Comparative study in which an equivalent sample (say, same age group) is selected each time the study is run – it is run at relatively long intervals	_____ _____ _____	time lag study

Exercises

Without looking back at the text (at first at least!) decide, for the following research projects, whether the design is *longitudinal*, *cross-sectional*, *cross-cultural* or a mixture of any of these (such as the cross-sectional short term longitudinal design described in the chapter):

1 Samples of children aged four, six and eight are given various Piaget-type problems to solve.

2 A sample of children are tested on Piaget-type problems when they are four-, six- and eight-years-old.

3 UK and Iranian five year-old children are compared on several Piaget-type tasks.

4 UK and Iraqi children are compared at four-, six- and eight-years-old on their development of story telling ability.

5 People of 54, 56 and 58 years old are studied for a period of six years as they approach retirement in order to assess changing attitudes towards the world of work.

6 In the last study, an extra cohort of 54, 56 and 58 year-olds is picked up at one, three and five years into the study. What name was given to this specific design in the text and what are its special advantages over simple cross-sectional and longitudinal designs?

7 A researcher decides to investigate how people from a newly discovered rain forest tribe will compete against each other in an individual problem-solving contest. Is the researcher making *emic* or *etic* assumptions about the research topic? In what way? Can you suggest a better way to go about investigating this topic with this community?

Answers

1 Cross-sectional design

2 Longitudinal design

3 Cross-cultural design

4 Cross-cultural and longitudinal

5 Cross-sectional short term longitudinal

6 Longitudinal cohort sequential design (Breakwell and Fife-Schaw); can compare same aged cohorts in different years; can compare the change from, say, 54 to 56 different cohorts; can detect whether certain common events affect different age groups in the same or different ways.

7 Researcher is making an imposed etic assumption about competition. Not all societies see a value in individual competition. Better, perhaps, to make an in-depth, ethnographic or participant observation study of the tribespeople's every day and collective behaviour in order to determine where, if at all, and in what ways, competition occurs between individuals or groups.

9

New paradigms and qualitative approaches – problems with measurement

This chapter presents a summary of recent strengthening in the use of methods often known as 'qualitative' and introduces recent efforts to introduce into psychology a general 'new paradigm' for research. Here, methods are not just an alternative set of procedures but incorporate a fundamental philosophical critique of the traditional 'positivist', hypothetico-deductive paradigm within psychological research. *Positivism* is the philosophy which sees only (numerically) measurable events as the possible objects of scientific study. *Constructivism* sees knowledge as relative and socially constructed by individuals in a social context.

- Traditional quantitative methods have often produced relatively artificial and sterile results, inapplicable to the realities of everyday human life.
- The alternative approaches presented here emphasise closeness to participants and the richness of information produced when unstructured data gathering methods are applied. *Inductive analysis* – permitting new themes and theories to *emerge* from gathered data – is stressed in many qualitative methods.
- *Grounded theory* is an import from sociology and is discussed in Chapter 21, as is *thematic analysis*.
- Participative research involves participants in the research process and validates findings against their recognition.
- *Ethnography* also hails from sociology and is the basis for participant observation.
- *Endogenous* approaches aim to help participants evolve their own research in their own community.
- *Action research* involves intervention aimed at change.
- In *collaborative research*, participants largely conduct their own research under the guidance of the researcher who acts more as consultant.
- *Feminist psychological research* emphasises qualitative and participative research methods relatively neglected by the male establishment which has dominated psychological research development.
- *Discourse analysis* focuses on the ways people construct individual versions of events, and perform 'speech acts', through their conversation.
- *Reflexivity* demands that readers of research reports are made aware of the relative nature of scientific views of the world through the author's discussion of their work with the reader by some appropriate 'reflexive' mechanism.

PSYCHOLOGY AND THE POSITIVIST PARADIGM

In Chapter 2 we encountered a controversy. The start of that Chapter took the conventional view that methods in psychology have a lot to do with finding appropriate measures of psychological variables so that we can test our hypotheses in a quantitative manner. The approach is modelled on the successful 'natural' sciences. The common sense notion that there are things in the world and that we can know about them *only* through measurement, applied in the world of scientific investigation, is roughly the position of POSITIVISM. Some thinkers, however, take a CONSTRUCTIVIST view of knowledge. They point out that everybody has a slightly different perceptual construction of, say, a concrete pillar. To most of us it *is* a concrete pillar, although our personal pictures of it will all be slightly different. To some (rare people) it might be a phallic monster, to others a ship's funnel. However, even to the relatively sober, it differs – to me it's an object to be avoided by my car's bumper; to another it's a blight, an eyesore and only made necessary by the curse of the car. To constructivists, this position on perception of the world leads to a conclusion that *all* knowledge is *relative* and a unique construction for each person – a position close to the *idealism* of Berkeley in the 18th century. From this perspective, *all* scientific activity would need re-assessment. However, others take the view that the problem of relative knowledge is only acute in the *social* sciences. In psychology, for instance, the objection, for some, is *not* to positivistic 'hard' science as such, but particularly to the *transfer* of those methods and ideas of knowledge and theory construction to the world of people and their ideas. To be specific: one can measure a concrete pillar publicly to most people's satisfaction; however, the idea of similarly measuring 'extroversion', or of agreeing about observations of 'dependency', is a completely different ball game.

For now we shall stick mainly with this critique of the application of a 'hard' scientific, positivistic, quantitative model to the discipline of psychological research. The overwhelming *paradigm* in psychological research this century, particularly influenced by the early behaviourists from the 1920s onwards (but not Skinner), has been the use of the *hypothetico-deductive method* described in Chapter 1. A PARADIGM is the generally accepted method for conducting research and theory development. In practice, if you don't follow it you're less likely to get research grants or have your work taken seriously.

The debate within psychology is not new. It started as far back as 1894 when Dilthey criticised the experimental psychology of the time for copying the natural science model and for consequent reductionism in explaining mental process. It sometimes dies down but has been particularly potent during the last 20 years. Psychology's extreme concern to be thoroughly scientific in the above sense is often contrasted with traditional science's *lack* of concern over similar matters. It seems, sometimes, as though psychology has overreacted in its pressing desire to be recognised as a 'true' science, and has worried about things even 'hard' scientists are not so rigid about. Woolgar (1996) discusses this issue and argues that psychology has been guilty of pushing an *idealised account* of what scientists actually *do* in their daily research work. I have tried to reflect this at several points in this book and there is a clear example of this in the heated debate over the use of one- or two-tailed tests – see p. 292. Scientists are pragmatic in their progress of knowledge, rather than following the rigid code which is often presented as the ideal to work towards in psychology methods courses.

It somewhat over-polarises the debate to talk of 'qualitative' researchers opposed to quantitative researchers. Many qualitative researchers have no particular objection to quantification in its appropriate place, and many of the arguments raised against the conventional scientific model in psychological research have been used by traditional quantitative researchers within their own paradigm. However, for the sake of ease of communication I will generally use the term 'qualitative researcher' to refer to a strong proponent of qualitative methods and one who generally rejects the conventional scientific paradigm as restrictive on progress within psychology. A 'quantitative' researcher will be one who generally accepts the status quo and sees no great advantage in qualitative approaches, probably remaining rather sceptical about their worth and concerned about numerical support for reliability and validity of findings.

THE PROBLEM WITH QUANTIFICATION IN PSYCHOLOGICAL RESEARCH

A major objection to use of the quantitative paradigm in psychology is this. If we carry out research using the highly controlled procedures and exact quantification of operationalised variables recommended by 'traditional' science, will we not be gaining only very narrow, perhaps sometimes useless knowledge of human behaviour and experience? Allport (1963), often quoted, as in Chapter 1, as a strong promoter of psychology as a conventional science, says:

> We should adapt our methods so far as we can to the object, and not define the object in terms of our faulty methods. (cited in Smith et al., 1995a, p. 2)

Consider an experiment where the independent variable is 20 common and uncommon words in a mixed list, presented one per second via computer screen. The final results table will be two sets of numbers, a pair for each participant, representing the number of words they correctly recalled during 60 seconds after exposure of the last item.

This provides us with the not unsurprising information that infrequently met words are harder to recall. The quantitative researcher argues that, nevertheless (and in the spirit of the points made in Chapter 1 about 'armchair certainties'), the research is required to back up what is otherwise only an unsupported, casual observation. A critic might argue as follows: only in psychology experiments and party games do people have to learn a list of 20 unrelated words. How can this relate to the normal use of human memory which operates in a social, meaningful context? The data difference may be significant but it tells us little of relevance. The study gives us no information at all about the participants' experiences. They all, no doubt, used personally devised methods and found their own unique meanings in the combination of words presented. This information is powerful and 'belongs' to the participants, yet is unused and is not asked for, which could even constitute something of an insult to 'subjects' who participated in what, for them, was to be 'an interesting experiment'.

It is also argued that memory experiments using unconnected words out of context, or even sets of nonsense syllables, which restrict the use of natural learning techniques, give rise to unnecessarily simplistic models of the person and of the nature and operation of cognitive processes.

EXAMPLES OF NARROWNESS AND ARTIFICIALLY IN THE ESTABLISHMENT PARADIGM

Measures in psychology can be very narrow indeed. For instance, many studies measure attitude using a scale of the kind we looked at in Chapter 7. On this, each participant ends up with a single numerical value. On political attitude, for instance, a person's position may be represented as 34, where 40 is the highest value a 'conservative' person could score, the other end of the scale being 'radical' (left-wing). Using this system, we are assuming political attitudes to lie along a unitary dimension, whereas, in fact, if we asked people in depth about their ideas and principles, we would uncover various unique combinations of left- and right-wing views which couldn't, meaningfully, be averaged down to a midpoint on the scale.

Harré (1981) argues that orthodox (positivist) research methods have led to a great deal of irrelevance in, for instance, social psychological research. He analyses an experiment in which women had to sit and look at themselves on a TV monitor for one minute. The IV was then applied in that they heard a lecture on venereal disease either straight away or four minutes later. They were then asked whether they would contribute to a venereal disease remedial programme under certain circumstances. The aim was to test the idea that heightened 'self-focus' would facilitate 'helping behaviour'. Harré argues that the 'self-focus' device (watching themselves) completely trivialised the complex concept of self originally proposed by G.H. Mead.

Henwood and Pidgeon (1995) argue that such narrowness is very much a result of the conventional paradigm, through its very nature, tending to *narrow down* the research focus and limit the potential for new perspectives, by always testing hypotheses from established prior theory, rather than *generating* hypotheses through new work. This is not strictly true, otherwise psychology could never have developed from anywhere to anywhere. However, it certainly is true that, having established the definitive topic areas for psychological research, it is very difficult to diverge and investigate entirely new areas of phenomena. It is also true that the quantitative paradigm forces the narrowing of variables such that an original proposed research topic becomes unrecognisably different from and intrinsically less interesting than its original form. Working to syllabus requirements, I have often been instrumental in such narrowing. For instance, two teenage students, intensely interested, understandably, in researching the self-concept among teenagers, have ended up counting how many more times girls used social terms to describe themselves compared with boys, because this was a numerically verifiable test of a hypothesis.

It is essential to be clear about what one wants to observe, otherwise communication suffers and researchers can be accused of engaging in quackery and a journalistic style. However, one must distinguish between being clear and being unrealistic. The requisite clarity of thought is achievable without an automatic knee-jerk reduction to numbers. Astronomers chemists and biologists don't always count – they look for patterns. So did Freud, Piaget, Bartlett, and many other psychologists whose insights do not fundamentally depend on strictly quantified data.

THE MAJOR OBJECTIONS TO THE TRADITIONAL PARADIGM

Some of these have already been touched upon in covering the more qualitative aspects of interviewing and observing, as well as in the case-study section, and in the argument above. However, let's put together the general case 'against'.

1. Traditional research treats people as isolatable from their social contexts. It even treats part of people (e.g. their memory or attitude) as separable. 'Subjects' are to be treated as identical units for purposes of demonstrating the researcher's preconceived notions about humans which the 'subjects' cannot challenge. They are manipulated in and out of the research condition.

2. Whereas we all realise that to know and understand even one's good friends one has to stay close, the researcher, in the interests of objectivity, strains to remain distant. The researcher's attitudes and motives are not recognised, revealed or seen as relevant to the research process. This cool distancing, however, is a real social relationship, responded to by participants in experiments but denied by quantitative researchers in the interests of variable control and reduction of 'error variance'.

3. This objectively is seen as mythical. The attempt to stay coolly distant blinds the researchers to his/her own influence and active role in the research process which is a social context. When students administer structured questionnaires to peers, for instance, the respondents usually want to know what the student *thinks* and whether they *believe* all those statements which the respondent had to check.

4. The experimental situation or survey interview can only permit the gathering of superficial information. In the study of person perception and interpersonal attraction, for instance, mainly first impressions have been researched with traditional methods.

5. Experimental procedures restrict the normal powers of 'subjects' to plan, react and express appropriate social behaviour in the context of the research topic. Yet the investigator uses the results to make statements about human nature in that area. The resulting model of the person is simplistic and mechanistic. Heather (1976) has claimed that:

> human beings continue to be regarded by psychologists as some kind of helpless clockwork puppet, jerked into life only when something happens to it. (p. 20)

6. Deception can only falsify the research context and give quite misleading results, besides treating the participant with contempt.

7. The relationship between experimenter and 'subject' is like that of employer–employee. It is dominating and elitist. Hence, behaviour exhibited will mirror this particular social context. This will also contribute to the resulting model of the person. Hampden-Turner (1971) states '... power over people in a laboratory can *only* lead ... to a technology of behaviour control'.

8. Highly structured research methods predetermine the nature of resulting information. Theoretical frameworks are imposed on the participants. Questionnaires, for example, singularly fail to extract the most important information from people. Information obtained is narrow, rarefied and unrealistic.

SO WHAT DO 'NEW PARADIGMS' PROPOSE?

Thomas Kuhn (1962) made the term PARADIGM popular when he discussed ways in which science goes through radical changes in its overall conception of appropriate models and methodology. A 'paradigm shift' occurred when Einsteinian physics replaced Newtonian.

The paradigm which 'new paradigm' psychological researchers are seeking to replace is the positivist, quantitative one, which embraces the traditional scientific (hypothetico-deductive) model. But there is not just *one* new methodology. The call for change crops up in several contexts. It occurs among groups with a variety of backgrounds, principles and aims but with most of the objections above in common. They also would agree with most, if not all of the following points:

1. Psychological research should concentrate on the meanings of actions in a social context, not on isolated, 'objective' units of behaviour – a 'holistic', not an 'atomistic' approach.

2. The research emphasis should also be upon *interaction*. Attribution, for instance, is not the work of one person, but the result of negotiation between observer and observed, the latter attempting to control or contradict attributions.

3. Meanings and interactions belong to social situations and contexts and can't be sensibly isolated from these.

4. To capture life as it is and to permit participants the greatest liberty to act as normal, research needs to be conducted in *naturalistic settings* and data gathered needs to be *qualitative*. However, Hammersley and Atkinson (1983) point out that to distinguish the 'artificial laboratory' from 'naturalistic' settings is 'to take the positivists' rhetoric for reality, to treat them as if they really had succeeded in becoming Martians, viewing society from outside' (p. 11). The laboratory *itself* is a social setting; it is *within* society, and this is a good perspective from which to view all the 'threats to validity' which concern demand characteristics and participant expectancy. There isn't a 'pure' experimental situation, devoid of 'nuisance' social variables, in which we could finally get at 'true', uncontaminated human behaviour. The notion is as other-worldly as an *actually* true null hypothesis – see Chapter 11.

5. Research is conducted as closely as possible *with* the person(s) studied. A quote from Hall (1975) makes this point:

   Social science research often appears to produce a situation in which a medical doctor tries to diagnose a patient's symptoms from around the corner and out of sight. The social scientist uses his 'instrument' to measure the response of the patient as though they were a kind of long stethoscope. The focus of the researcher has been on developing a better and better stethoscope for going around corners and into houses when the real need is for the researcher to walk around the corner, into the house and begin talking with the people who live there. (p. 30)

6. Participants' *own* terms and interpretations are the most central data or at least the most important starting point. This avoids the 'falsification of reality' mentioned by De Waele and Harré (1979) – see p. 134.

7. Some version of INDUCTIVE ANALYSIS is preferred to the hypothetico-deductive

approach. In the former, theories, models and hypotheses *emerge* from the data-gathering process rather than being confirmed by it – see the discussion of 'Grounded theory' in Chapter 21. Ironically, this is close to the philosophy of the early empirical method, where one was supposed to gather data from the natural, physical world with no preconceptions. Medawar (1963), however, has argued force-fully against the naïve assumption that one can approach any phenomenon, in order to study it, with *absolutely no preconceptions* as to its modes of functioning – certainly not in the social world anyway. We approach all new phenomena with our already acquired schemas for interpreting the world. Pidgeon and Henwood (1997) (see also Chapter 21) talk of a 'constructivist revision of grounded theory' in this context. The force of *inductive analysis* techniques is to constantly refine emergent categories and theory in the light of incoming data, rather than to define what can be observed and measured before the data gathering begins. The value of this approach is particularly seen in its ability to permit categories, processes, even hypotheses to emerge which might not have been envisaged as present before research began. By contrast, traditional research defines variables and dimensions *before* data collection – we already know what is there to measure.

8. Emergent theories are likely to be *local*, particular to the context studied, rather than massive generalisations about the nature of human thought or personality. Many times in this book I have warned about work (including student projects) which entirely blurs the crucial question of 'to *whom* in the world could these findings apply'? The 'scientific' model employed in much practical work leaves the question hardly tackled and the impression that what has been 'discovered' is true of the whole world. Many developmental textbooks, for instance, have assumed that the drive to become independent of one's parents is a universal feature of human development, rather than a feature of mainly industrialised, individualistic societies. Many effects studied in psychological research are a good deal more locally limited than this.

9. For the more radical departures from the traditional paradigm there is a high degree of *participation* by those researched in some or all of the development, running and analysis of the research project. The extreme version of this approach involves the target group acting as *collaborative researchers* with the original researcher as a form of consultant and data organiser/analyst. Any findings or interpretations are discussed and modified by the group as a whole in its own terms. Reality is 'negotiated'. The reason for this emphasis on participants' perspectives is not politeness or sheer humanism. Hammersley and Atkinson (1983) make this distinction here between the positivist and what they term the 'naturalist' (loosely, the qualitative proponent):

> Positivism treats the researcher – by virtue of scientific method – as having access to superior knowledge. The radical naturalist, on the other hand, views the social scientist as incapable of producing valid accounts of events that compete with any provided by the people being studied. (p. 234)

10. At the very least, most methods under the 'new paradigm/qualitative' umbrella involve the notion of a 'research cycle', gone round several times, in which an integral step is to consult with participants as to the acceptability and accuracy of

emergent theories, models and categories – see the issue of *respondent validation* in Chapter 21.

Qualitative research often has to define itself against the background of quantitative research as the norm. The issue of reliability is a good example with critics of qualitative research arguing that traditional science has provided a basis for checking the reliability of tests whereas there are no commonly agreed criteria for the reliability of qualitative findings. They forget that, in establishing the reliability of a test, a suspiciously circular method has developed, historically, which ignores item content completely, and which invests numbers with almost magical powers. The numbers in fact merely serve a purpose which is fundamentally expressed in qualitative terms – did we get similar results? A police investigation asks this of repeated interviews but does not resort to artificially created measures in order to appear 'scientific'.

QUALITATIVE APPROACHES

I had originally intended to head this chapter 'qualitative approaches' and take you through a distinct set of methods. As it turned out, it made more sense to deal with the quantitative–qualitative dimension as we went through observation, interview and the like, and to deal with data *analysis* in the later part of this book – Chapter 21. The *methods* we have encountered so far which could count as qualitative include:

- Open-ended questionnaires
- Unstructured and semi-structured interviews
- Qualitative observation
- Participant observation
- The diary method
- The clinical method (to some extent)
- Role-play and simulation (depending on particular research)
- Individual case-studies

Although these methods gather qualitative data, they are not all what one might call 'qualitative' in outlook, by which is meant that the research aim is to use the data in their qualitative form and not extract from them just that which can somehow be represented numerically. In qualitative *approaches*, the data are retained in their original form of *meanings*. Some traditional methods of analysis have accepted qualitative data as a legitimate product of research investigation but have then reduced these quantitative values in order to conduct statistical analyses. *Content analysis* is an example and is dealt with in Chapter 21.

It would be tempting to assume that all approaches which are qualitative in outlook would automatically fall into the category of 'new paradigm'. However, the subterfuge and secrecy of some participant observation studies runs counter to several of the principles outlined above. The people studied are often not participants in the research, only the researcher is. The presentation of results can tend to deliver the message 'what fascinatingly strange people, and they're organised too.' Hence, there is no great homogeneity among qualitative or so-called 'new paradigm' approaches. In 1990, Tesch was able to identify at least 26 varieties. There can be as much opposition between some of these as there is between all of them and the traditional paradigm.

GROUNDED THEORY

Probably one of the most influential qualitative approaches used, if not recognised as such by many psychological researchers, is a 'school' borrowed from a near neighbour – sociology. The major principle of grounded theory was outlined under point 7 – 'inductive analysis' – above. Since we also return to this in Chapter 21 in some detail we shall just mention the approach here and emphasise that it concentrates on permitting theory to *emerge* from gathered qualitative data. It resists the determination of 'results' by prior hypothesis making, and it expects theory to be 'local' to the research context.

THEMATIC ANALYSIS

In Chapter 21 we shall see that qualitative data *can* be used to test hypotheses. This is something that occurs every day. You check to see whether someone feels much the same way as you do about racism by having a discussion and assessing the content of what is said, not by counting the number of times they make the right noises. Again, hypothesis testing with qualitative data is discussed more fully in Chapter 21 so we shall just mention the possibility here.

PARTICIPATIVE RESEARCH

The idea of people participating in research and collaborating with the researcher in evolving the project is not new. Here is a quote from Madge (1953):

> The techniques of experimentation which have so far been discussed are based on those evolved in the natural sciences. Can it be that a radically different approach is required in social science? Can the human beings who constitute the subject-matter of social science be regarded, not as objects for experimental manipulation, but as participants in what is being planned? If this can be so, it requires a transformed attitude towards social experiment. Traditionally, attention is concentrated on the precautions needed to objectify results, and this entails treating the participants as lay figures to be observed before and after subjection to a series of external stimuli. In contrast, the new approach entails the acceptance and encouragement of conscious co-operation by all concerned. There are then no longer an investigator and his passive subjects, but a number of human beings, one of whom is more experienced than the others and has somewhat more complex aims, but all of whom are knowingly collaborating in a research project.

What increased, towards the end of the twentieth century, was the actual practice of such research and the recognition of people as active enquirers in the research process, so much so that the establishment body for academic psychology, the British Psychological Society, recommended, in 1992, that the term 'subjects' be dropped in favour of 'participants'. Things have changed. In the second edition of this book I wrote that 'there was just one use of the term "participants", in over 30 opportunities in the *British Journal of Psychology* from 1992 to mid-1993.' In Chapter 1 of this edition it was noted that the term virtually dropped out of use during 1996.

ETHNOGRAPHY

This is an import from anthropology, the originators of participant observation on a big scale, and sociology. Ethnography as a recognised research method stems from the social anthropologists' attempts to generate an understanding of a society from substantial experience of living within it. The method was taken up by various sociologists as a way to counter stereotypical assumptions about groups under study. Going among them might help curb preconceptions and develop empathy with the community from their own perspective. The approach was seen at one time to sociology as qualitative work often is to contemporary psychology – a kind of 'palace rebellion'. From this we have largely inherited the tradition of participant observation. The specific methods involved are very close to those of grounded theory and indeed Glaser and Strauss's model can be seen as a direct off-shoot.

ENDOGENEOUS RESEARCH

'Endogeneous' is sometimes used to refer to research where, rather than living with a community for a year or so, coming away, then publishing a report, the researcher involves members of the community in a research project on their own customs, norms and organisation, in their own terms.

ACTION RESEARCH

First proposed by Kurt Lewin in the mid 1940s, this approach basically called for research to be applied to practical issues occurring in the everyday social world. The idea was to enter a social situation, attempt change, and monitor results. This might be setting up or contributing to a programme designed to raise awareness on dietary needs or the dangers of smoking. The approach has been used extensively in the area of occupational psychology concerned with organisational change. Associated examples come from the work of the Tavistock Institute and their concentration on 'socio-technical systems'. The emphasis here is on facilitation of a work-group in developing human systems which counteract the otherwise dehumanising influence of machinery and technology. A guiding principle is that the researcher involves the work-group, or representatives of it, in the process of change. There are examples as far back as Trist and Bamforth (1951) who recognised workers in the Durham coalfields, and Rice (1958) who did the same in Ahmedabad, India. Obviously, here is an approach where the research aim and area lend themselves to a qualitative and participative approach. We are most likely to see it in action in areas of applied psychology, such as education, work and health.

COLLABORATIVE RESEARCH

Roughly speaking, putting endogeneous and action research together, we get the basis for COLLABORATIVE RESEARCH, in which participants are involved as fully as possible in research on their own organisation or group. The researcher may have to lead at the beginning, but as participants realise the nature of the game they become more centrally involved in the progress of research. In some cases the research is initiated by an already existing member of the organisation or group.

This is particularly suitable where the group is planning or undergoing change and requires evaluation. Participants take up data-gathering ideas, develop their own, consider the researcher's findings or analyse their own, and debate progress, directions and results in group meetings. Collaborative research is not without confrontations, but the idea is to build on these natural differences constructively. A major goal is for participants to direct their own change, rather than be told by an outside expert what is wrong and what might be changed, after that expert has conducted research on those participants.

Sims (1981) set out to study 'problem-generation' in health service teams and found that, as the participants became interested in the issues, they took on their own lines of investigation. This caused them to consider group dynamic issues they'd never thought about and created an atmosphere of awareness raising and constructive change. With the researcher they were able to develop many categories of processes in problem construction which could be transferred (not without addition and modification) to other group situations.

A COMPLETE ALTERNATIVE?

Patton (1980), an evaluation researcher who advocates the use of a wholly qualitative approach, argues that the hypothetico-deductive method is not bad or wrong, but has simply overwhelmed research in psychology to become not just a major paradigm, but the *only* paradigm of which new researchers are aware. In advocating the qualitative approach he argues that the new paradigm is a 'paradigm of choice' between the traditional hypothetico-deductive and the alternative holistic, inductive one.

Latour (1987) argues that quantification is only one example of a more general process of deriving order and meaningful abstractions from data in science which can be transferred. Quantitative and qualitative procedures are just different forms of the analytic practice of 're-representation' in science. In other words, whether I measure what you say numerically, or re-describe it, what results is my summarised *version* of what you actually said.

Flick (1998) points out that, in some research, qualitative results are allowed to exist alongside quantitative ones but only the latter are thought to 'lead to results in the actual sense of the word' (p. 258) because sample sizes are so small. On the other hand, other writers cited by Flick argue that qualitative methods can live without quantitative methods but the reverse is not true. Qualitative methods are required to explain the relations found by the quantitative methods. In general, many authors take the view of 'different horses for different courses' – the nature of the research problem, not political dogma, should determine what methods are appropriate for its solution.

A FEMINIST PERSPECTIVE

A further recent and powerful force within psychological research methods has been the arrival of serious challenges to the traditional research paradigm from the point of view of the politics and ideology of the women's movement. Some would argue that a large part of the driving force behind the rapid 'normalisation' of qualitative research methods has been the appropriateness that feminist researchers found within them in researching their particular themes.

It is now hard to believe that women did not until fairly recently, 'own' research into themselves. It is about as stunningly inappropriate that a male should author research on *The Psychology of Women* (I still have the Penguin paperback!) as that white psychologists should conduct studies on 'the Negro' (as they once did and as does Richard Lynn – see Chapter 8). The early stages of women's research involved studies, under a conventional paradigm, which destroyed (or should have) traditional stereotypes of women's nature or deficits relative to men. Research literature now contains a fair amount of stereotype challenging and consciousness-raising work. This period also challenged the lack of female authorship and visible presence within the research community. Parallels with racism occurred in that even where women had produced scholarship this had somehow become marginalised or obscured. The overwhelmingly male-oriented and -dominated research community had edged such work to the periphery.

However, the content-oriented period just described, though continuing, has led on to a realisation by women involved in the research process that the conventional methods which they had been using to develop the content were themselves largely the product of a male research perspective and thought-base. This is not to say that women would think, reason and conduct their research *utterly* differently, given the opportunity. It would fall back onto old stereotypes to suggest that women didn't *tend* to use quantification or feel happy testing hypotheses statistically. The logic underlying chess, computer programming and the statistical tests in this book are in a major sense neutral. But they have been 'owned' and promoted for so long by men that it is hardly surprising that when women came to assess their values in the research process they were alerted to methods and research relationships neglected or never taken up by male researchers, and felt by many female researchers to be more valid and more authentic in representing women's experience. The position is exemplified in Sue Wilkinson's *Feminist Social Psychology* (1986).

Recognised as characteristic of a male approach to research and understanding the world are: preoccupation with quantifying variables; an emphasis on control, mastery and manipulation; a tendency to remain distant rather than be involved with the subjects of research; a preference for gadget-oriented research over naturalistic enquiry; competition and ego building. The issue of power is raised above under participative research. The contemporary recognition of power relations in the research context is very much a product of feminist psychology – see Paludi (1992) whose title is *The Psychology of Women*, but this time by a woman! She argues that the terms 'control', 'manipulate', 'subject' are symptomatic of the 'masculinist' nature of the cool, distant, white-coated image of science that the main body of psychological research tried to project, particularly in the middle period of the twentieth century. Keller (1985) argued persuasively that being objective has been associated with being male and that to be objective one must take up a distant, uninvolved position. Feminist researchers challenge this assumption, as do qualitative researchers in general, arguing that this stance projects a deceptive image of neutrality; it cashes in on the socially accepted view of science as a world of expert 'truth' where challenges to this method are somehow 'biased'. Hence, to get involved, to listen, to treat interaction with the research participant as an everyday social encounter, will 'contaminate' the research process and findings. Women will be very familiar with being told that their judgements are unsound because they permit emotion to cloud their perception of the situation!

As qualitative research often has to define itself against quantitative methods as the norm, so feminist researchers describe having to define their position against the norm of maleness (aggression is normal – females just happen to have 'less' of it). A background norm in sex and gender research has been to find *differences*. Hence, the many studies actually carried out which *don't* find differences, plus those not attempted because it is not even suspected there *might* be differences, are absent from the literature (Tavris, 1993). The unwary psychology student will be aware *only* of 'sex-difference' research, not of sex similarity findings. A further related conceptual trap formed by this perspective is that by testing for significant *difference*, an impression of *group difference* is created. This is inherent in the decision to conduct research in this significance testing manner. In Chapter 3, I tried to highlight in a technical way the grossly misleading ideas that can be generated by conducting a *group difference* study, particularly if such a study is given 'scientific' endorsement by being termed an 'experiment'. Even with a *highly significant difference* there can be a very large *overlap* between populations – see Chapter 11. What is more important, the overlap or the difference? If we leave casual psychology users and readers with the impression that women do worse on X than men, will they then, in some future position of power, act upon the assumption that nearly *all* women are poor at X? It is not just feminist and anti-racist psychologists who should be aware of the biases inherent in different methodological approaches, We all have this duty and we should be particularly wary of apparently 'value free', 'neutral' and 'universally applicable' methods and systems.

DISCOURSE

Qualitative researchers have for some time become interested in various aspects of human interchange, through Conversation Analysis (see Sacks, 1992) and more recently and controversially through an emergent 'school', from the 1980s onwards, of Discourse Analysis (DA) (Potter and Wetherell, 1987; Edwards and Potter, 1992; Middleton and Edwards, 1990). Discourse analysis, like most approaches mentioned here, extends beyond specific method to an overarching research paradigm, this one often called 'Discursive Psychology' (the Edwards and Potter 1992 publication title). The approach wholeheartedly treats psychological topics, such as memory and attribution theory (two mainstream heartland topics), as processes of *discourse* between people. Memories are not seen as close attempts to recall 'the facts' but are reconstructions in a social context. One might recall the office party differently for an absent colleague and for the managing director. Memories are motivated constructions by people with a 'stake' in producing an 'account' which suits circumstances. These are not necessarily *conscious* constructions but they may, for instance, suit defences against blame or accountability, or may promote one *perspective* of a situation. What people say, when memorising, cannot be taken as a rather opaque window onto actual cognitive memory processes within the organism. The scientific chase after these underlying processes is seen as producing much arid theory and many artificial results.

Much of the controversial debate is beyond the scope of this book. The debate, at times, carries the image of David and Goliath. The flavour of the toing and froing of debate can be gained from a read of *The Psychologist*, October 1992. The reason for giving the issue some prominence here is that DA specifically discredits the *methods* used in experimental psychology, in particular, and blames these for what they feel is a distorted model of human cognition and social judgement. They place language as *action*, ahead of language as *representation*. Language cannot be used as a trusty, objective route to 'what people really think'. DA treats language as the constructor of *versions* of truth as the language occurs. There are an infinite number of ways in which I can describe to you my (negative) views on, for instance, traditional behaviourism or privatisation of welfare services. DA's view is not that these are all versions of some ultimate reality inside my head but that I would redefine and negotiate my view each time I attempted to explain it, dependent on the challenges I receive, my listeners' views, who else can hear, how formal we are and so on. Above all, my production is social action.

One of DA's major points against highly controlled experimental approaches is that the materials often used (word lists in memory; 'vignettes' in social perception) take away the very essence of what people normally *do* when remembering or judging – we engage in discourse with others or even with ourselves. It is not that DA sees everyone as little Machiavellis, constantly plotting and creating self-interested accounts. Their emphasis is on studying memory and other traditional topic areas as *the way things are done*. We normally memorise or attribute with a *purpose*, in a *context* that matters to us.

Although the DA 'movement' is as yet still promoted by a small group, and there do not appear to be *any* 'how to do it' books available, the approach has quite healthily rattled the establishment (see *The Psychologist* articles) and produced innovative work, with valuable human applications, hardly likely to have appeared but for its approach – for instance, the reminiscence work with the elderly of Middleton, Buchanan and Suurmond (1993). Baddeley (1992) wonders whether DA may be producing 'common sense dressed up as jargon', and whether all answers in DA are treated as equally true since none is perfectly true. Hitch (1992) argues that DA is valuable but should be seen as complementary, not an overthrowing alternative, answering its own questions about memory in ways that other researchers should recognise along with their own. A further critique (Silverman, 1993) has been that DA often deals, not with 'everyday conversation' but with 'exotic' or institutionalised exchanges (e.g. teacher–pupil; doctor patient; politicians' speeches – much of the 1992 book, above deals with Nigel Lawson, Margaret Thatcher and the media). Although teacher-pupil conversations *do* occur every day, Silverman's recommendation is to look at less social rule-driven exchanges in everyday conversations between people of equal status.

REFLEXIVITY

One of the strong currents within DA and similar approaches, which to some extent protects it from the criticism of being hard to refute, is its strong relationship and commitment to the self-critical theme of REFLEXIVITY. This is a term developed within modern sociology in the area of studies of scientific knowledge (Woolgar, 1988), but some of its effect is felt in psychology. To appreciate the felt need for reflexivity in research it is necessary to return again to the notion of knowledge of the world as *socially constructed*, not 'out there', fixed and grabbable if only the right method is used.

Sociologists (especially Woolgar) studying the process of 'doing' natural science (producing theories, studies, conferences, journals, etc.) concluded that the notion of an individual studying and discovering natural, objective 'facts' was an illusion and that any body of scientific knowledge is the product of social, cultural, historical and political processes. When we attempt to describe or explain something, especially something new to us, we are forced to employ analogies, models, similarities that are readily available. These are certain to be culturally bound and to be the contemporary concepts of your particular cultural group, where 'culture' can be quite small scale – your local community, your 'clique' at school and so on. Think how recent language of computing has infiltrated our descriptions of things in general: 'virtual', 'chips', 'programmed', 'mega', 'micro', 'interface', 'on-line' and so on. New 'explanations' depend upon available constructs. Schizophrenia is a 'disease', people are 'controlled by their genes', atoms are 'balls' and so on.

The central point, which I hope I can make clear, is that these 'models' of reality are used in scientific discourse and that scientific discourse is as much a social interaction, a psychological event, as any other social context. There are a multitude of social and psychological forces which might lead to one view being better accepted by a peer group than another. The relativist (or 'constructionist') view is that scientists don't discover pure, cold, unarguable facts at a distance; rather, they construct *versions* of the facts according to a host of schemata, pressures, socially accepted values and so on.

Having analysed the discourse and thinking of *natural* scientists in this way there was an inevitable consequence. Rather like the monster in *Yellow Submarine* which sucks up its own tail and thence itself, the spotlight, in turn, fell on the construction of social science. Writers became sensitive to their own construction of knowledge as they produced and wrote it. They became acutely self-conscious about the process of writing and analysing because they could see that they were just as 'guilty' of appearing to produce compartmentalised and 'objective' knowledge, with the stamp of authority, whereas their own knowledge must be as 'relative' as any other. One technique to prevent readers accepting as fact what was being socially produced was to make readers aware of this as they read. Texts were then produced which carried markers to highlight this process and overall philosophy. Latour (1988) defines a reflexive text as one which, '... takes into account its own production and which, by doing so, claims to undo the deleterious effects upon its readers of being believed too little or too much.'[1]

A general principle, then, is to take 'methodological precautions' which ensure somehow that readers are aware of your own role in constructing what they are reading, of your own possible 'stake' and so on. Challenging the conventional researchers' pose of neutrality, Reinharz (1983) argues that researcher's attitudes should be fully discussed and their values revealed and clearly located. This reflexive philosophy is a strong theme in

---

[1] Latour (1988) argues that even the Bible was meant to be read this way, and was, until readers in the age of empiricism started taking it literally.

feminist psychological research. Some texts include commentaries by the authors or peers after each section. As we shall see in Chapter 21, grounded theory and similar approaches recommend that researchers submit a diary of their thoughts as they gathered data, analysed them and constructed theory during their research project. They comment on their own attitudes and possible biases in coming to this or that conclusion or in proceeding this or that way in the research process. Rather than footnotes, or doubts admitted to trusted colleagues in the pub, this material is seen as equivalent in importance to the raw, summarised and analysed data.

One of the difficulties with the development of this approach has been deciding when enough reflexion is enough. There has been a tendency to reflect upon reflexion ('meta-reflexivity'), creating the obvious possibility of an infinite regress. A further difficulty is that, if a writer is telling you about such constructionism in academic texts, their own text is included in the analysis, and the position becomes something like that of trying to deal with the Cretan liar: if *all* Cretans are liars, and a Cretan tells you this, what are you to believe?

Some writers, as we shall see in Chapter 21, also use the term 'reflexivity' to refer to a process of self appraisal on the part of participants in research, for instance, those keeping long-term diaries or those engaged in forms of participative or collaborative research.

THE CURRENT STATE OF PLAY

The qualitative research debate has established a strong seam of interest and practice, now itself well on the way to becoming 'mainstream'. There has been immense change, even in the period from the first edition of this book to now – 1990–1999. Whereas such research was 'radical' in 1989, examination boards now include the terms and qualitative articles appear in most journals (though Chapter 5 argued that certain case studies have *always* been accepted as part of 'science'). It will now be interesting to see how the promoters of the radical views themselves cope with becoming conventionalised. How will students be stopped from mere journalism? How will radicalism in research be graded? Will the tables turn (as with long and short hair) so that students will soon be rebuked for having too *precise* a hypothesis? The experimental and quantitative approach will no doubt 'prevail' for some time, especially in its strongholds and where quantification is clearly useful and productive. We need to know whether a child's language is seriously delayed, for instance, or whether perceptual task performance is affected in such and such an environment, and what to do about it, and we need to operate with publicly agreed definitions of these terms.

In general, though, the debate will not now die away. Most see the growth surge in use of, and debate about, qualitative methods as a very healthy development which should enrich *all* research, rather than in the confrontational terms of a coming *coup d'etat* where quantitative methods are consigned to history. Richardson (1996) outlines the history of these changes within the UK psychological establishment. As late as 1991, the Scientific Affairs Board of the British Psychological Society received from Paula Nicolson a report it had commissioned on the use and relevance of qualitative methods. The report proposed wider teaching and use of such methods to facilitate development. Research departments have recognised how few psychologists are properly trained for qualitative work. In 1992, Henwood and Pidgeon produced a seminal review paper 'Qualitative research and psychological theorising', appearing in the *British Journal of Psychology* and constituting what Richardson describes as 'one of the first papers on qualitative research methods to be published in a mainstream psychology journal in the UK'. This article starts with the fundamental point that the qualitative–quantitative debate is not just about preferable methods for varying research contexts. It engages all the debate about experimentation, positivism, artificiality, political power of the establishment mainstream and the wrongness of 'natural science envy', which has been aired often but increasingly by qualitative writers. This author would prefer to see a less adversarial atmosphere in which each side agrees to work with and appreciate the value of the other. Both sides seem to succumb far too easily to simple, insular stereotypes and old-fashioned, non-academic, supremely counter-productive hostility.

Recommended further reading

There is a comprehensive list of more practically oriented texts at the end of Chapter 21. The only texts included here are those which do not appear there and which are largely theoretical.

Banister, P., Burman, E., Parker, I., Taylor, M. and Tindall, C. (1994) *Qualitative Methods in Psychology*. Buckingham: Open University.

Edwards, D. and Potter, J. (1992) *Discursive Psychology*. London: Sage.

Henwood, K. and Pidgeon, N. (1992) Qualitative research and psychological theorising. *British Journal of Psychology*, 83, 97–111.

Neisser, U. (1978) Memory: What are the important questions? In M.M. Gruneberg, P.E. Morris, and R.N. Sykes (Eds) *Practical Aspects of Memory*. London: Academic Press.

The Psychologist – special issue on qualitative methods, 1995, 8(3), 115–18.

Reason, P. and Rowan, J. (Eds) (1981) *Human Enquiry: a sourcebook in new paradigm research*. Chichester: Wiley.

Smith, J.A., Harré, R. and Van Langenhove, L. (Eds) (1995) *Rethinking Methods in Psychology*. London: Sage.

Strauss, A.L. and Corbin, J. (1990) *Basics of Qualitative Research: Grounded theory Procedures and Techniques*. Newbury Park, CA: Sage.

Tavris, C. (1993) The mismeasure of woman. *Feminism and Psychology*, 3(2), 149–68.

Ussher, J.M. (1991) *Women's Madness: misogyny or mental illness?* London: Harvester/Wheatsheaf.

Wetherell, M. and Potter, J. (1993) *Mapping the Language of Racism: discourse and the legitimation of exploitation*. London: Harvester/Wheatsheaf.

Wilkinson, S. (1986) *Feminist Social Psychology*. Milton Keynes: OUP.

Glossary

Practical intervention in everyday situations, often organisations, using applied psychology to produce change and monitor results	_____ _____	action research
Research in which participants are fully involved to the extent of organising their own processes of research and change	_____ _____	collaborative research
Theory holding knowledge to be relative and 'facts' to be social constructions, not permanent realities	_____	constructivism
Qualitative analysis of interactive speech which assumes people use language to construct the world as they see it and according to context and interests	_____ _____	discourse analysis
Research involving group members in study of their own customs, organisational norms and so on	_____ _____	endogenous research
Studying a culture intensively from within	_____	ethnography
Emphasis on women's perspective and on methods suitable to research which integrate gender politics	_____ _____	feminist psychology
Theory 'grounded in' specific qualitative data; patterns *emerge* from the data and are not imposed on them before they are gathered	_____ _____	grounded theory
Work with qualitative data which permits theory and hypotheses to evolve from the data rather than hypothetico-deductive *testing* of hypotheses set before data are obtained	_____ _____	inductive analysis
A prevailing agreed system of scientific thinking and behaviour within which research is conducted	_____	paradigm
Research in which participants are substantially involved in the investigative process as active enquirers	_____ _____	participative research
The scientific belief that facts in the world can be discovered only through measurement of what is observable	_____	positivism

Work (research or theoretical text) which includes self criticism and alerts the reader to the human subjective processes involved in production of the text; it warns the reader that knowledge is relative to the writer's perspective	_____	reflexivity
Belief that objective facts are an illusion and that knowledge is constructed by each individual	_____	relativism
Use of qualitative data to test hypotheses; in this approach, theory still drives analysis but examples of meaning rather than quantitative data are used as support	_____	thematic analysis

10
Descriptive statistics – organising the data

Precision in research requires quantitative measurement which is carried out at various *levels*. There is a strong debate about whether any variable, properly so-called, can escape some form of quantitative measurement. Qualitatively different events can at least be counted or categorised and, strictly speaking, a variable must vary in some quantitative manner. The levels at which data can be measured are: *nominal, ordinal, interval* and *ratio*. The latter is a specific form of interval scaling.

- *Nominal* level is simple classification. At *ordinal* level, cases are ranked or ordered. *Interval* scales should use equal intervals. *Ratio* scales are interval but include a real zero and relative proportions on the scale map to physical reality. Attempts are made to convert many psychological scales to interval level using *standardisation*. Many scales used in psychology can be called *plastic interval* because numerically equal appearing intervals on the scale do not measure equal amounts of a construct.

- All variables can be classified according to whether they are *categorical* or *measured*. *Measured* variables may be measured on a *discrete* or a *continuous* scale. Many variables in psychology are measured on discrete scales, where there are only a limited number of separated points, but are treated as continuous for statistical purposes.

- Higher levels of measurement give more information about the original data or phenomenon measured. Level of measurement limits choice in treatment of data, especially in terms of the statistical significance tests which may legitimately be carried out.

- *Descriptive* statistics are summaries of gathered data. *Sample* statistics usually include a measure of *central tendency* (*mean, median, mode*) and a measure of *dispersion* (*variation ratio, range, semi-interquartile range, mean deviation, standard deviation* and *variance*, the last two being most common for interval level data).

- *Sample* statistics, at interval level, are often used to make estimates of *population parameters*. This is a powerful technique employed in *parametric tests*.

- The appropriateness of the statistic depends upon the *level of measurement* of the data. Large sets of data form a *distribution* and these may be represented in several ways. They may be divided into categories and presented as a *frequency table*. A frequency distribution may be represented graphically as a *histogram*, where all data in a set are displayed by adjacent columns.

- In a *bar chart* only discrete categories of data are presented for comparison and this must be done fairly, without visual distortion.

- Other graphical forms include the *frequency polygon, line chart, time series chart* and *ogive*. In recent years the techniques of *exploratory data analysis* have been promoted with an emphasis on thorough examination of patterns before submitting data sets to tests of statistical significance. Two methods are included here: *stem* and *leaf* diagrams, and *box-plots*.

- The *normal distribution* is an extremely important distribution shape. Data approximating to this shape can be tested with the most powerful significance tests and techniques to estimate underlying *population parameters* from *sample statistics* are readily available.
- z scores are *deviations* from the mean measured in numbers of standard deviations and on the normal distribution they cut off known percentages of the whole distribution.
- Statistics of distributions include *percentiles*, *quartiles* and *deciles*.
- Distributions with substantially more scores at the high end of the measurement scale are said to be *positively skewed*. The opposite is a *negatively skewed* distribution. If a skewed distribution shows bunching at the top end because too many people score the maximum or very near it, then the variable measure shows a *ceiling effect*. Its opposite is a *floor effect*.
- Distributions with two distinct 'humps' (higher frequencies) are known as *bi-modal*.

PART 1 – MEASUREMENT

HOW DATA ARRIVE

In this chapter we move carefully into the world of numbers and describing measurements and findings in numerical terms – that is, using *statistics*. As with other concepts in this book, many of the ideas here will be known to you or at least you will find that you have used the concepts in your life already many times but perhaps not in a formal way. I will attempt throughout to stick closely to the everyday experience of statistical things (for instance, working out your average shopping bill or estimating whether we've had a particularly rainy month).

The reason you need to be familiar with statistics in psychology is that it is broadly an empirical science. In studying psychology you will read about all sorts of studies that compare sets of data. You will probably have to work on data you have gathered yourself in practical investigations. We have already seen that it appears that people drop more litter when others have done so. How do we know whether the extra amounts dropped are sufficient to support this sort of claim? People are apparently more worried after being exposed to negative news bulletins. How should we measure 'worry' numerically? We will gather a lot of data. How will we organise people's scores so we can report them effectively to others? How will we show that the 'worry' scores after negative news were a lot higher than the scores after a positive bulletin?

In this first section of the chapter, before we deal with organising and analysing data or 'results', we start out by simply looking at the different ways in which we can gather data. That is, the different *scales* that might have been used to acquire the raw data with which we start assessing results. RAW DATA are the participants' actual responses (e.g. 'yes' or 'no'; words recalled) before they are organised or treated. Very often these will be in a rather rough form. You may have the total scores of all your participants on a questionnaire, perhaps grouped into the categories of the independent variable – male/female or older/younger student, etc. You may have two columns of paired scores – scores for each person on both self-esteem rating and estimate of IQ, for instance. We need to decide what *kind* of data we have gathered before deciding what are the most appropriate procedures to deal with them – to summarise them, present them and analyse them according to the hypothesis we wished to test in the first place.

STARTING OUT ON MEASURES

The previous chapter looked at ways in which quantitative methods can fall short of giving realistic or 'rich' information. We also looked at theoretical objections to basing psychology on numerical measurement. The case *for* numerical measurement, as a part of psychological research, is simply that many things *can* be measured and people (who may be vehemently opposed to counting and measuring, who may hate maths) actually do use quantitative judgements in their everyday conversation. Take for instance:

- Helen is more artistic than Clare
- George is a contemplative type whereas Rick is practical, energetic and impulsive.

It may appear that a difference of quality, such as that expressed about George, does not need numerical values to confirm it, but how exactly do we know Rick is 'energetic' or 'impulsive'? We must be comparing some things he does (how strongly and how often) with their occurrence in others. We must define what *counts* as energetic and impulsive and show that Rick is like this more often or to a greater degree than is George. Hence, to demonstrate a difference, we would need some numerical measure or at least a *count*. What many people feel uncomfortable about in psychological measurement is the *crudity* of the measures and the *transparency* of the attempt. Nevertheless, it is hard to see how someone could claim that Rick is more energetic or more impulsive, or even that George falls into a 'contemplative' category, without some *description* that would come close to measurement, or at least to *categorising* – surely we at least claim that Rick does X while George does not?

CATEGORICAL AND MEASURED VARIABLES

Let's follow up that last point and introduce two major types of variable that can produce two different forms of data – CATEGORICAL and MEASURED. Suppose your friend Christina says:

> Marvyn is a Pisces, extremely extroverted and six foot tall.

Christina has introduced three variables on which she has assessed Marvyn. The first is a *category system* – people fall into one category or another and they can't be placed in between (forgetting, for now, all that stuff about 'cusps'!). You can't be half a Pisces or 2.7 Aries, in the same way as you can't have voted 0.7 Labour. You may not fully agree with Labour's policies but the system provided for voting forces you to choose one category or another. In these cases, the set of star signs or political parties would be called a CATEGORICAL VARIABLE. It is useful to call any other sort of variable, which operates *above* the level of mere categorising, a MEASURED VARIABLE. This is the sort of scale Christina used for her second two measures. The first is not on a quantified scale but she has placed Marvyn as 'more extreme' than many other people. She must therefore have some crude concept of *degree* of extroversion by which people can be separated. On the last measure of course there is no argument. Feet and inches are divisions on a publicly agreed, standardised and therefore checkable scale of measurement.

In very many experimental studies the independent variable is categorical and the dependent variable is a measured variable. Have a look at Table 10.1 which shows this

Table 10.1 Categorical and measured experimental variables

Independent variable	Categorical/ measured	Dependent variable	Categorical/ measured
Good or bad news bulletin	categorical	Worry score	measured
Imagery or rehearsal	categorical	Number of items correctly recalled	measured
Perform in front of audience or alone	categorical	Number of errors made	measured
Number of pieces of litter already on ground	measured	Dropped leaflet or not	categorical

distinction for several of the experiments we have discussed so far in this book. Cover up columns 2 and 4 if you wish to test yourself.

Notice that the only categorical dependent variable in the table is the dropping or not of the leaflet in the Cialdini *et al.* study and that, in this study, the independent variable was measured. However, for data analysis purposes, we shall *treat it* as categorical, as did Cialdini.

A QUICK INTRODUCTION TO DIFFERENT LEVELS OF MEASUREMENT

In order to introduce these in a simple and brief manner, before elaborating on each, let's run through an imaginary classroom scenario.

Suppose it's a snowy day and only eight people have turned up for your psychology class. Your tutor decides to abandon plans for a 20 participant experiment and decides on a quick demonstration of *levels of measurement* instead. She instructs you to divide into two groups, one 'short' and one 'tall'. After some shuffling around, two groups are formed – see the bottom of Figure 10.1. Suppose you are in the tall group. As a measure of height in the class, for the moment, all we know about you (we can't see into the classroom) is that you have the value 'tall'. We can't separate you from the other three people in your group. All four get the *equal* value 'tall'. We have used a simple categorical variable. The categorisation into 'short' and 'tall' uses a form of measurement scale known as NOMINAL and we will investigate that term further in a few moments. Some people think that the 'nominal scale' is not a scale at all since it involves categorising rather than 'measuring' *along* a scale. We shall absorb that point and move on, recognising that 'nominal scale' can be short for 'use of a categorical classification system'

Your tutor now asks you to get into a line in *order* of height. This causes some more shuffling and a couple of back to back contests before the line is finally formed (see middle of Figure 10.1). Your position in this line is seventh, next to the tallest person. This

Interval level

gives measured, real differences in height between people

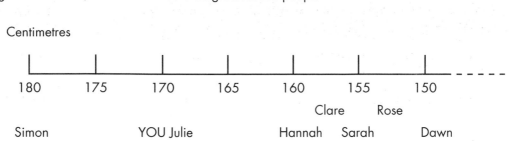

Ordinal level

only gives *position* of each person; we don't know that YOU are a lot shorter than Simon

Nominal level

only classifies each person as 'tall' or 'short'; no distinction *at all* between 'tall' people

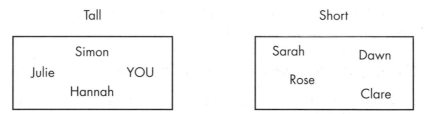

Figure 10.1   Levels of measurement and information obtained

ordering of items, by using *ranks*, demonstrates use of what is termed an ORDINAL level of measurement. When we were using only the nominal level for information we had no way to separate members of the 'tall' group from one another. However, now we know what position or rank you occupy in the group, relative to the rest. We are now measuring along a scale, in that there is one and only one order in which the students can be arranged. We are using a *measured variable* – height order – but the scale is rather crude. It does not take into account the fact that you are *way* below the eighth person in the line (Simon) but only a smidgin above the sixth (Julie). The ordinal level gives us more information than the nominal, but not the most.

To get the most subtle measure of class height we need a tape measure or wall chart. Of course the tutor has one and we now produce the familiar measurement of height in feet and inches (or centimetres) which is an example of an INTERVAL scale (and also a RATIO scale – to be explained later). Now we can say, accurately, whether the tallest person is a little above you or tends to gather snow on top (see top of Figure 10.1). We can also compare you to the *general* measure of height used everywhere else. We can tell whether you are tall relative to the general population. That is, the measurement scale is *standardised*.

The nominal level of measurement

Categorical data

For some differences of quality we do not need numbers in order to distinguish one item from another. For instance:

- male and female
- red, green and blue objects
- Roman noses and other noses.

Here we simply compare each item with some learned concept – what counts as green, a Roman nose (shape) or a male. On occasion we may count number of features present before categorising, for instance, when deciding whether to categorise a car as 'luxury' – how many luxury features does it have? In psychological research participants might be categorised into 'figure dependent' or 'figure independent' categories, decided by the number of 'embedded figures' they can detect.

What matters with categorisation, however, is that we must be able to place each item or person in just one category, for purposes of comparison. We might decide to categorise people as 'energetic', 'average' and 'slow' for instance. A person is either male or female and can't, when we use a nominal system, be included in both categories because he/she is a bit of both. Difficulties may arise in categorising a person as smoker or non-smoker, extrovert or introvert, optimist or pessimist, but nominal categories are *mutually exclusive*. People and things are bunched together on the basis of a common feature – Jason is not the same as Jonathan but they have maleness in common. All irrelevant differences are ignored for the measurement purpose at hand.

Coding of categories

If we conducted a survey which investigated use of the college refectory, we might like to count the number of people using it and categorise these. When preparing the data for entry into a computer statistics program (such as *SPSS*) we *must* give each category a *code*. If we are simply making up a table it is also very often neater and more useful to give each category a number, that is, a code. Table 10.2 shows the categories with their codes that might be drawn up from our refectory survey raw results.

Here we can see the origin of the term 'nominal' – the numbers or codes given to the categories here are only *names*. Code 1 (students) is not half of code 2 (teaching staff) or in

Table 10.2 Codes and frequencies of people surveyed using the college refectory

Code				
1 Students	2 Teaching staff	3 Non-teaching staff	4 Visitors	5 Other
650	34	43	17	2

any way prior to or less than the others in quantity. The numbers are simply convenient but arbitrary *labels* for identifying each category of person. We could have used 'A', 'B', 'C' etc. We are using numerals (the figures 1, 2, 3 etc.) as labels only and not as real numbers – they don't in any way stand for *quantities*. Likewise, numbers on office doors don't represent quantity but places to find people in. Your student number or exam number is also just a 'name' made up of numbers that computers adore.

The numbers within each category are known as FREQUENCIES or FREQUENCY DATA. They represent the number of times an event in each category occurred – the number of events given code 1. These numbers are being used to count, they do stand for quantities and are known as CARDINAL numbers. Note that, from the description of nominal data above, each person counted can only go in one category. Hence, a member of staff also undertaking a course as a student at the college can only go in one category, student *or* staff. Some examples of psychological data at a nominal level are given in Table 10.3.

Table 10.3 Examples of frequency data in nominal categories

Number of children (average age 4.5 years) engaged in type of play				
non-play	solitary	associative	parallel	cooperative
8	5	17	23	6
Oldtown by-election: number of voters by political party				
Communist	Conservative	Labour	Lib. Dem.	Other
243	5 678	15 671	4 371	567

Do we really have to bother so much about data types?

At this point the reader may start to feel, 'are we just splitting hairs over names or what?' I assure you we're not, otherwise we certainly wouldn't bother. The essential point is that if you want to use statistical techniques to *analyse* your data, you must decide what type they belong to before you can sensibly proceed. In fact, it is a golden rule to consider the type of data you will end up with before you even start to gather any and before you finish creating your variable measures. Why? Let's go back to the salutary tale concerning a recent student's project – the case of the questionnaire item about responsibility for an attack (p. 163). Here, the student chose a *dichotomous* categorical variable measure (i.e. one with only two fixed alternatives). Participants had to decide whether the man or the woman 'was most responsible for the attack'. Because the question was set in this way, the form of the data was already determined as categorical/nominal and the student could do nothing with the rather useless data gathered. 100% of participants of course saw the man as *more* responsible. Had the question been altered to asking for *degree* of responsibility along a 1 to 10 point scale, the variable would then have become a *measured* one and the gathered data would be treated as ordinal or even interval. This, in turn, would have led to an analysis where it would have been possible to see whether participants attributed *more* responsibility to the woman when she was dressed in a way that men saw as 'inviting' than when she was not so dressed. As it was, the scale chosen completely prevented this possibility (in fact, the student was lucky enough to be able to go back later and ask most of her participants again – but this was not really the most unbiased way to obtain her measures!).

Table 10.4 An example of ranking – changing interval level data to ordinal level

Person	Score	Rank of score
1	18	5.5
2	25	7
3	14	1
4	18	5.5
5	15	3
6	15	3
7	15	3
8	29	8

Ordinal level of measurement

ORDINAL numbers do not represent quantities or counts; they represent *rank position* in a group. They tell us who came first, second, third and so on in a race or test. They do not tell us how far ahead the winner was from the second placed. They tell us nothing at all about distances between positions. It may be annoying to be beaten by one-tenth of a second in a cycle race when you and the leader were ten kilometres ahead of the rest of the 'bunch', but what goes on your record is just 'second'. To the horse race punter it doesn't matter by what margin Golden Girl won – it won!

How to rank data

Giving ranks to scores or values obtained in research is very easy but must be done in a precise, conventional manner, otherwise the various significance tests based on ranks will give misleading results. Suppose we have to rank the scores of eight people on a general knowledge test shown in Table 10.4.

The score of 14 is lowest and gets the rank one. In competitions we usually give the winner 'first' but in statistics it is less confusing to give low ranks to low scores.

Persons five, six and seven 'share' the next three ranks (of second, third and fourth). In sport we might say 'equal second', but in statistical ranking we take the *median* value (see next chapter) of the ranks they share. If the number is odd, this is just the *middle* value. From 2 3 4 the middle value is 3. If the number is even we take the number midway between the two middle ranks shared. Persons one and four share the ranks 5 and 6. The point midway between these is 5.5. If four people shared 6 7 8 9, the shared rank would be 7.5.

Here we have converted data which were at a higher, more informative level (interval data, which we will discuss below), into *ordinal level* data. The *scores* are interval level; the *ranks* are ordinal.

Comparison of ordinal level with nominal and interval levels

Figure 10.1 shows that you are a *lot* shorter than Simon and similar to Julie. If you were sensitive about your height the nominal level classification would not have pleased you, since you would have been given the category 'tall'. All we'd know is that you were somewhere in the 'tall' group. The ordinal level hasn't helped much since now you are given a position of seventh – that's all we know; you are the second tallest in your group. Ordinal scales, in a sense, take frequencies out of their nominal box and onto a dimension, so we know the *positions* of people, but they don't give us the vital information about *distance between* positions.

Interval level of measurement

At the INTERVAL LEVEL of measurement you would feel a lot happier. As this level of measurement uses a scale with *equal units*, we can show now that you are a lot closer to sixth than eighth in your group on height. The distance on the scale from 160–165 cms is the same as that between 170–175 cms, for instance. But what about *psychological* scales? If these were interval scales then it ought to be true that:

a) Two children scoring five and eight respectively on an achievement scale are as far apart in motivation to achieve as two children scoring nine and 12.

b) Jane, whose IQ is 100, is as far ahead of John (IQ 80) in intelligence as Jackie (IQ 120) is ahead of Jane.

In practice it is hard to believe that most psychological measures operate in this seemingly accurate and scientific manner. However, it is the job of psychometrists to ensure that scales approach this criterion as closely as possible and that was one of the main objectives of *standardisation* procedures covered at the end of Chapter 7. It should be that intervals on a good test operate like intervals on the publicly accurate measures we are used to in everyday life – rulers, scales, air pumps, thermometers – where equal intervals represent equal changes in the phenomenon which is measured. Test creators attempt to standardise, often to a *normal distribution* – see p. 251 – so that the test produces the same *proportions* of people along the points of a scale as would any physical measure.

However, we must be careful not to be seduced by the seemingly clinical accuracy of numbers used as measures. Suppose you receive 60 for your essay whilst Tim gets 50 and Sean gets 40. This does not mean that the difference between Tim's and Sean's essays is equal to the difference between yours and Tim's. In UK higher education establishments, essays are very often graded on a time-honoured but actually rather peculiar scale that has a wider area for failed work – 0 to 40 – than it does for the whole range from barely passable to the start of the first class category, 40–70! On this sort of measure, even where tutors standardise very carefully, it would be safer to assume that the grades are really on an *ordinal* scale. It would probably be uncontroversial to claim that your essay is *better* than Tim's and that Tim's is better than Sean's. In the same way, although the temperature scale certainly uses equal intervals (based on expansion of mercury, for instance), the *experience* of heat changes would be better treated as an ordinal measure. An increase of 3° in a room originally at 14° will be noticed as more of a change than the same increase from 33°. Many psychological measures behave in a way that prompted Wright (1976) to call them 'plastic interval' scales. For instance, on an attitude item, it might well take a bigger shift for someone to move from 'agree' to 'strongly agree' than from 'undecided' to 'agree'. Intervals along the scale are not equal yet the familiarity of numbers can induce us to treat them as such.

So what sort of scale were my questionnaire data on then?

As a general rule of thumb, wherever data are gathered on an unstandardised, invented scale of human judgement – such as rating an observed aggressive act on a scale of 1 to 10, or adding up response codes to several Likert type items – it would be safer to treat the data as being on an ordinal scale. This simply means ranking the numerical data as explained earlier.

Ratio level of measurement

We saw above that it would be odd to treat the intervals on an essay marking scheme as equal. It would be odder still to talk as if *ratios* of marks on the scale made the kind of sense that number ratios usually make. For instance, would it make sense to say that your mark of 60 shows that your essay was one and a half times better than Sean's at 40? Or that a 40 mark essay is twice as good as a 20 mark essay. Even the temperature scale won't work like this. Can we say that 30°C is twice as hot as 15°C? Although the *number* 30 is twice 15, on a Fahrenheit scale the temperatures represented by these numbers would be 86°F and 59°F and the second is now no longer half of the first. This is simply because both these temperature scales (and several others) do not start from an *absolute zero* point. Similarly, even if we accept IQ as measured on an interval scale, it makes no sense to say that a person with an IQ of 120 is twice as intelligent as a person with 60, since IQ scales are not calibrated from a true zero point. Likewise, an introversion score of zero doesn't permit us to talk of a person having a complete absence of extroversion, to such an extent that no person could ever have less extroversion!

Ratio scales are interval type scales that start from a real and absolute zero point and on these scales ratios of values *do* make sense – six pounds is twice three pounds in the absolute sense, otherwise we couldn't argue with a shopkeeper over short weight. Typical ratio scales are all the measures of physical quantities we are familiar with, including weight, length, time, pressure, and so on.

The unremarkable difference between interval and ratio scales (for the psychologist)

A writer once enquired in *The Psychologist* (the bulletin of the British Psychological Society) why a psychologist would ever need to distinguish between interval and ratio level data. Would this make any difference in terms of what statistical test or treatment should be applied to their data? No one, so far as I know, has ever replied. In practice, as a student of psychology, you will not need to worry about the difference between interval and ratio scales except perhaps to state what the difference is. For the purposes of choosing an appropriate statistical test, covered in Chapter 20, they can be treated as exactly the same thing and you need only justify your data as being of *at least* interval level status.

Reducing data from one level to a lower one

We have seen above, with the example of attributing responsibility for an attack, that data originally collected at a certain level *cannot* be elevated to a higher level. Information which has not been gathered at the time of collection cannot usually be added later when data are being analysed. What you took is all you use. However, the reverse process

Table 10.5 Reducing data from interval to nominal level

Number of anxiety indicators observed:					
	Level of competitiveness			**Level of competitiveness**	
	High	**Low**		**High**	**Low**
			Position on anxiety indicators		
	14	10			
	21	6	Above mean (>11.8)	4	1
	7	13	Below mean (<11.8)	1	4
	13	5			
	18	11			
Mean	14.6	9.0			
Mean for all children = 11.8					

is very common – that of *reducing* data from a higher level in order to treat them at a lower and simpler level. We saw an example of this – reducing interval level data to ordinal – in Table 10.4. It is quite common to reduce interval level data like that shown in Table 10.5 to a nominal level. This is done by grouping together those above and below the overall average for the whole sample and comparing this with another variable, in this case, high and low competitiveness (the mean average will be dealt with technically on p. 228). The values on the left of the table have been categorised as above/below the mean of all anxiety values (11.8) and these frequencies are shown on the right of the table. These right hand frequencies are obtained by noting that four children in the high competitive group are above 11.8 and only one below, whereas only one of the 'Low competitive' children is above the anxiety indicator mean.

Continuous and discrete scales of measurement

A further division of scales is possible, into DISCRETE or CONTINUOUS. On discrete scales each point is entirely separate from the next; there are no real points in between. It is not possible to have two-and-a-half children, for instance. In a memory experiment you can only recall a discrete number of words – although the *mean* may take a non-real value of 14.3. On *continuous* scales there is no limit to the sub-divisions of points which are possible and meaningful, though there will be limits in practice, depending on the type of measuring instrument used, e.g. down to millimetres on a household ruler. It is theoretically possible to measure your height to the nearest thousandth of a millimetre; technically this might be difficult and in practice, hardly likely to be useful. In practice, interval and ratio scales can be either continuous or discrete. Nominal categories can only be discrete. Ordinal scales generally have 0.5 as the smallest division. Figure 10.2 gives examples of some different types of measure.

In general, psychological scales, such as IQ, and measures like number of words recalled from a 20-word list, are treated as continuous for statistical purposes and generally this has little effect, if any, on statistical analysis. It is important to note that with a truly interval scale we avoid the issue of measuring to the nearest thousandth of a millimetre

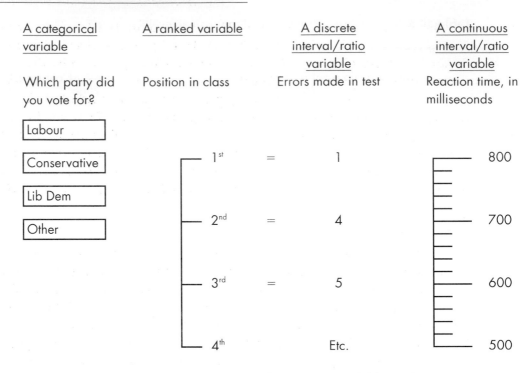

Figure 10.2   Categorical, ranked, discrete and continuous variables

or whatever by using *intervals*. We say that someone's height is between 174.5 and 175.5 cm rather than that they are exactly 175 cm tall (explained further under 'Range' in the next chapter). There would rarely be anyone *exactly* 174.50000 cm tall, falling precisely on the interval boundary, so, should this rare event occur, we could place them in this interval, or the preceding one, by the toss of a coin.

PART 2 – DESCRIPTIVE STATISTICS

SUMMARISING DATA – STATISTICS ARE A SELECTION

In this section, we are looking simply at the ways in which statistical information can be summarised and presented to a reader. Statistical information follows from organising the numerical data gathered during quantitative research. Most research gathers far too much information for every little bit of it to be presented. When a survey of political attitude is conducted, or an experiment is run on 35 participants, we end up with a DATA SET. This would be the individual scores on each item of the attitude questionnaire or the scores of the experimental participants on the dependent variable(s). These are the RAW DATA gathered in the study which we wish to summarise and analyse. Tables 10.2, 10.3, 10.5, 10.6 and 10.7 show *data sets*, though the *raw data* for Table 10.2, Table 10.3 and Table 10.7 would *originally* have been the tallies taken as cases were counted.

We summarise data because it is not useful to be given all the untreated and unorganised raw data. The whole data set doesn't tell us much without looking very carefully. If it is a large data set it can just be overwhelming. Hence we need to abstract and highlight from the data set any major trends or differences. However, it is important to note that the very act of summarising introduces distortions. We will be given what the researcher *decides* is the most important information and this will be presented in what is believed to be the most appropriate manner. Politicians and companies, among others, are renowned for presenting data in the best possible light. *A psychologist should be looking at the best way to present data **only** in terms of what gives the clearest, least ambiguous picture of what was found in a research study.* What is more, the raw data set should be kept available for any other researcher to query and perhaps look at in a different, selective way in order to argue against some of the original researcher's initial conclusions. This is what companies very often do *not* do, and politicians would be very often *loathe* to do!

But I can't do sums!

As with many ideas in this book, the things we will study are based on everyday common-sense notions you have undoubtedly used before. Even if you hate maths, dread statistics and have never done any formal work in this area, you have undoubtedly made statistical descriptions many times in your life without necessarily being aware of it. You may believe that only clever, numerically minded people do this sort of thing, but consider this. Imagine you have just come home from your first day on a new college course and I ask you what sort of age are your class colleagues. You would not proceed to tell me the exact age of each class member. This could take far too long. You'd be likely to say something like 'Well, most people in the class are around 25 years old but there are a couple of teenagers and one or two are over 40.' You have in fact summarised the class ages statistically, albeit rather loosely. First you gave me a rough *average*, the typical age in the group, then you gave me an idea of the actual *variation* from this typical age present in the group. These two concepts are absolutely *fundamental* to statistical description of measured data. Here we have an example of going from concepts which *naturally* occur to you in everyday life to a more formalised version of the same thing for statistical purposes, using the terms:

CENTRAL TENDENCY   This generally refers to the *centre* of the data set. It is the value in a group of values which is the most *typical* for the group, or the score which all other scores are evenly clustered around. In normal language, this is better and more loosely known as 'the average'. In statistical description, though, we have to be more precise about just what *sort* of average we mean.

DISPERSION   This is a measure of the extent to which all the values in a set tend to *vary* around the central or typical value.

Let's look at these aspects of description in a little more detail. Have a look at the data in Table 10.6.

> Before looking at the comments which follow this box, see what conclusions you can come to about the talking of girls and boys.

Overall, the girls speak just about twice the amount that boys do. We would see this if we calculated the *average* for each group. But not only this, the boys' times vary very

Table 10.6 Time spent talking during 10 minutes of observation of five-year-old male and female nursery children (in seconds)

Male children	Female children
132	332
34	345
5	289
237	503
450	367

widely compared with those of the girls', from as little as five seconds to nearly the highest girl's time.

MEASURES OF CENTRAL TENDENCY

The mean

In normal language we use the term 'average' for what is technically known as the ARITHMETIC MEAN. This is what we get when we add up all the values in a data set and then divide by the total *number* of values. Hence, if five people took 5, 2, 12, 1 and 10 seconds to solve an anagram, the mean time taken is:

$$\frac{5 + 2 + 12 + 1 + 10}{5} = \frac{30}{5} = 6 \text{ seconds}$$

The symbol used to denote the mean of a **population** is μ

The symbol for a **sample mean** is $\bar{x}$

Usually in psychological studies we treat the data we have as a *sample* of a population (see Chapter 2). The formula for calculating the mean is:

$$\bar{x} = \frac{\Sigma x}{N}$$

Finding the mean

This is our first encounter with a formula. A formula is only a short hand set of instructions, rather like following a recipe or instructions for Dr Jekyll's magic potion. In the example above we are told to:

1. Add up all values in the data set (Σx)
2. Divide by the *total number* of values (N)

Σ is a symbol which simply means 'add up each of what follows' and in the formula for the mean above what follows is x. For x you can read 'each score'. So we simply add up all the scores and divide the result by N – but you probably knew this, at least in an informal way. There is a section at the end of this chapter on notation and the rules for following a formula. I hope this will help you if it's some time since you did any 'sums' or hated them (or thought they were pointless). Rest assured that the *only* mathematical operations you need to perform, in going through this book, are the four junior school operations ('+' '−'

Figure 10.3   One rogue value can distort the mean

'×' '÷') and squares (which are multiplication anyway) and square roots (which are always found at the touch of a button). All work *can* be done on the simplest of calculators but, of course, and certainly towards the end of the book, computer programmes can make life a lot easier.

A note on decimals and spurious accuracy, before we go any further

Very often, in a student report, and sometimes because unformatted computer programmes are to blame, the mean of 9, 7, 7, 5, 4, 3 might be reported as '5.8333'. The last three decimal figures add nothing at all to accuracy since the original numbers were *whole*. They represented *intervals* like 6.5 to 7.5, so the answer just cannot be that accurate, i.e. to ten thousandths of a whole! A general rule of thumb is to round to *one place below* the original intervals. Hence, here the appropriate mean value would be 5.8 At times this book breaks this rule, usually just to show that two calculations give the same answer. Rounding processes can sometimes make this not appear to be so.

Advantages and disadvantages of the mean

The mean has the particular property of being the exact mid-point of all the combined scores. It acts rather like the fulcrum of a scale as I hope Figure 10.4 will demonstrate. If you balance equal weights on a pivoted 12 inch ruler at the points marked 1, 2, 5, 10 and 12 (our set of data points above) you will find that the ruler balances at the point designated by our mean i.e. 6.

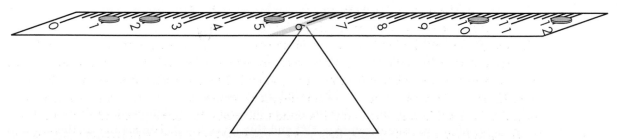

Figure 10.4   The mean as a central balancing point among values

Advantages

- The mean is a powerful statistic used in estimating *population parameters* (see page 238) and this estimation is the basis for the more powerful tests we can use to look for significant results – *t* tests (Chapter 14), Pearson's correlation (Chapter 15) and the ANOVA procedures (Chapter 17).
- It is the most sensitive and accurate of the three measures described here (because it works at an *interval* level of measurement and uses the greatest amount of information available).
- It is very quick to calculate and available on many calculators.

Disadvantages

- Because the mean *is* so sensitive there is also a problem that it is easily distorted by one, or a few, 'rogue' and unrepresentative values. For instance, if we had six people doing our anagram task (p. 228)and the sixth person took 60 seconds to find the solution, then the total would now be 90 seconds and our mean would become 15 seconds. This value for the mean is quite unrepresentative of the group as a whole. No one from the other five people actually scored even as high as this new mean.
- Single 'rogues' or 'outlier' values can distort the mean; *equal* rogues, but in opposite directions, tend to cancel one another out.
- A further small disadvantage of the mean is that with *discrete* variables we get 'silly' values for the mean and this is sometimes misleading or at least distracting – for instance the notorious case of parents with 2.4 children.

The median

Using the median gets us around the main disadvantage of the mean – that extreme scores give a distorted value. The mean is particularly sensitive to these. The median is the *central* value of a set. If we have an odd number of values in a small data set then this couldn't be easier to find. The central value of our first five anagram solution times above is the third one. To find this we must first put all five in numerical order. This gives:

1, 2, 5, 10, 12   The median is **5**   (1)

If there is an even number of values, as with our sixth person's time added, we take the mean of the two central values, thus:

1, 2, 5, 10, 12, 60   The median is $\dfrac{5 + 10}{2} = \mathbf{7.5}$ (2)

Notice that this value is still reasonably representative of the group of values.

Finding the median

If there are an *odd number of values in the data set:*

1. Find the MEDIAN POSITION or LOCATION. This is the place where we will find the median value. This is at $(N + 1)/2$. Call this position '*k*'
2. *k* will be a whole number. The median is the score at the *k*th position. In the set of 5 scores above we would get: $(5 + 1)/2$ and this gives $k = 3$. The median is the score in the *third* position when the data are ordered.

If there are an *even number of values in the data set:*
1. Find the median position, as above. It will be midway between two whole numbers. Where we had six values above we would get $k = (6 + 1)/2 = 3.5$.
2. The median is midway between the third and fourth values.

If there are *several* tied values *in the data set (e.g. 7, 7, 7, 8, 8, 8, 9, 9, 10, 10)*

Here, there are two possible approaches – the rough and ready, and the fastidiously correct. Which you use depends on the purpose at hand and also on the collection of values in your data set. The rough and ready approach says use the usual formula. Here we have an even set of numbers, ten in all, so the median is midway between the fifth and sixth values, i.e. 8. This will do for many purposes and even the statistical programme *SPSS* goes no further. After all, 8 is pretty representative of the set.

However, technically, what we require for the median is a position, *within the interval* 7.5 to 8.5, where the median would fall, based on the proportions of scores either side of it. To be absolutely accurate then we would use the procedure below. However, this procedure, though complicated, is also very useful (in fact necessary, unless you're doing computerised statistics) where you have a very large data set and the results are organised into frequency categories as in Table 10.7.

Table 10.7 Large frequency table – number of people smoking *N* cigarettes per day

N =	None	1–5	6–10	11–20	21–30	31–40	41+
	65	45	78	32	11	4	3

The formula to find the median here is:

$$\text{Median} = L + \frac{N/2 - F}{f_m} \times h$$

where:
L = exact lower limit of interval containing median
F = total number of values below L
f_m = number of values in interval containing median
h = size of class interval
N = total number of values in data set

So, for the cigarette smoking data in Table 10.7, we would need to substitute values. The categories 1–5, 6–10, 11–20 etc. in Table 10.7 are called CLASS INTERVALS. Notice that in this example they are not all the same size. Here, it is difficult to see where the median could be. There are 238 cases altogether so the median is the value above and below which 119 of all cases fall. This must be somewhere in the 6–10 category. The formula assumes that values in this category are evenly spread throughout it. So L is 5.5: this is the exact start of the 6–10 interval – see the point made towards the end of the section on the range, below. F is 110, f_m is 78, h is 5 and N is 238. Putting these values into the formula we get:

$$\text{median} = 5.5 + \frac{238/2 - 110}{78} \times 5 = \mathbf{6.08}$$

I'll leave you to calculate the median for the small set of tied values above. The answer you should get, if you feel it is worthwhile having a go at this, is **8.16**

Advantages and disadvantages of the median

Advantages

- Unaffected by extreme or 'rogue' values in one direction. Hence, better for use with 'skewed' distributions – see later in this chapter.
- Easier to calculate than the mean (as long as there are small groups and no ties or the tied scores situation is overlooked).
- Can be obtained when the *value* of extreme scores is unknown.

Disadvantages

- Doesn't take into account the exact values of each item in the data set.
- Can't be used in estimates of population parameters.
- In a small data set, can be unrepresentative; for instance, with 2, 3, 5, 98, 112 the median would be 5.

The mode

If we have data on a nominal scale, as with categories of play in Table 10.3, we cannot calculate a mean or a median. We can, however, say which type of play was engaged in most, i.e. which category had the highest frequency count. This is what is known as the MODE or MODAL VALUE. It is the most frequently occurring value and therefore even easier to find than the mean or median. The mode of the set of numbers:

1, 2, 3, 3, 3, 4, 4, 4, 5, 5, 5, 5, 5, 5, 6, 6, 7, 7, 7, 8

is therefore **5** since this value occurs most often. For the set of anagram solving times there is no single modal value since each time occurs once only. For the set of numbers 7, 7, 7, 8, 8, 9, 9, 9, 10, 10, there are two modes, 7 and 9, and the set is said to be BI-MODAL (see Figure 10.25). For the table of play categories, the modal value is parallel play. Be careful here to note that the mode is *not the number of times* the most frequent value occurs but that value itself. Parallel play occurred most often.

The mode is the *only* measure of central tendency that can be used with nominal level data but is also often a more comfortable alternative with discrete measurement scales, avoiding the gruesome unreality of '2.4 children' and giving us the *typical* family statistic of, say, 2 children.

Advantages and disadvantages of the mode

Advantages

- Shows the most frequent or 'typical' value of a data set.
- Unaffected by extreme values in one direction.
- Can be obtained when extreme values are unknown.
- Often more informative than mean when scale is discrete.

Disadvantages

- Doesn't take into account the exact value of each item.
- Can't be used in estimates of population parameters.

- Not at all useful for relatively small sets of data where several values occur equally frequently (1, 1, 2, 3, 4, 4).
- For bi-modal distributions (see p. 257), two modal values need to be reported.
- Can't be estimated accurately when data are grouped into class intervals. We can have a modal interval – like 6–10 cigarettes in Table 10.7 – but this may change if the data are categorised differently.

Central tendency measures and levels of measurement

Interval/ratio

The mean is the most sensitive measure but should only be used where data are at least at the interval level of measurement. Otherwise, the mean is calculated on numbers which don't represent equal amounts and is misleading.

Ordinal

If data are not at interval level but can be ranked then the median is the appropriate measure of central tendency.

Nominal

If data are in discreetly separate categories, then only the mode can be used.
The mode *may* also be used on ordinal and interval level data.
The median *may* also be used on interval level data.

MEASURES OF DISPERSION

Think back to the description of new college classmates. The central tendency was given as 25 but some 'guesstimate' was also given of the way people spread around this central point. Without knowledge of spread (or, more technically, DISPERSION), a mean can be very misleading. Take a look at the bowling performance of two cricketers shown in Figure 10.5. Both average around the middle stump but (a) varies much more than (b). The attempts of (a) are far more widely dispersed. Average wages in two companies may be the same but distribution of wages may be very different.

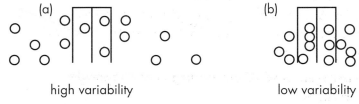

high variability   low variability

Figure 10.5 Dispersion in bowlers' deliveries

Variation ratio

This measure of dispersion is appropriate for data where the central tendency used is the mode. **5** was the mode of the set of data given opposite and the variation ratio is simply the proportion of the total number of values which are not at the modal value. There were 20 values and 14 of these were not the modal value of 5. That is:

$$\text{VARIATION RATIO} = \frac{\text{number of non-modal values}}{\text{total number of values}} = \frac{14}{20} = 0.7$$

Advantages and disadvantages of the variation ratio

Advantage

Unaffected by extreme values in the data set.

Disadvantage

Takes no account of grouping around centre *or* of range of spread.

The range

Remember that we said that the talking times of girls in Table 10.6 tended to vary far less than did the boys. The simplest way to measure the variation among a set of values is to use what is called the RANGE. This is simply the distance between the top and bottom values of a set.

Finding the range

1. Find top value of the set
2. Find bottom value of the set
3. Subtract bottom value from top value and add 1

For Table 10.6 this gives:

Boys $(450 - 5) + 1 = \mathbf{446}$
Girls $(503 - 289) + 1 = \mathbf{215}$

Why add 1?

The addition of 1 may seem a little strange. Surely the distance between 5 and 450 is, straightforwardly, 445? The addition of 1 allows for possible measurement error. When we say that a child spoke for 5 seconds, if our lowest unit of measurement is 1 second, then we can only claim that the child spoke for something between 4.5 and 5.5 seconds, the limits of our lowest measurement interval. If we had measured to *tenths* of a second then 4.3 seconds represents a value between 4.25 and 4.35. Hence, the range is measured from the lowest possible limit of the lowest value to the highest limit of the highest value. In the case of boys' talking times this is 4.5 to 450.5

Advantages and disadvantages of the range

Advantages

*   Easy to calculate.
*   Includes extreme values.

Disadvantages

*   Distorted by, and unrepresentative with, extreme values.
*   Unrepresentative of any features of the distribution of values between the extremes. For instance, the range doesn't tell us whether or not the values are closely grouped around the mean.

The interquartile range and semi-interquartile range

So far our measures have not taken account of the *distribution* of scores within the two extreme limits, apart from knowing, with the variation ratio, what proportion of scores were not modal. The interquartile range deals specifically with the *central* grouping of values in a set. Specifically it represents the distance between the two values which cut off the bottom and top 25% of scores. These two values are known as the twenty-fifth and seventy-fifth PERCENTILES, or the first and third QUARTILES respectively. (We shall deal with these more precisely in a while.) The *semi*-interquartile range is *half* of the distance between these two values.

In the following data set:

3, 3, 4, 5, 6, 8, 10, 13, 14, 16, 19

4 is the first quartile and 14 the third quartile. The distance between these is **10** (the INTERQUARTILE RANGE) and half this (the SEMI-INTERQUARTILE RANGE) is **5**.

Finding the interquartile and semi-interquartile range
The inter-quartile range is: $Q^3 - Q^1$

The semi-interquartile range is half of this value, that is: $\dfrac{Q^3 - Q^1}{2}$

The procedure is as follows:
1. Find the first quartile (Q^1) and the third quartile (Q^3). For most purposes (as with the rough and ready median) you can use the twenty-fifth and the seventy-fifth highest scores respectively. A formula for finding exact percentiles is given later.
2. Subtract Q^1 from Q^3 – this gives the interquartile range.
3. Divide the result of step two by 2 – this gives the semi-interquartile range.

Advantages and disadvantages of the semi-interquartile range
Advantage
Is representative of the central grouping of values in the data set.

Disadvantages
● Takes no account of extreme values.
● Inaccurate where there are large class intervals (i.e., where first and third quartiles cannot be accurately identified.

The mean deviation

An important way of looking at the spread of scores in a set is to use the concept of DEVIATION. A DEVIATION VALUE is simply the amount by which a particular score deviates from the mean. This is the *difference* between any particular value and the mean. For instance, if the mean average shoe size in your class is 6 and you take a 4, your deviation score is **−2** (note the negative value as you are *under* the mean – we always take $x - \bar{x}$, e.g. $4 - 6$, in this case, which comes to −2).

Table 10.8 Deviations of IQ scores from the mean

Score (x)	Mean ($\bar{x}$)	Deviation (d) (x − $\bar{x}$)	Squared deviation (d^2) (x − $\bar{x}$)^2
85	100	−15	225
90	100	−10	100
100	100	0	0
110	100	10	100
115	100	15	225
		$\Sigma d =$ 0	$\Sigma d^2 = 650$

The MEAN DEVIATION is then the mean of all the deviations. Let's do an example. Suppose you and five others took an IQ test with the following results:

Hugh	Helga	Harry	Helena	You
85	90	100	110	115

The mean is 100 and your personal deviation score is 115 − 100 = **15**.

If we are going to *summarise* dispersion in terms of people's deviations from the mean, it seems sensible to report the *average* of all the deviations in the set. The set of deviations for the IQ scores above is shown in Table 10.8 – ignore the column headed 'squared deviation' for now.

The sum of these deviations is zero and therefore the mean of the deviations would also be zero. This isn't what we wanted. If you look back to Figure 10.4 you can see why this has happened. The means sits precisely in the centre of all the deviations around it. Values above the mean have a positive (+) deviation and those below have a negative (−) value. When added together all these will exactly cancel each other out. The deviations from Figure 10.4, where the mean is 6, are, from left to right: **−5 −4 −1 +4** and **+6**; both the negative and positive sets add to 10 and cancel each other out. What we want is the average of those deviations, *ignoring their sign*. This value is known as their ABSOLUTE VALUE. This is represented mathematically by two vertical bars either side of a number – e.g. $| -10 | = 10$. So, for the absolute value of a deviation score we would write $| x - \bar{x} |$ or just $| d |$ if we already know the value.

Finding the mean deviation

The *formula* for the mean deviation is

$$MD = \frac{\Sigma | x - \bar{x} |}{N}$$

To step through this equation, calculate as follows:
1. Find the mean ($\bar{x}$).
2. Subtract the mean from each score or value in the data set (x − $\bar{x}$) to obtain a set of *deviations* (d).
3. Add up all these deviations taking no notice of any minus signs, i.e. find $\Sigma | d |$.
4. Divide result of step three by N.

Using this on our IQ data we get:

$\Sigma | d | = 15 + 10 + 0 + 10 + 15 = 50$;

$$MD = \frac{50}{5} = 10$$

Advantages and disadvantages of the mean deviation
Advantage

Takes account of all values in the data set.

Disadvantage

Not possible to use in making estimates of population parameters – see *standard deviation*, to follow.

The standard deviation and variance

We saw above that the average of all deviations in a data set comes to zero, since the positive and negative signs all balance and cancel out. Another way to remove the negative signs in Table 10.8 is to add up the *squares* of each deviation, that is each d^2. The mean of all these values (i.e. $\Sigma d^2 / N$) is a rather large figure and is known as the VARIANCE of the data set. To return to the same level of value we were at originally, we calculate the *square root of the variance* and this is known as the STANDARD DEVIATION of the set.

Populations and samples

The standard deviation and variance play a central and extremely important role in statistics, particularly in the estimation of *population parameters* – that is estimating from a sample how the scores of a population are distributed. They are also used in *inferential testing* – where we make judgements about the *significance* of differences or correlations. Because of this important role for these statistics, there are two versions of the variance and the standard deviation, the 'uncorrected' and the 'unbiased (population estimate)' versions. These are explained in the boxes below.

The 'uncorrected' or 'population' variance and standard deviation

This version is used when you treat your data set as an isolated group. i.e., you are *not* involved in making a population estimate, you are not using the statistic as part of a significance test, and you are only interested in the data set itself, not in any generalisations from it. You just want the standard deviation of the group and no more.

The 'unbiased' population estimate variance and standard deviation

This version is the most commonly used and it is usually best to use this version if you're unsure. It is used when the data set is treated as a *sample* of a population from which it was drawn. This is almost always the case in psychological studies. The variance and standard deviation are a powerful part of significance testing – assessing whether a difference between samples can safely be assumed to represent a difference between underlying populations. See the section below on population parameters.

Symbols

Sample standard deviation	S	Sample standard deviation	s
Sample variance	S^2	Sample variance	s^2
	Population standard deviation	σ	
	Population variance	σ^2	

Finding the standard deviation

Let's calculate both versions of the variance and standard deviation for the data set in Table 10.8:

Formula for standard deviation ('uncorrected')	Formula for standard deviation ('unbiased estimate')
(Note that the formula for variance in each case simply omits the square root sign)	
$$S = \sqrt{\frac{\Sigma d^2}{N}} \quad (1)$$	$$s = \sqrt{\frac{\Sigma d^2}{(N-1)}} \quad (2)$$
1. Calculate the mean of the data set: = 100	= 100
2. Subtract the mean from each value in the data set: see Table 10.8	see Table 10.8
3. Square each deviation: see Table 10.8	see Table 10.8
4. Find the sum of the squared deviations: 650	650

5. Divide result of step 4 by N
  $S^2 = 130$
	5. Divide result of step 4 by $N - 1$
	  $s^2 = 162.5$

You have now found the *variance* of the data set. Continue to find the standard deviation:

6. Find the square root of step 5: $S = 11.4$	$s = 12.75$

Variance calculation without finding deviations

There is a version of the formula for sample variance ('unbiased estimate' version) which avoids the calculation of deviations and for which you only need the set of scores and their total:

$$s^2 = \left(\frac{\Sigma x^2 - (\Sigma x)^2/N}{N - 1} \right)$$

The standard deviation would be the square root of this value. In later work this is a highly important equation, especially in the whole area of significance testing using *Analysis of Variance* (Chapters 20–22).

If you do use this formula, beware of the difference between Σx^2 and $(\Sigma x)^2$ (explained at the end of this chapter).

POPULATION PARAMETERS, SAMPLE STATISTICS AND SAMPLING ERROR

The consideration of two different variance calculations above introduces a central notion in statistical work. Measures of a *sample*, known as SAMPLE STATISTICS, are very frequently used to *estimate* the same measures of a *population*, known as POPULATION PARAMETERS. The measures concerned are most often the mean and variance. We are not

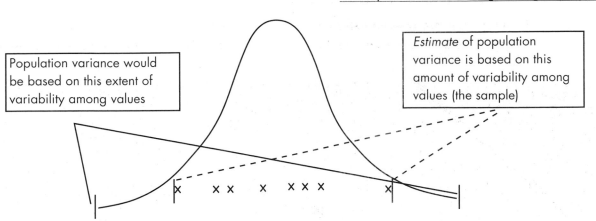

Figure 10.6 Variability of sample and population

usually able to assess whether two populations differ on a certain variable. Either populations are too large, or they may be infinite (such as all the scores we could ever gather on a memory task). We draw samples and assume that the sample statistics reflect the populations as a whole. Whenever we do this we will naturally be a bit out. This 'bit' is known as SAMPLING ERROR. Population estimates are used in conducting certain kinds of *parametric test* which are very powerful and most likely to give us an accurate assessment of whether or not we should accept sample differences as significant, representing a real difference between the underlying populations, given certain assumptions about our data. We shall discuss the role of these estimates further when we encounter the '*t* tests' in Chapter 14.

For now, notice from Figure 10.6 that the variance of a sample will almost always be smaller than the variance of the population it is drawn from, because the sample is *most likely* to draw individual values from near the centre of the distribution – see next section. The general spread (or 'variability') of the sample will be narrower than that of the population. Hence, to make some correction for this we divide by $N - 1$ in the variance equation, rather than just N. Since we are now dividing by a smaller number, the resulting value for variance will be larger and this to some extent compensates for the 'error' in estimating the population variance from the sample variance. When N is very large, the subtraction of 1 will make very little difference at all.

Advantages and disadvantages of the standard deviation or variance
Advantages
- Can be used in population parameter estimates.
- Takes account of all values.
- Is the most sensitive of measures covered.
- Can be calculated directly on many calculators.

Disadvantage
- Somewhat more complicated to calculate (if you don't have an appropriate calculator!).
- Distorted by extreme values in one direction.

Dispersion measures and levels of measurement

Interval/ratio

The *variance* and *standard deviation* are most appropriate for interval level data and above and are associated with the mean. Where populations are particularly *skewed* (see p. 256) a ranked measure might be preferred.

Ordinal

The interquartile range and semi-interquartile range depend upon ranked positions and are not affected by extreme values. They are associated with the median.

Nominal

The variation ratio depends upon the mode and non-modal frequencies.

The mean deviation is associated with the mean but the range is not associated with any central tendency measure.

DISTRIBUTIONS

So far we have looked at summaries of data only in terms of their numerical central tendency and dispersion. This is usually all that is necessary for a small data set, for example, scores on a memory task for 10 experimental participants, though we might like to inspect the set for extreme values which are distorting the mean. However, where a large data set has been gathered we would often like to look more closely at the overall DISTRIBUTION formed by our data. We can pick out patterns here which cannot be seen in a small sample simply because there are not enough repetitions of the same or similar values for us to be able to consider the *frequency* with which these occur. With a large enough sample, we can estimate the shape of the distribution for the whole population from which the sample was drawn and this is central to the development of psychological and educational tests.

In Table 10.9, on the left hand side are the raw scores of 30 participants who have been given an extroversion test. On the right hand side, these have been drawn up into a FREQUENCY DISTRIBUTION (or 'frequency table') which shows the score category (column 1 – sometimes called 'bins'), the number or frequency of people obtaining that score (column 2 – the number in the 'bin'), and the CUMULATIVE FREQUENCY which is the total *so far* of all the frequencies up to and including that category.

The data in Table 10.9 are grouped into categories representing a single score on the extroversion test. Where data are spread across very many possible values, this may not be a very useful approach. If, for instance, we gathered data from parents on the number of telegraphic utterances their 21 month-old children made in a single day we might obtain values ranging from 1 to 78 utterances. This could produce a very long frequency table with 78 categories, yet there might be only one or two occurrences in each one. Here we would group the data into broader categories as has happened in Table 10.10.

Notice here that, technically, each class interval has limits half an interval *beyond* the range of values given for each category. That is, the 10–19 interval, strictly speaking, runs from 9.5 to 19.5 so that if we had a value somewhere *between* 9 and 10 we would know how to decide into which category interval it fell. However, since 'number of utterances' is measured on a *discrete* scale (we can only have a whole number of utterances), this is not

Table 10.9 Frequencies of extroversion scores

Raw individual extroversion scores (N = 30)			Frequency table		
			(1) Score	**(2)** Frequency	**(3)** Cumulative frequency
8	9	9	8	1	1
10	10	10	9	2	3
10	11	11	10	4	7
11	11	11	11	6	13
11	12	12	12	5	18
12	12	12	13	3	21
13	13	13	14	2	23
14	14	15	15	2	25
15	16	16	16	3	28
16	18	18	17	0	28
			18	2	30
			$N = \Sigma =$ **30**		

Table 10.10 Frequencies of 21-month-old children by number of telegraphic utterances in one day

No. of telegraphic utterances	No. of children	Cumulative frequency
0– 9	3	3
10–19	0	3
20–29	15	18
30–39	43	61
40–49	69	130
50–59	17	147
60–69	24	171
70–79	4	175
$N = \Sigma = 175$		

Table 10.11 Frequencies of search times by 10 second intervals

Time taken to locate 'Y' in a search list			
Time interval (secs)	Frequency (participants)	Cumulative frequency	Class interval limits
10–19	3	3	9.5 to 19.5
20–29	7	10	19.5 to 29.5
30–39	19	29	29.5 to 39.5
40–49	21	50	39.5 to 49.5
50–59	26	76	49.5 to 59.5
60–69	8	84	59.5 to 69.5

a problem here, and calling the intervals 10–19 presents no decision difficulties. However, where we use a *continuous* scale we must be very careful to recognise class interval limits. In Table 10.11 we see a summary of participants' times taken for a visual search for a 'Y' hidden among a page of 'X's. Times are measured on a continuous scale so a value of 19.4 falls into the '10–19' category, whereas 19.7 falls into '20–29'. For the very rare value that falls right on the division when rounded (e.g. 19.50), we simply toss a coin to decide in which category it should be counted.

GRAPHICAL REPRESENTATION

To demonstrate to our readers the characteristics of a distribution more clearly, we can draw up a pictorial representation of the data. One of the advantages of doing this is that the mode will be immediately apparent, as will other features, such as the rate at which numbers fall off to either side and any specially interesting clusters of data. A graphical presentation can also be justified by its immediate appeal to the eye.

Charts are summaries – do not draw the raw data!

Many students like to draw a chart of their results with a single column representing each participant's score. **Please don't be tempted to do this.** The resulting chart has no order – participants could be arranged in *any* order along the *x*-axis – their position is arbitrary and the chart resembles an unruly set of mountain peaks and valleys. Worse, the chart tells us nothing we don't already see from the raw data set. It shows us everything in a way that tells us nothing general. What we want from a chart is an overall picture of any *pattern* in our data.

The histogram

A histogram is a way of showing the pattern of the *whole* data set to a reader. It communicates information about the *shape* of the distribution of scores found. The extroversion score data from Table 10.9 are depicted in a histogram in Figure 10.7.

Note that each category (or 'bin') of the frequency table is represented by one vertical bar. Frequency is usually shown on the *y*- (vertical) axis and the scale or class intervals on the *x*-axis. All the bars are joined because the chart represents a continuous and whole group of scores, and therefore a gap must be left where a category is empty (see the column for 17), except at the ends of the distribution. Each column is the same width, and since the height of each column represents the number of values found in that category, it follows that the *area* of each column is proportional to the number of cases it represents throughout the histogram. It also follows that the total of all column areas represents the whole sample. Conventionally we call the whole area *one unit*. The column for 16 in our histogram represents 3 of the 30 people in the entire group so the column for 16 is 10% of the whole in area, that is, 0.1 units if the whole area is 1. This is also true for the column representing people scoring 13, whereas the column for scores of 11, being 6 of the 30 scores, is 20% or 0.2 of the whole area 'under the curve'. Statisticians like to talk of a 'curve' even where a chart has jagged edges like this one. Most charts of large distributions *are* more curved than jagged, as we shall soon see.

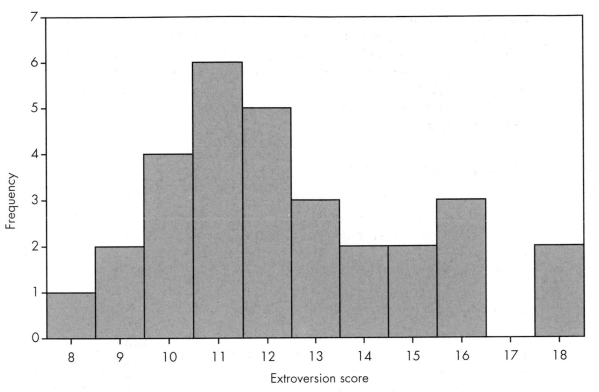

Figure 10.7   Histogram of extroversion scores

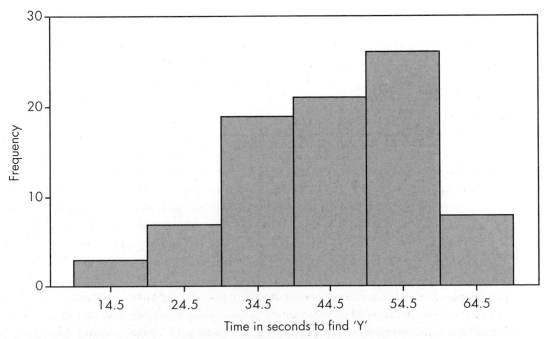

Figure 10.8   Frequencies of search times by 10 second intervals

A histogram of the distribution of search time scores in Table 10.11 is shown in Figure 10.8. Notice here that the *centre* of each column is marked by the mid-point of that category, since here each category does not represent a single value but a *range* of values. Hence, 14.5 is the mid-point of the category 9.5 to 19.5 and these are the extremes of the interval, as explained above.

Features of the histogram

- Columns are equal width per equal category interval
- Column areas are proportional to the frequency they represent and they sum to the total area which is considered as *one* unit
- Columns can *only* represent frequencies
- No space between columns (they are not separate bars as would appear in a regular bar chart – see below)
- All categories are represented *even if empty*, except at the two extremes of the distribution.

The bar chart

The histogram displays *all* of a data set and *all* relevant categories in a continuous manner. A bar chart is nothing like as restricted and usually displays a categorical variable – such as the mean score of several groups. Unlike the histogram, it can also display percentages, ratios, proportions, ranks and so on. The categorical variable is usually placed on the *x*-axis (horizontal) while the value for each category is placed on the *y*-axis.

- Because the *x*-axis variable has *categorical* values the columns of a bar chart should be separated (no matter what your computer does!)
- Not all the values of the categorical variable need be shown on the *x*-axis. For instance, we may only show, by way of contrast, the number of psychological articles published on AIDS in 1988 and 1998.

As an example, the lower bar chart in Figure 10.9 shows the percentage of females and males gaining a GCSE pass in Mathematics, grade A to C, in 1994 (for the most popular version of the SEG exams). Note that the bars are separate, since the categories of male and female are separate and unrelated. There is no technical reason, for instance, why 'female' should be on the left. With a histogram the positioning of the columns cannot be arbitrary in this way.

Misleading bar charts

It is very easy to mislead with unfairly displayed bar charts. Newspapers do it very frequently. Take a look at Figure 10.9. These percentages are for SEG's most popular version of Maths at GCSE, taken by 106,000 students in Summer 1994, almost twice as many as the next most popular exam. A die-hard sexist journalist might present the top chart, along with the headline **'Boys still outstrip girls at maths'**. In fact the correct, lower chart shows clearly the situation that brought these data to my attention in the first place. In 1994, headlines were more likely to be saying **'Girls finally catch up to boys in maths'**, which is just what *had* happened that year. The cheating journalist has chopped off the scale from 0 to about 49.18. This chart is an unfair representation of the

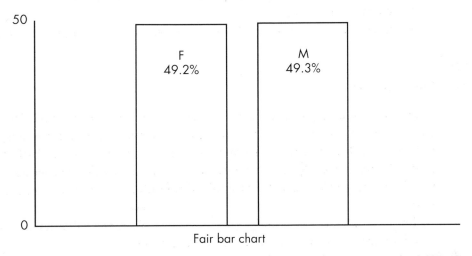

Figure 10.9 Percentage of females and males obtaining grade A–C passes in GCSE
Mathematics – Summer 1994

facts and shouldn't be used at all. The convention for avoiding this possible misrepresen-
tation, when you need to economise on space in your diagram, is shown in the chart produced by David *et al.* (1986) – Figure 10.10. Notice that the vertical scale has been
chopped between 0 and 15 but this is made obvious to the reader.

Combined bar charts

A bar chart can display two values together. Figure 10.11 shows the results of an experiment by Gordon, Bindrim, McNicholas and Walden (1988) in which participants were
asked to give a jail sentence to a fictitious person who had either committed burglary or
embezzlement and who was either black or white, giving four conditions in all under
which different participants were tested. Mean sentences are shown in Figure 10.11 and
note that the chart requires a 'legend' to explain the differing columns.

Frequency polygon

If we redraw our histogram of search times (Figure 10.8) with only a dot at the centre of
the top of each column we would get what is known as a FREQUENCY POLYGON when we
joined up the dots, as in Figure 10.12.

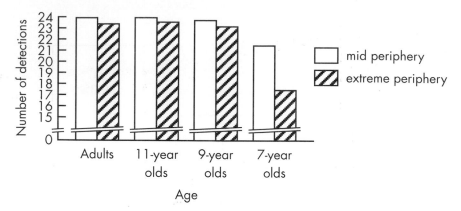

Figure 10.10 Mean number of apparent movement detections made by the four age groups in mid and extreme periphery (from David *et al.*, 1986)

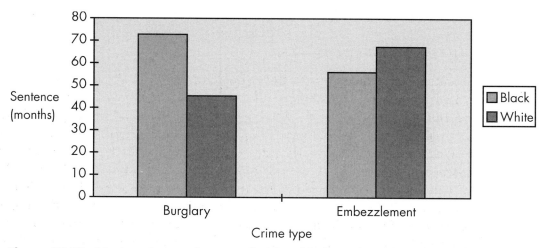

Figure 10.11 Mock sentences given to a fictitious black or white burglar and embezzler (data from Gordon *et al.*, 1988)

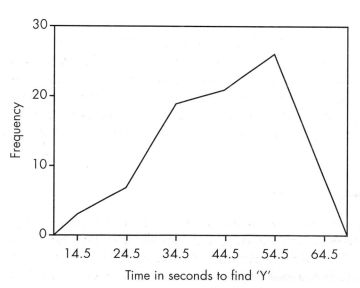

Figure 10.12 Frequency polygon of search times by 10 second intervals

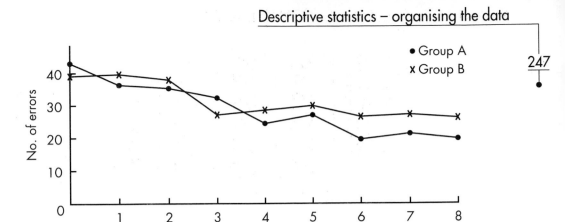

Figure 10.13 Line chart showing reading error scores for two groups of children progressing through two different training programmes

Line charts and time series

LINE CHARTS can be versions of the frequency polygon, though they often are not presented in this way. For instance, the chart in Figure 10.13 is very useful as a visual description of the comparison between regular progress for two groups of children who received different training-to-read programmes. Here, regular (e.g. daily) measures of reading error have been grouped into monthly intervals as the programme continued.

Line charts can also be drawn where the horizontal scale is *not* continuous. The horizontal axis might carry the values of several trials in an experiment or testing of children only at, say, two months, four months, six months etc. from the start of a programme. The TIME-SERIES chart in Figure 10.14 shows the clear change in road accident casualties following intense and well publicised use of the breathalyser in the UK in October, 1967. These data were referred to in discussing natural quasi-experiments in Chapter 3.

Ogive

This is obtained by plotting a *cumulative* frequency distribution, as shown in Figure 10.15 for the search time scores in Table 10.11. The dots show the number of cases which are below the scale point (e.g., the dotted line shows that 29 cases are below 39.5). It is therefore possible to read off the number of cases above or below any scale point, by following this example. The shape of Figure 10.15 would be particularly 'S' shaped if the histogram for the distribution were 'normal' – a special curve which we shall meet fairly soon.

EXPLORATORY DATA ANALYSIS

Within the last two decades or so the emphasis on good, informative display of data has increased, largely due to the work of Tukey (1977) whose book introduced the title of this section. Tukey argues that before submitting data to significance tests we should spend more time and effort than has been the case in *exploring* the patterns within our data set.

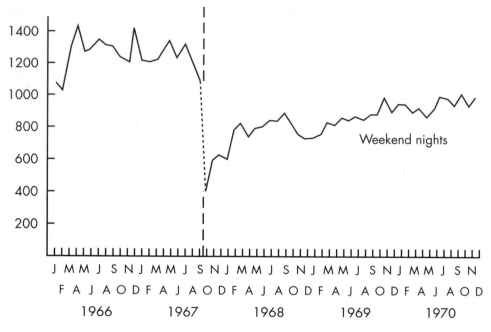

Figure 10.14 Time-series chart – Casualties (UK) before and after the 1967 breathalyser crackdown – from Ross *et al.*, 1973

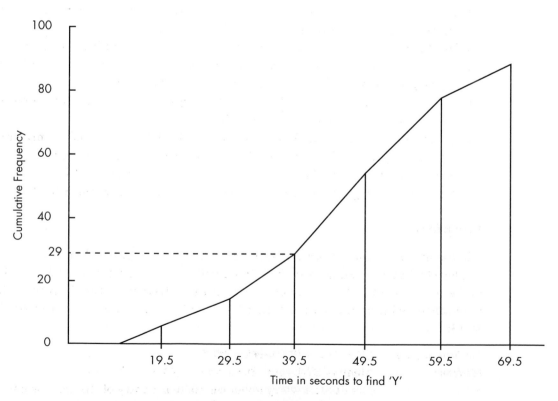

Figure 10.15 Ogive – Cumulative frequency of search time scores

Cum	Stem	Leaf
1	0	5
1	1	
4	2	129
11	3	3445569
25	4	00122235667778
47	5	011222333344455667789
65	6	0001124566777777899
72	7	1344578
74	8	01

Data for the 30–39 stem:

33 34 34 35 35 36 39

Figure 10.16 Stem and leaf display of exam results for 74 students

He has introduced a number of techniques, and we shall cover two of the most common ones here. The main aim is to present data in visually meaningful ways whilst retaining as much as possible of the original information.

The stem and leaf display

One way to achieve this aim is with this highly cunning, horticultural sounding diagram. We may as well look at one straight away and then discuss it. Have a look at Figure 10.16:

- The *stem* is the tens digit of each score (but this could differ with different scales)
- The *leaves* are the units of each score – hence, if you look to the right of stem '2', you can see that there was a 21, a 22 and a 29 in the set
- The diagram takes up the shape of a sideways histogram with the same intervals
- Note that we obtain this general histogram-like shape but retain each of the original individual scores which are lost in a traditional histogram
- The column headed 'cum', which is not always included, gives the cumulative frequency of cases – there are 25 people with 49 or less
- If there are too many data for each stem, *or* if the data are limited to only three stems, and the display would have only three lines, we can use * to represent the 0 to 4 leaves of each stem to 'flesh out' the chart into more detail – Figure 10.17 shows a stem and leaf diagram for our telegraphic utterances data in Table 10.10.

Box plots

These are based on *ordinal* measurements of the set of data. They give us a graphical display of what approximates to the interquartile range – the spread of the middle section of the data – whilst also giving us a view of the extremities. The following values have been calculated from the data in Figure 10.16 and produced the box plot shown in Figure 10.18:

Median position: $(N + 1)/2 = (74 + 1)/2 = $ **37.5**

Median: Mean of 37th and 38th scores = $(54 + 54)/2 = $ **54**
(we needn't worry about complete accuracy of the true median with tied values since this is a chart, not a fine calculation)

Hinge position: (Median position + 1)/2 = (37 + 1)/2 = **19**
                            (we drop decimal values)

Lower hinge: 19th lowest score = **45**

Upper hinge: 19th highest score = **66**

Hinge spread: upper hinge − lower hinge = 66 − 45 = **21**

Outer fences: low: lower hinge − (1.5 × hinge spread) = 45 − (1.5 × 21) = **14**
                            high: upper hinge + (1.5 × hinge spread) = 66 + (1.5 × 21) = **97**

Adjacent values: lower (= first *inside* low outer fence, nearer to median) = **21**
                            upper (= first *inside* high outer fence, nearer to median) = **81**

Cum	Stem	Leaf
2	0*	13
3	0	6
3	1*	
3	1	
11	2*	00123344
18	2	5567899
38	3*	0011112233333444444
61	3	555555555667778889 99999
96	4*	000000000011111111122222222333334444
130	4	5555555566666666777777777888899999
137	5*	1223334
147	5	5556677789
161	6*	00011122233444
171	6	5566678899
174	7*	001
175	7	5

Figure 10.17   Stem and leaf chart for telegraphic utterance data

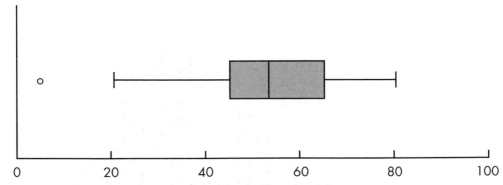

Figure 10.18   Box plot of exam results data in Figure 10.16

Explanatory notes

The box represents, roughly, the middle 50% of scores, shows the median, and is bounded by the two 'hinges'. The 'hinge spread' is the *range* from lower to upper hinge. The 'fences' are $1\frac{1}{2}$ times the hinge spread away from the hinges. The 'adjacent values' are those scores furthest from the median yet still inside the fences. These are shown on the plot by the 'whiskers' at the ends of the thin lines coming away from the hinges. Finally, any extreme values are shown where they fall or, when showing them would make the plot awkwardly squashed because of a huge scale, they are simply given at the edges with their actual values. Extreme values are probably obvious from the raw data without inspection of a box plot. Here, perhaps the extremely low score of 5 indicates someone who was sick at the start of the exam or who had 'spotted' the wrong questions in advance – a very dangerous practice!

The normal distribution

Earlier in this chapter, I pointed out that a measurement value, such as a person's height of, say, 163 cm, is really a statement that the value falls within a class interval. We are saying that the person, for instance, is closer to 163 cm than 162 or 164 cm, rather than that they measure 163 cm exactly. They are in the interval between 162.5 and 163.5 cm. In effect, if we measure to the nearest centimetre, we are placing individuals in class intervals 1 cm wide. It happens that if we take a large enough random sample of individuals from a population and measure physical qualities such as height (or weight, or length of finger), especially if we use a fine scale of measurement (such as to the nearest millimetre), we get a distribution looking like Figure 10.19.

The curve which typically results from such measurements *closely approximates* to a very well-known 'bell-shaped' mathematical curve, produced from a shockingly complicated formula (which you or I need not bother with) devised by Gauss. The curve is therefore known as 'Gaussian' but in statistical work we more commonly refer to it as a 'NORMAL DISTRIBUTION curve' (Figure 10.20), i.e. it plots a NORMAL DISTRIBUTION.

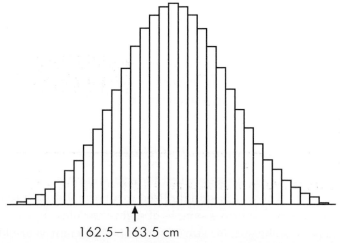

162.5–163.5 cm

Figure 10.19 Frequency distribution of heights in one centimetre intervals

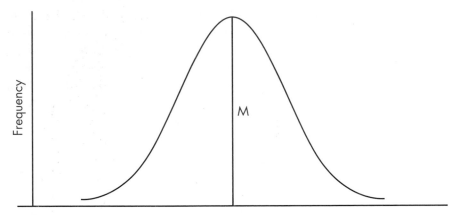

Figure 10.20 A normal distribution curve

Characteristics of a normal distribution curve

1. It is symmetrical about the mid-point of the horizontal axis.
2. The point about which it is symmetrical (the line marked 'M' in Figure 10.20) is the point at which the mean, median and mode all fall.
3. The 'asymptotes' (tail ends) of the perfect curve never quite meet the horizontal axis. Although for distributions of real large samples there are existing real limits, we can always hypothesise a more extreme score in a theoretical population.
4. It is known what area under the curve is contained between the central point (mean) and the point where one standard deviation falls. In fact, working in units of one standard deviation, we can calculate *any* area under the curve.

Approximations to the normal curve – and normal people

It's very important to remember, in all that follows, that when psychological variables are said to be 'normally distributed', or 'standardised to fit a normal distribution', that we are always talking about *approximations* to a pure normal curve. People *en masse* always differ a bit from the ideal. This matters, because, when we come on to testing significance, the statistical theory sometimes assumes a normal distribution for the population from which samples were drawn. If population scores on the variable form nothing like a normal distribution, then the conclusions from the significance test may be seriously in error. It's also important not to be morally outraged by the use of the term 'normal' or to balk against calling people 'normal' or not. The curve is called 'normal' for purely *mathematical* reasons (you may remember the use of the term 'normal' as meaning 'perpendicular' in geometry).

Area under the normal distribution curve

Suppose we devise a reading test for eight-year-olds and the maximum score possible on the test is 80. The test is standardised to a normal distribution such that the mean score, for a large, representative sample of eight-year-olds, is 40 and the standard deviation is 10. I hope it is obvious, for starters, that 50% of eight-year-olds will therefore be above 40 and 50% below. The area for the top 50% is *all* the shaded area in Figure 10.21.

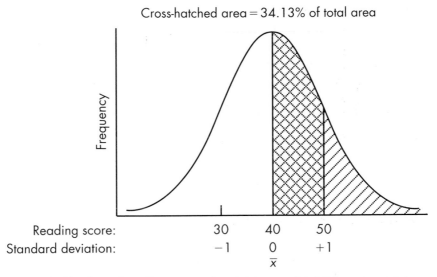

Cross-hatched area = 34.13% of total area

Reading score: 30 40 50

Standard deviation: −1 0 +1

$\bar{x}$

Figure 10.21 Distribution of reading scores for eight-year-old children

What we know, from the theory of the normal curve, is that one standard deviation, *on any normal distribution curve*, falls at the position shown by the line above 50 on Figure 10.21. This is the point where the downward curve inflects from an inward to an outward direction. We also know that the area trapped between the mean and this point is 0.3413 of the whole, shown cross-hatched. Hence we know that 34.13% of children score between 40 and 50 points on this test, since the standard deviation is 10 points. Figures worth noting are that:

- 34.13% of all values fall between ($\bar{x}$) and +1 (or −1) standard deviations (area = 0.3413)
- 47.72% of all values fall between ($\bar{x}$) and +2 (or −2) standard deviations (area = 0.4772)
- 49.87% of all values fall between ($\bar{x}$) and +3 (or −3) standard deviations (area = 0.4987)

The positions of these standard deviations are shown in Figure 10.22. Note the values above are doubled for areas between −n and +n standard deviations. For example, 34.13% of all values fall between the mean and +1 standard deviation, but double this to get 68.26% of all values between −1 and +1 standard deviations.

z Scores (or 'Standard scores')

In the reading test example above, in Figure 10.21, a child with a score of 50 lies one standard deviation above the mean. We could say that the number of standard deviations she is from the mean is +1 (the '+' signifying 'above'). If we measure number of standard deviations from the mean in this way we are using z scores or standard scores. There is a formula for z scores but it is always worth repeating to yourself that *a z score is the number of standard deviations a score is from the* mean. The formula is:

$$z = \frac{x - \bar{x}}{s}$$

where s is the standard deviation and $x - \bar{x}$ is, you'll notice, the deviation score. Dividing the deviation score by the standard deviation answers the question 'How many standard deviations is this deviation from the mean?' Let's say the mean for shoe size in your class is 8, with a standard deviation of 1.5. If your shoe size is 5 and I ask you how many standard deviations your size is from the mean you would probably have no difficulty in saying that your size is 2 standard deviations below the mean – a z score of -2. You actually followed the formula above. The only reason we need it is for when calculations involve not so friendly numbers. Let's check using the formula:

$$z = \frac{5 - 8}{1.5} = \frac{-3}{1.5} = -2$$

If z scores bother you at all then you should try to use the formula to check that a child with a score of 25 on the reading test discussed above, would have a z score of -1.5

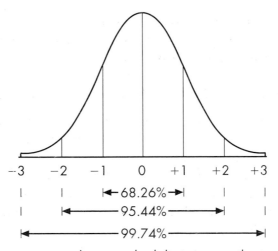

Area between $-n$ and $+n$ standard deviations on the normal curve.

Figure 10.22 Positions of standard deviations and the areas they enclose on the normal distribution

z scores and the normal distribution

We saw above that standard deviations cut off various known proportions of the area under the normal curve. Since z scores are just numbers of standard deviations, they too must cut off the same proportions. Therefore we know the percentage of the population enclosed between the mean and any z score. For instance, consulting Table 2 in Appendix 2, the area between the mean and a z score of $+1.5$ is 0.4332 or 43.32%, shown by the right-hand shaded pattern in Figure 10.23. In Table 2 of Appendix 2 we look up the value 1.5, under the left hand column (titled 'z') and take the figure in the next column on the right. The final right hand column contains the percentage between the z value and the *extreme right* of the distribution. Values for *negative* z scores are calculated using a mirror

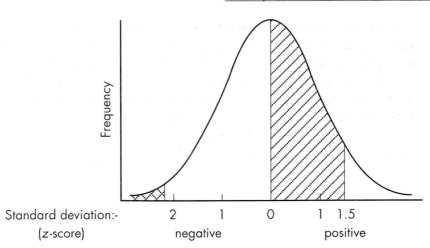

Figure 10.23 Area between the mean and z scores of +1.5 (right-hand shaded area) and −2.2 (left-hand cross-hatched area)

image. A z score of −2.2 traps 0.486 of the area between it and the mean on the left-hand side. Since the *whole* of the left-hand side of the mean is 0.5 of the area, then by subtracting 0.486 from 0.5, we find that only 0.014 is left at the left hand extreme beyond −2.2 standard deviations. This is shown by the cross-hatching in Figure 10.23, and by consulting the right-hand column of the z score table.

Standardisation of psychological measurements

This relationship between z scores and area under the normal curve is of crucial importance in the world of testing. *If* (and it is a big 'if') a variable can be assumed to distribute normally among the population, *and* we have a test standardised on large samples, then we can quickly assess the relative position of people by using their raw test score converted to a z score. This is valuable when assessing, for instance, children's reading ability, general intellectual or language development, adult stress, anxiety, aptitude for certain occupations (at interview) and so on. However, always recall that the 'if' is big and much work must go into the justification of treating a test result as normally distributed – see the points made on p. 175. Note that psychologists have not *discovered* that intelligence has a normal distribution in the population. The tests were created to *fit* a normal distribution, basically for research purposes and practical convenience. Usually, an IQ test is *standardised* (raw scores are adjusted) to produce a mean of 100 and a standard deviation of around 15 points.

Percentiles, deciles and quartiles

When tests are *standardised* they are piloted on very large samples of the intended population and various norms are calculated. These are similar to those you encounter when taking a baby to the health visitor. She will have a chart showing average heights and weights at various ages and she can tell at a glance where the baby is relative to these norms. She will use the term PERCENTILE. This is a point which cuts off a certain percentage of the population.

The 'tenth percentile' is the point on a scale which cuts off the bottom 10% of cases. In Table 10.12 you can see that the bottom 10% (34 out of 340 cases) are contained in the categories from 13 to 16 months. We can take 17 as the tenth percentile so long as we recognise that every child *under* 17 months is in the bottom 10% (or we can be strict and say 16.95 is the more accurate figure). The median (19.95) is the fiftieth percentile. It is also the fifth DECILE, because deciles cut off the distribution in 10% units; the third decile cuts off the bottom 30% for instance. The median is also the second QUARTILE because quartiles cut off in 25% (or quarter) units.

Table 10.12 Age (in months) at which parents report first telegraphic utterance

Age (months)	13	14	15	16	17	18	19	20	21	22	23	24	25	26	Total
Frequency	3	0	8	23	37	64	35	83	21	37	20	0	4	5	340

As with the median, if we want to calculate a percentile which is somewhere *within* a class interval, we need a formula:

$$Percentile = L + \frac{(Np/100) - F}{f_m} \times h$$

where p is the percentile required and the other symbols are the same as for the previous median calculation on p. 231.

> Note that the twentieth percentile is somewhere in the 17 month interval. Taking L to be 16.95, try calculating the twentieth percentile for this distribution. You should get an answer of 17.87 months.

Skewed distributions

Some distributions obtained from psychological measures which might be expected to be normal in fact turn out SKEWED. That is, they are 'lop-sided', having their peak (mode) to one side and a distinctive tail on the side where more than half the values occur. Have a look at Figure 10.24.

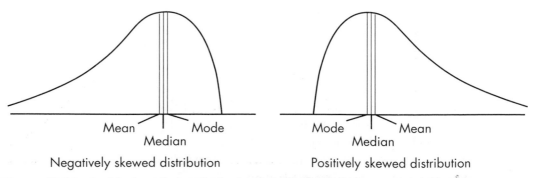

Negatively skewed distribution   Positively skewed distribution

Figure 10.24 Positively and negatively skewed distributions

How would you construct a test which produced a *negative skew* – make it very hard or very easy?

A negatively skewed distribution can be produced where a test is relatively *easy*. Most scores are clustered around the top end of the distribution. Such a test produces what are known as CEILING EFFECTS. People can't score much *higher* than the mean if the mean is, say, about 17 out of 20, but a substantial number of people can still score a lot *lower* than the mean. This greater number of lower scores below the mode has the effect of shifting the mean towards the tail. The mean, you may recall, is said to be most sensitive to extreme values. This is why the median or mode would be preferred here as a more appropriate and useful measure of central tendency. The opposite phenomenon, a hard test producing mostly low values and a positively skewed distribution, is said to have a FLOOR EFFECT.

Suppose we were measuring reaction time for responding to words displayed one at a time on a computer screen. Participants have to decide as quickly as possible whether the word is real or non-English. The reaction times recorded tend to centre around 0.7 seconds. Over many trials, what type of skewed distribution might develop?

It is possible to be very much slower than the majority of scores, but is it possible to be very much faster, when the majority of scores are around 0.7 seconds? This is like the situation in athletics where times can be quite a bit slower than the current good standard but not a lot faster. We would get a positively skewed distribution then. Notice that a positive skew has its *tail* up the *positive end* (higher values) of the horizontal axis.

Central tendency of skewed distributions

Notice where the mean, median and mode fall on each type of skewed distribution. The mode obviously still falls at the top, where the majority of scores are. In each case the mean is furthest from the mode – not surprising really, since we said that it was the most affected by extreme scores in one direction. The median is in between.

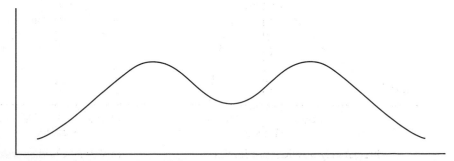

Figure 10.25 A bi-modal distribution

Bi-modal distributions

Some distributions are known as BI-MODAL and, like Bactrian camels, have two distinct humps. We noted in the section on standardisation in Chapter 7 that some measures of psychological variables may well produce such a distribution. Attitude measurement on a controversial issue (like privatisation of health services) where not many people are neutral might produce bi-modal distributions. So might a measure of job satisfaction in a company where there are a large number of well-paid white collar workers along with a similar number of poorly paid manual workers.

Glossary

Value of a number, ignoring its sign	_____ _____	absolute value
Full name for average at interval level – sum of scores divided by number of scores	_____ _____	arithmetic mean
General term for central tendency	_____	average
Chart in which (usually) the horizontal axis represents a categorical variable and the y-axis can represent frequency, average, percentage etc	_____ _____	bar chart
Exploratory data chart showing median, central spread of data and position of relative extremes	_____ _____	box plot
Number being used in a counting function, not as label or rank indicator	_____	cardinal number
Variable where cases are merely placed into independent, separate categories	_____	categorical variable
Phenomenon where measure produces very many high scores	_____	ceiling effect
Formal term for any measure of the typical or middle value in a group	_____	central tendency
Categories into which a continuous data scale can be divided in order to summarise frequencies	_____ _____	class intervals
Group of data points to be summarised/analysed	_____ _____	data set
Point on a measured scale which marks off 10% of the data set or population	_____	decile
Amount by which a particular score is different from the mean of its set	_____	deviation score
Technical term for any measure of the spread of scores in a sample of data or population	_____	dispersion

Shape and spread of data sets/populations		**Distributions**
Distribution with two prominent frequency peaks	__ – _____	bi-modal
Distribution showing total numbers above or below each class interval	_____ _____	cumulative frequency
Distribution showing how often certain values occurred	_____	frequency
Description of distribution which is not symmetrical about the vertical centre and which contains a lot more lower than higher values	_____ _____	negatively skewed
Continuous distribution, bell-shaped, symmetrical about its mid-point	_____	normal
Description of distribution which is not symmetrical about the vertical centre and which contains a lot more higher than lower values	_____ _____	positively skewed
Close examination of data by a variety of means, including visual display, before submitting them to significance testing – recommended by Tukey	_____ _____ _____	exploratory data analysis
Phenomenon where measure produces very many low scores	_____ _____	floor effect
Numbers of cases in specific categories	_____ _____	frequency data
Chart showing only the peaks of class intervals	_____ _____	frequency polygon
Chart containing whole of continuous data set divided into proportional class intervals	_____	histogram
Distance between first and third quartile in a distribution	_____ _____	interquartile range
Levels at which data are categorised or measured; relates directly to appropriateness of statistics to calculate and significance tests used		**Levels of measurement**
Level at which each unit on a scale represents an equal change in the variable measured	_____	interval
Level at which numbers, if used, are mere labels for discrete categories	_____	nominal
Level at which cases are arranged in rank positions	_____	ordinal

Interval type scale where proportions on the scale are meaningful because a real and absolute zero exists	_____	ratio
Chart joining continuous values (e.g. frequencies in class intervals or performance at various time intervals) in a single line	_____ _____	line chart
Variable where cases measured on it are placed on some sort of *scale* which has direction	_____ _____	measured variable
Measure of central tendency – middle value of data set	_____	median
Place where median is to be found in an ordered data set	_____ _____	median position/ location
Measure of central tendency – sum of scores divided by number of scores	_____	(arithmetic) mean
Measure of dispersion – mean of all absolute deviations	_____ _____	mean deviation
Measure of central tendency – most frequent value	_____	mode/modal value
Chart showing cumulative frequencies	_____	ogive
Point on a measured scale which marks off certain percentage of cases in a data set	_____	percentile
Statistical measure of a population (e.g. mean)	_____ _____	population parameter
Psychologist who develops and attempts to standardise psychological scales up to interval level	_____	psychometrist
Point on a measured scale which marks off a 25% segment of the data set	_____	quartile
Measure of dispersion – top to bottom value	_____	range
Untreated values obtained directly from measuring process used in a study	_____ _____	raw data/scores
Difference between a sample statistic and the true population statistic, usually assumed to be random in origin	_____ _____	sampling error
Statistical measure of a sample (e.g. mean)	_____ _____	sample statistic
Instrument for assessment of measured variable		**Scale**

Scale where there are no discrete steps; theoretically, all points along the scale are meaningful	_____	continuous
Scale where the underlying construct to be measured can only come in separate units (e.g. 'number of children')	_____	discrete
Half the distance between first and third quartile in a distribution	___-_____ _____	semi-interquartile range
Measure of dispersion – the square root of the sum of all squared deviations divided by N or $N-1$	_____ _____	standard deviation
Number of standard deviations a particular score is from its sample mean	_____ _____	standard score
Exploratory data analysis tool showing every value in a data set but organised into class intervals to give a histogram shape	_____ ____ _____	stem and leaf chart
Line chart showing measures of variable at progressive time intervals	_____ _____	time-series
Measure of dispersion – square of standard deviation	_____	variance
Measure of dispersion – proportion of non-modal values to all values	_____ _____	variation ratio
Same as standard score	_ _____	z score

Exercises

1. Find one example of each level of measurement from any textbooks (on psychology) you have available.

2. When judges give their marks in an ice-skating contest for style and presentation, at what level of measurement is it safest to treat their data?

3. A set of surgical records classifies patients as 'chronic', 'acute' or 'not yet classified'. What level of measurement is being used?

4. At what level are the measurements in Table 10.13 (a, b, c and d) below being made?

5. Which of the boxes, a) to d), in Table 10.13 below, contains the most sensitive or informative level of measurement?

Table 10.13 Exercises 4 and 5

a) Placings of top five riders in Tour de France – 29 July, 1998		b) Time taken on whole race so far	c) Popularity rating (max. 20) fictitious	d) Riders still in race	Riders dropped out
Pantani	1	77h 38m 24s	19	121 (fictitious)	77
Julich	2	77h 44m 6s	12		
Ullrich	3	77h 44m 20s	18		
Escartin	4	77h 44m 27s	15		
Rinero	5	77h 46m 25s	13		

6   Your daughter argues that, since she came top in each of the three maths tests held in her class this year, she must be *far* better than all the other pupils. What might you point out to her? (Would you dare?)

7   Think of three ways to measure driving ability, one using nominal level data, one ordinal and one interval/ratio.

8   Can you change the data in Table 10.14 first to ordinal level, then to nominal level? The blank tables are for you to fill in. **Hint:** For ordinal level, treat all the scores as *one* group.

Table 10.14 Exercise 8

a) Time taken to read (seconds)		b) Ordinal level		c) Nominal level
Consistent story	Inconsistent story	Consistent story	Inconsistent story	
127	138			
136	154			
104	138			
111	117			
152	167			
111	117			
127	135			
138	149			
145	151			
Mean of all times: $(\bar{x}) = 134.3$				

9   Below are several methods for measuring dependent variables. For each measure decide what level of measurement is being used. Choose from:
    1: Nominal 2: Ordinal 3: Interval 4: Ratio

    a. People are interviewed in the street and, on the basis of their replies, are recorded as either: pro-hanging, undecided, or anti-hanging.

b. Stress questionnaire for which various occupational norms have been established.
c. Photographs organised by participants according to level of attractiveness as follows:

Photos	F	C	B	G	E	A	H	D

← most attractive   least attractive →

d. Participants' estimates of various line lengths.
e. Time taken to sort cards into categories.
f. People's choice of: *The Sun, The Times*, or *The Guardian*.
g. Participants' sense of self-worth, estimated on a scale of 1–10.
h. Participants' scores on Cattell's 16PF questionnaire.
i. Distance two participants stand apart when asked to take part in an intimate conversation, measured from photos.
j. Critical life events given positions 1–10 according to their perceived importance to each participant.

10. Find the mean and median of the two sets of talking times in Table 10.6.

11. Consider the following set of times, measured in 1/100ths of a second:

62 65 71 72 73 75 76 77 79 80 82 83 92 100 106 117 127
65 70 72 72 74 75 76 77 79 80 82 88 93 102 110 121 128
65 70 72 73 74 76 76 78 80 81 83 90 95 103 112 122 135

a. Sketch a distribution for the data and decide which would be the most appropriate measure of central tendency for it. Calculate this measure and also a measure of dispersion.
b. Design a stem and leaf chart for this data.
c. Draw a box plot for the data set.

12. Draw a histogram for the data in Table 10.12. Calculate the mean for this data.

13. Sketch two roughly normal distributions which have the same mean but quite different standard deviations. Also sketch two normal distributions with the same standard deviation but different means.

14. You are told that a set of seven scores includes one score which is 0.8. The standard deviation for the set is 0. Can you give the mean of the set and say anything else about the six other scores in the set?

15. In an IQ distribution, where the mean is 100 and standard deviation 15,

a. what IQ score are 95% of people above?
b. what percentage would score less than 90?
c. what z score does a person have who scores 120?

16. What sort of skew is present in a distribution which has the following characteristics?

a. Mean = 50 b. Median = 60 c. Mode = 70

17　In Table 10.15 put values in the missing spaces.

Table 10.15 Exercise 17

Mean	SD	Specific value	Deviation	z-score	% above	% below
40	10	25	−15	1.5	93.3	6.7
100	15	135	35			
17.5	2.5			2		
	4	57		−1.75		
21		25	4		30.85	
15.6	3.47					56

Answers

2　Ordinal.

3　Nominal.

4　a. Ordinal.
　　b. Ratio.
　　c. Interval-like but safer treated as ordinal.
　　d. Nominal (or categorical).

5　Box b.

6　'Top' is a measure on an ordinal scale. We don't know how far ahead of the others she was.

7　Examples: Nominal – did/didn't hit kerb; Ordinal – positions after exercise on smoothness;
　　Interval/ratio – measure speed in race.

8

Ordinal level	
Consistent	Inconsistent
6.5	11
9	17
1	11
2.5	4.5
16	18
2.5	4.5
6.5	8
11	14
13	15

Nominal level		
	Consistent	Inconsistent
above mean	4	7
below mean	5	2

9   a. Nominal (or categorical).
    b. Interval (because standardised).
    c. Ordinal.
    d. Interval-like but unstandardised human judgement; best to convert to ordinal.
    e. Ratio.
    f. Nominal (or categorical).
    g. Interval-like but unstandardised human judgement; best to convert to ordinal.
    h. Interval (because standardised)
    i. Ratio, if measured using rule.
    j. Ordinal.

10 Males: mean = 171.6; median = 132. Females: mean = 367.2; median = 345.

11 a. Data are skewed, therefore use median. Median = 79 (or 79.25 if the precise formula is used).
    b. Stem and Leaf diagram:

Stem	Leaf
6	2555
7	0012222334455666677899
8	000122338
9	0235
10	0236
11	027
12	1278
13	5

    c. Box plot details:

Median position: 26   Median: 79
Hinge position: 13   Lower hinge: 73   Upper hinge: 95
Hinge spread: 22   Low outer fence: 40   High outer fence: 128
Outlier: 135   Adjacent value: 62   Adjacent value: 128

12 Mean = 19.35

14 Since there is absolutely no variation, all scores must be the same; all scores are therefore 0.8 and the mean is 0.8.

15 a. 75.31   b. 25.14%   c. 1.33

16 Negative skew.

Mean	SD	Specific value	Deviation	z-score	% above	% below
40	10	25	−15	−1.5	93.3	6.7
100	15	135	35	2.33	0.99	99.01
17.5	2.5	22.5	5	2	2.28	97.72
64	4	57	−7	−1.75	95.99	4.01
21	8	25	4	0.5	30.85	69.15
15.6	3.47	16.12	0.52	0.15	44	56

NOTATION

Statistical symbols

N is the number in a sample

N_A is the number in sample A

X is a value from the sample, such as Jane's score (can be lower case: x)

Y is also a value where there are two measured variables (or lower case: y)

Σ Greek letter S ('sigma') – means 'add up each of what follows'. For instance:

     ΣX means 'add up all the Xs in the sample'

     ΣXY means 'multiply all the Xs by their paired Ys and add up all the results'. Notice that XY means 'multiply X by Y'. Always do what's *after* the Σ before proceeding to add up, for instance:

     ΣX^2 means 'square all the Xs, *then* add them all up'. *Be careful* to distinguish this from:

     $(\Sigma X)^2$ which means 'find the total of all the Xs and square the result'.

11

Significance – was it a real effect?

Differences (or correlations) need to be submitted to a *test of significance* in order for a decision to be made concerning whether the differences are to be counted as showing a genuine effect or dismissed as likely to represent just chance fluctuation.

- Significance decisions involve rejecting or retaining a *null hypothesis* (H_0). A null hypothesis usually claims that underlying populations are identical or that population means are equal or correlations are zero. If the *probability* of a result occurring under H_0 is low, then H_0 is rejected in favour of the *alternative hypothesis* (H_1).

- *Probability* of events occurring is measured on a scale of 0 (not possible) to 1 (must happen). *Logical probability* is calculated from first principles as the ratio of the number of ways our predicted outcome can happen divided by the number of possible outcomes. *Empirical probability* uses the same ratio but puts the number of target events which *have* happened on top of the equation, and the total number of relevant events on the bottom. A *probability distribution* is a histogram with columns measuring the likelihood of occurrence of the events they represent.

- Social scientists reject the null hypothesis when the probability of a result occurring under it is less than 0.05 (the conventional set level of *'alpha'* – the level of probability acceptable for rejection). This is often called the *'5% significance level'*. The area of the probability distribution for a particular statistical test cut off by the set level of alpha is known as a *rejection region*. If a result falls into this area we may reject H_0.

- If the null hypothesis is true but has been rejected because $p < 0.05$, it is said that a *type I error* has been made. *Replication* is a safeguard against the acceptance of such 'fluke' significant results. A *type II error* occurs when the null hypothesis is retained, because $p > 0.05$, yet there is a real underlying effect.

- When the hypothesis tested is controversial, either theoretically or ethically, it is usual to seek significance with $p < 0.01$ or still better. A result with $p < 0.1$ might warrant further investigation, tightening of procedures, altering of design and so on.

- If the hypothesis investigated was directional then a *one-tailed test* of probability may be used, but there is controversy surrounding this issue. For *non-directional hypotheses* the test *must* be *two-tailed*. Results tested with a one-tailed test are more likely to reach significance than with a two-tailed test for the same sample size, but if the direction of results is opposite to that predicted, even if the difference is *past* the significant *critical value*, the null hypothesis *must* be retained.

- The general procedure for using a statistical test of significance is introduced.

Guys or Dolls? – Which do you want?

A couple of years ago there was a news report about a private clinic which claimed to be able to assist couples in producing a baby with the sex they would prefer. At the end of an interview, both technical and self-promotional, the director was asked how successful the clinic had been so far. 'Well,' he said, 'we've had six couples through and four of these have left with the result they wanted.'

Decide whether or not you are convinced, from this performance report, that the work of the clinic has been shown to be effective.

I have said earlier that many of the concepts in basic methods and statistics are those that most people operate with on an everyday basis, admittedly without necessarily being able to spell them out exactly. Here is a prime example. Many people concerned with psychology methods and statistics courses will claim that the logic of significance testing is rather tricky and obscure for students new to the subject. In fact, when you have at least basically grasped the concepts of the *null hypothesis*, the *alternative hypothesis*, *probability* and *levels of significance* covered in this chapter, I think you will agree, if you return to this page, that you have already employed those concepts (and so do most lay people) in evaluating the 'guys and dolls' clinic.

What most people say, when they are confronted with the extremely weak Guys and Dolls evidence (and similar claims based on pitifully few examples) is roughly the following: 'That's not very convincing, only four out of six? If they were complete charlatans and did nothing *at all* they'd be likely to get three satisfied clients out of six.'

Most people know that if you say to a parent who wants a girl baby 'Rest assured, you'll have a girl', then you have (close to) a 50–50 chance of being correct (equal probability). Hence, if we take these six cases as a *sample* of the clinic's overall (future) performance, we will probably assume that they are performing at a chance level – they may just as well say to each client 'Rest assured, you'll have the boy/girl you desire'. What is meant by 'performing at a chance level' here is that, for every client trial, there is an equal chance of a success (a 'hit') or a failure (a 'miss') for the clinic. Overall, their rate of success is only marginally higher than what we'd expect if this were true, and their method is ineffectual.

We are often faced with informal significance decisions in everyday life. Suppose you received 62% for your last essay and 60% for the one you've just had marked. Are you doing worse or is this just forgettable fluctuation in your tutor's grading? If you got 45% next time, you'd know there was a difference which mattered. The current difference, however, is unlikely to bother you. So, we are often certain that a difference indicates a real change and often certain that it doesn't. That's the easy part. When do we change from one decision to the other? How far below 62% indicates a real drop in your standard (or in your tutor's)? This is the fundamental question of significance testing.

DID IT WORK OR DIDN'T IT? – THE HEART OF THE SIGNIFICANCE TESTING MATTER

What potential clients have to do with the Guys and Dolls clinic is to decide whether they will use it or not. In other words, they cannot say something like 'Well, it's performing a little bit above chance level so *maybe* we'll use it', or 'we'll use it a little'. In practice, we have to say 'Either it's doing well above chance level – in which case we'll use it – or it's performing too close to chance level – in which case we're not convinced and we *won't* use it.' We must either reject the notion that the clinic's treatment is ineffective, and risk using the clinic, or stay with the assumption that the treatment is, indeed, useless, and hence, not use it.

This is much the same as the logic of significance testing for hypotheses. Take a look at the data in Table 11.1. Assume that both sets were gathered as part of an independent group project on social facilitation/inhibition in a psychology methods class. Participants were asked to perform a 'wiggly wire' task (attempting to take a hoop along a wiggly wire without touching it) either alone or in front of an audience. Your group (B) obtained the data shown on the right of the table. Using a different method, another group (A) in the class obtained the data on the left of the table. Typically, both groups were only able to use small samples of people. However, in your data, an EYEBALL TEST[1] indicates that the mean time touching the wire for the 'audience' condition is much higher than the mean for the 'alone' condition, but is it high enough to assume that the experimental 'treatment' – adding an audience – did 'work', that is, produced longer touching times? Shall we call this difference between group means 'significant'? For the other group's data it appears obvious that there is *no* significant difference.[2]

Table 11.1 Time(secs) spent touching wire whilst performing alone and in front of an audience

Student practical Group A Experimental conditions		Student practical Group B Experimental conditions	
With audience	Alone	With audience	Alone
9.9	5.2	14.8	4.1
15.1	3.3	13.5	3.2
16.2	9.1	9.6	5.7
11.7	6.1	8.7	9.0
11.1	16.2	12.2	11.3
9.1	2.7	15.3	2.8
10.0	7.8	18.6	5.1
8.5	18.2	12.1	6.1
1.3	10.3	15.8	3.3
2.4	9.0	17.1	7.2
Mean = 9.53	Mean = 8.79	Mean = 13.77	Mean = 5.78

[1] We can never *rely* on an 'eyeball test'. A formal statistical test must always be applied to the main data set if a claim of significance is to be made. 'Eyeballing' the data though is a useful exercise where, with a large set of results, we do not wish to dally with differences that are clearly unworthy of testing, ones that are very close indeed.

[2] Note that, to gain these impressions, we do not only look at the *size* of the difference between the means. We also take into account the *variation between individual scores* in each group to get a feel for what sort of difference between means would be a large one.

How do we approach these differences? We proceed as for the clinic. We must decide whether to accept, provisionally, that the treatment 'worked', or stay with the sceptical position that it didn't. If it did work, then the two sample means should be pretty far apart. If it didn't work, then the difference between the two means is within the range that we might expect *if audiences have absolutely no effect on performance* – i.e. performances in general do not differ. At this point you could say 'Well clearly even the two performances in practical group A do differ'. However, we need to think back to Chapter 2 where the point was made that we are not usually interested in the samples of data we gather as such, but in the *populations* from which they have been drawn. We want to estimate, using these sample data, whether there would be a real difference between the two *populations* of scores that could be gathered under the two conditions (each of which could be infinite). In other words, does an audience *generally* worsen performance? If we draw any two samples from the same population (for instance, two samples of 8 year-old reading scores) there will almost always be a finite difference between the two sample means. In a significance test, we need to decide between two possible alternatives: (a) was the obtained difference so small that we should remain conservative and assume that the two samples come from the *same* population, or, (b) was the difference so great that we can assume that the two samples come from two populations *with different means* (the two groups of reading scores are *really* far apart).

Deciding between these two alternatives (as with the 'Guys and Dolls' clinic) is known as a SIGNIFICANCE DECISION. Now let's summarise more formally.

THE NULL HYPOTHESIS – H_0

The position we have been describing as 'conservative' (no difference at all between populations) is that assumed by the so-called NULL HYPOTHESIS – symbolically written as H_0. The underlying assumption is that, in *loose* terms, nothing is going on, there is no actual effect. The null hypothesis that statisticians work with, however, is a 'tight' version of this assumption in operationalised terms. Table 11.2 gives the exact null hypothesis for the examples we have encountered above. For the Guys and Dolls clinic we assume, under H_0, that the probability of the clinic being right on each trial is equal to the probability of their being wrong – and we shall deal more fully with probability issues and calculations in a very short while.

Table 11.2 The Null and Alternative Hypotheses

	The NULL HYPOTHESIS – H_0 Verbal	Symbol H_0	Symbol H_1
Baby sex guessing	Frequencies of hits and misses are equal in the population *or* Probability of a hit is equal to probability of a miss	$p = q$	$p \neq q$
Wiggly wire experiment	Population means for the alone and audience conditions are equal	$\mu_1 = \mu_2$	$\mu_1 \neq \mu_2$

THE ALTERNATIVE HYPOTHESIS – H_1

The ALTERNATIVE HYPOTHESIS – symbolically written H_1 – covers every possibility that the null hypothesis does not. H_0 and H_1 are *mutually exclusive and exhaustive*. What we usually want to support is the alternative hypothesis, since this echoes our research prediction, and we do this by discrediting the null hypothesis. In the simple cases introduced above, the alternative hypothesis claims that there *is* a difference between population means or between frequencies of hits and misses, with the underlying assumption that there *is* an effect (samples are not drawn from the same population). In Table 11.2, the verbal version of H_1 would simply be the H_0 versions with the word 'not' appearing before the word 'equal' in each case.

A concrete example – the psychology/sociology chip shop

In an attempt to clarify the notions of null hypothesis and alternative hypothesis let me ask you to read the very unlikely tale that I have related in Box 11.1.

Box 11.1   The psychology/sociology chip shop – a concrete example of null and alternative hypotheses

Imagine one lunchtime you visit the local fish and chip emporium near the college and get into conversation with the chippy. At one point she asks you: 'You're from the college then? What do you study?'. Upon your reply she makes a rasping sound in her throat and snaps back. 'Psychology?!!! Yeughhh!!! All that individualist, positivistic crap, unethical manipulation of human beings, nonsensical reductionism rendering continuous human action into pseudo-scientific behavioural elements. What a load of old cobblers! Give me sociology any day. Post-Marxist-Leninist socialism, symbolic interactionism, real life qualitative participative research and a good dollop of post-modern deconstructionism'. You begin to suspect she may not be entirely fond of psychology as an academic subject. You meekly take your bag of chips and proceed outside only to find that your bag contains far too many short chips, whilst your sociology friends all have healthy long ones.

We must at this point stretch fantasy a little further by assuming that this story is set in an age where, post-salmonella, BSE and genetically modified food, short chips are the latest health scare; long chips are seen as far healthier since they contain less fat overall (thanks to my students for this idea).

Being a well-trained, empirically based psychology student, you decide to design a test of the general theory that the chippy is biased in serving chips to psychology and sociology students. You engage the help of a pair of identical twins and send them simultaneously, identically clothed, into the chip shop to purchase a single bag of chips. One twin wears a large badge saying 'I like psychology' whilst the other twin wears an identical badge, apart from the replacement of 'psychology' with 'sociology'. (OK! OK! I spotted the problem too! Which twin should go first? Those bothered about this can devise some sort of counterbalanced design – see p. 60 – but for now I really don't want to distract from the point of this example). Just as you had suspected, without a word being spoken by the twins beyond their simple request, the sociology twin has far longer chips in her bag than does the psychology twin!

Now, we only have the two samples of chips to work with. We cannot see what goes on behind the chippy's stainless steel counter. We have to entertain two possibilities. Either the chippy drew the two samples (fairly) from one big chip bin (H_0) or the bags were filled from two separate chip bins, one with smaller chips overall and therefore a smaller mean chip length than the other bin (H_1). You now need to do some calculations to estimate the *probability* of getting such a large difference between samples if the bags were filled from the same bin (i.e. if the null hypothesis is true). If the probability is very low you might march back into the shop and demand redress (hence you have rejected H_0!). If the probability is quite high – two bags from the same bin are often this different – you do not have a case. You must *retain* the null hypothesis – see below.

In this example, our *research hypothesis*, or *research prediction*, would be that the sociology student will receive longer chips than the psychology student. Our *alternative hypothesis* is that the psychology and sociology chip population means are different; the null hypothesis that the population means are the same (i.e. the samples were drawn from the same population).

SIGNIFICANCE DECISIONS

When we make a significance decision we have to decide whether to:

a) *retain* the null hypothesis – differences were small enough for us to find it quite likely that samples were drawn from the same or identical population(s); or

b) *reject* the null hypothesis – in favour of the alternative hypothesis – if H_0 is true this difference would occur *very* rarely.

In order to make this decision we take two steps:

1. We calculate the probability of obtaining our result *if the null hypothesis is true* (from now on we will often refer to this as 'the probability of the results under H_0').

2. On the basis of this probability estimate *we decide whether to retain or reject H_0*.

As we saw above, in the case of the Guys and Dolls clinic, most people, without necessarily being fully aware of it, make a rough calculation of the probability of obtaining the 4 hits/2 misses result if the frequency of hits and misses *is equal* (i.e. if the null hypothesis is true). They mostly decide that this probability is too high and too close to what would happen if the clinic was ineffective and only random selection was operating as usual. If, on the other hand, you read that the same clinic, some years later, now had a record of 132 hits out of 150 trials, I'm sure you'd feel intuitively that the probability of *this* happening under H_0 must be extremely low indeed. I hope you'll agree in general that it would make sense if we:

reject H_0 when, *if it were true*, the probability of getting our results is *very low*;
retain H_0 when, *if it were true*, the probability of getting our results is *very high*.

PROBABILITY

The problem we are faced with now is: just what level of probability is going to be counted as 'very low'? What size of difference between chip length is one we would be very *unlikely* to obtain 'by chance' (that is, if H_0 is true)? How improbable is the difference in social inhibition sample times if an audience makes no difference to performance? For this we need an introduction to notions and methods of calculating probability in general, with apologies to those of you who might recently have covered this more formally in a mathematics or statistics course.

Moving towards exact probability and significance – another baby-sexing problem

Let's use a practical problem in order to get to grips with significance testing.

Suppose a friend said she could reliably forecast the sex of unborn babies by swinging a stone pendulum above the mother's womb. Let's assume she guesses your baby's sex correctly. Would you be impressed? Your personal involvement might well cause you to react with 'amazing!' or at least, 'well it is interesting; there might be something in it.' Stepping back coolly from the situation you realise she had a 50–50 chance of being correct. Nevertheless most people would begin to think she had something going if she managed to go on to predict correctly the sex of two or three more friends' babies. Suppose we give her a sample of ten babies' sexes to guess. How many would you expect her to predict correctly in order for you to be impressed that she's not just guessing and being lucky? For instance, would 7 out of 10 convince you? Or would you want more or would fewer do?

The decision of a vast majority of students here is that eight or nine correct out of ten would convince them and this, as we shall see, pretty well coincides with the result that social scientists would want in order to record her result as 'significant'. A few generous people tend to choose 7 or even 6, and there is always the odd cynic who claims that even ten out of ten is not strong enough evidence. In fact we are moving slowly towards a formal exposition of the criteria that social scientists use in deciding whether to reject a null hypothesis and we shall see that requiring all ten guesses correct out of ten trials would usually be considered *too* conservative.

Let's suppose that, in fact, she got eight correct out of ten. We want to reject the null hypothesis that her 'sample' of correct and incorrect results is drawn from a 'population' containing equal numbers of each. We want to say that the result is just too unlikely to occur if she were just guessing. So what we need is:

1. the probability of her getting eight out of ten just by guessing (i.e. under H_0);
2. a decision on whether that probability is low enough to reject H_0.

Types of probability

Let's deal with probability calculations first. Most people have a fairly good sense of how probable various events are and yet many people are also loathe to get involved in giving such probabilities a numerical value, either because it seems complicated or because one then seems committed to mysterious 'laws of chance'. This was a conversation I once had with a friend's 11-year old son whilst driving him and his family to an airport:

Child: But planes do crash.

HC: Yes, but you only hear about the accidents. Thousands of flights run safely and the odds of you crashing are hundreds of thousands to one.

Child: I know but it still *could* be our plane.

... and so on, as if this were an argument when, really, we were both saying the same thing but with different emphasis and personal involvement. Nowadays a positive version of this occurs with the National Lottery: 'It *could* be me', 'You haven't a snowball's chance in Hell!', 'Yes, but . . .'. And for quite a few people who have thought this, it has indeed become reality, but we still *know* it will never be us! Kerlinger (1973) makes the following observations on probability:

> Probability is an obvious and simple subject. It is a baffling and complex subject. It is a subject we know a great deal about, and a subject we know nothing about. Kindergarteners can study probability, and philosophers do. It is dull; it is interesting. Such contradictions are the stuff of probability.

It is often said that there are three types of probability:
- logical probability
- empirical probability
- subjective probability

Although we shall deal with formal calculations of probability for most of this chapter, it is worth dallying for a moment with the notion of subjective probability – the cognitive estimates we make of probability, based on particularly salient experiences, no matter what the mathematicians or statisticians tell you. It's hard to stay convinced, as your return flight from Athens drops a sudden 800 feet through turbulence, that this really is safer than travelling by road. During the holidays my family and I have just come back from we had to travel to an island, and return, on a twin propeller plane. On both occasions, quite independently, we were given row 5 out of 30 rows (what's the odds on that happening?). Row 5 happens to be beside the propellers, each about ten foot in diameter. When those massive things wind up for take off, knowing that instant oblivion for the family is just three feet outside the window, it truly is hard to accept that 'it's millions to one against' a serious accident!

Some statistical facts are hard to accept subjectively. How many people do you think would have to be in a room in order for there to be a 50–50 chance that two of them share the same birthday? The answer, to most people's incredulity, is a mere 23. You can try this one in your local or at parties. So long as there are a few more than 23 people present, and, if you're a gambling type, you would end up making a bob or two in the long run. For a light-hearted look at the testing of subjective probability, take a look at Box 11.2.

Box 11.2 Sod's Law – or Murphy's Law as the Americans so politely put it

Do you ever get the feeling that fate has it in for you? At the supermarket, for instance, do you always pick the wrong queue, the one looking shorter but which contains someone with 5 unpriced items and several redemption coupons or with the check-out clerk about to take a tea-break? Do you take the outside lane only to find there's a hidden right-turner? Sod's law (known as Murphy's law in the USA), in its simplest form states that whatever can go wrong, will. Have you ever returned an item to a shop, or taken a car to the garage with a problem, only to find it working perfectly for the assistant? This is Sod's law working in reverse but still against you. A colleague of mine holds the extension of Sod's law that things will go wrong even if they can't.

An amusing QED (BBC) TV programme (Murphy's Law, 1991[3]) tested this perspective of subjective probability. The particular hypothesis, following from the law, was that celebrated kitchen occurrence where toast always falls

[3] Available from BBC Education and Training, 80 Wood Lane, London, W12 0TT.

butter side down – doesn't it? First attempts engaged a University Physics professor in developing machines for tossing the toast without bias. These included modified toasters and an electric typewriter. Results from this were not encouraging. The null hypothesis doggedly retained itself, buttered sides not making significantly more contact with the floor than unbuttered sides. It was decided that the human element was missing. Sod's law might only work for human toast droppers.

The attempt at more naturalistic simulation was made using students and a stately home now belonging to the University of Newcastle. Benches and tables were laid out in the grounds and dozens of students asked to butter one side of bread then throw it in a specially trained fashion to avoid toss bias. In a cunning variation of the experiment, a new independent variable was introduced. Students were asked to pull out their slice of bread and, just before they were about to butter a side, to change their decision and butter the other side instead. This should produce a bias away from butter on grass if sides to fall on the floor are decided by fate early on in the buttering process. Sadly neither this nor the first experiment produced verification of Sod's law. In both cases 148 slices fell one way and 152 the other – first in favour of Murphy's law then against it. Now the scientists had one of those flashes of creative insight. A corollary of Sod's law is that when things go wrong (as they surely will – general rule) they will go wrong in the worst possible manner. The researchers now placed expensive carpet over the lawn. Surely this would tempt fate into a reaction? Do things fall butter side down more often on the living room carpet (I'm sure they do!)?

I'm afraid this was the extent of the research. Frequencies were yet again at chance level, 146 buttered side down, 154 up. (Incidentally what test would be done on these frequencies? – see page 302).

Murphy, it turned out, was a United States services officer testing for space flight by sending service men on a horizontally jet propelled chair across a mid-Western desert to produce many Gs of gravitational pressure. I'm still not convinced about his law. Psychologists suggest the explanation might lie in selective memory – we tend to remember the annoying incidents and ignore all the unnotable dry sides down or whizzes through the supermarket tills. But I still see looks on customers' faces as they wait patiently – they seem to *know* something about my queue . . . .

Giving probability a value

There is in fact a conventional system for the measurement of probability and we shall move towards this using the following exercise:

Have a look at the statements below. For most of them, you'll find you have some idea of how likely or not it is that these events will occur. Try to give a value between zero (not at all likely) and 100 (highly likely) to each statement, depending on how likely you think it is to occur:
1. It will rain on Wednesday of next week
2. You will eat breakfast on the first day of next month
3. Your psychology tutor will sneeze in the next lesson
4. You will be given a million pounds next year
5. The sun will rise tomorrow morning
6. You will think about elephants later today
7. Someone will bump into you later today
8. A coin tossed fairly will come down showing tails
9. Two coins tossed fairly will both come down tails
10. If there were 20 students in your class and the tutor was about to pick one of them to talk about this week's reading, what is the probability that she will choose you? What is the probability that she will (phew!) choose someone else?

For number one, if you live in the UK, whatever the time of year, you may have answered with 50, whereas if you live in Bombay, and the month is October, you'd say about 3. Numbers two and seven depend on your habits and the time of day it is. I would be interested in what happens with number six, now I've said it!

Now divide all the values you gave by 100. So, if you answered 20 to number seven, for instance, then divide 20 by 100 and you get 0.2. Probability is denoted by '*p*' and is measured on a scale of:

0 ◄─────────────────── to ─────────────────► +1
NOT possible   MUST happen

. . . usually in decimal values, like 0.3, 0.5 and so on. Notice that you can't give zero to item four above, nor even 1 to item five, since there's always a *very slight* chance that item four could happen and item five might not! These are not *logical* impossibilities or necessities. They are simply very likely/unlikely based on prior events and experiences.

Logical and empirical probability

If you buy a ticket in a raffle where 100 people buy tickets altogether, you know *logically* that you must have a 1/100, or 0.01 chance of winning first prize. We shall deal further with *logical probability* in a moment. In many real life situations however, we cannot calculate probability on this logical basis. With real life events, such as the chance of an earthquake, a plane crash or of England beating Australia in cricket, we can't make such calculations. There are just too many variables to account for. Instead, in these circumstances, statisticians rely on 'actuarial' data – that is, data which are already available. The process is backward rather than forward looking. We say, to estimate the probability of X happening, 'how many X-type events have happened so far out of the total number of relevant events?' This is the basis for calculation of your car insurance premium. The company assesses the risk you pose based on the accidents of people with your characteristics (age, experience, residence and so on). Predicting the EMPIRICAL PROBABILITY of your tutor sneezing next lesson has to be calculated using:

$$p = \frac{\text{number of lessons in which tutor has sneezed so far}}{\text{total number of tutor's lessons so far}} = \frac{30}{100} = 0.3$$

(if your tutor has so far sneezed in 30 out of 100 classes).

Probabilities of selecting children with particular IQ or reading scores (a fictitious example will be worked on below) are based on the known *population of* IQ or reading scores. If we know the parameters of these populations we can calculate how likely it is to randomly select a 7 year-old child with, say, a reading age of 8.3.

Calculating logical probability from first principles

Your answer to item eight in the exercise above was almost certainly 50 – which becomes a probability of 0.5 If your probability answer to item nine was the correct 0.25 you can already calculate probability (probably!). Items eight, nine and ten are different from the others because we can calculate the probabilities *exactly* from first principles. Excluding those very rare occasions when the coin falls on its edge, we say for item eight:

- there are just two possible outcomes (a head or a tail)
- one of these is the target outcome (a tail)
- therefore, there is one chance in two that a tail will occur.

This leads to the empirical prediction that if you toss an unbiased coin fairly 1000 times it will come up tails about 500 times (and it will!).

For item ten we say:

- there are 20 possible outcomes (the teacher will pick someone)
- one of these is the target outcome (you!)
- there is one chance in 20 that you will be picked and 1/20 = 0.05
- there are 19 chances in 20 that someone else will be picked; 19/20 = 0.95

Note that the last two probabilities add up to 1 and so they should – your teacher is *certainly* going to pick *someone* in the class!

If it is a while since you converted figures like 5% or 5/100 to 0.05, or if anyway you have trouble with such conversions, take a look at Box 11.3 and I hope this will help you.

Box 11.3 Sums for the rusty – converting percentages to (probability) decimals

From percentage to decimal	**From decimal to percentage**
5% to $p = 0.05$	$p = 0.05$ to 5%
1. Remove the '%' sign (= 5)	**1.** Move the decimal point two places to the right (005.)
2. Put decimal point after the whole number (= 5.)*	**2.** Lose any zeros to the left of the first left hand whole digit (= 5.)
3. Move the decimal point two places to the left, inserting zeros as you go where necessary (i.e. first move 0.5, second move 0.05)	**3.** Lose the decimal point if there is nothing to the right of it (= 5)
	4. Add the '%' sign (= 5%)
* If there already is a decimal point, leave it where it is, and go straight to step **3**, e.g. $2.5\% \to 2.5 \to 0.25 \to 0.025$	e.g. for 0.025: $0.025 \to 00.25 \to 002.5 \to 2.5 \to 2.5\%$

When we come to multiple tosses, as in item 9, we need to resort to a *general* formula for probability which holds for cases like ours where each *trial* (toss of a coin) has two equally likely outcomes:

$$p = \frac{\text{number of permutations producing target outcome}}{\text{total number of permutations possible}}$$

Notice this is generally the same as the fraction we used above for empirical probability – the ratio: *target events/total events*. A 'permutation' is a particular set of tosses. For instance, a tail followed by a head is a different permutation from a head followed by a tail. We used the formula above for items eight and nine but hardly needed to refer to it consciously. In item eight there is one target outcome on the top of the equation (a tail) and two possible outcomes altogether on the bottom (a head or a tail). For item ten there is one target outcome (you) and 20 possible outcomes altogether.

For item 9 we refer to Table 11.3. There is just one permutation which satisfies our 'target' outcome of two tails, so the top of the equation takes the value 1. There are four permutations altogether, so four goes on the bottom of the equation. Hence the probability of two tails occurring in two tosses is $\frac{1}{4}$ or 0.25. Note that there are *two* permutations which produce the outcome of one tail only (the middle two in Table 11.3), so the probability of obtaining *just one tail* from two coin tosses is 2/4 which is $\frac{1}{2}$.

Table 11.3 Possible permutations of events in tossing two coins together

a		b	c	d	e
Toss number			**Number (*n*) of tails in outcome**	**Number of permutations**	**Probability of occurrence**
First		**Second**			
Head		Head	0	1	0.25
Head		Tail	} 1		
Tail		Head		2	0.5
Tail		Tail	2	1	0.25
			Total number of permutations 4		

Frequency distributions and probability distributions

The probabilities that we have just calculated are reflected in the PROBABILITY DISTRIBUTION shown in Figure 11.1b. Note that the probability distribution gives us *proportions* of outcomes which *should* happen over very many trials. Given those proportions, if we bothered to toss two coins 1000 times, we would expect to obtain no tails 250 times, one tail 500 times and two tails 250 times. When I asked my computer to (virtually) 'toss 2 coins 1000 times' it blinked and came up with the *frequency distribution* shown in Table 11.4, also plotted as a histogram in Figure 11.1a. The eerie thing about probability is that,

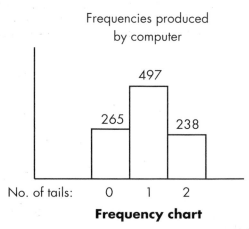

Figures produced by computer

497
265   238

No. of tails: 0   1   2

Frequency chart

Figure 11.1a

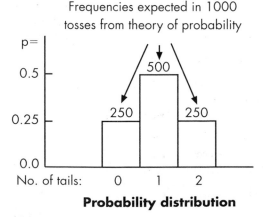

Frequencies expected in 1000 tosses from theory of probability

p=
0.5   500

0.25   250   250

0.0
No. of tails: 0   1   2

Probability distribution

Figure 11.1b

Table 11.4 Expected and obtained frequencies of numbers of tails in tosses of two coins

No. of tails	Probability × total	Expected frequency	Obtained frequency
0	0.25 × 1000	250	265
1	0.5 × 1000	500	497
2	0.25 × 1000	250	238

although we can never be certain *exactly* what frequencies will come up, we can be *absolutely* certain that something *near* the theoretically predicted frequencies will occur (almost all of the time). Out of 1000 tosses of two coins there could *never* be no tails ... or couldn't there?

What was the probability of the sex-guesser doing so well then (if she's a con-artist)?

We now have a formal system for calculating such events as the baby sexer getting two babies' sex right out of two trials, or only one right, or none right. To discover the probability of her guessing the sex of two babies correctly we treat 'correct guess' and 'incorrect guess' like heads and tails in tossing two coins. However, we need to move on to a system for dealing with ten trials, not just two. We could do it the long way by literally counting up all the possible permutations of outcomes for ten guesses or ten coin tosses, but there are over 1000 of these! Note that the *order* of guesses is important. For instance there are ten ways that she could get nine right and 1 wrong. She could be wrong on the first trial, or on the second, or on the third and so on. The number of possible permutations for just

Table 11.5 Possible permutations of events in tossing three coins together

a			b	c	d
Toss number			Number (n) of tails in outcome	Number of permutations	Probability of occurrence
1	2	3			
Head	Head	Head	0	1	0.125
Head	Head	Tail			
Head	Tail	Head	1	3	0.375
Tail	Head	Head			
Head	Tail	Tail			
Tail	Head	Tail	2	3	0.375
Tail	Tail	Head			
Tail	Tail	Tail	3	1	0.125

Total number of permutations 8

three trials is given in Table 11.5. Clearly, for ten trials the table of permutations is going to be huge. However, as you might have guessed, there is a quick way.

At this point I should point out very clearly that you are *not ever* going to be involved in elaborate calculations of probability of this kind (unless you want to be!). I am going through this example just to show that the whole process isn't magic. If I just give you the probability of guessing the sex of eight, nine or ten babies, you would just have to believe me. I would rather that you saw, in this introductory example, the whole process of finding probabilities and deciding what is extreme enough to reject H_0. After you get a basic understanding of this process (and trust in its non-magical nature), you will use calculators or computers, and prepared table values. Psychology students do not and should not need to be involved in a great deal of number crunching calculations.

Pascal's triangle – a quick way to probability

The mathematician Pascal developed an interesting little pattern of numbers shown in Figure 11.2. For our purposes, if we are tossing two coins (or making two baby sex guesses) just consult row number 2. You'll see that we get the row of values: 1 2 1. These are the frequencies of outcomes with no tails, one tail, two tails, just as shown in Table 11.3, column d. That is, of all the possible permutations of events which could occur, there is only one way to get no tails, two ways to get one tail (the single tail can come up on the first or the second toss) and just one way to get two tails, as we have already seen. For three events (three coins or guesses) we consult row three and obtain 1 3 3 1. Table 11.5, column c shows that of the eight possible permutations which could occur, only one will contain no tails, three will involve one tail, three will involve two tails, and just one will have three tails. So Pascal's triangle provides these frequencies and it will also give us the appropriate frequencies for tosses of ten coins. However, at this point we'll switch from heads and tails to correct and incorrect predictions of a baby's sex. Exactly the same logic and probabilities apply.

We can therefore move directly to row ten of Pascal's triangle. This tells us that there is

Row No.																					Total
0										1											1
1									1		1										2
2								1		2		1									4
3							1		3		3		1								8
4						1		4		6		4		1							16
5					1		5		10		10		5		1						32
6				1		6		15		20		15		6		1					64
7			1		7		21		35		35		21		7		1				128
8		1		8		28		56		70		56		28		8		1			256
9	1		9		36		84		126		126		84		36		9		1		512
10		10		45		120		210		252		210		120		45		10		1	1024

Figure 11.2 Pascal's triangle

Table 11.6 Frequencies of outcomes with *n* tails when tossing ten coins together

No. of correct predictions (*N*)	Probability of *N* occurring by chance (guessing) alone	
	Fraction	Decimal
0	1/1024	0.001
1	10/1024	0.01
2	45/1024	0.044
3	120/1024	0.117
4	210/1024	0.205
5	252/1024	0.246
6	210/1024	0.205
7	120/1024	0.117
8	45/1024	0.044
9	10/1024	0.01
10	1/1024	0.001

one way to get an outcome with no correct predictions. In other words, of all the 1024 permutations possible, only one of these has none right/ten wrong. As we said above, there are ten ways to get an outcome with 1 right/nine wrong. There are 45 permutations which contain two correct guesses and so on. Table 11.6 lists all the possible outcomes (one correct guess, two correct guesses etc.) along with the probability of getting this outcome, first as a fraction, following our formula above, then as a decimal as is the more usual way to express probability. Now we're close to home!

Suppose that our baby-sexer had guessed all 10 sexes correctly. Consulting Table 11.6, we now know that the probability of this occurring is 1/1024 or a probability (*p*) of around 0.001! Now, as I said earlier, there is always a cynic who says 'well it *could* just be a fluke!'. Well yes it could, but we must remember that if we tossed ten coins at a time thousands and thousands of times over, less than one time in a thousand would the ten coins all come up tails. Yet this is the result which our baby-sexer would have achieved on the *one* occasion that we decided to test her! We set up a sample and the *prediction* was that she would do well. She did. An equivalent situation that will emphasise just how well she did is this: imagine I ask a volunteer from the audience to think of, but not reveal, a number between 1 and 1000. I then ask *you* to pick a number from 1000 raffle tickets, already checked and shuffled in a bag. If I 'get' you to pick the same number as the volunteer is thinking of you'd think I was a pretty good conjuror, *not* just lucky! We can rely on the rarity of probability extremes so much that, at a recent village fete, a local garage safely offered a free new car if anyone threw seven 6s with seven dice.

Most people would conclude then, that if all ten babies' sexes are guessed correctly, we are fairly confident that something *is* going on here. We *reject* the idea that she is just guessing. If she *is,* the odds on her performance being that good are less than a thousand to one. We could still remain cynical about the actual *cause.* It may not be the stone pendulum. Perhaps she uses body shape or has access to hospital scanner records! A supported H_1 does not 'prove' that the underlying theory is correct. There are usually several possible explanations of a predicted outcome.

No one's that perfect!

What if our baby-sexer had only predicted nine correct sexes out of ten? Well, Table 11.6 tells us that the probability of *this* happening under H_0 (when she's just guessing) is 0.01. The probability of what she *did* produce – eight sexes correct – is $p = 0.044$.

Did we say exactly 8 or better than 7?

Actually, it would be odd if you said 'I'd be convinced if she got eight right out of ten,' but then went on to say that you would *not* be convinced if she got nine or ten right out of ten. What you meant initially was that you'd be convinced if she got *at least* eight right out of ten. To calculate the probability of this happening, if she's only guessing, we need only add up the probabilities of her getting eight, nine or ten right – that's $0.044 + 0.01 + 0.001$ and this comes to 0.055. Similarly, the probability of her getting nine right or better is 0.011.

Where shall we decide it wasn't a fluke?

We have now narrowed our problem right down and we're getting to the heart of the matter. Most people are convinced the baby-sexer is genuine when she guesses all ten correctly and the probability of her producing her results just by guessing would be less than 0.001. Many people are convinced with nine correct guesses and a p around 0.01. Not so many are too sure with eight correct guesses and p at 0.055. What did you opt for? If you said you'd be convinced with eight correct guesses out of ten, for instance, are you now comfortable with the knowledge that, even if she were guessing, she'd get this result by luck more than one time in every 20 that she attempted to predict the sex of ten babies (0.055 is a bit bigger than 1/20)? On the other hand, if you demanded she get all ten predictions correct, do you now think this was a little harsh? At some point between seven correct and ten correct most of us switch from being unconvinced to being convinced. Where, then, do we draw a line and say, 'No, this probability is too low – I doubt she could produce this performance by guesswork alone'?; alternatively, where is the point where we say, 'This probability is too high; the performance is too close to "chance" level'? In other words, at what point of probability of the results (under the assumption that she's guessing) do we opt to reject or retain H_0?

The standard level of significance – $p < 0.05$ or the '5% significance level'

Statisticians do have a standard cut-off point for making this decision, for deciding when to retain or reject H_0. Both lay people and social scientists would reject H_0 when p is less than 0.001 and when p is around 0.01. However, those accepting a probability of more than 0.05 (i.e. accepting 8 correct as convincing) would make the social scientist wince. Have a look at the exercise in Box 11.4 if you'd like another demonstration of how our intuitive sense of probabilities tends to concur with social science decisions.

The rule which social scientists follow is, quite simply:

if the probability of our result occurring under H_0 is not greater than 0.05, reject H_0;

if the probability of our result occurring under H_0 is greater than 0.05, retain H_0.

Some observations are necessary.

- Rejection of H_0 can never mean that we have 'proved H_1 true'
- Retention of H_0 cannot mean that we *know* H_0 is true
- If we reject H_0 we are simply stating that the probability of getting our result, *if the null hypothesis is true*, is so low that we are inclined to believe it *isn't* true and that we have conditional support for H_1
- If we retain H_0 we are saying that the probability of our result occurring, *if the null hypothesis is true*, was too high; it was too likely to occur just 'by chance', by mere sampling error. We are not confident that the result was extreme enough to make us very much doubt the validity of H_0. We are *not* saying, at all, that we have 'proved the null hypothesis true'.

In these circumstances then, getting eight correct sexes out of ten would *not* count as a significant result. p is 0.055 and just greater than 0.05 In short-hand we say '$p > 0.05$'. Getting nine or ten correct certainly would be a significant result. In either of the latter two cases we might say, more formally:

the difference between hits and misses was significant ($p < 0.05$),

or just,

the number of correct guesses was significant ($p < 0.05$)

Box 11.4   Knowing the limit with cards

This exercise should convince you that people operate naturally, with no statistical expertise, with the same significance level used in social science testing. Suppose I hand you a pack of cards and say one of two things is true – *either* all the red cards are on top *or* the pack is randomly shuffled. The second alternative is equivalent to the null hypothesis. Your job is to decide which of these two alternatives is the truth by turning over one card at a time from the top. We are interested in how many red cards you would want to turn over before being fairly convinced that all the reds are on top. There is a catch. To stop you going for an absolute but not very useful certainty, imagine you start with £1000. Every time you turn over a card this amount halves. If your guess is correct you get to keep all the cash. When would you make your guess? If you wait, very conservatively, to the seventeenth card, for instance, you would win just 1p! On the tenth you'd only win £1. After how many red cards would you first feel fairly confident that the probability of getting that many is too low, *if the pack is shuffled* (and H_0 is true)? DECIDE NOW!

The probability of drawing a red card off the top of a full, shuffled pack is 0.5 (there are two possible colours, equally represented, and we want one of these). Doing this four times in succession, without replacing the drawn card, gives a probability of 0.055.[4] A large number of people say that by five reds they feel pretty confident that the pack is fixed, not shuffled. In other words, they reject the (null) hypothesis that this run could have occurred with a shuffled pack, once the probability of it doing so has dropped well below 0.05. However, they are usually not doing any calculations in their heads!

---

[4] $26/52 \times 25/51 \times 24/50 \times 23/49 = 0.055$ – these fractions are the proportion of red cards to all cards after each turnover of a red card from the top.

Critical values

We have just found that the baby-sexer must reach a *minimum* of nine sexes correct for us to count her result as significant. Hence, the value nine here is a CRITICAL VALUE for this particular test of significance – it is a cut-off point. If she equals this or does better we reject H_0. If she does not reach it we retain H_0. For significance, her performance must be in the top 5% of outcomes that could be expected under H_0. With this rather crude distribution of outcomes (because we are using only 10 right/wrong *nominal level* outcomes) we find that 8 correct or better embraces 5.5% of the possible outcomes but 9 correct or better embraces just 1.1% of outcomes. In this latter *region* of outcomes we reject H_0 because we are in a region of less than 5%. We now move on to looking at these regions for rejecting H_0 in more detail.

Rejection regions

Returning to an example from Chapter 1, suppose you are out to demonstrate that Vitamin K5 (which, we shall assume, exists abundantly in spinach) has an enhancing effect on reading ability. Be assured this is completely in the realm of fantasy – I can read fine and I hate the stuff! You find an eight year-old child who absolutely adores spinach and has eaten acres of the stuff. Your theory now predicts that this child should have an exceptionally high reading score. She (Natasha) should appear very much to the right of the fictitious distribution of eight year-old reading scores shown in Figure 10.21 on page 253. This gives 40 as the overall population mean on the test. Suppose her score is 58. How can we assess whether this apparently large difference between her score and the population mean is *significant*?[5] We have to decide between the two possibilities depicted in Figure 11.3 (don't worry about 'α' for the moment).

To test the theory that vitamin K5 improves reading ability you would form the research hypothesis that a spinach eater will have a superior reading score. Formally, you would argue:

- H_0 is that the child's score is drawn from the population of normal eight year-old reading scores
- H_1 is that the child's score comes from a population of reading scores with a higher mean[6]
- if H_0 is true, what is the probability of drawing this score at random? If p is lower than 0.05 we shall reject H_0 and accept H_1: if p is higher than 0.05 we shall retain H_0.

If Natasha's score had been plucked at random from a barrel containing the entire population of normal eight year-old reading scores (a version of H_0), we know from the significance criterion established above that if it fell in the top 5% of scores we would

---

[5] For this sort of test we would not usually work with just one score. We would use a sample of scores and carry out a test on the mean or the median of this sample – see chapters 13 and 14. However, a single case is used here to aid explanation and clarity.

[6] In technical terms this would mean we are conducting a one-tailed test on a directional hypothesis – see p. 289. Although this is a controversial area among statisticians, the example is put this way for the sake of simplicity and explanation.

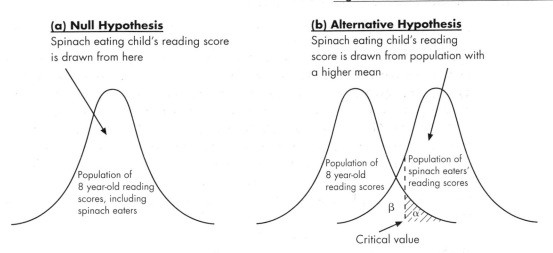

Figure 11.3 Null and alternative hypotheses for the effect of spinach on reading

reject H₀. We would argue that such an extreme score was too unlikely to have occurred 'just by chance'. The top 5% has been shaded in Figure 11.4 and we may now refer to this as the 'rejection region'; scores in this area cause us to reject H_0, as explained on the diagram.

From page 253, we can see that a score of 58 would mean the child was 1.8 standard deviations above the eight year-old mean score. This value of 1.8 is her z score. Referring to Table 2 in Appendix 2 we find that this value cuts off 0.0359 of the area to the right of the normal distribution, roughly the highest 3.6% of scores. It is therefore well within the

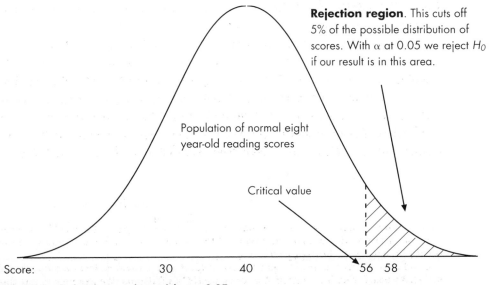

Figure 11.4 Rejection region with $p < 0.05$

top 5% of scores. We can reject H_0 and claim support for the alternative hypothesis which in turn supports the research proposal that spinach enhances reading (because it contains K5).

But couldn't it still be a fluke? – the crucial role of replication

Yes indeed it could! This is the whole point of setting a significance level. We leave ourselves a 1 in 20 chance that the result would occur randomly even if H_0 is true. Referring back to Box 11.4, about one time in 20 you *will* deal four red cards off the top of a shuffled pack. I can hear students going home, playing snap with their younger sister or brother and saying, 'There! Four reds! ... and that Coolican says it's rare.' Well, we *expect* you to get this result around one time in 20 deals of four cards, remember. So now you can hear a little voice (like my 11 year-old friend) saying, 'Well that means, if social scientists accept results less likely than 0.05 by chance, that one time in 20 they're accepting fluke results!' And the voice is right! (In a way.) Let's think about this:

> What steps can be taken to ensure that, when a researcher finds a difference significant with $p \le 0.05$, the finding is not a fluke occurrence (caused only by random error)?

What researchers do is to *replicate* studies. If an effect is taken as significant, and consequently published, someone else would try to obtain the same results in a repeat of the original study. The probability of two 'significant' differences occurring under H_0, simply through sampling error, is far smaller than the probability of just one occurring. Natasha *could*, then, have simply been an unusually good reader in the normal population of readers – an incidence of 'sampling error' (see p. 239). Vitamin K and/or spinach may not make a scrap of difference. Likewise, if the baby-sexer got nine out of ten sexes correct, she could just have had a lucky day. Replication would boost confidence in these results.

Type I and type II errors

We have a decision rule which says that if a sampled score falls above the point that cuts off the 5% of the distribution of normal reading scores, reject the null hypothesis and assume this score comes from a population with a higher mean. The trouble is that, if the null hypothesis is true, and all spinach eating scores are randomly distributed within the normal population (see the left hand side of Figure 11.3), when we select a spinach eater at random we have a 0.05 probability of selecting them from the rejection region. We would consequently reject the null hypothesis when it is, in fact, true. This is conventionally know as committing a TYPE I ERROR – see Table 11.7.

Table 11.7 Type I and type II errors

		Null hypothesis is:	
		Retained	Rejected
Null hypothesis is actually:	True	✓	Type I error
	False	Type II error	✓

Statisticians use the symbol 'α' (alpha) to refer to the probability of making a type I error *when H_0 is true* (i.e. getting a 'fluke set of results that will cause us to reject H_0 when it's true'). Technically, before doing any statistical analysis, we must decide what level of α is acceptable. Statisticians talk of 'setting α at 0.05' as the conventional level – see Box 11.5.

Suppose an audience has absolutely no effect on people's wiggly wire task performance (remember that?). If we carry out the experiment described earlier in exactly the same way 20 times over we are, in effect, simply drawing two random samples from the *same population* each time. Therefore, we would be likely to obtain just one 'significant' effect (which in fact would be a type I error). If we carry it out 100 times we should obtain, on the basis of probability 'law', just five type I errors leading to incorrect rejection of H_0.

Reducing the probability of a type I error – increasing type II error

How could we reduce the possibility of type I errors in the spinach eating example? Well, we could simply reduce α to 0.01 – see Figure 11.5. Then, where the null hypothesis is true, we shall only reject true null hypotheses 1% of the time. We shall feel safer that ours was not a 'fluke' result. However, we incur a complementary disadvantage in doing this. We increase the probability of *retaining* a null hypothesis when it is in fact false and not obtaining evidence for an effect or difference that is *actually there*. This mistake is known as a TYPE II ERROR. We become rather too conservative in our judgements. To support our spinach case, we now require a score of at least 63 for our result to count as significant and Natasha has only 58. We would have to report that her score did not differ significantly from the mean of normal scores and we would therefore have to retain the null hypothesis that Natasha's is a normal score. There is no support for the research

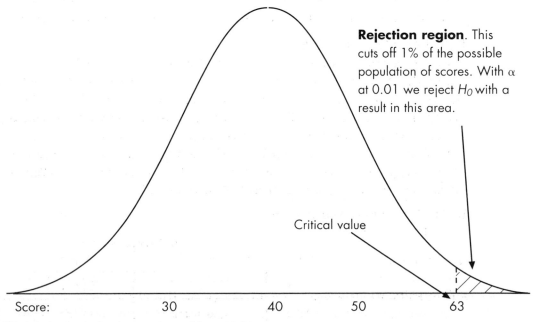

Rejection region. This cuts off 1% of the possible population of scores. With α at 0.01 we reject H_0 with a result in this area.

Critical value

Score: 30 40 50 63

Figure 11.5 Rejection region with $p < 0.01$

hypothesis that spinach improves reading ability. Figure 11.3 shows that if a score is higher than the critical value at α it falls in the rejection region of the normal population and we shall reject H_0 in favour of H_1. But what if the alternative hypothesis is in fact true? Some of the time we will select a spinach eater with a reading score to the left of α, in the area marked 'β. Because this person's score is *below* the critical value for rejection of H_0 (they are an unusually low scoring spinach eater) we would *retain* the null hypothesis. We would assume, incorrectly, that the person's score has been drawn from the normal population. We would make a type II error. β is in fact the probability that we will make a type II error *when the alternative hypothesis is true*.

If we make α, our significance level, a very strict value (e.g. lower it from 0.05 to 0.01), in order to lower the risk of making type I errors, we automatically increase the risk of making type II errors.

Faced with this dilemma, a simple answer is to increase sample size. The mechanics behind this are explained in Chapter 14 under the topic of 'Power'.

Different levels of significance – changing the value of α from 0.05

If the baby-sexer had got all ten predictions correct it would seem necessary to say that she didn't produce a result which was *just* significant at 5%. The probability of her result occurring if the null hypothesis was true was less than 0.001 ('$p < 0.001$'). When results are this strong, psychologists, in their final report, tend to point out the level obtained. Although this an area of debate (see Box 11.5), there is a tendency to use the following language in reporting results:

Significant at 5% – 'The difference was significant'
Significant at 1% – 'The difference was highly significant'

p $\leq$ 0.1 (the 10% level)

A researcher cannot be confident of results, or publish them as an effect, if the level achieved is only $p < 0.1$ But if the probability is in fact close to 0.05 (like the sex guesser's results if she gets eight predictions correct) it may well be decided that the research is worth pursuing. Procedure would be tightened or altered, the design may be slightly changed and sampling might be scrutinised, with an increase in sample size.

p $\leq$ 0.01 (the 1% level)

Sometimes it is necessary to be more certain of our results. If we are about to challenge a well-established theory or research finding by publishing results which contradict it, the convention is to achieve $p < 0.01$ significance before publication. A further reason for requiring this level would be when the researcher only has a one-off chance to demonstrate an effect. Replication may be impossible in many field studies or 'natural experiments'. In any case, significance at 1% gives researchers greater confidence in rejecting the null hypothesis.

Levels lower than p < 0.01 (<1%)

In research which may produce applications affecting human health or life changes, such as the testing of drugs for unwanted psychological or behavioural effects, we'd want to be even more certain that no chance effects were being recorded. Hence, researchers might even seek significance with $p < 0.001$ (0.1%).

When we want *to* retain H₀ with p > 0.05 (above the 5% level)

A researcher may be replicating a study which was a challenge to their work. It may be that showing there *isn't* a difference is the research aim. This would be the case with a lot of modern studies aimed at demonstrating a lack of difference between men and women on various tests and tasks. In this case the prediction is that the null hypothesis will be supported. The probability associated with results must now fall in the less extreme 95% area under the probability curve. However, Harcum (1990) argues that significance testing is *conservative* and various conventions tend to *favour* retention of the null hypothesis so that chances of a type I error are minimal. This creates a bias if the null hypothesis is what a researcher wants to support. Harcum's article contains various criteria that should be met by the data where research predicts support for H_0.

Box 11.5   Setting the significance level before or after results are in

There is a long-running debate between statistical 'purists' and practical researchers. Purists argue that the 'rules' of the significance testing game say that you should state before testing what level is acceptable and that is the only level you can then legitimately report. For instance, assume that you start research with α set at the usual 0.05. Suppose it turns out that your result is really extreme – it 'beats' the critical value for $p < 0.01$ for instance. According to this view you can't report anything other than that your results were significant at the level set (0.05). However, in practice, most students, and research psychologists, would report the 'better' value obtained. For instance, in the sign test just calculated, the researcher might report that the difference was significant with $p < 0.025$ because, if you look at the tables again you'll see that 1 is also the critical value in the 0.025 (one-tailed) column. I think I'm not a purist on this. It seems to me there is no harm in saying, 'Our result was, in fact less likely to occur under H₀ than 2½ times in 100'. It's important to remember, however, that a result significant at $p < 0.001$ is not necessarily 'better' than one at $p < 0.05$. A highly significant effect can nevertheless be quite weak, if the sample is very large. This is a further argument against over-large samples and is explained more fully in the correlation chapter.

Directional and non-directional hypotheses – one-tailed and two-tailed tests

Suppose, in the reading test example above, we actually have no particular prediction about the effects of K5 in spinach. Perhaps one group of theorists holds that it enhances reading ability while another group says that it actually slows up reading ability. In this case, we must decide between the two following alternatives:

- H_0 is that Natasha's score is drawn from the population of normal eight year-old reading scores
- H_1 is that Natasha's score comes from a population of reading scores with a *different* mean (it might be higher or *lower*)

Note that we now just claim that Natasha's score comes from a population with a *different* mean, not a *higher* one. The hypothesis tested is *non-directional*.

Using a one-tailed test

When we were deciding whether the spinach eating child's score came from a population with a *higher* mean, we were working with a *directional hypothesis* and we referred to

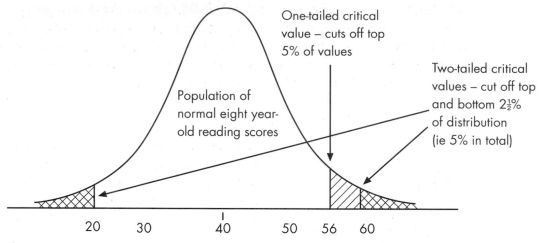

Figure 11.6   One and two-tailed critical values

only *one tail* of the distribution of means under H_0 – the right hand tail – see Figure 11.4. If our child's mean came from the top 5% of that distribution we would reject H_0.

A directional hypothesis *may* be tested with such a ONE-TAILED TEST but this can be controversial and we shall return to this point.

A non-directional hypothesis <u>requires</u> a two-tailed test

If, however, we only claim that the child's score is from a population with a *different* mean, then the rejection region *must* include the possibility that the child's score came from a distribution with a *lower* mean as well as from a distribution with a *higher* mean. As before, we reject H_0 only when the child's score falls in the extreme 5% of the distribution, but, in this case, the extreme 5% is taken as being at *either end* of the distribution; that is, the most extreme 2½% at each end. I hope Figure 11.6 makes this clear. We can see here that we now require a score of 60 in order to count Natasha's score as significant and, unfortunately, she is short of this. We must retain H_0

It is important to remember that a non-directional hypothesis must always be tested with a two-tailed test.

Returning to the baby-sexer for just a moment, suppose our friend had got every single prediction wrong. Would we say she was a hopeless baby-sex guesser? Or would this be a fascinating result? After all, the probability of her doing *this* 'by chance' is also 0.001. We might suspect that she has indeed got a valid method but that she has her instrument round the wrong way or is reading it incorrectly! Since everything is symmetrical (see Table 11.6), the probability of guessing ten sexes correctly is the same as the probability of guessing ten sexes *incorrectly*. The probability of each is 0.001. The probability of getting *either* ten right *or* ten wrong is .001 + .001 = .002. Here we are adding the probabilities in both ends of the probability distribution. If we want the probability of getting *at least* 9 right or wrong, we must add the two extreme probabilities at either end, that is: 10 right + 9 right + 9 wrong + 10 wrong. This is 0.001 + 0.01 + 0.01 + 0.001. Hence, the probability of getting nine or more right or wrong is 0.022 – still significant. Getting eight right was not significant, even using a one-tailed approach. For a two tailed approach we need to add on the probabilities of her getting either eight right or eight wrong. This is 0.044 + 0.044 added to 0.022. This total probability of her getting eight or more *right* or *wrong* is 0.11. As you'd expect, this is double the probability of her getting 8 or more correct and way above 0.05. So, a two-tailed test here produces the same result as a one tailed test – she must get nine or more right to convince us.

Why not always do one-tailed tests?

If we use a two-tailed test on the spinach eating score, we cannot report a significant difference between Natasha's score and the general mean. If we use a one-tailed test we *can*. Why not always do a one-tailed test then? Well, if we use a one-tailed test we cannot have our cake and eat it too. We must put all our eggs in the one basket – all the 5% at one end – and accept that if the result were *extreme* in the *opposite* direction, we'd still have to treat this as just a chance occurrence, support for H_0.

If your result for a one-tailed test is extreme in the *opposite* direction from that predicted by the hypothesis, you cannot report a significant result.

You cannot suddenly switch and say 'Ah it's significant but the other way!'. This is because you would then really be working with a significance level of 0.1 – the 0.05 you chose to work with and the new 0.05 you've just included.[7]

The critical value for a one-tailed test is always less extreme than the value for a two-tailed test. In crude terms, 'it is easier to obtain'. I say 'crude' because it is easy to slip into the habit of thinking something like 'Oh let's get a result, whatever. Surely there's some way this result is significant? It is for a one-tailed test.' This is kind of dangerous because what we really want is *confidence* that we really do have an effect, not 'something concrete to report in our assignment' or to get us into a journal. Nowhere should students lose marks solely because they do not obtain a result. The important thing to do on such 'failure' is to analyse critically both the design of the study and the theory which led to it. A failure to produce a significant difference may well be a very important outcome, especially if prior research predicted a difference.

However, because it is often so rewarding to 'get a result', the question some of you will no doubt be asking now is: 'Who would ever know we started with a prediction in the opposite direction?' Well, it's not that simple. When you present a piece of research work you rarely just present an isolated hypothesis and a test of it. The hypothesis needs to be a logical outcome of theoretical reasoning behind your overall research work. As we said in the introduction, a theory for which evidence of an effect in either direction would count as support is a pretty useless theory. However, if we are simply *exploring* data for differences we *must* use two-tailed tests. So, to summarise the 'rules' outlined above:

- if you use a one-tailed test and the result is extreme in the opposite direction from that predicted you may *not* claim a significant effect
- a one-tailed test is only appropriate with a directional hypothesis (but even then some theorists argue against their use in psychological research – see Box 11.6)
- if you test a non-directional hypothesis you *must* use a two-tailed test.

---

[7] This would be 0.075 if the result has come out significant in the opposite direction at the two-tailed value – your initial 0.05 and the new 0.025 at the other end.

It is safer then, overall, to always use two-tailed tests. No one can then accuse you of switching sides. The disadvantage of two-tailed tests is that we need to obtain a larger difference in order to make it into the rejection region. However, you will still obtain significance, assuming there *is* an effect to be found, *if you use a large enough sample*. If you want to use a one-tailed test do be aware of the debate outlined in Box 11.6.

Box 11.6   Please sir, may we use a one-tailed test, sir?

It is hard to imagine that statisticians would get passionately heated up about issues in their subject. However, they're scientists and of course they do. Odd, though, are the sorts of things they fall out over. Whether it is legitimate to do one-tailed tests in psychology on directional hypotheses is, believe it or not, one of these issues. Here are some views *against* the use of one-tailed tests on two-group psychological data:

A directional test requires that no rationale at all should exist for any systematic difference in the opposite direction, so there are very few situations indeed where a directional test is appropriate with psychological data consisting of two sets of scores. McRae, 1995

I recommend using a non-directional test to compare any two groups of scores . . . Questions about directional tests should never be asked in A level examinations. McRae, 1994

I say always do two-tailed tests and if you are worried about β, jack the sample size up a bit to offset the loss in power. Bradley, 1983

And some arguments *for* the use of one-tailed tests:

To generate a theory about how the world works that implies an expected direction of an effect, but then to hedge one's bet by putting some (up to $\frac{1}{2}$) of the rejection region in the tail other than that predicted by the theory, strikes me as both scientifically dumb and slightly unethical . . . Theory generation and theory testing are much closer to the proper goal of science than truth searching, and running one-tailed tests is quite consistent with those goals. Rodgers, 1986

. . . it has been argued that there are few, if any, instances where the direction [of differences] is not of interest. At any rate, it is the opinion of this writer that directional tests should be used more frequently. Ferguson and Takane, 1989

McRae is saying that any result in the non-predicted direction would have to be seen as a chance outcome since the null hypothesis for directional tests covers all that the alternative hypothesis does not. To justify use of a one-tailed test, you must, in a sense, be honestly and entirely uninterested in an effect in the opposite direction. A textbook example (one taken from a *pure* statistics book, not a statistics-for-social-science textbook) would be where a government agency is checking on a company to see that it meets its claim to include a *minimum* amount of (costly) vitamin X in its product. It predicts and tests for variations *below* the minimum. Variations above are not of interest and almost certainly are relatively small and rare, given the company's economic interests. A possibly equivalent psychological example could be where a therapist deals with severely depressed patients who score very much up the top end of a depression scale. As a result of therapy a decline in depression is predicted. Variations towards *greater* depression are almost meaningless since, after a certain degree of serious depression classification, the idea of becoming even more depressed is unmeasurable and perhaps unobservable.

Rodgers, however, says what most people feel when they conduct psychological projects. Why on earth should I check the other way when the theory and past research so clearly point in this one direction? In a sense, all McRae and Bradley are asking is that we operate with greater surety and always use the 2.5% level rather than the 5% level. If we've predicted a result, from closely argued theory, that goes in one direction, use two-tailed values and find we are significant in the opposite direction, we're hardly likely to jump about saying 'Eureka!'. Probably we will still walk away glumly, as for a failure to reach significance, saying 'What went wrong then?' It will still feel like 'failure'. If we had a point to make we haven't made it so we're hardly likely to rush off to publish now. Our initial argument would look silly.

During this argument it always strikes me as bizarre that textbooks talk as if researchers really do rigidly stick to a hypothesis testing order: think through theory, make a specific prediction, decide on one- or two-tailed test, find out what the probability is, make significance decision. The real order of events is a whole lot more disjointed than that. During research, many results are inspected and jiggled with. Participants are added to increase *N*. Some results are simply discarded. Researchers usually know what all the probability values are, however, before they come to tackle the niggling problem of whether it would be advisable to offer a one-or two-tailed analysis in their proposed research article. *When* the one-tailed test decision is made is a rather arbitrary matter. In some circles and at some times it depends on the received view of what is correct. In others it depends upon the actual theory (as it should) and in others it will depend upon who, specifically, is on the panel reviewing submitted articles.

So what *would* happen, realistically speaking, if a researcher or research team obtained an opposite but 'significant' result, having made a directional prediction? In reality I'm sure that if such a reversal did in fact occur, the research team would sit back and say 'Hmm! That's interesting!'. They're not likely to walk away from such an apparently strong effect, even though it initially contradicts their theorising. Theories and research findings rarely follow the pure and simple ideal. It is rare in psychology for a researcher to find one contrary result and say 'Oh well. That blows my whole theory apart. Back to the drawing board. What else shall I turn my hand to today then?' The result would slot into a whole range of findings and a research team in this dilemma might start to re-assess their method, look at possible confounding variables in their design and even consider some re-organisation of their theory in order to incorporate the effect. It is important to recognise the *usefulness* of this kind of result. Far from leaving the opposite direction result as a 'chance event', the greater likelihood is that this finding will be further investigated. A *replication* of the effect, using a large enough sample to get $p < 0.01$, would be of enormous interest if it clearly contradicts theoretical predictions – see p. 288 and 'the 1% level'.

So should you do one-tailed tests? This is clearly not a question I'm going to answer, since it really does depend upon so many things and is clearly an issue over which the experts can lose friends. Personally, I can see no great tragedy lying in wait for those who do use one-tailed tests so long as they are conscientious, honest and professional in their overall approach to research, science and publishing. As a student, however, you should just pay attention to three things:

- follow the universally accepted 'rules' given in the main text
- be aware that this is a debate and be prepared for varying opinions around it
- try to test enough participants (as Bradley advises), pilot your design and tighten it, so that you are likely to obtain significance at $p < 0.01$, let alone 0.025!

USING TESTS OF SIGNIFICANCE – THE GENERAL PROCEDURE

Significance tests are used when you've collected and organised your data and have come to a point where you're asking questions like, 'Well, we got a difference just as we predicted but is it a big enough one not to be a fluke?' or, 'It obviously worked (the independent variable); but where do I go from here?' Writing the statistical test section of practical reports is one of the hardest tasks for new students of psychology, often because the full logical process hasn't been completely absorbed, so I would recommend that you turn to this section whenever, in the early days, you want to organise this part of your practical write-up.

Let's look at what we did with the baby-sexer's test in brief terms.

	right	wrong

1. We obtained a difference. A description of our raw data was: 8   2
2. We calculated a 'critical value' – the maximum number she could get wrong (out of 10) that would give a result less likely to occur than five times in 100 under H_0. This value was 1.
3. We compared our friend's result with this 'critical value'.
4. We decided which side of the critical value our result was on – the non-significant side, because we wanted 1 for significance but obtained 2 (known as 's' in the *sign test* to be encountered in the next chapter).
5. We consequently reported significance or not at the level of probability set (0.05) – in this case, a non-significant result and we retained H_0. Officially, this level should be set before testing but $p \leq 0.05$ is the conventional maximum. This is a way of stating a lack of credibility for the null hypothesis. If the result is not significant we retain the null hypothesis as credible or not sufficiently undermined.

Table 11.8 Conventional procedure in conducting and reporting results of a statistical test of significance

Choose appropriate statistical test	When we've covered all the tests, Chapter 20 will help you through this step
Calculate test statistic	In our sex-typing case this was 2, the number our friend got wrong. In all cases the statistic will be denoted by a letter, for instance t or U. In our test, **s** = 2 (see p. 300)
Compare test statistic with critical value in tables Take account of: **1** Number of cases in sample (N) or df **2** Whether one- or two-tailed test **3** Maximum probability level acceptable	Tables are provided at the back of the book for all the tests introduced. In calculating our critical value, we took account of: **1** $N = 10$ **2** One-tailed test **3** $p \leq 0.05$ Critical value was 1
Decide which side of the critical value your result is on – pay attention to instructions accompanying the table	Our result of 2 was on the non-significant side of the critical value of 1
Report the decision – whether to retain or reject the null hypothesis and at what level of confidence (significance)	We retained the null hypothesis. We found a probability >0.05 that our results could occur if it was true. Therefore we didn't have sufficient confidence to reject it.

This is the logical sequence behind *any* test of significance, no matter how complicated they get. In fact, one aspect of the above sequence is even easier. We don't *calculate* the critical value – we look it up in tables. You'll see from the calculation of the sign test in the next chapter, that the value of 1, which we calculated as the critical value, is given directly by tables at the back of this book. If you're using a computer program you will usually be given the exact probability of the result occurring under the null hypothesis and you won't even have to consult tables. Table 11.8 puts the whole process in formal terms.

Glossary

Percentage of the probability area under H_0 which forms the 'rejection region'. Commonly known as the *significance level* set for the test	_____	alpha (α)
Assumption that populations differ (or that a population correlation <> 0 exists)	_____ _____	alternative hypothesis H_1
If the null hypothesis is *not* true, this is the probability that a type II error will be made	_____	beta (β)
Value used to decide whether a null hypothesis should be rejected or accepted. In an inferential test the obtained statistic is compared with this critical value	_____ _____	critical value
Hypothesis which states in which direction differences (or correlation) will occur	_____ _____	directional hypothesis
Informal test of data made simply by inspection and mental calculation plus experience of values	_____ _____	eyeball test
Hypothesis which does not state in which direction differences (or correlation) will occur	____-_____ _____	non-directional hypothesis
Assumption of no difference (or correlation) in the population(s) from which samples are drawn	_____ _____	null hypothesis H_0
A numerical measure of pure 'chance' (randomly based) occurrence of events	_____	**Probability**
A measure of probability based on existing data and comparing number of target events which have occurred with total number of relevant events	_____	empirical
A measure of probability calculated from logical first principles using the ratio of target possibilities to total possibilities	_____	logical
A measure of probability made on the basis of human internal, and often emotional assessment	_____	subjective

A histogram of the probabilities associated with a complete range of possible events	_____ _____	probability distribution
Area of (sampling) distribution which, if a result falls within it, determines rejection of H_0; the area cut off by the critical value	_____ _____	rejection region
Levels of probability at which it is agreed to reject H_0. If the probability of obtained results under H_0 is less than the set level, H_0 is rejected	_____ _____	**Significance levels**
Significance level generally considered too high for rejection of the null hypothesis but where effects 'significant' at this level might merit further investigation	_____	$p \leqslant 0.1$ (10%)
Conventional significance level	_____	$p \leqslant 0.05$ (5%)
Significance level preferred for greater confidence than that given by the conventional one and which should be set where research is controversial or unique	_____	$p \leqslant 0.01$ (1%)
Test performed in order to decide whether the null hypothesis should be retained or rejected	_____ _____	significance test/decision
Test referring to both tails of the probability distribution under H_0; must be used if alternative hypothesis is non-directional	___-_____ _____	two-tailed test
Test referring to only one-tail of the distribution under H_0; may be used if alternative hypothesis is directional	___-_____ _____	one-tailed test
Mistake made in rejecting the null hypothesis when it is true	_____ ____ _____	type I error
Mistake made in retaining the null hypothesis when it is false	_____ ____ _____	type II error
Procedures for making inferences about whole populations from which samples are drawn, e.g. significance tests	_____ ____	inferential test/statistics

Exercises

1. State whether the following values of z (on a normal distribution) are significant or not ($p < 0.05$) for:

   a. One-tailed tests:
      1.32   1.75   −1.9   −0.78
   b. Two-tailed tests:
      −2.05   1.89   −1.6   1.98

2. State whether tests of the following hypotheses might permit one- or two-tailed tests:

   a. Diabetics will be more health conscious than other people.
   b. Extroverts and introverts will differ in their ability to learn people's names.
   c. Job satisfaction will correlate negatively with absenteeism.
   d. Self-esteem will correlate with outward confidence.

3. A student sets out to show that attitude change will be greater if people are paid more to make a speech which contradicts their present attitude. Her tutor tells her that this runs directly counter to research findings on 'cognitive dissonance'.

   a. What would be the appropriate significance level for her to set?
   b. If she had originally intended to use the 5% level, is she now more or less likely to make a type II error?

4. A z score of 2.0 is significant (two-tailed), with $p \leq 0.05$ because it is greater than the critical value of 1.96 for $p \leq 0.05$. This is why the first line of the table below is marked 'true'. Can you complete the rest of the table with ticks or crosses?

z	One- or two-tailed test	$p \leq$	true or false
a. 2.0	Two	0.05	true
b. 1.78	One	0.05	
c. 2.2	Two	0.025	
d. 2.88	One	0.002	
e. 3.35	Two	0.001	
f. 2.22	One	0.01	

Answers

1. a. 1.32 and −0.78 are not significant. 1.75 and −1.9 are (*critical value* = 1.65).
   b. 1.89 and −1.6 are not significant. −2.05 and 1.98 are (*critical value* = 1.96).

2. a. possibly one   b. only two   c. possibly one   d. only two

3. a. 1%   b. more likely

4. b. true   c. false   d. true   e. true   f. false

12
Nominal level tests – analysing categories

The tests presented in this Chapter are at the *nominal* level of measurement. They are:

1. *The binomial sign test* (better known as just 'sign test').

   This tests for a difference between pairs of *related data,* by calculating the probability that the proportion of positive and negative differences would occur if H_0 is true – that positive and negative differences are equally distributed.

2. *Chi-square* (χ^2) – test of association between two *categorical* variables; the 2 × 2 or $R \times C$ versions can be used to test for *difference* between one distribution and another (e.g. males' and females' distributions across car driver and non-car driver); can also be seen as a 'collapsed' correlation (association) across two categorical variables. Versions of chi-square covered are:

   - one variable, two categories
   - 2 × 2 frequencies
   - $R \times C$ (more than two rows or columns)
   - one variable, more than two categories ('*Goodness of fit*' test)

   There are limitations on the use of χ^2: data must be frequencies, not ratios, means or proportions, and must belong exclusively to one or another category, i.e. the same case (person) must not appear in more than one 'cell' of the data table. There is statistical debate about what to do when expected cell frequencies are low. Preferably avoid low expected cell frequencies where possible, but if low frequencies occur, sample sizes above 20 make the risk of a type I error acceptably low.

INTRODUCTION TO SIMPLE TESTS OF STATISTICAL SIGNIFICANCE

The next four chapters cover all the basic test of significance you are likely to encounter on an initial psychology research methods course. Mostly these are appropriate where you have two data samples (chi-square can be an exception) and you want to test for differences or correlation. Each calculation on your samples ends with finding a *test statistic* which then has to be checked against tabled *critical values* in Appendix 2. You will need to know how many were in your samples and what level of significance you want to check at. In each chapter we shall then start with a brief explanation of the test, some sample data to be tested, followed by the calculations. Problems, limitations and issues are then discussed. Finally, the specific conditions for which the test is appropriate are tabled, along with any limitations.

For the current chapter you should be consulting these tests only if your data are *categorical* (i.e. *'nominal'* level) or have been *reduced* to categories from an initial measured level (see the first part of Chapter 10).

RELATED DATA – THE (BINOMIAL) SIGN TEST

RATIONALE

Suppose that, in order to assess the effectiveness of therapy, a psychotherapist investigates whether or not, after three months of therapy, clients feel better about themselves. If therapy improves people's evaluation of themselves then we would expect clients' self-image ratings to be *higher* after three months' therapy than they were before. Take a look at the data in Table 12.1, showing clients' self-image ratings on a scale of 1–20, where a *high* value relates to a very *positive* self-image. Here we would expect the scores (clients' rating of their own self-image) to be *higher* in column C than they are in column B. Therefore we would expect *positive* differences in column D. If we ignore the *size* of each difference, and put the *sign* (or direction) of each difference into column E, what would we expect to find if the therapy is working? We would hope to obtain a large number of positives and a small number of negative signs, if any. The SIGN TEST gives us the probability of finding this number of negative signs (or fewer), given that the null hypothesis is true. That is, it tells us how likely it is that such a large (or even larger) split between positive and negative signs would be drawn 'by chance' under the null hypothesis. What *is* the null hypothesis? It is the assumption that there are equal numbers of positive and negative signs in the 'population' we have sampled from – and we assume we have sampled from that population at random – see Figure 12.1. This is exactly the position we were in with the baby sexing result in the last chapter and, in effect, we went through the details of a sign test there. Here, we simply present the 'cookbook' method of conducting a sign test on a set of this kind of paired data.

Figure 12.1 The sign test gives us the probability of drawing a certain number of negative signs (or fewer), given that we have randomly sampled from a 50–50 distribution

DATA

Table 12.1 Self-image scores before and after three months' therapy

A	B		C	D	E
Client	Self-image rating			Difference (C−B)	Sign of difference
	Before therapy	After 3 months' therapy			
a	3	7		4	+
b	12	18		6	+
c	9	5		−4	−
d	7	7		0	
e	8	12		4	+
f	1	5		4	+
g	15	16		1	+
h	10	12		2	+
i	11	15		4	+
j	10	17		7	+

Procedure	Calculation on our data
1. Calculate the difference between columns B and C always subtracting in the same direction. If a directional prediction has been made, it makes sense to take the expected smaller score from the expected larger one. Enter difference in column D.	Find difference between scores in columns B and C of Table 12.1. We expect column C scores to be higher. Hence we take C–B in each case.
2. Enter the *sign* of the difference in column E. Leave a blank where the difference is zero and ignore these in the analysis.	See column E of Table 12.1. N becomes 9 because the result for client d is zero. This case is dropped from any further analysis.
3. Count the number of times the less frequent value occurs. Call this 's'.	Negative signs occur less frequently, so $s = 1$
4. Consult Table 3, Appendix 2. a) Find the line for N (the *total* number of signs not including zeros). b) Consult 1- or 2-tailed values.	a) $N = 9$ (see step 2, above). b) Therapy should only improve. Make the test one-tailed.
5. Compare s with the critical value for the significance level set. For significance, s must be equal to or less than the appropriate critical value.	Our s is 1. The critical value under the column headed $p < 0.05$ (one-tailed) is 1. Therefore, our result is not greater than the critical value and meets the criteria for significance.
6. Make statement of significance.	Our result is significant with $p < 0.05$. We may reject the null hypothesis.

SUMMARY

The sign test looks only at the *sign* or *direction* of differences between pairs of data. The critical value tells us the *maximum* number of signs we can have in one of the groups (positives or negatives) in order for us to claim that, overall, our set of differences is significant. We shall leave this test here since it was in fact this test that we were developing from first principles, using the baby-sexer data, whilst introducing significance in the last chapter.

THE BINOMIAL SIGN TEST – CONDITIONS FOR USE

Difference or correlation	Level of data	Related or Unrelated design
Differences	**Nominal** (or above, if reduced to nominal)	**Related**

Notes and special conditions: only the *sign* of the difference between each pair of values is used.

H_0: population contains equal numbers of positive and negative differences

UNRELATED DATA – THE CHI-SQUARE (χ^2) TEST

Note: 'chi' is pronounced 'kye' in English. The Greek 'χ' is like the 'ch' of (Scottish) 'Loch'.

RATIONALE

> Please start by reading Box 12.1 and trying to answer the questions set at the end of the passage.

In the marketing survey described in Box 12.1, 56% of women spontaneously reporting a loss of up to one inch from their thighs, and 52% reporting the same for their hips, after just one month's use of a gel seems, at first sight, very impressive (one colleague I spoke to over this said, 'Never mind the stats, Hugh, where do I get hold of the stuff?'!). However, we really need to compare this result with the prediction under the null hypothesis. What would happen if the women were choosing a response at random? If we assume that choices of 'gained' and 'lost' occur with equal frequency, then we would expect, from 550 choices, 275 'gains' and 275 'losses'. In chi-square terminology, these frequencies predicted under the null hypothesis are known as EXPECTED FREQUENCIES – they are what we typically *expect* to occur with our overall frequencies if the null hypothesis is true. Note that the frequencies we actually obtained from our study are referred to as OBSERVED FREQUENCIES. Our data for our first simple chi-square test on the hip data, then, would be as follows.

DATA (FOR SIMPLE ONE VARIABLE/TWO-CATEGORY TEST)

Table 12.2 _Observed frequencies_ of women reporting losses and gains in hip fat

	Lost up to 1"	Gained up to 1"	Total
Number of women choosing:	a 286	b 264	550

Table 12.3 _Expected frequencies_ of women reporting losses and gains in hip fat

	Lost up to 1"	Gained up to 1"	Total
Number of women choosing:	a 275	b 275	550

The chi-square test simply makes a calculation based on the distance each observed cell frequency is from its partner expected cell – what would be _expected_ under the null hypothesis. It uses the following general formula:

$$\chi^2 = \Sigma \frac{(O - E)^2}{E}$$

Procedure	Calculation on our data
1. Give each corresponding observed and expected cell a letter.	Letters 'a' and 'b' are shown in Table 12.2 and Table 12.3.
2. Calculate expected frequencies according to the null hypothesis (here we assume equal frequencies in each cell).	See Table 12.3. Each cell = total averaged across cells = 550 ÷ 2

3. Calculate according to χ^2 formula:
  a) Subtract expected from observed frequencies.
 	
  b) Square each cell result.
  c) Divide each result by E.
 	
  d) Sum all results.
	Cell a **Cell b**
	$O - E$ 286–275 264–275
	          =11 =−11
	$(O - E)^2$ =121 =121
	$(O - E)^2/E$ =121/275 =121/275
	          =0.44 =0.44
	$\Sigma(O - E)^2/E$ =0.44 + 0.44 = 0.88
	    hence χ^2 =**0.88**

4. Calculate 'degrees of freedom'[1] which here will be one less than the total number of cells.	$df = 2 - 1 = 1$
5. Using the result of χ^2 and the calculated df, consult Table 4, Appendix 2 and find the relevant critical value.	For $df = 1$ we find that, for $p < 0.05$, we need a χ^2 value of _at least_ 3.84.
6. Make significance decision.	Our calculated χ^2 value 0.88 is well below the required figure of 3.84. Hence our result is not significant ($p > 0.05$) and _we retain the null hypothesis._

[1] See 'Notes on chi-square' at the end of the chapter.

What about the result for thighs?

You might think we cheated a little there by dealing only with the less impressive hip data. OK. Let's look at the result for the thigh data.

> Calculate the chi-square value for the thigh data, following the procedure above but substituting the observed frequencies of 308 losses and 242 gains. The expected frequencies will remain the same.

You should have obtained the result that chi-square is 7.92. This value is well above the required critical value of 3.84. In fact, it is also above the value required for significance at $p < 0.01$ where χ^2 must be at least 6.64, so we certainly have a significant result here.

Box 12.1 Does the magic ointment really work?

A few years ago Christian Dior ran an advert in a colour supplement claiming that, of 550 women asked to use a fat reducing gel ('Svelte') for one month, upon a later survey, 52% claimed that they had lost 'up to one inch' off their hips during that period, whilst 56% had lost the same amount off their thighs. Now this might sound very impressive indeed except that we do not know what questions were asked in the survey. This is a perfect example of the need to know what question was asked before being able to fully interpret an apparently strong piece of evidence. It is unlikely that the women were simply asked to give open-ended responses. It is very likely indeed that they were asked to respond to multiple choice items, such as 'Over the last month did you:

a. lose up to one inch off your hips
b. gain up to one inch off your hips
c. notice no change at all on your hips?'

For simplicity's sake let's ignore the latter alternative since there would *always* be some, perhaps very tiny, change over one month. Here then, let's imagine we have 52% of the sample of 550 saying 'lost fat' and 48% saying 'gained fat' in reference to their hips. That's 286 positive and 264 negative outcomes from the Dior marketing perspective.

Questions for you to ponder are:
1. How many women would respond 'positive' and how many 'negative' if they were simply tossing a coin (i.e. selecting an alternative at random)?
2. On the basis of your answer to the question above, are the 286 vs 264 results *impressive* (i.e. will we consider them to be a *significant difference*) or are they within the range we might reasonably expect 'by chance' if the women are selecting at random (a form of the null hypothesis)?

Taking the slightly more impressive 56% losing up to one inch from their thighs, you might ponder the same questions.

A MORE COMPLEX (BUT MUCH MORE COMMON) EXAMPLE – THE 2 × 2 CHI-SQUARE

Must we accept then, that the gel does indeed work on thighs at least? Life is never that simple (you probably guessed that I wouldn't have used this example if it were!). Let's reconsider what we did with the gel survey figures above. For the null hypothesis we assumed that, in the absence of using Dior's gel, women would select *at random* from the two choices 'did you *gain* up to 1 inch ...' and 'did you *lose* up to 1 inch ...'. In fact, this is not good science. This is what we *might* assume if we could know no better – if we had no chance of determining what would happen under a free choice. But we *can* find out what would happen. What we need is a *control group* with whom to compare our 'experimental' group – see p. 55. On one occasion I did informally ask all the women in a lecture audience to answer the question 'cold' (with no prior information about the gel advert, but with assurances that the purpose was statistical demonstration!). 53% reported a loss and 47% reported a gain, when forced to choose between these two alternatives. If we assumed these same percentages would be found with a control group of 550 women, equal in number to the Dior survey group, then we would obtain the (rounded) figures shown in Table 12.4.

Table 12.4 *Observed frequencies* (fictitious) for the number of gel using and control group women reporting a loss or gain of up to 1 inch in the month prior to survey

	Lost up to 1"	Gained up to 1"	Total
Gel group choices:	a 308	b 242	550
Control group choices:	a 292	b 258	550
	600	500	1100

What we have in Table 12.4 is a classic form of data table on which we would perform a 2×2 chi-square in order to discover whether there is an association between using gel and losing fat ('2×2' because there are two columns and two rows). Note that we are assuming that the independent variable (using gel or not using it) is having a causal effect on a dependent variable (loss or gain of fat). Note also that these two variables are *both* at a *categorical* or *nominal* level because they are not measured on any sort of scale and each has just two qualitatively separate values. It is not necessary, however, for there to be an *experimental* independent variable and dependent variable (see p. 51). We could be interested, for instance, in whether introverts are more likely to feel awkward on a nudist beach than extroverts – see Table 12.5. Introversion need not *cause* introverts to feel awkward; awkwardness may be related to or simply a part of the overall personality characteristic.

Table 12.5 Frequencies of introverts and extroverts who would/would not feel awkward on a nudist beach

A	Observed frequencies			B	Expected frequencies		
	Extrovert	Introvert	Total		Extrovert	Introvert	Total
would feel:				**would feel:**			
Awkward	a 10	b 40	50	Awkward	a 25	b 25	50
not awkward	c 40	d 10	50	not awkward	c 25	d 25	50
Total:		50	50	100	**Total:**		50	50	100

Expected frequencies for the new gel data

The null hypothesis for the new (fictitious) gel study is based on the assumption that there is absolutely no association, in the population as a whole, between using the gel (or not) and changes in amounts of fat. More technically, it assumes that frequencies in the population are arranged as are the frequencies for our two variables separately, with no relationship between the two. Let's put that into concrete terms for our example. In our fictitious study, 550 women used gel and 550 women did not.

> If there is absolutely no association between using gel and losing fat, then how many of the 600 who 'lost up to one inch', shown in Table 12.4, should appear in cell A (gel users) and how many in cell C (non-gel users), given there were equal numbers of gel and non-gel users?

I hope you decided that just half the fat losers (i.e. 300) should be gel users and half should be non-users. There were equal numbers of users and non-users and, *if gel use has nothing to do with fat loss*, then about half those who lose weight would be from each group. The expected frequencies are shown in Table 12.6.

Table 12.6 *Expected frequencies* for the number of gel-using and control group women reporting a loss or gain of up to 1 inch in the month prior to survey

	Lost up to 1"		Gained up to 1"		Total
Gel group choices:	a	300	b	250	550
Control group choices:	c	300	d	250	550
		600		500	1100

This is the reasoning that all expected frequencies are based on. The formula for calculating an expected frequency cell is:

$$E = \frac{R \times C}{T}$$

where R is the total of the row, and C is the total of the column in which the cell is situated. T is the overall total. However, you did in fact use a version of this in your head in deciding that 550/1100 (R/T, or a half) of the 600 fat losers (C) would be expected in cell a. The general formula is used because, in most cases, the numbers are not quite as simple as the ones I've partly invented here.

It is important to remember that 'expected frequencies' are those 'expected' under the null hypothesis, not those (in fact the opposite of those) that the researcher usually expects (or would like) to occur in the research study.

Let me try to outline a visual example of what a 2×2 chi-square does (roughly speaking) by referring to Table 12.5, where 50 introverts and 50 extroverts have been asked whether they would feel awkward on a nudist beach. 50% of *all* participants reported feeling awkward. Hence, half the introverts and half the extroverts should, in turn, report feeling awkward if there is no link between awkwardness and introversion. The expected

Random bounce
into any cell

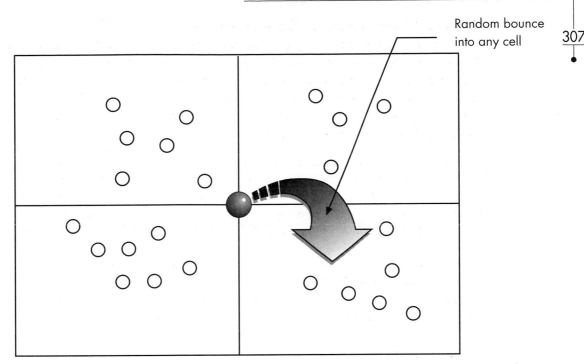

Figure 12.2 Chi-square assumes random 'bouncing' into the cells, given the row and column

frequencies for this example then are 25 in each cell. For a significant result, indicating an association between awkwardness and introversion, we would want the *observed* frequencies in cells a, b, c and d to depart a good deal from the *expected* frequencies predicted under the null hypothesis. In Figure 12.2 we have an imaginary box with four compartments into which we 'drop' the results in a random manner. Imagine each one of the 100 results is a little ball dropped onto the centre spot and bouncing randomly into one of the four equal sized compartments. There is a limitation to the randomness here – when any row or column adds to fifty we stop permitting balls into that row or column. If we dropped the 100 balls many many times then, roughly speaking, the results would vary around those in Table 12.5, mostly by only a little but sometimes (less frequently) by quite a lot. If we calculate chi-square for every drop of 100 balls, then through this largely random process we will create a distribution of chi-square values. For a significant result, what we are interested in is obtaining a chi-square value that is in the top 5% of this random distribution of values – that is we want a chi-square value that would occur less than 5 times in 100 *if the null hypothesis were true* (if the balls were bouncing randomly).

DATA (FOR REGULAR 2 × 2 CHI-SQUARE TEST)

Now let's calculate a 2 × 2 chi-square on a set of actual data gathered in a psychology practical workshop investigating the proposal that women are better drivers in terms of obeying traffic rules, in particular that of stopping when a traffic light is on amber. Have a look at the data in Table 12.7.

Table 12.7 Numbers of drivers stopping or not at an amber traffic light by sex

Behaviour at amber light	Sex of the driver		Total
	Female	Male	
Stopped	a 90	b 88	178
Did not stop	c 56	d 89	145
	146	177	323

NOTE: If you are about to use this procedure to calculate chi-square for your own gathered data, do consult the 'limitations on the use of chi-square' at the end of this chapter (page 310) before proceeding. Your data may not be suitable and/or may produce a quite unreliable result.

Procedure	Calculation on our data
1. Give each corresponding observed and expected cell a letter.	Letters a, b, c and d are shown for the observed frequencies in Table 12.7
2. Calculate expected frequencies using the equation: $$E = \frac{R \times C}{T}$$ where R is the total of the row in which the cell appears, C is the total of the column in which it appears and T is the overall total.	**Cell a** $(146 \times 178)/323 = $ **80.46** **Cell b** $(177 \times 178)/323 = $ **97.54** **Cell c** $(146 \times 145)/323 = $ **65.54** **Cell d** $(177 \times 145)/323 = $ **79.46**

3. Calculate according to the χ^2 formula given earlier:

Step in formula:	Cell a	Cell b	Cell c	Cell d	
i. $O - E$	$90 - 80.46 = 9.54$	$88 - 97.54 = -9.54$	$56 - 65.54 = -9.54$	$89 - 79.46 = 9.54$	
ii. $(O - E)^2$	$(9.54)^2 = 91.01$	$(-9.54)^2 = 91.01$	$(-9.54)^2 = 91.01$	$(9.54)^2 = 91.01$	
iii. $(O - E)^2/E$	$91.01/80.46 = $	$91.01/97.54 = $	$91.01/65.54 = $	$91.01/79.46 = $	total
iv. Σ results:	1.13	0.93	1.39	1.15	= **4.6**

4. Calculate 'degrees of freedom'[2] using: $df = (R - 1)(C - 1)$ where R is the number of rows and C the number of columns.	$df = (2 - 1) \times (2 - 1) = 1$
5. Using the result of χ^2 and the calculated df, consult Table 4, Appendix 2 and find the relevant critical value.	For $df = 1$ and using two-tailed values[2], we find that, for $p < 0.05$, we need a χ^2 value of *at least* 3.84
6. Make significance decision.	Our calculated χ^2 value of 4.6 is above the required figure of 3.84. Hence our result is significant ($p < 0.05$).

Here then, if sex is not related to stopping at the amber light (the loose null hypothesis), the expected frequencies were that just 80 of the 146 women drivers should stop whereas, in fact, 90 did so. About 50% of the male drivers stopped, compared with a far greater

---

[2] See 'Notes on chi-square' at the end of the chapter.

proportion of women drivers. The observed frequencies vary far enough away from the expected frequencies for the chi-square value to be a relatively rare and high one, *if the null hypothesis is true*.

Quick 2 × 2 formula

This can be used only where there are two columns and two rows, as in the example above. It saves the labour of calculating expected frequencies and, if you're handy with a calculator, you'll find this can be done in one move from the cell totals:

$$\chi^2 = \frac{N(AD - BC)^2}{(A + B)(C + D)(A + C)(B + D)}$$

where N is the total sample size.

MORE COMPLEX CHI-SQUARE DATA ($R \times C$ DESIGNS)

Each of the two variables in a chi-square table might have more than two values. We might for instance have introduced a *placebo group* to the gel study (see p. 55). We could give an inert cream to a third group of participants in order to account for any psychological effect that simply tending to one's body might have on one's retention of fat. We might have used the categories 'stopped', 'slowed down' and 'kept on going' in the sex and traffic light observations. Cialdini *et al.* (1990) varied the amount of litter placed by the investigators on a path down which unwitting participants would walk after they had received a leaflet from research assistants. The design tested the proposal that more litter already present on the path would prompt a greater amount of littering by participants. The results appear in Table 12.8.

Table 12.8 Amount of existing litter and frequency of consequent littering (Cialdini *et al*, 1990)

Observed person	Amount of existing litter		
	0 or 1 piece	2 or 4 pieces	8 or 16 pieces
dropped litter	17	28	49
didn't drop litter	102	91	71

Cialdini, R.B., Reno, R.R. and Kallgren, C.A. (1990) A focus theory of normative conduct: Recycling the concept of norms to reduce litter in public places. Journal of Personality and Social Psychology, 58, 1015–26. Copyright © 1990 by the American Psychological Association.

df here are $(3 - 1) \times (2 - 1) = 2$. The chi-square result is 22.43 and easily exceeds the required value of 13.82 for $p < 0.001$ – a 'highly significant' result might be reported.

THE 'GOODNESS OF FIT' TEST – χ^2 ON A SINGLE VARIABLE

We started this section on chi-square by considering frequencies for a single variable – numbers of people reporting a loss or gain of fat. This single variable might have had several categories, not just two. We might for instance be interested in the number of births at a particular hospital in each quarter of the year, as arranged in Table 12.9.

Table 12.9 Number of babies born per quarter year

Jan–Mar	Apr–Jun	Jul–Sep	Oct–Dec	Total
129	297	165	133	724

The higher number of babies born in April–June might be support for the suggestion that more babies are born in the second quarter of the year, just nine months after the warmest and most body-exposing quarter the year before!

The chi-square calculation for this table is performed in exactly the same way as that shown at the beginning of the section for the two-category test, except that here we must calculate for cells a, b, c, and d (not just a and b). The expected frequencies, as before, will be the total of the frequencies averaged across all the cells. We have 722 births overall and four cells. So, 724/4 gives 181 as the expected frequency for each cell. *df* are again (and for all single variable tests) one less than the number of categories, giving us a value of 3. You might like to calculate the result and, if so, don't look at the answer I'm about to give, which is: $\chi^2 = 103.43$ and is significant with $p < 0.01$.

The 'goodness of fit' test is sometimes used in the estimation of whether a large sample approximates to a normal distribution (a requirement for some significance tests – see p. 339). Here expected frequencies would be calculated using Table 2, Appendix 2 to determine the number of scores which should fall between, for example, the mean and half a standard deviation, half a standard deviation and one standard deviation, and so on. Using these known proportions under the normal curve the goodness of fit test can tell us whether our observed frequencies depart from these ideal frequencies to a significant degree.

LIMITATIONS ON THE USE OF CHI-SQUARE

Observations must be unique to one cell

If we were to look for a relationship between social class and participation in football or cricket we might find that some participants would appear in more than one preference cell, because they participate in both sports. This would invalidate assumptions made on the chi-square findings.

Only frequencies can appear in cells

Chi-square *cannot* be calculated where the cell contents are: means, proportions, ratios, percentages or anything other than a frequency count of the number of instances in the data of an occurrence described by the particular cell.

Low expected frequencies

There is a problem with accepting a chi-square result where expected frequency cells

Table 12.10 Low expected frequencies – too few data in one category

Observed frequencies				Expected frequencies			
	Preferred hand				**Preferred hand**		
	Left	**Right**	**Total**		**Left**	**Right**	**Total**
Better ear				**Better ear**			
Left	2	6	8	Left	0.8	7.2	8
Right	0	12	12	Right	1.2	10.8	12
Total	2	18	20	**Total**	2	18	20

are low. How low though is a subject of much debate among statisticians. A rule of thumb given by Cochran (1954) and used for many years was that *no more than 20% of expected frequency cells should fall below 5*. This would rule out any 2×2 calculations where a single expected frequency cell was below 5. Low expected frequencies often occur where too few data have been collected in one of the rows or one of the columns – see for instance Table 12.10.

Some statisticians feel Cochrane's rule is too 'conservative' – it leads to retention of the null hypothesis too often for a particular significance level. That is, there is a danger of too many type II errors (the original problem was that low expected frequencies could produce too many type I errors). Camilli and Hopkins (1978) argue that 2×2 chi-square tests are accurate and 'safe' even when one or two of the expected frequencies are as low

Table 12.11 Data producing weak evidence for age differences in conservation

Age	Conserved	Didn't conserve	Total
5 years	2	6	8
7 years	6	2	8
Total	8	8	16

as 1 or 2, so long as the total sample size is greater than 20. With both these criteria unmet it's easy to produce an example where the chi-square calculation appears untrustworthy. Calculation on the data in Table 12.11 gives a chi-square value of 4 which is 'significant' with $p < 0.05$. The expected frequencies here would be 4 in each cell – the null hypothesis says there are equal numbers of seven-year olds who conserve and don't conserve, likewise for five-year olds. Without statistical sophistication one can see that it would be relatively easy 'by chance' to obtain these results. Even if the proportion of conservers and non-conservers is 50–50 and the same for the 5 and 7 year old populations, it would not be remarkable to select 6–2 instead of 4–4 for seven year-olds and the reverse for five year-olds. One can, in fact, quite easily calculate the probability of doing so by simply counting all the possible combinations of cell data, keeping the row and column totals fixed at eight. We then compare this figure with the number of combinations which are as far from the expected frequencies as are our data or further. Working from first principles in this way gives a probability of occurrence substantially greater than 0.05. However, you don't want to be forced into the position of making such laborious and time consuming calculations.

Avoiding the problem – check before you gather data

In order to avoid worries about low expected frequencies there are three basic precautions you can take:

- *Avoid low samples for one category.* Use a design which is unlikely to produce low frequencies in one row or column – be wary of gathering data on left-handers, conservers among younger age groups, single parents, people with a particular disorder such as dyslexia (apart from ethical considerations) unless you know in advance you can get enough of these.

- *Avoid low samples.* As we saw, samples of at least 20 reduce the problem of low expected frequencies for 2×2 tables but far more is better.

- *Obtain significance at p < 0.01.* The original worry was over too many type 1 errors at the 5% level of significance. Where significance at 1% is achieved, the decision to reject the null hypothesis is far more secure.

One and two-tailed tests

The one-tailed/two-tailed debate mentioned in Chapter 11 need not concern us very much here. Even if the hypothesis tested is directional *we must always use two-tailed values* for a chi-square square test, *except* for the special case with which we started this section – the simple one variable, two category test. In this special case only, the same arguments apply as were covered on p. 289.

Degrees of freedom

This is a rather complicated notion in its full version but it generally has to do with the extent to which data are free to vary. For the chi-square test, this amounts to the number of cell frequencies you need to know, given that the row and column totals are fixed, before you can work out what all the other cell frequencies must be. For a 2×2 table, if we know the row and column totals then we need know only *one* cell value in order to calculate all the others – in Table 12.7, since we know that the number of female stoppers was 90, the number of male stoppers must be 88 in order for the total to be 178, and so on. With the *t* tests, Pearson's correlation and ANOVA we shall also have to calculate degrees of freedom before consulting our critical value tables.

SUMMARY

The chi-square test looks at the variation between observed and expected frequencies for data gathered using categorical variables. For cases where an association between two variables is investigated, the expected frequencies are based on the assumption that there is absolutely no association, in the overall population, between one variable and the other (the loose null hypothesis). Where variations among the categories of a *single* variable are investigated, the expected frequencies *usually* (but not always) are based on the assumption that the total number of observations is randomly spread across categories. Using tables, the chi-square value found will give the probability that the observed frequencies would occur (or an even greater variation from the expected frequencies) if the null hypothesis is true. The null hypothesis is that population data mirror the expected frequency cell proportions.

THE CHI-SQUARE TEST – CONDITIONS FOR USE

Differences or correlation	Level of data	Related or unrelated design
The test is one of *association* between variables, but *differences* between groups can be investigated.*	Nominal	Unrelated

Notes and special conditions: data *must* be in the form of frequencies; test is of association between frequency row and column categories

H_0: no relationship between variables. Population frequencies are distributed in the same proportions as are the *expected frequencies*. For single row data tables, H_0 is usually that population frequencies for each cell are equal.

In a study where two groups (e.g. extroverts/introverts) form the rows of a 2 × 3 data table, and the columns are values of an association variable (such as 'high anxiety', 'moderate anxiety', 'low anxiety'), χ^2 tests for a difference between the extrovert and introvert distributions on this anxiety variable.

Glossary

Test of association between two categorical variables, using unrelated data at a nominal level; can also test for departure from expected variation among frequencies in categories of a single variable	___-_____	chi-squared
Number of cells in frequency table which are free to vary if row and column totals are known; also used in other tests where it defines the number of individual values free to vary when a group total is known	_____ __ _____	degrees of freedom
Frequencies expected in table if no association exists between variables – i.e. if null hypothesis is true	_____ _____	expected frequencies
Test of whether a distribution of frequencies differs significantly from a theoretical pattern	_____ __ _____	goodness of fit
Frequencies obtained in a research study using categorical variable(s)	_____ _____	observed frequencies
Nominal level test for difference between two sets of paired/related data using *direction* of each difference	_____ _____	sign test (binomial)

Exercises

1. Nine people are sent on an interpersonal skills training course. They are asked to rate their opinion of the need for this type of course both before and after attendance. Having attended, seven people rated the need lower than previously, one rated it higher and one didn't change in opinion.

    a. What test could be used to test for significance between the higher and lower ratings?
    b. Use the test you chose to decide whether this apparent negative effect of the course is significant.

2. Carry out a χ^2 test on the data below:

Politics:	Pro-hanging	Anti-hanging
Left	17	48
Right	33	16

3. Should a χ^2 test be carried out on the following data table?

7	1
2	7

4. A (fictitious) survey shows that, in a sample of 100, 91 people are against the privatisation of health services, whereas 9 support the idea.

    a. What test of significance can be performed on these data?
    b. Calculate the χ^2 value and check it for significance.
    c. Can this type of chi-square test be one-tailed?
    d. If, for a large sample of unknown size, we knew only that 87% of the sample were against the idea and 13% were for it, could we carry out the same test to see whether this split is significant?

5. A field study produced the following table of results:

Observed frequencies				Expected frequencies			
	Taste preferred				Taste preferred		
	A	B	C		A	B	C
Age:				Age:			
Under 14	3	8	4	Under 14	2.5	5.25	7.25
14–30	4	6	2	14–30	2	4.2	5.8
Over 30	3	7	23	Over 30	5.5	11.55	15.95

    a. How many degrees of freedom are involved here?
    b. Does it look safe to conduct a χ^2 test on these data?

Answers

1. a. The sign test.
   b. $N = 8$; $s = 1$. Result *would* be significant for a one-tailed test but we cannot predict *only* a negative outcome. Hence a two-tailed test is appropriate and the result is not significant ($p > 0.05$).

2. $\chi^2 = 19.25$

3. Unwise since all expected frequencies less than 5 and sample is small (<20).

4. a. Chi-square one variable, two-category test.
   b. $\chi^2 = 67.24$; $p < .001$.
   c. Yes.
   d. No. χ^2 cannot be performed on percentages or proportions.

5. a. $df = 4$
   b. More than 20% of expected frequency cells are less than 5 *and* data are skewed. However, result gives significance with $p < 0.01$. Worries about type 1 errors generally concern the $p < 0.05$ level. Hence, safe conclusion of significance.

13

Ordinal level tests – analysis with ranks

Tests presented here are used on data at the *ordinal* level of measurement. In this case data may originally have been at interval level or apparently so. If this is the case they would first be converted to rank values. These ranks are the data used by the significance tests. The tests are:

- **Wilcoxon matched pairs signed ranks (*T*)** – Related data
- **Mann–Whitney *U*** – Unrelated data
- **Wilcoxon rank sum (*T*)** – Unrelated data (simpler to calculate than Mann–Whitney)

Formulae are provided for when *N* is large, where the ordinal level test statistic can be converted into a z score and checked for significance in normal distribution tables.

RELATED DATA – THE WILCOXON (*T*) MATCHED PAIRS SIGNED RANKS TEST

This is one of two major tests used at the *ordinal level* for testing *differences*. This test is used with *related* data (from a repeated measures or matched pairs design). The other major test we will look at will be the Mann-Whitney for *unrelated* data. There are two points to be careful of with the Wilcoxon matched pairs test:

1 The Wilcoxon statistic is known as '*T*' and this is extremely easy to confuse with the (little) '*t*' test to be met later on.

2 There is also a Wilcoxon '*rank sum*' test (also calculating a *T*) which works on unrelated data and can be used instead of the *Mann-Whitney test*, as we shall see.

RATIONALE

Suppose we ask students to rate two methods of learning which they have experienced for one month each, a traditional lecture based approach and an active assignment based method. We might hypothesise that students would be very likely to prefer a more active, involved approach. If you look at the data in Table 13.1 you'll see that, for each student, we know which they preferred by looking at the sign of the difference between their two ratings (column C). In column D, the *size* of the differences has been *ranked*, ignoring the sign. This turns the differences between the absolute score values into *ordinal* data. Just three students prefer the lecture method to the assignment method and this is shown by

Table 13.1 Student ratings of a lecture and assignment based teaching approach

Student (N =15)	Rating of traditional lecture	Rating of assignment based method	Difference (B–A)	Rank of difference
	A	**B**	**C**	**D**
Abassi	23	33	10	12
Bennett	14	22	8	9.5
Berridge	35	38	3	3
Chapman	26	30	4	5
Collins	28	31	3	3
Gentry	19	17	−2	1
Higgs	42	42	0	
Laver	30	25	−5	6
Montgomery	26	34	8	9.5
Parrott	31	24	−7	8
Peart	18	21	3	3
Ramakrishnan	25	46	21	14
Spencer	23	29	6	7
Turner	31	40	9	11
Williams	30	41	11	13

the fact that their differences are *negative*. If we are to convince ourselves and others that the preference for an assignment approach is real and that we can dismiss the idea that the ratings fluctuate only randomly, we need, as with the sign test, more positive than negative differences. However, here, *because we are also taking **size** of difference into account*, we want the *size* of any negative differences (i.e. the 'unwanted' ones) to be small. More specifically, we look at the *ranks of sizes* rather than the sizes themselves. Hence, *we want a small rank total for the negative (unwanted) differences.*

Like the sign test, the WILCOXON MATCHED PAIRS SIGNED RANKS TEST looks at differences between paired values. The sign test looks only at the probability under H_0 of the *number* of differences in the less frequent direction. If this probability is low, a significant difference is declared. In addition to looking at the *direction* of differences, the Wilcoxon test also looks at the *rank* of these differences relative to the other differences. It adds up the ranks of the positive and negative differences. One of these totals will usually be lower than the other. The Wilcoxon test tells us, in effect, how unlikely we were to get such a low rank total for one group, if the null hypothesis is true (i.e. there is no real difference between the populations sampled). If we have made a prediction that scores in one condition will be higher than scores in the other, then any negative ranked differences are 'unwanted'. The Wilcoxon test assesses, in a sense, whether or not these 'unwanted' ranks are small enough to ignore. If they are, we can declare a significant difference.

DATA

Procedure	Calculation on our data
1. Calculate the difference between the pairs of scores (columns A and B), always subtracting in the same direction. As with the sign test, with a directional hypothesis it makes sense to subtract in the direction differences are predicted to go, i.e. predicted smaller from predicted larger value.	See Table 13.1, Column C
2. Rank the differences in the usual way (see page 222). Ignore the sign of the difference. For instance, Laver's difference (-5) is given rank 6 because it is the next largest, in absolute size, after the value $+4$. Also ignore any zero values. These results are omitted from the analysis.[1]	See Table 13.1, Column D Note that Higgs' results are dropped from the analysis
3. Find the sum of the ranks of positive differences, and the sum of ranks of negative differences. The *smaller* of these[2] is T. If the sum of one set of ranks is obviously smaller, you need only add these.	Sum of ranks of negative signed differences (22, 25, and 27) will obviously be smaller. Therefore add their ranks: $1 + 6 + 8$. Hence, $T = 15$.
4. Find relevant line (using N which doesn't include zero differences) in Table 7 (Appendix 2) and decide whether to pay attention to one- or two-tailed values.	Relevant line is $N = 14$ (remember one result has been dropped). Conservatively stick to 2 tailed test.
5. For significance, T must be *less than or equal to* a table value. Find lowest critical value which T does not exceed.	T equals the table value of 15. This appears under '0.02'.
6. Make statement of significance.	Difference is significant ($p < 0.02$). Usually reported as '$p < 0.05$'

[1] *Almost all writers tell you to ignore zero differences so you'll be in safe company if you do. However, a small bias is incurred and Hays (1973) advises the following: with **even** numbers of zero differences, give each the average rank that all the zeros would get (they get the lowest ranks, before you move onto values of 1 and 2) and arbitrarily give half a negative sign. Do the same with an **odd** number, but randomly discard one of them first. This might make some results significant that wouldn't otherwise be. Notice, this has no effect on our calculation above because, with **one** zero difference the methods are the same.*
[2] *Some textbooks say T is the sum of the ranks of the least frequent sign. This is because that usually is also the smaller sum of ranks. When it isn't, you can be sure that differences were not significant at 5%. If you want to know the exact probability of occurrence (with a little error for small samples) then you can use the formula on page 324 to convert to a z score. Using one sum of ranks will give you the same z value as the other, except with an opposite sign. Oddly, MINITAB always gives you the sum of the positive ranks (but it also gives you the exact probability of T occurring at this value under H_0). SPSS does not provide T at all but gives you the z score and its probability of occurrence under H_0.*

Power and the weakness of ordinal level tests

Power, as we shall see in the next chapter, has to do with the ability of a test to detect an effect if it is really there. We also do not want to detect apparent effects that are not

Table 13.2 Increases in co-operation and decreases in aggression after therapy

	Decrease in aggressive responses after therapy	Rank	Increase in cooperative responses after therapy	Rank
Archie	17	8	16	7.5
Bill	13	2.5	2	3
Colin	−12	1	−14	5
Derek	18	9	1	1.5
Eric	13	2.5	1	1.5
Francis	15	6	4	4
George	14	4.5	19	10
Hugh	14	4.5	18	9
Ian	16	7	16	7.5
John	−43	10	−15	6

there. In the Wilcoxon test, where $N = 10$, the critical value for T (one-tailed) with $p < 0.05$ is 11. We can tolerate a *small* number of *large* negative differences, or a *larger* number of *smaller* differences, whilst still achieving a significant result. Take a look at the data in Table 13.2. We can have almost half the group 'go the wrong way' on co-operation (Bill, Colin, Derek and Eric) and still T would only be 11, so a significant increase in co-operation would still be reported. For the aggression scores, though, we have the two extreme scores going the wrong way and T is 11. John has increased in aggression more than anyone else has decreased, yet this information is lost when we rank the data and he simply comes out tenth. Colin's increase in aggression is similar to other group members' decrease. With John and Colin worsening to this degree, the result remains significant in favour of the success of the therapy. Whereas the Wilcoxon leads us to reject the null hypothesis for both these results, a t test would not, thus suggesting that to reject the null hypothesis might be a type one error, since t tests are generally more powerful. Notice that we can also have two middle rankers go 'the wrong way' and stay significant, as in the co-operation results.

SUMMARY

The Wilcoxon test looks at the differences between related pairs of values. It ranks these according to absolute size, ignoring the direction of the difference. Statistic T is calculated by adding the ranks of the positive and negative differences separately and taking the smaller sum. Critical values are the maximum value T can be for the particular significance level. In a sense it asks 'How likely is it that differences this size, relative to all other differences, would occur in the "wrong" direction, if H_0 is true?'

WILCOXON MATCHED PAIRS SIGNED RANKS (T) TEST – CONDITIONS FOR USE

Differences or correlation	Level of data	Related or Unrelated design
Differences	**Ordinal** (or above, if reduced); it must be meaningful to rank the data.[3]	**Related**

Notes and special conditions: only the *rank* and *direction* of the differences between each pair of values is used. Where N is large (>20) see 'When N is large', p. 324.

H_0: two related samples are drawn from symmetrical populations with the same mean (or differences are symmetrically spread around zero)

---

[3] *It is not legitimate to rank data where one difference is not meaningfully higher than another. This can occur where there are ceiling (or floor) effects. For instance, if Jane improves from 10 to 15 points on a reading test, but Jason increases from 17 to the text maximum of 20, it is not reasonable to claim that Jane's increase is 'better' or greater, since Jason has no chance to show his potential increase.*

UNRELATED DATA – THE MANN-WHITNEY (U) TEST

RATIONALE

THE MANN-WHITNEY TEST can be related to a very familiar situation in which we look at the performance of two teams. Suppose you were in a five-person school cross-country team, competing against a local school. You would have to be impressed if the other school took, say, the first four places with the last of their team coming seventh. The sum of their places is $1 + 2 + 3 + 4 + 7 = $ **17**. The total sum of *available* places (1 to 10) is 55. Your team's rank sum is $55 - 17 = $ **38.** The test asks, in a sense, what is the probability of this difference in ranks occurring if there is no real difference between the teams. How do we assess this probability?

Imagine, instead, that the members of the two teams each drew from the numbers one to ten placed in a hat. The Mann–Whitney, in a sense, looks at all the combinations of rank sums that are possible when doing this. It tells us whether our split in rank sums (17 against 38) is one which would occur less than 5% of the time, if we repeated the number drawing exercise many times. That is, it tells us the probability of drawing 5 numbers at random which total only 17, leaving 38 as remainder. In other words, the critical value of U is the point below which we start saying 'The other school's apparent superiority was not a fluke!', something which of course we would rush to admit!

Again we have the weakness that the test deals only with relative positions and not absolute scores. If all the first eight runners were neck and neck at the tape (rare in cross-country), then we would not feel so ashamed, at least, not in front of those watching the race. The printed result sheet would not be so kind to us. The weakness is, again, that we are losing information in dealing with ordinal, rather than interval level data. If we knew the runners' times, we could carry out a more sensitive test of significance, such as the t test dealt with in the next chapter.

Figure 13.1 The B team position looks good! – The logic of the Mann-Whitney test

DATA

Children's tendency to stereotype according to traditional sex roles was observed. They were asked questions about several stories. The maximum score was 100, indicating extreme stereotyping. Two groups were used, one with mothers who had full time paid employment and one whose mothers did not work outside the home.

Note that, since the design is independent samples, the two samples do not need to be equal in size.

Table 13.3 Stereotyping levels of children with employed and non-employed mothers

Scores of children whose mothers had:			
Full time jobs $(N = 7)$	Rank	No job outside home $(N = 9)$	Rank
17	1	19	2
32	7	63	12
39	9	78	15
27	4	29	5
58	10	35	8
25	3	59	11
31	6	77	14
		81	16
		68	13
Sum of ranks:	$R_A = 40$		$R_B = 96$

Procedure	Calculation on our data
1. If one group is smaller call this group A.	Call full-time job mothers group A – Table 13.3.
2. Rank all the scores as one group. If there are many TIED RANKS you should use the formula given under the heading 'When N is large' further on.	See Table 13.3.
3. Find the sum of the ranks in group A (R_A) and group B (R_B).	See Table 13.3. $\quad R_A = 40$ $\quad\quad\quad\quad\quad\quad\quad R_B = 96$
4. Use the following formula to calculate U_A: $$U_A = N_A N_B + \frac{N_A(N_A + 1)}{2} - R_A$$	$U_A = 7 \times 9 + \dfrac{7 \times (7 + 1)}{2} - 40$ $= 63 + \dfrac{56}{2} - 40 = 63 + 28 - 40 = \mathbf{51}$
5. Then calculate U_B from: $$U_B = N_A N_B + \frac{N_B(N_B + 1)}{2} - R_B$$	$U_A = 7 \times 9 + \dfrac{9 \times (9 + 1)}{2} - 96$ $= 63 + \dfrac{90}{2} - 96 = 63 + 45 - 96 = \mathbf{12}$
6. Select the smaller of U_A and U_B and call it U.	Since $12 < 51$ then $U = \mathbf{12}$.
7. Check the value of U against critical values in Table 5, Appendix 2.	Our two sample sizes are 7 and 9. For demonstration purposes we'll treat the test as one-tailed. For $p < 0.01$ the U has to be equal to or less than 9. Our value is not this low. The $p < 0.025$ critical value is 12 so our U just reaches this level.
8. Make statement of significance.	The result is significant with $p < 0.025$. If the test had been two-tailed this would be $p < 0.05$. Either way, conventionally, '$p < 0.05$' is reported.

SUMMARY

The test looks at differences between the sums of two sets of ranks. The value U is calculated from the two rank sums. The critical value gives the value of U, for the particular numbers in each group, below which less than 5% (or 1% etc.) of Us would fall if members of each group acquired their rank on a completely random basis.

MANN-WHITNEY (*U*) TEST – CONDITIONS FOR USE

Differences or correlation	Level of data	Related or Unrelated design
Differences	**Ordinal** (or above, if reduced); it must be meaningful to rank the data.[4]	**Unrelated**

Notes and special conditions: only the *ranks* of values, ranked as one group, are used. Where N_A0, N_B is large (>20) see 'When *N* is large', p. 323.

H_0: the two samples are drawn from the same population or identical populations. If populations are symmetrical, the two samples are drawn from populations with equal means.

[4] *See note 3 on p. 320.*

THE WILCOXON RANK SUM TEST

Conditions of use for the WILCOXON RANK SUM TEST are the same as for the Mann-Whitney. So is the calculation up to and including Step 3 on p. 322. Then, simply take the rank sum of the smaller group – that's R_A in our example, i.e. 40. Call this *T* and consult critical values in Table 6 (Appendix 2) for n_1 (number of scores in the larger sample) and n_2 (number of scores in the smaller sample). This means we would use 9 and 7 respectively for these values. We find, for a one-tailed test at $p < 0.05$, our *T* needs to be under 43, and for $p < 0.025$, our rank sum just matches the critical value. This is reassuring, since the calculation with *U* gave a similarly close finish. Where a smaller group has the larger rank sum either reverse the rank order or let $T = N_A(N_A + N_B + 1) - R_A$.

Beware of getting this test mixed up with the *Wilcoxon matched pairs signed ranks test*! If you remember there's only one of these two Wilcoxon tests in which *signs* are relevant, you should be OK. Even better if you remember that 'matched pairs' (of data) can only occur in a *related design*.

When *N* for either sample is greater than 20, use the z score conversion for large samples shown below.

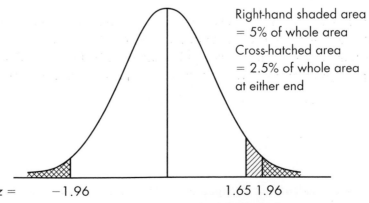

Figure 13.2 z scores forming one-tailed and two-tailed critical values on a normal distribution

Mann-Whitney or Wilcoxon Rank Sum?

Obviously the Wilcoxon test just given is a lot simpler than the Mann-Whitney. Is one preferable to the other? Not really. The reason Mann-Whitney is included is that it is popular, being the only test mentioned or included in several syllabuses and in many computer programmes.

When N is large

Non-parametric rank tests use tables in which N, for either group, only goes up to a modest value of 20 or 25. For larger values there is usually a conversion formula which gives a z score. The value of z then has to be large enough to cut off less than the final 5% of the normal distribution at the predicted end (one-tailed tests) or less than 2.5% at either end (two-tailed tests). From the normal distribution table in Appendix 2 and Figure 13.2 on p. 323, I hope you'll agree that a z score of 1.65 does the former and 1.96 the latter.

The relevant formulae are:

Mann-Whitney

$$z = \frac{U - \dfrac{N_A N_B}{2}}{\sqrt{\left(\left[\dfrac{N_A N_B}{N(N-1)}\right] \times \left[\dfrac{N^3 - N}{12} - \Sigma T\right]\right)}}$$

where N = the sum of N_A and N_B and

$$T = \frac{t^3 - t}{12}$$

each time a number of values are tied at a particular rank and t is the number of times the value occurs. For instance, for the data in Table 14.2, the score 8 appears three times. $t = 3$ and $T = (3^3 - 3)/12 = 2$. This would then be repeated for 9, which occurs twice. This time $T = (2^3 - 2)/12 = 0.5$. This would be repeated for 10, 12 and so on.

Wilcoxon signed ranks (related)

$$z = \frac{N(N+1) - 4T}{\sqrt{\left(\dfrac{2N(N+1)(2N+1)}{3}\right)}}$$

where T is Wilcoxon's T calculated in the usual way.

Wilcoxon rank sum (unrelated)

$$z = \frac{2T - N_A(N+1)}{\sqrt{\left(\dfrac{N_A N_B(N+1)}{3}\right)}}$$

where T is calculated as explained in the rank sum method, N_A is the number of values in the smaller sample and N_B is the number in the larger sample.

Glossary

Ordinal level test for differences between two sets of unrelated data – using U	____-_____	Mann-Whitney
Feature of data when scores are given identical rank values	_____	ties (tied ranks)
Ordinal level test for differences between two sets of unrelated data – using T	_____ ____ _____	Wilcoxon rank sum
Ordinal level test for differences between two related sets of data – using T	_____ ____ _____ _____ _____	Wilcoxon matched pairs signed ranks

Exercises

 1 Find out whether the test statistics in examples a, b, c and d in the table below are significant, and at what level, for the one- or two-tailed tests indicated. You are given the numbers in groups and the appropriate test. You can put the probability value (p) achieved in the blank columns under 'sig'.

	Number in each group			Sig			Significant					Sig	
	N_A	N_B	$U =$	one-tailed	two-tailed	$T =$ (WRS)*	one-tailed	two-tailed		N	$T =$ (WMP)*	one-tailed	two-tailed
(a)	15	14	49			158			(c)	18	35		
(b)	8	12	5			68			(d)	30	48		

* Note: 'WRS' = *Wilcoxon rank sum* 'WMP' = *Wilcoxon matched pairs signed ranks.*

2 Carry out the appropriate test (either Mann-Whitney or Wilcoxon signed ranks) on the data in:

    a. Table 14.1
    b. Table 14.2

and test the results for significance using one-tailed values.

Answers

 1 a. U: 0.025 (one-tail), 0.05 (two-tail); T(WRS): 0.025 (one-tail), 0.05 (two-tail).
    b. U: 0.005 (one-tail), 0.01 (two-tail); T(WRS): Not sig. (one- or two-tail).
    c. T(WMP): 0.025 (one-tail), 0.05 (two-tail).
    d. T(WMP): 0.001 (one-tail), 0.002 (two-tail).

2 a. Table 14.1 – use Wilcoxon signed ranks: $T = 1$, $N = 12$, $p < 0.001$.
    b. Table 14.2 – use Mann-Whitney or Wilcoxon Rank Sum.
       Mann-Whitney: $U = 49$; Wilcoxon: $T = 140$; both not significant ($p > 0.05$).

14

Interval level tests – using *t* tests for interval level data

This chapter introduces the *t* tests which are a type of *parametric test*. The tests are:

- *t test for related data* or *related t test*. This tests the differences between pairs of data, typically taken from two repeated conditions of an experiment. It assumes under the null hypothesis that the mean of these differences should be zero (i.e. if there is no real difference between conditions). A large *t* means that the mean difference found was a long way from the value of zero expected if the null hypothesis is true.

- *t test for unrelated data* or *unrelated t test*. This tests the difference between means of unrelated groups, typically where each has participated in just one condition of a two condition experiment. It assumes under the null hypothesis that any difference between the two means is only sampling error. The true difference between means should be zero (i.e. if there is no real difference between conditions/groups). A large *t* means that the difference found between means was, in fact, a long way from the value of zero expected if the null hypothesis is true.

- *single sample t test*. This is used where we take a single sample and wish to show that it is unlikely to have been drawn at random from a population with a known mean. We hope to establish that it is from a *different* population.

- *t* tests are generally considered more *power efficient* (better at detecting genuine differences) than their non-parametric equivalents but this is paid for with certain restrictions on the features of data that can safely be submitted to these tests (often called 'parametric assumptions'). The restrictions are that:
  – data should be at interval level or above
  – samples should be drawn from normally distributed populations
  – for unrelated designs with uneven sample numbers, there should be *homogeneity of variance* (variances should not be significantly different).

- The tests are also *robust* – meaning that these asumptions about data may be violated substantially whilst still obtaining fairly accurate probability estimates.

- *Power* (probability of *not* making a type II error with a false null hypothesis) can be improved by taking larger samples. Use of the concept of *effect size* can, in certain circumstances, give an estimate of the sample size required to demonstrate an effect.

PARAMETRIC TESTS (OR 'DISTRIBUTION DEPENDENT TESTS')

t tests are a type of PARAMETRIC TEST. Some way back we discussed 'parameters'. Perhaps you'd like to try and remember what these are before reading any further, or to remind yourself by looking back to Chapter 10. Here, anyway, is a redefinition. *Para-*

meters are measures of populations, in particular the mean and variance. Remember that the variance is the square of the standard deviation. Parametric tests are so called because their calculation involves an *estimate* of population distribution parameters made on the basis of sample statistics. The larger the sample, the more accurate the estimate will be. The smaller the sample, the more distorted the sample mean will be by the odd, extreme value. Some people prefer to talk of *'distribution dependent'* and *'distribution free'* tests, rather than 'parametric' and 'non-parametric' tests. The meanings are very close. The reason we must pay attention to the fact that such tests make population estimates is that we must be fairly sure that our data satisfy the assumptions behind these estimates, so that our test results can be considered valid – see p. 339.

THE *t* TEST FOR RELATED DATA – (RELATED *t* TEST)

RATIONALE

To understand clearly what is going on in a *t* test you need to be familiar with the work covered in Chapter 11 on significance and hypothesis testing so it might be a good idea to refresh your memory on this now, if you have the time, by reading pp. 272 to 286 at least.

Take a look at the data in Table 14.1 where our old friend the imagery and memory experiment has been conducted. Let's just think step-by-step through what we expect to happen here, if there is an 'effect' from imagery. We expect the imagery scores to be higher. Note that, in general, they are but, as ever, we cannot just say 'it worked', we need a significance test to demonstrate to the research world that the probability of our result occurring, if the null hypothesis is true, is less than 0.05.

To do this we need to think about what *would* happen if the null hypothesis were true. Let's start by looking, not at everyone's two scores, one with imagery and one without, but at the *difference* between the two scores. Since this is a *repeated measures* design we can look at the *difference* for each person as the amount they improved or worsened with imagery. If there is an effect, most people should *improve*. In turn this means, as with the Wilcoxon matched pairs, that differences (the *d* values in Table 14.1) should generally go in one direction. Taking the control score from the imagery score, the differences should mostly be positive and the larger they are the better for our research hypothesis. This is a *directional* approach. In a non-directional approach we would simply be saying that the differences should go in *one* direction, without specifying which. Again, they should not be close to zero. On the other hand, what we'd expect if H_0 is true would be that the differences would all centre around zero and mostly be small. Remember, this would happen if the imagery condition produces just the same sort of scores as the control condition.

Introducing the difference mean

We can't do much with the individual results. What we need to do is to look at the sample as a whole. What happened in general? A way to do this is to look at the *mean of all the differences*. In this sort of design, this is known as the DIFFERENCE MEAN. Table 14.1 tells us that this is 4.54. We need to know whether 4.54 is a likely or an unlikely difference mean to occur if H_0 is true. We know that most difference means would centre around zero if H_0 is true, since most scores are small and centre around zero. On the other

Table 14.1 Words correctly recalled under related imagery and control memorising conditions

Participant number	Number of words recalled in:		Difference	
	Imagery condition (A)	Control condition (B)	d	d^2
1	6	6	0	0
2	15	10	5	25
3	13	7	6	36
4	14	8	6	36
5	12	8	4	16
6	16	12	4	16
7	14	10	4	16
8	15	10	5	25
9	18	11	7	49
10	17	9	8	64
15	12	8	4	16
12	7	8	−1	1
13	15	8	7	49
	$\bar{x}_A = 13.38$	$\bar{x}_B = 8.85$	$\Sigma d = 59$	$\Sigma d^2 = 349$
	$s_A = 3.52$	$s_B = 1.68$	$(\Sigma d)^2 = 3481$	

Mean of differences ('difference mean') $\bar{d} = 4.54$
Standard deviation of differences $s_d = 2.60$

hand, if imagery has an effect, we expect a *positive* difference mean substantially greater than zero.

So how do we know what 'substantial' is then? We need to know how other difference means would fall under the null hypothesis, and then compare ours with this. How could we find out what the *distribution* of difference means would look like if H_0 is true? It would be handy if we could conduct an experiment, with people performing in the control condition *twice*, over and over again. If we took the difference mean each time we would build up a distribution of difference means. They should centre around zero and basically would form the distribution that the null hypothesis predicts – see Figure 14.1. From then on we'd be on the home run. We would use the same reasoning as for z scores in Chapter 12. With a z score we can assess how far a particular score is from the mean *in numbers of standard deviations*. This is exactly what we can do with our difference mean here. We can see how many standard deviations it is from zero on the sampling distribution of difference means under H_0. If it is within the extreme 5% of values we can say it is significant – that is, it would be one of the most extreme 5% of difference means we'd get if we stayed up all night doing our two control group experiment.

You might be relieved to hear that you won't be staying up all might obtaining a distribution whenever you want to conduct a t test. A distribution of sample means is known as a SAMPLING DISTRIBUTION OF MEANS and there are ways to *estimate* what any particular one would look like. We can estimate the features of the distribution from our sample data. Now we are at the heart of what are called 'parametric tests', in that they estimate population parameters from sample statistics.

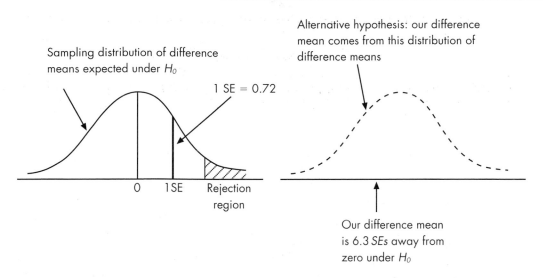

Figure 14.1 Hypothetical distribution of difference means under H_0

How can we estimate what the distribution of difference means would look like under H_0? Have a look at Figure 14.1. The left hand curve is what we would expect under H_0. What can we say about it? First, we said above that the distribution should centre around zero. That is, its mean (the mean of difference means) will be zero – this is actually the null hypothesis. The *shape of* this distribution is determined by the sample size. It is flatter and wider with smaller N. The only thing we don't know at this moment then is the *spread* of the curve. More technically you would know this as the standard deviation but for sampling distributions we use a different term – STANDARD ERROR (or SE for short). The term 'error' is used because the taking of a sample is seen as a way of *estimating* the population mean and there will always be a certain amount of error involved. The sample mean will rarely be the same as the population mean. What we have is a distribution of 'errors' in estimating the *true* distribution mean and the standard error is, roughly speaking, the 'average error'.

To recap. We know our difference mean. We want to know where it would fall on a hypothetical sampling distribution of difference means under H_0. We need to know how many standard errors our mean is from the distribution mean. We know that the distribution mean is zero. We just need to know the size of one standard error and divide this into our mean to know how many standard errors it is from zero. If it is more than about 2 standard errors away, cutting off less than the extreme 5% of means, we will be able to claim significance.

So, we need to find the standard error of the distribution of difference means. This seems an unlikely venture since the distribution is hypothetical and infinite. However, we can resort to a statistical principle known as the CENTRAL LIMIT THEOREM. This says that the distribution of means, formed by taking samples from a population of size N, has a standard error equal to the standard deviation of a sample divided by $\sqrt{N}$, that is, for a sampling distribution of means of samples of size N:

standard error $(SE) = s/\sqrt{N}$

From Table 14.1 we see that the standard deviation of our sample of differences was 2.6. So, an estimate of the standard error of the distribution of difference means is:

2.6/√13, and this is .721

How many of these standard errors, then, is *our* difference mean from zero? Just like a z score calculation, we divide *our* deviation by the standard deviation, that is, the *standard error*. We have a mean which is 4.54 away from zero.

4.54/.721 gives 6.297   We have just conducted a *t* test!

t is simply the number of *SE*s a difference mean is from zero on the estimated distribution of difference means.

Our difference mean then would be 6.3 *SE*s from the mean of zero *if the null hypothesis is true.* Now that's an awful long way. If you recall, on a normal distribution, a z score of 2 cuts off around the top 2.5% of the distribution. Although the *t* distribution for $N = 13$ would be a bit broader than a normal distribution, the difference is not that great. Six standard deviations or *SE*s would be a very long distance to the right – see Figure 14.1. This position would cut off an infinitesimal area of the curve representing even more unlikely results than ours under H_0. Such an extreme result would prompt us to reject H_0 and claim support for the alternative hypothesis, a version of which is that our difference mean comes from a distribution with a mean above zero – see the right hand side of Figure 14.1.

Although it is obvious that our value of *t* will give us a significant result, we need to check *t* in Table 8, Appendix 2. In general, if it exceeds the appropriate critical value, then we know that our result was one of the most extreme 5% of difference means that would occur if H_0 is true. We can then confidently reject H_0. Here, we need to 'beat' 3.055 for significance at $p < 0.01$, two-tailed, which we easily do.

We are indebted to William Gosett for the theory behind *t* and its distributions. He worked for Guinness who, at that time, did not permit its workers to publish findings connected with their company work. Hence, he published under the pseudonym of Student and the distribution statistic is known as Student's *t*.

DATA

Participants were given two equivalent sets of 15 words to memorise under two conditions. In condition A they were instructed to form visual imagery links between each item and the next. In condition B they were instructed only to read the words for learning. Conditions were counterbalanced. Participants had two minutes immediately after list presentation, to 'free recall' the words (recall in any order).

FORMULA

$$t = \frac{\Sigma d}{\sqrt{\left(\dfrac{N\Sigma d^2 - (\Sigma d)^2}{N - 1}\right)}}$$

Note: This formula does not produce the steps we just worked with. These appear below where we go through the procedure to use if your calculator calculates standard deviations directly. The version of the formula given above is common and is easier to use with only a simple calculator.

Procedure	Calculation on our data
1. Calculate the mean of the scores in each condition.	See Table 14.1, foot of second and third columns.
2. Arrange the final results table such that the first column has the higher mean and call this group (or column) A. Call its mean $\bar{x}_A$. Call the other mean $\bar{x}_B$ and the group (or column) B (see note below).	See Table 14.1, second and third columns.
3. Subtract each participant's B score from their A score. Call this *d*.	See Table 14.1, fourth column.
4. Square the *d* for each participant.	See Table 14.1, fifth column.
5. Add up all *d* (Σd) and all d^2 (Σd^2).	$\Sigma d = 59$ $\Sigma d^2 = 349$
6. Square Σd. Note this is $(\Sigma d)^2$. Be careful to *distinguish* between Σd^2 and $(\Sigma d)^2$!	$(\Sigma d)^2 = 3481$
7. Multiply N (the number of pairs of scores there are) by Σd^2.	$13 \times 349 = 4537$
8. Subtract $(\Sigma d)^2$ from the result of step **7**.	$4537 - 3481 = 1056$
9. Divide the result of step **8** by $N - 1$.	$1056/12 = 88$
10. Find the square root of step **9**.	$\sqrt{(88)} = 9.38$
11. Divide Σd by the result of step **10** to give *t*.	$59/9.38 = 6.29$
	t = 6.29
12. Find degrees of freedom (*df*). For a related design this is $N - 1$ where N is the number of *pairs of values*.	$df = 13 - 1 = \mathbf{12}$
13. Find the largest value of *t* in Table 8, Appendix 2, given the degrees of freedom and appropriate number of tails, which does not exceed our obtained value of *t*. Make significance statement.	Critical value for $p < 0.01$ is 3.055, two-tailed test and 2.681, one-tailed. The table goes no higher than these. Our value of 6.29 easily exceeds them both. Therefore, the probability of our *t* value occurring under H_0 is at least as low as 0.01 and probably a lot lower. The difference is therefore (highly) significant.

Note on step 2: If your hypothesis is directional (you already expect one mean to be higher than the other from your research theory and aims) then there is no need to arrange the columns this way (which was just for the convenience of not having negative signs in our later calculations). Just take the column of values you predict to be lower from the other set. If you're wrong, and the results, in fact, go the other way (the other mean is the higher) then your t value will arrive with a negative sign (and you can't, anyway, have a significant result, because you 'put all your eggs in one basket' by making a directional prediction).

Procedure with automatic calculation of standard deviation

If your calculator gives you the standard deviation of a set of values directly there is a far easier route to t. It is, in fact, the procedure we went through in the 'rationale' above. This is:

$$t = \frac{\bar{d}}{s/\sqrt{N}}$$

Procedure	Calculation on our data
1. Find the standard deviation of the differences, using the population estimate version in the example above.	$s = 2.6$
2. Divide s by $\sqrt{N}$	$= 2.6/3.61$ $= 0.72$
3. Divide the mean of the differences ($\bar{d}$) by the result of step **2**.	$t = 4.54/0.72$ $t = 6.31^*$

* Don't be disturbed that this is not exactly the result obtained above. The (trivial) difference is caused by decimal rounding. *Both* results round to 6.3.

SUMMARY – RELATED *t* TEST

This looks at the mean of differences between pairs of related values (the 'difference mean'). Using the variance of the differences, it estimates the standard error of a sampling distribution of similar difference means. The null hypothesis assumes that the mean of this sampling distribution would be zero. The *t*-value given is the number of standard errors the obtained difference mean is from zero. The critical value from tables is the value *t* must reach or exceed for significance.

THE *t* TEST FOR RELATED (PAIRED) DATA – CONDITIONS OF USE

Differences or correlation	Level of data	Related or Unrelated design
Differences	Interval/ratio	Related

Notes and special conditions: data must be sampled from a normally distributed population*
Data must be truly measured at an interval level*
H_0: population difference mean is zero. $\mu_d = 0$ (*or* the two samples of scores are drawn from populations with the same means)

Parametric assumptions

The assumptions marked * above are the 'parametric assumptions' for this test that have already been referred to. That is, the *t* test is powerful but certain conditions must be met *because* the test makes estimates of features of the parent *population(s)* from which it is assumed the samples of data were drawn. If the population doesn't have pretty well the normal distribution shape, then these estimates may well be in error. A second parametric assumption is that the data are at true interval level or above. See the notes on parametric *t* test assumptions on p. 339.

THE *t* TEST FOR UNRELATED DATA (UNRELATED *t* TEST)

RATIONALE

The reasoning behind the unrelated *t* test should be fairly familiar by now, being somewhat similar to the reasoning of the related *t* test, but also being very close to what we discussed in the significance chapter concerning the chip shop and the psychology/sociology twins, the social facilitation/audience inhibition experiment and the vitamin K5 example.

Let's go back to the chippy then. We suspect she draws the sociology and psychology chip samples from two populations with a different mean length of chip. This position asserts the alternative hypothesis. The chippy maintains that they were both drawn (at random) from the same bin (population). This position asserts the null hypothesis. It proposes that the difference between the means of the two chip samples is caused *only* by random sampling error, mere chance variation in chip length, bin distribution and scoop action.

Suppose we did the following many times:

1. Take two random samples from the same population of chips – i.e. from the bin claimed by the chippy to be the *only* bin she draws chips from.
2. Take the mean of each sample.
3. Take the *difference* between these two means, taking the second mean from the first.
4. Repeat steps **1** to **3** *very many times*, always taking the second mean from the first.

Notice that this is slightly different from what we did with the related *t* example. Here we cannot take differences between pairs of scores. We take two independent samples and take the difference *between each pair of means*. If we plotted all the differences between the two means each time we would obtain a sampling distribution of the differences between two means, looking pretty much like Figure 14.1 again, but this time depicted on the *left* of Figure 14.2. The differences between sample means would mostly be small, rarely large, and could be in either direction, negative or positive. Again, they would centre around zero.

This time we would want to know where our difference between means fell on *this* distribution of differences between two means. Again, all we need is the value of the standard error of this distribution and here is where we depart from the related *t* thinking. This time we have *two* independent samples of scores, not one sample of differences. What the independent *t* formula does is provide a 'pooled' estimate of the standard error of the sampling distribution. It uses the central limit theorem again but calculates from *both* the samples of data. This is why the two samples need to have similar variances (the

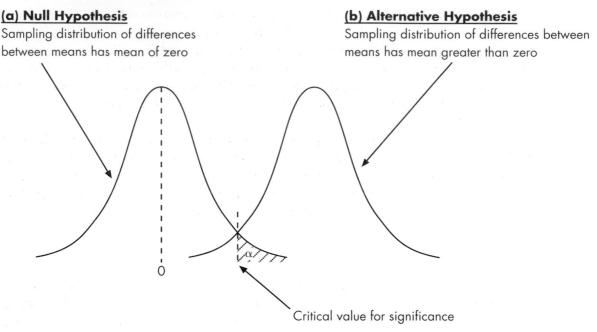

(a) Null Hypothesis
Sampling distribution of differences between means has mean of zero

(b) Alternative Hypothesis
Sampling distribution of differences between means has mean greater than zero

0

Critical value for significance

Figure 14.2   The null and alternative hypothesis assumptions for the unrelated t test

'homogeneity of variance' criterion mentioned in the special conditions for the test, below: this is one of the 'parametric assumptions'). The nasty bit on the bottom of the t equation on p. 336 is this estimate of standard error from the two sample variances. Finally, as with the related t, we divide *our* difference between means by the estimated standard error of the sampling distribution and hope to get a large figure, beyond the tabled critical value, which tells us that *our* difference between means is too improbable; it would be very unlikely to occur if H_0 is true.

Looking at Figure 14.2, we see that if our difference between means is beyond the appropriate critical value, we reject the null hypothesis that the two samples were drawn from the same population (left hand side) and claim support for the *alternative* hypothesis that the mean of the sampling distribution is above zero. This reflects the reality proposed by the alternative hypothesis, that the two samples are drawn from populations with different means. This proposal is depicted in Figure 14.3.

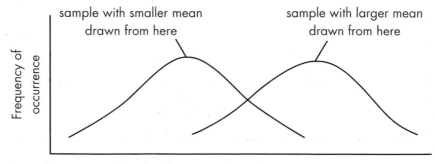

sample with smaller mean drawn from here

sample with larger mean drawn from here

Frequency of occurrence

Figure 14.3   The reality proposed by the alternative hypothesis

Notice here that although the simple form of the alternative hypothesis is that the two populations differ, the unrelated *t* test has tested a different version of this – that the sampling distribution of differences between means has a mean different from zero (in this case, *greater than* zero). Don't worry that null and alternative hypotheses can be stated in different ways. To say that two populations have different means *implies directly* that differences between means of pairs of samples drawn from them would not centre round zero.

In this case, if the chippy is prepared to accept the quantitative paradigm (doubtful) *and* a one-tailed test of our hypothesis (psychology chips from a 'shorter chip' bin), by the general rules of statistical testing we would have a case against her. However, if it were a very close call, as for the memory data below, we may like to attempt a replication of the result before de-briefing her on the nature of our experimental intervention!

DATA

To keep things relatively simple, we use the same experiment as for the related *t* except that here we pretend that 12 experimental participants were asked to use visual image linking in memorising 15 words, while 13 *different* control participants were asked to learn the list without specific instructions. Participants used free recall to demonstrate retention.

Table 14.2 Words correctly recalled by two unrelated groups, one using imagery and one acting as a control group

Number of words correctly recalled in:			
Group A (Imagery)		**Group B (Control)**	
$(N = 12)$ (score $= x_A$)	x_A^2	$(N = 13)$ (score $= x_B$)	x_B^2
12	144	12	144
18	324	9	81
12	144	12	144
10	100	8	64
10	100	10	100
14	196	8	64
14	196	7	49
18	324	13	169
12	144	16	256
8	64	11	121
14	196	15	225
14	196	13	169
		9	81
$\Sigma x_A = 156$	$\Sigma x_A^2 = 2128$	$\Sigma x_B = 143$	$\Sigma x_B^2 = 1667$
$\bar{x}_A = 13$		$\bar{x}_B = 11$	
$(\Sigma x_A)^2 = 24336$		$(\Sigma x_B)^2 = 20449$	
$s_A = 3.02$		$s_B = 2.80$	

FORMULA

$$\text{Unrelated } t = \frac{|\bar{x}_A - \bar{x}_B|}{\sqrt{\left[\dfrac{\left(\sum x_A^2 - \dfrac{(\sum x_A)^2}{N_A}\right) + \left(\sum x_B^2 - \dfrac{(\sum x_B)^2}{N_B}\right)}{(N_A + N_B - 2)}\right]\left[\dfrac{N_A + N_B}{(N_A)(N_B)}\right]}}$$

This is a very complex formula with the greatest number of steps so far, so do try to be careful and patient!

Procedure	Calculation on our data
1. Add up all the group A scores (x_A) to give $\sum x_A$.	See Table 14.2, first column.
2. Add up all the *squares* of group A scores (x_A^2) to give $\sum x_A^2$.	See Table 14.2, second column.
3. Square the result of step **1** to give $(\sum x_A)^2$. Again, be careful to distinguish this from $\sum x_A^2$.	See Table 14.2, first column.
4. Divide the result of step **3** by N_A (number of results in group A).	$24336 \div 12 = 2028$
5. Subtract result of step **4** from result of step **2**.	$2128 - 2028 = 100$
Steps **6–8** Repeat steps **1–3** on the group B scores to give: $\sum x_B$ (step **6**), $\sum x_B^2$ (step **7**) and $(\sum x_B)^2$ (step **8**).	See Table 14.2, third and fourth columns.
9. Divide the result of step **8** by N_B (number of results in group B).	$20449 \div 13 = 1573$
10. Subtract result of step **9** from result of step **7**.	$1667 - 1573 = 94$
11. Add the results of steps **5** and **10**.	$100 + 94 = 194$
12. Divide the result of step **11** by $(N_A + N_B - 2)$.	$194 \div (12 + 13 - 2) = 194 \div 23 = 8.435$
13. Multiply the result of step **12** by $\dfrac{N_A + N_B}{N_A \times N_B}$	$8.435 \times \dfrac{12 + 13}{12 \times 13} = 8.435 \times 25/256$ $= 8.435 \times 0.16 = 1.35$
14. Find the square root of the result of step **13**.	$\sqrt{1.35} = 1.162$
15. Find the difference between the two means: $\bar{x}_A - \bar{x}_B$	$13 - 11 = 2$
16. Divide the result of step **15** by the result of step **14** to give *t*.	$2 \div 1.162 = 1.72$ Therefore ***t* = 1.72**
17. Calculate degrees of freedom when $df = N_A + N_B - 2$	$df = 12 + 13 - 2 = \textbf{23}$
18. Consult Table 8, Appendix 2 and make significance statement as for related *t*.	For a two-tailed test, with df 23, *t* must be $\geqslant 2.069$ for significance with $p < 0.05$. Hence we would not have a significant result here. However, for a one-tailed test, critical value is 1.714. Hence, one-tailed, the result would be significant by a very narrow margin!

SUMMARY – UNRELATED *t* TEST

This looks at the difference between the two means of two sets of unrelated values. It estimates, using the *pooled variance* of both sets, the standard error of a sampling distribution of differences between two means. The null hypothesis proposes that the mean of this hypothetical distribution is zero. *t* is the number of standard errors away from zero the obtained difference between means is on this distribution. The critical value from tables is the value *t* must reach or exceed for significance.

t TEST FOR UNRELATED DATA – CONDITIONS FOR USE

Differences or correlation	Level of data	Related or Unrelated design
Differences	Interval/ratio	Unrelated

Notes and special conditions: Data must be sampled from normally distributed population(s)*
Data must be truly measured at an interval level*
If sample numbers are very uneven, the variances in the two samples should not be significantly different (there should be *'homogeneity of variance'*)*

H_0: Population means are equal $\mu_1 - \mu_2 = 0$ (or sampling distribution of differences between means has mean of zero)

These are the parametric assumptions for this test. See page 339 for qualification of these criteria.

The single sample t test

If you look back to the vitamin K5 example in Chapter 11 on significance, you will see a footnote that warned that such a test would normally be carried out, not on one child but on a *sample*. We can easily extend to a sample now, knowing what we do about the *t* test introduced above. If we already *know* the parameters of an underlying population, as we do for the *normal* 8 year-old reading population, we can use a single sample *t* test to assess the probability of drawing *our* sample at random from that population. Let's say we find that a sample of 20 spinach eaters have a mean reading score of 48 and a standard deviation of 6. We know that the mean of normal 8 year-old reading scores is 40. We need to know what sort of sampling distribution of means we would get if we took many samples of 20 normal readers. We know it would centre round 40. Again the central limit theorem will tell us that an estimate of the *SE* of this distribution will be $s/\sqrt{N}$, that is, $6/\sqrt{20} = 1.342$. Our sample differs from 40 by 8 points. That's 8/1.342 *SE*s from the mean, which is 5.96 *SE*s and this is our value for *t*. *df* here are $N - 1 = 19$ and our *t* is well above the critical value of 2.861 for significance with $p < 0.01$, two-tailed. We may reject H_0 that this sample was drawn from a population with a mean of 40.

POWER

Parametric tests are said to have more POWER. Power is defined as *the likelihood of the test detecting a significant difference when the null hypothesis is false*, i.e. there really *is* a difference associated with the independent variable. Put another way, it is the probability

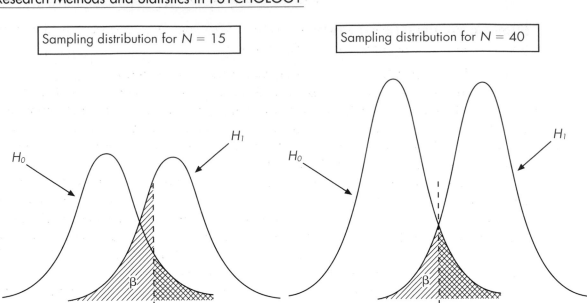

Figure 14.4   Increasing the sample size to increase power

of *not* making a type II error. Looking at Figure 14.4 (left-hand side, where $N = 15$) you'll see that if a result falls to the left of the critical value represented by the dotted line, as we now well know we consider this too weak a difference to count as significant and we will retain H_0. However, suppose there *is* an effect. Suppose our result did in fact come from the distribution predicted by the alternative hypothesis but it was a rather low one and fell to the left of the dotted line *within* the H_1 distribution. The light shaded portion where this result falls represents β, the percentage of results which will fall below the critical value and which will therefore result in a type II error being made. β is therefore the probability of a type II error, *if the alternative hypothesis is true*. Power, then, is therefore the value $1 - \beta$, since it covers all the rest of the distribution where we would reject H_0.

Increasing power – increasing sample size

How can we increase power? One way would be to increase our value of α, that is our level of significance. If we rejected the H_0 when p falls below 0.1 instead of 0.05, our dotted critical value line would move to the left and the probability of a type II error would decrease. Trouble is, the probability of a type I error would *increase* and we have already seen that the scientific community would not be at all impressed with the 'significant' results we report. There is one uncontroversial way to increase power and that is to increase the sample size. Look what happens to the two sampling distributions when we increase the sample size to 40 (the right hand side figure) – the distributions become narrower in range. This is because N is larger in the equation which estimates the SE. As we hinted in Chapter 2, if samples are large, the errors produced in estimating the population mean from the sample means must be a lot smaller than when samples are small.

If you are trying to estimate the average weight of tomatoes in a large sack you'll do a lot better with samples of 20 than with samples of four.

Power of parametric *t* tests and non-parametric rank tests

Non-parametric rank difference tests usually require more data (more sets of scores, so more participants in the study) to reach the same power as their equivalent parametric tests. Several things affect the power of tests, including the sensitivity of the test (*t* tests assume interval level data, for instance), the sample size, as we have seen, and the direction of our test (e.g. one- or two-tailed).

The comparison of the power of, say, a parametric test and its equivalent non-parametric test is known as POWER EFFICIENCY and is expressed as a ratio. You would encounter the mathematics behind this in a more advanced text. Non-mathematically speaking, efficiency is, in a sense, the savings made by the more powerful test in terms of finding more differences that are non-random differences and in, therefore, helping to dismiss type II errors; also in retaining the null hypothesis when there is no real effect.

It is important to remember, however, that parametric tests can't undo damage already done. If data have been collected poorly and/or there are just too few data (*N* is very low) then the greater sensitivity of the parametric test will not compensate for this. Very often the slight advantage of the *t* test can be neutralised, using a rank type test like those in the last chapter, by simply taking a few more participants for testing. Non-parametric tests also have the advantages of being usually easier to calculate and being more widely usable. They don't require the sorts of assumptions encountered in the *t* tests concerning normally distributed data, homogeneity of variance and interval level data.

The greater power of parametric *t* tests comes from their greater sensitivity to the data. This in turn is because they use *all* the information available. They look at *size* of differences and values involved, not just ranks (order of sizes). They are more subtle, then, in their analysis of data. This power and accuracy, however, has to be paid for. The tests make estimates of underlying population parameters.

The data assumptions for t tests

Because the *t* test makes these assumptions about population parameters – it is a 'parametric test' – there are certain limitations on the form that our data may take in order that the test gives a good estimate of *p* under the null hypothesis. First, ***we must assume that the level of measurement for the data is at least interval***. Parameter estimates depend on the mathematics of equal interval scales.

The normal distribution

For both tests we met the requirement that data samples should have been drawn from a normally distributed population[1]. We very often can't ascertain that this is so but we can inspect our sample data, if large enough, and look for obvious quirks, such as floor or ceiling effects or any other sort of skew. The sample itself need not be normal, in fact it

---

[1] In fact, there are ways around this, such as taking the log of scores and consequently producing a normal distribution. Also, there is no real problem as long as the appropriate *sampling distribution of means* would be close to a normal distribution.

can't be, since we need a very large number of data points in order to achieve a near-normal distribution. If we are unsure, it is possible to test a large enough sample of data using the χ^2 'goodness of fit' test covered in Chapter 12. This can tell us the likelihood of obtaining this shape distribution if it *did* come from a normal distribution. In practice, for small samples, we have to *assume* that the population they were drawn from is normal on grounds of past experience or theory. It may be known, from other research, that the variable tested is normally distributed, or it may be possible to argue that, given what we do know, the assumption is reasonable.

Homogeneity of variance

Statisticians have further investigated this requirement, which used to demand very similar variances in the two samples. Fortunately, we can now largely ignore it when dealing with *related* designs without any great risk of distortion in our result. For *unrelated* designs (mostly independent samples) we need to be more careful *where sample sizes are quite different*.

A simple check for variance difference between two samples can be made by checking the variances 'by eye' or even just the two ranges. A thorough check involves use of the *F*-test, (see Chapter 20) which tests for the difference between two sample variances in much the same way as a *t* test checks for a significant difference between the two means. Even this test is considered unsafe when the populations depart from normal distributions. (See Howell, 1992, from which you can get pretty complicated but reliable tests by O'Brien or Levene). *SPSS* automatically calculates the Levene test when you conduct an unrelated *t* test. It gives the probability that your two variances would be so different if the null hypothesis is true. With significance here, use the 'unequal variance' result. However, the safest thing is to try to get almost identical sample sizes in your project!

Parametric t tests are robust (or are they?)

The parametric assumptions for *t* test principles above are not set in concrete. One can do a *t* test on data which don't fit the assumptions exactly. The fact that the tests, under such conditions, still give fairly accurate probability estimates has led to them being called ROBUST. They do not break down, or produce many errors in significance decisions, unless the assumptions are quite poorly met. An alternative interpretation of this term 'robust' sometimes occurs however, where defenders of non-parametric tests argue that, since rank tests, for instance, can be carried out on *any* form of measured data, and are not sensitive to measurement level, distribution shape or variance differences, *they* are more 'robust' in this sense of wide applicability. The robustness of *t* tests refers only to the fact that one may break the data assumptions quite substantially, yet still obtain a fairly accurate estimate of probability for the difference found.

Comparison of t tests and their non-parametric equivalents

	Parametric	Non-parametric
Equivalent tests:		
Related designs	related *t*	Wilcoxon *T* (matched pairs)
Unrelated designs	unrelated *t*	Mann-Whitney *U*
		Wilcoxon *T* (rank sum)
Strengths	More power	Power often not far from parametric equivalent
	More sensitive to features of data collected	No need to meet data requirements of parametric equivalent at all
	Robust – data can depart somewhat from assumptions	Simpler and quicker to calculate
Weaknesses	Limited to data that satisfy parametric assumptions of the test	May need higher *N* to match power of parametric equivalent

COMPARING OUR *t* TEST RESULT WITH A NON-PARAMETRIC TEST

Power-efficiency concerns the relative sensitivity of tests in detecting an effect. Where the margin of significance is quite small (our obtained value only just exceeds the critical value), the non-parametric test equivalent may not show significance, hence we may make a type II error with the latter test.

If you rank the values in Table 14.2, and then add the ranks up for each group, you will find that the lower of these two sums is 140. If you look in the tables for the Wilcoxon rank sum test, with smaller *N* being 12 and larger *N* being 13, you'll find that we must not exceed 125 for significance with $p < 0.05$, one-tailed. The Mann-Whitney also gives a non-significant result. Yet the *t* test we conducted told us that the result was just significant for a one-tailed test. In some circumstances it is also possible for a non-parametric test to show significance when a *t* test wouldn't.

As an exercise for the end of this chapter, try conducting the appropriate *t* test and a Wilcoxon rank sum test on the table of data shown here which is for two unrelated samples.

13.4	13.1
13.6	13.1
13.2	13.1
13.7	13.6
13.7	13.4

You'll find that here the non-parametric test gives significance (1 tailed) where the *t* value just fails to reach the critical value. What kind of error would a researcher be making if the (true) null hypothesis were rejected after use of the Wilcoxon?[2]

---

[2] Type one error.

Notice that this error is possible because the rank test doesn't 'know' that the actual values are so close. Again we see the value of interval/ratio level data in taking account of actual distances between values, rather than mere positions.

Power, effect size and the ideal sample number

EFFECT SIZE is a measure of the (usually unknown) distance between the sampling distributions for H_0 and H_1, in other words, the size of the effect of a 'treatment', assuming it works. It would be the distance between the means of the two distributions shown in Figure 14.2 for instance. Howell (1992) defines this as:

$$d = \frac{\mu_1 - \mu_0}{\delta}$$

where μ_0 is the mean of the control population, μ_1 is the mean of the treatment population and δ is the standard error of the control population. In other words we have the distance from μ_0 to μ_1 measured in standard deviations of the control distribution. d is a kind of z score and it would be a constant value, whatever size samples we take from the overall populations.

Suppose an applied educational psychologist is keen to demonstrate that a teaching programme can increase students' grades on a set of tests taken at 16 years old (e.g. GCSEs in England) and that the overall achievement is measured in points. Let's say the county average is 100 and that the psychologist will receive funding from the local education authority only if an increase of about 5 points could be made by one class of students ($N = 30$). She wonders what size sample she needs to be fairly sure of getting this 'effect'. We know, from the consideration of *power* above, that the larger the sample the better will be the power and the lower will be the risk of a type II error, if the effect 'works'. In this case, the psychologist knows the effect does work but needs to be sure of selecting a sample large enough, given her estimate of the effect size, to avoid a type II error.

She knows that the general standard deviation on the tests is 15 points. Her effect size of interest then is: $d = (105-100)/15 = $ **.33**. Now she needs to relate this to sample size.

Howell defines statistic δ, for the one sample t test, as $\delta = d\sqrt{N}$ and this statistic can be used to look up 'power' in tables. For instance, here, $\delta = .33 \times \sqrt{30} = 1.81$. With $\delta = 1.81$ for a two-tailed test at $p < 0.05$, power, according to Howell's (1992) tables, would be .44. This means that, *if the teaching programme works*, the psychologist has only a .44 probability $(1 - \beta)$ of demonstrating this 5 point increase using 25 students – less than half a chance. The chances of a type II error (β) are .56 and this isn't good enough. She may not get her research grant. She needs to increase the sample size, but to what? Well, let's say she wants power around 0.8, reducing her probability (β) of making a type II error to 0.2. δ (from Howell's table) then needs to be 2.8, so $d\sqrt{N}$ needs to be 2.8 and $\sqrt{N}$ therefore needs to be 2.8/.33 = 8.48 N therefore needs to be 71.99 which we must round up to 72 to get whole students. She needs well over twice the number of students she was going to use to be that *much* surer of demonstrating her effect satisfactorily.

Glossary

Statistical theory which includes estimation of standard error of sampling distribution from standard deviation of a sample	_____ _____ _____	central limit theorem
Mean of differences between pairs of scores in a related design	_____ _____	difference mean
Estimation of extent of effect of an independent variable or 'treatment'.	_____ _____	effect size
Parametric assumption to be satisfied by data before proceeding with an unrelated *t* test (if sample numbers are quite different) – this condition occurs when the two sample variances are not significantly different	_____ __ _____	homogeneity of variance
Relatively powerful significance tests which make estimations of population characteristics; the data tested must usually therefore satisfy certain assumptions; also known as '*distribution dependent tests*'	_____ _____	parametric test
Likelihood of a test finding a significant difference when the null hypothesis is in fact false	_____	power (of test)
Comparison of the power of two different tests of significance	_____ _____	power efficiency
Parametric difference test for related data at interval level or above	_____ __ - _____	related *t*-test
Tendency of test to give satisfactory probability estimates even when data assumptions for the test vary somewhat from the ideal	_____	robustness
Hypothetical distribution (often of means or differences between means) features of which can be estimated from sample statistics	_____ _____	sampling distribution (of means)
Standard deviation of a sampling distribution	_____ _____	standard error
Parametric difference test for unrelated data at interval level or above	_____ __ - _____	unrelated *t*-test

Exercises

1   Comment on the wisdom of carrying out a t test on *each* of the following two sets of data:

	a.			b.		
	17	23		17	23	
	18	9		18	11	
	18	31		18	24	
	16	45	(unrelated data)	16	29	(related data)
	16			12	19	
	18			15	16	
	17					
	6					

For each of a and b, what is an equivalent non-parametric test?

2   Brushing wisdom aside, calculate the t values for the data in 1a and 1b above any way you like.

3   A report claims that a t-value of 2.85 is significant ($p < 0.01$) when the number of people in a repeated measures design was 11. Could the hypothesis tested have been two-tailed?

4   At what level, if any, are the following values of t significant? The last three columns are for you to fill in. Don't forget to think about degrees of freedom.

	t =	N	Design of study	One- or two-tailed	$p \leqslant$	Significant at (%)	Reject null hypothesis?
a)	1.750	16	related	1			
b)	2.88	20	unrelated	2			
c)	1.70	26	unrelated	1			
d)	5.1	10	unrelated	1			
e)	2.09	16	related	2			
f)	3.7	30	related	2			

5   Two groups of children are observed for the number of times they make a generous response during one day. The researcher wishes to conduct a t test for differences between the two groups on their 'generosity response score'. A rough grouping of the data shows this distribution of scores:

Group	Number of generous responses						
	0–3	4–6	7–9	10–12	13–15	16–19	20–22
A	2	16	24	8	3	0	1
B	5	18	19	10	5	1	3

Why does the researcher's colleague advise that a t test might be an inappropriate test to use on this occasion?

Answers

1. a. Variances not at all similar, unrelated design and very different sample numbers. Hence, unwise.
   Non-parametric equivalent: Mann–Whitney/Wilcoxon Rank Sum.
   b. Lack of homogeneity of variance but related design. Therefore, safe to carry on with *t*.
   Non-parametric equivalent: Wilcoxon Signed Ranks.

2. a. *t* (unrelated) = .53 (or −.53)   b. *t* (related) = 1.57 (or −1.57)

3. No. *df* = 10. *cv* (two-tailed) at $p < 0.01 = 3.169$

4. a. NS, keep NH
   b. 0.01, 1%, reject NH
   c. NS, keep NH
   d. 0.005, 0.5%, reject NH
   e. NS, keep NH
   f. 0.01, 1%, reject NH

5. Distributions are skewed. As samples are large, the whole population may well be skewed too, and this is contrary to normal distribution assumption.

15 Correlation and its significance – do they go well together?

Correlation is the measurement of the extent to which pairs of related values on two variables tend to change together or 'co-vary'. It also gives a measure of the extent to which values on one variable can be predicted from values on the other variable. If one variable tends to increase with the other, the correlation is *positive*. If the relationship is inverse, it is a *negative* correlation. A lack of relationship is signified by a value close to zero. Two major calculations for correlation are introduced:

- *Pearson's (r) product moment correlation* – based on variance in two sets of scores. *r* is high when large deviations are paired with large deviations.
- *Spearman's rank correlation* – a Pearson calculation on the ranks of the values in the data set.

Important points about correlations are:

- *Cause* cannot be inferred from the existence of a strong correlation between variables.
- *Strength* is a measure of the correlation but *significance* assesses how unlikely such a correlation was to occur under the null hypothesis (usually that the population correlation is zero). This assessment depends on the size of N.
- *Scattergrams* can demonstrate the strength of correlation, and can identify unusual relationships among the pairs of data.
- *Sampling* weaknesses may artificially increase or decrease a correlation coefficient – one particular phenomenon is the *restriction of range* caused by only correlating scores for certain categories of people, often only those available.
- Correlations for *dichotomous variables* are covered briefly (*point biserial correlation*, *biserial correlation* and the *Phi coefficient*).
- *Common uses* of correlation in psychology are:
  – non-experimental studies on two measured variables
  – reliability testing of scales, tests and questionnaires
  – factor analysis
  – twin studies
- The procedure of *regression analysis* estimates the best fit of a line through a scatter of related score pairs such that *residuals* (the distances between actual score on *y* and scores *predicted* by the regression line) are minimised. Regression is used in the prediction of *criterion variable* scores from *predictor variables*, particularly in practical, applied fields of psychology, such as personnel selection and educational assessments.

- *Multiple regression* uses the technique of regression with several predictor variables. It gives the best prediction possible (R^2) of a criterion variable from this set of predictors. This technique is also extensively used in applied psychological fields.

THE NATURE OF CORRELATION

POSITIVE AND NEGATIVE CORRELATIONS

Have a look at the following statements:
1. The older I get, the fewer things I remember.
2. The more you give kids, the more they expect.
3. Taller people tend to be more successful in their careers.
4. The more physical punishment children receive, the more aggressive they become when they're older.
5. Good musicians are usually good at maths.
6. People who are good at maths tend to be poor at literature.
7. The more you practise guitar playing, the fewer mistakes you make.

These are all examples of relationships known as CORRELATION. In each statement it is proposed that two variables are correlated, i.e. they 'co-vary' in the sense that:
a) as one variable increases so does the other. These are called POSITIVE CORRELATIONS. For instance:
- the further you walk, the more money you collect for charity.
- the more papers you have to deliver, the longer it takes you.
b) as one variable *increases* the other variable *decreases* – a NEGATIVE CORRELATION. For instance:
- as temperature increases, sales of woolly jumpers decrease.
- the more papers you have to carry, the slower you walk.

Someone once suggested the following memory 'hook' for negative correlation: 'as rain comes down so umbrellas go up', a common enough *negative* experience for British people! There is a more graphic example in Figure 15.1.

Decide which of the proposed correlations (1–7) above are positive and which are negative. (Answers below[1].) Think of other examples of positive and negative correlation, in particular, two of each from the research you have studied so far.

SETTING UP A CORRELATIONAL STUDY

It is fairly easy to see how we could check out the validity of statement **6** above. We could have a look at school class-test grades or exam results for people who have taken both subjects. To test statement **3** we have a straightforward measure of one variable

[1] 1-negative; 2-positive; 3-positive; 4-positive; 5-positive; 6-negative; 7-negative

Figure 15.1 A perfect negative correlation between *d*1 and *d*2

(height) but how do we go about measuring the second variable, 'career success'? Do we measure only salary or should we include a factor of 'job satisfaction' – and with what sort of weighting? We would need to *operationalise* our variables.

> Operationally define the two variables to be compared in each of statements 1 to 7 above, and decide how exactly you might measure these in a study looking at correlation.

MEASUREMENT OF A CORRELATION

Statements like 'there is a correlation between severe punishment and later delin-quency in young boys' or 'severe punishment and delinquency in young boys tend to corre-late' are often made in theoretical literature. Actually the golden word 'significant' is missing from the first statement and 'significantly' from the second. Both also fail to report the STRENGTH of the relationship. As we shall see, a *strong* correlation may not be significant, yet a weak correlation *may* be significant. So, *strength* and *significance* are not the same thing. We can actually calculate the *strength* of correlation between any two measurable variables under the sun so long as there is some way of pairing values. Values may be paired because they belong to the same individual (for instance, maths and liter-ature mark in class), or to larger or more abstract units (for instance, resources of schools and their exam passes, average temperature for the week and number of suicides in that week). When researchers announce the finding of a correlation, however, we generally assume that the relationship is not a chance affair – it is strong enough to be unlikely under H_0, given the specific data conditions.

The calculation of correlation between two variables is a *descriptive* measure. We measure the 'togetherness' of the two variables. Testing the correlation for significance is *inferential*.

The *strength* of the relationship between two variables is the degree to which one vari-able does tend to vary with the other. This strength is expressed on a scale ranging from

−1 (perfect negative) through zero (no relationship) to +1 (perfect positive). The figure arrived at to express the relationship is known as a CORRELATION COEFFICIENT or COEFFICIENT OF CORRELATION. It is not possible to obtain a coefficient less than −1 or greater than +1. If you do obtain such a value, there is a mistake somewhere in your calculations (but this can't indicate an error in your raw data). The interpretation of the correlation coefficient scale is, in general:

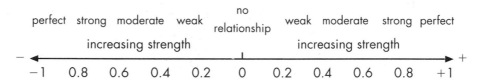

Figure 15.2　Correlation is measured on a scale from −1 to +1

Something might jar here. How can something getting more negative be described as getting stronger? Well it can. The sign simply tells us the *direction* of the relationship.

Warning for tests and exams!

It is very easy to interpret a *negative* correlation as 'no correlation', probably because the two terms 'negative' and 'no' are sometimes equivalent, particularly among US servicemen in war films. Here, beware! To assess strength of correlation *ignore the sign*. Negative correlation means the two variables are *inversely* related. Zero correlation means there is no relationship *at all*.

Scattergrams

A powerful graphical technique for demonstrating correlational relationships is the SCATTERGRAM. This plots pairs of values, one for variable A, the other for variable B, on a chart, thus demonstrating the scattering of paired values. The extent to which pairs of readings are not scattered randomly on the diagram, but do form a consistent pattern, is a sign of the strength of the relationship. I hope the scattergrams in Figure 15.3 to Figure

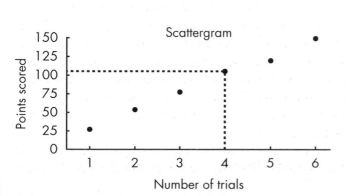

Data	
Number of trials	Points scored
1	27
2	54
3	78
4	105
5	120
6	149

Figure 15.3　Perfect positive correlation: Data pairs for number of practice trials and points scored on a driving task

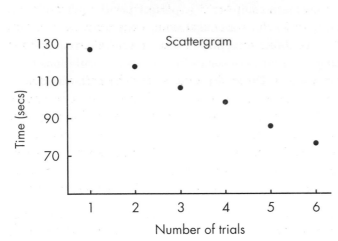

Data	
Number of trials	Time to complete route (secs.)
1	127
2	118
3	106
4	98
5	85
6	76

Figure 15.4 Perfect negative correlation: number of practice trials and time taken on a driving task

Consumption of red wine correlates negatively
with what?

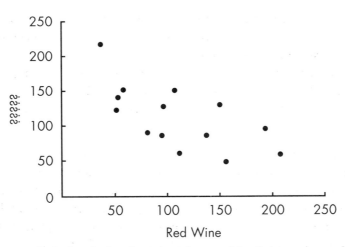

Figure 15.5 Consumption of red wine (across various residential areas) correlates with what?

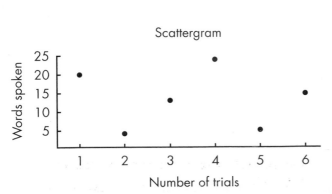

Data	
Number of trials	Number of words spoken
1	20
2	4
3	13
4	24
5	5
6	15

Figure 15.6 No correlation: number of practice trials and words spoken during the driving task

15.8 will demonstrate this. The first two represent fictitious data from one person taken after each trial on a simulated driving task. The trials represent an operational measure of practice – the greater the practice, the better the performance and the shorter the time taken.

In the first example (Figure 15.3) you'll see that the marker for the pair of values 4 trials/105 points is placed on a vertical line up from 4 on the 'number of trials' axis and on a horizontal line from 105 on the 'points' axis. All points are plotted in this way. For number of practice trials/points we get a picture of a perfect positive correlation, value $+1$. For number of practice trials against time taken (Figure 15.4), a perfect negative correlation occurs, value -1. Notice that the pattern here is a mirror image of the positive correlation pattern. Negative correlation scattergrams run from top left to bottom right.

> An interesting negative correlation pattern is shown in Figure 15.5. Each pair of values is taken from a different residential area, ranging from 'affluent suburban housing' to 'poorest council estates'. Can you guess what might decrease as consumption of red wine increases across areas? (Answer at the foot of the page[2].)

For number of practice trials against number of words spoken throughout the trial (Figure 15.6) we get no relationship at all. The value of the correlation coefficients is -0.02. Again, these data are fictitious.

Do not be tempted to draw a 'line of best fit' on scattergrams like Figure 15.5 and Figure 15.6. The 'best fit' line *must* be calculated mathematically and is known as a 'regression line'. It has powerful properties, introduced at the end of this chapter, but it cannot be judged by eye.

Interpretations of $r = 0$

When there is no relationship at all between two variables, we end up with a scattergram like that in Figure 15.6. In this scattergram we have no relationship because variable Y (number of words spoken) does not change in any way that is related to changes in variable X (amount of practice on the task). Another way of putting this is to say that changes in Y are not at all predictable from changes in X. In Figure 15.7 we have zero correlation because variable Y stays the same value no matter what changes occur in variable X. Y is predictable, but not from the *value* of X. Y might be volume of a burglar alarm

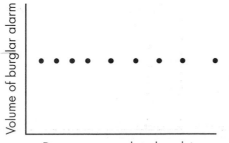

Damage caused on break-in
$r = 0$

Figure 15.7 A special form of no relationship (r = zero)

[2] Answer: Consumption of brown sauce! (Number of families with 'frequent use'.)

and X might be the amount of damage caused by each illegal entry. The only predictable event is that if there is an X there is also a Y. The value of X is also not at all predictable from the value of Y.

Does $r = 0$ always mean no predictive relationship?

If the size of r tells us the strength of the relationship, is there any point in plotting a scattergram? There are several patterned relationships which might show up on a scattergram when our calculation of r gives us near zero. Instead of having the random relationship indicated in Figure 15.6, for instance, we might have the kind of CURVILINEAR RELATIONSHIP between variables shown in Figure 15.8. We could also obtain the reverse

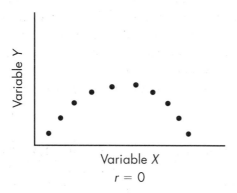

Figure 15.8 A curvilinear relationship between two variables

pattern, an upright 'U'. Here, although $r = 0$, there *is* a predictable relationship between X and Y.

What might show this inverted 'U' relationship? What about temperatures and months of the year? Is there a good psychological example? One's interest in a task might increase then wane with increasing practice. People perform worse on memory tasks both when there has been extreme sensory deprivation and with sensory overload.

---

1. Draw the scattergrams for the other tables of data in this chapter (Table 15.2, Table 15.5 and Table 15.6).
2. Can you think of other relationships between variables which might be curvilinear?

Calculating correlation coefficients

The two most frequently used coefficients are:

Name	Symbol	Level of data used with	
Pearson (product moment)	r	Interval/Ratio	(a type of parametric test)
Spearman	ρ^* or r_s	Ordinal	(a non-parametric test)

* pronounced 'ro', this is the Greek letter rho.

PEARSON'S PRODUCT–MOMENT CORRELATION COEFFICIENT

RATIONALE

Pearson's correlation calculation is based on the idea of *dispersion*, in particular, *deviations from the mean* in each group of data (check back to Chapter 10 to revise these notions). Think of all scores in terms of their deviation from the group mean. If there is a strong correlation then if a person is far above the mean on one variable they should also be far above on the other. Similarly, anyone way below the mean on one should be way below on the other. In general, there should be a match between each person's deviation from the mean on both variables. If we *multiply* each person's deviation on one variable by their deviation on the other, then, with a strong correlation, we would get a very high result because high deviations will be multiplied with high. Where two deviations are both large and negative, the multiplication will again produce a high positive result. Look at the arrangements in Table 15.1 and you can see this happening with the different totals of the multiplied deviations. Note that deviations on the A variable are the same in each example.

Table 15.1 Multiplying pairs of deviations

	PERFECT POSITIVE			PERFECT NEGATIVE		WEAK RELATIONSHIP	
	Deviation			Deviation		Deviation	
A	B	$d_A d_B$		B	$d_A d_B$	B	$d_A d_B$
3	3	9		−3	−9	2	6
2	2	4		−2	−4	−1	−2
1	1	1		−1	−1	1	1
−1	−1	1		1	−1	−2	2
−2	−2	4		2	−4	−3	6
−3	−3	9		3	−9	3	−9
Totals		28			−28		4

For the perfect positive relationship, the highest deviations are multiplied by the highest and vice versa, resulting in the maximum product possible of 28. For the perfect negative, the opposite occurs. The first person, for instance, has a deviation of +3 on A but −3 on B and −9 on multiplication. This gives the maximum possible *negative* total of −28. These two results, when the correlation is calculated as explained below, would produce the highest and the lowest possible *r* values respectively (+1 and −1). A random mixing of deviations gives an intermediate value of 4 which would produce a very low value for *r* (around zero).

In fact, the Pearson formula doesn't just multiply deviation by deviation because the size of these depends upon the particular measure. It uses *standard scores* (p. 253) so that whatever the actual measures, correlation coefficients are on a standard scale.

Calculating Pearson's product moment correlation coefficient

The grand title of this coefficient might make you feel that this could just be a little complicated ... and you'd be right! There is, however, a simple way of starting out. One formula for Pearson's *r* is:

(a) $\quad r = \dfrac{\Sigma(z_x z_y)}{N - 1}$

where z_x is the standard score (or z score) for the first value (variable X) in each pair, and z_y is the z score for the second value (variable Y).

Table 15.2 Scores on old and new reading test

Child	Score on test	
	Old test	**New test**
A	67	65
B	72	84
C	45	51
D	58	56
E	63	67
F	39	42
G	52	50

The data in Table 15.2 are scores for 7 children on old and new versions of a reading test. As a test of *concurrent validity* (Chapter 7) we would expect the pairs of scores to correlate together. All we have to do, looking at our formula for *r*, is to find the z score for each child on each set of test scores, then multiply each pair together, add this lot up and divide by $N - 1$.

In Table 15.3 each z score on X is multiplied by each z score on Y and the result is seen in the right-hand column. The sum of these (5.6) is shown at the bottom of this column and this figure is divided by $N - 1$ to give us a Pearson's correlation value of 0.93.

There is a complicated-looking formula for Pearson's *r* which can be used if you don't wish to calculate z scores and/or you have a non-statistical calculator. If you don't have standard deviations then use formula b) below:

(b) $\quad r = \dfrac{N\Sigma(xy) - \Sigma x \Sigma y}{\sqrt{[N\Sigma x^2 - (\Sigma x)^2][N\Sigma y^2 - (\Sigma y)^2]}}$

If you have already calculated the standard deviations it's probably easier to use the z score version above, but a direct calculation, using *deviations* is:

(c) $\quad r = \dfrac{\Sigma(x - \bar{x})(y - \bar{y})}{(N - 1)(s_x)(s_y)}$

Note that s_x and s_y are the 'unbiased' population estimate versions of the standard deviations outlined in Chapter 10 – they use $N - 1$ in the denominator rather than N.

Table 15.3 Calculation of Pearson's r using the data in Table 15.2

Score on old test (x)	Deviation from mean (d)	z_x (d/11.9)*	Score on new test (y)	Deviation from mean (d)	z_y d/13.9	$z_x z_y$
67	10.4	0.87	65	5.7	0.41	0.36
72	15.4	1.29	84	24.7	1.78	2.29
45	−11.6	−0.97	51	−8.3	−0.60	0.58
58	1.4	0.12	56	−3.3	−0.24	−0.03
63	6.4	0.54	67	7.7	0.55	0.30
39	−17.6	−1.48	42	−17.3	−1.24	1.84
52	−4.6	−0.39	50	−9.3	−0.67	0.26
$\bar{x} = 56.6$			$\bar{y} = 59.3$			$\Sigma(z_x z_y) = 5.6$
$s_x = 11.9$			$s_y = 13.9$			

Pearson's $r = \dfrac{5.6}{6} = 0.93$ using formula (a)

You may need to check back to Chapter 10 to remind yourself about z scores. A z score is the number of standard deviations a particular score is from the mean of its data set. In Table 15.3 we see that the standard deviation for the old test scores is 11.9. For child A's z score here we need to know how many 11.9s her deviation of 10.4 is from the mean. We convert her 10.4 to standard deviations by calculating 10.4/11.9 – this is her z score.

Table 15.4 Reading test values for calculating Pearson's r by hand

Column: Child number	A Score x	B (Score x)²	C Score y	D (Score y)²	E (x × y)
1	67	4489	65	4225	4355
2	72	5184	84	7056	6048
3	45	2025	51	2601	2295
4	58	3364	56	3136	3248
5	63	3969	67	4489	4221
6	39	1521	42	1764	1638
7	52	2704	50	2500	2600
	$\Sigma x = 396$ $(\Sigma x)^2 = 156816$	$\Sigma x^2 = 23256$	$\Sigma y = 415$ $(\Sigma y)^2 = 172225$	$\Sigma y^2 = 25771$	$\Sigma xy = 24405$

Procedure using Formula b	Calculation on our data
1. Find Σx and $(\Sigma x)^2$	See column A, Table 15.4
2. Add all x^2 to get Σx^2	See column B, Table 15.4
3. Multiply Σx^2 (step **2** result) by N	$23256 \times 7 = 162792$
4. Subtract $(\Sigma x)^2$ from step **3** result	$162792 - 156816 = 5976$
5. to 8. Repeat steps **1** to **4** on the Y data	See columns C and D, Table 15.4 $25771 \times 7 = 180397$ $180397 - 172225 = 8172$
9. Multiply step **4** result by step **8** result	$5976 \times 8172 = 48835872$
10. Take square root of step **9** result	$\sqrt{48835872} = 6988.27$
11. Multiply Σx by Σy	$396 \times 415 = 164340$
12. Find Σxy (multiply *each* x by its y and add the results)	See column E, Table 15.4
13. Multiply step **12** result by N	$24405 \times 7 = 170835$
14. Subtract step **11** result from step **13** result	$170835 - 164340 = 6495$
15. Divide step **14** result by step **10** result	$6495 \div 6988.27 = 0.929 = 0.93$ $r = \mathbf{0.93}$
To check this result for significance* see Table 10 in Appendix 2 using $df = N - 2$	$df = 5$; $p < 0.01$ critical value $= 0.875$ (2-tailed – though 1-tailed would also be appropriate here. It would be a useless new test that correlated negatively!)

Note that in all other tests, the test statistic (t, U, etc.) is only used on the way to determining significance. Correlation coefficients are also often used as descriptive statistics to indicate the strength of the relationship and may be used in other calculations as well (e.g. as part of a multiple regression procedure used to select candidates for military training or for a course in applied psychology).

As an exercise, try checking that Formula c produces the same result as Formula b.

SUMMARY

Pearson's correlation coefficient (r) shows the degree of correlation, on a scale of $+1$ to -1, between two interval level variables where each value on one variable has a partner in the other set. The higher the value of r, the closer the correlation between values. The lower the value (below zero) the more inverse the correlation. See **Conditions for Use** opposite.

SPEARMAN'S RHO (ρ)

EXPLANATORY NOTES

The Spearman correlation looks at the *rank* a person receives for their score on one of the two variables and compares this with the rank they received for their score on the other variable. What should happen if there is a good correlation? One's rank on one variable should be pretty well equal to one's rank on the other. It might help then to look at the *difference* between these pairs of ranks.

PEARSON'S PRODUCT MOMENT CORRELATION COEFFICIENT – CONDITIONS FOR USE

Differences or correlation	Level of data	Related or Unrelated design
Correlation	Interval/ratio	Related (by definition)

Notes and special conditions: Data must be sampled from a normally distributed population[3]
Data must be truly measured at an interval level

H_0: Population correlation is zero

Before moving on, take a look at the rank differences and their squares in Table 15.5 (columns E and F). If we are expecting students to score about the same on both tests (Maths and Music), what size would we expect these values to be, large or small? What size would we expect (Σd^2) to be then, if there is to be a strong positive correlation?

I hope you agree that, if there is to be a strong correlation between pairs of values, the *differences between each pair of ranks* (d) should all be small or zero. This will indicate that students are scoring at about the same *position* on both tests. Σd^2 should therefore also be small. Let's see how Spearman's approach incorporates this expectation.

DATA

The following fictitious data give students' maths and music class test grades. Columns C and D give the results in rank order form.

Table 15.5 Class tests results for Maths and Music

Student	Maths mark (x)	Music mark (y)	Maths rank	Music rank	Difference between ranks (d)	d^2
	A	**B**	**C**	**D**	**E**	**F**
John	53	34	5	2	3	9
Julia	91	43	7	3	4	16
Jerry	49	73	4	5	−1	1
Jean	45	75	3	6	−3	9
Jill	38	93	2	7	−5	25
Jonah	17	18	1	1	0	0
Jasmine	58	71	6	4	2	4
						$\Sigma d^2 = 64$

[3] Again, there are ways around this, such as taking logs.

The formula for Spearman's correlation is:

$$r_s = 1 - \frac{6\Sigma d^2}{N(N^2 - 1)}$$

Procedure	Calculation on our data
1. Give ranks to values of x.	See column C, Table 15.5.
2. Give ranks to values of y.	See column D, Table 15.5.
3. Subtract each rank for y from each paired rank for x.	See column E, Table 15.5.
4. Square results of step **3**.	See column F, Table 15.5.
5. Add the results of step **4**.	Total of column F = 64
6. Insert the result of step **5** into the formula for r_s above where N is the number of pairs*.	$r_s = 1 - \dfrac{6 \times 64}{7(7^2 - 1)} = 1 - \dfrac{384}{336} = -0.143$ $r_s = \mathbf{-0.143}$
7. Calculate r_s and consult Table 9 in Appendix 2; r_s has to be equal to or greater than the table value for significance at the level consulted.	Critical value for $p < 0.05$, where $N = 7$ and test is two-tailed is 0.786 -0.143 is lower than this critical value.
8. Make significance statement.	Coefficient is not significant**.

Do watch the figure 1 in this formula. Students often report wonderfully 'successful' results, about which they are understandably pleased, only to find that their result of, say, 0.81 has yet to be subtracted from 1!
**If we'd made a one-tailed prediction that the correlation would be positive, there would be no point even consulting tables since the negative sign here tells us that, whatever the size, the relationship found is negative.*

When there are tied ranks (Spearman is really a Pearson!)

The Spearman formula above is technically for use *only* when there are no tied ranks. If ties occur the statistic becomes a weaker estimate of what it is supposed to measure. The Spearman test is actually a Pearson calculation on the *pairs of ranks*. The Spearman formula is only a short-cut for doing this. If there are too many ties you should carry out the Pearson calculation long-hand. In Table 15.5 we would calculate a Pearson correlation on columns C and D. The resulting coefficient is still referred to as Spearman's r_s. Actually, the difference between the Spearman formula and using Pearson on the ranks, when there are ties, is rather slight, especially with large samples. For instance, with $N = 40$ and 75% of values tied, the difference between the formula calculation and using Pearson on the ranks is around 0.001 or less. Statisticians, however, are correct in insisting that the formula for Spearman is not correct when ties occur. This will not trouble the computer user but means a bit more work with a calculator.

When N is greater than 30

The table of critical values for r_s stops at $N = 30$. If N is larger than 30, r_s (or Pearson's r) can be converted to a t value using:

$$t = r_s \sqrt{\frac{N - 2}{1 - r_s^2}}$$

t is then checked for significance with $N - 2$ degrees of freedom, as in Chapter 14.

SUMMARY

Spearman's Rho, ρ or r_s, shows the degree of correlation by using the Pearson correlation on paired, ranked values, rather than on the values themselves.

SPEARMAN'S RANK CORRELATION COEFFICIENT (RHO) – CONDITIONS FOR USE

Differences or correlation	Level of data	Related or Unrelated design
Correlation	Ordinal	Related (by definition)

Notes and special conditions: Data must be in the form of related pairs of scores

Spearman's *rho* is a Pearson's correlation calculated on the *paired ranks* of the data in each set.

H_0: Population correlation is zero

Does the formula work?

If you look at the Spearman formula you'll see that Σd^2 is the only value that can change. 6 is a constant number and N is fixed by the number of pairs of ranks in the sample. If there are no differences between pairs of ranks, Σd^2 is zero and the value to be subtracted from 1, in Spearman's equation, becomes zero, because $N(N^2 - 1)$ divided into zero is zero. Hence we get the perfect correlation coefficient of $+1$.

Let's look at a perfect negative correlation. In Table 15.6 you'll see that the *more* anagrams people solved the *less* time they took to solve the first one. Inserting Σd^2 into the formula we get:

$$r_s = 1 - \frac{6 \times 40}{5 \times 24} = \frac{240}{120} = 1 - 2 = -1$$

A perfect inverse relationship gets the value -1.

Pearson's r or Spearman's r_s?

Being *non-parametric*, Spearman's *rho* loses information from the data and sometimes may not be as sensitive in detecting significance as Pearson's r. This could lead to either type I or type II errors depending on the data circumstances. However it is easier to calculate and can be used on any rankable data, whereas Pearson's r requires certain restrictions on the sort of data which may be safely correlated.

Table 15.6 Number of anagrams solved and time to solve first anagram – a perfect negative correlation

Participant	Anagrams solved	Rank	Seconds to solve first anagram	Rank	Rank difference d	d²
1	19	5	8	1	4	16
2	17	3	24	3	0	0
3	18	4	15	2	2	4
4	15	1	45	5	−4	16
5	16	2	32	4	−2	4
					$\Sigma d = 0$	$\Sigma d^2 = 40$

SIGNIFICANCE AND CORRELATION COEFFICIENTS

Now we turn to a familiar theme. Consider the results for maths and music results in Table 15.5 and the reading test results in Table 15.4 above. I hope you'll agree that, whereas for maths and music it's pretty obvious (by an 'eyeball test') that nothing at all is going on in terms of a relationship, for the test scores above it's equally obvious that there *is* a relationship. The scattergrams in Figure 15.9 show this too.

The theme is that we can tell when a correlation is obviously significant (just as you could tell when the baby-sexer was successful) and you can tell when there is clearly no significance. How do we decide when a coefficient of correlation becomes significant? We need to know, for a particular number of score pairs (i.e. $N = 7$ in the two examples) the value of r above which just 5% of coefficients would occur if we were doing our calculations on randomly associated pairs. Let me clarify.

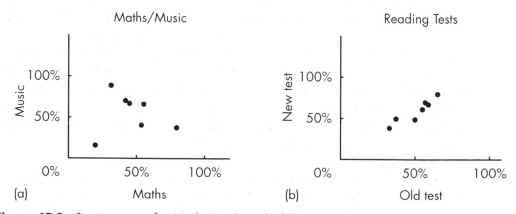

Figure 15.9 Scattergrams for Maths/Music and Old/New reading tests

Suppose we have obtained for some participants a piece of writing on 'Myself and my family'. You are to rate each piece for *self-confidence* whereas I will rate them for *warmth* in the feelings expressed by each participant towards their parents and siblings. We are predicting that the two ratings will be positively correlated. We rate by placing the pieces of writing in rank order on our two variables. We rate three participants and get the results shown on the left-hand side of Table 15.7. We treat these as ordinal, ranked data.

Table 15.7 Ranks of three participants' writing on self-confidence and warmth

Participant	Your ranking on Self-confidence	My ranking on Warmth	Rank orders I *could* have produced					
A	1	1	1	1	2	2	3	3
B	2	2	2	3	1	3	1	2
C	3	3	3	2	3	1	2	1

The *strength* of the correlation is +1, perfect. But is it *significant*? How likely is it that my rankings would agree exactly with yours simply by *coincidence*? In other words, what is the probability of a perfect rank match if the null hypothesis is true that the population correlation is actually zero? Given that your ratings are 1, 2 and 3, the probability we're after is exactly the same as the probability that I would draw the numbers 1, 2 and 3 *in the same order* from a hat containing only these numbers. Remember that probability is

number of desired outcomes
──────────────────────────
number of possible outcomes

We 'desire' only one specific outcome (1, 2, 3 in that order). What is the number of *possible* outcomes? These are shown on the right-hand side of Table 15.7. There are six possible orders for 1, 2, 3. The probability that I would produce the particular order I did (at random) is therefore 1/6. Expressed in the usual way, probability (p) of this result under H_0 (that my selection was random) was therefore 0.167. This is not low enough to permit us to say that the correlation of +1 was significant. We require a p value less than 0.05.

What happens if there are *four* participants and our two sets of rankings match perfectly? The ranks one to four can be arranged in 24 different ways. Therefore, the probability of a perfect match under H_0 is now 1/24 and this gives $p = 0.042$ – a value low enough for significance.

In the case of five participants, the probability of a perfect match is 0.008. The probability of being just one rank out, as in Table 15.8, for instance, is $p = 0.033$.[4]

---

[4] There are just four ways in which the warmth ranks can be arranged such that they are only one rank different from the self-confidence ranks. There are 120 ways of arranging ranks one to five altogether: 4/120 = 0.033.

Table 15.8 Perfect and near-perfect correlations with five participants

	Self-confidence	Warmth
Participant A	1	1
Participant B	2	2
Participant C	3	3
Participant D	4	4
Participant E	5	5
	$r_s = 0.9$	$(N = 5)$

Probability of correlation of 0.9 = 0.033
Probability of correlation of +1 = 0.008
Therefore, total probability of either 0.9 or +1 occurring is: 0.041

Hence, the probability of getting either a correlation of +1 *or* of 0.09 is a total of 0.041. We can count the correlation in Table 15.8 as significant then (one-tailed), since the probability of it, or a higher correlation, occurring if the null hypothesis is true is, in total, less than 0.05. The next possible value for the coefficient is 0.8 and the probability of this value occurring is far higher than 0.05.

The *critical value* for Spearman's r_s, when $N = 5$ then, is 0.9 (one-tailed), $p < 0.05$.

When $N = 6$, the Spearman table gives the critical value as 0.829 (one-tailed). If we had numbers one to six in two separate hats and drew one from each hat to create six pairs, the probability of achieving a correlation between these pairs of more than 0.829 is 0.05 or less. Another way of saying this is that if we were perverse enough to repeat this pairing operation very many times we would get a great number of low correlations and only 5% of the correlations would be above 0.829.

For $N = 20$, however, the value which only 5% of results would exceed is as low as 0.38. As N increases so the distribution of the frequency of correlations lessens or 'bunches up', as I hope Figure 15.10 makes clear. The values for $N = 6$, particularly, would not form such a smooth curve in fact. There would actually be a discrete number of steps – values which r_s can take. But the figure gives the rough outline of the shape the curves would take.

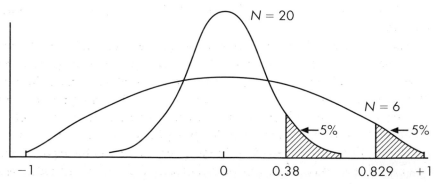

Figure 15.10 Distribution of random correlations when $N = 6$ and $N = 20$

Notice that as N increases so the critical value for 5% significance decreases. This is, in itself, a negative correlation. Note, too, that if, with $N = 6$, you predicted a negative correlation, as you might between, say, self-confidence and feelings of dependence, then your calculated correlation coefficient must be *absolutely* greater than 0.829. For example, -0.93 would count as significant, so long as a negative correlation was predicted, since it is more extreme, on the negative end of the curve, than -0.829.

But surely a strong *correlation* must be significant?

Our natural inclination, I'm sure, is to feel this must be so. But reconsider what we've been looking at. It's *easy* to get a high-valued coefficient with low N even when the null hypothesis is true and there is really no relationship at all. With three pairs of data we'd get $+1$ or -1 every one time in three trials, simply on a random selection basis, so, by the rules of social science research and of common sense, we cannot call these results *significant*, even though they're as strong as is possible. On the other hand, as we saw just above, for the moderate sample size of 20, correlations above 0.38 will not be expected more than 5% of the time, and are therefore significant when they do occur, though weak. With very large sample numbers (e.g. a survey of 2000 consumers) even a correlation of 0.1 will be 'significant', yet it is a very weak correlation indeed. This is what is meant when you read in a newspaper report that there was a 'small but significant' trend – often in connection with a type of food and a particular health condition.

Variance estimate and coefficient of determination

We have two problems now. One is that a rather low coefficient can tell us that two variables are only weakly connected but to a significant degree. What does this weak relationship mean? What can we infer from it? The other problem is that correlation coefficients don't lie on a ratio scale. A correlation of 0.6 is not twice as 'good' or predictive as one of 0.3. One way of converting these figures to a ratio scale is to square the value of the coefficient i.e. find r^2. Statisticians use this as a VARIANCE ESTIMATE, arguing as follows.

Any set of scores (for instance, the set of old reading test scores) has a variation within it – what we know as the *variance*. The new reading test scores also have a variance. Our r for these two sets of scores was 0.93 and r^2 would therefore be 0.86. It is now said that 86% of the variance in Y is predictable from the variance in X. The other 14% of the variance must be accounted for either by random performance errors or some difference between the new test and the old. The variance estimate is made using the COEFFICIENT OF DETERMINATION. This value is: $r^2 \times 100$, which is simply our value r^2 above, expressed as a percentage.

As another example of variance estimation, suppose you heard of a study which showed a correlation of 0.43 between amount of physical punishment given to a child (assessed by observation and interview, say) and a measure of aggression in the child. You could assume that 0.18 (0.43×0.43) or 18% of the variation in aggression amongst the children studied was linked with ('explained by') the variation in the amount of physical punishment they had received. However, tempting though it might seem, using *only* the results of a correlation, we *can't* say that the punishment *causes* the aggression, only that the two are linked and aggression can be predicted, to a certain extent, from the punishment scores – see the next section.

WHAT YOU CAN'T ASSUME WITH A CORRELATION

Cause and effect

See if you can detect flaws in the following statements:
- Research has established a strong correlation between the use of physical punishment by parents and the development of aggression in their children. Parents should not use this form of discipline then if they don't want their children to end up aggressive.
- There is a significant correlation between early weaning and later irritability in the infant, so don't hurry weaning if you want a good-tempered child.
- Poverty is correlated with crime, so if you can achieve a higher income, your children are less likely to become law-breakers.

In each case above it is assumed that the first variable is a *cause* of the second. With any significant correlation there are several possible interpretations:

1. Variable A has a causal effect on variable B.
2. Variable B has a causal effect on variable A.
3. A and B are both related to some other linking variable(s).
4. We have a type I error (i.e. a fluke coincidence and there is no real correlation in the population).

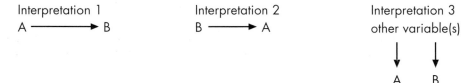

Figure 15.11 Possible interpretations of a correlation

Interpretations 1 to 3 are visually presented in Figure 15.11. A good example of interpretation 3 would be the perfect correlation of two adjacent thermometers, one in °C and the other in °F. The common factor causing *both* to vary together is, of course, heat – one thermometer cannot affect the other. Both use of physical punishment and aggression in children may be a product of the same environment. Physical punishment may not cause aggression but may be commonly used in the sort of environment that also tends to produce aggressive children. Very often it is worth challenging a claim that A causes B with the question, could B cause A instead? Perhaps physical punishment doesn't cause aggression but innately aggressive children provoke parents to move to this extreme! Likewise, perhaps children born irritable induce mothers to give up on weaning.

When cause is more likely

1 The prior variable

One variable may be *prior* to the other. For instance, if tall people were found to be more successful, success could hardly have affected their height. It may of course make them 'walk tall' and it certainly affects others' *perception* of their height as shown by US research indicating that people consistently tend to overestimate the winning candidate's height in presidential elections. But later success can't influence the genetic blueprint for the physical development of height.

Interpretation 3 is possible, however. Other genetic qualities of tall people might contribute to success in later life, not the height factor itself.

2 In experiments

In a non-experimental correlation between two measured variables it is hazardous to claim that one of the variables is the cause of the other.

However, when a researcher conducts a highly controlled experiment in the laboratory, for instance on hours of food deprivation in rats and their errors in learning to run a maze, the independent variable can take several values and hence a scattergram of results like those shown in Figure 15.12 might emerge:

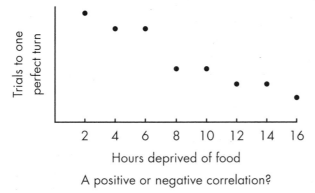

Hours deprived of food

A positive or negative correlation?

Figure 15.12 Trials to make a perfect maze run by hours of food deprivation

Similarly we might display words at varying brief intervals and measure the number correctly recognised each time. Here we can be more confident that A causes B, even though we've used a correlation. The correlation simply serves a statistical purpose – it demonstrates *common* variation between IV and DV. In this example, as display period increases, so do the number of words correctly recognised. The *design* is still experimental. We can make the same assumptions we make in a traditional two condition experiment about the independent variable affecting the dependent variable. Since the IV is altered first, the DV can't be causing changes in the IV, though, of course, a confounding variable is still not ruled out.

The missing middle

By selecting certain groups to be included in a correlational study, a researcher could appear to demonstrate a strong correlational effect. For instance, such a correlation might be announced between financial status and unwanted pregnancies, in that more unwanted pregnancies were reported from lower income households. This could be used politically either to blame the poor for a higher birth rate (along with the sin of being poor) or for a campaign against low incomes and for better sex education. The actual facts, however, may have been obscured by biased sampling of only particularly low- and high-income families. Have a look at Figure 15.13:

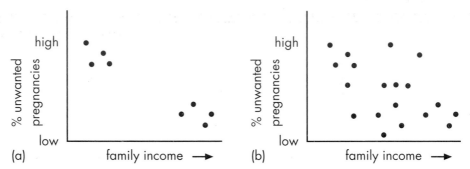

Figure 15.13   Unwanted pregnancies by financial status – two versions

The selective samples drawn (Figure 15.13a) may show a strong correlation, but a more representative sample (Figure 15.13b) may not.

An opposite effect may occur when the range is restricted in a different way, the 'range' meaning the whole possible continuum of scores on either variable. Suppose a company employed an occupational psychologist to help select candidates for posts using a battery of psychometric tests and also to compare these tests later with the productivity of those employed after one year in the job. For this latter correlation the psychologist can only use those who passed the entry criteria and were taken on. These would be those people represented on the right-hand side of Figure 15.14. Since there is no obviously strong correlation for these data, the psychologist might conclude that the test does not predict later productivity. However, had it been possible to measure the productivity after one year of *all* candidates, including those *rejected*, the correlation would have been a lot stronger.

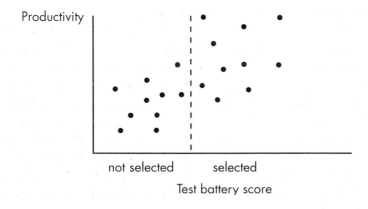

Figure 15.4   Restricted range of test-productivity correlation

Correlation when one variable is nominal

In general, if one variable is a purely nominal category type measure then correlation cannot be carried out, unless the variable is *dichotomous* (two values only, like

Table 15.9 Type of car owned by trustworthiness ratings

Car owned	% rating on trustworthiness	N	Number above mean	Number below mean
			(Trustworthiness mean = **58.99**)	
Vauxhall	78	12	8	4
BMW	65	15	9	6
Rover	51	14	6	8
Citroen	62	17	9	8
Porsche	49	21	7	14
Jaguar	56	16	7	9
Totals		95	46	49

male/female). We will deal with this special case later on. For now, consider the data in the first two columns of Table 15.9. Assume that we have asked separate people to rate different car owners for trustworthiness. The variable of car type is nominal. We can't *order* the car types meaningfully (unless cost is relevant, in which case we could rank the cost prices). The correlation of car type with average rating can't be carried out as the data stand.

Warning for computer users

Because categorical data, such as make of car or marital status, must be *coded* (see Chapter 7) into programs such as *SPSS*, it is very easy to click away and obtain completely meaningless correlations. I have seen students struggling to understand a correlation between attitude to social welfare benefits (a genuine measured variable) and, for instance the codes 1, 2, 3, 4 representing 'Single mother', 'Unmarried childless', 'Married mother with partner' and 'Divorced, no children'. It is easy to mistake numbers used as labels for numbers acting as quantities.

What can we do with the car make and trustworthiness data?

Recall from Chapter 12 that χ^2 was called a *test of association*. As we've seen in this chapter, correlation is *also* a measure of association between two variables. What we can do with nominal categorical data, such as that on car ownership, is to reduce the *other*, measured variable also to nominal level and conduct a χ^2 test on the resulting frequency table. This is only possible, however, where you have gathered *several cases* in each category. Imagine that 12 people assessed the Vauxhall owner, 15 the BMW owner and so on. We can find the *overall* mean trustworthiness rating (58.99 in Table 15.9) and, for each car category, record how many judgements were above and below this mean. These fictitious frequencies are shown on the right-hand side of Table 15.9. We could now proceed with a 2×6 χ^2 test – six rows of car types and two columns of trustworthiness, 'above mean' and 'below mean'.

Correlation with a dichotomous nominal variable – the point biserial correlation

We said above that on special occasions we *can* correlate using a dichotomous variable. The special case is when the categorical variable has just two all-inclusive values. Examples would be male/female, car owner/non-car owner and so on. Here, we may give an arbitrary value according to membership of the categories, e.g. '0' for female and '1' for male. The number can be any value, so 5 = 'car', 10 = 'no car', will do. We then proceed with the Pearson correlation as usual. This *point biserial correlation* is written as r_{pb}. This value can be turned into an ordinary t using the formula on page 359 which turned correlation into a t value. Significance is then found using $df = N - 2$. This may sound like a cheat because we emphasised earlier that Pearson's was a parametric type of statistic and that the level of measurement should be at least interval. This is true *only* if you want to make certain assumptions from your result about underlying populations which are mostly too complex for the level of this book. We will mention this again briefly though when looking at the assumptions underlying multiple regression.

To check this works, try calculating r_{pb} and the resulting t value, using columns 1 and 2 of Table 15.9, and giving one value (e.g. 1) to each of the European cars (BMW, Porsche, Citroen) and another value (e.g. 2) to the remaining ex-UK cars. *Then*, calculate an independent t test on the same two groups. You should find that the t values are very close – not really surprising. Saying there is a significant association between category of car (European, ex-UK) and trustworthiness scores (DV) is the same as saying there is a significant difference in trustworthiness rating between the two categories.

Truly or artificially dichotomous? – the biserial *correlation coefficient*

You might have reduced what was once interval level data down to a dichotomy, as we did earlier with the 'above mean/below mean' calculation for trustworthiness – see Table 15.9. Here the dichotomy is said to be 'artificial' (rather than 'true') because there is an interval scale lying underneath. If you wish to calculate a correlation where one of the variables is formed into this sort of dichotomy, with a *normally distributed variable lying underneath*, then you could use the BISERIAL CORRELATION COEFFICIENT. This would occur where, for instance, height or IQ score had been 'collapsed' so that each person is coded as being '1' for below the mean value and '2' for above the mean. The appropriate formula is:

$$r_b = \frac{r_{pb}\sqrt{p_1 p_2}}{y}$$

where r_{pb} is calculated as just above, p_1 is the proportion of people falling into the lower category of the dichotomous variable (e.g. 60% of participants below the mean would be .6) and p_2 is the proportion in the upper category. y is the height of the normal distribution (the 'ordinate') at the point where z divides the distribution into the proportions of p_1 and p_2. To get this last value you would need to consult a text, such as Howell (1992), containing the y ordinate values in its normal distribution tables. It is safer to use r_{pb} where you are unsure of the normality of the distribution underlying the dichotomous variable.

Both truly dichotomous – the **Phi coefficient**

If the dichotomies for two variables are *both* 'true', however (such as male/female and employed/not-employed), there is even a correlation for these. Values for both variables can be given two arbitrary values, as we did for the cars, and a Pearson calculated again. The result is called ϕ, the PHI COEFFICIENT, and significance is even easier to test with this one because we get $\chi^2 = N\phi^2$, and we check in the usual way using $1df$. The resulting χ^2 is the same value we'd get from a $2 \times 2 \chi^2$ calculation on the data.

Why bother with association when difference tests give the same result?

We noted earlier that a $2 \times 2 \chi^2$ is like a collapsed correlation. Correlations and χ^2 are tests of association between two variables. In a 2×2 frequency table we simply don't have information about how the cases are separated (ranked or measured) or they can't be separated. The point of finding ϕ or r_{pb} is to look at the *degree of association* between our variables, on a $+1$ to -1 scale, rather than the *differences* (or the χ^2 value). Reassuringly, if we test either the association or the difference for significance we come to the same decision. There are also other, more advanced statistical reasons why these association statistics come in useful.

COMMON USES OF CORRELATION IN PSYCHOLOGY

Apart from the several uses already described, there are particular areas of research where a correlation is especially useful and popular.

Non-experimental studies

By far the most common use of correlation is in the sort of study where a sample is drawn and two variables are measured which already exist, i.e. the study is non-experimental. Examples have been given in this chapter but others might be: amount smoked and anxiety level; attitude on sexism and attitude on racism; locus of control and stress felt in job. This is why non-experimental studies are sometimes referred to as 'correlational' but, as I said in Chapter 3, this can be misleading because not all such studies use correlation, and correlation may be used in experiments.

Reliability

When testing for reliability, the test–re-test method would involve taking a set of measurements on, say, 50 people at one time, then re-testing *the same people* at a later date, say six months later. Then we perform a correlation between the two sets of scores. Tests between raters (people who rate) for their reliability of judgement would also use correlation, as would a comparison between two halves or two equivalent forms of the same test (see Chapter 7).

Factor analysis

This uses a matrix of all correlations possible between several tests (a 'battery') taken by the same individuals. Factors statistically derived from the analysis are said to 'account for' the relationships shown in the matrix – see Chapter 7.

Twin studies

Identical twins (and to some extent, fraternal twins) form an ideal *matched pairs* design. Very often scores for twin pairs are correlated. This is of particular use in heritability estimates and was relied on very heavily in the IQ inheritance debate where a strong correlation between twins reared apart was thought to be powerful evidence for a genetic contribution. It was the *strength* of correlation for high numbers of twin pairs which first encouraged Leon Kamin (1977) to investigate Sir Cyril Burt's famous flawed data, but it was the uncanny coincidences in getting *exactly* the same coefficient, *to three decimal places*, with differing numbers of pairs (N) in different reports through the years, which led to allegations of fraud and final dismissal of the data.

REGRESSION AND MULTIPLE REGRESSION

Regression

Regression (rather than 'correlation') is the term used for what we have been studying where the specific aim is to predict values on a 'criterion' (or 'target') variable from a 'predictor' variable. It will help to look at another scattergram, this time representing the correlation between students' numeracy scores on joining a psychology course, and their achievement on the course one year later. Let us suppose that some zealous tutors are conducting this kind of research in order to highlight factors that would help them raise their students' pass levels. Tutors do very many things in between the times when they are seen in a classroom!

The scattergram is shown in Figure 15.15. The idea behind regression is that, if we

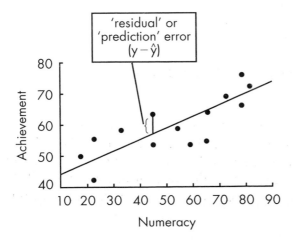

Figure 15.15 Numeracy on enrolment and end of year psychology achievement

know scores on one variable (the PREDICTOR VARIABLE), we can, to an extent dependent on the size of r^2, predict scores on the other variable (the CRITERION VARIABLE). This is done by using a regression line, which is the line of 'best fit' placed among the points shown on our scattergram. On this line will lie all our predicted values for y (known as $\hat{y}$) made from our knowledge of the x *values*. *The vertical line shown on the chart between an actual y value and its associated $\hat{y}$ value is known as a 'PREDICTION ERROR'* (also called a 'RESIDUAL) because it represents how wrong we are in making the prediction. The 'best fit', then, is a line which *minimises* these prediction errors. The calculations involved are somewhat complex and involve the use of calculus. However, for those readers with a vague memory of school algebra, you might remember that the equation of a straight line can be written as: $\hat{y} = bx + a$. Here, b is the *slope* of the line and a is the point where it cuts the y axis (i.e. when $x = 0$). Statistical programmes will kindly calculate a and b for us from a set of data pairs. In our example, a takes the value 42.5, b is 0.318. Substituting any value for x gives us two points (the first was the point on the y axis where $x = 0$ and y therefore $= 42.5$) With these we can now draw accurately the line shown in Figure 15.15 which gives us the *regression of y upon x*.

Multiple predictions

Multiple regression can be used when we have a set of variables (x_1, x_2, x_3, etc.) each of which correlates to some known extent with a criterion variable (y) for which we would like to predict values – see Figure 15.16. Suppose our tutors have information, not only on

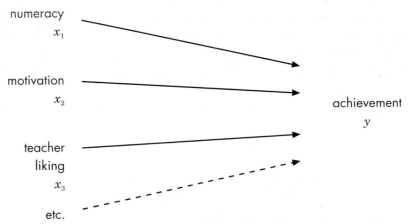

Figure 15.16   Predictors of a criterion in multiple regression

initial numeracy, but also on each student's motivation, on the liking for their tutor and so on. We have seen that values on one variable can be used to predict values on another. The tutors may think 'Well, if *all* these variables predict end-of-year achievement to some extent, what a pity we can't *combine* all the regression coefficients and predict end-of-year achievement from the combination of predictors. Well, we *can*. This is exactly what MULTIPLE REGRESSION is used for.

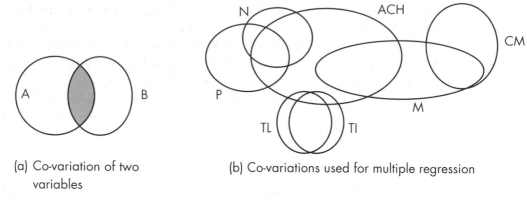

(a) Co-variation of two variables

(b) Co-variations used for multiple regression

Figure 15.17   Covariation and overlap in multiple regression prediction

In Figure 15.17a we see a representation of the situation when two variables, A and B, vary together to some extent. The shaded portion represents the amount of correlation, or rather, the variance which they share in common. Remember that the *square* of the correlation coefficient is used to estimate how much variance in one variable is 'explained' by variance in the other. In Figure 15.17b the big circle, labelled 'ACH', represents the variance of our students' scores on the end-of-year test (the 'achievement' criterion). The overlap of numeracy (N) with achievement represents the variance in achievement 'explained' by its correlation with numeracy. Other predictor variables, such as teacher liking (TL), teacher interest (TI) and motivation (M) will also correlate with achievement and therefore overlap somewhat. There are two more variables on Figure 15.17b. One is 'P' which represents scores on a test which measures people's ability with patterns (recognising them when rotated, imagining abstract relationships visually, and so on). We will assume that numeracy and pattern recognition are somewhat correlated and that both correlate more strongly with achievement than with each other. CM stands for career motivation and for the sake of this example we'll assume that, whilst motivation in general *does* correlate with achievement, career motivation does not at all. Teacher liking and teacher interest turn out to be almost the same thing in terms of their correlation with one another and achievement. Assume that the tutors have test assessments for all their students on *all* these variables.

In multiple regression *a statistical prediction of one variable is made using the correlations of other known variables with it*. The extent that *each* predictor variable predicts values of the criterion (achievement, in this case) is known as its REGRESSION COEFFICIENT. Here, N is a good predictor of ACH, and so is P to a slightly lesser extent.

The very important point, however, is the issue of how much *extra* P contributes to the prediction of ACH. This is the amount of variance it shares with ACH *but not with* N. You'll see that TL doesn't tell us much more about ACH than TI does. M's contribution is unique. What is CM appearing for then? Well, the motivation test will have variance in common with career motivation but career motivation (we're assuming) has nothing in common with achievement on the end-of-year test. Hence, if we set up a test of career motivation we can assess the contribution of this to overall motivation and then subtract this out of the contribution in variance that motivation makes to test achievement. Career motivation is known as a 'SUPPRESSOR VARIABLE' because, if not accounted for, it suppresses the amount by which we can predict achievement from motivation as a whole. The regression coefficient for each predictor variable is related to its correlation with the criterion variable but also takes into account these inter-correlations between all the predictors.

In multiple regression then, there is an equation which predicts y, not just from x as in simple correlation and regression, but from the regression coefficients of x_1, x_2, x_3 ... and so on, where the xs are predictor variables whose correlations with y are known. The equation would take the form:

$\hat{y} = b_0 + b_1 x_1 + b_2 x_2 + b_3 x_3$ ... and so on,

where the bs are the regression coefficients for each of the predictors (xs) and b_0 plays the role of a in the simple regression equation. Programs for multiple regression calculate R, the MULTIPLE REGRESSION COEFFICIENT (you can of course do this by hand!). R is a measure of the correlation between $\hat{y}$ and the actual values of y. The more predictors we have, which share some *unique* variance with y, the more variance in y we can account for. As with simple correlation, R^2 is an estimate of the amount of variance in y which we have 'explained', this time using a combination of predictors, not just one x variable. This technique is typically employed when occupational psychologists are attempting to construct predictive measures of job performance by combining the predictive power of variables such as: years of experience, age, qualifications, test scores and so on. In the same context, it is also used in the construction of a single test to decide which combination of many items are the best predictors of a criterion. A 'stepwise' program will offer the value of R^2 as each extra item is added to the overall predictive equation. We might find, for instance, that item 23 of a test of computing aptitude (potential) is the strongest predictor, on its own, of test results after one year of computer training. Item 19 adds more predictive power, so do items 12, 6, 28 and so on, whereas, later on in the analysis we find additional items adding virtually nothing of significance (in the technical sense) to the prediction of y. It is important to remember that this does *not* make item 19 the 'second-best predictor' because this is only true in the context of taking item 23 first. Multiple regression calculations take into account the inter-correlations between all predictor variables. Also, it does not mean that any *one* individual's score can be predicted to the level of general accuracy found. As ever, with psychological variables, the predictive accuracy refers to samples as a whole. A large company may well decide, though, that over large numbers, they would be fairer and more efficient in their selection if they used this form of analysis of their selection resources.

Glossary

Correlation used where one variable is artifically dichotomous, formed by categorising from an underlying continuous and normal distribution	_____ _____ _____	biserial correlation coefficient
Proportion of variance in one variable predictable from another, using the squared correlation coefficient x 100 as a percentage value	_____ __ _____	coefficient of determination
Relationship of co-variance between two variables	_____	**Correlation**
Number signifying strength of relationship between two variables	_____	coefficient
Relationship between two variables which gives a low value for *r* because the relationship does not fit a straight line but a good curve	_____	curvilinear
Relationship where, as values of one variable increase, related values of the other tend to decrease	_____	negative
Relationship where, as values of one variable increase, related values of the other variable also tend to increase	_____	positive
Decision made when the probability of a correlation occurring, if the population correlation were zero, is less than 0.05 (or the set level of α)	_____	significance
Closeness of relationship between two variables	_____	strength
Variable which is being predicted in regression procedures	_____ _____	criterion variable
Technique in which the value of one 'criterion' variable is estimated using its known correlation with several other 'predictor' variables	_____ _____	multiple regression
A value indicating the strength of prediction of the combined set of predictor variables being used in multiple regression	_____ _____ _____	multiple regression coefficient
Parametric measure of correlation	_____ _____-_____ _____	Pearson's product-moment coefficient
Measure of correlation between two *true* dichotomous variables	_____ _____	Phi coefficient

Measure of correlation where one variable is truly dichotomous	_____ _____ _____	point biserial correlation
Difference between an actual score and what it would be as predicted by a predictor variable using a regression procedure $(y-\hat{y})$ (same as 'residual')	_____ _____	prediction error (or residual)
Variable used in combination with others to predict values of a criterion variable in multiple regression	_____ _____	predictor variable
Procedure of predicting a criterion variable $(\hat{y})$ from a predictor variable (x) using the 'line of best fit' around which correlated pairs of x and y scores are arranged	_____	(linear) regression
Value indicating the extent to which each predictor variable predicts scores on a criterion variable	_____ _____	regression coefficient
Diagram showing placement of paired values on a two-dimensional grid	_____	Scattergram
Non-parametric, ordinal level measure of correlation; Pearson correlation on ranks	_____ _____	Spearman's Rho
Variable whose common variance can be partialled out of the variance of a predictor variable so that the latter can more accurately predict values of a criterion variable (in multiple regression procedures)	_____ _____	suppressor variable
Estimate of predicted variance in one variable using the square of its correlation with another variable	_____ _____	variance estimate

Exercises

1. From an article in the *Times Educational Supplement*, 3 June 1988:

   . . . teaching the sound and shape of letters can give pre-school children a head start . . . children who performed best at the age of seven tended to be those who had the most knowledge and understanding of the three Rs at the age of four.

   In the case of reading, the strongest predictor of ability among seven-year-olds was 'the number of letters the child could identify at the age of four-and-three-quarters' . . . Tizard concludes that nursery teachers should give more emphasis to literacy and numeracy skills . . .

   a. What conclusion, other than the researcher's, could be drawn from the last paragraph of the passage?
   b. Briefly describe a study which could help us decide between these alternative interpretations.
   c. What sort of correlation would the researchers have found between number of letters identified at four and number of reading *errors* at seven – *positive* or *negative*?
   d. Suppose the correlation between adding ability at five and mathematical ability at seven was +0.83. How would you describe the strength of this coefficient verbally?
   e. What level of significance would the (Pearson) correlation of 0.83 be at (one-tailed) if the sample of children had numbered 33?

2. Several students in your group have carried out correlations, got their results, know what significance level they need to reach, but have sadly forgotten how to check in tables for significance. They agree to do calculations on your data if you'll just check their results and tell them whether to reject or retain their null hypotheses. The blank column in Table 15.10 is for you to fill in. Assume one-tailed tests where a direction has been predicted.

   Table 15.10 Incomplete correlation results for exercise 2

	Coefficient obtained	$N =$	Significance level required	Direction Predicted	Retain or reject H_0?
a)	$r = 0.3$	14	$p < 0.01$	+	
b)	$r = -0.19$	112	$p < 0.01$	–	
c)	$r_s = 0.78$	7	$p < 0.05$	+	
d)	$r = 0.71$	6	$p < 0.05$	+	
e)	$r_s = 0.9$	5	$p < 0.05$	+	
f)	$r = 0.63$	12	$p < 0.01$	no prediction made	
g)	$r = 0.54$	30	$p < 0.05$	–	

3. Spearman's correlation may always be used instead of Pearson's. Is the reverse of this true? Please give a reason.

4. A researcher correlates participants' scores on a questionnaire concerning 'ego-strength' with measures of their anxiety level obtained by rating their verbal responses to several pictures. Which measure of correlation should be employed?

5. If a student tells you she has obtained a correlation coefficient of 2.79, what might you advise her to do?

6. Another student friend has carried out a practical project in which she asked people whether they went to state school, private school, public school or some other type of school. She also asked them to fill out her attitude to study questionnaire. She now wishes to correlate these two sets of data. What would you advise her to do?

Answers

1. a. Early letter recognition at four years old *correlated* with reading ability at seven years old but may not have *caused* the superior reading. It may be general home environment that affects both early letter recognition and seven-year-old reading ability. Encouraging the recognition of letters may *not* automatically lead to an increase in reading ability at seven.
   b. Could take experimental group at age four, matched with a control group, and train for letter recognition. Then follow through to seven and compare groups on reading. Could also attempt to balance out all conceivable third factors (thought to possibly cause both better letter recognition at four and better reading at seven), then follow groups from four to seven on reading.
   c. Negative.
   d. Strong/very strong.
   e. $p < 0.0005$.

2. a. Retain b. Retain c. Reject d. Retain e. Reject f. Retain g. Retain (wrong direction)

3. No. For Pearson, data must meet certain parametric requirements.

4. Spearman. Data should be treated as ordinal since human judgement ratings are used.

5. Check her calculations – highest possible value for r is 1.

6. One of her variables is categorical so a correlation cannot be conducted. She can:
   a. collapse her attitude data into two groups (e.g. above below median) and her school categories into two groups (e.g. state/private) and calculate chi-square or a phi-coefficient.
   b. just collapse the school categories as in a. and calculate a point-biserial correlation.
   c. calculate a one-way ANOVA (see Chapter 16) using the four categories as independent variable and the attitude score as dependent variable.

16 Multi-level analysis – an introduction (with non-parametric tests)

This chapter introduces a major step into the sort of significance testing which is more likely to be used in practical research. Researchers rarely use just two samples to test for differences. A very large number of projects make use of ANOVA techniques, to be encountered in the next chapter. However, the focus here, early on, is the warning that making multiple two sample test from complex data (e.g. several *t* tests to cover all combinations in a four condition experiment) will be treated as *'capitalising on chance'* or *'fishing'* for results and is flawed in terms of the basis of significance testing. This permits us to reject H_0 when our statistic is lower than the value that would occur 1 time in 20 *by chance* under H_0. If we make *several* tests we have several opportunities to 'find' this 1 in 20 and *p* is consequently a lot higher than 0.05. Fishing increases the probability of type I errors.

This chapter then proceeds with the introduction of four new non-parametric tests for more than two samples, categorised as follows:

- **Unrelated**
  - Differences: *Kruskal–Wallis* one-way analysis of variance
  - Trend: *Jonckheere*
- **Related**
  - Differences: *Friedman*
  - Trend: *Page*

The *difference* tests are used when we move beyond two sample designs. They will give the probability that two *or more* samples were drawn from identical populations.

The *trend* tests assess the probability that the sample ranks increase significantly in the direction predicted.

All the rank tests lose a certain amount of power, weighed by the advantage that they are 'distribution free' – they can be used on data from any shape of distribution whereas parametric tests require a near-normal distribution pattern for the underlying population.

INTRODUCTION TO MORE COMPLEX TESTS

Three students are discussing a practical project which has to be of their own design. They've decided to investigate whether knowing a person's attitude to the environment affects our overall assessment of them, measured as 'liking'.

Adrian: So one group will hear that our fictitious person (let's call her 'Jane') cares about global warming and the other group will hear she's sceptical, doesn't care.
Dina: Yes! erm, but . . . hold on a minute; wouldn't it be important, well, more interesting to have a control group, you know, a 'baseline measure' wow! Posh word!
Lynsi: OK, so the third group hears nothing about Jane's attitude . . . or should they have a 'neutral' bit of information – that Jane is undecided on the issue – like a placebo group? [Now level with Dina on Brownie points for jargon.]
Dina: Maybe we should have the group with no information *and* the sort of placebo group . . . but hang on! How can we test for significance between more than two groups?
. . . and so on. Having more than two conditions in your research is pretty common. Very often it makes sense to have 'treatment' A, 'treatment' B, no 'treatment' at all and even the placebo 'treatment'. The students here want to use four values for their independent variable (Jane is worried by global warming, Jane doesn't worry, Jane is undecided and no information about her attitude at all). Their dependent variable will be a measure of 'liking' for Jane. There are two problems, however, which Lynsi, Dina and Adrian are going to face, one practical and one (more seriously) theoretical.

Problem 1 – inconvenience

Think what test would be appropriate for testing for significant difference between liking scores in the first two conditions which Adrian mentions, before reading any further. The appropriate interval and ordinal level tests are mentioned at the foot of this page[1]. Now, if the students are going to use this test for looking at significance between *all* their four possible conditions, they will have to test two conditions at a time. Count the number of tests they'll have to conduct. The number of different pairs of conditions is six, but they might also like to look at the difference between, say, the don't care-about-global-warming condition and all the other three together. Perhaps the other three are similar whereas the negative information produces lower evaluations of Jane.

The first, and less important problem which the students face, then, is the sheer inconvenience and time involved in conducting so many *t* tests – not a huge problem if they can use a computer.

Problem 2 – capitalising on chance

The *fundamental* problem concerns what is often termed 'capitalising on chance'. If we conduct several significance tests we increase the probability of getting type I errors when the null hypothesis is actually true. We saw in Chapter 11 that if we repeat 20 times the testing of randomly drawn samples under circumstances when H_0 is true (for instance, no

---

[1] interval = unrelated *t* test; ordinal = Mann–Whitney or Wilcoxon Rank Sum

sex difference in memory), we would expect to reach 5% significance on one of these tests. This is because that's just what our original significance estimate is based on – the critical value we have to reach (from tables) is calculated as that value which only 5% of tests would reach *if the null hypothesis is true*. We will discuss this issue a little further on under the heading of 'Error rates' on p. 399. If you do a lot of tests on various aspects of a gathered data set you can be accused of 'fishing' for results or 'capitalising on chance'. You are increasing the probability of creating a type I error. To avoid this criticism you need to use tests designed for the purpose of looking for significance among several (more than two) conditions.

Multi-level tests

All the tests we are going to mention in this section are designed to take this reasoning into account and to tell us when a *group* of samples (i.e. three or more) differ significantly among themselves. The tests we have already used for two samples are mostly just *special* cases of the more general tests introduced here. Some tests, properly called 'multi-variate tests' or 'multi-factorial tests', deal with the situation where a researcher uses more than one independent variable simultaneously. These 'factorial approaches' will be encountered in Chapters 18 and 19. For the non-parametric tests in this chapter we will not dwell on the background theory for each test. We will simply learn how to use the tests and when they are appropriate. Readers wishing to go further should consult any of the commonly available books mentioned in the reference section at the end of Chapter 19. On page 443 there is a table indicating the appropriate use of multi-level tests. Because ANOVA ('Analysis of Variance') is so widely and popularly used, I have included fuller explanations of the versions and calculations of this technique for investigating statistical differences among multiple samples and variables.

Trends

The fact of having three or more conditions in a research study introduces a new concept concerning the results. Not only might we wish to see whether the samples differ significantly among themselves, we might also wish to test the prediction that, as the level of the independent variable alters in one direction, so does the value of the dependent variable. We might predict, for instance, that as doses of coffee or amphetamines increase, so do periods of staying awake or levels of accuracy in vigilance tasks – a mini-correlation in fact. We might predict that the therapy we are promoting produces more effective client improvement than, say psychoanalysis, and that a control group with no treatment would fare worst of all. Such dependent variable relationships are known as *trends*.

Through most of this section we will work with the same set of data. Let's assume the students could test only four people in each condition. Obviously you would be advised to use more than this in your own investigations, but this low number will make all calculations a lot simpler to understand and learn from. Let's also assume the students finally settled on only three conditions and used:

Condition A – person doesn't care (is sceptical) about global warming.

Condition B – no information about person's attitude on global warming given.

Condition C – person does care about global warming.

The data they obtained are displayed in Table 16.1

Table 16.1 'Liking' assessments of Jane by type of information given on Jane's attitude to global warming

	Type of information on Jane's attitude:		
	Condition A (doesn't care)	**Condition B** (no information)	**Condition C** (cares)
	3	2	10
	5	7	8
	6	9	7
	3	8	11
Sum:	17	26	36
Mean:	4.25	6.5	9

Liking scale: 0 = don't like at all   to   12 = like very much

NON-PARAMETRIC TESTS FOR MORE THAN TWO CONDITIONS
UNRELATED DESIGNS

KRUSKAL-WALLIS ONE-WAY ANALYSIS OF VARIANCE

This is a generalised version of the Wilcoxon Rank Sum test, dealt with earlier. If we used the test, as described here, on the data in Table 13.3 we should come to the same conclusion about significance as we did when using the Rank Sum test. However, this test will tell us whether *three or more* samples differ significantly among themselves. It tells us the probability that the samples would differ as they do if they were all drawn from the same population (the null hypothesis). If this probability is lower than the usual alpha level of 0.05, we can reject the null hypothesis. Have a look at our data as arranged in Table 16.2:

Table 16.2 'Liking' assessments of Jane from Table 16.1, ranked as one group

1	2	3	4	5	6
Condition A (doesn't care)	**Rank**	**Condition B** (no info)	**Rank**	**Condition C** (cares)	**Rank**
3	2.5	2	1	10	11
5	4	7	6.5	8	8.5
6	5	9	10	7	6.5
3	2.5	8	8.5	11	12
Sum	$R_A = 14$		$R_B = 26$		$R_C = 38$

CALCULATION OF THE KRUSKAL-WALLIS TEST

Procedure	Calculation on our data
1. Rank all scores irrespective of sample.	See columns 2, 4 and 6 in Table 16.2.
2. Add the ranks for each condition and use them in the following equation: $$H = \frac{12}{N(N+1)} \sum \frac{R_k^2}{n_k} - 3(N+1)$$ k refers to *each* column in turn. $\sum \frac{R_k^2}{n_k}$ means, *for each condition* square the sum of ranks and divide by the number of values in that condition, then add all three of these results. n_k is the number in the specific condition being dealt with, while N is the total number of values altogether.	See the 'Sum' row in Table 16.2. $$H = \frac{12}{12(12+1)} \sum \frac{14^2}{4} + \frac{26^2}{4} + \frac{38^2}{4} - 3(12+1)$$ $= (12/156 \times (49 + 169 + 361)) - 3 \times 13$ $= (0.077 \times 579) - 39$ $= 44.583 - 39$ $= \mathbf{5.583}$
3. H is treated as a χ^2 value with $df = K - 1$ where K is the number of conditions.	With $2df$, χ^2 must be ≥ 5.99 for significance ($p < 0.05$). Hence we cannot reject H_0 that all these samples come from the same or identical populations.

SUMMARY

Kruskal-Wallis tests for significance among three or more unrelated, ranked samples of data. A significant result tells us the probability of all samples coming from an identical population. It does not tell us exactly where the greatest variation is occurring, i.e. which samples differ most from the rest. Further analysis is required for this.

KRUSKAL-WALLIS ONE-WAY ANALYSIS OF VARIANCE – CONDITIONS FOR USE

Differences or correlation	Level of data	Related or Unrelated design
Differences	Ordinal	Unrelated

Notes and special conditions: Data must be meaningfully ranked

Do not confuse with ANOVA (analysis of variance) procedures for interval level data – to be encountered in the next chapter.

H_0: Distributions from which samples are drawn are identical.

JONCKHEERE TREND TEST

This is appropriate when we not only want to know whether three or more unrelated samples are likely to have come from different populations but also whether there is a significant TREND as the rank totals increase from lowest to highest. Of course, we need to predict here that the trend would go in a specific order and direction, i.e. lowest rating for 'doesn't care' and highest rating for 'does care'. We can't observe a trend *post hoc* (after the event) and then test for it. *It must follow from the theory we're attempting to support.* The reasoning is the same as for one-tailed tests. The calculations in this test involve you in quite a lot of simple counting and not a lot of difficult formula work.

Table 16.3 'Liking' assessments of Jane from Table 16.1 arranged for Jonckheere test calculation

1	2	3	4	5
Condition A	No. of greater values to right	Condition B	No. of greater values to right	Condition C
3	7	2	4	10
5	7	7	3	8
6	7	9	2	7
3	7	8	2	11
Sum	28		11	

CALCULATION OF THE JONCKHEERE TREND TEST

Procedure	Calculation on our data
1 For each score, count how many scores exceed it in any of the columns to its right. It's easier to start this process from the extreme left hand column first.	The first score in column 1 is exceeded by 7, 9, 8, 10, 8, 7, 11 in columns 3 and 5. Hence enter 7. The score of 7 in column 3 is exceeded only by 8, 10, 11 in column 5 – don't count the tied score of 7. Hence give 3. Etc.
2 The sums of these count columns are added to give a value called **X**.	Sum of columns 2 and 4: $X = 28 + 11 = 39$
3 Now find the highest value that **X** could have been using the formula: $$Y = k(k-1)/2 \times n^2$$ where k = number of conditions and n = number of people in each condition.	$Y = (3 \times 2)/2 \times 4^2$ $= 3 \times 16$ $= 48$
4 Calculate: **P = 2X − Y**	$P = 78 - 48 = 30$

Table 13, Appendix 2 shows that with $k = 3$ and $n = 4$, **P** must be >24 ($p < 0.05$), so here we can *reject* the null hypothesis that the trend is a chance relationship from identical populations. Note we do not 'beat' the critical value of 32 for $p < 0.01$.

Unequal or large sample sizes

If the number of values in each condition is not always the same, or if n exceeds 10, you'll have to use the forbidding formula:

$$z = \frac{2X - \Sigma(n_i n_j) - 1}{\sqrt{\frac{1}{18} \{N^2(2N + 3) - 3\Sigma(n^2) - 2\Sigma(n^3)\}}}$$

where N is the total number of values, n is the total in any particular sample and where $\Sigma(n_i n_j)$ means multiply all possible combinations of sample sizes, two at a time, and add results. So, if the sample sizes were 4, 6 and 7, we would get $(4 \times 6) + (4 \times 7) + (6 \times 7) = 94$. Note, also, that here $\Sigma(n^2)$ is $4^2 + 6^2 + 7^2 = 101$. z is a z score and gets checked for significance, referring to normal distribution areas in the manner described under 'When N is large' on p. 323.

SUMMARY

Jonckheere's test looks for a specified ascending relationship between means, although it works on ranked *unrelated* data only. As with one-tailed tests, if means do not rise in the relationship predicted in the first place, there is no point in using the test.

JONCKHEERE TREND TEST – CONDITIONS FOR USE

Differences or correlation	Level of data	Related or Unrelated design
Differences but in the form of a directional trend	Ordinal	Unrelated

Notes and special conditions: The specific trend must be predicted (similar to one-tailed test requirement)

H_0: $\mu_1 > \mu_2 > \mu_3$ (or the same relationship for population medians)

RELATED DESIGNS

FRIEDMAN TEST FOR RELATED SAMPLES

This will be appropriate when the data are *related*. Assume that the data in Table 16.4 are from the *same* sample of four people but taken in three conditions. The test can be thought of as similar to the Wilcoxon signed ranks test but for three or more conditions.

Table 16.4 'Liking' assessments of Jane from Table 16.1 arranged as repeated measures for Friedman's test

Participant	Score A	Rank A	Score B	Rank B	Score C	Rank C
1	3	2	2	1	10	3
2	5	1	7	2	8	3
3	6	1	9	3	7	2
4	3	1	8	2	11	3
Sum:		$R_A = 5$		$R_B = 8$		$R_C = 11$

CALCULATION OF FRIEDMAN'S χ^2 ON DATA IN TABLE 16.4

Procedure	Calculation on our data
1. Here, we first rank each person's scores *across the three conditions*. The first horizontal line (row) in the table represents the first person's scores and each row represents a different person's set of scores.	See columns 3, 5, 7. Note: for person 1, their score of 2 (condition B) was lowest and gets rank 1, the score of 3 gets rank 2 and the 10 gets rank 3.
2. Find the sums of the columns of ranks.	See 'Sum' row in Table 16.4. $R_A = 5 \quad R_B = 8 \quad R_C = 11$
3. Insert the sums of the rank columns into the equation: $$\chi^2_F = \left(\frac{12}{Nk(k+1)} \sum R_k^2 \right) - 3N(k+1)$$ where k is the number of conditions, N is the number of rows (sets of related scores, i.e. people, in this case) and R_k is the sum of ranks in each condition χ^2_F represents Friedman's χ^2 treated as any other χ^2 from this point. $df = k - 1$	$$\chi^2_F = \left(\frac{12}{4 \times 3(3+1)} \times [5^2 + 8^2 + 11^2] \right) - 3 \times 4(3+1)$$ $= [12/48 \times (25 + 64 + 121)] - 48$ $= [0.25 \times 210] - 48$ $= 52.5 - 48$ $\chi^2_F = \mathbf{4.5}$ $df = 2$, so the critical value required is 5.99 and our result is not significant for $p < 0.05$

SUMMARY

Friedman's test is used with three or more related, ranked samples of data. A significant result tells us the probability of the rank totals being so different if scores come from identical populations. It does not tell us exactly where the greatest variation is occurring. Further analysis would be required.

FRIEDMAN'S TEST – CONDITIONS OF USE

Differences or correlation	Level of data	Related or Unrelated design
Differences	Ordinal	Related

Notes and special conditions: Calculates a χ^2 known as Friedman's χ^2 or χ^2_F

H_0: Distributions from which samples are drawn are identical

PAGE'S TREND TEST – TREND ACROSS SAMPLES

This is appropriate when we not only want to know whether three or more *related* samples are likely to have come from different populations but also whether there is a significant *trend* as the rank totals increase from lowest to highest. As with the Jonckheere test, it makes sense to conduct the Page test only if the samples have produced total rank scores which increase in the *predicted order*. Let's suppose we predicted that, in Table 16.4:

condition A scores < condition B scores < condition C scores

CALCULATION OF PAGE'S TREND TEST ON DATA IN TABLE 16.4

Procedure for Page's *L* trend test	Calculation on our data
1. Rank data as in Table 16.4.	
2. Use the formula: $L = \Sigma(R_k \times k)$ where R_k = the sum of a column of ranks and k is the predicted order number of that column – we predicted condition A scores (and therefore rank total) would be lowest, hence the predicted order for the A rank total is 1, for B it is 2 and for C it is 3.	From Table 16.4: $L = (5 \times 1) + (8 \times 2) + (11 \times 3)$ $= 5 + 16 + 33$ $= \mathbf{54}$ From Table 14 we find that with $k = 3$ and $n = 4$ we need to equal or exceed 54 for significance $(p = <0.05)$.

This trend test also just makes it to significance. Notice here that L gets larger as it approaches significance because the higher numbered rank totals get multiplied by the higher numbered column numbers. If scores in column 2 had been, contrary to our expectation, higher than those in column 4, then a relatively high rank total would have been multiplied by 1 rather than 2, thus lowering the possible value of L.

Large samples

If N is greater than 10 use:

$$z = \frac{12L - 3nk(k + 1)^2}{\sqrt{nk^2(k^2 - 1)(k + 1)}}$$

where n is the number in the sample and k is the number of conditions.

SUMMARY

Page's test looks for a specified ascending relationship between means, although it works on ranked *related* data only. As with one-tailed tests, if means do not rise in the relationship predicted in the first place, there is no point in using the test.

PAGE'S TREND TEST – CONDITIONS FOR USE

Differences or correlation	Level of data	Related or Unrelated design
Differences but in the form of a directional trend	Ordinal	Related

Notes and special conditions: The specific trend must be predicted (similar to one-tailed test requirement)

H_0: $\mu_1 > \mu_2 > \mu_3$ (or the same relationship for population medians)

Glossary

Conducting several significance tests on the same data (or parts of it) so that the probability of obtaining a type I error increases well above 0.05	_____ __ _____	capitalising on chance
Test for significant differences between two or more related samples; data at ordinal level	_____	Friedman
Test for trend across three or more independent samples; data at ordinal level	_____	Jonckheere
Test for significant differences between two or more independent samples; data at ordinal level	_____-_____	Kruskal-Wallis
Test for trend across three or more related samples; data at ordinal level	_____	Page
Tendency for scores to rise in a predicted direction across several conditions	_____	trend

Exercises

What non-parametric test is appropriate in the following circumstances?

a. A researcher wants to know whether there are significant differences between a group given a stimulant, a group given a placebo pill and a control group, in the number of errors they make in recognising briefly presented words.

b. Participants are asked to sort cards into category piles, first, when there are only two category piles, then when there are four categories and finally into eight categories. It is expected that sorting time will increase across the three conditions.

c. Three groups of children are given sets of nonsense words, with typically French spellings, and later tested for recall. It is expected that French children will recall best, English children worst, with English children of one French parent falling in between these.

d. A group of participants are tested for hearing sensitivity in the morning, at midday and in the evening. Significant differences are expected between the sets of scores.

Answers

a. Kruskal–Wallis one-way analysis of variance.
b. Page trend test.
c. Jonckheere trend test.
d. Friedman χ^2_F.

17

Analysis of variance (ANOVA) – introduction and the one-way unrelated model

ANOVA (analysis of variance) procedures are powerful parametric methods for testing the significance of the differences between sample means where more than two conditions are used, or even when several independent variables are involved.

- Methods with more than one independent variable are known as *Multi-factorial ANOVA designs* and are dealt with in Chapter 18

- *One-way ANOVA* is dealt with here and tests the null hypothesis that two or more samples were drawn from the same population by comparing the variance of the sample means (*between groups* variance) with the 'error' or *within groups* variance (an average of the variances *within* each sample around its mean). If means differ among themselves far more than people differ within groups then the *F ratio* will be higher than 1 to a significant extent.

- Tests of specific comparisons (such as mean$_A$ against mean$_C$, or mean$_A$ and mean$_B$ *combined* against mean$_C$) are either *a priori* ('planned' before testing because predicted from theoretical reasoning) or *post hoc* (tested only because the difference looks significant once results are in).

- One or possibly two simple comparisons can be made using *t* tests and *linear contrasts*, which make possible the testing of *combined* means where a set of coefficients must be calculated.

- Making several tests on data raises the probability of obtaining a 'significant' result on a chance basis alone ('capitalising on chance'); the *family-wise error rate* can rise unacceptably and must be attended to. Either the significance level for *each* test can be lowered or several types of test, devised for multiple testing, can be resorted to.

- Post hoc tests include *Bonferroni t* tests, the *Newman–Keuls* test, *Tukey's honestly significant difference* test, and *Scheffé's* test.

ANOVA MODELS – CONDITIONS OF USE

Differences or correlation	Level of data	Related or Unrelated design
Difference (between several means)	Interval/ratio	Unrelated* Mixed Related

Notes and special conditions: * One-way *unrelated* ANOVA procedures are dealt with in this chapter. ANOVA procedures are general and can be used on unrelated designs, related designs or a mixture of the two. There can be more than one independent variable (or 'factor') as we shall see in subsequent chapters. Certain parametric assumptions about data must be met:

- samples drawn from normal distributions[1]
- sample variances are homogenous – see p. 340

H_0: Population means are equal (samples drawn at random from the same population, or from populations with the same mean).

---

[1] *With the same flexibility here as outlined on p. 340.*

WHAT'S ANOVA ALL ABOUT THEN?

Suppose Dina recalled from her A-level learning that t tests were more powerful and robust than non-parametric tests. She might (quite correctly) assume that the Kruskal-Wallis test for differences described in the last chapter, because it only uses ranked data, might well fail to produce a significant result in her global warming attitude practical, even though there is an effect to be found (i.e. she suspects the danger of a type II error). She would be well advised to turn to the extremely popular and powerful set of methods which come under the general heading of ANALYSIS OF VARIANCE (ANOVA for short), *so long as her data satisfy the associated parametric test assumptions.*

The general idea

The thinking behind the most simple 'model' is relatively easy to comprehend. In the chip shop example of Chapter 11, suppose the sociology twin had received a bag of chips which not only had a greater mean length but in which *most* of the chips were long. Suppose the psychology bag had a lower mean length but *also* contained fairly consistently small chips. You would be far more convinced *here* that there was a significant difference than if there was a good deal of *overlap* between the lengths in the two bags. In other words, if there is very little variation *within* each group of scores, but a lot of difference *between* group means, we are more convinced of a significant difference than when the means differ by the same amount but there is a lot of variation within groups. Figure 17.1 shows the means for *three* chip bags, the third belonging to a (triplet?) Geography student whom the chippy neither favours nor dislikes. Note that the means are the *same* in the two diagrams but (b) convinces us more that there is an effect.

If we now turn to the data in Table 16.1 (p. 381) on liking assessment for Jane, we see, in Figure 17.2, the way in which those data were spread for groups A, B and C. The sample means *do* increase but sample B rather messes things up by being more dispersed, overlapping with both the other two samples (but mainly because of one low 'rogue'

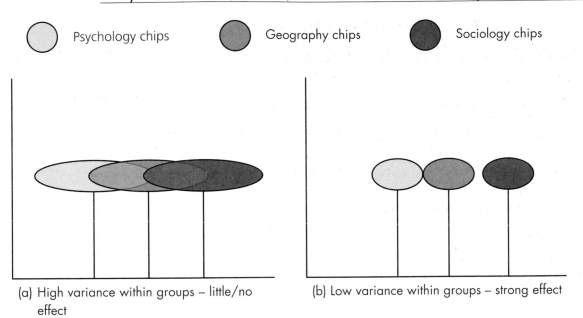

(a) High variance within groups – little/no
effect

(b) Low variance within groups – strong effect

Figure 17.1 High and low variance within groups and the significance of differences between group means

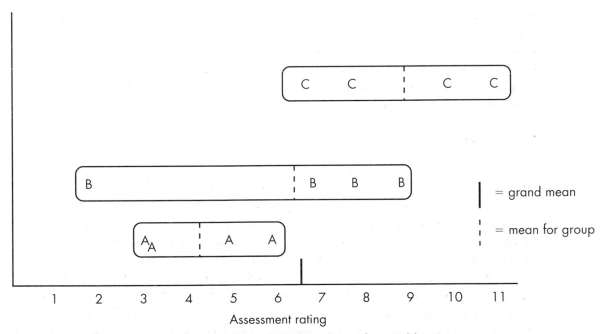

Figure 17.2 Spread and mean of 'liking' assessments of Jane from Table 16.1

value). Here it is not at all obvious that the means are far apart enough for significance. Given the overlap of scores from the different groups, we would not be sure that we have support for H_1 – that the parent populations have different means, nor are we sure we should retain H_0. These two hypotheses are depicted in Figure 17.3.

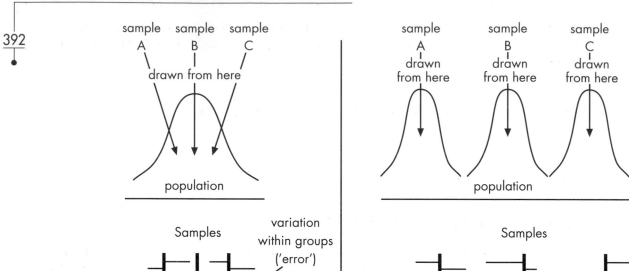

Figure 17.3   The null and alternative hypotheses for a one-way ANOVA with three samples

THE THEORY UNDERLYING THE ANOVA APPROACH

Our sample means have the following relationship: $\bar{x}_A < \bar{x}_B < \bar{x}_C$. We wish to know whether this is a reflection of the relationship between the means of their parent *popula-tions* (H_1) or whether we should treat the relationship as non-significant and retain the null hypothesis that the population means are identical. We saw that the non-parametric test dictated the latter option. What we need from a significance test then is the probability that we could obtain means as varied as these, *if the null hypothesis is true*. We expect this probability to be small for a significant result.

The position of the null hypothesis is depicted on the left hand side of Figure 17.3. If sample means are close together we have little support for rejecting the notion that the samples were all drawn from the same 'pile' or population. However, as explained loosely above, the notion of 'close together' depends upon the variation *within* the groups. In Chapter 11 on significance, we looked at Table 11.1 and saw that the difference (for group A) between two means of 9.53 and 8.79 did not look intuitively impressive. How did we make that judgement? Well, if you agree, then consciously or not, you would have had to take into account, in a rough way, the sort of *dispersion* there was *within* the samples. Suppose we had the same difference between means but that *all* the scores for the audience condition ranged between 9.4 and 9.7, and *all* the alone scores ranged between 8.6

and 8.9. Now we're in a different league and the difference *does* look large. This is because we've taken into account the difference between means *relative to the variation within the samples.*

The heart of the matter – separating the variation

This is indeed the heart of the matter.

The ANOVA test makes a direct comparison between the amount by which sample means vary and the amount that values in each sample vary around the group mean.

HOW DOES ANOVA MAKE THE COMPARISON?

As we know from Chapter 10, variation of values within groups can be measured in terms of *deviations* of values from their mean. If we take all the values in the Jane table (16.1) as one group, we find that they *all* vary around a GRAND MEAN which is the mean of the whole set, ignoring any conditions they are in. This value is shown in Figure 17.2 as 6.58. Let's suppose Amar gave the rating, of 10 in group C. This deviates by $(10 - 6.58)$ points, that is **3.42** from the grand mean. Amar's rating, however, can be split into the amount by which it deviates from *its own group mean* $(10 - 9 = 1)$ and the amount by which group C's mean deviates from the grand mean $(9 - 6.58 = 2.42)$. We can visualise this as:

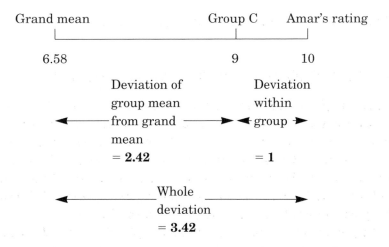

Every value can be treated in this way. Therefore we would find that:

A	B	C
sum of whole deviations	= sum of deviations of group means from grand mean*	+ sum of deviations within groups

* *There would be one of these for* **each** *value so we'd need to multiply each mean's deviation from the grand mean by* **n** *(number in each group) to make this add up.*

It is also true that:

A	B	C
the sum of squares of whole deviations =	**the sum of squares of deviations of group means from the grand mean*** +	**the sum of squares of deviations within groups**

Again, there would be one of these for each participant's deviation and therefore n in each group

This equation is central to ANOVA thinking and from here on we'll refer to it as the *'main equation'*, and we'll use headings 'A', 'B' and 'C' to refer to different parts of it.

If an independent variable has an effect we have said that we would expect the total variation *within groups* (C) to be small compared with the total variation *among group means* (B). We can measure this variation in terms of sums of deviations or in terms of *sums of squares* of deviations. The expectancy for an effect remains the same.

There is of course a reason for introducing sums of squared deviations. These ought to sound familiar to you from Chapter 10. They are the statistical measures on which the *variance* of values is based. To remind you, the formula for the variance of a set of values is

$$s^2 = \frac{\Sigma d^2}{N-1}$$

which can also be written as:

$$\frac{SS}{df}$$

The latter short hand version just shows that variance is the *sum of squares* (of deviations of scores about their mean) divided by their *degrees of freedom*.

Following the main equation above, it might be tempting to wonder whether the *total variance* of all values (A) would be equal to the *variance of the means* (B) plus the *variance within groups* (C). We've seen that the top parts of the variance equations (*SS*) behave in this way. Well, the variances don't add up in this way and this is because the *degrees of freedom* in the variance equation would be different for each component. However, ANOVA does make a comparison between the variance of the means and the variance within groups. It uses a statistic known as the *F* RATIO and this is:

$$F = \frac{between \text{ groups variance}}{within \text{ groups variance}}$$

This is the variance associated with the B part of the main equation, divided by the variance associated with the C part. Following the reasoning above, for an effect we would expect the variance *between groups* (B) to be large, *relative to* the variance *within groups* (C). In saying this we are in fact creating the *F* ratio. Hence, if there is an effect, *F* will be a relatively large value above 1. However, if the two variances are similar, means are not particularly far apart and *F* will be close to 1.

The F ratio compares population estimates

In fact, both the top and bottom parts of this fraction are *estimates of the variance in the population the samples were drawn from*. The bottom part simply estimates the population variance as similar to that within groups. This is why *'homogeneity of variance'* is important (see p. 340) because we assume each sample has roughly the same variance and is a reflection of the population variance. The top part of the fraction is an estimate of the population variance based on the set of means. We start, under the null hypothesis, by assuming that the means are drawn from the same population. *If this null hypothesis is true*, the estimate based on means should be the same as the estimate based on variance within groups (the B estimate should be equal to the C estimate). The more the means vary among themselves, however, the more the top part of the fraction will increase and we become increasingly less sure that the means could vary this much 'by chance' if they're drawn from the same population. At a certain point F becomes so large that it is a highly unlikely ratio under H_0 and we eventually reject this null hypothesis. For the situation depicted in Figure 17.1b, or Figure 17.3b, we should get a high F and, when it is higher than the table critical value, we would reject the null hypothesis that the population means are equal.

CALCULATIONS IN ANOVA

The calculations in ANOVA can get rather complicated – a lot of number crunching rather than anything mathematically sophisticated – and it is to be hoped that the reader using this section will have access to one of the commonly used computer programmes available these days, such as *SPSS* (for *Windows* or *MAC*) and *Minitab*. I have, however, included calculation of the simpler models in recognition of the view that calculating the formulae of tests by hand leads to greater understanding of what the test is actually doing. For the more complex models an outline is provided, but if you require the by-hand calculation, please consult one of the texts indicated at the end of Chapter 19.

Calculating sums of squares

ANOVA involves calculation of several variance components. If you look back to Chapter 10 we said there that one version of the variance formula was very important and used as the model in ANOVA calculations. Well, here we are! The equation is:

$$s^2 = \frac{\Sigma x^2 - (\Sigma x)^2/N}{N - 1}$$

Notice that we still have 'SS' on top and 'df' underneath.

When we calculate sums of squares in ANOVA we have to use the top part of this equation:

$$\Sigma x^2 - (\Sigma x)^2/N$$

and substitute various values in place of the first x, depending on which part of the *main equation* we are working on. Note that the second part

$$(\Sigma x)^2/N$$

(sometimes called a 'correction factor') is common to all calculations except SS_{error} and keeps the same value. The calculations of sums of squares of deviations use the following values (but only look at this table in conjunction with calculating the ANOVA below, otherwise it will hardly make sense!):

A	B	C
Total sum of squares SS_{total}	**Between groups sum of squares** SS_{groups}	**Error** SS_{error}
Σx^2 means take all the scores in all the samples, square each one and add them all up.	$\Sigma \bar{x}^2$ means perform the operation on the *means* of the samples. It is easier however to take the *totals* of all the scores in each group, square these, add them up and then divide by the number (n) there were in each group.	The short cut[1] here will be to calculate $SS_{total} - SS_{groups}$ This is not a fiddle because we are simply following the *main equation* where we saw that: $SS_{total} = SS_{groups} + SS_{error}$

[1] *The long method is to calculate $\Sigma x^2 - (\Sigma x)^2/N$ for each sample, where x, in both cases, refers only to the scores within that sample and N to the number in the sample. Finally, the result for each sample would be summed, e.g. for sample A we would get: $(3^2 + 5^2 + 6^2 + 3^2) - 17^2/4$.*

CALCULATION OF ONE-WAY UNRELATED ANOVA ON DATA FROM TABLE 16.1

Procedure	Calculation on our data	
1. Calculate SS_{total} using the standard sum of squares formula which we shall refer to as 'formula A' from now on: $\Sigma x^2 - (\Sigma x)^2/N \qquad (A)$ where 'x' is each of the 12 scores in Table 16.1. Here we calculate the SS of all the whole deviations. Be careful not to confuse Σx^2 with $(\Sigma x)^2$	$\Sigma x \quad = 3 + 5 + 6 + 3 + 2 + 7$ $\quad\quad\quad 9 + 8 + 10 + 8 + 7 + 11$ $(\Sigma x)^2 \quad = 6241$ $(\Sigma x)^2/N = 6241/12$ $\Sigma x^2 \quad = 3^2 + 5^2 + 6^2 + 3^2 + 2^2 + 7^2$ $\quad\quad 9^2 + 8^2 + 10^2 + 8^2 + 7^2 + 11^2$ $SS_{total} \quad = 611 - 520.08$	$= \mathbf{79}$ $= \mathbf{520.08}$ $= \mathbf{611}$ $= \mathbf{90.92}$
2. Calculate SS_{groups}. Now we are calculating the SS for the deviations of the group means, so each x should be a sample mean, but we use total (T) and get back to means by dividing by n – the number in each group. We use[2]: $\dfrac{\Sigma T^2}{n} - (\Sigma x)^2/N$	$\Sigma T^2/n \quad = (17^2 + 26^2 + 36^2)/4$ $(\Sigma x)^2/N = \text{(as above)}$ $SS_{groups} \quad = 565.25 - 520.08$	$= \mathbf{565.25}$ $= \mathbf{520.08}$ $= \mathbf{45.17}$
3. Calculate SS_{error} using: $SS_{error} = SS_{total} - SS_{groups}$ (see above)	$SS_{error} \quad = 90.92 - 45.17$	$= \mathbf{45.75}$

4. Calculate df for:

SS_{total} : $N - 1$
SS_{groups} : $k - 1$ (k = number of conditions)
SS_{error} $df_{total} - df_{groups}$

df_{total} = 12 − 1	= 11
df_{groups} = 3 − 1	= 2
df_{error} = 11 − 2	= 9

5. Calculate each *mean sum* of squares by dividing each sum of squares by its appropriate df

MS_{total} = 90.92/11	= 8.26
MS_{groups} = 45.17/2	= 22.59
MS_{error} = 45.75/9	= 5.08

6. Calculate F which is $\dfrac{MS_{groups}}{MS_{error}}$

$F = \dfrac{22.59}{5.08}$

F = 4.45

7. Check significance of F in Table 11, Appendix 2, as described in the paragraph below. Write $F_{(effect, error)}$.

Critical value for $F_{(2,9)}$, with $p < 0.05$ = **4.26**

[2] *Instead of $\bar{x}$ we use T/n, therefore, in the formula, this becomes T^2/n^2. If you look back to the partition of whole deviations on page 393, you'll see that there would be a deviation of the group mean from the grand mean, for each value in the in the data set. For each sample then there would be n of these. So, since we have n times T^2/n^2, this term becomes T^2/n. Note that $\sum (T^2/n) = (\sum T^2)/n$*

Finding the significance of F

We need to consult F ratio tables (pp. 564–5) and use these as follows. First go to the table for $p < 0.05$, since this is the highest value for probability with which we can claim significance. To find the critical value we must use the degrees of freedom for the effect concerned (= 2) – this is the *numerator* (since it goes on the top of the F ratio equation) and the degrees of freedom for the error term (= 9) – this is the *denominator* in the equation. As usual, if we achieve significance with $p < 0.05$ we could consult further to see whether our F value is greater than critical values for smaller values of p. In the F tables this means moving to the next whole page of table values (but see p. 289).

ANOVA TABLE OF RESULTS

It is conventional to lay out the full results of an ANOVA test as in Table 17.1.

Table 17.1 One-way ANOVA test results

Source of variation	Sum of squares	df	Mean sum of squares	F ratio	Probability of F under H_0
Between groups*	45.17	2	22.59	4.446	$p < 0.05$
Error	45.75	9	5.08		
Total	90.92	11	8.26		

* *Often referred to as the variation for the 'effect'.*

Conclusion from our test (interpreting the ANOVA result)

Using ANOVA we are justified (by the narrowest of margins, assuming $p < 0.05$ is acceptable) in rejecting the null hypothesis that the population means are equal.

Interpreting the F test result in ANOVA

What we know from this result is that *at least one mean differs significantly from at least one other mean*. We don't know which means these might be but we can see from the group means (group A: **4.25** group B: **6.5** group C: **9**) that the most likely significant difference is between group A and group C, with the next likely contender being the difference between group B and group C. In order to decide which groups differ significantly from which, without *capitalising on chance* (see p. 379) and just conducting several *t* tests, we need to consider what are known as A PRIORI and POST HOC COMPARISONS.

A PRIORI AND POST HOC COMPARISONS

Have a look at the results (Table 17.2) from a fictitious study on memory where the cell means represent mean recall of items from a 25-word list by different groups of participants being tested on Monday to Friday.

Table 17.2 Mean recall by day of the week tested

(a) Monday	(b) Tuesday	(c) Wednesday	(d) Thursday	(e) Friday
$\bar{X}_m$	$\bar{X}_t$	$\bar{X}_w$	$\bar{X}_{th}$	$\bar{X}_f$
16.71	14.56	10.45	13.78	14.23

Let's suppose that the 'complete' null hypothesis is true and that, for the population sampled, recall does not differ across days of the week ($\mu_m = \mu_{tu} = \mu_w = \mu_{th} = \mu_f$). In other words, the population means for each weekday are all the same value. Suppose *also* that on this particular occasion of testing (taking specific samples) we had a fluke result where the sample mean for Monday does differ significantly from the sample mean for Wednesday, using an unrelated *t* test. On this occasion a type I error has occurred if we reject the null hypothesis that these two samples come from populations with the same means.

POST HOC COMPARISONS

Post hoc comparisons are those we make *after* inspecting the results of our ANOVA test. Suppose, having obtained the overall results in Table 17.2, we decided to make all possible tests between pairs of means and count any significant differences as justification for rejecting the null hypothesis. In this case, we would be *bound* to make a type I error since we are bound to test Monday and Wednesday's means along with all the others.

A PRIORI COMPARISONS

On the other hand, if we had decided, on the basis of our general theory, that only

Monday's and Friday's means should be tested, because we believed people would, say, be more tired at the end than at the beginning of the week, we would not make this type I error. In fact, *whichever two samples we chose to test in advance*, since there are 10 possible pairs, we only had a 1 in 10 ($p = 0.1$) chance of making a type I error given the results occurred as they did. Only one of the differences between pairs that we *could* have predicted as different was spuriously 'significant'. This assumes that the prediction concerned just two means (known as PAIRWISE COMPARISON). A PRIORI ('PLANNED') COMPARISONS, then, are comparisons we can make, having made a specific prediction, based on theoretical argument, *before* conducting our ANOVA test. This should remind you of one and two-tailed tests because, in the simple two condition experiment, a one-tailed hypothesis is a kind of a priori planned comparison.

Making all possible comparisons produces a far higher probability of making a type I error than occurs if we make selected and predetermined a priori comparisons. In fact, deciding, in advance, to make all possible comparison tests is the same thing as conducting post hoc tests. The latter involves inspecting everything and testing what looks likely. The former amounts to the same thing because the prior plan is to test everything and see what turns up as 'significant'. Generally, these global approaches are seen as 'fishing' for results and viewed with suspicion unless there are strong theoretical reasons for predicting all possible differences.

FAMILY-WISE ERROR RATE

We have said before that if you make 20 tests of significance on randomly drawn data you are likely to get one 'significant' difference. That is the logic of significance testing. We look for results which would occur less than five times in 100 under H_0 and count them as significant if we predicted them before testing. If we set significance at $p \leq 0.05$, then, and make multiple tests on randomly drawn data, we know that there is a 0.05 probability, *since the null hypothesis is true*, that any comparison we make will be wrongly assumed to be significant, i.e. we will have made a type I error. We are said to be working with an ERROR RATE PER COMPARISON of 0.05. If we are making several tests on our data it is possible to calculate something known as the FAMILY-WISE ERROR RATE which is the probability of making *at least one* type I error when making multiple tests, if H_0 is true.

TESTS FOR A PRIORI COMPARISONS

If you have justifiably predicted just one significant difference ('planned one comparison') then there is no problem in testing this with a special t test (as used by 'LINEAR CONTRASTS' – see below), since you have a 0.05 chance of a type I error. If you make two tests your chance of making *at least one* type I error rises to near 0.1. You can compensate by setting your significance level, *prior to testing*, at 0.025. The new test will be:

$$t = \frac{\bar{x}_1 - \bar{x}_2}{\sqrt{\dfrac{MS_{error}}{n_1} - \dfrac{MS_{error}}{n_2}}}$$

using df_{error}, where MS_{error} comes from the overall ANOVA result and n_1 and n_2 are numbers in the samples.

Bonferroni t tests

Rather than doing this, however, you can use Bonferroni t tests. They are only recommended though if you are making a *few* comparisons. If you want to test *all* possible comparisons then you should use one of the tests required for post hoc comparisons. These tests are not dealt with here but will be found on computer programs, such as *SPSS* in the ANOVA sections.

Linear contrasts – testing combinations of means

There may be occasions when you want to test for significance between *combinations* of means, for instance, from Table 17.2, between the combined mean for Monday and Tuesday against the combined mean for Thursday and Friday. When this occurs you need to make use of the LINEAR CONTRAST approach. The mathematics are not covered in this text but, assuming you are using a commercial statistics package (such as *SPSS*), the only tricky calculation you'll have to perform is to provide a set of LINEAR CONTRAST COEFFICIENTS to let the program know, using numerical codes, which combinations of means you wish to test between. The tests themselves will use the F ratio on relevant sums of squares. You can also use linear contrasts to test simple comparisons between just two means – basically a t test. So, when you need to tell your computer which combinations of means you wish to test, here's what you need to do to give a coefficient (code) to each mean:

Rules for determining contrast coefficients
1. All coefficients must sum together to zero.
2. You will want to test one mean or group of means (group 1) against another (group 2). A 'group' could be just one mean. The sum of coefficients for group 1 must equal the sum of coefficients for group 2, but have the opposite sign.
3. The coefficient for any mean not tested must be zero.

Table 17.3 Coefficients used for groups of means tested with linear contrasts

Test of:	Mon	Tues	Wed	Thur	Fri	Explanation using rules
$\bar{X}_m$ against $\bar{X}_w$	1	0	−1	0	0	Rule **1** numbers sum to zero Rule **2** 1 and −1 sum to zero Rule **3** other numbers are 0
$\bar{X}_m + \bar{X}_t$ combined against $\bar{X}_{th} + \bar{X}_f$	1	1	0	−1	−1	Rule **2** the two means marked '1' will be taken together and contrasted with the two marked '−1'. Other rules as above
$\bar{X}_m + \bar{X}_t$ combined against $\bar{X}_w$	−1	−1	2	0	0	Rule 2: −1 + −1 = −2; Wed has +2 and will be contrasted with the other two together

Choosing coefficients is something of an intuitive task. There is no one right answer. For instance, in the third row of Table 17.3 we *could* have chosen: −2 −2 4 0 0.

TESTS FOR POST HOC COMPARISONS

These would be used in either of two situations:

1. Where *all* possible comparisons are desired, and this has been decided a priori.
2. Where comparisons are only being made *after* examination of the differences between means and *not* because of any theoretical prediction.

There are several tests, each with variations and complications, for carrying out post hoc comparisons. I am just going to mention two of the most popular, with their associated characteristics.

Newman–Keuls test

This alternative is generally controversial because, under certain circumstances, the family-wise error rate gets high. This will only happen in studies with quite a lot of conditions, and, for studies involving only three conditions, the Newman–Keuls gives a greater chance of showing real significant differences, with only slightly more risk of making type I errors than the Tukey$_a$ test, below. Again, the calculations for the Newman–Keuls and Tukey's test, below, are not dealt with here but the test can be automatically carried out using *SPSS* and similar.

Tukey's$_a$ (honestly significant difference) test

This engagingly titled test is generally considered the safest you can use if you wish to carry out all possible 'pairwise' (two means at a time) comparisons and keep the family-wise error rate down to 0.05. The price you pay is that the test is 'conservative' – you might miss real differences in keeping your interpretations safe.

Examples of Tukey$_a$ results

If we had conducted a Tukey$_a$ HSD on our sample data, following the ANOVA result in Table 17.1, we would have obtained the result below (Table 17.4), which is part of the *SPSS (Windows)* output:

Table 17.4 Results of Tukey$_a$ test in SPSS (version 6)

Homogeneous subsets (highest and lowest means are not significantly different)					Grp 1	Grp 2	Grp 3
Subset 1							
Group	Grp 1	Grp 2					
Mean	4.2500	6.5000					
				Mean	Condition		
Subset 2							
Group	Grp 2	Grp 3		4.2500	Grp 1		
				6.5000	Grp 2		
Mean	6.5000	9.0000		9.0000	Grp 3	*	

The asterisk on the right shows us that the means for group 1 and group 3 *are* significantly different but that no other difference is. The left hand side tells us that groups 1 and 2 can be assumed to belong in the same 'subset' – their means do not differ significantly. This is also true of groups 2 and 3 taken as a pair. But, as we know, the overall variation in means is unlikely if all three samples come from the same population.

Whether group 2 'belongs' in reality with group 1 or group 3 we can't say on this occasion, but look at the data in Table 17.5. Here, again, the ANOVA result is significant. Here the Tukey result tells us that groups 1 and 2 belong together and their means are *both* significantly different from group 3's mean.

Table 17.5 SPSS (version b) Tukey results showing a clear group difference

	Group 1	Group 2	Group 3	Homogeneous subsets		
	←	(scores)	→	Subset 1		
	12.00	14.00	16.00	Group	Grp 1	Grp 2
	14.00	15.00	20.00	Mean	13.2500	14.7500
	13.00	14.00	18.00	Subset 2		
	14.00	16.00	19.00	Group	Grp 3	
Means	13.25	14.75	18.25	Mean	18.2500	

GENERAL OPTIONS FOR COMPARISONS IN ANOVA

- For one *planned* comparison (or possibly two if alpha is lowered) between pairs of means ('pairwise') use *individual* (special) *t* tests or *linear contrasts*.
- Where these one (or two) comparisons involve the means of *combinations* of groups, use *linear contrasts*.
- If several *planned* comparisons are to be made (pairwise or with combinations) use a *Bonferroni* t *test method*.
- If you want to compare all possible pairs of means, post hoc, or make more than two pre-planned comparisons where there are several groups, use *Newman–Keuls* (or *Tukey's HSD* for safety).
- If you want to compare all possible pairs of means, post hoc, where there are quite a few groups (five or more), use *Tukey's HSD*.
- If you want to make all possible contrasts (i.e. not just 'pairwise' but including all possible *combinations* of means against others), use the *Scheffé* test (not described here).

Where are all these alternatives?

There are other specific alternatives depending on the particular design of the study and on your specific purposes. The above comparisons are all found in statistical programmes like *SPSS* but you really should check in one of the advanced texts mentioned at the end of Chapter 19 before proceeding, in order to know that your analysis is valid.

Unequal numbers in the samples

Usually it's safest to attempt to get the same number of people in each sample but sometimes one is stuck with unequal numbers – we couldn't know, in advance, how many would answer a questionnaire in a certain way, for instance. People's results may be unusable or they may fail to show up for testing. In the case of one-way ANOVA this isn't *too* difficult. In step **2** of the one-way ANOVA calculation above, we don't find the sum of all T^2, *then* divide by n. We divide *each* T^2 by its associated n and add the results. In the case of multi-way ANOVA tests, to be dealt with later, it is beyond the scope of this book to provide the relevant calculations. You could either consult one of the more detailed texts referenced at the end of Chapter 19, or check that your software deals with different numbers in each sample. *SPSS* just steams ahead and copes.

MANOVA – MULTIVARIATE ANALYSIS OF VARIANCE

Put simply, this is a set of statistical procedures which tests the significance of *multiple dependent variables* as a set. Suppose you had gathered data evaluating your college course where students assessed 'usefulness', 'interest', 'enjoyment' and so on. With MANOVA it is possible to test these several dependent variables as a set across the various conditions of the independent variable, which, in this case, might be part-time, full-time and evening students. It would be possible here to conduct a one-way ANOVA for each of the assessment scores separately, or *t* tests if only two types of student were involved. MANOVA does this but also estimates the significance of any difference across levels of the IV *taking all assessments (DVs) together*. The general rule is, if you want to conduct an ANOVA test of means on several dependent variables, in order to avoid type I error (you are 'cheating chance' by doing several tests with alpha at 0.05), conduct a MANOVA test first (it is an option in *SPSS* and other programmes). If this shows significance then it is legitimate to investigate and take as significant any of the individual ANOVA results which the MANOVA procedure has shown to be significant.

ANCOVA – ANALYSIS OF CO-VARIANCE

This will be easier to explain using an example first. Suppose we conduct a quasi-experiment using two groups of students, one a day-time class and one a part-time evening group. This evening group are going to use a new interactive computer package for learning statistics and research methods. We want to see whether they do as well as the day-time class who will be taught conventionally. The trouble is that the groups did not start off equal in competence in numeracy. We have not allocated our participant 'pool' to conditions at random. Suppose the evening group, who use the computer package, contained more adults returning to education after several years. They are generally weaker on maths and statistics, though there is a lot of overlap between the two groups and the range within each group is wide. In addition, when we investigate end-of-year test results as a whole, we find that initial numeracy level correlates quite strongly with 'final achievement', no matter what class the student was in. We suspect that the independent learning package *did* help the evening group but the difference between groups is not significant. Our results are *confounded* by the initial numeracy difference which we *know* will produce a systematic bias. However, unlike other extraneous variables, we have an element of control over this variable because we happen to know how it correlates with final achievement scores. ANCOVA permits us to 'partial out' the effect of the numeracy differences (known as the CO-VARIATE). It gives us an estimate of the means of the two groups which would occur *if*, in a sense, both groups started from equal positions on numeracy.

It is important to note that ANCOVA does *two* things. First, if groups start out similar on the co-variate it only takes out the variance which is assumed to be caused by the co-variate. This reduces the error term of the standard ANOVA calculation. That is, we've reduced the 'unexplained' error in the bottom half of the F ratio calculation and we're more likely to see a significant result if there is a real population difference. Second, if the groups *differ* on the co-variate to start with, as in our example, ANCOVA is used to conduct the analysis of variance on the estimate of what the means would be if they *didn't* differ on the co-variate. This latter use can be controversial.

Glossary

Statistical procedure used to investigate differences between two means which may be adjusted to allow for the fact that the two groups differ on a variable which correlates with the dependent variable (the 'co-variate')	_____ __ ___-_____	analysis of co-variance (ANCOVA)
Differences between means, or combinations of means, which were predicted from theory before the data were collected	_ _____ _____	a priori comparisons
Statistical technique which compares variances within and between samples in order to estimate the significance of differences between sets of means	_____ __ _____	analysis of variance (ANOVA)
Sum of squares of deviations of group means from the grand mean; used to calculate the variance component related to the 'effect', i.e. distance between group means	_____ _____ __ ___ _____	between groups sum of squares
Procedure for testing several *planned comparisons* between (groups of) means	_____ __ _____	Bonferroni *t* tests
$(\Sigma x)^2/N$ – the second term in all ANOVA sum of squares equations	_____ _____	correction factor
A variable which correlates with a dependent variable on which two groups differ; the biasing effect of this confounding variable can be adjusted for in ANCOVA when conducting ANOVA analysis across the group means	__-_____	co-variate

Probability of making type I errors if H_0 is true		**error rates**
Given the significance level set, the likelihood of a type I error in *each* test made on the data	_____	(error rate) per comparison
The probability of having made *at least one* type I error in all the tests made on a set of data	_____	family-wise error rate
Sum of all the squares of deviations of each score from its own group mean; used to calculate an estimate of the 'unexplained' variance with which to compare the 'explained' variance of group means around the grand mean; when divided by *df*, becomes the *MS* on the bottom part of the *F* ratio	_____ __ __ _____	error sum of squares
Ratio of two variances; used in all ANOVA tests; top of ratio fraction is the 'effect' variance; bottom is the 'error' variance	__ _____	F test/ratio
Mean of all scores in a data set, irrespective of conditions or groups	_____ _____	grand mean
Values to be entered into an equation for calculating *linear contrasts* – see below	_____ _____	linear coefficients
Procedure for testing between individual pairs of means or combinations of means when *planned comparisons* (see below) have been made	_____ _____	linear contrasts
Statistical procedure for testing the effects of one or more independent variables *on more than one* dependent variable	____-_____ _____ __ _____	multi-variate analysis of variance (MANOVA)
Sum of squares divided by *df*; a particular component's variance estimate in ANOVA	____ ___ __ _____	mean sum of squares
Procedure for testing many or all possible pairs of means in a data set for significance, so long as number of groups is relatively low	_____ _____	Newman-Keuls test
Comparison of just two means from a set of means	_____ _____	pairwise comparison
Tests which it was intended to make, because of theoretical predictions, *before* data were collected	_____ _____	planned comparisons
Tests between means, or groups of means, only decided upon *after* inspection of data	____ __ _____	post hoc comparisons
Addition of the squares of deviations around a mean	____ __ _____	sum of squares

Procedure for testing all possible pairs of means from a data set where there are a relatively large number of groups; with low number of groups, considered rather conservative	_____ (_____) _____	Tukey's$_a$ (HSD) test
Procedure for testing all possible combinations of means	_____ _____	Scheffé test
Alternative name for the F test – see above	_____ _____ _____	variance ratio test

Exercises

1. Produce three samples of eight values by using the random numbers in Table 1, Appendix 2 (start anywhere, for each sample, and select the next eight numbers in any direction). Calculate a one-way ANOVA (unrelated) and check the F ratio for significance. If it is significant, tell your tutor you're a little more sceptical about the 5% significance level convention!

2. Imagine that you conduct an experiment with five people in one condition, six in a second condition and eight in a third condition, and that you are going to conduct a one-way ANOVA analysis. Produce the outline 'source of variance' table, including the degrees of freedom for each component.

3. In the experiment in question 2, if the null hypothesis has already been rejected and you *now* decide to test all the paired comparisons, what test would be appropriate? Tukey$_a$ *or* set alpha at 0.01 and do *t* tests?

4. Suppose, in the experiment of question 2, you had predicted in your introduction that only the first and third conditions would differ. What test might it now be legitimate to conduct?

5. In the experiment in question 2, we wish to use a linear contrast to test for a difference between conditions one and two *together* against condition three. What would be the simplest set of coefficients to use?

Answers

2   Table is as Table 17.1 in the chapter with df: total = 18; between groups = 2; error = 16.

3   Tukey is safest, but for three conditions there are six possible (special) t tests (1v2, 1v3, 2v3, (112)v3, 1v(213), (113)v2) and $6 \times 0.01 = 0.06$, which is a *rough* estimate of the likelihood of a type I error if H_0 is true, and this is an almost acceptable level.

4   Special t test preferable (i.e. linear contrast), but Bonferroni t test also possible.

5   1 1 −2

18

ANOVA designs – multi-factorial ANOVA for more than one independent variable

The chapter deals with multi-factor ANOVA where more than one independent variable is involved. Each independent variable is known as a *factor* and each condition of one independent variable is known as a *level* of that factor.

A design where all factors are between groups is known as *unrelated* or *between subjects*. When at least one factor is repeated measures, the design is *mixed*, unless all factors are repeated measures, in which case the model is *repeated measures* or *within subjects*.

The use of more than one factor raises the possibility that each factor may have different effects on different levels of a second factor. This effect is known as an *interaction effect*. For instance, extroverts might exhibit poorer memory in the morning than in the afternoon, whereas the reverse might be true for introverts.

The effect of one factor over all levels of another factor taken together is known as a *main effect*. Effects of one level of one factor across the levels of another are known as *simple effects* (e.g. effect of morning learning across extroverts and introverts).

Total sum of squares (*SS*) in a multi-factor ANOVA analysis, is divided into:

- *Between groups SS* (the 'explained' variation) which divides into:
  - *Between groups SS* – for each factor plus
  - *Interaction SS* – for each possible combination of factors
- *Error SS* – the 'unexplained', within-groups variation

USING TWO OR MORE INDEPENDENT VARIABLES

THE STUDENT PROJECT EXPANDS

Let's suppose Adrian, Dina and Linsi (remember them?) have pushed their ideas even further. One of them has realised that the people they tested, being students, were *likely* to hold strong views about global warming. Helen suggests that if they'd tested people who don't care about global warming then perhaps the results would have been different. Perhaps people who don't care would have disliked the person who *did* care and seen the person who, like themselves, didn't care as positive. They realise that what they should have done was to take samples from among a group known not to care about global warming, and a group who do care, in order to test this more complicated hypothesis.

The example of ANOVA which we have already considered involved the manipulation of just *one* independent variable (with three values). Very often, researchers test the effect of *two* independent variables at the same time.

FACTORS AND LEVELS

In a classic study, Godden and Baddeley (1975) asked scuba divers to learn a list of words either on dry land or under water. Subsequently, the divers in each group were divided again and half of each original group was asked to recall the words on dry land and the other half while under water. Here two independent variables are manipulated simultaneously. Since things can get complicated when we move into the world of multiple independent variables, there is a consistent language to be used. In multi-factor ANOVA language, independent variables are known as FACTORS and the different values each can take are known as LEVELS. If we manipulate the *factor* of caffeine, we might use four *levels*: no caffeine, placebo (salt pill), 50 mg and 100 mg. In Godden and Baddeley's design we have two factors – learning environment and recall environment. Each of these has two levels: on land or under water. Consequently there were four groups of participants, as shown below:

Factor 2 Recall environment ⇓ (levels)	Factor 1 Learning environment ⇓ (levels)	
	Dry land	**Under water**
Dry land	learned on land and recalled on land	learned under water and recalled on land
Under water	learned on land and recalled under water	learned under water and recalled under water

The means of words correctly recalled in each set of conditions are plotted in Figure 18.1 where it can be seen that learning and recalling in the same environment produces superior recall to conditions where the two environments are different. This type of chart is very common for plotting the means in studies such as these. The effect shown is known as an INTERACTION EFFECT. This is because the effect of one factor changes for different levels of the other factor. We shall return to this point in a moment.

Multi-factorial ANOVA designs are often referred to by their factor structure. Godden and Baddeley's design is a 2×2 *factorial design* (two factors, each with two levels).

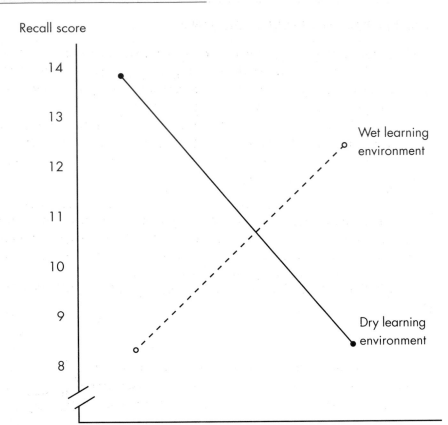

Figure 18.1 An interaction effect – learning and recall on dry land or under water (from Godden and Baddeley, 1975)

Let's look now at a slightly more complex design. In 1986, Alexander and Guenther reported a study in which they manipulated the moods of three groups of participants by getting them to read statements. They proposed that this led to states described as either 'elated', 'depressed' or 'neutral'. They then read participants a list of equal numbers of positive and negative personality traits to see whether mood affected the type of trait recalled. Apparently it did – 'depressed' participants recalled more negative traits, for instance. This is an example of a 2 × 3 factorial design (two types of trait; three types of mood).

Designs can become very complicated indeed. Samuel and Bryant (1984) tested four ages of child (Factor 1) on three types of task (Factor 2) using three types of material (Factor 3) – a 4 × 3 × 3 design. David *et al.* (1986) used a 4 × 2 × 16 design in the investigation of road accidents and Gulian and Thomas (1986) used a 2 × 2 × 3 × 4 design where males and females were tested in high or low noise, under three different sets of instructions about the noise across four different periods of testing! There is no limit to the complexity of designs which can be used apart from the researchers' patience with data analysis and the size of the willing participant pool.

UNRELATED AND RELATED DESIGNS

If a factor involves independent samples, for instance one group learns on land, a *different* group learns under water, then the factor is known as a BETWEEN GROUPS FACTOR. If it is a repeated measures factor, such as different levels of coffee given to the *same* participants, then it can be called a WITHIN GROUPS FACTOR.

If *all* the factors of a complex ANOVA design are *between groups*, it is known as an *unrelated design*. If *all* factors are within groups factors it is a *related* or *repeated measures* design. If at least one of the factors is between groups, and at least one within, then we refer to it as a MIXED DESIGN.

> The designs of our 'global warming' attitude study, and of the mood manipulation one just described, are outlined on the left hand side of Table 18.1 (overleaf). See if you can fill in the information required for the other designs in the table. Answers appear at the end of the chapter as answers to 'Question 1'.

INTERACTION

A powerful and central feature of 'multi-factorial designs is the possibility of detecting *interaction effects*. In the Godden and Baddeley diving study there are really two experiments in one. Had we only asked divers to learn some words, then tested them on land and under water, we might have come to the erroneous or at least incomplete conclusion that water interferes with learning. The complementary, but odd, study would have been to have divers learn under water, then be tested 'wet' or 'dry' – the dotted line in Figure 18.1. However, by using two *learning* environments *and* two *recall* environments, we complete the combinations and unearth the much more general principle that performance is better if both learning and recall environments are similar – a point to remind your tutors of when exams are set in the great hall! An extremely important point here is that we have *more* than the power of two separate experiments. The participants here are all *allocated randomly* from the same 'pool' (pun not intended!) whereas there could be a stronger possibility of participant differences between two quite separate studies.

Very often, in testing the effect of a single variable, one is drawn to the speculation that an apparent *lack of effect* may be obscuring a difference in performance between types of people or on different sorts of tasks. If we did not know that the divers had learned in different environments, and only looked at the overall mean recall performances under water and on land, we would conclude that differences in recall environment have no effect – the points midway between the two right hand dots in Figure 18.1 (mean wet recall performance) and between the two left hand dots (mean dry recall) represent quite similar means. Here we know about the learning environment difference. However, consider a study where people are asked to memorise in the morning and in the afternoon. Suppose no overall difference is found. It could be that extroverts memorise better in the afternoon, whereas introverts memorise better in the morning. Overall, differences are cancelled out across time of testing and across personality type, but the interaction effect in a 2×2 study (two testing times, two personality groups) would illuminate this complex

Table 18.1 Exercise on identifying factors, levels and designs in multi-factorial research

Description of study	Levels	Factorial design
1 Effect on perception of a person of knowing whether they are concerned or unconcerned about global warming and when no such information is given.	level 1 – knowing person is unconcerned level 2 – knowing person is concerned level 3 – no information	one way unrelated ANOVA; three levels of single IV
2 Effect of mood (depressed, neutral, elated) on recall of positive or negative traits.	Factor 1: Mood (unrelated) level 1 – depressed level 2 – neutral level 3 – elated Factor 2: Trait type (repeat measure) level 1 – positive level 2 – negative	3 × 2 ANOVA mixed design
3 Investigation of different times taken by same people to name colours of colour patches, non-colour words or colour words.		
4 Effect of psychoanalysis, humanist therapy or behaviour modification on groups of male and female clients.		
5 Effect of age (old vs. young) on recall performance using three different memorising methods on each group of participants.		
6 Effect of either coffee or alcohol or a placebo on performance of a visual monitoring task under conditions of either loud noise or moderate noise or intermittent noise or no noise.		
7 Extroverts and introverts are given either a stimulant, placebo or tranquilliser and observed as they perform an energetic and then a dull task.		
8 People with either high or low race prejudice observe either a black or a white person performing either a pro-social, neutral or hostile act. Their ratings of the person observed are compared.		

effect. Below are two other examples where interaction effects illuminate processes which might otherwise remain hidden.

Students were given arguments to convince them that their college should initiate a new, harder exam system. They were given either three or nine weak or strong arguments. This produces four conditions. Overall, nine strong arguments produced greater agreement than did three. Surprisingly though, nine weak arguments produced even *less* agreement than did three weak arguments (Petty and Cacioppo 1984 – see Figure 18.2).

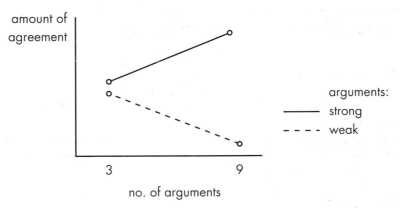

Figure 18.2   Agreement after three or nine weak or strong arguments (after Petty and Cacioppo, 1984, in Atkinson *et al.*, 1993)

Gordon, Bindrim, McNicholas and Walden (1988) asked students to give sentences to a fictitious defendant. One factor was the defendant's 'race', either black or white. The other factor was the type of crime committed – either burglary or embezzlement. This gives a 2×2 unrelated design. One might expect, with an investigation into prejudice using white students, as this study did, that the black defendant would get a higher sentence whatever the crime. In fact, Gordon *et al.* were also looking at *attribution*, where people tend to blame more if a crime can be attributed to one's *regular personality* rather than to *external environmental* factors. Coupling this with social stereotyping trends, they predicted that the black defendant would receive a higher sentence than the white defendant for burglary, this being seen, in the US, as a stereotypically 'black' crime, whereas the white defendant would receive a higher sentence than the black defendant for embezzlement. The findings confirmed these predictions with mean sentences of: black burglar 72.8 months; black embezzler 55.3 months; white embezzler 66.4 months; white burglar 45 months.

An interaction effect, then, occurs when the effect of one factor is dependent upon which levels of other factors are considered. In the diving example, whether recall on land is superior to recall under water depends on the place of learning. In Gordon's example, the black defendant does indeed get a higher sentence than the white defendant as a burglar but a *lower* sentence as an embezzler.

MAIN EFFECTS

The astute reader might have noticed, with Gordon's crime attribution research just mentioned, that the black defendant, though receiving a lower sentence than the white defendant for embezzlement, nevertheless came off worst overall, with mean sentences of 72.8 and 55.3 months relative to 66.4 and 45 months.

In this design, if we ignore the factor of crime type, and concentrate solely on the 'race' difference factor, we are considering what is known as a MAIN EFFECT. These are the sorts of effect we have considered almost exclusively in the book up to now – a single factor focus. In ANOVA language, a main effect occurs when one of the factors, irrespective of any other variable, has an overall significant effect. For instance, in the Petty and Cacioppo example above, strong arguments produced significantly more agreement by students *overall* (disregarding number of arguments given) – consider the mid-point (roughly the mean) of the solid line relative to the mean of the dotted line.

SIMPLE EFFECTS

A SIMPLE EFFECT occurs when we extract a *part* of a multi-factor ANOVA result and look at just the effect of *one* level of one factor across one of the other factors. For instance, in the Petty and Cacioppo example, there appears to be a simple effect if we only consider the different effects of nine strong arguments and nine weak arguments. We certainly can't see this effect for the *three* strong and weak arguments. Simple effects are like the simple experiments we have been used to so far, *extracted* from the overall multi-factorial ANOVA results. They can be investigated for significance using *t* tests, planned contrasts or even a one way ANOVA. For instance, if, in the mood and memory study, we predicted that positive traits (only) would be recalled most by elated, less by neutral, and least by depressed participants, we could conduct a one-way ANOVA across these three conditions of just the one level of the factor 'traits'. But the investigation of simple effects must still avoid 'capitalising on chance', as with all other comparisons and contrasts.

> Various kinds of interaction and main effect are possible. Have a look at Figure 18.3 and try to interpret what has happened. Note that it is possible to have main and interaction effects occurring together.

DATA IN A TWO-WAY UNRELATED ANOVA DESIGN

Let's assume that our students decided to press ahead with a more complex design and that they obtained data from 12 students and 12 loggers. They hypothesise that students will be more positive about Jane when she cares about global warming, whereas loggers (not renowned for environmental care) will prefer the Jane who *doesn't* care about global warming. The data obtained are arranged in the 'cells' shown in Table 18.2. Don't be put off by this table. It is more 'busy' than it needs to be because each cell is labelled in order to be absolutely clear about what is being calculated in the ANOVA procedure below. Factor A ('Jane'), across the top, has three levels, in columns: 'Jane doesn't care', 'Jane is neutral' and 'Jane does care'. Factor B ('occupation' or 'occ' for short) has two levels, in rows: 'students' and 'loggers'. A 'cell' (each outlined block in Table 18.2) occurs for each level of one factor crossed with each level of the other factor. Hence cell A1B1 contains the

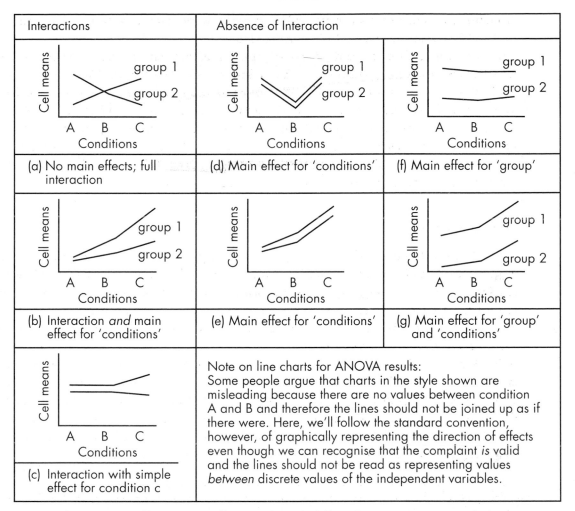

Interactions	Absence of Interaction	
(a) No main effects; full interaction	(d) Main effect for 'conditions'	(f) Main effect for 'group'
(b) Interaction *and* main effect for 'conditions'	(e) Main effect for 'conditions'	(g) Main effect for 'group' and 'conditions'
(c) Interaction with simple effect for condition c	Note on line charts for ANOVA results: Some people argue that charts in the style shown are misleading because there are no values between condition A and B and therefore the lines should not be joined up as if there were. Here, we'll follow the standard convention, however, of graphically representing the direction of effects even though we can recognise that the complaint *is* valid and the lines should not be read as representing values *between* discrete values of the independent variables.	

Figure 18.3   Interaction effects, main effects and simple effects in two-way ANOVA designs

scores of the students told 'Jane doesn't care'. In this study, a representative sample of students has been randomly allocated to the three conditions and the same is true for the loggers.[1]

PARTITIONING THE SUMS OF SQUARES

When we calculated the sums of squares for the one-way ANOVA we had three terms: 1. SS_{total}, 2. SS_{groups}, and 3. SS_{error}. For two-way unrelated ANOVA, we divide the sums of squares up as shown in Figure 18.4. Here, the split is just the same as in the one-way version – we have the same three elements – except that SS_{groups} has been subdivided to take account of the *two* between groups factors and the interaction between them. Each of

---

[1] Technically, one should not test some participants then, later, add some more in new conditions, since, this way, the same 'pool' has not been randomly allocated to all conditions. However, here, since the added group would have to be different sorts of people anyway, this addition of participants is not really a 'crime', as long as the loggers too were randomly allocated to the three 'Jane' conditions.

Table 18.2 Assessments of Jane described as concerned, neutral and unconcerned ('Jane') about global warming by students and loggers ('occ')

	Jane's attitude to global warming (Factor A – 'Jane')		
	Doesn't care **A1**	**Neutral** **A2**	**Does care** **A3**
Participant occupation (Factor B – 'occ')	Liking score	Liking score	Liking score	**Total$_{occ:}$**
Student (B1)	A1B1 3 5 6 3 $T_{A1B1} =$ **17** $\bar{x}_{A1B1} =$ **4.25**	A2B1 2 7 9 8 $T_{A2B1} =$ **26** $\bar{x}_{A2B1} =$ **6.5**	A3B1 10 8 7 11 $T_{A3B1} =$ **36** $\bar{x}_{A3B1} =$ **9**	**79**
Logger (B2)	A2B1 5 4 7 7 $T_{A1B2} =$ **23** $\bar{x}_{A1B2} =$ **5.75**	A2B2 6 5 6 5 $T_{A2B2} =$ **22** $\bar{x}_{A2B2} =$ **5.5**	A2B3 5 3 5 4 $T_{A3B2} =$ **17** $\bar{x}_{A3B2} =$ **4.25**	**62**
Total$_{Jane}$:	**40**	**48**	**53**	**141**

these factors accounts for some of the otherwise unexplained variance of all scores around the grand mean. What's left – the 'unexplained variation' – is, again, the variation of people *within* their groups ('cells') and is the error SS.

As I said earlier, I would hope that readers will not need to calculate tests at this level or higher by hand. Most would, I hope, be using a computer program. Consequently, I have included here a step-by-step approach to the calculation of two-way ANOVA, with explanation, but excluding some of the arithmetic detail. The calculations are, in any case, already familiar, since the same formula for calculating variance components – used in

TOTAL SS

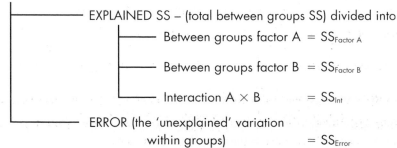
EXPLAINED SS – (total between groups SS) divided into

Between groups factor A = SS$_{Factor\ A}$

Between groups factor B = SS$_{Factor\ B}$

Interaction A × B = SS$_{Int}$

ERROR (the 'unexplained' variation within groups) = SS$_{Error}$

Figure 18.4 Division of sums of squares in a two-way unrelated ANOVA

the one-way example – is used throughout. What the reader *does* need to pay attention to is the meaning of each of the components and their role in the overall analysis.

CALCULATION OF TWO-WAY UNRELATED ANOVA ON DATA FROM TABLE 18.2

Procedure	Calculation on our data
1. Calculate SS_{total} as before using formula A, page 396.	$\Sigma x^2 = 3^2 + 5^2 + 6^2 + \dots$ etc. $= 947$ $\Sigma x = 141$ $(\Sigma x)^2 = 19881$ $(\Sigma x)^2/N = 828.375$ $SS_{total} = 947 - 828.375$ **= 118.625**
2. Calculate SS_{Jane} using equation B, page 396, where T is the total in each condition of Factor A (Jane) and n is the number in each condition. Note that we aren't dealing with cells yet, but overall conditions. 8 people (4 students and 4 loggers) participated in condition 1 of Factor A	$\Sigma T_{Jane}^2 = 40^2 + 48^2 + 53^2 = 1600 + 2304 + 2809$ $= 6713$ $SS_{Jane} = 6713/8 - 828.375$ **= 10.75**
3. Calculate SS_{occ} using equation B where T is $Total_{occ}$; $n = 12$.	$\Sigma T_{occ}^2 = 79^2 + 62^2 = 10085$ $SS_{occ} = 10085/12 - 828.375$ **= 12.042**
4. Calculate SS_{cells}, the total between groups SS; that is, the variation produced by all the groups, i.e. the variation of the cell totals around their mean. Here T is T_{cells}, the values 17, 26 etc., that are the cell totals in Table 18.2; n in each cell is 4.	$17^2 + 26^2 + 36^2 + 23^2 + 22^2 + 17^2 = 3563$ $SS_{cells} = 3563/4 - 828.375$ **= 62.375**
5. Calculate $SS_{Jane \times occ}$ (the interaction SS) by subtraction: $SS_{Jane \times occ} = SS_{cells} - SS_{Jane} - SS_{occ}$	$SS_{Jane \times occ} = 62.375 - 10.75 - 12.042$ **= 39.583**
6. Calculate $SS_{error} = SS_{total} - SS_{cells}$	$SS_{error} = 118.625 - 62.375$ **= 56.25**
7. Calculate df which is (levels -1) for each factor. For the interaction term, multiply together the df for each factor involved Total df is $N - 1$ as before Error df is again the remainder	$Factor_{Jane} = 3 - 1 = 2$ $Factor_{occ} = 2 - 1 = 1$ $= 2 \times 1 = 2$ $= 24 - 1 = 23$ $(23 - 1 - 2 - 2) = 18$
8. Calculate the MS as in the one-way example by dividing each SS by its associated df.	
9. Calculate F as before by dividing the effect MS by the error MS. This time, however, we do this for Factor $_A$, Factor $_B$ and the interaction effect.	See results in Table 18.3

These results are now organised into a typical ANOVA summary layout shown in Table 18.3.

Table 18.3 Summary of results for two-way unrelated ANOVA

Source of variation	SS	df	MS*	F	Probability of F under H_0
Total	118.625	23			
Main effects:					
Jane	10.75	2	5.375	1.72	NS
occ	12.042	1	12.042	3.853	NS
Interaction					
Jane × occ	39.583	2	19.79	6.333	$p < 0.01$
Error	56.25	18	3.125		

* To make things a little less cluttered, unnecessary total MS and between groups MS are omitted here and in further tables.

Finding the significance of F

We need to consult *F* ratio tables as explained for the one-way example. Here, we consult for *all* our effects – that's the three *F* values shown in Table 18.3. In each case the effect *MS* (mean sum of squares) is the *numerator* and the error *MS* is the *denominator*. For our example:

Effect	Obtained value	df	Critical value	p
Jane	1.72	2, 18	$F_{0.05}(2, 18) = 3.55$	NS
Occ	3.853	1, 18	$F_{0.05}(1, 18) = 4.41$	NS
Jane × occ	6.333	2, 18	$F_{0.01}(2, 18) = 6.01$	<0.01

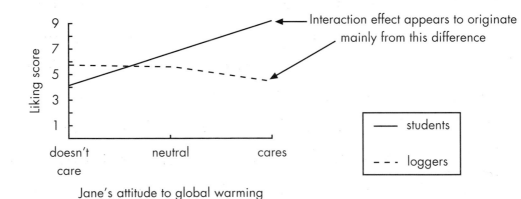

Figure 18.5 Means of liking scores of students and loggers given varying information about 'Jane's' attitude to global warming

INTERPRETING THE RESULT

It appears that neither independent variable had a significant effect, taken in isolation, across all of its levels, and ignoring the other independent variable (i.e. there was no 'main effect'). That is, varying the information about Jane's global warming attitude had no consistent effect on all the people tested taken as an undivided group. Nor did the students differ from the loggers overall, if we ignore individual Jane conditions.

There *is*, however, a significant *interaction* effect (see Figure 18.5). The two groups of participants *do* differ in attitude to Jane when we take into account the separate conditions of attitude to global warming factor. It appears that the strongest effect comes from the difference between the two groups when they are told that Jane is extremely concerned about global warming. The students like her the most here and the loggers the least, with a stronger divergence than that between them when Jane doesn't care. If predicted, the *simple effect* of 'knowing Jane is concerned' could be tested across the two participant types, students and loggers, as a simple comparison.

THREE-WAY ANOVA CALCULATION

I hope you would never be unfortunate enough to find yourself needing to calculate a three-way unrelated ANOVA *by hand* (not a likely event in the twenty-first century). I will list here the components that would need to be found, however, so that you can understand what a computer printout is telling you. It's important to lay out your data clearly *even if* you're using a computer, since otherwise you'll get in a mess wondering what all the components of the results table are. Imagine that our dogged students used a further condition (C) which is a new 'public' condition where participants either do or don't have to declare their ratings to an audience! In this three-way design you'd need to find the following components:

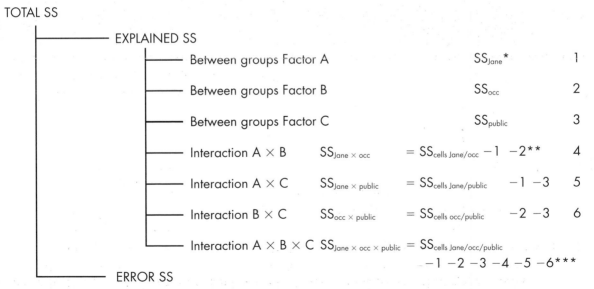

Figure 18.6 Division of sum of squares in a three-way unrelated ANOVA

*As before, use overall totals of condition A ('Jane') *ignoring* the other two factors.

**$SS_{cells\ Jane/occ}$ is found using the totals of conditions A (Jane) and B (occ) ignoring C (public) as a factor. In a three-way table, the cell A1B1 from the two-way table would be subdivided into two groups of C (public and private declaration). Here, these two C sub-groups are treated as one group and $SS_{cells\ Jane/occ}$ uses the totals of A1B1, A1B2, A1B3, A2B1, A2B2, A2B3. The notation '-1-2' means you find $SS_{Jane/\ occ}$ by finding $SS_{cells\ Jane/occ}$ and subtracting lines 1 (SS_{Jane}) and 2 (SS_{occ}).

***$SS_{cells\ Jane/occ/public}$ uses the total of *all* cells, A1B1C1, A1B1C2, A2B1C1 etc.

Glossary

An ANOVA design using only unrelated factors	_____ _____	unrelated design (model)
One of the independent variables in a design with more than one independent variable	_____	factor
A research design involving more than one independent variable	_____ _____	factorial design (multi-factor/variate design)
Significant effect where effect of one factor depends upon specific levels of another factor	_____ _____	interaction effect
The different values (conditions) of an independent variable or 'factor'	_____	levels
One factor alone has a significant effect across all its levels, irrespective of any other factors	_____ _____	main effect
An ANOVA design using at least one repeated measures factor and at least one unrelated factor	_____ _____	mixed design (model)
An ANOVA design using only repeated measures factors	_____ _____ _____	repeated measures design (model)
One level of one factor *alone* has a significant effect across levels of another factor	_____ _____	simple effect

Exercises

1. Do the exercise on page 412 if you haven't done it already!

2. Imagine that two groups of students, one vegetarian, the other meat-eating (Factor 1 – groups 1 and 2) are asked to memorise animal words, vegetable words and flower words (Factor 2 – conditions A, B and C). There's no research I know of to predict any particular result so suppose, in each example below, that the stated results occurred. Pick out the diagram from Figure 18.3 which you think best depicts the result obtained. Assume that 'differences', when mentioned, are significant.

a. Vegetarians and meat-eaters differ. No other effect.
b. Vegetarians and meat-eaters differ and there are differences across conditions as a whole. No interaction.
c. There are overall differences across conditions only.
d. There is a difference between groups on one condition only and no other effects.
e. There is *only* an interaction effect between eating style and memory condition. There is no overall difference between eating styles or between memory conditions.
f. There is an overall difference across conditions but this is more extreme for one of the groups.

3 Suppose the following data were obtained from a study of the sociability of boys and girls with no siblings who have or haven't attended pre-school of some kind before starting school. Calculate the two-way ANOVA and comment on the effects.

	Preschool children Sociability scores						No preschool children Sociability scores				
Boys	45	23	25	56	49		12	14	21	18	9
Girls	35	48	45	42	39		35	34	35	38	48

4 Suppose we measure people on a variable called 'sociability' – 'S' for short. We then investigate their performance on a wiggly-wire task where touching the wire with a ring-on-a-stick causes a buzzer to ring and records an error. Suppose it is true that high S people perform well in front of an audience but poorly alone and that low S people perform well the other way round. Overall, high and low S people tend to perform at about the same level. What effects would you expect from ANOVA? Sketch the expected effects or choose the appropriate diagram from Figure 18.3.

Answers

1 3) Factor: colour task (three levels); one-way repeated measures.
4) Factor 1: type of therapy (three levels); Factor 2: sex of client (two levels); 2 × 3 unrelated.
5) Factor 1: age (two levels, unrelated); Factor 2: memorising method (three levels, repeated measure); 2 × 3 mixed design.
6) Factor 1: stimulant (three levels, unrelated); Factor 2: noise level (four levels, unrelated); 3 × 4 unrelated.
7) Factor 1: personality type (two levels, unrelated); Factor 2: drug (three levels, unrelated); Factor 3: task type (two levels, repeated measure); 2 × 3 × 2 mixed design.
8) Factor 1: prejudice level (two levels); Factor 2: 'race' of target person (two levels); Factor 3: type of social act (three levels); 2 × 2 × 3 unrelated.

2 a. f
b. g
c. d or e
d. c

e. a
f. b

3 See table below.

Source of variation	Sum of squares	df	Mean sum of squares	F	Probability of F
Total	3582.950	19			
Main effects:					
School	1022.450	1	1022.450	13.601	$p < 0.01$
Sex	806.450	1	806.450	10.728	$p < 0.01$
Interaction	551.250	1	551.250	7.333	$p < 0.05$
School × sex:					
Error	1202.800	16	75.175		

4 No main effects; significant interaction effect. Diagram a) from Figure 18.3.

19
ANOVA designs – repeated measures ANOVA designs

This chapter deals with one-way or multi-factor ANOVA when at least one of the factors is *related*, *repeated measures* or *matched pairs*.

- The one-way repeated measures model *partials out* the variation which relates to variation among the individuals in the sample.
- It may be that individuals differ very much from one another. This variation is known as the *between subjects* variation. If, nevertheless, they all differ *in the same way* across conditions, i.e. *between conditions*, then most of the *total* variation will be accounted for by the *between conditions variation* and the *between subjects variation*, leaving very little residual *'error'* (which is actually the *interaction* of participants with conditions – the extent to which participants do not vary consistently across conditions). When this residual is small relative to the effect SS, a high value of *F* will occur.
- In *multi-factor repeated measures* designs, each main effect, and each interaction, has its own associated error term.
- In a *mixed design* unrelated factors are dealt with much as in the unrelated model dealt with earlier. Their *main effects*, plus *interaction for the unrelated factors* only, plus *error* together make up the *between subjects variation*. The *within subjects* variation is made up of the *main effects of the repeated measures factors* plus their *interaction*, plus their *interactions with the unrelated factors*, plus the residual *error for within subjects*.

At the end of this chapter some recommended further and more technical reading on ANOVA procedures is included.

Up till now we've worked in detail on designs which use only independent samples throughout, known as 'unrelated designs'. We now look at 'related designs' which very often are *repeated measures* but occasionally include *matched pairs*. We shall look at a repeated measures design in which a group of participants is tested at least twice in different conditions (levels) of an independent variable, using the same dependent variable each time. Our model study is a fictitious experiment based on an investigation of 'levels of processing' and as originally conducted by Craik and Tulving (1975). Participants are asked one of three possible questions about each of a set of presented words:

1. Is it in capitals?
2. Does it rhyme with ____?
3. Does it fit into the sentence ____?

These three conditions are known as 1 'physical', 2 'phonetic', 3 'semantic', based on the assumed type of processing the participants have to perform on the presented word for each type of question. There are 45 words altogether, 15 for each type of question. The conditions are presented in a randomised manner (see Chapter 3). The hypothesis is that participants will recall more items at 'deeper' levels of processing. We expect mean 1 < mean 2 < mean 3. Hence, the independent variable is the type of question and the dependent variable is items correctly recalled. The data in Table 19.1 might have been produced by such an experiment.

Table 19.1 Words recalled correctly in three conditions of a repeated measures design

Participant	Physical (1)	Phonetic (2)	Semantic (3)	T_{subs}
	Conditions			
1	5	8	9	**22**
2	3	5	10	**18**
3	4	8	12	**24**
4	6	6	11	**23**
5	5	4	10	**19**
T_{proc}	**23**	**31**	**52**	$\Sigma x = 106$

RATIONALE FOR ONE-WAY RELATED ANOVA

If you think back to Chapter 17 you'll recall that the one-way ANOVA is based on comparing the variation *within* samples with the variation *between* them (between their means). Above, we have three samples of scores (but each sample consists of the same people). As before, the more the scores vary *within* each condition, the less confident we are that the condition means differ significantly. But, in a repeated measures design, such as this one, the variation within each condition is *related to* the variation in all the others. Rather than the variation in each condition being thought of as three separate samples of the variation in the general population, we know that *part* of the variation in each column is predictable from knowing the variation in the other columns, because it's coming from the differences *between the same people*. These overall differences between people (in the '*T*subs' column in Table 19.1) are known as the BETWEEN SUBJECTS variation.

Please note here that I have kept to the use of the term 'subjects' because much other work you conduct with ANOVA will use this term and I wouldn't want to confuse people more than ANOVA tends to anyway. It is a generic term referring to animals or even plants (in biology) as much as to human results. *Some* computer software refers to 'cases', but not in a medical sense!

BETWEEN SUBJECTS VARIATION

Have a look at the fictitious and extremely idealised data in Table 19.3. In a crudely simplistic way, what repeated measures ANOVA does is to say we *know* participant 4 (let's call him Tim) is better than the rest. His score causes variation within each condition. But we can ignore this variation because it's completely regular – it is accounted for by the *between subjects variation*. We want to know if he varies *between conditions* in the same proportions as the others.

Imagine that Table 19.2, Table 19.3 and Table 19.4 represent three different sets of results which might occur with four participants. In Table 19.2 we have the persons-as-robots experimental dream result which scientific minds would adore! Each person performs at exactly the same level and only the 'treatment' (IV) has any effect on performance – the effect being perfectly regular. Here, the total variation (assessed, as always from sums of squares) is *completely* accounted for by the variation BETWEEN CONDITIONS. In Table 19.3, participant 4 performs two points better than the others, but is

Table 19.2 Three repeated conditions – no subject variation, no error

Participant	Condition			
	A	B	C	
1	2	4	6	**12**
2	2	4	6	**12**
3	2	4	6	**12**
4	2	4	6	**12**
	8	**16**	**24**	48

Total SS = 32
Between subs SS = 0
Between conds SS = 32
Error SS = 0

Table 19.3 Three repeated conditions – subject variation but no error

Participant	Condition			
	A	B	C	
1	2	4	6	**12**
2	2	4	6	**12**
3	2	4	6	**12**
4	4	6	8	**18**
	10	**18**	**26**	54

Total SS = 41
Between subs SS = 9
Between conds SS = 32
Error SS = 0

Table 19.4 Three repeated conditions – subject variation and error

Participant	Condition			
	A	B	C	
1	2	4	6	**12**
2	2	4	6	**12**
3	2	4	6	**12**
4	8	6	4	**18**
	14	**18**	**22**	54

Total SS = 41
Between subs SS = 9
Between conds SS = 8
Error SS = 24

affected by the treatment conditions just as they are. So here the variation *between conditions* and *between subjects together* completely explain all the variation among the scores. There is still no 'unexplained' error.

Finally, in Table 19.4, a trifle more like reality, participant 4 performs as in Table 19.3 except that the scores are in the reverse order. There is *interaction* between people and conditions here. This is exactly like the concept of interaction in the previous two-way unrelated example – see the exercise just below. Note that *between subjects SS* is unchanged from Table 19.3, but the *between conditions SS* is very much reduced. We can have little faith in the now narrow difference across conditions, especially considering the 'unexplained' variation (sometimes called RESIDUAL), left in the 'error' SS and unaccounted for by overall subject or condition differences. It is produced by the unsystematic ways in which people have varied across the conditions (in this case there's just one 'deviant' actually!).

One-way related ANOVA can be thought of mathematically as a two-way unrelated design, with the two factors being conditions and subjects. The 'cells' are then the individual scores by each person on each condition, so in Table 19.4 there are 12 'cells'. The 'error' term in the repeated measures table of results (see p. 428) is actually the interaction of subjects with conditions – the extent to which all 'subjects' don't go the same way as each other across the conditions.

As an exercise, and if you have the time and patience (or computer software), take each of the last three tables (19.2, 19.3 and 19.4) in turn and try calculating the two-way unrelated ANOVA which would result from treating the data as produced by *two* variables – one called 'conds' and the other called 'subs'. There will only be one result per 'cell' – that will be each individual score in the tables. Hence there are 12 'cells'. You should obtain the sums of squares shown below each table. In your results, the interaction between conds and subs should be the same as the error term in the tables. There will be no further error after calculating the interaction, as there would be in a normal two-way ANOVA, because for each 'cell' there is only 1 score here. Error usually comes from variation *within cells*, so there can't be any variation here amongst only one score. Hence F can't be calculated but you should get the same SS values.

The power of repeated measures design

The points made above demonstrate the true power of the repeated measures design. We are able to reduce the value of the bottom portion (denominator) of the F ratio – the 'unexplained variance' – by extracting the amount of variation *within conditions* which we can attribute to consistent differences between people. The smaller the denominator, the larger is F and the better estimate we have of the likelihood of the difference *between conditions* occurring if H_0 is true. That is, we can lower the probability of a type II error. In the one-way unrelated example, each score in each sample was in no way related to scores in the other samples. Hence, *all* the variation *within conditions* was 'error' or unexplained variation from any number of random variables. However, in the repeated measures design some of that variability, attributable to individual differences, is accounted for.

The division of variation – 'between subjects' and 'within subjects' variation

The *total variation* in related ANOVA is first split (see Figure 19.1) into the BETWEEN SUBJECTS *variation*, which is said to be 'partialled out', and WITHIN SUBJECTS *variation* which consists of:

1 BETWEEN CONDITIONS VARIATION: How the individuals differ as a result of the different conditions, irrespective of any differences between the individuals themselves – this is the *main effect* we're interested in.

2 ERROR REMAINING: The interaction of 'subjects' with conditions, that is, the extent to which different people respond unsystematically across the conditions. This is the residual or 'unexplained' variation and, the smaller it is, the greater confidence we can have in the effectiveness of the independent variable.

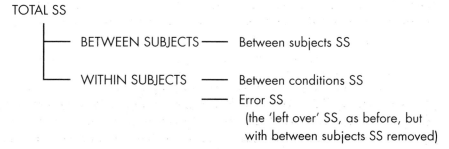

Figure 19.1 Division of sum of squares in a one-way related ANOVA

CALCULATION FOR ONE-WAY REPEATED MEASURES ANOVA – DATA IN TABLE 19.1

As with the two-way unrelated, I shall include the calculation steps and explanatory notes but not all the number crunching arithmetic steps:

Procedure	Calculation on our data
1. Calculate SS_{total} as before using formula (A): $\Sigma x^2 - (\Sigma x)^2/N$	$\Sigma x^2 = 862$ $(\Sigma x)^2/N = (106)^2/15 = 749.07$
Note: In related ANOVA, N is the number of values or scores, *not the number of participants*. Hence, here, $N = 15$.	SS_{total} = **112.93**
2. Calculate SS_{subs} using equation (B) $\dfrac{\Sigma T^2}{n} - (\Sigma x)^2/N$ Here T is T_{subs} and n is the number of conditions for each T_{sub}.	$\Sigma T^2/n = (22^2 + 18^2 + 24^2 + 23^2 + 19^2)/3$ $= 2274/3 = 758$ $SS_{subs} = 758 - 749.07$ = **8.93**
3. Calculate SS_{proc} (between conditions – levels of processing) using equation (B) as before T is T_{proc} and $n = 5$ (in each condition).	$SS_{proc} = (23^2 + 31^2 + 52^2)/5 - 749.07$ $= 4194/5 - 749.07 = 838.8 - 749.07$ = **89.73**
4. Calculate SS_{error} using: $SS_{error} = SS_{total} - SS_{subs} - SS_{proc}$	$SS_{error} = 112.93 - 8.93 - 89.73$ = **14.27**
5. Calculate MS as before (SS/df).	See Table 19.5.
6. Calculate F for the effect as before using: MS_{proc}/MS_{error}	$F = $ **25.21**
7. Calculate df: **Total** $= N - 1$ **Between subjects** $=$ subjects $- 1*$ **Between conditions** **Error** $=$ Total $-$ subjects $-$ conditions	$= $ **14** $= 5 - 1 \quad = $ **4** $= 3 - 1 \quad = $ **2** $= 14 - 4 - 2 = $ **8**
8. Check significance of F in Table 11, Appendix 2	Crit value for $F_{(2, 8)}$, with $p < 0.05 = $ **4.46** with $p < 0.01 = $ **8.65**

Treat 'subjects' as a factor with 5 levels;
Within subjects df (see Table 19.5) is then Total – Between subjects = 10

Table 19.5 Summary of results for one-way repeated measures ANOVA

Source of variation	Sum of squares	df	Mean sum of squares	F ratio	Probability of F
Between subjects	8.93	**4**	2.23		
Within subjects	104	**10**			
Between conditions (*proc*)	89.73	2	44.87	25.21	$p < 0.001$
Error	14.27	8	1.78		
Total	112.93	**14**			

Interpreting the result

Here, our research hypothesis, that the mean numbers of words recalled in each of the three conditions (*levels of processing*) would differ, is strongly supported by our repeated measures analysis. H_0 (that the population means are equal) is rejected.

TWO-WAY (RELATED) DESIGN

For this, and the mixed design which follows, the calculations get rather complicated and it is difficult to conceptualise how the variation components are being accounted for. Here, then, I haven't included the equations, since they are the same as those used before. I again hope you'll have access to computer calculations of ANOVA. Though you might wish to check the calculations, the important point is to understand what the different components are doing, as I emphasised earlier. If you can understand what you have to do in these two models, and the three-way unrelated, then you can manage and interpret all other possible combinations of ANOVA model (in terms of within or between subjects variables).

In this design, the *same* group of participants undergo *all* levels of *all* factors – if they have the energy and stamina! Although this is often not covered in introductory texts it is, in fact, quite a common design in projects, where people may be hard to come by and you can get your friends and/or family to do, say, two versions of the Stroop test under two conditions, say fast presentation and slow.

Imagine that the fictitious data in Table 19.6 are from a hypothetical study in which one group of air traffic controllers performs both a simple and a complex vigilance task (Factor A) under both quiet and noisy conditions (Factor B). Values shown are mistakes made. Counterbalancing would be employed, of course, to even out order effects.

Table 19.6 Mistakes made in simple and complex tasks under quiet and noisy conditions in a two-way repeated measures ANOVA design

Pt.	Simple task (A1) Quiet (B1) A1B1	Noisy (B2) A1B2	**A1 Total**	Complex task (A2) Quiet (B1) A2B1	Noisy (B2) A2B2	**A2 Total**	**B1 Total**	**B2 Total**	**Subs totals**
1	3	4	**7**	7	12	**19**	10	16	26
2	5	5	**10**	3	13	**16**	8	18	26
3	9	4	**13**	5	15	**20**	14	19	33
4	7	8	**15**	9	21	**30**	16	29	45
Totals:	24	21	**45**	24	61	**85**	**48**	**82**	130

Complications

What is new in the two-way related ANOVA calculation is the existence of an error term for *each* of the effects (two main and one interaction). We do with each effect what we did with the single effect, in the related one-way. We look at the interaction of subjects with the effect – how far their scores vary across the conditions in a way contrary to how the condition totals vary. We will simplify our subscripts here by referring to SS as, for instance, '$SS_{FactorB}$' rather than 'SS_{noise}'. SS_{AB} is the SS for the interaction of A with B.

For each effect we calculate the SS in the usual way, then calculate an error term which is the interaction of subjects with the factor. For instance, to calculate the error term for factor A (SS_{errorA}), we calculate the SS for interaction between Factor A and 'Subjects'. In other words, each 'subject' is a level of a factor called 'subjects'. Hence, for the appropriate 'cells' SS ($SS_{cellsAS}$), there are eight 'cells' to look at – those formed under the columns 'A1 total' and 'A2 total'. For each of these cells there are two scores, those taken under B1 and B2, so $n = 2$ for this calculation. We use

$$\frac{\Sigma T^2}{n} - (\Sigma x)^2/N$$

as ever.

The Ts are the eight cell totals, n is 2 as we said, and the 'correction factor' is the same as usual – square of the scores total over N. Remember, N is again the total number of values or scores, *not* the number of people involved. In fact, N is number of people × number of combinations of conditions and there are 4 combinations here (A1B1, A1B2, A2B1, A2B2), so $N = 16$.

CALCULATION OF TWO-WAY REPEATED MEASURES ANOVA ON DATA IN TABLE 19.6

Procedure		Calculation on our data
1. Calculate SS_{total} using formula (A) as before. Note: N is the total number of *values* = 16	SS_{total}	= **371.75**
2. Calculate SS_{subs} as before with $n = 4$ (conditions)	SS_{subs}	= **60.25**
3. Calculate $SS_{factorA}$. Use totals for A (45 and 85) in Table 19.6. $n = 4$	$SS_{factorA}$	= **100**
4. Calculate SS_{errorA} by finding $SS_{cellsAS}$ – see explanation above. Then $SS_{errorA} = SS_{cellsAS} - SS_{factorA} - SS_{subs}$	$SS_{cellsAS}$ SS_{errorA}	= **173.75** = **13.5**
5. Calculate $SS_{factorB}$. Use totals for B in Table 19.6. $n = 4$	$SS_{factorB}$	= **72.25**
6. Calculate SS_{errorB} as for SS_{errorA} but this time use cells for B × S. These will be the eight totals in columns B1 and B2. $SS_{errorB} = SS_{cellsBS} - SS_{factorB} - SS_{subs}$	$SS_{cellsBS}$ SS_{errorB}	= **142.75** = **10.25**

7. Calculate SS_{AB} – the interaction factor. For this, put the totals of A1B1, A1B2, A2B1 and A2B2 into the standard equation to find $SS_{cellsAB}$. n will be 4

$SS_{AB} = SS_{cellsAB} - SS_{factorA} - SS_{factorB}$

$SS_{cellsAB}$ $= \textbf{272.25}$
SS_{AB} $= \textbf{100}$

8. Calculate the error term for the interaction –
$SS_{errorAB} = SS_{total} - SS_{subs} - SS_{factorA} - SS_{factorB}$
     $- SS_{errorA} - SS_{errorB} - SS_{AB}$

$SS_{errorAB}$ $= \textbf{15.5}$

9. Degrees of freedom:

Total	$= N - 1 = 16$ values $- 1$	$= 15$
Between subjects	$= 4 - 1$	$= 3$
Between conditions (A)	$= 2 - 1$	$= 1$
$Error_A$	$= 1 \times 3^*$	$= 3$
Between conditions (B)	$= 2 - 1$	$= 1$
$Error_B$	$= 1 \times 3$	$= 3$
Interaction (AB)	$= 1 \times 1$	$= 1$
$Error_{AB}$ (Interaction $df \times$ Subjects df)	$= 3 \times 1$	$= 3$

$Error_A$ is the interaction of factor A with subjects; hence we multiply df for A $\times$ df subjects.

Table 19.7 Two-way related ANOVA test results

Source of variation	Sum of squares	df	Mean sum of squares (SS/df)	F ratio	Probability of F
Between subjects	60.25	3	20.08		
Within subjects					
Factor A (task)	100	1	100	22.22*	$p < 0.05$
$Error_{factorA}$	13.5	3	4.5		
Factor B (noise level)	72.25	1	72.25	21.13	$p < 0.05$
$Error_{factorB}$	10.25	3	3.42		
$Interaction_{AB}$ (task $\times$ noise)	100	1	100	19.34	$p < 0.05$
$Error_{AB}$	15.5	3	5.17		
Total	**371.75**	15			

Each effect is divided by its associated error MS.

INTERPRETING THE RESULT

We have significant main effects for both factors (task complexity and noise) and a significant interaction effect. In fact, it is the interaction which requires scrutiny since it appears to be the much worse performance by controllers on the complex task in noisy conditions, relative to all the other conditions, which has produced the significant results.

ANOVA MIXED DESIGN – ONE REPEATED MEASURE AND ONE UNRELATED FACTOR

In the example below, returning to the levels of processing experiment, assume that we now have two groups of participants doing the experiment described in the one-way repeated measures test. One group have the items presented visually, the others listen to them. We shall call the repeated measures factor LEVELS as before, and we shall call the new unrelated factor PRES (for 'presentation method'). Note that, in the calculations, an error term is found for both the between and within subjects effects. Note, also, that any effect which includes the repeated measure factor is also counted as 'within subjects'. In this example, therefore, the *interaction* between PRES and LEVELS gets counted as within subjects, since it includes the within subjects LEVELS factor.

Table 19.8 Words correctly recalled in three repeated conditions of levels of processing with visual or auditory presentation as an unrelated factor – mixed ANOVA design

	⟸ Repeated factor – 'levels' ⟹				
	Physical	**Phonetic**	**Semantic**		
Unrelated factor ('pres') ⇓					
Pres 1 (visual)					
Pt					T_{subs}
1	5	8	9		22
2	3	5	10		18
3	4	8	12		24
4	6	6	11		23
5	5	4	10		19
T_{cells}	**23**	**31**	**52**	T_{pres}	**106**
Pres 2 (auditory)					
Pt					
6	5	3	4		12
7	4	9	3		16
8	9	7	7		23
9	3	6	6		15
10	6	8	5		19
T_{cells}	**27**	**33**	**25**	T_{pres}	**85**
T_{levels}	**50**	**64**	**77**	$\sum x =$	**191**

Note: In the following calculations, the SS_{total} and SS_{pres} (SS for the main, unrelated effect) are the same figures we would get if we conducted a one-way ANOVA on the two group results for auditory vs. visual, ignoring the existence of the repeated measures conditions. See the top part of Figure 19.2.

CALCULATIONS FOR A MIXED ANOVA – ONE UNRELATED AND ONE REPEATED MEASURES FACTOR

Procedure	Calculation on our data
1. Calculate SS_{total} in the usual way using equation A.	$SS_{total} = 186.97$
2. Calculate SS_{subs} using equation B. T is T_{subs}; n is total for each $T_{sub} = 3$.	$SS_{subs} = 46.97$
3. Calculate SS_{pres}. T is T_{pres}; n = number of values per group = 15.	$SS_{pres} = 14.7$
4. Calculate the error term for the unrelated factor using: $SS_{error\ between} = SS_{subs} - SS_{pres}$	$SS_{error\ between} = 32.27$
5. Calculate the SS for the entire within subject division: $SS_{within} = SS_{total} - SS_{subs}$	$SS_{within} = 140$
6. Calculate SS_{levels} using equation B where T is T_{levels} and n = number of values in each condition = 10	$SS_{levels} = 36.47$
7. Calculate SS_{cells} using equation B; T is T_{cells}; n in each cell = 5	$SS_{cells} = 111.37$
8. Calculate $SS_{pres \times levels}$ from: $SS_{cells} - SS_{pres} - SS_{levels}$	$SS_{pres \times levels} = 60.2$
9. Calculate $SS_{error\ within}$ from: $SS_{within} - SS_{levels} - SS_{pres \times levels}$	$SS_{error\ within} = 43.33$

10. Calculate degrees of freedom:

df:

Total = total values − 1 = 30 − 1   **= 29**
Between subjects = subjects − 1 = 10 − 1   **= 9**
Between groups = groups − 1 = 2 − 1   = 1
Error/between = between subs − between groups = 9 − 1   = 8
Within subjects = total − between subjects = 29 − 9   **= 20**
Between conditions = conditions − 1 = 3 − 1   = 2
Interaction = groups × conditions = 1 × 2   = 2
Error/within = within subjects − between conditions − interaction = 20 − 2 − 2 = 16

Interpreting the result

Results are shown in Table 19.9. It looks as though levels of processing has an effect but that this effect is limited to the visual presentation group only. There is a main effect for levels but also a significant interaction and, by inspection, we can see the progression upwards of words recalled for the visual but not for the auditory presentation group.

Table 19.9 Mixed ANOVA results – one unrelated factor and one repeated measures factor

Source of variation	Sum of squares	df	Mean sum of squares (SS/df)	F ratio	Probability of F
Between subjects	46.97	**9**			
pres	14.7	1	14.7	3.648	Not sig
error/between	32.27	8	4.03		
Within subjects	140	**20**			
levels	36.47	2	18.24	6.731	$p < 0.01$
interaction pres × levels	60.2	2	30.1	11.107	$p < 0.001$
error/within	43.33	16	2.71		
Total	**186.97**	**29**			

These *are* fictitious data – if anyone actually *does* this study, please let me know the result! Note that there is no main effect for presentation type, the auditory group not doing worse overall than the visual group.

MORE COMPLEX ANOVA DESIGNS

We've reached a point where it makes sense to stop. You now have the principles for any more complicated design. As I've said once or twice, I doubt you'll be calculating at this level by hand. You should now be able to interpret the terms produced when submitting your data to software analysis. Should you need to carry out more complicated calcula-

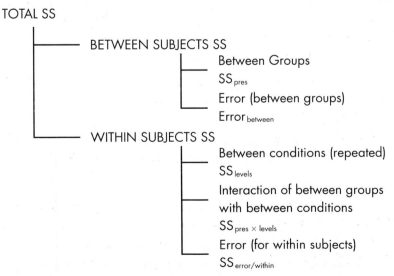

Figure 19.2 Division of sum of squares in a mixed design (1 unrelated factor, 1 repeated measures factor)

tions, the principles are just more of those presented. In a two-unrelated plus one-repeated measure design, for instance, you'll need to work out the SS for two unrelated factors, *and* their interaction, and subtract these from the between subjects SS, before proceeding to find the within conditions factor SS and the SS *for all* the interactions of it with the unrelated factors. The calculations are obviously lengthy, but if you are careful to lay out the data accurately and follow each step in the manner already explained you should get there in the end. If you require further theoretical understanding or need to check more detailed calculations then please consult one of the texts I've referred to below. The last mentioned, by Winer, is treated by many, in awe, as the 'bible' for ANOVA theory. Howell's is deep at times, but excellent, modern and uses actual research examples throughout.

Further reading on Anova techniques and theory

Ferguson, G.A., Takanae, Y. (1989) *Statistical Analysis in Psychology and Education.* New York: McGraw-Hill.

Hays, W.L. (1974) *Statistics for the Social Sciences.* New York: Holt Rinehart Winston.

Hays, W.L. (1988) *Statistics.* New York: Holt Rinehart Winston.

Howell, D.C. (1992) *Statistical Methods for Psychology.* Boston: PWS-Kent.

Winer, B.J. (1971) *Statistical Principles in Experimental Design.* New York: McGraw-Hill.

Glossary

Variation associated with the differences between participants' overall totals in a repeated measures design; this variation is partialled out of the overall error which would be used in an unrelated design	_____	between subjects variation
Variation, calculated in a repeated measures design, which comes from how scores between the conditions vary when the variation between participants' overall totals has been removed	_____	between conditions variation
Error term associated with the between groups (unrelated factors) portion of the sum of squares division in a mixed ANOVA design	_____	error between
Error term associated with the within subjects portion of variation in a mixed ANOVA design	_____	error within (also 'residual')
See 'error within'	_____	residual
Variation remaining in a mixed ANOVA design when the between subjects portion has been removed from the total; it contains between conditions factors, interactions involving these and the residual	_____	within subjects variation

Exercises

1. As in Chapter 17, use random number tables to generate three sets of eight scores. This time, assume that the three sets are from the same eight people and conduct a one-way repeated measures ANOVA. Again, complain to your tutor if the results are significant!

2. Produce an outline results table for a mixed design where there is one repeated measures factor with three levels and one unrelated factor with four levels, eight people in each. As in Chapter 17, put values into the 'degrees of freedom' column.

3. Below in Table 19.10 is an incomplete fictitious results table for a two by three ANOVA. For each statement below choose between true/false or choose the correct answer:

Table 19.10 Fictitious results for question 3

Source of variation	SS	df	MS	F	Probability of F
Between subjects		13			
Groups	14.88	1	14.88	4.55	0.054
Error between	39.24	12	3.27		
Within subjects					
Conditions	16.33	2	8.17	1.32	0.286
Groups × conditions	48.90	2	24.45	3.94	0.033
Error within	148.76	24	6.20		

a. There was a significant main effect for *groups*.
b. There was a significant main effect for *conditions*.
c. There was a significant interaction effect between *groups* and *conditions*.
d. The design was fully unrelated.
e. Total degrees of freedom were: 36 41 42 (choose an answer)
f. There were three groups.
g. There were three conditions.
h. The number of participants was: 7 21 14

Answers

2

	SS	df	MS	F	Prob. of F
Total		95			
Between subjects		31			
Between conditions (unrelated)		3			
Error between		28			
Within subjects		64			
Within conditions		2			
Between × within conditions		6			
Error within		56			

3　a. False　b. False　c. True　d. False　e. 41　f. False　g. True　h. 14

20

So what test should I use? – choosing the appropriate inferential test for your data

This short chapter takes you through the criteria for choosing an appropriate test of significance for the data you have obtained. It deals first with simple *two condition tests* and reminds you about certain parametric assumptions associated with certain tests. We then move on to *tests for more than two conditions*. Finally, some information is given on computer-based statistical analysis programmes, including a statistics teaching programme, and on where to obtain up to date information and help on similar software.

CHOOSING AN APPROPRIATE TEST

Trying to choose an appropriate test can leave you with a floundering feeling, since there are so many tests and there can be a lot of data and several hypotheses. The first golden rule is not to panic! Stay calm. Next . . .
- Take one hypothesis at a time
- Choose the test for this hypothesis
- Calculate the test
- Decide whether the result is significant

TESTS FOR TWO SAMPLES

The simpler tests covered in detail in this book, and assessed at A level, assume you have just two samples of values and that you want to test for a difference or a correlation between them. If this is your position then only consult the top section of Table 20.1 entitled 'Tests on two conditions'. Tests for more than two conditions, and for more than one independent variable, are dealt with after the general system for making decisions has been outlined.

The NEAB and International Baccalaureate Higher Level syllabuses include all the

Table 20.1 Choosing an appropriate statistical test of significance

| | Difference | | Correlation |
	Related	Unrelated	
LEVEL OF MEASUREMENT OF DEPENDENT VARIABLE **Categorical** Nominal	(Binomial) **Sign** test	**Chi-square**[1] χ^2	
Measured Ordinal (ranked data)	**Wilcoxon *T*** matched pairs signed ranks	**Mann-Whitney *U*** or **Wilcoxon** Rank Sum	**Spearman** (rho ρ)
Interval/ratio	***t* test**[2] (related)	***t* test**[2] (unrelated)	**Pearson**[2] ***r*** (product moment)
Ordinal – differences	**Friedman**	**Kruskal-Wallis**	
Ordinal – trends	**Page**	**Jonckheere**	
Interval/ratio – one or more similar 'factors' – at least one factor unrelated and one repeated measures	**ANOVA**[2] (repeated measures)	**ANOVA**[2] (unrelated)	
	ANOVA[2] (mixed design)		
Several correlations – one predicted variable			**Multiple regression**
Several ANOVA tests	**MANOVA**		
ANOVA with adjustment for the effect of a correlating variable (co-variate)	**ANCOVA**		

Left margin labels: TESTS ON TWO CONDITIONS / TESTS ON TWO OR MORE CONDITIONS

[1] *See the general hints on page 442 for an explanation of why χ^2 is placed here as a difference test.*
[2] *Certain parametric assumptions must be satisfied before these tests may be applied – see text.*

tests for two conditions apart from Wilcoxon's rank sum. The AEB would expect use of one of these tests in appropriate coursework. If you are unsure what your syllabus covers you should ask your tutor or seek information from the appropriate examining board.

Making a choice

So how do we choose the appropriate test? This really should be quite simple if you follow the three steps in Box 20.1 while you are consulting Table 20.1.

Box 20.1   Steps in choosing an appropriate two sample test

Decision:	In top section of Table 20.1:
1. Does the hypothesis predict **difference** or **correlation**?	Consult difference or correlation column.
2. At what **level of measurement** are the data?[1,2]	Choose appropriate row nominal, ordinal or interval.
3. If a difference is being tested, are the data in **related** pairs or **unrelated**?	Choose related or unrelated difference column.

1. Although you may have actual scores or ratings, looking like interval level data, you may wish to put these into *rank* form (see the first part of Chapter 10). If so you will then be dealing with *ordinal* data.
2. If you wish to conduct a *t* test or Pearson's correlation you will need to be able to satisfy certain parametric assumptions about your data – see Chapter 14 for *t* tests and Chapter 15 for Pearson. Briefly these are:
  ● data must be genuinely at interval level or above
  ● sample data should come from normally distributed population(s)
  ● homogeneity of variance – variances not too different (ignore for *related t* and if sample sizes for *unrelated t* test are equal, unless variance difference is extreme)
The result of the three decisions listed in Box 20.1 should specify a particular test.

EXAMPLES OF CHOOSING A TEST

Take a look at Table 20.2. The fictitious data were produced by asking male and female 17-year-olds to estimate their own IQ ('given that the national average is 100'), by measuring their actual IQ, measuring their height and measuring their mothers' IQs.
  ● Assume that mother and offspring can be treated as matched pairs
  ● Assume that *estimated* IQ *cannot* be treated as interval level data
  ● Assume that this researcher will treat *measured* IQ as interval level data
Using the decision chart (Table 20.1), try to select the appropriate test for each of the following hypotheses:
  1. Male IQ estimates are higher than female IQ estimates
  2. Female measured IQs are higher than male measured IQs
  3. The taller people are, the higher their IQ
  4. Female measured IQs are higher than their mothers' IQs

Table 20.2 Male and female participants' estimates of their own and their mothers' IQ

Males				Females			
Estimated IQ	Measured IQ	Height (cm)	Mother's IQ	Estimated IQ	Measured IQ	Height (cm)	Mother's IQ
120	107	160	100	100	97	155	105
110	112	181	105	95	92	165	97
95	130	175	102	90	104	177	115
140	95	164	97	110	112	162	96
100	104	163	120	85	130	173	100
120	92	158	131	100	95	159	120
110	97	172	115	105	107	164	102
105	101	171	96	100	101	165	131

Hypothesis 1

Decision 1: we are looking for a *difference*.

Decision 2: we shall have to convert the estimated IQs to ranked, *ordinal* data.

Decision 3: the design is *unrelated*; we have separate groups of males and females.

   Our choice is therefore *Mann–Whitney* (or *Wilcoxon rank sum*).

Hypothesis 2

Decision 1: we are again looking for a *difference*.

Decision 2: these data are being treated as *interval* level.

Decision 3: the design is *unrelated*, as before.

   Our choice is therefore a *t test for unrelated samples*.

   t test parametric assumptions must be met:

- The interval level data assumption has been made.
- IQ tests are standardised to ensure that scores for the general population are normally distributed on them. Hence, the samples come from a normally distributed population.
- Using an 'eyeball' test, variances are not too different. This is not a big problem anyway, since although we have an unrelated design, the numbers in each group are equal.

Hypothesis 3

Decision 1: a positive *correlation* is predicted between height and IQ. (We treat male and female as one group.)

Decision 2: IQ is being treated as *interval*. Height is ratio level and, therefore, at least interval level.

Decision 3: correlations are related designs.

   Our choice is therefore *Pearson's correlation coefficient*.

   Parametric assumptions must be met:

- arguments are the same as for hypothesis 2 except that the design is related
- height is known to be normally distributed.

Hypothesis 4

Decision 1: a *difference* is predicted.

Decision 2: measured IQ is being treated as *interval* level data.

Decision 3: matched pairs are a *related* design.

  Our choice is therefore a *t test for related samples*.

  Parametric assumptions must be met (as above).

Could we have chosen a rank test instead?

For each of the cases where a parametric type test is chosen you could of course have chosen a non-parametric (rank) test, if you just wanted to use a simpler but possibly less powerful test. Some theorists argue that very little power, if any, is lost using rank tests (see Meddis, 1984). It is rare that the choice makes a difference in practice, especially where samples are large.

Here are some **general hints** to keep in mind when choosing tests:

- Correlations are, by their nature, *related* designs.
- χ^2 tests the *difference* between one distribution (e.g. across one row of the frequency table) and at least one other. This is usually what we are interested in. This is why it is placed where it is on the chart. However, the net result is to tell us whether there is a significant association between one variable (say, being a smoker [or not] and having poor health [or not]). It is often called a 'test of association'. In *this* sense it can be viewed as a kind of nominal level correlation. If you look at Table 10.5 in Chapter 10 you'll see that two columns of data, ready for a *difference* test, have been reduced to categorical level by allocating each score in each group to 'above overall mean' or 'below overall mean'. The frequency table on the right, ready for a χ^2 test, can be viewed in terms of a categorical correlation (an 'association') between high/low competitiveness and high/low anxiety.
- If data appear as frequencies, in categories, a χ^2 test is indicated. Even though the frequencies are cardinal numbers, if all you know is that, say, 22 people are in one category, and you know no more about them and can't separate them in any way (by rank or score), the data are in frequency form and the categories concerned can be treated as a nominal (categorical) 'level' of measurement.
- If a test or other psychological measure has been *standardised*, it can usually be treated as producing interval level data. Do so unless otherwise advised.
- If the results in question are in the form of scores or numbers produced by humans estimating or 'rating' events or behaviour, on some arbitrary scale, it is almost always safest to convert the numbers to ordinal level (by ranking them). The same goes for scores on an unstandardised questionnaire or opinion survey.
- Ordinal data appear as a set of ranks ('ord' for order).

TESTS FOR MORE THAN TWO SAMPLES

To discover which test is appropriate you need to go through the three decisions already described for two sample tests. When you use Table 20.1, look in the section headed 'Tests on two or more conditions'. What is important, if you have more than two samples, is that you don't just split your samples into sets of two and carry out a *t* test, say, on all the various combinations. Each time you carry out a test the probability level for significance is 0.05 and if you do two tests you obviously increase your chance of getting a false 'significant' result – a type I error. This is known as 'capitalising on chance' and is discussed more fully in the introduction to Chapter 16 and in Chapter 17. Your decisions, in choosing a difference test for more than two samples, can be organised as shown in Table 20.3.

Table 20.3 Choosing a test for more than two samples

Are appropriate parametric assumptions met?		
YES:	Use ANOVA method unless non-parametric method preferred	
		ANOVA types:
	Single factor (one independent variable)	
	unrelated	– one-way unrelated
	repeat measures	– one-way repeated measure
	Multi-factor (more than one independent variable)	
	all factors unrelated	– unrelated
	all factors related	– repeated measures
	at least one factor unrelated and	– mixed; see Chapter 19; use
	at least one related	repeated measures design in SPSS
	More than one dependent variable	– use MANOVA version of above
NO:		**Non-parametric tests:**
	Unrelated differences	– Kruskal–Wallis
	trend	– Jonckheere
	Related differences	– Friedman
	trend	– Page
	Multiple correlations – one predicted variable	– use multiple regression procedure

SOME INFORMATION ON COMPUTER PROGRAMS

Computers have taken the donkey work out of statistical description and testing, of that there is no doubt. In preparing this book I have been able to calculate tests in a few seconds which would have taken me several minutes, or even hours, a few years ago, armed only with a calculator. However, as any experienced psychology tutor will argue, it is only by calculating at least the easier tests that you come to realise just what the test is doing, why it shows what it does, what its limitations are and so on. By grappling (or playing) with numbers you get to realise what's going on. I would definitely recommend therefore that you calculate some tests to begin with and check for significance in tables. By just taking what the computer says you can end up with only a passive and superficial understanding of statistical testing, and simple mistakes can easily be missed because final results don't strike you as obviously impossible.

That said, once you do understand what's going on, I see no point in masochism. Computers in this domain are doing just what they were intended for, not putting you out of work but leaving you free to concentrate on things which require new and creative thought. Computers used to be a luxury. Now they're ubiquitous and even the poorest college or school department can afford the cheapest program which will be adequate for A-level work. Below then, I've given a brief description of just one or two programmes I know of. However, since the last edition, the number of cheap practical statistics software packages has snowballed and it is impossible to keep track of these or to write about them all. I would recommend a call, letter or e-mail to:

CTI Psychology
Department of Psychology
University of York
York YO1 5DD
Tel: 01904 433156
Fax: 01904 433181
E-mail:ctipsych@york.ac.uk

This centre is *the* UK centre for psychology software, including quantitative and qualitative data analysis. They know just about all there is to know! Here is an Internet address for their directory of computer software for psychology in general but including statistics packages: http://www.york.ac.uk/inst/ctipsych/web/CTI/DirTxt/reviews/rcontents.html

STATPAK

Written by Concord Informatics Ltd. and distributed by the Association of Teachers of Psychology (ATP; your tutor should belong), this is cheap (£15 for members still), cheerful and written specifically for A-level psychology work. It runs on PCs. It uses all the A-level tests (Wilcoxon signed-ranks, Mann–Whitney, *t* tests, Pearson's and Spearman's correlation and Chi-square). A speciality, making it more useful for teaching than some of the others, is a print-out of the *calculation steps* in the test so you can see how the answer was obtained! It will mostly only work on two samples at a time and will hold only 20 columns of data at once so you can do several tests – but beware of 'capitalising on chance'.

For information on computer software for teaching, members of the ATP can contact Geoff Haworth whose number/address, or that of his successor, can be obtained from the British Psychological Society, 48 Princess Road East, Leicester, LE1 7DR – the ATP being an invaluable organisation in general for psychology teachers, *especially* those new to the subject.

STATUTOR

Written for PC by Peter Richardson and well reviewed in the CTI literature. You can read their review, and all the disc details, at the Internet site given above. The main review comment picked out by CTI was: 'A useful tool in teaching basic statistical methods'. The package does your statistics but also takes you through a teaching introduction to statistics and testing with interactive exercises throughout. At £25 it's therefore a bargain. It can be used by a complete novice, says the review, and it has quizzes and interesting demonstrations of statistical points. This is an extremely useful and effective disc for any student having a bit of a struggle with their course statistics, though you may need to check things out *with* your tutor having used the package. You can contact Peter Richardson through the CTI centre address above, or try to get hold of him at the Open University, Milton Keynes.

SPSS

This comes as a *Mac* or *Windows* product and there is a relatively affordable, yet still powerful, student version at around £40. Data are entered in spreadsheet format but every row is always a 'case' (participant). You need therefore to pay particular attention to the point on p. 65 about arranging unrelated data with codes. Fortunately *SPSS* will show you either the codes as numbers, *or* as the titles you have given that they represent (e.g. 'male', 'female' etc.). Even the student version will do everything in this book and far beyond, including factor analysis, reliability tests, item analysis, multiple regression, multi-factor ANOVA and so on. It is fairly friendly and 'talks' to other applications, such as word processors and spreadsheets. It produces wonderful editable charts but you must be careful to edit, since the bar chart for instance comes out in the misleading form described on p. 244, until you alter its scale.

MINITAB

This is an old favourite and also comes in spreadsheet format. Many complaints have been sorted out in the latest *Windows* version. It's pretty powerful, and does ANOVA, multiple regression, box-plots and so on. There is a student version at around £40.00 from Addison-Wesley publishers. The student version doesn't have quite the complexity, but is more than adequate for A-level and early degree work.

EXCEL etc.

If you have access to *Microsoft Office*, or just the *Excel* spreadsheet programme within that, you will be able to conduct chi-square, *t* tests, ANOVA tests and correlation. Other spreadsheets (such as Quatro-pro, will also do this). Unfortunately, in *Excel*, the rank tests are not included but you can create a macro or simply save the spreadsheet on which you calculated a Mann-Whitney and just enter your new data next time. You will have to use tables to check for *p* however.

Exercises

The following exercises are all based on tests for two samples only. Exercises involving choice of more complex tests are included at the end of the relevant Chapters (16–19) and also in the text of the Multi-factor ANOVA Chapter (18) – see p. 412.

 1. Height (in cm) of girls bred on:

All Bran	Bread and dripping
172	162
181	172
190	154
165	143
167	167

The researcher was interested in whether one of the diets tended to produce taller girls. What test should be carried out on the data? Choose the most powerful test available.

 2.

Table 20.4 Snooker players' position in league table

Smoking and drinking players		Abstemious players	
Stephen Parrott	2	John Hendry	8
Jimmy Ebdon	6	Peter White	1
Ronnie Williams	10	Mark O'Sullivan	5
Ken Lee	9	Stephen Docherty	3
Alan Drago	4	Tony McManus	7

In this case, we want to know whether abstemious players get higher placings. What test can be used to see whether there is a significant difference here?

 3.

	No. of businessmen standing on window ledges	No. of businessmen *not* standing on window ledges
Tokyo	46	598
New York	103	524

If this was what happened when the stock market fell sharply in September 1998, was the effect far worse in the USA? What test will tell us?

 4. Students observe whether males or females do or don't walk under a ladder. They want to see whether one sex is more 'superstitious' than the other. What test do they need to use?

5 20 people perform a sensori-motor task in two conditions, one in a quiet room, alone, the other in a brightly lit room with a dozen people watching. An electronic timer takes an accurate record of the number of errors made in each condition.

    a. What test would be appropriate for investigating the significance of the differences in performance between the two conditions?

    b. Assume everybody deteriorates in the second condition. What test would be appropriate for seeing whether individuals tend to deteriorate to the same degree?

6 A psychologist claims to have a very well standardised measurement scale. What statistical test would be used to check its test–retest reliability? What test would be used to check its validity on a criterion group who should score higher than a control group?

7 A set of photos of couples are rated for attractiveness by a panel of judges who rate the males separately from the females. The hypothesis tested is that people in couples tend to be of a similar level of attractiveness. What test would be used to compare the similarity of the two sets of ratings for male and female partners?

8 Question 5, Chapter 14, shows two distributions of scores (A and B). Suppose the researcher felt that these departed significantly from the pattern of a normal distribution. What test could be used to test for a difference between the two groups?

9 Two groups of people are selected. Scores have been used to place people in one of two groups – high 'initiative-taking' and low 'initiative-taking'. They are asked to select just one of three possible activities which they would prefer to do. The choices are: rock-climbing, dancing or reading a book. What test would demonstrate a significant difference between the choices of the two groups?

10 The time is recorded for the same group of participants to read out loud a list of rhyming words and a list of non-rhyming words. What test is appropriate for showing whether time differences are significant and that rhyming words take less time to read?

11 A group of management personnel undergo an intensive course on race issues. Essays written before and after the course are content analysed and rated for attitudes to race. What test would be appropriate for demonstrating a significant change of attitude as expressed in the essays?

12 A group of people attempting to give up smoking have been assessed for their progress on two occasions separated by six months. Raw scores have been discarded and we only know for each client whether they have improved, worsened or stayed about the same. What test would show any significant change over the period?

Answers

1. Unrelated *t* (most powerful); simpler alternative – Mann–Whitney or Wilcoxon Rank Sum.

2. Mann–Whitney or Wilcoxon Rank Sum.

3. Chi-square.

4. Chi-square.

5. a. Related *t*; ordinal alternative – Wilcoxon Signed Ranks.
   b. Pearson's correlation. Ordinal alternative – Spearman's rho.

6. Test-retest – Pearson; Validity test – unrelated *t*.

7. Spearman correlation. (Not Pearson because unstandardised human ratings.)

8. Mann-Whitney or Wilcoxon rank sum.

9. Chi-square (2×3 table).

10. Related *t*; ordinal alternative – Wilcoxon Signed Ranks.

11. Wilcoxon Signed Ranks (scores are unstandardised human ratings).

12. Sign test.

21 Analysing qualitative data

This chapter gives a brief introduction to the methods employed by qualitative researchers for collecting, analysing and reporting their data. The first argument is that one must consider the *purpose* of gathering the data (description, theory testing, theory generation or intervention) before deciding on an appropriate approach. One must also understand what it is that most qualitative writers find lacking or distorting in traditional quantitative approaches.

- *Content* analysis is a conventional approach and tends to reduce qualitative data to codes and frequency counts.
- Advice is given to the student wishing to embark on a qualitative data gathering project. Two relatively accessible approaches are concentrated upon:
  - *Thematic analysis* can test hypotheses whereas *grounded* theory is used to generate theory through the data collection and analysis. Data must be carefully sorted and re-sorted to produce a system of categories or themes. Emergent systems of 'explanation' can be supported by further data analysis and the whole process of analysis is iterative.

Advice is offered on the construction and form of *qualitative research reports*.

Issues of *reliability* and *validity* are discussed, from the position that these concepts cannot apply to research underpinned by a *constructivist* view of knowledge, through to discussion of various processes whereby the majority of qualitative researchers feel their findings are credible in terms of relative truth, rigour and good practice. Themes mentioned here are: *documentation*, *multiple records*, *training*, *'fit'* and *integration of theory*, *negative case analysis*, *respondent validation*, *triangulation*, *generalisability* and *transfer*, repetition of the *research cycle* and *reflexivity*.

ANALYSIS, WHAT ANALYSIS?

This chapter concentrates on the collection and analysis of qualitative data. However, since many of the modern qualitative approaches come embedded in their own chosen philosophy of truth, science and research motivation, it is not going to be possible to say that *this* is the accepted way to analyse data. There is far less agreement here than for quantitative methods (though even there, things are not as homogenous as they may sometimes appear). The philosophical issues involved in qualitative research and emerging paradigms were discussed in Chapter 9. However, there is an intimate link between the polemics of each approach and its preferred method of data collection and analysis. Here we can only hope to look at a few general common principles, some commonly used techniques associated with major approaches, and to give direction towards more substantial and varied resources.

DOING QUALITATIVE RESEARCH

This chapter is not intended to advise on the whole process of conducting a qualitative research project. That would take at least another whole book and several good ones exist already, of which a few are listed at the end of this chapter. However, since examination boards and enlightened university courses are rightly promoting the inclusion of qualitative projects in required coursework, I hope this section can prove useful in helping students decide roughly what kind of qualitative project they could conduct and I hope it can help answer the two agonising questions I hear so often these days: 'What do I do with the data and how do I report them? What does a good qualitative report *look* like?' This last question is a very vexed one, even for experienced qualitative researchers, a few of whom reject the very notion of fixed or conventional criteria. This stance, of course, leaves the student who wishes to do qualitative work in a vulnerable and worrying position, particularly if their tutors or supervisors are vague, unsure or dismissive about the standards to be met in qualitative reports. This can be a strong factor working against the promotion of qualitative projects and can send students hurrying back to the safety of the known and well documented quantitative project.

The situation is not helped by a dirth of texts with a very clear 'how to do it' structure and few at all with *examples* of good qualitative reports. It is interesting, and a statement on the position of qualitative approaches within psychology as 'rebel causes', that almost all qualitative research texts that I know of tend to start, and often return to, a philosophical rejection of various interpretations of positivism, scientific method in psychology or the conventional paradigm. Though they bear promising 'how-to-do-it' titles, they often spend much time on rather deep arguments which really can't be followed without the reader being already familiar with the language of social construction, relativism and post-structuralism. These serve to justify the promoted approach but one is often left screaming, 'Yes, but just tell me *how* you do it!'. Names will not be named here but the student taking care with cash would be well advised to look carefully, ask tutor advice, check in the library and so on before investment. Many academic articles themselves can be rather obscure and certainly too long for inclusion in this sort of text. A suck-it-and-see approach won't do when students have grades to think about so this chapter will try to provide some general practical guidelines. I have also included, not whole academic reports, but a commentary and some illustrative sections from two qualitative reports at the end of the next chapter.

COLLECTING QUALITATIVE DATA

This section will not describe specific data collection methods since these are embedded in the methods sections earlier in this text, particularly the work on interviewing methods, but also qualitative and/or participant observation, diary studies and so on. However, a question which certainly will be helpful to answer before setting out on a qualitative project will be: 'What is the major purpose of this project?' What will it attempt to achieve? How far will it go?' This is similar to thinking about the structure of measures and related data testing issues before starting to gather quantitative data.

Purposes for the data

As for quantitative studies, qualitative studies can be carried out for a number of research purposes. Some major non-exclusive categories include:

- descriptive/exploratory
- hypothesis testing
- theory/hypothesis generation
- intervention and change/action research

There may be overlap between these in any particular study. Things are immediately not as clear cut as for quantitative approaches in that many qualitative approaches involve theory generation *during* the gathering of data and a return for more, based on emergent insights and possibilities. Hence, reports do not always follow a 'this-is-what-we-did-and-here-are-the-results' format.

DESCRIPTIVE STUDIES

Some studies can attempt to be purely descriptive – an attempt to *start* investigating an area perhaps or an attempt to simply record and assess experiences of a particular group or progress in a specific intervention project. There are some problems with such an enterprise. First, qualitative approaches themselves emphasise the *relativist* nature of knowledge and the idea that 'facts' are social constructions. As I said in Chapter 1, we don't 'see' insecurity in a child as a universally available 'fact'. Much of qualitative research is about the recognition of different perspectives, different interpretations of 'reality' and so on. Hence, a descriptive study will have to take up a position on *whose* perspective it is reporting *from*.

A more pressing problem for students new to psychology will be trying to locate the difference between an acceptable report of psychological research and a piece of journalism or anecdotal account. In Chapter 23 there is a warning about 'day at the zoo' reports. A descriptive account, standing as a psychological report, simply *must* find daylight between itself and what would be acceptable for a magazine article. One danger is not to distinguish between a *social* problem and a *psychological* research problem. Hence, some (weak) psychology reports come in as 'an account of my friend's battle with anorexia' where the story may be fascinating but the reference to psychological issues, constructs, processes or relevant theory is minimal or stretched to fit. The student must ask 'In what way will this be psychology, not media reporting.' Silverman (1993) says:

> How could anybody think that what we ought to do [in social science] is to go out into the field to report people's exciting, gruesome or intimate experiences? . . . Naïve interviewers fail to recognise what they have in common with media interviewers (whose perennial question is 'How do you/does it feel?') and with tourists (who in their search for the 'authentic' or 'different', invariably end up with more of the same). (p. 199)

> Few contemporary social scientists have any stomach left for any remaining field researchers who might maintain that our only methodological imperative is to 'hang out' and to return with 'authentic' accounts of the field. (p. 156)

Although Silverman speaks from a sociological perspective the issue is the same for psychology – you need a *psychological research question* to answer. Simply reporting what you heard or saw, from your vantage point, or only trying to reflect others' perspectives, will not advance your knowledge of psychological processes, nor anyone else's.

Reason and Rowan (1981) make the point:

Once we start to do research which does not conform to the general requirements of experimental method, we run the risk of being accused of being mere journalists; indeed we run the risk of *being* mere journalists. (p. 247)

Even 'purely descriptive' work needs to be related at some point either to existing theory – one might relate children's sayings to cognitive stages – or to emergent theory. In several qualitative approaches the theory 'emerges' from the data analysis – one might arrange children's sayings and phrases into 'themes' around 'fairness' or 'animistic concepts'. Although the report summarised as an example (Kerwin *et al.*, 1993) on p. 525 is exploratory and largely descriptive, it generates many hypotheses and it challenges a background of theoretical assumptions that bi-racial children *must* have problematic experiences of self-esteem, cultural identity, marginality and conflict.

QUALITATIVE DATA AND HYPOTHESIS TESTING

The reader who has absorbed the main objections of qualitative researchers to the conventional paradigm might be surprised to see 'hypothesis-testing' in among the purposes of qualitative research. Because of the over-powering paradigm of natural science, it is often assumed that hypotheses can only be tested with quantified, empirical data. On the other hand, a major critique of the quantitative paradigm is that it stifles discovery and theory generation by concentration only on quantitative testing of hypotheses from *existing* theory (Henwood and Pidgeon, 1995).

However, we use qualitative data very often in supporting or contradicting our predictions and explanations. Much of our reasoning about people's motivations and decision-making is based on qualitative evidence. We may explain the unusual or depressive behaviour of a friend in terms of her unique situation in being a single parent and having just lost a supportive parent. In a courtroom there is little purely quantitative analysis (though there is often a lot of irrelevant numerical detail). Nevertheless the jury is there to weigh up evidence in a situation bearing uncanny resemblance to the testing of a null hypothesis. The jury *must* come down on one side, may be overly impressed by differences in 'their' direction, must apply well worn and professionally advised caution, and will be 'conservative' where there is doubt. Decisions are based, however, mainly on meanings and arguments, not on a statistical significance test.

We can predict that persistent young offenders will feel more alienated from middle-class society. We can demonstrate this with the sheer strength and animosity of the content of their accounts. We are not limited to simply counting the number of aggressive responses. No doubt it will be argued that 'strength and animosity' must come from comparison with other accounts, but what *informs* us here are the qualitative differences in content. The positivist may well feel tempted to create a standardised questionnaire from the offenders' data for use on offenders elsewhere, or on a control group. However, it is the unexpected *meaning* contained in offenders' accounts which will be of use, not the trivial but true fact that their accounts will somehow differ from non-offenders' accounts. It is what offenders say, which we may never have heard, that research uncovers and highlights for debate. Insights gained in interviewing a group of offenders can be incorporated into theory. Perspectives on the world, quite novel and unexpected, may emerge from the interviews and give another interviewer a new range of ideas to broach with different offenders, or with 'control' teenagers who don't share the ideas.

An example of hypothesis testing in qualitative research would be Hayes' (1991) research into two software companies. This approach can be termed 'theory-driven research' or THEMATIC ANALYSIS – see Chapter 9 glossary. Using background theory, including social identity theory and aspects of organisational culture research, she was able to analyse interview data in a manner which was *driven* by the theory and which enabled her to organise the causal attributions that employees made about their working environment and their employers to support hypotheses from the theory. This study (see Hayes, 1997, for an account) clearly demonstrates the way in which meaningful statements, not significance tests, can collectively support theoretical predictions.

QUALITATIVE DATA AND THEORY GENERATION

Contrary to the hypothesis testing role of qualitative data, many of the emerging methods within psychology (several have older roots in sociology) see the role of data analysis as a process in the *generation* and *construction* of theory. This principle is central to the GROUNDED THEORY approach (Glaser and Strauss, 1967; Strauss and Corbin, 1990; see Chapter 9 Glossary). It implies that the researcher should approach the data with a completely open, if not blank, mind. No pre-conceptual explanatory schema should be imposed on the data. Patton (1980), an evaluation researcher, states:

> The cardinal principle of qualitative analysis is that causal relationships and theoretical statements be clearly emergent from and grounded in the phenomena studied. The theory emerges from the data; it is not imposed on the data. (p. 278)

In Chapter 1 and above it was argued that to assume we could approach any new phenomenon completely without empirically based assumptions would be conceptually naïve. The idea is more that one should not permit initial theory to impose limits on what will be collected or on how the data will finally be organised and analysed. One reviews the data, trying to make sense of them, constantly aware of one's pre-conceptions about the topic and ready to be led away from these or even surprised by the revelation of a bias one did not know one had. Pidgeon and Henwood (1997) talk of the 'flip-flop' between known background theory and organisation of the new data. They suggest this approach might be a 'constructivist revision of grounded theory' (p. 255). Notice that Kerwin (in the qualitative report example, p. 525) had to start somewhere and she used all the questions she could generate from previous research, *not* as a limit to her investigation but as a framework to advance from. Liem (p. 530) does much the same thing in her research on shame and guilt, though she does not cite her influences.

A main aim, then, of theory generating qualitative work is to give participants the greatest opportunity to 'tell it like it is', to gather a broad and initially untreated set of information and then to gain thorough experience of the set of data, to get immersed in it, to organise it in a way which will produce higher order concepts (e.g. 'themes') which explain, make sense of or 'fit' as much of the whole collection as is possible. A major aim of this sort of research is to leave very few, if any, 'awkward' or 'rogue' raw data out of the final analysis.

As an analogy, it's a bit like knowing something vague about psychologists and 'conditioning' (seen perhaps as 'brainwashing'), immersing oneself in the various sources of information about conditioning (textbooks, TV programmes, what psychologists and/or your tutor say) and gradually developing a fuller but never complete picture of how the various forms are conceptualised and operated in practice. Even then, your view of conditioning will be a 'version', not *the* truth. Psychologists can argue viciously about the *real* nature, principles and worth of the same basic material.

INTERVENTION AND CHANGE/ACTION RESEARCH

The student new to psychology will be doing very little of this overtly. Of course, when we investigate anything at all we must create just the slightest bit of change around us; such is everyday life. But psychologists who carry out explicit change programmes, or 'action research' (see Chapter 9) need to be professionally trained and experienced. Besides, the methods used in such research will, to some extent, be the same as many covered here already (interview, questionnaire and so on). The action researcher might also employ collaborative practices (see Chapter 9) or run training sessions, but this has little, for now, to do with our aim here of dealing with qualitative data, so we will leave this particular research purpose alone for now.

QUANTITATIVE AND QUALITATIVE TREATMENT OF QUALITATIVE DATA

Most of this chapter will concentrate on the qualitative treatment of qualitative data. There are however some well-established traditions, in existence well before the contemporary expansion of qualitative philosophy, which gathered qualitative data and then subjected it to analysis to extract some form of quantitative summary. We have met several of these already in the form of rating schedules for the assessment of stories or dream content, coding schemes for analysing reactions to TAT tests – see Chapter 7. Those approaches, however, tend to pre-define what categories and themes will count for quantification, usually based on a mixture of prior research experience and background theory (e.g. psycho-analytic assumptions about dream symbol meanings). This rating of qualitative data is in the positivist tradition of simply seeking to measure 'slippery' phenomena in order to bring them into the 'legitimate' arena of scientific analysis.

CONTENT ANALYSIS

CONTENT ANALYSIS is a step away from this kind of pre-determination of data coding, but its roots remain in a quantitative, positivist approach to social science and measurement. Originally, the formalised method was devised for sampling and analysing messages from the media and other recorded material, such as literature, politicians' speeches, or wartime propaganda. Attempts to analyse media messages can be dated back to the turn of the century, when various writers were concerned about standards and about the influence of the press on society, crime and morals. In the 1930s and 1940s, however, content analysis 'took off', first because 'weighty' social psychological theory turned towards it for supporting evidence, second because propaganda became a serious threat before and during the war, and third because the electronic media (radio, TV, film) could no longer be considered an extension of the press. In this use it was seen as a quantifying instrument for descriptive information, as this definition demonstrates:

> . . . content analysis broadly describes a heterogeneous domain of techniques which are focused upon the (more or less) systematic, objective and quantitative description of a communication or series of communications. (Crano and Brewer, 1973)

This, then, is another way of observing, not people directly, but the communications they have produced. The communications concerned were originally those already published, but some researchers conduct content analysis on materials which they ask people to produce, such as essays, answers to interview questions, diaries and *verbal protocols* (described in Chapter 5).

Content analysis has been used on plays, folklore, legend, nursery rhymes and even popular music in order to demonstrate differences between cultures and subcultures, and within cultures over time. The preoccupations of various magazines, newspapers and journals have been linked, through content analysis, with the various political leanings of such publications. Changes in content have been used as indicators of change in public attitude (although they could indicate changes in the politics of the newspaper owner).

Box 21.1 Research examples using content analysis

Examples of analysis of existing materials

Shneidman (1963)

Analysed the speeches of Kennedy and Nixon in their televised presidential debates, demonstrating differences in their logical argument.

Ogilvie et al. (1966)

Analysed real and simulated suicide notes with some success in discriminating between the two. In this case the simulated notes did not exist naturally but were written by persons matched for the real note-writers' characteristics.

Manstead and McCulloch (1981)

Content analysed 170 British television advertisements for gender role portrayal and found several differences in accordance with traditional stereotypes. For a detailed discussion of this study, and the limitations of content analysis as a method, see Gross (1999).

Cumberbatch et al. (1990)

Analysed over 500 prime-time advertisements over a two-week period in 1990 involving over 200 character appearances. 75% of men but only 25% of women were judged to be over 30 years old. Men outnumbered women 2:1 and 89% of voice-overs, especially for expert/official information, were male. 50% of female voice-overs were categorised as 'sexy/sensuous'. The ratio of women to men rated as 'attractive' was 3:2. Men were as likely to be engaged in housework for friends as for their family, whilst females predominantly worked for their family and never friends.

A relatively rare example of qualitative content analysis

Bruner and Kelso (1980)

Reviewed studies of 'restroom' graffiti spanning 30 years. Most studies analysed the material either at a superficial level – the overt content of statements – or at an interpretive, often psychoanalytic level. Bruner and Kelso analysed the messages 'semiotically', concluding that women's graffiti were more interpersonal and interactive, tending to contain questions and advice about love, relationships and commitment. Men's graffiti tended to be egocentric and competitive, concentrating on conquests and prowess. Their messages served the function of confirming a position of control and the maintenance of power, whereas women's messages reflected the co-operation and mutual help strategies of the dominated.

Analysis of specially produced materials
Some studies use content analysis on open-ended interview data or on essays or stories written by participants.

Miller (1997)

Asked college social psychology students to keep journals in which they applied course concepts to their daily social experiences. Content analysis of the entries showed evidence of the acquisition of various forms of self-knowledge which provides tutors with a useful framework for assessing aspects of student psychosocial development.

Other examples from 1997
A review of literature produced the following uses of content analysis of the following materials in research articles published during 1997: female college students' talk into tape recorders whilst walking a route after dark, analysed for fear factors; television portrayal of the mentally ill associated with violence (10 times 'normal' association) and negative impact on society; letters to a newspaper editor during a town's anti-smoking campaign; interviews with athletes and coaches to assess competitive stress and coaches' expectancies; interviews with women leaders in Holland and Poland on their social identity as women in relation to their leadership positions; interviews with adolescents about caregiving in the family; several studies on textbook and research articles covering the following – environmental psychology, how B.F. Skinner's analysis of cognitive processes is portrayed, whether homosexuality is portrayed in abnormal psychology texts as illness, sin or minority group behaviour, personality theory concepts, reification of the use of the term 'variable' over three decades, representation of groups (females and certain ethnic groups still underrepresented in textbooks), childrens' responses to certain maths problems

THE PROCESS OF CONTENT ANALYSIS

Sampling

The researcher has the problem of deciding just what material to sample from all that exists. For newspapers, this will mean making a decision based on political leaning, price, target readership and so on. For visual media, a representative sampling of programmes, times, advertising slots and so on, must occur. Advertising is often linked to the content of adjacent programmes.

Coding units

These are the units into which the analysed material is to be categorised – see the examples in Box 21.2

Procedure

In the traditional model, the researcher will present coders with a pre-constructed system for categorising occurrences. This means that the researcher will have to become very familiar with the sort of materials likely to be encountered prior to the start of the content analysis exercise.

As with observation, coders may be asked to *categorise* only. They may be asked to rank items, for instance a set of participants' descriptions of themselves, ranked for 'confidence'. Alternatively, each item might be *rated*: aspects of children's drawings could be scored for 'originality'. In the interests of removing researcher bias, having developed the coding system on pilot material, the coding of the research data might be entirely completed by assistants who are unaware of the research hypothesis or aim. It has also been common to test for inter-coder reliability using correlational techniques, as for inter-observer reliability.

Box 21.2 Possible coding units for content analysis

Unit	Examples
word	Analyse for sex-related words in different magazines
theme	Analyse for occasions, in children's literature, on which boy/girl initiates and gets praised
item	Look for whole stories e.g. article on Northern Ireland
character	Analyse types of character occurring in TV cartoons
time and space	Count space or time devoted to particular issue in media

It became common in the 1980s to investigate children's literature and both children and adult television programmes for evidence of stereotyping, negative images or sheer omission of women or members of minority ethnic groups. Try the following exercise:

Imagine that you are going to conduct a practical exercise in which the aim is to investigate cultural stereotyping in children's books, old and new. We are interested in the extent to which, and ways in which, black people are portrayed. What units (words, themes, characters) might you ask your coders to look out for? Possible answers are shown at the bottom of the page.[1]

QUALITATIVE ANALYSIS OF QUALITATIVE CONTENT

The qualitative researcher almost always sees qualitative data as meaningful in its own right. In fact, the use of the term 'qualitative method' usually indicates a commitment to publish the results of research in qualitative terms, remembering, of course, that such a

[1] Here are some possible coding units:
black person in picture
black person in leading role
black person in subsidiary role
European features but face made darker
disappearance from story pictures of black person who appeared earlier
success/failure/trouble – black and white characters compared
inappropriate words: 'coloured', 'immigrant'
portrayed as foreign/savage/'primitive' etc.
portrayed as comic, troublesome or problematic
Note: content analysis can also highlight the *omission* of items, themes and characters.

researcher is not averse to looking at things quantitatively, should the opportunity arise and be found illuminating (see Silverman, 1993, p. 162–170). A blanket rejection of numbers needs to be treated suspiciously and probably masks a pathological fear and misunderstanding of what numbers can and can't do. Numbers are required if one is to refute claims of 'falling standards' or to demonstrate the reality of discrimination in jobs. At the very least, the qualitative researcher must *categorise* data.

The whole data set may have been produced from any of the following sources:

- participants' notes and diaries
- participant observer's field notes
- informal or semi-structured interviews
- open-ended questions (interview or questionnaire)
- in-depth case-study (mixture of interviews, observations, records)
- observation of advertisements, wall paintings, graffiti etc.

and might consist of speech, interactions, behaviour patterns, written or visual recorded material, filing systems, seating arrangements, slogans and so on. They might also include the researcher's own ideas, impressions and feelings, recorded as the research project was progressing.

The set of data will need order imposing upon it. It has to be organised so that comparisons, contrasts and insights can be made and demonstrated. The qualitative researcher, however, will not be categorising in order to *count* occurrences. One major aim of categorisation, in *grounded theory* analysis at least, is to reflect the *diversity* of participant perspectives, not their frequency (Pidgeon and Henwood, 1997, p. 261). This marks the approach out from content analysis (above) or protocol analysis (see Chapter 5). From interviews with drug addicts, for instance, on their experiences in trying to break the habit, various fears and perceptions of the 'straight' world may emerge which are unique and qualitatively different from others. Each has a special value in painting a picture of personal experience, invisible to non-addicts, but of great utility to a rehabilitation therapist. Examples of the categorisation process can be seen in the Kerwin synopsis (p. 525), in which interview content needed to be sorted according to 'themes' that respondents produced on the issue of bi-racial identity.

Qualitative work as a student project

Pidgeon and Henwood (1997) warn that qualitative research is, in general, 'highly labour intensive' and 'not for the faint hearted'. Students may well be drawn towards 'doing a qualitative project' because they feel unhappy with figures and are 'not mathematical'. This would be one of the worst reasons I can think of for doing a qualitative project. Because the methods are so tied up with the philosophy rejecting positivism, I believe that you can't really understand what qualitative research is trying to do without a good understanding of what it rejects in the quantitative approach. It would be silly, for instance, to start with a basically quantitative supposition (e.g. I believe smokers are more anxious than non-smokers) and then discount quantification for the sake of it or from number phobia. An understanding of quantitative weaknesses will strengthen a qualitative project, but the main reason I express caution is that doing a *good* qualitative project will be *hard*. It will use as much concentration and clear reasoning as does the average quantitative project, but it is also very likely to take a lot longer. The student will have to go through quite a few examples of the approach and may need to sift large amounts of verbal data before getting some idea of how the work typically proceeds (there is no one right or accepted way, and that's a lot of the difficulty here). Having said that, if the student is prepared to put in the time and effort then I'm sure many tutors would be delighted to see more qualitative work coming their way. Just don't do it as an easy option!

METHODS OF ANALYSIS

It is not possible to give precise guidelines on the analysis and presentation of qualitative data. There is no universally accepted paradigm. The decisions will be influenced by the theoretical background or model from which the researcher is working and there are many of these. Several quite specialised methods of analysis have been developed for different sorts of data: conversations (see Box 21.3), non-verbal communication, pedestrian behaviour and so on. What follows is a set of points applying to collections of data produced from the types of source mentioned above and drawing from quite commonly used approaches such as grounded theory and thematic analysis. After that, the reader will be directed to several specialised texts which have more to say on various qualitative or 'new paradigm' approaches, several of these based on conversations or 'discourse', as well as the content of interviews, responses to visual stimuli, discussions during participant observation, observational field notes, and so on.

Some approaches are more accessible than others. If you are considering discourse analysis for your project you will not be encouraged by the following from Potter and Wetherell (1993):

> Much of the work of discourse analysis is a craft skill, something like riding a bike or chicken sexing, which is not easy to render or describe in a codified manner. Indeed as the analyst becomes more practised it becomes harder and harder to identify explicit procedures that could be called analysis.

You will see below that researchers in this area often fully reject the 'positivist' notions of 'reliability' and 'validity'. However, this statement does raise great concern over how *any* reader, outside this 'guild' of craftsmen and women, would ever be able to distinguish good analysis from poor. The analogies are perhaps not well chosen – chicken sexing is surely not *that* difficult to explain to the naïve observer. A small number of quite clear and objective instructions are exceedingly helpful in learning to ride a bike first time. If the reference is to the practised art of 'clever' riding, then surely the 'apprentice' discourse analyst can be given, as forward guidance, the criteria that judges use. This is certainly possible for fancy biking.

To be fair, Potter (1996, p. 139) does answer the validity query raised later about the *representativeness* of statements by pointing out that in discourse analysis, contrasted with ethnography, readers can check out their own interpretations since the DA norm is to present all the original discourse along with the analysts' interpretations.

Box 21.3   Transcribing speech

Edwards and Potter argue that how one chooses to report or display recorded speech (TRANSCRIPTION) will depend upon, not just technical decisions, but a theoretical position. If only words are recorded, making the speech appear as text in a book, then this displays a lack of interest in what people do with speech or in the difference between talk and text. In turn, this might reflect the position of a researcher who sees the speech as a fairly direct reflection of internal mental processes. Analyses of discourse may vary somewhat but many researchers now stick fairly close to a system devised by Jefferson (1985). What follows is partly quoted (* to *) from Edwards and Potter's 1992 text and partly condensed.

/ / signifies overlapping or simultaneous speech:
(*)

Dean: That was the – impression that very / / clearly came out.
Gurney: In other words, your – your whole thesis

Alternatively, the start and end of overlapping speech may be marked with extended square brackets thus:

N: <u>Oh</u>:: do:ggone I [thought maybe we could]
E: [I'd <u>like</u> to get   ]   some little slippers but uh,

Numbers in round brackets indicate pauses, timed to tenths of seconds, while the symbol (.) represents a pause which is hereable but too short to measure:

now Prime Minister (.2) how you res↑po::nd (.) to this claim of <u>blame</u>(.) may be of <u>crucial</u> significance

A break in the voicing of sound is marked by a single slash:

as I reca::ll (1.0) with Mister Ghobanifa/r   (*)

:	single elongation of the previous sound
underline	added emphasis
↑/↓	upward/downward in turn intonation
-	abrupt stop
•hmm	• represents audible intake of breath berfore 'hmm'
</>	speeded up/slowed down pace of speech

Categorising

The qualitative researcher will inevitably begin with a large quantity of written notes and material (audio and video recordings will usually have been transcribed). In thematic analysis the major category of statements of interest will have already been defined. For instance, Hayes (1991, described above) was specifically interested in *causal attributions* made by employees about their organisation. These were the data of interest and were separated out for analysis. In grounded theory approaches such a specific decision 'filter' would not be applied so early in the process. However, both approaches require aspects of the following procedures, in the Hayes example *after* the data of interest have been filtered out.

As notes or responses are read and re-read it should be possible to start grouping items together. As a simple example, if you had asked student colleagues to discuss, during informal interviews, reactions to their college course, statements they make might fall into the following groupings:

social contacts	timetable
link to career	available resources
quality of teaching	facilities (canteen, etc.)
fears (exams, work load etc.)	adjustments (e.g. homesickness)

. . . and so on.

Some statements will fall into more than one category. Traditionally, the researcher would make several copies of all data so that items can be cut and pasted into various categories and clusters and cross-referenced. The modern, labour-saving way is to use the computer and a flexible database system. Several systems now exist for the analysis of qualitative data. Some of these are listed in Box 21.4.

The iterative nature of qualitative analysis

Theory generating approaches stress that, during this stage, maximum flexibility needs to be maintained in naming and conceptualising the categories and themes emerging from the analysis. The process is *iterative* in the sense that early analysis will lead to themes and categories but will also perhaps highlight the need for further data. In most approaches this is recognised and further data collection, from original or new participants, will be guided by these early realisations. The process is also iterative in the sense that, as further information is analysed, categories may be changed, merged or further subdivided, and the whole system of category and sub-category may become reorganised.

What is essential during this whole process is that success with some form of organisation does not blind the researcher to other possibilities, and does not narrow down or force further data collection and analysis into the already formed schema. This is where Pidgeon and Henwood's constant 'flip-flop' notion should be most active – between data and theory, between research experience and older theoretical frameworks. There is a constant need for discipline in this reflective process, a need to keep away from a comfortable 'foreclosure', that is aided to a great degree by working as a team, constantly feeding ideas to a colleague who perhaps takes a cooler look at 'blinding light' discoveries.

Indigenous categories

Prior to, or in addition to, development of the researcher's own categories and groupings, the analyst usually looks at those used by the participants themselves. An example would be a group of students who call themselves 'the brains' whilst others get called 'the Neanderthals' by staff. Later on, the analyst might compare these titles and propose explanations of their derivation.

Researcher's categories

Some categories or 'themes' may emerge quite clearly on analysis or during data collection. In studying the organisation of a school, for instance, it might emerge that teachers are split into those who do and do not get involved in after-school activities. More likely, though, will be *dimensions* along which people vary, for instance, teachers in their attitude towards student discipline. These could range from the severe, through moderate to lax. This might sound like a quantitative dimension. However, the qualitative researcher is more interested in the *perspective* of each person, in their unique social construction. So the positions along the dimension from severe to lax are only roughly ordinal but are determined by specific reasons given. Quantification of the positions is often not useful or relevant. People are in a *category* along the dimension. 'Severe' would be those who say 'you have to show them who's boss' and the like. 'Moderate' teachers might say 'It's no good being the strict parent with them. They get enough of that at home and they don't respect it.'

Typologies

Where categories and dimensions are descriptions of people, some researchers may cross these in order to produce a matrix of 'types'. A teacher who is 'lax' on the discipline dimension, but also 'caring' rather than 'distant', may turn out to have an identifiable approach to students, different from all other staff, in that she particularly tries to raise self-esteem and enable students to take control of their own lives. Researchers sometimes give names to these types. In this case the type might be 'therapist'. It is important to remember, however, that the type is mere analogy. Any types created are products of the researcher's current scheme of looking at the data and not lasting realities.

All sciences use analogy and metaphor. In order to tell us what atoms are like, physicists describe electrons and neutrons as little balls. Electrical theory borrows the analogy of current 'flowing' like a river. Analogy is necessary in order to communicate under these circumstances. It tells us what something unique and novel is *like*, not what it *is*. Creating the matrix of types, however, is useful in several ways. The reasons why a person fits none of the types created might well be worth investigating and lead to fresh insights. Conversely, a type might be produced which no one fits.

Organising the categories and themes – 'memo writing'

Grounded theorists (and others) often use the term 'memo-writing' at this point – see Charmaz (1995) for a full account. As soon as categories and/or themes start to emerge, the idea is to start writing 'memos' which justify the use of a category or the allocation of certain data sections to that category, but which also, and far more importantly, start to link one category to another or which justify the fitting of a category within the emerging system or hierarchy of categories. This is, in fact, theory development – a conceptual system which binds together the data and which would, if finally completed and in an ideal case, 'explain' or account for *all* the observations gathered during the research.

Validity checking

A certain degree of validity for categories and typologies can be achieved during the middle and later stages of data analysis. In hypothesis testing approaches, a version of Analytic Induction (AI) can be employed (see Fielding, 1988) in which a hypothesis about the data is formed and then certain cases are selected to see whether they fit the 'explanation'. Those that do are no problem but those that do not cause the researcher to redefine categories and to reformulate hypotheses. According to Fielding and Fielding (1986), this is a parallel with statistical significance testing but with the difference that here no 'random error variance' is left over; statistical tests are not required; hypotheses are revised until *all* exceptions are eliminated and *all* the data fit the final 'explanation' or category system. In some ways it can be seen that this is going on whether or not the researcher admits to using hypothesis testing. In grounded theory and other approaches, as the process of re-organising and categorising proceeds, in very many small ways, the process just described is occurring. Examples of AI attempts are given below under the heading 'Negative Case Analysis'.

Quotations

The final report of qualitative findings will usually include verbatim quotations from participants which will bring the reader into the reality of the situation studied. At times, the researcher will, of course, be summarising the perspectives and understandings of participants in the study. But it is important that these summaries, which must, to some extent, be interpretive, or at least selective, are clearly identified as such. The quotes themselves are selections from the raw data which 'tell it like it is'. The quotations used are often chosen to *exemplify* a perspective or construction. Very often comments just stick with us because they typify perfectly a view or stance in life. Here are a few:

- 'Everybody else out there seems to be having a great time except me'
- 'It's no use me speaking out – nobody wants to listen and they'd tell me it was wrong anyway'
- 'Management here uses the classical mushroom principle – keep 'em in the dark but pull 'em out periodically to cover 'em in crap'

Mason (1996) makes the extremely important point that use of such 'slices' of the data should be carefully considered as to whether they are 'constitutive' or 'illustrative'. That is, did the sample data play a role in *forming* the idea, category or theme that is being discussed, or was that formed earlier and is this data slice just serving to *illustrate* the point? This difference should be made clear to the reader.

Many researchers see it as important that quotations, especially those intended for publication, are checked out first with the original speaker wherever this is feasible. If this is conscientiously done we at least have a check on their authenticity. The question arises though of how *representative* these statements are. How do we know that the cases selected for discussion in a qualitative research report are representative? This point, raised by many critics, is one which goes to the heart of qualitative 'weaknesses'. It concerns *validity* which we shall return to below. As we shall see, some writers (e.g. Bryman, 1988) argue for authors to make available their entire data collection so the reader can check on the full context in which statements were made and on their typicality among all statements made.

Box 21.4   Computer software for qualitative data analysis

There is a growing number of sophisticated qualitative data analysis packages now on the market. Some, such as Ethnograph and Nud*ist have been around for 10 years or more but the sophistication of modern desktop technology permits much faster and far more intricate searching, retrieval and organising. These are the main tasks of the packages. Smith (1996) outlines four major functions in fact:

1. **Frequency counting** A simple count of the number of times a word or phrase occurs in text. This prepares data for quantitative treatment and is not likely to be of wide interest to the qualitative researcher, though useful for content analysis.

2. **Concordance** Finds and prints every occurrence of a word or phrase *in the string of words in which it occurred*. This gives the varying contexts of occurrence and could be useful in discourse and conversation analysis work, as well as in general.

3. **Category selection** Searches and sorts coded data, rather than untreated text. Where the researcher has already coded various occurrences the programme will list and sort chunks of text occurring with the coded item and may even sort on multiple categories

4. **Theory building** These go one step further and will look for patterns and relationships across the contents of the various categories that have been coded.

Full information on a number of packages, including most of those listed below and more, is available from the CTI Centre at York University, whose address is provided on p. 444.

Code and retrieve
Ethno (PC)*
The Ethnograph (PC)
FolioVIEWS (PC, Mac)
Fuzzystat (PC)
GATOR (PC)
HyperFocus (Mac)
HyperQual (Mac)
Kwalitan (PC)
Martin (PC)
WINMAX (PC)
QUALPRO (PC)
Sonar (Mac)
SQL Text retrieval (PC, Mac)
Textbase Alpha (PC)

Content analysis
Textpac (PC, Mac)
WordCruncher (PC)
ZyIndex (PC)

Theory building
AQUAD (PC)
ATLAS/ti (PC)
HyperRESEARCH (PC, Mac)
Hypersoft (Mac)
NUD*IST (PC, Mac)
Qualog (PC)

*'PC' or 'Mac' refers to systems that ran the software at the time of going to press.

Adapted from: Grbich, C. (1999) *Qualitative Research in Health*. St Leonards, NSW, Aus: Sage, p. 241

Qualitative research reports

One of the most common appeals I have heard over the last few years, as examination boards and undergraduate courses have introduced qualitative research to their practical requirements or recommendations, is that for the very rare, simple text which says 'here is a qualitative report and here is how you can write one.' I don't know whether my attempt to include examples is going to be successful but I have tried to help with this plea by including two synopses of actual reports at the end of Chapter 23. I hope students wishing to submit qualitative work will find these useful, and also the pointers outlined below. It is not easy to state *the* final criteria for a *quantitative* report, still less for a qualitative one. There are a wide variety of qualitative approaches and some sharp differences of opinion among followers of these different 'schools' as to what will constitute a credible and fair report. I have attended workshops where some groups of qualitative researchers *refuse*, on theoretical principle, to accept the possibility of rough criteria for good research (reports) or to collaborate in devising a set of criteria useful as guidelines to less experienced researchers. However, such academics are few in number and the majority are prepared to agree on quite a number of guidelines for good research and reporting, the main aspects of which will be covered below.

A qualitative research report will very often follow much the same *overall* structure as the 'conventional' model presented in Chapter 23. However, depending on the philosophy and principles of the particular qualitative approach taken, a variety of important diversions from this overall pattern may appear. Typically the report will contain samples of the raw data in the form of illuminative and exemplary quotations or significant sections of the original diary or research log. In some cases it is thought necessary to include feelings and reactions of the observer at the time significant events occurred. These are all valid components for inclusion but it is important that analysis, inference, feeling and researcher insights are clearly separated and labelled as such.

The final qualitative research report, then, should give an account of early hypotheses, categories or themes that were formed and the extent to which these guided or changed the direction of further inquiry. Since most qualitative research encourages the iterative process of early analysis followed by further data collection, the final report can include an account of insights and question development. To the extent that the researchers attempt *reflexivity* (Chapter 9), the report will also contain an account of the researcher's questioning of their own decisions along the way and may contain discussion of the researcher's self-assessment of bias, emotion, doubts and misgivings.

What does the 'results' section look like?

Those already familiar with conventional reports will easily recognise the overall structure of the report and will readily be able to write an 'introduction' and 'method' section; also, possibly, the discussion and abstract, once the rest is completed. However, the unfamiliar territory will be the results section. There is usually no place for a statistical summary table (though for the eclectic researchers there is no objection to simple counting of frequencies) and certainly no 'treatment of results' where a significance test is conducted. In fact, qualitative reports can range from being similar in structure, at this point, to quantitative ones (see the Kerwin synopsis in Chapter 23) to a complete merging of the results and discussion sections, and perhaps parts of the method too (as in the Liem article summarised in Chapter 23). This is because the researcher has to develop an account of the *process* which led to theoretical or thematic organisation and insights. This may include cycling around the re-interviewing process described earlier. It certainly will mean a blurring of data reporting and theoretical conclusions and proposals.

This is going to be a hard area for students conducting their first attempts at qualitative research. The astute first year student can probably knock off the results section of a simple memory experiment in around half an hour and even in a quantitative degree dissertation there are conventions which already dictate much of the structure of this section. In a qualitative report the problem is to keep this section academic, analytic and well away from possible accusations of journalism.

Silverman (1993) warns that in reviewing qualitative reports in social science journals he was disturbed by the amount of 'anecdotal' quality in much of what he read. He found two recurrent problems, identified earlier by Fielding and Fielding (1986):

1. selecting data to fit an 'ideal conception'
2. selecting data which are 'conspicuous because they are exotic' (Silverman, p. 153)

Bryman (1988) too is concerned that 'snippets' are used to support contentions and that

the representativeness or generality of these fragments is rarely addressed. (p. 77)

Pidgeon and Henwood recommend for the new student in psychology that attempts at qualitative analysis might be usefully limited to the 'taxonomy development' stage (see 'categorising' above). Students will have usually gathered only a relatively small sample of data but can at least develop initial categories, perhaps also recording how these changed as later data were analysed. They might also attempt to explain how well all the data 'fit' the categories developed, identify where there are obvious deficiencies and try to develop tentative links between some of the categories.

A further course of analysis can be to investigate *individual cases* (i.e. the full sample of data from one person) and look for inconsistencies. This is part of the approach used in discourse analysis (other techniques are listed below). Variation in what people say about the same thing is not seen as 'error' here but as an indication that the issue is complex and each individual can hold several perspectives. In discourse analysis, variation can be an interesting pointer to what an individual might be trying to *do* with speech in varying their emphasis or their construction of an idea or report.

Smith (1995a, pp. 23–5) gives some useful advice on writing up the results of an interview based project and, as mentioned elsewhere, Smith's entire chapter here, is extremely useful as a guide to the conduct of research based on semi-structured interviewing.

Justification of method

Several qualitative research reports spend quite some time justifying the choice of a qualitative approach and the particular version used in the research. There are positive and negative reasons for such 'extra' justification, the negative first. It is sometimes a sign of the insecurity felt by a researcher new to, but interested in, qualitative methods, using an unfamiliar approach which is perhaps also not familiar to their supervisor, coursework marker or prospective journal reviewer. It is also in the nature of political pressure group minorities, working for change, to see themselves as little understood, discriminated against and to find themselves constantly referring back to the status quo in order to attempt to define themselves. This is something of an analogy with a tinge of actual real life in the contemporary psychology research world. Reading qualitative texts, one is often given this impression of the great fight to be fought against the tyranny of the quantitative establishment.

The first qualitative report synopsis (Kerwin) in Chapter 23 falls into the category of being perhaps over-cautious in this respect, at several points giving justification of the reasons for *not* taking a quantitative approach. The second synopsis makes no such 'apology' and assumes that the audience sees qualitative work as legitimate and credible alongside the other mainly quantitative articles in that particular journal.

The positive side of such justification is to argue that this is a 'jolly good thing' and why don't quantitative report writers feel they should do this too? The latter will occasionally justify their choice of a particular statistical analysis, but there is never a rationale offered for taking a quantitative approach – one which many qualitative writers would see as in danger of trivialising, of 'mechanising', of assuming that 'facts' have independent existence, or at least of seriously narrowing the possibilities for meaningful data analysis.

The time taken to justify methodological decisions, characteristic of most reports, is a necessity and a strength. A necessity because there is not *one* qualitative paradigm but several, often competing for primacy but certainly in need of careful definition in any particular project. It is a strength because it adds to the credibility of the work and this in turn has direct implications for the assessment of what 'positivists' would term *reliability* and *validity*.

EVALUATING QUALITATIVE RESEARCH – VERSIONS OF 'RELIABILITY' AND 'VALIDITY'

Because the variety of philosophical views represented across the spectrum of 'qualitative research' is not unified (except in its rejection of the positivist, quantitative model), we again encounter a discussion whose major perspectives depend upon *which* qualitative approach we are talking about. However, it is possible to present a brief look at the views which lead a minority of writers to reject conventional notions of reliability and validity entirely. We can then summarise various methods and techniques espoused by those who generally see a need to satisfy the mainstream of journal report readers that their work is credible, consistent and not mere fiction.

The rejection of reliability and validity

We discussed the conventional measures of reliability and validity in Chapters 4 and 7. Qualitative researchers generally use an argument that takes up the following position against these forms of evaluation of research quality. It argues that the conventional (quantitative, positivistic) paradigm assumes that 'error' is all there is between a descriptor (say an extroversion score) and the 'thing' described (actual extroversion as an entity in the world), or at least it acts as if this were the ideal. It also assumes that if only observers could hit on the most appropriate coding and scaling methods they would completely agree in their ratings apart from superfluous error (no different philosophically from the errors produced when several people attempt to measure average wind velocity over 12 hours, say). Pidgeon and Henwood (1997) argue as follows:

> . . . the constructivist view challenges the dualistic distinction between knower and known, leading to the realisation that personal and social forms of subjectivity are always present in research . . . On this view it follows that there are no methodological criteria for guaranteeing the *absolute* accuracy of research (quantitative or qualitative). (p. 268–9)

The use of the stressed 'absolute' in this statement seems to permit some *kind* of checking against sheer invention and completely individual perspectives. Silverman, discussing sociological research, points out that some researchers (e.g. Marshall and Rossman, 1989) reject notions of reliability altogether, on the constructivist viewpoint, and others reject validity, for example Agar (1986), who wants to dismiss conventional validity issues in favour of 'an intensive personal involvement' among other factors. Silverman argues that this works against credibility and just abandons any validity check on researchers' statements and claims:

> It simply will not do to accept any account simply on the basis of the researcher's claims to 'an intensive personal involvement'. Immediacy and authenticity may be a good basis for certain kinds of journalism but ethnography [the particular approach under discussion] must make different claims if we are to take it seriously. (p. 153)

QUALITATIVE CHECKS ON RIGOUR, GOOD PRACTICE AND RESEARCH EVALUATION

The terms in the title just given appear more often than do 'reliability' and 'validity' when qualitative research thinkers discuss these issues. Because of the varied nature of qualitative work there is not such a clear distinction between issues of reliability and validity as there was in our earlier quantitatively oriented discussion. However, we can start below with the sorts of methods recommended from several writers, which deal with the simpler issue of keeping consistent notes and making judgements that others would also make (forms of reliability checking), through to issues of veracity and 'fit', e.g. of derived categories to the original or newly gathered data.

Field notes and documentation

Several writers recommend keeping several forms of observational or diary notes where this is a main data gathering tool. Bryman (1988) argues for the researcher making available all their field notes or extended transcripts in order for the reader to make up their own minds about the experiences of the people studied. He also argues for data on *how* field notes were recorded. Spradley (1989) suggests that observers take short field notes at the time of an observation session, write up extended notes immediately after the session, keep a log of problems and ideas at each stage of the research and a fourth continuous record of analysis and interpretation (Silverman, 1993, p. 147). Lincoln and Guba (1985) recommend the keeping of a 'reflexive journal' (see 'reflexivity, below and Chapter 9) which includes these last two suggestions of Spradley's but also incorporates a log of one's own values and interests, where recognised, and their influence on the progress of the research. They argue for the provision of a 'paper trail' such that an independent 'audit' can be performed on the entire research process. Yin (1989) suggested that, even without an *actual* independent audit, a good validity checking discipline for the researcher is to file all data in a way that would permit, in principle, colleagues and others to follow the line of thinking and chain of evidence that has taken the original researchers through to their final conclusions.

Training and inter-rater reliability

Several writers accept that, though the project is basically carried out under qualitative principles, there is still the possibility of checking quantitatively for consistency among data analysers in the use of category or coding systems. Where, for instance, the project is large and several assistants are used to code data into emergent categories, it is still feasible to make a reliability check on these codings. In addition, assistants or research team members can undergo training in use of an interview schedule and in application of coding systems.

Fitting and integrating theory

Pidgeon and Henwood (1997) refer to these two features of the overall *grounded theory* analysis procedure. Both researcher and peers should be able to justify the 'fit' of their emergent theoretical system (e.g. the set of categories and their links) to the original data. In addition, the final theory should be 'rich, complex and dense, and integrated at diverse levels of generality' (p. 269). For instance, using the technique of 'negative case analysis' – see below – there should be few if any data left over and not incorporated into the derived explanatory system.

Analysis of negative cases

This approach was first formalised by Kidder (1981b). It is basically the consideration of why certain cases just don't fit the major patterns outlined as a result of analysis. The method was described above (AI) as a validity check *during* data collection and analysis. Others can accept the proffered explanation or not, and can call for re-analysis, analyse raw data themselves or attempt some form of replication.

The process followed by the researcher is to formulate a 'hypothesis' or general explanatory proposal as a result of data inspection. Individual new examples are then matched with the proposal. These can be data slices or separated case studies. The hypothesis or proposal is then modified in the light of each new sample or case, attempting at all stages to keep the explanation consistent with all the cases so far. Robson (1993, pp. 380–1) gives a clear example, adapted from Kidder, of the development of a hypothesis concerning the likely occurrence of embezzlement, based on interviews with convicted embezzlers. Smith (1995, pp. 193–198) gives a description of the development of local theory concerning expectant mothers' accounts of the later stages of pregnancy described at the time, then retrospectively several months after the birth. Interesting features emerge including the glossing of negative real-time accounts into positive memory reconstructions, and the counteracting of decline and divergence images with images of self-development and improvement.

Potter (1996) argues that in the discourse analysis model, a negative instance, or 'deviant case', can *confirm* the validity of the general pattern by demonstrating the unexpected problems which are produced when the deviant ('rule-breaking') piece of discourse 'throws' the participants in a discussion.

Respondent validation

In qualitative and 'new paradigm' approaches great stress is laid on the authenticity of the experience of the people under study, on the unique and genuine quality of their constructions of their own realities. Hence, figuring strongly in arguments concerning validity tend to be recommendations to check out findings and conclusions from research with those who served as data generators in the first place. Going back to check with participants is often called RESPONDENT VALIDATION, though it also appears as 'member validation' (Smith, 1996). Many writers express some hesitation about accepting this as an overriding criterion for validity. Most argue that the researcher cannot always be bound by participants seeing the whole picture as the researcher now can. People are not always aware of the reasons for their actions – that is partly the point of doing psychological research in the first place. They may well be foxed by the depth and specialism in the wording of a psychological report intended for fellow researchers in the specific topic area. In addition, there is the argument that participants will usually be somewhat respectful of the academic researcher and will not find it easy to articulate objections they may have to the analysis.

Triangulation

Borrowed from surveying and navigation, and used in evaluative research, this means comparing two different views of the same thing: interview with observational data, open with closed questions or one researcher's analysis with another's. In most qualitative research it is also used to urge that various *perspectives* be compared – different particip-ants in different roles (e.g. students, teachers), the perspectives of the researchers among one another and their views compared with the participants' views. Here the term 'trian-gulation' can be unfortunately misleading in that it connotes complete accuracy – one uses two or more points in navigation to get a perfect 'fix' on direction. However, the whole philosophical underpinning of qualitative research is that different people construct *dif-ferent* but *equally valid* perspectives of a situation. We would hardly expect accounts from differing perspectives to merge at all. It is the contrast which is of interest. For these reasons, not surprisingly, several writers (e.g. Silverman, 1993; Smith, 1996; Pidgeon and Henwood, 1997) express reservation about the concept. Smith argues that 'respondent val-idation' is also akin to triangulation and both are simply attempts to obtain a multiplicity of views. One possible conclusion from this line of reasoning on 'triangulation' is that if the fundamental purpose of a piece of research is to obtain different views, then triangula-tion (the obtaining of different views) cannot then be presented as a validation procedure. It is to some extent just *the* procedure, not a *check* on it.

Generalisation and transferability

Pidgeon and Henwood (1997) discuss the issue of 'transferability' in guarded terms because, to some extent, the point of grounded theorising, at least, is to keep theory 'local' to the context. However, there would be merit in showing that the research has come up with an explanatory system that is at least similar to others from previous research and/or in demonstrating how *some* of the findings might usefully transfer elsewhere. This would be particularly useful in applied settings where researchers can enter into dialogue and pick up 'best practice' from each other, *adapting* findings to their particular location and client group.

On generalisability of findings, Bryman (1988) makes a point which echoes that of Leary (1995) made in Chapter 4. The purpose of research is not always to generalise from findings directly to specific populations, new groups or new contexts. We generalise find-ings to *theory* and then apply the adapted theory to new circumstances. Hence, he points out (p. 91) that we need not be interested in whether a hospital studied is 'typical' but whether the thought processes of terminal patients are similar to the thoughts of other people in similar circumstances to which a theory of such thinking might apply.

Repetition of the research cycle

Reason and Heron (1995) argue that qualitative researchers go around the 'research cycle' several times. The researcher checks and rechecks the early assumptions and inferences made. As patterns and theories are developed, so the researcher goes back in again to gather more information which should confirm tentative hypotheses and/or help to further refine, deepen and clarify categories. This is also a main feature of grounded theory where the process is referred to as 'iterative', see above. In some ways, one could argue, as for triangulation, that if this process is part of the *procedure* of data gathering and analysis it can't *also* serve as an independent validity check. However, the counter-argument might be that qualitative approaches do not see a clear distinction between the truth 'out there' and independent researchers checking on it. Hence, validity is enhanced, they would say, by constantly checking that one view is not dominating or that the researcher is not getting 'carried away' on a tunnel vision perspective. Constant re-visitation of the research cycle maintains the possibility of gathering in new insights and further perspectives.

Reflexivity

Many writers refer to this concept, usually with reference to themselves but sometimes with reference to the stimulation of reflexivity in the participant or interviewee (see Smith, 1996, p. 195–9). The concept has been referred to elsewhere (see Chapter 9) and Lincoln and Guba's 'reflexive journal' was mentioned above. Here, we should just note that taking a continuous cool, hard look at what one is producing, as research proceeds, is seen as a kind of validity check in that it may serve to head off, for instance, early closure on a 'brilliant idea', or it may lead to the realisation that one is *not* getting to grips with an obvious block or problem in data collection and analysis. This activity is not unknown to quantitative researchers but the traditional paradigm has tended to keep the 'self' of the researcher out of the frame, whereas many qualitative researchers would want to keep a track of how personal biases and feelings are pushing progress one way or another. If a record is kept, later peer readers can appreciate the paths that led to perhaps surprising and unexpected conclusions.

Persuasiveness

Several writers (e.g. Pidgeon and Henwood, 1997) resort to the notion of overall persuasiveness as a criterion of validity equivalence in qualitative research findings. This rings alarm bells for me because as we all know from history, many speeches and writings are wonderfully and very effectively persuasive, but utterly perverse, misguided and sometimes evil. Persuasion is involved in seduction and seduction involves hearing what you want to hear. Rather than being seductive, I would hope that the persuasion comes from a good chemical mixture of several of the points made above (clear attention to counter-evidence, for instance) and that the persuasion is just an overall *effect*, not a *criterion* for validity.

FURTHER READING AND ASSISTANCE (SEE ALSO END OF CHAPTER 9)

Bromley (1986) Declared the partial aim of setting out rules of procedure for gathering and analysing case-study data.

Bryman and Burgess (eds) (1994) A useful practical volume.

Burgess (1984) Discusses the taking and organising of field notes in great detail.

Denzin and Lincoln (1994) I have not studied this text. It is again sociologically oriented, but it is considered a classic so is probably worth consulting for detail.

Edwards and Potter (1992) Very readable and contains the extract of analysed speech included in this chapter.

Flick (1998) A friendly new general guide, fairly practical in approach. Interesting to have a German perspective and one emanating from health and nursing. Nevertheless, very useful for the prospective qualitative researcher, written at an accessible level.

Grbich (1999) Although this text is geared to health research, much of the methodological content is easily applicable to psychological research, of which there are plenty of examples within the text. It has a comprehensive analysis of computer packages for the sorting and analysis of qualitative data. It gives detail on most of those shown in Box 21.4.

Hayes (1997) This is an extremely useful new text, with several 'how to' and hands on chapters. It has contributions from mainstream qualitative writers and examples of the more central contemporary approaches (including thematic analysis, grounded theory, case studies and discourse analysis) which students would be able to tackle in fairly early projects.

Mason (1996) A useful, committed qualitative how-to book.

Miles and Huberman (1994) States early on that 'Qualitative data are sexy'. A classic mid-90s sourcebook, completely 'hands-on'.

Patton (1980) Discusses in depth the content analysis of qualitative data.

Potter and Wetherell (1987) Includes a step-by-step guide to discourse analysis.

Richardson (ed) (1996) A recent set of edited chapters covering the qualitative-quantitative debate, and the critique of mainstream, 'old paradigm' research methods, written by mainly UK based authors.

Robson (1993) Covers well what its title suggests (*Real World Research*). Describes methods for field research and includes coverage of the more mainstream qualitative methods used in contemporary social and applied psychological research, along with conventional research designs.

Silverman (1993) Although addressing sociological research, much useful advice and how-to methodology can be applied to psychological research. In particular the arguments are useful and Silverman is not afraid to deal with numbers when appropriate, nor to call for rigour and public agreement on research findings. A particularly good discussion of reliability and validity.

Smith, Harré and Van Langenhove (eds) (1995a, b) Two central recent UK texts. Very comprehensive and very influential.

Glossary

Search of non quantitative materials (especially text) to find 'units' (usually words, phrases or themes. Analysis often concentrates on quantitative treatment of frequencies thus derived	_____ _____	content analysis
Analysis of reasons why single case does not fit patterns or categories so far identified; iterative process as hypotheses are adapted to fit deviant cases; similar to *Analytic Induction*	_____ _____ _____	negative case analysis
Attempt to validate findings and check on summaries and interpretations by presenting these to original participants	_____ _____	respondent validation
Comparison of at least two views/explanations of the same thing(s) – events, behaviour, actions etc	_____	triangulation

22

Ethical issues in psychological research

The chapter deals with two major sets of responsibilities carried by professional psychologists, whether their work is applied or research oriented.

- First, psychologists have responsibilities as a *research community* to publish only well-founded results with conventional support, open to analysis by colleagues. They also need to pay attention to possible social effects of research results and assess these in the prevailing moral and political climate.
- Second, they need to follow strict codes of conduct, devised by both the British Psychological Society and the American Psychological Association, when working with participants, including the recognition and promotion of equality of opportunity.

These codes cover: *confidentiality* (of results and those who produced them), *privacy, deception* (which can lower the public's trust in psychological research), *debriefing* (informing participants and returning them to their pre-test state), *mental* and *physical stress* and *discomfort, recognition of participants' rights to withdraw,* the *special power of the investigator* and problems with *involuntary participation* and *intervention*. There are various techniques which gain information but guarantee privacy and confidentiality and several have been suggested for avoiding the need to deceive, but psychology has the peculiar characteristic that informing people of what is being tested has the effect of altering their likely 'natural' behaviour.

The arguments *for* and *against animal research* are outlined.

INTRODUCTION

Both the British Psychological Society (BPS) and the American Psychological Association (APA) have agreed guidelines on the ethical issues involved in psychological research. The BPS currently has a booklet of statements (1998) covering a wide range of issues, including a general Code of Conduct (1993). The 1992 revision of an earlier code is entitled *Ethical Principles for Conducting Research with Human Participants*, the key terms here being the introduction of 'participants' to replace 'subjects', and the notion of researching 'with' rather than 'on' participants – not trivial amendments. The APA's (1992) *Ethical Principles of Psychologists and Code of Conduct* is an extremely comprehensive document which provides six General Principles for overall guidance towards 'the highest ideals of psychology'. These concern: *competence, integrity, professional and scientific responsibility, respect for people's rights and dignity, concern for others' welfare* and *social responsibility*. It also lists detailed Standards in specific areas of psychology which, unlike the general principles, are 'enforceable'. The general public can bring complaints to the ethics committee who then adjudicate. The psychologist concerned can be reprimanded, dismissed or required to alter behaviour or attend relevant training. This breadth of principles and disciplinary power reflects the far wider application of psychology to the general public as consumers in the USA. Most of the major *applied* principles are similar to those which are relevant in the doctor–patient relationship.

The 1992 BPS *Principles* cover the following areas: *consent, deception, debriefing, withdrawal from an investigation, confidentiality, protection of participants, observational research, giving advice (to participants) and monitoring of colleagues in the profession.* Section 2 of the *Principles*, entitled 'General', runs as follows:

> In all circumstances, investigators must consider the ethical implications and psychological consequences for the participants in their research. The essential principle is that the investigation should be considered from the standpoint of all participants: foreseeable threats to their psychological well-being, health, values or dignity should be eliminated. Investigators should recognise that, in our multi-cultural and multi-ethnic society and where investigations involve individuals of different ages, gender and social background, the investigators may not have sufficient knowledge of the implications of any investigation for the participants. It should be borne in mind that the best judge of whether an investigation will cause offence may be members of the population from which the participants in the research are to be drawn.

Both the British and United States' principles stress that psychological research should lead to better understanding of ourselves and to the enhancement of the human condition and promotion of human welfare. Both stress the need for an atmosphere of free inquiry in order to generate the widest, most valid body of knowledge. But both also stress that this free atmosphere requires a commitment to responsibility on the part of the psychologist in terms of competence, objectivity and the welfare of research participants.

Since 1987, the Royal Charter of the BPS has been amended, taking us some way towards the American model described above. The Society now maintains a 'register' of 'chartered psychologists'. These are people who practise psychology either in an applied or a research capacity. Members of the register use the formal letters 'C. Psychol', can be struck off for unprofessional behaviour and, it is hoped, will become recognised as bona fide 'trademarked' practitioners whom the general public can recognise and trust.

In the 1990s most research institutions had in place or created an ethics committee to vet research proposals (of staff and students) for unacceptable procedures in any of the areas which we are about to consider.

PUBLICATION AND ACCESS TO DATA

Before taking a look at the rights and protection of individual participants, we can consider how psychologists are expected to commit themselves to freedom of information. Recently, for instance, psychologists have discussed the problem of projective or personality tests being used by the lay selector for jobs or other positions.

In general, a psychologist cannot claim to have demonstrated an effect and then withhold raw data or information on procedures and samples used. Persons who do this are generally considered to be charlatans. Where psychologists are prepared, as most are, to be completely open with their data, they would still not allow the alleged results of their work to affect people's lives, by policy formulation for instance, before the research community has thoroughly verified, evaluated and replicated results where possible. They should not 'rush to publish'.

There are occasions, in fact, when any scientist may feel that publication of results is potentially harmful or even dangerous. (One is reminded of the scientists who first became fully aware of the horrendous power of the nuclear fission process.) In such cases, the investigator is expected to seek the opinion of 'experienced and disinterested colleagues', an option recommended several times in the BPS statement for various dilemmas.

It was noted in Chapter 3 that there are numerous incidents of withholding crucial data associated with the heated debate around the extent to which 'intelligence' (often limited to the narrow construct of IQ) might be inherited. The political implications here are profound. For example, do we nurture and provide compensatory support for 'slow' developers? Alternatively, do we simply accept that intellectual differences largely reflect unalterable genetic variations within society and consequently make arrangements by, for instance, providing different 'tiers' of education? The debate is also closely linked to the hottest potato of them all – race differences in IQ, the controversy sparked by Jensen (1969) and renewed quite recently by Herrnstein and Murray (1994). The debate is not just academic. Governments would like to know or, rather, would often like 'expert' support in their policies from psychologists. Burt's data appeared to provide very strong evidence for the genetic role in human intellectual abilities. The early findings played a part in the political debate which produced the British '11-plus' examination and a two (originally three) tier secondary education system, wherein the successful 20% of children passing the exam received a grammar school education. Only after Burt's death did Leon Kamin (1977) establish beyond doubt that Burt's data were inconsistent, to a degree way beyond acceptability and probably fraudulent. Kamin demonstrated that Burt was persistently vague about the exact tests in use and had not made it at all easy to check his raw data. The cult of the 'great expert' had also inhibited investigation of Burt's work by 'lesser' researchers. Although Burt's work has, to some degree, become rehabilitated in the psychological establishment during the 1990s, his contribution and data on IQ and inheritance will remain permanently unacceptable.

Burt's data have been far from the only problem in this area, however. It seems an unlikely coincidence that, in this same arena of debate, Kamin also experienced decades of resistance from Jensen in providing the data referred to in Chapter 1, and has more recently met with complete resistance from Bouchard *et al.* who claim (e.g. 1990) remarkable similarities between identical twins 'reared apart, from birth', a theme which has advanced well beyond sober psychological research to participants in the research having agents, wide media coverage and the making of Hollywood films. Kamin questions the extent to which the 'separated' twins really saw and knew nothing of each other, yet Bouchard consistently refuses to provide detailed case histories.

Psychological researchers, and science in general, just cannot afford to work with this kind of resistance to public check. Unfortunately, the general public are not always so astute or concerned about integrity. The drama of the identical twins can swamp the academic subtleties. Psychologists have an overriding responsibility to honour the scientific endeavour over the attractions of media exposure and fame.

Psychologists also need to exercise integrity over *where* they publish. Billig (1979) has produced evidence of clear links between certain publications in which psychologists publish articles and extreme racist opinions and activity. *The Mankind Quarterly*, whose editorial board has included Cattell, Jensen and Lynn, the latter as editor, was investigated in great detail and Billig's work is confirmed by Richards (1997). Tucker (1994) confirms many extreme racist connections and makes clear that the journal has long been supported, directly or indirectly, by the Pioneer Fund, a US white supremacist organisation, and has had a succession of far right editors and close associations with members of neo-Nazi organisations – see Tucker (1994). Contents concentrate on articles stressing 'race' difference, sometimes breathtakingly global and crude – see Lynn (1991b). Hence, UK psychologists would need to consider the conflict between their commitment to the British Psychological Society's multicultural and equal opportunity principles, and support, by publication, of a journal with such contrary motives.

Findings on 'racial' difference (in intelligence or personality, for instance) almost always stir up controversy, which is hardly surprising. For this reason some psychologists have been led to argue that a moratorium should be held on publication. They argue that, since 'race' is always inextricably bound up with culture and socio-economic position, most responsible researchers would announce results with great qualification. However, they cannot then stop the lay racist or ignorant reader from using the unqualified information in discriminatory or abusive practices.

Psychologists have also argued that professional psychological researchers should exercise integrity over the *sources of their funding*, increasingly likely to come from industry or other organisations with an interest in the non-academic use of findings. The Pioneer Fund, for instance, either directly or through intermediate organisations, is alleged to have funded Jensen, Shockley, Rushton, Hans Eysenck and Lynn, all to at least six figure sums (Richards, 1997; Connolly, 1994; Tucker, 1994).

CONFIDENTIALITY AND PRIVACY

We turn to researchers' treatment of, and guarantees to, participants. Apart from any ethical considerations, there is a purely pragmatic argument for guaranteeing anonymity for participants at all times. If psychologists kept publishing identities along with results, the general public would soon cease to volunteer or agree to research participation.

An investigator can guarantee anonymity or request permission to identify individuals. Such identification may occur through the use of video recordings, as in Milgram's film *Obedience to Authority*. Research participants who have been seriously deceived have the right to witness destruction of any such records they do not wish to be kept. If records are kept, participants have the right to assume these will be safeguarded and used as anonymous data only by thoroughly briefed research staff.

There are very special circumstances where an investigator might contravene the confidentiality rule and these are where there are clear dangers to human life. An investigator conducting participant observation into gang life would have a clear obligation to break confidence where a serious crime was about to be committed. A psychiatric patient's plan to kill himself or a room-mate would be reported. The ethical principles involved here are broader than those involved in conducting scientific research.

The participant obviously has the right to privacy, and procedures should not be planned which directly invade this without warning. Where a procedure is potentially intimate, embarrassing or sensitive, the participant should be clearly reminded of the right to withhold information or participation. Particular care would be required, for instance, where participants are being asked about sexual attitudes or behaviour.

This principle is difficult to follow in the case of covert participant observation, and serious criticism has been levelled at users of this approach on these grounds. In such cases it is also difficult to check out the final version of reports with participants in order to verify that an accurate account of their statements has been made.

MILGRAM – THE CLASSIC EXPERIMENT FOR ETHICAL DEBATE

Any discussion of ethical principles in psychological research inevitably throws up Milgram's famous demonstrations of obedience fairly early on in the proceedings. Several ethical issues are involved in this study so let me just describe it briefly and then ask you to think about what these issues are. Almost certainly you will have already heard about the experiment and fuller details are given in, for instance, Gross (1996).

Volunteers were introduced to another 'participant' who was actually an experimental confederate. The volunteer became a 'teacher' who was asked to administer electric shocks, increasing by 15 volts for each mistake made by the confederate. 375 volts was described as 'Danger: severe shock'. A tape recording of screams and refusals deceived the teacher–participant into believing the confederate was experiencing great pain and wished to end the session. The teacher–participant was pressured into continuing by 'prods' from the experimenter such as 'The experiment requires that you continue' and 'You have no choice but to go on'. To Milgram's surprise, 65% of participants delivered shocks to the end of the scale (450 volts) even though the confederate had ceased responding at 315 volts. Milgram had consulted 'experienced and disinterested colleagues' – psychiatrists predicted that no more than 0.1% would obey to the end. The teacher–participant often displayed extreme anxiety. One even suffered a seizure. An observer wrote:

> I observed a mature and initially poised businessman enter the laboratory smiling and confident. Within 20 minutes he was reduced to a twitching, stuttering wreck, who was rapidly approaching a point of nervous collapse. He constantly pulled at his ear lobe and twisted his hands. At one point he pushed his fist into his forehead and muttered, 'Oh God, let's stop it.' (Milgram, 1974)

The results of this demonstration were used to argue that many ordinary people are capable of behaving in a manner, under pressure, which is retrospectively considered cruel. Atrocities are not necessarily carried out by purely evil persons or 'cultures'.

List the aspects of this investigation which you consider to be unethical. Should the investigation have been carried out at all? Do the ends (scientific and surprising knowledge) justify the means?

DECEPTION

Milgram's participants were grossly deceived. Not only did they believe they were shocking an innocent victim and that the victim suffered terribly, but also the whole purpose of the research was completely distorted as concerning the effects of punishment on learning.

DECEPTION, or at least the withholding of information, is exceedingly common in psychology experiments. Menges (1973) reviewed about 1000 American studies and found that 80% involved giving participants less than complete information. In only 3% of studies were participants given complete information about the independent variable, and information about the dependent variable was incomplete in 75% of cases.

Some of this deception seems fairly innocuous. Some participants are told a baby is male, others that it is female, and their descriptions of it are compared. Participants performing a sensori-motor task, where the true aim is to record the effect of an observer on performance, are told that the observer is present to note details of the skilled behaviour involved. Children are told not to play with a toy because it belongs to another child who is next door. Students are told their experimental rats are 'bright'. Even the use of placebos is a deception.

Some deception is more serious. Participants have been told that test results demonstrate that they are poorly adjusted. Female participants are given feedback that they are considered attractive or unattractive by the men who will later interview them. Bramel (1962) gave male participants false feedback about their emotional reaction to photographs of men such that their responses seemed homosexually related. Participants in Latané and Darley's (1976) experiments thought they were overhearing an authentic epileptic seizure. The dependent variable was the speed or occurrence of reporting the seizure.

So what can the investigator do if deception is to be used? *First*, the 1992 BPS *Principles* recommend that, wherever possible, consultation should be conducted with individuals who share the social and cultural background of the participants. *Second*, debriefing should be very carefully attended to – see below. *Third*, in some cases it is possible to obtain permission to deceive. Volunteers can be asked to select what sort of research they would be prepared to participate in, from for instance:

- research on recognition of commercial products
- research on safety of products
- research in which you will be misled about the purpose until afterward
- research involving questions on attitudes

DEBRIEFING

In all research studies, the investigator has a responsibility to DEBRIEF each participant. The true purpose and aims of the study are revealed and every attempt is made to ensure that participants feel the same about themselves when they leave as they did when they arrived. In Johnston and Davey's (1997) experiment, described in Chapter 1, for example, the negative news tape was recognised by the researchers as possibly emotionally disturbing. For this reason they asked participants in that condition to listen to two minutes of a relaxation tape on a personal stereo before telling them all about the study and giving them their fee.

Where participants have been seriously deceived, this responsibility incurs a substantial effort in reassurance and explanation. The debriefing itself may have to involve a little more deception, as when children are told they 'did very well indeed' whatever the actual standard of their performance, and when any suspicion that a participant really *is* 'poorly adjusted' is not communicated to them. In Milgram's experiments, participants who went to the end of the scale were told that some people did this 'quite gleefully'. The idea was to help the obedient participants compare their own unwillingness to proceed, and experienced anxiety, fairly favourably with the fictitious happily obedient participants. (Milgram never reported that any participant *did* proceed happily.) Even with this comparison, at least 26 out of 40 participants knew, when they left, that they were capable, under pressure, of inflicting extreme pain, if not death, on an innocent human being. It hardly seems possible that these people left the laboratory feeling the same about themselves as they did before they entered.

Does debriefing work?

Milgram sent a questionnaire to his participants after the study and 84% said they were glad to have participated, whereas only 1% regretted being involved, the remainder reporting neutral feelings. 80% believed more research like Milgram's should be carried out. 75% found the experience meaningful and self-enlightening. Some writers discounted this broad range of appreciative and illuminating comments as an attempt by Milgram to justify an ethically unacceptable study. Ring *et al.* (1970) decided to evaluate the consequences to the participant in a study which, even though the investigators were critical of Milgram, not only included the deceptions of the original study but also used a dishonest primary debriefing before a second honest one. They showed that an initial, superficial debriefing dramatically reduces any negative participant evaluation of the research. However, they also found that one third of participants reported residual anger and disappointment with themselves even after the second, complete debriefing. The fact that even a few participants felt quite negative about themselves well after the experiment, and that many participants felt extremely upset during it, has led many researchers to the position that such extreme deception and stress is ethically unacceptable.

Besides the question of ethics, it is unwise of investigators to indulge in a great deal of deception. Students very often suspect that the manifest structure and explanation of a study in which they participate is false. Ring found that 50% of their participants claimed they would be more wary and suspicious of psychology experiments in the future. As Reason and Rowan (1981) put it, 'Good research means never having to say you are sorry.'

If you won't deceive, what can you do?

Several investigators, finding gross deception at the Asch or Milgram level quite unacceptable, have turned to role-play or simulation. A description of successful findings by Mixon, (1974) who used the heading above for his title, is given in Chapter 5.

Ring was among the advocates of role-playing, whereas Aronson and Carlsmith (1968) argued that essential realism would be lost. Horowitz and Rothschild (1970) conducted a replication of Asch's design using a 'forewarned' group, who were told that the experiment was a fake but were asked to play the part of a naïve participant, and a 'pre-briefed' group who knew the experimental aim in detail. The forewarned group 'conformed' at a similar level to the traditionally deceived group, whereas the fully informed group did not conform at all.

These latter participants seemed to behave in accordance with what most people believe would actually occur in the Asch set up. This is, after all, why Asch's study is so renowned, gripping and well-recalled by the psychology student. It defies common sense. The prognosis for role-play, on this evidence, in demonstrating such counter-intuitive effects, therefore, seems not so good. However, the capacity in normal students during role-play for aggressive authoritarianism and subservience was demonstrated convincingly and against prediction in Zimbardo's classic study described briefly below.

This does not mean that deception of the Milgram intensity is therefore ethically acceptable. Both the BPS and the APA ask that the uncertain investigator seek opinion, again, from those 'experienced and disinterested colleagues' who are not fervently committed to the investigator's chosen hypothesis and proposed method.

STRESS AND DISCOMFORT

There is no argument against the principle that psychological investigators should guarantee the safety of their participants and that everything possible should be done to protect them from harm or discomfort. The difficulty comes in trying to decide what kind of stress or discomfort, physical or mental, is unacceptable. Humanists and others might argue that *any* traditional experimental research on 'subjects' is an affront to human dignity. At a lesser extreme, those who see value in the human experimental procedure have nevertheless criticised some investigators for going too far.

Mental stress

Examples of studies involving a possibly substantial degree of mental stress were given above. These involved deterioration of a person's self-image or the strain of feeling responsible for action in the Latané and Darley study. A further example, causing some dissent, is that in which a child was asked to guard the experimenter's pet hamster, which was then removed from its cage through a hole in the floor when the child wasn't looking.

Not all mental stress emanates from deception. Participants may be exposed to pornographic or violent film sequences. Extreme psychological discomfort, in the form of delusions and hallucinations, was experienced by participants undergoing 'sensory deprivation' (deprived of sound, touch and sight) such that they often terminated the experience after three days. Zimbardo's (1972) simulation of authority and obedience had to be stopped after six days of the 14 it was supposed to run. Students played the part of aggressive, sadistic and brutal prison guards far too well. Their 'prisoners' (other students) became extremely passive and dependent. Within two days, and on the next few, participants had to be released, since they were exhibiting signs of severe emotional and psychological disorder (uncontrollable crying and screaming) and one even developed a nervous rash.

There is an obligation for investigators not only to debrief but also to attempt to remove even long-term negative effects of psychological research procedures. Forty of Milgram's participants were examined, one year after the experiment, by a psychiatrist who reported that no participant had been harmed psychologically by their experience. The 1992 BPS *Principles* urge investigators to inform participants of procedures for contacting them should stress or other harm occur after participation.

Physical discomfort

Many psychological experiments have manipulated the variables of, for instance, electric shock, extreme noise level, food and sleep deprivation, anxiety or nausea producing drugs and so on.

Watson and Rayner (1920), as is well known, caused 'Little Albert', a young infant, to exhibit anxiety towards a white rat he had previously fondled quite happily, by producing a loud disturbing noise whenever he did so. Apparently Albert even became wary of other furry white objects. His mother moved away and so Albert was removed from the project before he could be deconditioned. This procedure developed into that of 'aversive conditioning' which is intended to rid willing clients of unwanted or destructive behaviour.

The term 'willing' creates difficulties. In the sensitive cases which have occurred of gay men submitting themselves to aversive therapy, it has been argued that treatment is unethical, since the men are succumbing to a conventional norm structure which treats their sexual preference as undesirable or 'sick'. In general research work, a 'willing' participant may act under social pressure. They may wish to sustain a 'real man' image, to bear as much as, or 'beat', their peers. They may feel they are ruining the experiment or letting down the experimenter (the special power of the investigator is discussed below). For these reasons, the investigator has a set of obligations to participants to ensure they do not suffer unduly or unnecessarily. These are outlined in the following section. In any research where discomfort might be expected the investigator is expected to seek opinion and advice from professional colleagues before going ahead.

THE RIGHT TO NON-PARTICIPATION

In all research which involves individual participation the investigator is obliged to:
1. Give the participant full information as to the likely level of discomfort and to emphasise the voluntary nature of the exercise and the right to withdraw at any time.
2. Remind the participant of this right to withdraw at any point in the procedure where discomfort appears to be higher than anticipated.
3. Terminate the procedure where discomfort levels are substantially higher than anticipated and/or the participant is obviously disturbed to an unacceptable level.

Now we can see one of the most controversial aspects of Milgram's study. He was actually testing the power of the experimenter over the participant. His experimenter flagrantly contravened all three principles. The duty to respect the participant's right to withdraw and to remind the participant of this right are both now stressed by the APA and BPS. Contrary to this, and in a perhaps less humanistic era, each participant wishing to stop was commanded to continue in the interests of the research programme. Continuance was 'absolutely essential' and the participant had 'no choice but to go on'. The APA and BPS now also stress special vigilance when the investigator is in a position of power over the participant. This was, of course, the very position forcefully exploited and examined in the Milgram study.

It is usual to obtain the INFORMED CONSENT of research participants. As we shall see below, this isn't always possible before the research is conducted, though for laboratory experiments consent can always be obtained. In research with children, the informed consent of parents must first be obtained. For obvious reasons, children cannot be subject to great stress, even in the unlikely instance that parents agree (though little Albert's mother did). Two factors working against informed consent are the investigator's need to deceive on some occasions, and the significant power attaching to the investigator *role*.

THE SPECIAL POWER OF THE INVESTIGATOR

In general, then, the investigator is obliged to give the participant every chance not to participate, both before and during the experimental procedure. Working against this, as we have just said, is the position of influence, prestige and power of the investigator. Torbert (1981) says:

> . . . the unilaterally controlled research context is itself only one particular kind of social context and a politically authoritarian context at that. It should not be surprising that some of its most spectacularly well-conceived findings concern persons' responses to authoritarianism. (p. 144)

An additional dimension to this power emerges when we consider the common position of United States' psychology undergraduates who often face obligatory participation in a research project of their choice. In some cases an exemption is offered but it costs one additional term paper, making the choice more apparent than real.

A further issue for ethical concern has been the practice of obtaining prison inmates or psychiatric patients for stressful experimental studies, where inducements, such as a pack of cigarettes or temporary release from daily routines, are minimal and would not normally 'buy' participation outside the institution. The 1992 BPS *Principles* lay particular emphasis on the way in which consent is obtained from detained persons and also on the special circumstances of children and adults with impairments in understanding or communication.

INVOLUNTARY PARTICIPATION

In participant observation studies, and in naturalistic (covert) observation, the persons observed are quite often unaware of their participation. This seems fairly unobjectionable where completely unobtrusive observation is made and each person observed is just one in a frequency count; for instance, when drivers are observed in order to determine whether more males or more females stop at a 'stop' road sign.

In participant observation people's private lives may be invaded. Humphreys (1970) investigated the behaviour of consenting homosexuals by acting as a public washroom 'lookout'. Persons observed were completely unaware of the study and of the fact that their car registration numbers were recorded in order to obtain more background information through interviews later on.

Some field studies carried out in the public arena involve manipulations which interfere with people's lives. A street survey obviously delays each respondent but here consent is always sought first. In Piliavin et al.'s (1969) studies on bystander intervention, a person looking either lame or drunk 'collapsed' in a subway train. In one version the actor bit a capsule which produced a blood-like trickle on his chin. Predictably, the 'lame' person got more help than the drunk. The 'blood' condition also had a lowering effect on helping. Piliavin's study, in fact, contravenes the principles of openness (no deception), stress avoidance and informed consent before participation.

Doob and Gross (1968) delayed drivers at a traffic light in either a very smart, new car or an older, lower status one. Effects were predictable in that it took drivers longer to hoot at the smarter car! If these results are fairly unsurprising, couldn't willing participants simply be asked to imagine the situation and consider their likely response? Would simulation work here? Doob and Gross used a questionnaire as well, and found no difference between the times *predicted* by independent samples of students for hooting at either car. Oddly, of those who said they would not hoot, all six of those who would not hoot at the low status car were male, and all five of those not hooting at the high status car were female. The 'as if' findings were so different from actual behaviour that the defenders of field research seemed vindicated in their claim to more realistic data. However, by 1991, a computer simulation had been devised, and this produced results confirming the original findings.

INTERVENTION

Some aspects of brief INTERVENTION with naïve participants have been dealt with above. Several studies have involved intervention on a substantial scale but with willing participation. For instance, psychologists have worked with parents and children in the home in an effort to demonstrate the beneficial effects of parental stimulation on the child's learning and intellectual performance. In these studies a control group is necessary for baseline comparison. In hospital experiments with new drugs, trials are halted if success is apparent on the grounds that it would be unethical to withhold the new drug as treatment from the placebo and control groups. Unfortunately, in psychological intervention research, even if success is apparent, there would not usually be the political power and resources to implement the 'treatment' across *all* disadvantaged families. Ethical issues arise, therefore, in selecting one group for special treatment.

Where intervention occurs for research purposes only, and involves the production of behaviour usually considered socially unacceptable, ethical principles need very careful consideration. Leyens et al. (1975), for instance, raised levels of aggression in boys shown a series of violent films. They were observed to be more aggressive in daily activities compared with a control group shown non-violent films. It is quite difficult to see how debriefing alone could leave the boys just where they were before the study began.

RESEARCH WITH ANIMALS

There is nothing more certain of producing a lively debate among psychology students than the discussion of whether or not it is necessary or useful to experiment on defence-less animals. Many students are far more emotionally outraged about animal research than about some of the more questionable human studies, on the grounds that humans can refuse whereas animals have no such chance.

One cannot deceive animals, though one can fool them. Nor can they give their informed consent, be debriefed or ask for a procedure to be terminated, though only the most callously inhumane experimenter could ignore severe suffering. Animals can, however, be subject to exploitation, extreme levels of physical pain and mental stress.

Many students, to their cost, spend the whole of an essay on psychological research ethics discussing the plight of research animals, though Milgram will often be a secondary focus of attention. I don't intend to go through the innumerable examples of animals in pitiful situations in the psychological research laboratory. To list the kinds of situation is enough:

- severe sensory deprivation
- severe to complete social deprivation
- extirpation or lesion of the nervous system or body parts
- use of extremely aversive physical stimuli including electric shock, noise, poisonous or otherwise aversive chemicals, mood or behaviour altering chemicals
- starvation.

Why have psychologists found it useful or necessary to use these methods?

The case for animal research

1. Animals can be used where humans can't. For instance, they can be deprived of their mothers or reared in complete darkness. This point of course completely begs the question of whether such procedures are ethical.

2. Great control can be exerted over variables. Animals can be made to feed, for instance, at precise intervals.

3. Several generations can be bred where species have short gestation and maturation periods. This is useful in studying genetic processes and it also means that the whole process of development can be observed.

4. An effect shown or insight gained in animal studies, although not directly applicable to humans, may lead to fresh and fertile theories about human behaviour. Animal studies have contributed ideas to the debate on human adult–infant bonding and maternal separation, for example.

5. Comparisons across the phylogenetic scale are valuable for showing what humans *don't* have or *can't* do – what we have probably evolved away from or out of. Comparison is invaluable in helping us develop a framework for brain analysis based on evolutionary history. A seemingly useless or mystical piece of the nervous system may serve, or have served, a function disclosed only through the discovery of its current function in another species.

6. At a very elementary, physiological level, animals and humans have things in common. The nature of the synapse, neural connections and transmission for instance, are similar among higher primates.

7. Skinner argued that elementary units of learning would also be similar across most higher species. Hence, he mostly used rat and pigeon subjects in his research work, arguing that patterns of stimulus–response contingencies, schedules of reinforcement and so on were generalisable to the world of human behaviour.

The case against animal research

Theorists have argued that too much extrapolation from animal to human has occurred. Here are some reasons why such extrapolation is considered inappropriate.

1. Seligman (1972) has argued for the concept of *preparedness*. The concept is that, through evolutionary processes, some animals are born specially prepared to learn specific behaviour patterns of survival value to the species. Likewise, some patterns are difficult or impossible to learn at all – the animal is *contra-prepared*. This makes comparison between one species and another hazardous, let alone comparison between human and animal.

2. Kohler (1925) demonstrated in apes what he referred to as *insight learning* – solving a novel problem with a sudden reorganisation of detail, much like we do when we spontaneously solve one of those annoying match-stick problems. If apes can do what humans certainly can, then the validity of the traditional behaviourist rat model, transferred to human learning, when the rat doesn't show anything like the same level of insight, seems questionable.

3. The ethologists have shown that quite a lot of behaviour, subject to cultural variation and slow developmental learning in humans, is instinctive in animals, demonstrated as 'fixed action patterns'. Mating preludes and territorial defence are quite rigidly organised in a large number of species yet quite ungeneralised across the breadth of human cultures.

4. The ethologists, among others, have also questioned the validity of having animals do abnormal things in the laboratory and have concentrated on behaviour in the natural environment, only testing animals in the laboratory with variations of the stimuli which would be encountered normally outside it.

5. Language, *carefully* defined in terms of syntax and symbol, appears to be unique to humans. Language is the vehicle for transmission of cultural values, meanings and the individual's social construction of reality. Very much psychological research, consciously or not, assumes these values and meanings as integral to human awareness. The comparison with most animals seems at its weakest here.

The points above are all aimed at the rejection of animal research on *practical* grounds. It is argued that such research will not tell us what we want to know. Other arguments take a moral or humanitarian line.

6. Some argue that it is just categorically wrong to inflict pain and suffering on any living creature.

7. A more profound argument is that the experimenter's 'attack' on nature typifies the 'controlling' model of humankind associated with the psychologist as hard, objective,

neutral and distant scientist. This image of the scientist is currently rejected, not just by humanist and many other psychologists, but by many scientists across the disciplines who wish to project a model of environmental care.

Supporters of the points above would argue that kittens need not be deprived of visual experience in order to study the nature–nurture issue in perception. Field studies on children who unfortunately happen to have been so deprived would be considered more realistic and more ethical. Likewise, monkeys do not need to be deprived of their mothers. Plenty of children have been. The great debate in attachment theory has been over the number and quality of bonds necessary for optimum child development, and here monkey studies can hardly help us.

Whatever the rationale for animal studies, or the fierce, impassioned objections, it seems likely they will continue as an adjunct to psychological research, though perhaps not at their earlier intensity. British research is carried out under guidelines issued by the BPS (1998). In these the following points are made:

- Knowledge to be gained must justify procedure; trivial research is not encouraged; alternative methods are.
- The smallest possible number of animals should be used.
- No members of endangered species should ever be used.
- Caging, food deprivation, procedures causing discomfort or pain should all be assessed relative to the particular species studied. A procedure relatively mild to one can be damaging to another.
- Naturalistic studies are preferred to laboratory ones, but animals should be disturbed as little as possible in the wild.
- Experimenters must be familiar with the technical aspects of anaesthesia, pharmacological compounds and so on; regular post-operative medical checks must be made.

The guidelines also direct the psychologist to the relevant laws under which animal research is conducted and to the need for various licences.

CONCLUSION

All in all, it looks difficult to conduct much research at all without running into ethical arguments. Certainly it seems impossible to proceed with anything before considering possible ethical objections. But this is as it should be. Other sciences too have their associations and committees for considering social responsibility in scientific research. They argue about the use to which findings might be put or the organisations from whom it would not be prudent to accept sponsorship. They consider the likely impact of their work on society as a whole.

Similarly, psychology has to make these considerations. But, since humans, as individuals in society, are also the focal point of research, it is hardly surprising that psychology, as a research society, has to be far sharper on its toes in spotting malpractice, abuse, thoughtlessness and lack of professionalism. If psychologists prefer not to have people take one step backwards at parties and say things like 'I bet you're testing me' or 'Is this part of an experiment?', they need to reassure the public constantly that some excesses of the past cannot now happen and that deception really *is* only used when necessary.

The humanists and 'new paradigm' researchers appear to have gained the moral high ground on these ethical issues, not just because they put dignity, honesty and *humanity* first, but because they see their participative or non-directive methods as the only route to genuine, uncoerced information. According to Reason and Rowan (1981), Maslow has said, '... if you prod at people like things, they won't let you know them' (p. xviii).

Well, what do you think? You'll probably discuss quite heatedly, with co-students or colleagues, the rights and wrongs of conducting some experiments. I can't help feeling that the information from Milgram's work is extremely valuable. It certainly undermined stereotypes I had, a long time ago, about whole cultures tending to be more obedient or capable of harming others. But I also can't help thinking immediately about those participants who went all the way. Can we be so sure we'd be in the 35% who stopped? Not even all these stopped as soon as the victim was clearly in trouble. How would we feel the rest of our lives? Should we inflict such a loss of dignity on others? I haven't made any final decision about this issue, as about many other psychological debates and philosophical dilemmas. Fortunately, I'm not in a position where I have to vote on it. But what do you think?

Glossary

Informing participants about the full nature and rationale of the study they've experienced and attempting to reverse any negative influence	_____	debriefing
Leading participant to believe that something other than the true independent variable is involved or witholding information such that the reality of the investigative situation is masked or distorted	_____	deception
Agreement to participate in research in the full knowledge of the research context and ethical rights	_____ _____	informed consent
Research which makes some alteration to people's lives beyond the specific research setting, in some cases because there is an intention to ameliorate specific human conditions	_____	intervention
Research which intrudes into people's personal lives	_____ __ _____	invasion of privacy
Taking part in research without agreement or knowledge of the study	_____ _____	involuntary participation

23 Planning your practical and writing up your report

PLANNING YOUR PRACTICAL PROJECT

If you are going to be devising and running your own practical work in psychology, good luck! It is great fun, and highly satisfying, to be presenting a report of work which is all your own, rather than of a practical set by your tutor. However, beware! Your tutor almost certainly has a lot of experience in planning such exercises, such that you do not waste all your efforts and end up with useless data or find yourself running a project with hopeless snags or a completely inappropriate design.

Below I have jotted down most of the things I can think of which need attention before you start your data gathering. I've almost certainly missed some things but I hope these will be of some help. *Nothing I've written, however, can substitute for very careful planning, preferably in a small group, before you start your data collection.*

Remember that the 'practical' doesn't start when you actually begin running your trials or questioning your participants. That is a tiny part of the whole process. There is a large portion of time to spend planning and another large portion to spend analysing and (dare I say it) writing up your report!

I have written these notes with the traditional, 'tight' hypothesis test in mind. Hence there is emphasis on strict definition of variables and thinking about the system of analysis before starting. This obviously runs counter to the tenets of qualitative and 'new paradigm' research. However, most students will find that, through syllabus requirements or other forces, they will need to be familiar with this traditional design. Besides, since the 'old paradigm' is hardly likely to disappear overnight, I believe it is necessary to understand the approach fully in order to understand its weaknesses and to be able to take off in other directions.

The student wishing to conduct something more qualitative in design would need to consult thoroughly with their tutor in order to avoid ending up with a report which is fascinating but is seen as the work of a 'displaced novelist' and mainly anecdotal – see the previous chapter.

THE OVERALL AIM

- Did the idea just pop up in your head? You will need to investigate theory that backs up your proposals. This might give you firmer ideas. Most research follows from prior findings or speculative theory based on detailed arguments. You will probably be working to a syllabus which wants you to 'embed' the research aims in some form of background theory. There is nothing wrong in principle, however, in testing a personal idea which came to you unaided. Creativity is encouraging. However, it is likely that there *is* some related work on it, though perhaps hard to find in your college library. You can always phone up or write to other institutions or libraries. If you are in school or the further education sector you could try visiting your local university library to consult journals or wider literature. You could ask to use their *Psychlit* software which is on CD-ROM and contains a short summary of an enormous number of psychological research studies. Several journals are also now available on the Internet.

- *Now* is the time to state your hypotheses very carefully, not when you come to write up the report! If you think carefully about what you want to demonstrate, what effects would support your arguments, then the design, analysis and report of your study should all follow fairly logically from that.

- Choose a hypothesis that is possible or feasible to test. Try to avoid difficult data collection hurdles. If you need left-handers or dyslexics, think carefully whether you will be able to find enough for a reasonably sized sample.

- Don't choose a design where you will need to *correlate* too many variables. If you take measures on many characteristics of your sample and test them using several tests, each with several sub-scales, you may be tempted just to correlate everything together. If you do, you will be seen as 'fishing'. Remember that getting around one 'significant' correlation out of 20 Spearman tests is just what we'd expect if the null hypothesis is true for *all* of them – not at all impressive. The only useful significant correlations will be those specifically *predicted* significant on good theoretical argument, or those where you have had the opportunity to follow up on the 'fished' significant correlations to show that the finding can be replicated.

THE DESIGN

- Do you need to quantify your variables? Are there any existing measures or will you need to create them? Can this be done sensibly? How will 'self-concept', for instance, be assessed?

- In thinking of variables it will be useful to think about any *statistical analysis* you are going to employ. For instance, if you have been asked to use correlation then it is almost certainly intended that you should use Pearson or Spearman where both your variables should be measurable on at least an ordinal scale. Otherwise, if you tried to 'correlate sex with driving speed', for instance, you would end up with the difference between males and females, since sex is a nominal variable – it only has two qualitatively different values. There are the special procedures mentioned in Chapter 15 but you won't be able to produce a sensible scattergram when one variable has only two distinct values. With such variables it makes sense to test for difference.

- *Observation studies*: If you want to conduct one of these be very careful that it does not end up as what coursework moderators like to call a 'day at the zoo study' or 'my cute baby cousin'. You *must* develop adequate observation schedules or coding systems and/or plan exactly what it is your observation will focus upon. Almost certainly you will need to run a pilot observation to see how hard it is to gather useful information which you can write up into a report. The closer your report comes to what a journalist or animal lover might write, the further you are away from an adequate psychological practical report.

- Will you be able to develop a plausible *rating scale* for your variable(s)? Can people rate a photograph of a face on a scale of one to ten for 'happiness', for example? This will produce rank ordered data at best, and you will be limited to non-parametric rank tests – no problem but it's as well to be aware at this point that you are limiting your options for statistical analysis. Options are limited still further if, for instance, you measure driving ability by whether a driver stops or not. This is a categorical measure. Is that what you want? You may be limited to a chi-square analysis. Compare asking whether people passed their test first time with asking how long it took them to learn. The latter gives you at least ranked data.

- If you need to carry out an *experiment*, choose a very *clear* one, not one where you will worry over whether it really is an experiment or not, or where the independent variable is not fully manipulated. Piaget type demonstrations are very attractive to students but often aren't experiments at all. Where is the independent variable when 5 year-olds go through the orange-juice-and-different-sized-glasses routine?

- If you want to carry out a study of *group difference(s)*, e.g. a sex-difference study, you need to ensure that the two groups are very carefully matched on all the possibly relevant variables you can manage – see Chapter 3 on group difference studies.

- Are you dealing with *too many variables* to keep statistical analysis simple enough? Say you wanted to see whether introverts improve on a task without an audience, whereas extroverts deteriorate. You'd like to see whether this is more true for males than for females and perhaps whether age has an effect too. Admirable thinking on interacting variables, but the statistical analysis will get very complicated. You'll need to use ANOVA. Do you understand the procedure? Can you easily get computer assistance? Can you find enough participants per group?

- The last example was costly on participants. In general, will you be able to get enough people for your chosen design? Remember, an unrelated design requires twice the number of people, to get the same number of differences as a repeated measures design. Will you be able to match pairs appropriately? You may not be able to obtain the information you need for this (e.g. educational level). If you are going to use repeated measures, with tests on two different occasions, will everyone be available second time around?

- Have you got all the *control conditions* or *groups* you need? A pair of students once tried to test the matching hypothesis. They gave participants cards holding 10 photos of married women and 10 photos of the men they were married to. Participants had to attempt to match couples on physical attractiveness. Trouble was, when they came to present the 'success' rates of their participants there was no simple way to compare this with what would be expected from random pairing. A complicated probability calculation would have done it but would not account for slight variations in the cards. An empirical, practical and easy solution was to have a control condition in which people paired the photos when they were face down. So, will you need a condition for comparison? Could you use a placebo group? Think clearly about the exact *null hypothesis* you wish to reject in order to support your alternative hypothesis.

- Is there a likelihood of any obvious *confounding variables*? If the general public are to be approached, will it matter that most of the researchers are female? Some students I knew were going to say 'hello' to passers-by under two conditions, with and without a smile. It struck them that all of them were female and that there could be a differential response from male and female passers-by!
- Are *conditions equivalent*? If the experimental group have longer, more intricate instructions and introduction to their task, could this act as a confounding variable? Should the control group get equivalent but 'dummy' introduction and instructions, and/or equivalent time with the experimenters?

THE SAMPLE(S)

- Will you have to use the same old 'friends and acquaintances' or students in the college canteen? If so, will they be too well aware of your previous deceptions?
- Will they reveal the nature of the research to naïve participants you still wish to test?
- Even though the sample can't be truly random or representative, can you balance groups for sex, age etc.?
- Should you ask whether they've participated in this before? You can't ask beforehand, in many cases, such as when you're showing an illusion. You'll have to ask afterwards and exclude them from the results if they weren't 'naïve'.
- If you suspected some participants of 'mucking around' or of already knowing the aim and perhaps trying to 'look good', you'll have to decide, having asked them afterwards, whether it is legitimate to drop their results. You can discuss this with colleagues.
- Make sure samples are of an adequate size for the job. If they just can't be large enough, then think of another hypothesis. Some students once presented, quite seriously, the results of a project which they claimed supported their hypothesis that northerners (in the UK) were less racist than southerners, having used one or two questions about tolerance for racist jokes. Trouble was, they had tested just eight northerners and five southerners!

THE MATERIALS

First of all, make a very careful note that any materials you produce have a direct effect on the sort of statistical or other analysis you can perform on the data you gather. If you look back to p. 163 you'll see there that the phrasing and structure of a crucial question could have led to disaster in a student's dissertation. A slight change and she could gather data with which sensible comparisons could be made.

- Are materials *equivalent* for both conditions? A group of students were doing a version of the Asch 'warm–cold' study. People in one group were shown a set of terms: *intelligent*, *shy*, *confident*, *warm*, *practical*, *quick*, *quiet*. The other group were shown the same terms except that 'cold' was substituted for 'warm'. The people had to judge other characteristics of the hypothetical person. One student had missed a class and had no 'cold' forms, so she changed the word 'warm' in ink and photocopied. This gave a not-too-subtle clue to her second group as to what the important word in the set was.

● Can two memory word-lists be equivalent? Can you say that the words in each are equally frequent in normal language use, or that two sets of anagrams are equally hard to solve? You can use *pre-testing* of the materials to show there is no real difference or you can get hold of word frequency lists.

● Are *instructions* to participants *intelligible*? If you're unsure of the wording in a questionnaire, do get the help of someone who's good with language. Respondents will not respect or take seriously a badly-written questionnaire with several spelling mistakes.

● Are there too many units in the material? Will it take too long to test them all on each participant? Can the list of items or questions be shortened?

● If you want to construct a *questionnaire* (see Chapter 9) remember, a test of an attitude is often made not with questions but with *statements* for people to agree/disagree with or say how far it represents their view. Don't say 'Do you believe in abortion/nuclear power/strikes?' These things exist! We want to know what people *think* about them.

● *In all cases, pilot! Try out materials on friends and relatives.*

It takes many years to train in the psychoanalytic interpretation of projective tests, such as the Rorschach and TAT. Their validity is very much questioned within the academic world. Therefore it would be extremely unwise to attempt to incorporate the use of these instruments in a student practical.

If you are focusing on a specific group of people, such as a minority ethnic group, then please read 'doing a "race" project' in Chapter 8 and be extremely careful with your choice of terms. If possible, check with members of the group concerned, other 'experts', your tutor and/or your classmates. This applies wherever a specific group is the focus, whether members of that group will *themselves* be questioned or not (e.g. a nationality, gay people, people with disabilities or specific illnesses or difficulties such as dyslexia, and so on).

THE PROCEDURE

● There may well be several of you going out to gather data. Make sure you *standardise your procedure* exactly before you start. The most common problem I have seen amongst a group of students doing a practical together is that they didn't have a final check that they had all got exactly the same steps of procedure. Don't be shy to ask your friends to do a final check before they rush off after a lot of hurried changes. Don't feel stupid if you don't feel confident about exactly what you have to do. Ask your friends or the tutor where appropriate. It's better to take a little more time, and admit you're not perfect, than to end up with results that can't be used or with having to do things over again.

● Decide what *extra data* are worth recording (sex, age). These might show up a relationship which wasn't part of the original hypotheses, but which can be discussed with a view to new future research. However, don't overdo it – see p. 154.

- *Record all the information on the spot.* If you decide to wait till later to record age or occupation of your interviewee, you may well forget. Then the result may be wasted. *Remember to note which group a participant was in.* If you forget, your efforts are wasted!
- Be prepared to put participants at their ease and give an encouraging introduction.
- Work out the *exact instructions* to participants. Have a simulated run through with a colleague. What have you failed to explain? What else might people need/want to know?
- Decide how you will answer questions your participants might ask. Will you have stock answers or will you ask them to wait until after the testing?
- If the study is an *observation*:
  – Will the observations really be unobtrusive? Check out the recording position beforehand.
  – Will *recording* be easy? Does talking into a tape recorder attract too much attention for instance? Does the coding system work? Is there time and ample space to make written notes?
  – Will more than one person make records simultaneously in the interests of reliability?

ETHICS

As a student, it is unlikely that you have been trained sufficiently to be able to conduct satisfactory *debriefing* sessions. Professional research psychologists themselves often argue these days about the adequacy of debriefing in returning people to their starting point and 'undoing' any psychological harm done. It is also unlikely that you'll have the time or resources to debrief properly. Therefore it is extremely important that your proposed research project will not involve any of the following:

- Invasion of privacy
- Causing participants to lose dignity
- Causing participants to think less of themselves
- Deception which causes resentment or hostility (check that any deception used is absolutely necessary and is benign)
- Unnecessary withholding of information
- Pain or discomfort
- Breaking of local prohibitions (for instance, drinking alcohol on college premises)
- Anything at all about which participants feel uncomfortable.

There are a couple of examples I have come across recently in course assessment work which are quite unacceptable. Students investigated bystander intervention in a shopping mall by falling and including the use of imitation blood. One student conducted an 'observation' by making covert notes on one class colleague, whom she described as 'disturbed and anti-social', over a period of six weeks. The notes included information on the girl's 'disruptive' class activities, including pseudo-psychiatric descriptions, and an account of the girl's apparent anorexic tendencies.

It is to be hoped that, as psychology continues to grow in the pre-University sector, tutors will monitor student practical work very closely indeed for its adherence to the standards now required by the public examining bodies. Ask your tutor for the information given out by these organisations, or contact them directly for help. They will be only too pleased to advise what is acceptable, what is educationally and ethically appropriate, and what is strictly out of bounds, though this should really be obvious upon sober reflection.

Assure participants that anonymity will be maintained, and *maintain it*! It is discourteous and bad practice even to talk with close colleagues in the project, or very best friends, in a derogatory manner about participants, even if anonymous. It develops an elitist, manipulative approach to people who have tried to help you in your work.

Also assure participants that they will not feel or look stupid, or reveal anything they don't wish to reveal about themselves – and make sure this also is true! Assure them that they can have destroyed any record of behaviour, in particular any they feel very uncomfortable about. Remind them they can stop if they wish to.

On approaching unknown members of the public, tell them who you are, where you're from and the reason for doing research (part of your required coursework, for instance). Make sure your tutor and college are happy about any approach to the public, since they will receive complaints if you use the college name. If you have any doubts at all discuss the proposal with your tutor and/or another responsible person whose opinions you respect. Remember that you are, in a small way, an ambassador for your college and for psychology, and the general public can already have a quite distorted view of what psychologists are about.

NOW HAVE FUN!

WRITING YOUR PRACTICAL REPORT

If you carry out some practical work, you will find yourself faced with the onerous task of writing it all up. My first piece of advice is *don't put it off*! You'll find it much harder to come back to when any initial enthusiasm you had for the project will have worn off, and you won't be able to understand why certain precautions were taken or just what certain conditions were all about. You'll find essential details of data and analysis are missing and you may need the help of your class colleagues who've now lost their raw data or are too busy to help.

If it's any consolation, as you slog away through the small hours finishing your work, consider the *general* skills you are acquiring which will help you through your working life. Our Applied Science department, where students, as in psychology, generally take a dim view of report writing, recently carried out a survey on graduates of ten years ago. Very high on the list of things from their course that they had found most useful, on entering and progressing in their working lives, was ... yes, you guessed it – report writing! It is the one thing you are very likely to do, in some form or another, in a professional career, in further study, or even as a member of a local community or interest group. Reports are all about clear communication to others.

WHAT IS THE PURPOSE OF A REPORT?

There are two main purposes, neither of which is to do with keeping your tutor happy. First, you are telling your reader just what you did, why you did it and what you think it adds to the stockpile of knowledge and theory development. Second, you are recording your procedures in enough detail for some of those readers, who are so inclined, to *replicate* your work. We have seen elsewhere why this is so important to scientific method. Golden rule number one for report writing, then, is:

Make sure you write with enough depth and clarity for a complete stranger to repeat exactly what you did in every detail.

A useful criterion for tutors who mark reports is to consider how many extra questions a naïve reader would have to ask you in order to get on with a fair replication of what you did. Think of this as you write and you really can't go far wrong.

WHAT ARE THE RULES?

There are none. However, your tutor will often act as if there are when commenting on your work. This is because there are fairly generally accepted *conventions*. Most of these make sense and work in the interests of good report organisation and communication between researchers. Have a look at some journals in your college library, if that's possible, or ask to borrow a copy of one volume from a local academic institution. Your tutor may well have copies of old student work, though very often only the poorer work gets left. (Why this systematic bias?) The Associated Examining Board (now part of the Southern Examining Group) will send examples of marked work. Other boards will probably do the same. The International Baccalaureate includes examples in their internal assessment guide for teachers. I have included two fictitious reports on the same practical, one with commentary, at the end of this chapter. I have also included two synopses of actual qualitative articles, with brief comments.

What follows, then, is the generally accepted format, around which most articles vary quite a bit. Qualitative, inductive work will follow much the same format but will not have a specific hypothesis to test. However, it will have overall aims clearly set out. Another major difference will be that the 'results' section will tend to merge with the discussion. Otherwise, reporting of procedures and evaluation of findings, overall design and method should all be similar.

Plagiarism

Perhaps I was wrong about rules above. Plagiarism is copying directly from another's work *or* paraphrasing it so closely that it is recognisably similar. This includes taking other people's data. When formally published this is illegal and people can be sued for it. On college courses, if coursework counts towards final marks then plagiarism is exactly the same as cheating in an exam. On many courses the ruling is stiff – one substantial piece of copying fails the entire work and perhaps that whole element of coursework. The main point is that coursework marked as individual *must be your own work*. Don't attempt the 'I copied notes from Gross then didn't realise when I copied from the notes' gambit. Plagiarism is plagiarism, intentional or not. Copying notes directly from texts is, in any case, quite pointless. Educationally we learn very little from copying, as you'll know from your psychological studies of memory and learning processes. The ethical point is that copying is *stealing*. Just don't ever copy from texts. Of course you can't invent your ideas. Learning is about appreciating what has gone before, then, hopefully, adding to it. The best procedure is to read, *make your own notes*, close any books, ask yourself questions to see how far you've understood, *then* attempt to write out the ideas as you now see them. If you use a direct quotation you *must* make this clear. This is just as important in the introduction and discussion sections of practical reports as in any essay.

THE SECTIONS OF A STANDARD REPORT

Box 23.1 shows a skeleton scheme of the various sections of a report.

Box 23.1

Title
Abstract/summary
Introduction/aims/literature review
Hypotheses
Method: Design
Participants
Materials/Apparatus
Procedure
Results: Description/Summary
Analysis/Treatment
Discussion
Conclusion
References
Appendices

THE TITLE

This should be as concise as possible. You don't need 'An investigation to see whether . . .' or similar. You just need the main variables. Very often, in an experiment, you can use the IV and DV. For instance, 'The effect of imagery and rehearsal methods on recall of verbal material' will adequately describe a (probably familiar) study. For a field investigation using correlation, 'The relationship between age and attitude to environmental issues' says enough.

ABSTRACT

Your abstract should stand out from the rest of the report by being in a box, in a different colour, indented or in a different font. It is a skeleton of the main features of the work, 'abstracted' from it, in around 200 words at most. Yours do *not* need any detail of methods for instance. Have a look at the 'good report' example. Abstracts are very hard indeed to learn to write. Just stick to the essential points – the aim/hypothesis, the main design, the groups, the results, main conclusion(s). The abstract is *also* known as the 'summary'.

Why on earth do we have a *summary* at the *beginning*? Well, suppose you were interested in whether anyone had done work on your proposed topic: anxiety and jogging behaviour in red-bearded vegetarian East Londoners. As you flip through dozens of journals looking for related work, how much easier it is to see the summary of findings right at the beginning of the article, without having to wade through to the end.

INTRODUCTION

I like to think of this as a funnel:

Start with the general psychological subject area.
Discuss theory and research work which is
relevant to the research topic. Move from
the general area to the particular
hypotheses to be tested via a
coherent and logical argument
as to why the specific predictions have been
made. State the
s p e c i f i c
HYPOTHESIS

You must refer to some relevant research from the literature here, if only from your general psychology textbook. You should research other texts if possible. You can use *Psychlit*, mentioned above, and you could also make good use of the Internet, if available. *Be sure to make a note of every reference you wish to use.* Make a note that every name and date mentioned here *must* appear in your reference list at the end of the report. 'Gross', 'Hayes' or 'Cardwell *et al.*' are not 'references' if they are not mentioned here.

As an example of the funnelling argument required, let's run through the introduction to our imagery experiment described briefly in Chapter 3. The introduction to a study testing this hypothesis need not contain a five-page essay on the psychology of memory, including Ebbinghaus' work and the performance of eye-witnesses in court. The hypothesis test belongs within a specialised area of memory research. We can move our reader through the introduction in the following steps:

- The concepts of short- and long-term memory stores
- Outline of the two-process memory model
- Phenomena the model explains, such as primacy and recency in free-recall tasks
- Focus in on the model's emphasis on rehearsal as the process by which material is transferred to the long-term store
- Introduce the 'cognitive' objection that humans always attempt to construct meaning out of incoming sensory data; give an example of what this means

- From this theory it follows that an attempt to give an unconnected word list some 'life', by visualising the items and connecting them, should be more successful for memory than the rehearsal that we assume occurs when participants just read for learning
- Additional support could be given here, referring to previous similar studies and the work on imagery in the literature.

We have argued through to our specific prediction. It only remains to state the aims and hypothesis in the clearest terms so there can be no doubt about what are the expected outcomes.

STATING AIMS

One aim of our research is to provide evidence to support our hypothesis, using a free-recall experiment under two conditions. An overall aim is to challenge the traditional two-store memory model. Aims are what the research project is for, what it is supposed to do. In qualitative projects, aims may be more wide ranging, more exploratory and therefore less specific than those in a hypothesis-testing project. However, they still must be clearly stated and referred back to when the time comes to discuss overall findings.

THE HYPOTHESIS

What you should write here is your *research hypothesis* (see Chapter 1). It contains your research predictions – what you expect to happen. Some texts treat the *research* hypothesis and the *alternative* hypothesis as the same thing. However, the alternative hypothesis is a claim about *underlying* (and hypothetical) *populations*. This is rarely what is written in research reports. What is required here is a clear statement, in specific terms, of *what you expect to happen* or what difference/ correlation is to be tested. For instance, our hypthesis in the memory experiment might be that *mean correct recall scores will be higher in the imagery condition than in the reading condition*.

There is a tradition, which you may encounter, of attempting to write out the *null hypothesis* at this point. This is an odd requirement. Almost all 'null hypotheses' written here in student work are not a null hypothesis but the research hypothesis as described above with the word 'not' inserted somewhere. The null hypothesis, should you be required to write it, is *not* a prediction of what will happen but a claim about underlying populations, often that means are equal or that the population correlation is zero. Re-read Chapter 11 if necessary in order to reinforce these concepts. Note that the strict null hypothesis and alternative hypothesis cannot contain the term 'significant' since this would be illogical. The null hypothesis is what we assume is true in order to *assess* significance so it can't, in turn, predict 'no significance'. However, a prediction of what will happen in a research study may contain the term 'significant'. Most psychological reports don't, in fact, use the term because they take it for granted that any reported difference cited as 'evidence' will have been tested for significance. Tutors may insist on your use of the term in order to reinforce teaching of the point that *any* old difference just will not do!

Either way, what is essential is that variables are precisely defined and predictions made absolutely clear. Remember, your results analysis must relate back *directly* to the exact predictions made here. It will be uninformative to say 'people will remember better after caffeine'. The hypothesis or prediction should also not contain the underlying rationale. For instance we do not say 'There is a correlation between self-esteem and academic achievement because people feel better when they are successful' – this is more a description of the *aim* of the study. We simply hypothesise or predict a correlation between self-esteem scores and a precise measure of academic achievement – say, number of GCSE and A level passes. Sometimes it would be awkward, in your hypothesis, to spell out exactly what will be the operational definition of a construct to be measured. In such cases psychologists refer to the term specifically but leave detailed operationalisation until the 'design' or 'materials' heading of their 'method' section – see below. Here is an example we encountered in Chapter 1:

> Relative to a control group receiving no training, participants trained in the extension rule [will] commit fewer conjunction errors. (Fisk and Pidgeon, 1997)

Fisk and Pidgeon make quite clear what their dependent variable is but the detailed description of their measure of a 'conjunction error' will appear in the 'method' section of their report.

Table 23.1 contains loose statements of some hypotheses from the Chapter 20 exercises with possible wordings of the alternative hypothesis and prediction for the study. You might like to try writing out column two or three whilst only looking at column one.

THE METHOD

It is customary and convenient, but not absolutely necessary, to break the method used down into the following four subheadings. Materials and procedure may often be one

Table 23.1   Loose, alternative and research hypotheses

Loose	Alternative	Research
5. People will be worse on a sensori-motor task in front of an audience	The mean number of sensori-motor task errors made in front of an audience is higher than the mean number of errors made when alone.	Participants in the audience condition will make more errors on the sensori-motor task than will participants performing alone.
7. Members of couples will have similar attractiveness ratings because like attracts like.	The population correlation between ratings of male and female partners on attractiveness is greater than zero.	There will be a (significant) positive correlation between attractiveness ratings of male and female partners.
10. Non-rhyming words are harder to read.	Mean time to read non-rhyming words is higher than mean time to read rhyming words.	A (significant) difference will be found between mean times for reading rhyming and non-rhyming words.

heading. Different research journals have very different traditions for their methods sections.

Design

This describes the 'skeleton' outline of the study – its basic framework. For instance, is it an experiment or not? If it is, what design is used (repeated measures, etc.)? What conditions are there, and how many groups are used? What is the purpose of each group (control, placebo etc.)? How many participants are in each group (though this information can go in the 'participants' section below)? In many cases, describing the groups will be a way of describing the IV. In any case, both the IV and DV should be specified exactly here.

What controls have been employed? Is there counterbalancing and, if so, of what form? In our experiment on imagery, we could say:

> We used a repeated measures design with one group of 15 participants who were presented with a 20-item word list in two conditions. In one condition, participants were instructed to use image-linking and in the other they were told only to read each word for learning. Order of taking conditions was reversed for half the participants. The DV was number of correct items produced under free recall conditions.

. . . and that's about enough. You don't need to give any details of procedure or materials used, otherwise you'll find yourself laboriously repeating yourself later on.

If the study is non-experimental, its overall approach (e.g. observational) can be stated along with design structures such as longitudinal, cross-sectional etc. There may be independent and dependent variables which are uncontrolled, such as number of pedestrians waiting at a crossing and whether a drivers stops or not. Controls, such as measures of inter-observer reliability, may have been incorporated. Don't mention details here, just that the control was employed.

Participants

Give numbers, including how many in each group, and other details relevant to the study. If someone wishes to replicate your findings about 'adolescents' and their self-concepts, it is important for them to know exactly what ages and sex your participants were. These variables are less important in technical laboratory tasks, though general age range is usually useful and handedness may be relevant. Other variables, such as social class or occupation might be highly relevant for some research topics. Certainly important is how naïve participants were to psychology. Otherwise, keep details to a minimum. How were participants obtained? How were they allocated to the various experimental groups (if not covered in your 'design')? It is unlikely that participants will be a 'random sample'.

Materials/Apparatus

Again, apply the golden rule: *give enough detail for a proper replication to be possible*. This means giving specifications of constructed equipment (finger-maze, illusion box) and source (manufacturer, make, model) of commercial items (tachistoscope, computer). Exact details of all written materials should be given here or in an appendix, including: word lists, questionnaires, lists people had to choose from, pictures and so on. You *don't* need to give details of blank paper or pencils!

In our memory study we would need two lists of words because we can't have people learning the same list twice without a mammoth confounding variable. We would state in this section how we justify the equivalence of our two lists – selected from word frequency list, same number of concrete and abstract terms, etc.

It may be useful to include a diagram or photo of an experimental set-up or seating arrangements.

The source of questionnaires should be cited (and referenced later). If questionnaires are 'home-grown' then there should be a description of how the measure was developed and any information, if possible, on its reliability or validity. A sample questionnaire can be included in the appendix section, unless it is a very well known instrument.

Procedure

The rule here is simple. Describe *exactly* what happened from start to finish in testing. This must be enough for good replication. Any standardised instructions should be included here or in an appendix, including any standard answers to predicted questions from participants. The exact wording used in training participants to use imagery in our memory experiment should be included, together with instructions for the reading condition and any practice trials included.

It is very tempting to 'skim' the materials and procedure sections and give far too little detail. My advice if you're not sure you've written enough is:

GIVE IT TO A FRIEND OR RELATIVE TO READ!

If your mother or boyfriend can understand exactly what happened, if they could go off and do it, then it's clear enough. (They might not get on too well with the other sections without some psychological knowledge.)

RESULTS

Description

Very many early psychology practical reports simply present a table of data or statistical summary here and no verbal description. It is very important to realise that one's description of results at this point carries on the verbal style of the previous sections of the report. *You tell your reader, in words, what you found*. Tables and charts are supplementary aids to communication. Raw data generally go in an appendix. A *summary table* of these (only) is presented here, including frequencies or means and standard deviations or their equivalents. You should not include every measure of central tendency and dispersion you can think of. Marks are awarded for *appropriate* selection of statistical summaries not every summary possible. The mean or the median or the mode will be appropriate, depending on how you have gathered and treated/arranged your data. Any tables (appearing here or in the appendix) should be well headed and labelled. For instance, a summary of our experimental result starting like Table 23.2 is inadequate. What do the numbers stand for? We need a heading like 'Number of words recalled in two recall conditions'. If results are times, state 'seconds' or 'minutes'; if they are distance measurements, state the units.

Table 23.2 Inadequate results table

Participant	Imagery	Rehearsal
1	12	8
2	15	12
etc.	etc.	etc.
:	:	:

You might wish to present a chart of your data, such as a histogram or scattergram. Make sure these are clearly headed too, and that the vertical and horizontal axes have titles. If there are multiple columns in coded shading, for instance, your chart will also require a 'legend'.

Tables and charts should occur in the text of the report where they are relevant, not in an appendix. They will also need numbering for reference purposes. The number goes with the title. Note that charts are 'figures' and tables of data (like Table 23.2) are *not* 'figures'.

Don't litter your work with charts looking at the data from various angles. Only one chart is usually useful in a simple experiment, one which demonstrates the main effect found. Why should the reader be interested in a chart showing a column for each individual's score (see p. 244)? Why would they want to see a pie chart, bar chart and line chart of the same data? Why would they want to see the distribution of all scores unless this is referred to in deciding which test to use, for instance? Ask yourself, 'What does my reader *need*?', not 'How can I make the report look as stunning or pretty as possible?' Markers will not give extra marks for superfluous charts.

Don't trust computers to draw your charts for you. Without an understanding of what the chart should be representing you are very likely to produce a naff graph. *SPSS*, for instance, will produce the misleading kind of bar chart presented on p. 244 unless you tell it not to. Computer drawn charts still require full labelling and heading. Charts with 'Variable 0001' on one axis are not terribly useful.

Analysis or 'treatment' of results

It is best to *tell* your reader when you've finished describing your data and are about to analyse them, e.g. by using an inferential statistical test. If there are several hypotheses to test, or different treatments, take one at a time and divide this section into subsections ((a), (b), etc.) with a heading for each one stating which hypothesis is being tested in each case. *State which statistical test is being applied, to which data, and justify the application*, using the sorts of decision procedure outlined in Chapter 20. Never say 'the results were tested . . .'. State exactly *which* results. The simplest table of data can be tested in several ways.

State the result of the test clearly and compare this with the appropriate critical value. Justify the choice of this critical value, including N or degrees of freedom, number of tails, and the corresponding level of probability under H_0 (e.g '$p < 0.05$'). Box 23.2 is a quick exercise in noting what can be missing from statements of significance.

Box 23.2   Incomplete significance statements

Significance statements	What's missing
'The *t* test showed that differences were significant.'	Usually only *one* difference is tested at a time. *Which* difference? Significant at what level? How many degrees of freedom? 1- or 2-tailed test?
'There was a strong correlation between the two variables.'	*Which* two? Positive or negative? What value? Was it significant? If so, at what level? 1- or 2-tailed?
'There was a significant difference between the two conditions at the 1% level.'	*Which* conditions? 1- or 2-tailed?

State whether the null hypothesis is being rejected or retained. If required, define each null hypothesis (here rather than at the end of the introduction – see above). If there are a number of test results, these could be presented in a clear summary table.

Calculations of your tests, if you wish to include them, should appear only in an appendix. Many calculations these days will be performed by computer or dedicated calculator. The software used, and intermediary results, can be mentioned in an appendix but are not really relevant except for specialist data treatments.

Actual journal articles never show calculations or include raw data and rarely justify the statistical test chosen. However, this information is always available through private correspondence. Students are often asked to substitute for the real-life situation by including these as appendices, though tests should always be justified.

DISCUSSION

Do *not* be tempted to give brief attention to your findings here then revert back to another essay on your topic. In general, *very little new research or background theory should be introduced into your discussion.* You should rely on what you wrote in your introduction. Here you discuss your findings in the light of the argument in the introduction. On occasion, because of what has shown up in your study, or as an overall comment, you might include a new reference, but these should be absolutely minimal.

Summarising the findings

The first step here is to explain in non-statistical language just what has happened in the results section. These results must then be related to the hypotheses you set out to test, and to the original aims of the research. These in turn are then related to the background theory, showing support or a need to modify theory in the light of contradictory or ambiguous findings. Unexpected findings or 'quirks' in the results can also be discussed as a secondary issue. From time to time, such 'oddities' lead in novel research directions. You can try to offer some explanations of these if you have good reasons. A verbal summary of statistical findings may be useful where several tests in the results analysis have been treated one by one in the discussion.

Evaluating the method

The conscientious researcher always evaluates the design and method, picking out flaws and areas of weakness. This isn't just to nitpick. A reader of the report might well come back and accuse the researcher of not considering such weaknesses. The researcher can forestall such criticism by presenting a good argument as to why the weakness should not have serious effect. The emphasis of the evaluation depends partly on the outcome:

a) If we got the result we expected, we should look carefully at the design for possible confounding variables producing a type I error. If we were hoping to find no difference, (e.g. to reject an earlier finding), we should look for ways in which the design and procedures may have hidden differences or relationships.

b) If we failed to get a predicted difference, we should look for sources of random variables (though research with a successful outcome may also have been affected by these). What aspects of the design, procedures and materials used did we find unsatisfactory? We should also look for any confounding variable which might have acted in a direction which *obscures* our predicted effect.

Not everything in an experiment or investigation can be perfect. There is no need to talk about not controlling temperature or background noise unless there is good reason to suppose that variation in these could have seriously affected results. Usually this is quite unlikely. Have a look back to Hovey's study in Chapter 3.

Suggest modifications and extensions

Most research leads on to more research. From the considerations made so far you should be able to suggest modifications of this design, or quite new directions, which will follow up on or check the critical points and new speculations made.

If you find yourself stuck for something to say, do avoid the kneejerk reaction of 'We should have tested more participants'. This is often said under a misapprehension of the purpose and nature of experiments and sampling. Chapter 2 explains why, to some extent, larger samples aren't always better. If you tested 30 participants in two conditions of a tightly controlled experiment then you shouldn't require more. If you *do* say you needed more participants then you should explain exactly *why* you think so and the same goes for the suggestion that a sex difference for the effect should now be investigated.

Conclusion

Most reports wind up with some form of 'final comment'. Avoid repeating a summary or abstract at this point. That is not necessary. What you can do is to make some summarising comment in terms of overall findings, their relationship to the relevant model or theory and implications for the future.

REFERENCES

This can be a finicky aspect of writing a report, especially if you've referred to a lot of different research in your work. It is also the section which will infuriate tired tutors most if omitted or poorly done. There is often a lot of confusion over what exactly counts as a reference. Exactly what should be included?

Golden rule number 2 is:

If you referred to it directly somewhere in your text, include it. If you didn't refer to it, don't include it!

If you wrote '. . . Gross (1992) argues that . . .'. this *is* a reference. The date means you're telling the reader where you got the information from. If you happened to read Gross' textbook whilst preparing your practical or trying to write it up – it may be where you got Bower (1977) from, for instance – then Gross is *not* a reference but Bower will be, if you included it. Strictly speaking, if you read about Bower *only* in Gross, it is a secondary reference. You can say 'Bower (1977) as cited in Gross (1996)' in your text, then give the Bower and Gross references in the 'References' section.

In fact there are various systems of secondary referencing and what counts as secondary can be debatable. What is essential is simply that the reader should be able to locate precisely the work you have referred to. This is the one and only purpose of referencing. Quotations should be referenced, *with the page number*. If you want to tell your reader what you read but didn't specifically refer to in your text, put these titles under 'Bibliography'. Your 'references' are what and only what your text literally refers to, not what you read in total.

Most psychologists write references in the way they appear at the back of this book – the Harvard system of referencing, using the format and punctuation shown below:

For a **book**: Author's name, initials, (year), *title*. Place of publication: publisher.

For an **article**: Author's name, initials, (year), title. *Journal*, vol, part, page numbers.

Notice that journal articles have the journal title in italics (you can use underline). The article is in ordinary print. For books the book title gets special treatment and is italicised. There can be a few awkward ones which were articles in someone else's collection of articles, government reports, MSc theses and so on. In all cases the important criterion is simply that your reader can easily locate the specific work.

APPENDICES

These might contain: calculations, instructions given to participants, memory list items, questionnaires and so on. These continue your normal page numbering. Separate topics go in separate, numbered appendices ('Appendix 1', 'Appendix 2', etc.).

GENERAL PRESENTATION

It is useful to have page numbering throughout. You might find it convenient to refer to pages in your text. A title page sets the whole project off well and a contents page helps the reader go to specific sections. If you have presented a set of projects together, it might help to begin the whole set with a contents page and to have a 'header' on each page telling the reader what particular practical they're in.

CHECKLIST FOR WRITING A PRACTICAL REPORT

(Note: some of these points will not apply to non-experimental or qualitative work)

TITLE   Does your title give a brief, but clear indication of the content, including the specific variables studied?

CONTENTS   Have you numbered every page? Have you included a contents page listing main sections of the report?

ABSTRACT/SUMMARY   Does your summary cover the aims, IV, DV, participants, design, measures, main statistical results and conclusions of the research project? Does it convey a brief, essential impression of the research in less than 200 words?

INTRODUCTION   Have you given a brief general overview of the issues and concepts that are relevant to the topic which places the research in context? Is there an account of similar or related studies? Have you explained why your study was undertaken? Have you explained the main aims of the investigation? Are hypotheses (if any) clearly stated in a straightforward, measurable form?

METHOD   Will your readers have enough detail to repeat the study exactly as you did it? Have you chosen a suitable set of subheadings which organise the information clearly?

DESIGN   Have you stated the main design form (field observation, repeated measures experiment, etc.)? Have you explained briefly why this design was selected? Have you explained the purpose of the different groups and given numbers in each? Have you identified the IV and DV, *if there are any*, and described conditions? Have you listed controls introduced ('blinds', counterbalancing)?

PARTICIPANTS   Is it clear who they were, why and how they were chosen or obtained? Have you provided any additional information which may be relevant to the research (age, sex, first language, naïveté)?

MATERIALS/APPARATUS   Have you described these in sufficient detail for replication? Have you made use, where necessary, of drawings and diagrams? Have you described any technical apparatus? Have you included word lists, questionnaires etc. (in an appendix)?

PROCEDURE   Have you explained, in sequence, exactly what the researcher did and what each participant experienced? Have you reported in full any important instructions given? Have you given a clear impression of the layout and arrangement of events? Are there details of your debrief session or procedure?

RESULTS   Have you written clearly about main findings? Is there a summary table of results giving totals, means, standard deviations or their equivalents? Are lengthy, raw data in an appendix? Have you exploited an opportunity for visual presentation? Are tables and figures fully and clearly labelled and numbered? Have you given each a title and are units clearly shown? Have you clearly explained any coding or rating systems, scoring of questionnaires or other ways data were manipulated before final analysis?

ANALYSIS/TREATMENT Have you explained and justified your choice of statistical test for analysis? Have you stated clearly which 'results' (i.e. which data in what form) are being tested by each test you introduce? Have you listed the results of the tests, their significance, the degrees of freedom, number of tails? Are calculations in the appendix, or an explanation of how they were performed (e.g. computer)? Are statements made about rejection or not of each null hypothesis?

DISCUSSION Is there a verbal description of statistical findings? Do you explain how the results relate to your hypotheses and any background theory or prior research? Can you explain any unexpected results? Have you evaluated the design and procedures used? Have you considered alternative explanations of results? Have you suggested modifications, extensions or new research to deal with these last three points?

REFERENCES Have you listed all and only the studies which were mentioned in your text (with a date in brackets)? Have you used the standard Harvard format for references?

APPENDICES Have you labelled each appendix clearly? Do the appendices continue the page numbering? Are the appendices included on your contents page and referred to at appropriate points in the text?

COMMENTS ON A STUDENT PRACTICAL REPORT

What you see below are two *fictitious* student reports. *The first is not a good report*, so please use it carefully as a model, taking into account all the comments I've made beside it. My reasoning was this. If I comment on a perfect report the recent newcomer to psychology and its practical writing conventions would have little clue as to what typically goes *wrong* in report writing. To include all possible mistakes would be to produce an unreadable piece of work serving little purpose. In this third edition, however, I have succumbed to persistent pleas to include a 'good' version of the report and this follows the 'average' version below. I resisted this for a while because I would be concerned that the 'good' version might be seen as *the* model, with tutors having constantly to explain that, although a student's report follows all the points in the 'good' version, it still has faults in the context of the particular assignment that has been set. So please see this as a fair example for specific circumstances and not a gold standard model that can serve all purposes.

The 'average' report below would be roughly in the mid-range at A-level, perhaps a little lower at first year degree level (I think), but its exact mark would depend upon the level or particular syllabus. Hence, I've refrained from assessing it formally. It contains quite a lot of omissions and ambiguities, but few outright mistakes. Too many of these might be misleading. I have coded comments as follows:

✓ A good point

✗ An error, omission, ambiguity; in general, a point which would count cumulatively to lower the overall mark for the report

? An ambiguity or odd point which would not lower the mark on its own but could contribute to an overall lower mark if it were repeated. This is also used for grammatical and conventional style points which, again, are not terribly bad on their own but which may accumulate into a feeling of 'not quite so good' (but this *does* depend on your level of study).

Assume that materials mentioned as being in appendices *were* included (often they aren't!).

For ease of reference, the comments are laid out progressively, side by side with the report.

AN EXPERIMENT TO SHOW WHETHER PEOPLE ARE[1] AFFECTED BY KNOWING A WRITER'S SEX WHEN THEY JUDGE A PIECE OF WRITING

ABSTRACT

We[2] set out to see whether people make sexist assumptions about an author when they read their writing. We asked 39 participants to read an article and told half of them (19) that the author was a man and the others that it was a woman. We did this by making the writer's name 'John Kelly' for one article and 'Jean Kelly' for the other.[3] Because of stereotyping we expected the 'Jean Kelly' group to think worse of the article's quality.[4] Results were not significant[5] and the null hypothesis was kept. It was thought that the article was too neutral and women might have voted lower on a technical article and men lower on a child-care article. If results were valid this could be interpreted as a change in attitude since Goldberg's (1968) work.[6]

INTRODUCTION

People use stereotypes when they look at other people. When we perceive people it's like looking at things in the world. We look through a framework of what we've learnt and we don't see the real thing but our impressions of it are coloured by what we expect and our biases. Bruner (1957) said we 'go beyond the information given';[7] we use what's there as 'cues' to what we interpret is really there. For example, when we see a car on the road and a mountain behind it, the mountain might look only twice as high as the car but because we know how far away the mountain is we can estimate what size it really is. When we take a picture of a pretty sight we often get telephone wires in the way because we've learnt not to see what isn't important. Also, we take a shot of Uncle Arthur on the beach and he comes out really small because we thought he looked much bigger in the viewfinder because he's important to us. Bruner and his friends started the 'new look' in perception where they experimented with perception to show that we're affected by our emotions, motivation and 'set'. In one experiment they showed sweet jars to children that were either filled with sand or sweets.[8] The children saw the jars with sweets as larger, so we are affected by our past experience and what we *want*. (Dukes and Bevan, 1951.)[9]

To show that a small bit of information affects our judgement of persons, Asch (1946) gave some people some words to describe a person. The words were the same except that 'warm' and 'cold' were different. This even works when the person is real because Kelley (1950) introduced students to a 'warm' or 'cold' person and they liked the 'warm' one more. The 'warm' person was seen quite differently from the 'cold' one.

Sex differences are a myth.[10] Condry and Condry (1976) showed people a film of a nine-month-old child reacting to a jack-in-the-box. If they were told he was a boy the reaction was thought of as 'anger' but for a 'girl' it was thought of as 'fear'. Deux (1977) reviewed several studies and found females often explain their performance as luck, even if they do well, but men say their ability helped them. This was where the task they did was unfamiliar. This means that men and women accept their stereotype and go along with it in

1. ? Don't need 'An experiment . . .'; title could be shorter, 'The effect of author's sex on evaluation of an article'.

2. ? Conventional reports are written in *passive* not *personal* mode; e.g. 'The theory was tested that author's sex affects judgement of writing.' '39 participants were asked . . .'

3. ✓ IV is clearly described.

4. ✗ DV is not at all defined. How was 'thinking worse of' measured?

5. ✗ Results very poorly reported. What data were tested and how?

6. ✓ Some brief statement of conclusions included.

7. ✓ Quoted phrase is in quote marks and attributed to an author, with date – this *must* be referenced at the end of the report.

8. (Poor children! – you wouldn't think they'd let psychologists do that sort of thing!)

9. ✓ A broad start about factors which affect judgement in perception. The introduction should now introduce *person* perception and narrow down to sex-role stereotype effects.

10. ✗ !!! A gigantic and unjustified assumption made here; there are *some* differences (e.g. reading development rate); the claim needs qualifying with the use of 'some', 'many' or examples and trends.

their lives.[11] Maccoby and Jacklin's experiment[12] in 1974 showed that males describe themselves with independent terms (e.g. intelligent, ambitious) but females use more social terms (e.g. co-operative, honest).

A psychologist called[13] Goldberg (1968) got female students to read articles written by a man or a woman (they thought). The articles written by a man were rated as better. This is the experiment we're doing here.[14]

Hypothesis

People thinking an author is male will think some articles are better written than people thinking the author is female.[15]

METHOD[16]

Design

The experiment was independent samples.[17] There were two groups. The independent variable was the sex of the author and the dependent variable was the way they judged the article.[18]

Participants

We used a random sample of 39 participants from the college canteen.[19] Originally there were 20 in the male author condition and 20 in the female author condition but the results for one in the male author condition went missing. The participants were all students except for one who was a friend of one of the students.

Materials

We used an article from *The Guardian Weekend* magazine about travelling in Tuscany. This is in Appendix 1. It was 908 words long and was printed on two sheets of A4 paper. We also used a rating sheet (in Appendix 2) where participants recorded their rating of the article for quality and interest on a 10-point scale.[20,21] This also had some questions on it to make sure the participants had noticed the name of the author.[22]

Procedure

We sat each participant down and made them feel at ease. We told them there would be no serious deception and that they would not be 'tested' or made to feel stupid in any way. We said we just wanted their opinion of something and that their opinion would be combined with others and their results would be anonymous.[23] We then gave them the instructions shown below. All this was done in a standardised way.[24]

> 'We would like you to read the article we are about to give you. Please read it once quickly, then again slowly. When you have done that, please answer the questions on the sheet which is attached to the article. Try to answer as best you can but please be sure to answer all questions *in the order given.*'[25]

If the participant's number was odd they received the female author where the article

11. ✗ Another grand assumption here, following a very specific result; needs qualification.

12. ✗ It wasn't an experiment; it was a review of mostly *ex post facto* studies.

13. ? Don't need 'A psychologist called ...'

14. ✗ The leap into the hypothesis is *far* too sudden here; we lurch from good background description straight into the hypothesis without some introduction to the (different) nature of the study being reported.

15. ✗ Hypothesis a bit vague; states the independent variable but should also specify the DVs of 'quality' and 'interest'. Hence there are *two* hypotheses – one for quality and one for interest.

16. ✓ Good that all sections of the method are present and correctly titled.

17. ✓ Correct design and this *is* an experiment.

18. ✗ Again, DV not specified; it doesn't need complete description here but there should be an operational definition of the measure – 'quality was measured by scores given on a 10-point scale' or similar. Other controls have not been specified.

19. ✗ Almost certainly *not* randomly selected from the canteen; no mention of the sex of participants and this might be important in this particular study.

20. ✓ Materials well described.

21. ✗ Notice that tucked away here is the first, and only, mention of the 10-point scale; we could have heard about this earlier; we still don't know which way the scale runs – is 10 high or low quality?

22. ✗ The technique of asking questions, including dummy ones, in order to ensure participants noticed the sex of the author, deserves clearer presentation, possibly in the design (as a type of 'control') or procedure. It is tucked away here in the materials section.

23. ✓ Ethical considerations well implemented here.

24. ? Ambiguity; was the initial rapport session standardised, or just the instruction giving?

25. ✓ Exact instructions given are included.

was written by 'Jean Kelly'. The other participants were given 'John Kelly' sheets. In one case this order was reversed by mistake.[26]

Participants were then left to read the article and no questions were answered by the experimenters unless it did not concern the reading at all, for instance, if they wanted the light turned on or heater turned off. Questions about the reading were answered 'Please answer as best you can and we can talk about ("that problem") after you've finished. That way, all our participants do exactly the same thing. Thank you for your co-operation.' The experimenters kept a watchful eye to ensure that instructions were followed in the correct order.

RESULTS

Data obtained

The results from the two groups were collected and organised into the table of raw data shown in Appendix 3. The averages and standard deviations were calculated and these are shown in Table 1.[27]

	Author	
	Female	**Male**
Quality		
Mean	6.7	6.3
SD	1.5	2.3
Interest		
Mean	4.3	5.2
SD	1.1	1.3

You can see from this Table[28] that the male got a lower rating on quality but a higher rating on interest. This may be because people think men *can* write more interestingly, in general, but women are more likely to be accurate and are generally better with language and the rules of grammar.[29]

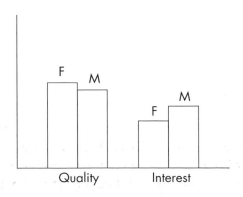

Figure 1[30]

26. ?   This system of allocation of participants might have been mentioned in the
    ✓   'design' or 'participants' sections; good that the mistake was reported however.

27. ✗   Table has no title; it does not state what the values 6.7 etc. *are*; it should refer to
        these as mean ratings on quality and interest at least.

28. ?   Should describe and summarise *for* the reader, not refer to them in this personal
        way.

29. ✗   Any interpretation or speculation belongs in the 'Discussion' section; here, just
        the factual results should be reported.

30. ✗   Chart has no title; 'M' and 'F' have no key (yes, it's obvious what they mean but
        clarity is the keyword here); the vertical scale has no values; the chart is correctly
        drawn as a bar chart (not histogram); hair-splitters may argue that, since male
        and female are qualitatively separate, there should be space between the M and F
        bars, but the approach used here is common and usefully illustrative.

Analysis

We decided to use an unrelated t test on this data to test for difference between the male and female quality and interest means. t tests are parametric and there must be a normal distribution from which the sample comes. Also, there must be homogeneity of variance and the level of measurement is interval.[31,32]

The calculation for t is shown in Appendix 4. [33]

Our t was 0.97 for quality and 1.43 for interest. Neither of these is significant and in both cases we retained the null hypothesis.[34]

DISCUSSION

As we see above, there were small differences between the male and female author groups but the tests showed there was no significance. It could be that there is a difference but our design has failed to show this.[35] Or else there really is no difference in the way people judge this article according to the sex of the author. If this is true then we have contradicted Goldberg's results but these were done in 1968. Perhaps things have changed since then and people no longer judge according to sex on writing. First we will look at the things that could be wrong with our design.[36]

We asked participants to answer some 'dummy' questions so that we could be sure they'd noticed the sex of the author before they rated the article.[37] When we thought about it afterwards, we decided perhaps we should have got them to do the questions (or some of them) *before* they read the article so that they would be aware of the author's sex *while* they were reading it. This might have made a difference and we could do another study like this sometime.[38] We didn't take any notice of the sex of our participants but obviously this might make a difference.[39] Perhaps males would downrate female authors and maybe vice versa. In a future study we could take groups of men and women separately. Another problem was that not everybody would use our scale in the same way. 'Good' might be 7 to one person and 9 to another. We could perhaps have standardised by getting them to rate something else first and then discussing the points on the scale with them.[40] Also, we should have used more participants[41] and participants may have guessed what was going on and there may have been demand characteristics.[42]

We felt that the article used was on a very neutral subject. Goldberg used a selection of articles. Some were on traditionally male subjects and some of the subjects would be more associated with females. We could do the study again using, perhaps, an article on car

31. ✓ Good that test data and *t* test criteria are recognised and described fairly well.

32. ✗ The use of the *t* test here has not been justified – there should be an answer to the criteria given here, showing that *these* data are therefore suitable for a *t* test. The student writing the 'good' report thinks they were not.

33. ✓ Doing calculations *may* help understand the test, and mental effort, in general, is usually rewarded; however, not strictly necessary for A-level and in many other syllabuses; check whether you *need* to show working.

34. ✗ How many degrees of freedom? Was the test one or two-tailed? What level for *p*?

35. ✓ Recognition that a type II error could have occurred and that the outcome, if genuine, needs interpretation in the light of its contradiction of other work.

36. ✓ Deals with type II error possibility first, i.e. looks critically at the method.

37. ? Again, role of dummy questions should have been made clear earlier but we have already taken this weakness into account in our assessment – not a double penalty.

38. ✓ Suggests modifications based on an analysis of the present study's outcomes and weaknesses.

39. ✓ Good! This point from our earlier debits has now been picked up so we can balance this in our assessment.

40. ✓ This point has also been picked up but it's a pity the implications for parametric *t* test assumptions aren't spotted here; should the data have been accepted as interval level then? Really, this is a partial ✗.

41. ✗ Should avoid this knee-jerk point, unless there is a good reason to include it; there were a fair number of participants and with no reason given this is rather an empty point, 'thrown in'.

42. ✗ A difficult one; is the point that people may have guessed *and* there could have
    ? been 'demand characteristics'? If so, there should be an explanation of *why* the effect of demand characteristics is suspected; in what way? If people's guessing was meant *as* a demand characteristic, is this *feasible*? It must always be remembered in independent samples designs of this kind that *you* know what the IV is but how can the participants know? Why should *they* suspect that another author will be a different sex? This is an example of 'ego-centrism' to some extent (not seeing others' perspective), and being wise after the event.

maintenance and one on child-care to see whether this made a difference, like Mischel did.[43]

If our result is genuine then perhaps times have changed since 1968. These days there are female bus drivers, fire-fighters and even boxers.

Bem sees sex stereotypes as a 'straight-jacket'[44] (Gross, 1996, p. 696) and argues that society would improve with a shift towards 'androgyny'. This is where a person has the strengths of both traditional sex-roles. In order to 'discover' androgyny, it was necessary to see masculinity and femininity as not mutually exclusive but as two *independent* dimensions and to incorporate this into a new sort of test which would produce two logically independent scores. Bem developed such a test (1974).[45] It has been shown that people scoring high on Bem's Sex Role Inventory report higher levels of emotional well-being than others (Lubinski *et al.*, 1981 in Gross, 1996[46]) and show higher self-esteem (Spence *et al.*, 1975). Perhaps, from our results, we have shown that people are less likely today to take sex into account when judging the quality of writing because androgyny is more acceptable.[47]

REFERENCES[48]

Asch, S.E. (1946) Forming impressions of personality. *Journal of Abnormal and Social Psychology*, 4, 258–90.

Bem, S.L. (1974) The measurement of psychological androgyny. *Journal of Consulting and Clinical Psychology*, 42(2), 155–62.

Bruner, J.S. (1957) Going beyond the information given. In *Contemporary Approaches to Cognition: a symposium held at the University of Colorado*. Cambridge, MA: Harvard University Press.

Condry, J. and Condry, S. (1976) Sex differences: A study in the eye of the beholder. *Child Development*, 47, 812–19.

Deux, K. (1977) The social psychology of sex roles. In L. Wrightsman, *Social Psychology*, Monterey, CA: Brooks/Cole.

Dukes, W.F. and Bevan, W. (1951) Accentuation and response variability in the perception of personally relevant objects. *Journal of Personality*, 20, 457–65.

Goldberg, P. (1968) Are women prejudiced against women? *Transaction*, April, 1968.

Gross, R.D. (1996) *Psychology: The Science of Mind and Behaviour* (third edition). Hodder and Stoughton Educational: London.

Kelley, H.H. (1950) The warm–cold variable in first impressions of people. *Journal of Personality*, 18, 431–9.

Lubinski *et al.* (1981) as cited in Gross, R.D. (above).

Maccoby, E.E. and Jacklin, C.N. (1974) *The Psychology of Sex Differences*. Stanford, CA: Stanford University Press.

Spence, J.T., Helmreich, R.L. and Stapp, J. (1975) Ratings of self and peers on sex-role attributes and their relation to self-esteem and concepts of masculinity and femininity. *Journal of Personality and Social Psychology*, 32, 29–39.

Atkinson, R.L., Atkinson, R.C., Smith, E.E. and Bem, D.J. (1993) *Introduction to Psychology*. Fort Worth: Harcourt Brace Jovanovitch[49].

43. ✓ Good extension of study proposed – but looks dangerously like an ANOVA design! Are we ready for the testing involved? Remember, we can't just do several t tests (or Mann–Whitneys – see introduction to Chapter 16).

 ✗ 'Mischel' has no date and does not appear in the reference list.

44. ✓ Has quoted and acknowledged, with page number, Gross's specific term here.

45. ✗ !!! This suddenly technical and academic sounding piece of text, compared to most of the rest of the report, should set alarm bells ringing for the marker. Most markers, after only a little experience, can spot this kind of change and will reach for the most likely textbooks to check for plagiarism. It is, in fact, cribbed straight from Gross (1992), page 696 – a clue is given just above! This really would be a shame in an otherwise fair report.

46. ✓ An appropriate secondary reference. The writer obtained the information from Gross and doesn't have access to the original. Technically that would be true for many of these 'references' but this is a can of worms we'll leave aside for now. What is essential at this level is that the reader can trace every reference.

47. ✓ Good attempt to feed the result into general context. Some of these results are up to 20 years old. However, in some colleges it's difficult to get hold of more up-to-date research to relate to but try, if you can, to include more recent work.

48. ✓ Good references, put in conventional style and most in alphabetical order. One missing.

49. ✗ 'Allo, 'allo! What's this one doing here? It's not in alphabetical order and, much more important, it *wasn't* referred to in the text of the report at any time. It's probably been read to do the report but it *isn't* a reference. It could be included as 'background reading' or, sometimes 'bibliography'. (But beware! Sociologists use 'bibliography' in much the same way as psychologists use 'references'!)

A better report of the same practical now follows overleaf.

EFFECT OF AUTHOR'S APPARENT SEX ON ASSESSMENT OF A WRITTEN ARTICLE

ABSTRACT

In an attempt to assess current effects of sex-role stereotyping on judgement of writing skill, Goldberg's (1968) study was partially replicated. 25 participants were asked to read an article. 12 participants were told the author was male whilst 13 were told the author was female. Whilst the 'female' author was rated higher on quality and lower on interest than was the 'male' author, neither difference was significant ($p > 0.05$). The neutrality of the assessed article is discussed and the suggestion made that judgements might vary according to author's sex if the supposed authored articles had themselves been sex-typed (e.g. technical or child-care related). The result is only tentatively accepted as evidence of a change in social attitude since Goldberg's work.

INTRODUCTION

Just as our perception of the physical world is affected by the subjective, interpretive and constructive nature of perception, so is our perception of people. In Bruner's (1957) words we 'go beyond the information given' in constructing our perceptual world of objects. Our interpretation of physical stimuli is constantly affected by prior knowledge and expectancy. For example, when we see a car on the road and a mountain behind it, the direct visual stimulus of the mountain might be only twice the height of the car stimulus, yet, because we have experience of interpreting other cues to distance and size, and because we therefore know that the mountain is, in fact, much further away from us than the car, we instantly interpret the mountain as far taller than the car. Our perceptual processes are *selective* in that we can ignore present stimuli – for instance, the telephone wires crossing a photograph of a pretty sight. Bruner and his colleagues were responsible for the 'New Look' movement in perception which demonstrated experimentally the effects of emotions, motivation and 'set' on physical perception. For instance, Dukes and Bevan (1951) showed sweet jars filled with either sand or sweets to 5 year-old children. The children's estimates of the sizes of sweet filled jars were higher than their estimates of the sizes of sand-filled jars, supporting the hypothesis that associated value affects estimations of physical size.

It is of interest whether our perception and impressions of people are affected by the same sorts of processes as are our perceptions of the physical world. To show that varying a small piece of information can affect our judgement of persons, Asch (1946) gave some people a list of terms which described an imaginary person. In two conditions the word lists were identical except for the replacement of 'warm' by 'cold'. The imaginary person described by the words was judged quite differently in the two conditions, with the word 'cold' apparently producing a more negative appraisal on quite a number of other characteristics. This even seems to works with a person who is physically present. Kelley (1950) introduced students to a person previously described to them as either 'warm' or 'cold', along with several other traits which were the same for both descriptions. Having been spoken to by the 'visiting professor', the students in the 'warm' condition assessed him more positively than did those in the 'cold' condition.

Expectancies about sex associated behaviour and traits also seem to affect strongly our perception of people. Condry and Condry (1976) showed people a film of a 9 month-old child reacting to a jack-in-the-box. If they were told he was a boy the reaction was more likely to be reported as 'anger' whereas for a 'girl' the more common description was that of 'fear'. Stereotypical assumptions then appear to affect people's judgements of the *same* target person. This could even be a factor in people's assessments of their *own* characters. Maccoby and Jacklin (1974) showed that males tend to describe themselves with independent terms (e.g. intelligent, ambitious) whereas females tend to use more social terms (e.g. co-operative, honest).

The studies above suggest that a target person's known sex may affect people's direct assessment of that person's character or personality. Being students whose performance is often assessed, we were interested in whether knowledge of a person's gender might influence judgements of their written work. This is obviously an important question since, in a climate of equal opportunity, a person's gender or sex ought not to be relevant to the assessment of their ability. Torrance (1986) found teachers rewarding creative behaviour of boys three times more often than the equivalent behaviour in girls. Goldberg (1968) showed that female students rated several articles more highly when the article indicated a male author than when the apparent author was female. To discover whether this effect might still occur, 30 years on, we attempted a partial replication of this study using just one 'gender-neutral' article, where Goldberg had used several, some more male oriented and some more female oriented. He found that ratings did *not* differ for some of these articles and on at least one, allegedly with more female-oriented content, the female author was rated more highly. For this reason, our hypothesis is not directional, though the main result of Goldberg's study was a male author bias. We asked participants to rate the article on both 'quality' and on 'interest' and we used a mixed-sex sample.

Our hypothesis was that people thinking the author was male would rate the article differently (on interest and on quality) from those thinking the author was female.

METHOD

Design

We used an independent samples experimental design with two groups. The independent variable, being apparent sex of the author, was manipulated so that one group was informed that the author was male while the other groups was informed that the author was female. Dummy questions were used to ensure that the participant was made aware of the sex of the author. Dependent variables measured were quality and interest of the article, both assessed on a 10 point scale.

Participants

We used a sample of 39 participants from the college canteen, selected as haphazardly as possible. There were 12 males and 8 females in the male author condition, 9 males and 10 females in the female author condition. Participants were allocated to conditions on an alternate basis, as selected, and were all students except for one who was a friend of one of the students. Numbers in each condition were originally equal but one participant's results were subsequently mislaid.

Materials

We used an article from *The Guardian Weekend* magazine about travelling in Tuscany. This is provided in Appendix 1. It was 908 words long and was printed on two sheets of A4 paper. One version gave the author's name as 'John Kelly' while the other version used 'Jean Kelly'. We also used a rating sheet (in Appendix 2) where participants recorded their rating of the article for quality and interest on a 10 point scale where 10 signified high value. This also included dummy questions (such as the title of the article, the number of pages, and so on) in order to make sure that participants were aware of the name, and therefore the sex, of the author, when they were making their assessments.

PROCEDURE

We sat each participant down and made them feel at ease. We told them there would be no deception and that they would not be 'tested' or made to feel stupid in any way. We said we just wanted their opinion of something and that their opinion would be combined with others and their results would be anonymous. We then gave them the instructions shown below. The instructions and all statements used in the preliminary briefing were standardised.

Instructions used

'We would like you to read the article we are about to give you. Please read it once quickly, then again slowly. When you have done that, please answer the questions on the sheet which is attached to the article. Try to answer as best you can but please be sure to answer all questions in the order given.'

If the participant's number was odd they received the female author version where the article was written by 'Jean Kelly'. The other participants were given 'John Kelly' sheets. In one case this order was reversed by mistake.

Participants were then left to read the article and no questions were answered by the experimenters unless it did not concern the reading at all, for instance, if they wanted the light turned on or heater turned off. Questions about the reading were answered 'Please answer as best you can and we can talk about that (problem) after you've finished. That way, all our participants do exactly the same thing. Thank you for your co-operation.'

The experimenters monitored participants and checked that instructions were followed in the correct order.

RESULTS

Data obtained

The results from the two groups were collected and organised into the table of raw data shown in Appendix 3. Summary statistics are given in Table 1. The male author received a lower mean rating than the female author on quality, but a higher mean rating on inter-

Table 1 Mean and sd of quality and interest ratings for male and female authors

| | Apparent sex of author | |
	Female	Male
Quality		
Mean	6.7	6.3
SD	1.5	2.3
Median	6	6
Interest		
Mean	4.3	5.2
SD	1.1	1.3
Median	4.5	5

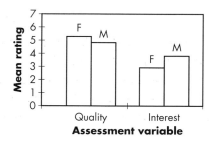

F = Female author condition
M = Male author condition

Figure 1 Mean ratings on quality and interest for female and male author

est. Variation among ratings was higher for the male author on both dependent variables, but particularly so for the quality rating (male sd = 2.3; female sd = 1.5).

Analysis

We decided to use a Mann-Whitney test, since this is appropriate where we wish to test for differences between data in two unrelated groups with data at an ordinal level. Although an unrelated t test would also have been appropriate, we were not confident that our data satisfied assumptions necessary to conduct that test. In particular, since we invented the unstandardised 10 point scale, we did not believe our measurement scale to be at a truly interval level and so our data are converted to ranks in order to calculate U. The calculation is shown in Appendix 4.

U for quality was 183 and U for interest was 164

For significance with $p < 0.05$, where $n_1 = 19$ and $n_2 = 20$, U must be no greater than the critical value of 119 (two-tailed). Therefore neither difference is significant at the $p < 0.05$ level. Both null hypotheses are retained.

DISCUSSION

Although there were small differences between the male and female author groups on quality and interest, inferential analysis showed that these were not significant. In fact, although the mean interest rating for the male author was higher, the rating for quality was higher for the female author. However, for the inferential test used, the median ratings are more relevant and these show no difference all for the quality ratings. The only conclusion possible from the present study is one of no effect of author's sex on article rating. This failure to support Goldberg's work may be related to real changes in the effects of sex-role stereotyping since the time of his study. On the other hand, it may well be that our design has failed to identify an existing difference and we should look now at several weaknesses which could possibly have contributed to this outcome.

We asked participants to answer some 'dummy' questions so that we could be sure they had noticed the sex of the author before they rated the article. In fact, this does not ensure that participants' stereotype schemas are operating *as they read and interpret* the article, only when they are asked to assess it. A solution would be to present some of the dummy questions, including the crucial author name item, *before* participants read the article so that they would be aware of the sex *during* the reading.

Goldberg's participants were all female college students. It could be that females will tend to rate male authors higher and vice versa. However, in our study, with participant sex not separated, any male author bias by female participants could be counteracted, within the results, by female author bias from male participants. We could re-analyse the results separately but then there would be rather a small number of results in each category (male ratings of female author, etc.). There could also be an interaction here with the masculinity or femininity of the article's content. A more complex study could look for participant sex, author sex and article content effects. Mischel (1974) found that participants of both sexes rated a male author more highly on a male dominated topic and a female author more highly on a female dominated topic. We could repeat the study using unambiguously male and female oriented articles, such as one on car maintenance and one on child care (though even these topics are challenged these days as being typically 'male' or 'female'). We had no measure of the 'femininity' or 'masculinity' of the content of our article. We could have partially achieved this either by asking other participants to rate it on this dimension, or by investigating any difference in ratings between male and female participants in a control group not given any author name.

Since our scale was invented for the study we have no evidence of it being used in a standard way by all participants. 'Good' might be 7 to one person and 9 to another. We could perhaps have standardised the scale by getting other participants to rate the same article and then discussing the points on the scale with them.

It is difficult to see how demand characteristics could have operated here to produce a result of no difference. It is unlikely that naïve participants would have guessed the purpose of this experiment or the nature of the hypothesis, given they served in only one condition. However, some students may have served in similar designs elsewhere and many are suspicious of psychology experiments in general. They may just have suspected an independent variable of author sex but they might just as well have suspected a hypothesis based on ethnicity or nationality, given the 'author's' surname. A solution would be to test a non-student sample and/or to include questions about these suspicions in the de-briefing session.

Bem (1975) sees sex stereotypes as a 'straight-jacket' (Gross, 1996, p. 696), and argues that society would improve with a shift towards 'androgyny'. Perhaps, from our results, we might tentatively speculate that such a shift may now have occurred, or at least that people are less likely today to take sex into account when judging the quality of writing. There may have been no shift but simply a weakening of the strength of sex stereotyped assumptions in snap judgements.

REFERENCES

(Assume these were perfect! [most appear in the adequate report, above])

SYNOPSIS OF TWO QUALITATIVE RESEARCH REPORTS

As explained in Chapter 21, the reports below were selected, not as 'models', but as convenient (and relatively short) samples of qualitative reporting styles and techniques. They are not chosen as 'perfect', nor as typical of a type. They are just intended as useful materials for students and tutors.

KEY:

'. . .' = Direct quotation from study
All italics are added
bracketed points [. . . .] indicate my personal comments
*** = Could easily be quantified or tested in quantitative study

Report 1

Christine Kerwin, Joseph G. Ponterotto, Barbara I. Jackson and Abigail Harriss (1993) Racial identity in biracial children: A qualitative investigation. *Journal of Counselling Psychology*, 40(2), 221–231

Abstract

'This article describes a *qualitative* study of issues salient in the development of racial identity for schoolchildren of Black/White racial heritage. *Semi-structured interviews* were conducted individually with *9 Black/White biracial children and their parents* (a total of 6 families). Major findings from this study tend to run counter to problems conjectured in the counselling and related literature. For example, in contrast to deficit models, participant children and adolescents *did not appear to perceive themselves as 'marginal' in two cultures*. The majority of participant children, adolescents and adults demonstrated sensitivity to the views, cultures and values of both the Black and the White communities. Developmental transitions associated with different ages were identified. *Emergent themes yielded hypotheses with implications for future research.'*

INTRODUCTION

$1\frac{1}{2}$ sides on the literature concerned with the identities and adjustment problems of children born to parents from two 'racial' groupings. 'little is known . . .', 'limited research . . .', 'early status of theory . . .' so authors justify qualitative approach to (a) identify critical identity issues . . . (b) . . . generate hypotheses for future qualitative and *quantitative* research.

METHOD

Heading on qualitative research and a justification for the approach in exploratory work; introduction of the 'long interview method' and a reference to an expert commentary on its use and strengths

Sample

Description of children and parents interviewed, including area, ages, 'racial' composition of family. Cites expert on qualitative interview study samples who recommends small N, strangers with no special knowledge of the research topic and a contrast within the sample of age, sex, gender education etc. [little cross-sectional variation possible with small N]. Small N is then justified using several experts who argue that in qualitative methodology 'less is more' and that the crucial factor is the 'potential of each "case" to aid the researcher in developing theoretical insights.' Most participants recommended from school staff. Better response when intermediary used to recruit. Used 'snowballing' strategy to obtain some potential families (see p. 38). High refusal rate. Researchers agreed to use a family if at least one parent agreed to participate and other parent agreed they could. Sampling strategy produced participants above economic and educational average. Limitations of sample discussed. However, 'expert' review of transcripts (the other three article authors) confirmed that 'a range of perspectives had been obtained and that additional data were simply confirming previously gained insights'.

Procedure

All interviewed at home except one at researcher's house. Interview guide developed through literature review to generate 50 questions which were piloted on one non-participant family. Guide also reviewed by research team (who were 'well published in the topic area'). Details of question topics and areas provided and arrangements for probes and prompts (see pp. 145–6). Prompts tailored individually during interview. Many parents covered topics spontaneously. Questions phrased in language appropriate to age, made more natural for younger children.

DATA ANALYSIS

Contrasts qualitative analysis to be used with conventional quantitative methods. Follows stages recommended by expert:

'(a) initial sorting out of important from unimportant data, (b) examination of the slices of data, logical relationships and contradictions, (c) re-reading of transcripts to confirm or disconfirm emerging relationships and beginning recognition of general properties of data, (d) identification of general themes and sorting of the themes in a hierarchical fashion, while discarding those that prove useless in the organisation, (e) review of the emergent themes for each of the interviews and determination of how these can be synthesised into theses.'

Justifies use of audio-recordings [belongs with procedure rather than analysis?]; states that transcripts were made.

'From the approximately 300 pages of typed transcripts, [note this is with just 9 children and 10 parents!] portions of the transcripts were identified that related to the research topic. This was accomplished by highlighting sections . . . related to biracial identity development and transferring these sections to index cards [can be done electronically using the software described on pp. 463–4]. These "data slices" were then further analysed through re-reading and logical relationships were identified. Transcripts were re-read to confirm or disconfirm the emerging possibilities. At this step . . . General themes were identified and the sorting process determined major and minor themes as well as those that did not fit into the hierarchy. From the sorting of findings across the interviews emerged the general theses . . . presented in the Results section [akin to presenting statistical summaries not raw data; but whereas we would all find the same mean, would we all develop the same themes etc.?] . . . Comparisons across parent and child interviews are presented in the Discussion section.' [somewhat arbitrary; could be contrasted in the results section as quantitative data are]

QUALITATIVE VALIDITY PROCEDURE

Argument that validity is strived for through constant collaboration with experts in the department (the other article authors), the effect of this on the researcher's self-monitoring throughout the project, the 'triangulation' of views by interviewing parents and children separately, and re-phrasing of participants' statements during the interviews to clarify positions and consistency. [good to see a specific section which tackles issues of validity. Some of these are akin to quantitative procedures – similar to inter-rater reliability – but more depth and breadth here]

ETHICAL CONSIDERATIONS

Goals, methods and sample questions all agreed with parents beforehand. Just one parent asked that no race issues be raised unless her daughter initiated. All participants expressed comfort with questions, suggesting none be omitted but also suggesting additional ones for future interviews.

RESULTS

Major themes are those identified as important by the 'great majority'. Minor themes were so identified by less than half the respondents. Results for parents are followed by those for children, as parents have provided the major contextual background for the children.

Parents

Labels: decried society's need for a single label; census and monitoring forms as a nuisance; explanations devised by parents to explain their origins and identities; parents unsure how their child would respond to a race category question unless they had discussed this and provided a label. Non-discussing parents tended (***) to have children who used colour terms ('tan', 'coffee' etc.). *Preparation for anticipated discrimination*: difference between white and black parents; black parents more conscious of need to have a perspective in order to survive; more ready to prepare children overtly for dealing with prejudice (***). Parents also saw it as positive that their children uniquely prepared to deal with issues concerning differences between people.

Location: 'racial' composition of area lived in is important; need mixed, open environment; child needs exposure to role models and cultural values.

Children

'Trends were noted that often parallel the children's ages' [*** considering overall low numbers this seems an insupportable statement; four children 5–9 years and five children 10–16]. **Labels**: 'about half' the children [shouldn't be hard to be exact with $N = 9$!] reported not being asked by anyone about their racial background [probably the younger ones – pity this isn't specified. One was 7 and one was 10; the 9 year-old *was* asked.] Some children give religion as main characteristic to 'What are you?'***. Younger children use colour terms (e.g. 'tan'), older use societal group terms (e.g. 'black') (***). Some peer pressure from older children to select 'racial' group, e.g. in school groups. **Self-description**: all but one used skin colour in a description of themselves to a stranger sent to meet them(***). Long description here of features chosen by children but a consistent pattern here. **Racial awareness**: all but the 5 year-old showed awareness of social grouping by 'race'(***). None could clearly recall when they first became aware but several mention the possibility of a change of school (e.g. to mainly white) or move to different area. 16 year-old boy makes strong statement that girls do the splitting into Black/White/Hispanic groups whereas boys play team games and are less divided (***).

DISCUSSION

Strength of result: findings *counter* to conjectures made in counselling literature for this group. [i.e. major role of science is to disconfirm shaky or non-empirically based theories]. No great sense of self-perception as marginal in two cultures was found (but this is assumption in counselling literature). Majority more sensitive to values of both cultures and saw more commonality. No alienation of family from extended families. All six participant girls identified with mother not same-race parent. Therefore gender more salient than race in identification [***small N for this sort of claim]. Most families happily discussed race issues but in two families who didn't, mothers saw child as belonging more to one race and children identified that way also, unlike the rest(***). In both these families, one Black, one White, the father refused to be interviewed.

LIMITATIONS

Admits small, biased sample (e.g. most were familiar with social science research) and says difficult to determine whether a full range of perspectives was uncovered since refusal rate was high (this is somewhat inconsistent with point made at end of 'Sample' section about expert review and exhaustion of perspectives). Reliance on verbal reports, especially feeling that some parents were 'trying to present their child's or children's experiences in an overly positive light.' Suggests possible desire to counteract negative stereotypes of biracial children. Tailoring questions for level of younger children may have restricted participants' responses.

DIRECTIONS FOR FUTURE RESEARCH

The author explains that a major aim (of this and other exploratory qualitative studies) is to generate hypotheses for further qualitative and quantitative investigation. Several of the latter are outlined and all have been identified by *** above, though the author doesn't include all of these.

COMMENTS ON THE REPORT

The report follows quite closely the familiar framework for a traditional psychological research report. In several places the author is at pains to compare her chosen strategies favourably with traditional quantitative ones, almost as an apology or an appeal to antici-pated hostile review. This is a possibility because the work comes direct from her doctoral thesis; it appears that the co-authors are tutors in her department. The report often sounds tentative. Other qualitative reports make no such apology or hesitant claim for parity with traditional quantitatively based reports. However, they often do make the con-trast, whereas traditional paradigm reports see no need to, being the 'norm' or dominant force. If you *are* going to use a particular approach (semi-structured interview; repertory grid; diary method; content analysis of any of these), it does no harm to add some justifica-tion of the method chosen, if only to set it in the context of the research topic and aims, showing that the choice is considered in this light.

The report tends to avoid specific numbers even where, with only nine children inter-viewed, the number would be very easy to give. Silverman (1993) and many others see no problem with using quantification where it is appropriate. Ironically, almost all the derived hypotheses for further testing would be easily and most appropriately researched on a quantitative basis. However, there are insights within the research which may well not have occurred to the creator of a questionnaire so the value of the study is in bringing out issues and perspectives which the *respondents* could provide, and in challenging coun-sellors' untested beliefs and assumptions.

Because the work cannot avoid counting at times, and because the topic lends itself to identifying differences, it sounds all the more unconvincing to use terms like 'the great majority of participants', 'most of the children', 'trends were noted that often paralleled the children's ages', with such small numbers. On the credit side, one must consider how little *more* we would know from a typical quantitative study which might assess rather more children on, say, some variables like self-esteem, identity formation, and perhaps a specially formatted form of the standard racial identity scales which exist. The numbers might have told us 'no difference' 'just like others' or 'worth looking at the "awareness of racial issues" sub-scale; mean scores were higher here but not for self-esteem' and so on. *This* research provides many directions for new quantitative or qualitative research projects.

Report 2

Ramsey Liem (1997) Shame and guilt among first- and second-generation Asian Americans and European Americans. *Journal of Cross-Cultural Psychology*, 28, 4, 365–392

Abstract

'Shame and guilt narratives of first- and second-generation Asian Americans and multigeneration European Americans were collected in semi-structured interviews to learn how respondents perceive the phenomenology, function and interpersonal dynamics of these emotions. This article focuses on the formal characteristics of shame episodes reported by members of these groups and offers an interpretive explanation for differences that involve respondents' conceptions of the self and related cultural practices. The analysis proposes that shame is at times embedded in a triadic structure for first-generation Asian Americans comprised of the actor, a shamed other and an audience. European American shame experiences, however, typically conform to a dyadic structure of actor and audience. Shame stories of second-generation Asian Americans contain elements of both emotion ecologies that may reflect a unique bicultural adaptation. These findings are consistent with a cultural constructionist view of the emotions.'

INTRODUCTION

This uses four and a half sides [journal pages are narrow!]. First, Liem says interest in shame waned because the older approach saw shame as a more 'primitive' emotion, relative to guilt and therefore typified cultures that were more shame driven as emotionally somewhat immature and less advanced – an ethnocentric view which needed to collapse in a post-colonial world. Arguing from clinical experience and self theory, it is claimed that shame now has an almost equal status with guilt, although normal conversation tends to avoid it and people often do not recognise it. Shame is constructed differently in different societies, more positively in Japan for instance. Shame can depend on a real or symbolic *audience* (but not so much in individualistic cultures) and can also be more internal (when one has hurt another) in which case it overlaps somewhat with guilt. Some research points to less differentiation between guilt and shame in societies like Japan.

Within American society the language of emotion is shared but underlying this may be quite different social constructions of specific types. Liem takes *guilt* to arise from transgressions of *conscience* – the repository of ethical and moral standards. *Shame*, more concerned with the *ideal self*, is provoked by exposure to an audience/someone else through whose eyes the person experiences themselves as seriously flawed. Shame prompts feelings of immaturity before a 'parental' adult. Guilt makes one seek forgiveness whereas shame urges one to flee. Liem's research is also prompted by stories of emotional dilemmas from Asian American students, from fiction and from clinical work with Asian American clients.

RESPONDENTS AND INTERVIEW STRATEGY

This title replaces the conventional 'method' section. Age and culture details of respondents interviewed so far are given. Liem interviews all Asians and four Euro Americans, the rest of whom are interviewed by a trained assistant. The interview uses guided open-ended conversation around experiences of shame and guilt by getting the respondent to recount stories involving these emotions. The interview is guided where respondents fail to cover central aspects of the research. A 'Who am I' inventory (quantitative) was introduced late in the research for two thirds of participants consequent upon findings in early sessions.

GUILT AND SHAME AS REPORTED BY EUROPEAN AMERICANS

There is no 'results' section as such. This part of the report presents short extracts from interviews where respondents describe guilt and shame experiences. The two Euro American ones are presented as 'typical' and as representing very closely the mainstream psychological constructions of the terms. A student who worked as a waiter describes cheating a 'bragging' colleague out of the weekly prize for getting the most charges by pooling other colleagues' bills. He felt guilty about this, then ashamed when the boss found out and exposed him publicly. A woman (Clare) describes guilt concerning familiar professional work conflicts with child care but finds *shame* difficult to identify until the interviewer uses 'ashamed or embarrassed'. She recounts discovering a typo in a conference paper she had handed out.

REPORTS FROM FIRST-GENERATION (KOREAN) ASIANS

The guilt story concerns difficulty faced by the student ('Young') in calling his tutors by their first names. This seriously transgresses a code of duty and obligation. This is contrasted with Clare's *individualised* ethics concerning her child. The Korean's is situated in the formal status of student, culturally prescribed, and its relationship with superior roles. Young's shame story makes it clear that *others* would also be shamed by his actions, as he would be shamed by his sister failing an exam. [Compare Young's shame in telling friends his sister had failed with how most Western brothers would break this news to friends; they usually wouldn't *share* her failure; they may well dismiss or *blame* her.]

Here, there is a long discussion (more than two sides) of the clear differences between Young's stories and the Euro-Americans', with new literature references included. That is, at this point in the report, theory discussion and data are completely merged. This is because the writer is establishing the central notion that the 'non-western' shame stories include a 'shamed other' along with the shamed self, *both* of whom are shamed in front of a real or imaginary audience.

At this point there is a tiny piece of quantification as Liem says that seven out of ten first-generation Asian Americans incorporate the triadic structure in their stories. One of these seven first-generation respondents also refers to shaming himself and the Korean culture in front of (white) Americans as audience, and is in turn shamed in front of (white) Americans by news events from Korea (i.e. political repression).

REPORTS FROM A SECOND-GENERATION (FILIPINA) ASIAN

Mariflor describes an incident where she recognises that her mother will be worried about shame (that Mariflor was locked out of the house and talked with a boy on his porch until midnight when her father found her). However, she feels mainly anger at her mother for considering her behaviour shameful. She recognises her mother's sense of shame but doesn't feel this herself, more a sense of frustration with her mother's power to make her feel ashamed when she has a more self-righteous analysis of the event. Liem interprets this, somewhat hesitantly, as a form of midway position between the individualistic Western constructs (shame in front of an audience) and the 'positioned' self of Asian cultures, self defined in relation to others not as completely independent. Liem finds six of the 12 second generation Asians producing 'this triadic/anger pattern' and finds it interesting that, asked for an incident where the *respondent* felt shame, respondents like Mariflor, and then Sophia, choose a shame related incident in which they do not, but know they could have, felt shame, whereas their parent *does* feel shame. Comparing this with normal Western parent-child conflicts, Liem says 'In the mainstream (USA) culture, adolescent struggles over autonomy take place within a shared understanding of separation and independence as the hallmark of psychological maturity. Adolescence is a difficult period precisely because both parent and child value this outcome and share the anxieties of letting go. Sophia's and Mariflor's experiences, on the other hand, suggest a different kind of conflict, in which the idealized, mature selves envisioned by parents and daughters are incompatible.' Liem argues that the second generation respondents do not simply have an American self conflicting with parental tradition but a 'hybrid of the independent and interdependent selves'.

At this point the report concentrates on the well researched constructs of the independent and 'positioned' self-concepts familiar within cross-cultural psychology writing. It particularly leans on the seminal Markus and Kitayama (1991) paper identifying ways in which the experiences of emotion, operation of motivation and of cognition might be different depending on the way one construes one's self – as an entirely independent being or as a person-related-to-others with attendant duties and formal responsibilities – the latter typified in 'we [family members] are like the fingers on a hand, each with its own shape and purpose, yet essential to the whole'. The rest of the discussion explores the 'hybrid self' construct, dependent upon stages of enculturation to American society.

The small sample size is recognised. Note the term 'sample' is used, so there is an aim here to generalise to populations. The limitation on excerpts from the interviews is also recognised but the author provides a summary table of all the interviews conducted so far in the as yet unfinished project, in a very brief coded format, as an appendix. The inclusion of limited quantitative data from the 'Who am I' inventory (the ratio of independent to interdependent statements about oneself) is rationalised as providing weak 'concurrent validity' for the existence of differing self schemas – positioned (interdependent), independent and transitional ('hybrid').

COMMENTS ON THE REPORT

The Journal of Cross-Cultural Psychology contains a large proportion of quantitative, conventional reports. Even a recent article on 'Love songs in the United States and China' uses ratings and a chi-square analysis! It is striking then that this report departs so far from the 'standard' report structure. Possibly, with so few qualitative articles, there are as yet no firmly established norms for presentation. Noticeable are the lack of specific aims for the study and a very limited 'method' section (there is no 'method' heading). The interview procedure is rather loosely described and there is no rationale provided for the interviewing of most, but not all, of the 'Caucasian' respondents by a Euro American and the remainder by Liem. This method section would probably be found wanting by A level and first year undergraduate methods tutors! The interview segments provide clear examples which support Liem's main thesis of a transitional self among enculturing Americans. This is not the sort of 'grounded' study where themes emerge from the data, however. The segments are specifically chosen to support a clear prior theory and hence it is notable that the introduction could have ended with far more specific aims for the study. The report *could* be seen as containing, if written in far less technical jargon, not a lot more in empirical data and speculation than might appear in an intellectually oriented magazine article on 'How the new South East Asians cope with the old and the new' or similar. However, it is situated among carefully described and organised background research and competing theory. It also integrates other classic studies and constructs into the data as they are analysed and discussed. It also, unlike journalism, discusses weakness of method and aspects of validity, room for improvement, further research and so on. Its richness is in the clarity and power of the ways in which the second generation respondents describe a dilemma which would otherwise remain hidden to researchers from the mainstream culture, and yet begs for explanation in terms of already developed constructs of the self, constructs which can be subtly modified and extended by the reported research.

Appendix 1

STRUCTURED QUESTIONS WITH ANSWERS

The following structured questions should give the reader experience in the type of assessments often used in examinations and class tests. I have tried to indicate some of the kinds of guidance given to markers. Marking is usually lenient where one part of a question is answered in another (e.g. in 7b where the answer to i. might partly cover the answer to ii). None of the wordings below is absolute. There are many ways to say the same thing. In some cases, additional points are possible, not listed here. If in doubt, please consult your tutor or ask your tutor to consult me!

QUESTION 1

A psychologist wished to find out whether there was any relationship between the use of physical punishment by mothers and the levels of aggression in their children. Questionnaire scores were obtained on a scale from 0 to 20, for each mother's level of physical punishment use. Levels of aggression in the mothers' children were assessed using naturalistic observation at the children's schools at playtime. The correlation between physical   5
punishment scores and aggression scores was 0.6.

Marks

a. State one strength of the use of questionnaires in psychological assessment.   1
b. State one difficulty with the method of naturalistic observation as used in this
    study and explain why you think this is a difficulty.   2
c. The correlation found was *positive* (line 6). State what is meant by a *positive*
    correlation between two sets of scores.   1
d. A newspaper article described the research as showing that physical
    punishment caused aggression in children. Explain why this interpretation
    of the result is incorrect.   3

QUESTION 2

In a psychology experiment participants are asked to listen to a talk. During the talk a stranger holding an object bursts in and shouts at the speaker. In one condition the object is a gun while in the other condition it is a pen. Participants are later asked if they can recall the colour of the stranger's hair. It is predicted that fewer people would notice the stranger's hair colour when he is holding a gun. Results are shown on the next page: 5

Table 1 Number of people correctly recalling stranger's hair colour in gun and pen conditions

	Participant recalled hair colour:		
	correctly	incorrectly	total
stranger holding:			
gun	17	33	50
pen	27	23	50
Total:	44	56	100

Marks

a. State which statistical test would determine whether the difference in recall success for the gun and pen conditions is significant. 1

b. State the independent variable in this experiment and give a reason for your answer. 2

c. The experiment uses an *independent samples* design. Explain one *advantage* and one *disadvantage* of using an independent samples design. 4

d. State one ethical issue clearly involved in the *design* and *procedure* of this study. 1

QUESTION 3

Marks

a. Describe what is meant by the *reliability* of a psychological measure. 2

b. Describe what is meant by the *validity* of a psychological measure. 2

c. State one major advantage of the use of interviews in psychological research compared with the use of structured questionnaires. 1

d. Describe how content analysis could be used to deal with data gathered from informal interviews with hospital staff on the nature and causes of stress in their jobs. 3

QUESTION 4

In an experimental study which predicts that anagrams of uncommon words will take longer to solve, participants are given a list of anagrams containing 6 which are of common words and 6 of uncommon words. Both sets are mixed together randomly into one list of 12 anagrams. The researcher records the mean time taken by each participant to solve the two sets of anagrams.

Marks

a. State which is the *independent variable* and which is the *dependent variable* in this experiment. 2

b. State the type of experimental design used in this study. 1

c. State one advantage of the experimental design used in this study. 1

d. Explain why the common and uncommon word anagrams are randomly mixed together (*line 3*). 2

e. State an appropriate null hypothesis for this study. 2

QUESTION 5

A researcher attempts to assess the effectiveness of two different programmes intended to improve children's reading ability. She matches each child in one class with a child in another class at the same school. All the children in both classes are 8 years-old. Each class receives just one of the two programmes. After 6 months the children's reading scores are obtained and a comparison between the two groups is made. 5

Marks

a. State two *relevant* variables on which the children might be matched. 2

b. i. Suppose the children's reading scores are *ranked*. State a statistical test which would be appropriate for testing for a significant difference between the reading scores of the two classes. 1

   ii. Give *two* reasons for your choice of test. 2

c. State whether the hypothesis tested in this study is directional or non-directional. 1

d. One mother asks for specific information on how her child performed. Explain how the psychologist might react to this request. 2

QUESTION 6

An investigation is carried out to test the hypothesis that young teenage mothers are more controlling with their children than older mothers. Two groups of mothers, younger and older, are visited in their own home. A thirty minute video tape recording is made of each mother at play with her two year-old child. Several raters, unaware of the research hypothesis, are asked to rate the mothers' child discipline behaviour using a rigorous 5 coding system. One of the measures is verbal control. The mean for the younger mothers on this variable is 35.8 and the standard deviation is 6.5. For the older mothers the mean is 28.6 and the standard deviation is 8.3.

Marks

a. Add all labels to the outline chart below which is intended to show the central tendency measures for the two groups. 3

Mean verbal control scores for younger and older mothers

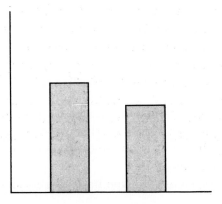

b. State what the standard deviation tell us about a set of values.   1

c. Explain why the raters are kept unaware of the research hypothesis (*line 4*).   2   **537**

d. Explain why a 'rigorous coding system' (*line 5*) is used to analyse the video taped mothers' behaviour.   2

QUESTION 7

In an experiment the same group of participants is asked to perform a motor task requiring care and concentration under two different conditions. In the experimental condition they are given a strong cup of real coffee and in the control condition they are given decaffeinated coffee. These conditions are *counterbalanced*. Differences in performance are found to be significant with $p < 0.05$.   5

Marks

a. State one advantage of the *repeated measures* experimental design.   1

b. i. State what is meant by 'counterbalanced' (*line 4*).   1

    ii. Explain why counterbalancing is used in this design.   2

c. Explain what is meant by the term 'significant with $p < 0.05$' (*line 5*).   2

d. Explain why the participants are given decaffeinated coffee in the control condition.   2

QUESTION 8

Two groups of babies are observed in a play situation in a specially designed observation room. One group have been reared in an institutional setting while the other group have been reared with two parents at home. The researchers are interested in how securely attached the babies are. All the babies have a female main carer. 'Attachment' is operationalised for this study in terms of their specific reaction to a stranger, their behaviour when their main carer departs and their reaction on her return. In order to assess these reactions, procedures in the play situation are completely standardised.   5

Marks

a. State what is meant by saying that the variable of attachment is 'operationalised' for this study (*line 5*).   1

b. i. State what is meant by a 'standardised procedure' (*line 7*).   1

    ii. Explain why a standardised procedure is used in this kind of study.   2

c. One critic of the study argues that it very much lacks 'ecological validity'. Explain the meaning of *ecological validity* in the context of this study.   2

d. Each baby is given an overall 'attachment level' score.

    i. State the statistical test which would be appropriate for testing the difference between the two groups' attachment scores.   1

    ii. Give, briefly, one reason for your choice of test.   1

QUESTION 9

Clients attending a drug rehabilitation unit are asked to take part in research aimed at improving the treatment offered. For technical reasons it is necessary to use a group attending on Mondays as the experimental group, who are trained in the special techniques of the programme, while a group attending on Wednesdays serves as the control group. At the end of the programme a measure is taken of each participants' 'self-esteem' on a 1 to 10 scale. The scores for the experimental group are given in the following table: 5

Self-esteem scores for experimental group participants:

3   4   4   4   5   5   5   5   6   6   7   8

Marks

a. i.   Give a reason why this research design would be called a *'quasi-experiment'*.   1
   ii. Describe a disadvantage that a *quasi-experiment* has when compared with
        a *true experiment*.   2
b. Describe the purpose of the control group used in this study.   2
c. State the mode of the set of scores shown in the table of self-esteem scores
   above.   1
d. The variation ratio of the scores above is .67 Explain what is meant by the
   term 'variation ratio'.   2

QUESTION 10

In a study designed to compare sex role stereotyping in television drama today and ten years ago, a researcher uses a 'content analysis' technique to analyse several hours of television film from both periods. Part of the analysis gives the frequencies shown in the table below for numbers of main character women in senior role positions (such as manager, prison governor and so on). The chi-square test performed on these data produced a result which was not significant ($p > 0.05$). 5

Main characters in senior role		Main characters in non-senior role	
1987	7	1987	43
1997	15	1987	38

Marks

a. Describe how the researchers would obtain the data shown in the table from
   content analysis of the television film they observed.   2
b. State two factors that the researchers might have to take into account when
   choosing the film to be analysed.   2
c. i   State the statistical test which would be used on the data in the table in
        order to decide whether the change from 1987 to 1997 is significant.   1
   ii   Give *one* reason for your choice of test.   1
d. Explain what is meant by saying that the test result was 'not significant' (*line 6*).   2

QUESTION 11

Mothers are interviewed in order to discover the quality of the diet they provide for their children and also the extent to which they provide extra vitamins. The research is aimed at the theory that extra vitamins and other dietary factors can enhance children's mental ability. The children's scores on a mental ability test are correlated with an overall 'healthy eating' score derived from the mothers' interview responses. The value of the correlation coefficient is 0.35 and is significant ($p < 0.05$). A local newspaper claims in a report on the research that 'healthy eating improves your child's mental ability'. The psychologist replies in a letter that this is *only one* possible conclusion from the research.

Marks

a. i. State the *strength* of correlation when the 'value of the correlation coefficient is 0.35' (*line 6*). 1

   ii. Explain what is meant by saying that a correlation is 'significant' (*line 6*). 2

b. i. Explain why the researcher argues there are other possible conclusions from the research, *other than* that healthy eating improves a child's mental ability (*line 7*). 2

   ii. State *one* other possible conclusion from the result. 1

c. i. A critic argues that 'social desirability' might have affected the validity of the interview data. State what is meant by 'social desirability'. 1

   ii. State briefly how social desirability might affect the validity of this study. 1

QUESTION 12

Participants are asked to perform a very difficult task requiring a great deal of concentration and patience. Even so the task is made so difficult that few participants can complete it without a great deal of frustration. Times taken to complete the task are correlated with the number of errors made. These results are shown in the chart below. Immediately after the task is finished the participants are asked to complete a psychological test which is intended to assess levels of anger. It is found that those making more errors scored more highly on the anger test.

Marks

a. State the *strength* and *direction* of the correlation shown in the scattergraph below. 2

b. Explain how 'demand characteristics' might be involved in the apparent relationship between number of errors and anger level. 2

c. The person administering the anger test was kept unaware of the task results. Explain why this precaution might be taken. 2

d. The researchers predicted a correlation between levels of anger and errors made. Write out a *null hypothesis* associated with this prediction. 2

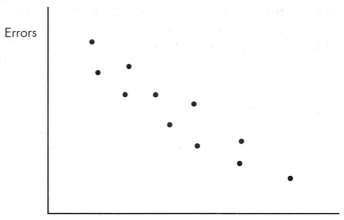

Time to complete task

QUESTION 13

A field experiment is conducted in which one group of factory workers is given a stress reduction training programme for two months. They are selected randomly from among all the workers in one large department. A second control group is also selected at random from the same department. Participants are asked to assess their stress levels both before and after the training period and the researchers use the median value of these assess-   5
ments in their analysis.

		Marks
a.	i. Describe a method for selecting a *sample* at *random* from the department.	2
	ii. Explain the importance of drawing a *random sample*.	2
b.	Describe the advantage that a *field experiment* (*line 1*) might have over a *laboratory experiment*.	2
c.	i. State exactly what is meant by the term 'median' of a set of scores (*line 5*).	1
	ii. Give a reason why the median would be preferred to the mean when describing a set of test scores.	1

QUESTION 14

A psychologist tests the research hypothesis that the more experience people have had with computers the less anxious they will be. Psychology students are interviewed about their experience with computers and are then asked to complete a short computer anxiety scale. The raw scores on the anxiety test are given below.

Raw scores for computer anxiety (*N* = 26)
1   2   2   2   3   3   4   5   5   6   6   6   7   7   7   7   7   8   8   8   8   8   9   9   9

Marks

a. Name a statistical test which could be used to support the *research hypothesis* (*line 1*).   1

b. State the *range* of the raw scores for computer anxiety.   1

c. Complete the histogram of anxiety scores shown in Figure 1 by adding information at points A to D. (Points A and D are labels; B is a value and C is a column).   4

d. A local computer company is interested in the results and intends to use them in adjusting their recruitment policy. Describe *one* limitation there might be in *generalising* the results to computer company applicants.

2

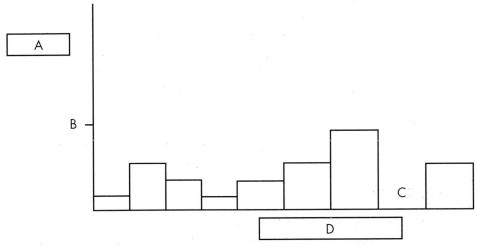

Figure 1 Distribution of computer anxiety scores

QUESTION 15

A clinical psychologist publishes results of a case study on one client who had received a programme of therapy designed to alleviate the problems he was experiencing in leaving his home and getting back to normal working life. Together the therapist and client drew up a list of behaviour patterns which they intended to improve. They gave each of these behaviour patterns a rating from 1 to 10 at the start of the therapy and at the end of a three month period. These behaviour patterns are labelled 'A' to 'J' in the table below where the start and finish ratings are also shown.

5

Behaviour pattern	A	B	C	D	E	F	G	H	I	J
rating at start	1	3	5	7	5	3	4	4	2	4
rating at end	3	5	5	9	4	7	8	8	6	5
improvement	+	+	0	+	−	+	+	+	+	+

Marks

a. The therapist decided to use a *sign test* on the start and finish ratings to see whether there was significant improvement across all the behaviour categories. Give two reasons why this test is appropriate for the data in the bottom row of the table.

2

b. State the range of the 'rating at start' data.

1

c. State two ethical principles which the psychologist should observe before publishing the results of this therapy programme.

2

d. Describe the value of case studies in psychological research.

3

ANSWERS

QUESTION 1

a. Produce quantitative data; can be made reliable; standardised method of data collection; reduce researcher bias (compared with interview).

b. Can't control observing situation; different children might or might not provoke aggression in observed child. In general, lack of control of extraneous variables.

c. Variables increase together; if one of a pair is high, tendency for the other to be high also and vice versa. (Must explain 'positive' for two marks.)

d. Correlation only shows a relationship, it doesn't account for the direction of *cause* and effect, e.g. perhaps naturally aggressive children, or children who have learned to be aggressive at school, *provoke* physical punishment from parents. 'Cause' is the central point and must be addressed in some way.

QUESTION 2

a. Chi-square.

b. Gun or pen since this is the variable *manipulated* by the experimenter ('controlled' may not be a clear enough reason).

c. Advantage – no order effects which occur in repeated measures design where participants may improve through the unwanted variable of practice, for instance. Disadvantage – participant variables; groups may differ and this may be responsible for any differences found.

d. Participants were deceived; *all* ethical issues (confidentiality, anonymity etc.) are *possibly* involved but deception is inherent in the *design* of this experiment. 1 mark for a connected issue, e.g. 'genuine fear caused in participants'.

QUESTION 3

a. The measure is *consistent*. Extra mark for a fuller explanation or appropriate example, e.g. accurate reference to *inter-rater/observer* reliability or *internal* reliability, *external* reliability.

b. That it measures what it is intended to measure. Could refer to any of the validity types (face, content, criterion etc.) for the extra mark.

c. Interviewer can clear up ambiguities, perhaps gain more relevant information (*or* questioning can be flexible; richer information may be obtained and so on).

d. Researcher would need to identify appropriate categories and provide coding for placing information in each category. The coding might be carried out by coders unaware of the research hypothesis but certainly they would need to be well trained in the use of the coding system.

QUESTION 4

a. Independent variable – common or uncommon words. Dependent variable – (mean) time taken for solution.

b. Repeated measures; between subjects.

c. Avoids problem of participant variables. Also needs fewer participants for same amount of data.

d. To avoid order effects from practice, fatigue or from guessing what the experiment is about. 'So they are randomised' would be given one mark.

e. There is no difference between mean times to solve common and uncommon word solutions. Predictions *from* H_0 obtain only 1 mark (e.g. there will be no [significant] difference . . .).

QUESTION 5

a. Initial reading level; other academic ability indicator; sex; socio-economic factors. (Note: sex is relevant because it is known that girls are generally superior in reading during the school years. Variables *must* be relevant; there would be no *obvious* rationale for choosing 'race', height or distance lived from school.)

b. i Wilcoxon signed ranks. ii The data are ranked, the test is of differences between groups and the design is related (matched pairs).

c. Non-directional. She does not predict the direction of the difference. Either programme might be more effective than the other.

d. Psychological ethics demand that participants be given full information on data collected about them. Therefore, unless there are prior restrictions agreed to by participants, the information should be made available along with any appropriate counselling or advice. *Refusal* by the psychologist only credited (1 mark) if some good hypothetical reason given (e.g. the mother had already signed a consent form to this effect). The answer *must* recognise right to information, even so.

QUESTION 6

a. Central tendency used is the mean. Hence taller column on chart should be labelled 'younger mothers' and the other column should be labelled 'older mothers' – both on horizontal axis at bottom of chart. The vertical axis should be labelled 'mean verbal control score' or similar. 1 mark for each correct label.

b. The spread or *dispersion* of the set of values. No mark for the 'range' as this is an alternative technical term.

c. Avoids the possible criticism that they could be biased in their rating and help support the research hypothesis. 'Because it is a single blind procedure' would get 1 mark.

d. A rigorous system helps maintain objective assessment. It will at least aid in reliability if not validity of ratings.

QUESTION 7

a. Differences between conditions cannot be the result of differences between two sets of participants (i.e. participant variables are ruled out). Could refer to economy of participants in obtaining the number of results in the data set.

b. i Involves having some (usually half) participants perform conditions in one order while the other half perform in the opposite order.
   ii Reduces confounding from order effects (practice effects, fatigue, guessing hypothesis).

c. If the null hypothesis is true (and there is actually no difference in population scores for the two conditions) then the probability of obtaining samples this different is less than 0.05. 1 mark for the likes of: 'only a 5% probability of these results occurring by chance'; 1 mark for a *consequence* of the significance decision, such as 'the null hypothesis is rejected'. (This isn't the *meaning* of 'significance'.)

d. To ensure *all* variables are as identical as possible *except* the independent variable. Here, only coffee content is absent from the control condition. All participants have a coffee-tasting drink. Answers referring to a 'placebo' condition can be credited. Answers such as 'to avoid bias' are too vague in this context but 'to make things equal' or similar would receive 1 mark.

QUESTION 8

a. A psychological variable term is defined precisely in terms of what will be done to measure it for this particular study. Any answer concerning strictness of definition or 'operations' of measurement is satisfactory.

b. i All procedures are exactly the same for each participant. ii This reduces any bias possible from researcher-participant interaction or error from extraneous variables which might cause differences in children's play behaviour.

c. Would the attachment behaviour transfer from the observation room? The question is whether the findings would transfer to natural situations, outside the observation setting, when a stranger is involved. Perhaps this particular play set-up produces only behaviour special to the test situation (e.g. some element may be particularly frightening, or comforting, to some of the children.)

d. i Mann-Whitney. ii The children are given scores so data are at least ordinal and not just frequencies. The design is unrelated and we are testing for differences. (Note: *one* of these last two points would be sufficient for the single mark available.) (*t* test for unrelated samples is also appropriate if data meet parametric requirements for this test; data would have to be treated as being at least at interval level of measurement.)

QUESTION 9

a. i Researcher is not able to allocate participants to conditions at random. ii Any difference found *might* be the result of differences between the groups unrelated to the independent variable. True experiment answers this threat through random allocation to conditions.

b. To provide a base-line measure (1 mark). We can see whether self-esteem might have increased during the period *without* the special training and hence see whether the programme has any real effect. (Needs full description for 2 marks.)

c. 5.

d. It is a measure of *dispersion* and is the proportion of scores which are not of the modal value. (Note: two marks available so best to make the general point about dispersion as well as giving a specific definition.)

QUESTION 10

a. See answer to 3d.

b. Sampling would need to be *representative* and *balanced* across the two years. Samples would need to come from equivalent slots and would be chosen *randomly* within the slots.

c. i Chi-square. ii Data are *frequencies*, we seek differences in role categories across two years or an *association* between these two variables; the design is *unrelated*. (Note: only one of the italicised terms would be required.)

d. The probability is greater than 0.05 that these frequencies would occur through random sampling if the null hypothesis is true (no association exists at all). 'The frequencies are likely to occur by chance' receives only 1 mark.

QUESTION 11

a. i. Weak (possibly 'moderate'). Note: *direction* was not asked for.
   ii. Probability is less than 0.05 that this correlation would occur by chance *if the population correlation is zero*. The point in italics must be addressed for 2 marks. 1 mark for 'correlation unlikely to have occurred by chance' or similar.

b. i. Correlations do not indicate cause and effect. Various explanations are possible.
   ii. Perhaps families with higher mental abilities are more likely to see the value of healthier eating. Again, such families may be better off and can *afford* healthier eating habits. (Note: one reason will do.)

c. i. Conforming to social values and presenting oneself in this light.
   ii. Here, mothers may have *said* they used healthier foods because they know this is socially desirable – the 'right thing to do'.

QUESTION 12

a. Strong (1); negative (1).

b. Participants might guess that the questionnaire has something to do with the emotional experience they have just had with the task. Hence this might affect the way they answer. Any answer which demonstrates knowledge that demand characteristics have to do with participants responding to *cues* from the experiment as to its aims.

c. So that there can be no suggestion that knowing the desired outcome for the research, the test administrator could have biased the results, consciously or not. Brief answers like 'to avoid bias' receive just 1 mark.

d. The correlation between number of errors and anger level is zero.

QUESTION 13

a. i. All names in box and shuffle; then pick sample. Give each person a random number then take the highest/lowest 20 numbers if 20 required in sample. Put all names in computer and let it generate random order. Take first 20 if 20 required. (any of these three methods will do).
   ii. To make sure each person has an equal chance of being in sample (1) – gives good chance of a representative group and no sampling bias. (1)

b. Less artificial so behaviour more likely to be affected by normal social and physical context. Greater realism. Participants less inhibited by strange, formal situation and (possibly) demand characteristics (though these are possible in field studies too). (*One of these points would do.*) Understanding of 'field' must be clear.

  c. i.   The central value in a data set. ii. Not affected by extreme scores (in one direction).

QUESTION 14

a. Spearman's rho; Pearson.

b. $9 [= (9 - 1) + 1]$.

c. Point A – 'Frequency' (or similar); point B – '5'; point C – column should be just one unit higher than the column to its left, double the one to its right; point D – 'Computer anxiety scores'. 1 mark for each correct point only.

d. Problem of generalising results. Computer company applicants are not necessarily interested in psychology and are not students. Limitation of construct measure – anxiety only assessed by paper test and not with actual computers.

QUESTION 15

a. The bottom row data are the signs (i.e. directions) of the differences between start and end ratings. Since we only have positive or negative signs the data are *nominal*. The design is *related*. We are looking for differences. (*Two* of these points would do.)

b. 7.

c. Any two of: client should be assured of anonymity and confidentiality of any information on him; client should be asked whether he is in agreement with publication; he should be able to check any data and to withdraw permission at any time before final publication; no information published should threaten his psychological health or make him feel uncomfortable. (Other points are possible if made relevant.) 1 mark for each point, not 2 for a well made point.

d. Three of the points on pages 126–7, or two, with one expanded, should gain full marks here.

Appendix 2

Table 1 Random numbers

03 47 43 73 86	39 96 47 36 61	46 98 63 71 62	33 26 16 80 45	60 11 14 10 95
97 74 24 67 62	42 81 14 57 20	42 53 32 37 32	27 07 36 07 51	24 51 79 89 73
16 76 62 27 66	56 50 26 71 07	32 90 79 78 53	13 55 38 58 59	88 97 54 14 10
12 56 85 99 26	96 96 68 27 31	05 03 72 93 15	57 12 10 14 21	88 26 49 81 76
55 59 56 35 64	38 54 82 46 22	31 62 43 09 90	06 18 44 32 53	23 83 01 30 30
16 22 77 94 39	49 54 43 54 82	17 37 93 23 78	87 35 20 96 43	84 26 34 91 64
84 42 17 53 31	57 24 55 06 88	77 04 74 47 67	21 76 33 50 25	83 92 12 06 76
63 01 63 78 59	16 95 55 67 19	98 10 50 71 75	12 86 73 58 07	44 39 52 38 79
33 21 12 34 29	78 64 56 07 82	52 42 07 44 38	15 51 00 13 42	99 66 02 79 54
57 60 86 32 44	09 47 27 96 54	49 17 46 09 62	90 52 84 77 27	08 02 73 43 28
18 18 07 92 46	44 17 16 58 09	79 83 86 16 62	06 76 50 03 10	55 23 64 05 05
26 62 38 97 75	84 16 07 44 99	83 11 46 32 24	20 14 85 88 45	10 93 72 88 71
23 42 40 64 74	82 97 77 77 81	07 45 32 14 08	32 98 94 07 72	93 85 79 10 75
52 36 28 19 95	50 92 26 11 97	00 56 76 31 38	80 22 02 53 53	86 60 42 04 53
37 85 94 35 12	83 39 50 08 30	42 34 07 96 88	54 42 06 87 98	35 85 29 48 38
70 29 17 12 13	40 33 20 38 26	13 89 51 03 74	17 76 37 13 04	07 74 21 19 30
56 62 18 37 35	96 83 50 87 75	97 12 25 93 47	70 33 24 03 54	97 77 46 44 80
99 49 57 22 77	88 42 95 45 72	16 64 36 16 00	04 43 18 66 79	94 77 24 21 90
16 08 15 04 72	33 27 14 34 90	45 59 34 68 49	12 72 07 34 45	99 27 72 95 14
31 16 93 32 43	50 27 89 87 19	20 15 37 00 49	52 85 66 60 44	38 68 88 11 80
68 34 30 13 70	55 74 30 77 40	44 22 78 84 26	04 33 46 09 52	68 07 97 06 57
74 57 25 65 76	59 29 97 68 60	71 91 38 67 54	13 58 18 24 76	15 54 55 95 52
27 42 37 86 53	48 55 90 65 72	96 57 69 36 10	96 46 92 42 45	97 60 49 04 91
00 39 68 29 61	66 37 32 20 30	77 84 57 03 29	10 45 65 04 26	11 04 96 67 24
29 94 98 94 24	68 49 69 10 82	53 75 91 93 30	34 25 20 57 27	40 48 73 51 92
16 90 82 66 59	83 62 64 11 12	67 19 00 71 74	60 47 21 29 68	02 02 37 03 31
11 27 94 75 06	06 09 19 74 66	02 94 37 34 02	76 70 90 30 86	38 45 94 30 38
35 24 10 16 20	33 32 51 26 38	79 78 45 04 91	16 92 53 56 16	02 75 50 95 98
38 23 16 86 38	42 38 97 01 50	87 75 66 81 41	40 01 74 91 62	48 51 84 08 32
31 96 25 91 47	96 44 33 49 13	34 86 82 53 91	00 52 43 48 85	27 55 26 89 62
66 67 40 67 14	64 05 71 95 86	11 05 65 09 68	76 83 20 37 90	57 16 00 11 66
14 90 84 45 11	75 73 88 05 90	52 27 41 14 86	22 98 12 22 08	07 52 74 95 80
68 05 51 18 00	33 96 02 75 19	07 60 62 93 55	59 33 82 43 90	49 37 38 44 59
20 46 78 73 90	97 51 40 14 02	04 02 33 31 08	39 54 16 49 36	47 95 93 13 30
64 19 58 97 79	15 06 15 93 20	01 90 10 75 06	40 78 78 89 62	02 67 74 17 33
05 26 93 70 60	22 35 85 15 13	92 03 51 59 77	59 56 78 06 83	52 91 05 70 74
07 97 10 88 23	09 98 42 99 64	61 71 62 99 15	06 51 29 16 93	58 05 77 09 51
68 71 86 85 85	54 87 66 47 54	73 32 08 11 12	44 95 92 63 16	29 56 24 29 48
26 99 61 65 53	58 37 78 80 70	42 10 50 67 42	32 17 55 85 74	94 44 67 16 94
14 65 52 68 75	87 59 36 22 41	26 78 63 06 55	13 08 27 01 50	15 29 39 39 43

Abridged from R. A. Fisher and F. Yates, Statistical Tables for Biological, Agricultural and Medical Research, (6th ed.) Longman Group UK Ltd (1974).

Table 2 Areas under the normal distribution

z	0 z	0 z	z	0 z	0 z	z	0 z	0 z
0.00	0.0000	0.5000	0.40	0.1554	0.3446	0.80	0.2881	0.2119
0.01	0.0040	0.4960	0.41	0.1591	0.3409	0.81	0.2910	0.2090
0.02	0.0080	0.4920	0.42	0.1628	0.3372	0.82	0.2939	0.2061
0.03	0.0120	0.4880	0.43	0.1664	0.3336	0.83	0.2967	0.2033
0.04	0.0160	0.4840	0.44	0.1700	0.3300	0.84	0.2995	0.2005
0.05	0.0199	0.4801	0.45	0.1736	0.3264	0.85	0.3023	0.1977
0.06	0.0239	0.4761	0.46	0.1772	0.3228	0.86	0.3051	0.1949
0.07	0.0279	0.4721	0.47	0.1808	0.3192	0.87	0.3078	0.1922
0.08	0.0319	0.4681	0.48	0.1844	0.3156	0.88	0.3106	0.1894
0.09	0.0359	0.4641	0.49	0.1879	0.3121	0.89	0.3133	0.1867
0.10	0.0398	0.4602	0.50	0.1915	0.3085	0.90	0.3159	0.1841
0.11	0.0438	0.4562	0.51	0.1950	0.3050	0.91	0.3186	0.1814
0.12	0.0478	0.4522	0.52	0.1985	0.3015	0.92	0.3212	0.1788
0.13	0.0517	0.4483	0.53	0.2019	0.2981	0.93	0.3238	0.1762
0.14	0.0557	0.4443	0.54	0.2054	0.2946	0.94	0.3264	0.1736
0.15	0.0596	0.4404	0.55	0.2088	0.2912	0.95	0.3289	0.1711
0.16	0.0636	0.4364	0.56	0.2123	0.2877	0.96	0.3315	0.1685
0.17	0.0675	0.4325	0.57	0.2157	0.2843	0.97	0.3340	0.1660
0.18	0.0714	0.4286	0.58	0.2190	0.2810	0.98	0.3365	0.1635
0.19	0.0753	0.4247	0.59	0.2224	0.2776	0.99	0.3389	0.1611
0.20	0.0793	0.4207	0.60	0.2257	0.2743	1.00	0.3413	0.1587
0.21	0.0832	0.4168	0.61	0.2291	0.2709	1.01	0.3438	0.1562
0.22	0.0871	0.4129	0.62	0.2324	0.2676	1.02	0.3461	0.1539
0.23	0.0910	0.4090	0.63	0.2357	0.2643	1.03	0.3485	0.1515
0.24	0.0948	0.4052	0.64	0.2389	0.2611	1.04	0.3508	0.1492
0.25	0.0987	0.4013	0.65	0.2422	0.2578	1.05	0.3531	0.1469
0.26	0.1026	0.3974	0.66	0.2454	0.2546	1.06	0.3554	0.1446
0.27	0.1064	0.3969	0.67	0.2486	0.2514	1.07	0.3577	0.1423
0.28	0.1103	0.3897	0.68	0.2517	0.2483	1.08	0.3599	0.1401
0.29	0.1141	0.3859	0.69	0.2549	0.2451	1.09	0.3621	0.1379
0.30	0.1179	0.3821	0.70	0.2580	0.2420	1.10	0.3643	0.1357
0.31	0.1217	0.3783	0.71	0.2611	0.2389	1.11	0.3665	0.1335
0.32	0.1255	0.3745	0.72	0.2642	0.2358	1.12	0.3686	0.1314
0.33	0.1293	0.3707	0.73	0.2673	0.2327	1.13	0.3708	0.1292
0.34	0.1331	0.3669	0.74	0.2704	0.2296	1.14	0.3729	0.1271
0.35	0.1368	0.3632	0.75	0.2734	0.2266	1.15	0.3749	0.1251
0.36	0.1406	0.3594	0.76	0.2764	0.2236	1.16	0.3770	0.1230
0.37	0.1443	0.3557	0.77	0.2794	0.2206	1.17	0.3790	0.1210
0.38	0.1480	0.3520	0.78	0.2823	0.2177	1.18	0.3810	0.1190
0.39	0.1517	0.3483	0.79	0.2852	0.2148	1.19	0.3830	0.1170

Table 2 Continued

z	0 z	0 z	z	0 z	0 z	z	0 z	0 z
1.20	0.3849	0.1151	1.60	0.4452	0.0548	2.00	0.4772	0.0228
1.21	0.3869	0.1131	1.61	0.4463	0.0537	2.01	0.4778	0.0222
1.22	0.3888	0.1112	1.62	0.4474	0.0526	2.02	0.4783	0.0217
1.23	0.3907	0.1093	1.63	0.4484	0.0516	2.03	0.4788	0.0212
1.24	0.3925	0.1075	1.64	0.4495	0.0505	2.04	0.4793	0.0207
1.25	0.3944	0.1056	1.65	0.4505	0.0495	2.05	0.4798	0.0202
1.26	0.3962	0.1038	1.66	0.4515	0.0485	2.06	0.4803	0.0197
1.27	0.3980	0.1020	1.67	0.4525	0.0475	2.07	0.4808	0.0192
1.28	0.3997	0.1003	1.68	0.4535	0.0465	2.08	0.4812	0.0188
1.29	0.4015	0.0985	1.69	0.4545	0.0455	2.09	0.4817	0.0183
1.30	0.4032	0.0968	1.70	0.4554	0.0446	2.10	0.4821	0.0179
1.31	0.4049	0.0951	1.71	0.4564	0.0436	2.11	0.4826	0.0174
1.32	0.4066	0.0934	1.72	0.4573	0.0427	2.12	0.4830	0.0170
1.33	0.4082	0.0918	1.73	0.4582	0.0418	2.13	0.4834	0.0166
1.34	0.4099	0.0901	1.74	0.4591	0.0409	2.14	0.4838	0.0162
1.35	0.4115	0.0885	1.75	0.4599	0.0401	2.15	0.4842	0.0158
1.36	0.4131	0.0869	1.76	0.4608	0.0392	2.16	0.4846	0.0154
1.37	0.4147	0.0853	1.77	0.4616	0.0384	2.17	0.4850	0.0150
1.38	0.4162	0.0838	1.78	0.4625	0.0375	2.18	0.4854	0.0146
1.39	0.4177	0.0823	1.79	0.4633	0.0367	2.19	0.4857	0.0143
1.40	0.4192	0.0808	1.80	0.4641	0.0359	2.20	0.4861	0.0139
1.41	0.4207	0.0793	1.81	0.4649	0.0351	2.21	0.4864	0.0136
1.42	0.4222	0.0778	1.82	0.4656	0.0344	2.22	0.4868	0.0132
1.43	0.4236	0.0764	1.83	0.4664	0.0336	2.23	0.4871	0.0129
1.44	0.4251	0.0749	1.84	0.4671	0.0329	2.24	0.4875	0.0125
1.45	0.4265	0.0735	1.85	0.4678	0.0322	2.25	0.4878	0.0122
1.46	0.4279	0.0721	1.86	0.4686	0.0314	2.26	0.4881	0.0119
1.47	0.4292	0.0708	1.87	0.4693	0.0307	2.27	0.4884	0.0116
1.48	0.4306	0.0694	1.88	0.4699	0.0301	2.28	0.4887	0.0113
1.49	0.4319	0.0681	1.89	0.4706	0.0294	2.29	0.4890	0.0110
1.50	0.4332	0.0668	1.90	0.4713	0.0287	2.30	0.4893	0.0107
1.51	0.4345	0.0655	1.91	0.4719	0.0281	2.31	0.4896	0.0104
1.52	0.4357	0.0643	1.92	0.4726	0.0274	2.32	0.4898	0.0102
1.53	0.4370	0.0630	1.93	0.4732	0.0268	2.33	0.4901	0.0099
1.54	0.4382	0.0618	1.94	0.4738	0.0262	2.34	0.4904	0.0096
1.55	0.4394	0.0606	1.95	0.4744	0.0256	2.35	0.4906	0.0094
1.56	0.4406	0.0594	1.96	0.4750	0.0250	2.36	0.4909	0.0091
1.57	0.4418	0.0582	1.97	0.4756	0.0244	2.37	0.4911	0.0089
1.58	0.4429	0.0571	1.98	0.4761	0.0239	2.38	0.4913	0.0087
1.59	0.4441	0.0559	1.99	0.4767	0.0233	2.39	0.4916	0.0084

Table 2 Continued

z	0 z	0 z	z	0 z	0 z	z	0 z	0 z
2.40	0.4918	0.0082	2.72	0.4967	0.0033	3.04	0.4988	0.0012
2.41	0.4920	0.0080	2.73	0.4968	0.0032	3.05	0.4989	0.0011
2.42	0.4922	0.0078	2.74	0.4969	0.0031	3.06	0.4989	0.0011
2.43	0.4925	0.0075	2.75	0.4970	0.0030	3.07	0.4989	0.0011
2.44	0.4927	0.0073	2.76	0.4971	0.0029	3.08	0.4990	0.0010
2.45	0.4929	0.0017	2.77	0.4972	0.0028	3.09	0.4990	0.0010
2.46	0.4931	0.0069	2.78	0.4973	0.0027	3.10	0.4990	0.0010
2.47	0.4932	0.0068	2.79	0.4974	0.0026	3.11	0.4991	0.0009
2.48	0.4934	0.0066	2.80	0.4974	0.0026	3.12	0.4991	0.0009
2.49	0.4936	0.0064	2.81	0.4975	0.0025	3.13	0.4991	0.0009
2.50	0.4938	0.0062	2.82	0.4976	0.0024	3.14	0.4992	0.0008
2.51	0.4940	0.0060	2.83	0.4977	0.0023	3.15	0.4992	0.0008
2.52	0.4941	0.0059	2.84	0.4977	0.0023	3.16	0.4992	0.0008
2.53	0.4943	0.0057	2.85	0.4978	0.0022	3.17	0.4992	0.0008
2.54	0.4945	0.0055	2.86	0.4979	0.0021	3.18	0.4993	0.0007
2.55	0.4946	0.0054	2.87	0.4979	0.0021	3.19	0.4993	0.0007
2.56	0.4948	0.0052	2.88	0.4980	0.0020	3.20	0.4993	0.0007
2.57	0.4949	0.0051	2.89	0.4981	0.0019	3.21	0.4993	0.0007
2.58	0.4951	0.0049	2.90	0.4981	0.0019	3.22	0.4994	0.0006
2.59	0.4952	0.0048	2.91	0.4982	0.0018	3.23	0.4994	0.0006
2.60	0.4953	0.0047	2.92	0.4982	0.0018	3.24	0.4994	0.0006
2.61	0.4955	0.0045	2.93	0.4983	0.0017	3.25	0.4994	0.0006
2.62	0.4956	0.0044	2.94	0.4984	0.0016	3.30	0.4995	0.0005
2.63	0.4957	0.0043	2.95	0.4984	0.0016	3.35	0.4996	0.0004
2.64	0.4959	0.0041	2.96	0.4985	0.0015	3.40	0.4997	0.0003
2.65	0.4960	0.0040	2.97	0.4985	0.0015	3.45	0.4997	0.0003
2.66	0.4961	0.0039	2.98	0.4986	0.0014	3.50	0.4998	0.0002
2.67	0.4962	0.0038	2.99	0.4986	0.0014	3.60	0.4998	0.0002
2.68	0.4963	0.0037	3.00	0.4987	0.0013	3.70	0.4999	0.0001
2.69	0.4964	0.0036	3.01	0.4987	0.0013	3.80	0.4999	0.0001
2.70	0.4965	0.0035	3.02	0.4987	0.0013	3.90	0.49995	0.00005
2.71	0.4966	0.0034	3.03	0.4988	0.0012	4.00	0.49997	0.00003

The left-hand column in each set of three shows the particular z-value. The centre column shows the area contained between the mean and this z-value. The right-hand column shows the area left in the whole distribution to the right of this z-value. The whole area is one unit and values shown are decimal portions of it. These are also the probabilities of finding a value within the area concerned. For percentages, multiply all area values by 100. For areas between −z and +z, double the values shown.

SOURCE: R. P. Runyon and A. Haber, **Fundamentals of Behavioral Statistics**, *3rd Ed. Reading, Mass.: McGraw-Hill, Inc. (1976) Used with permission. Artwork from R. B. McCall.* **Fundamental Statistics for Psychology**, *Second Edition, New York: Harcourt Brace Jovanovich, Inc. (1975).*

Table 3 Critical values in the Binomial Sign Test

	Level of significance for a one-tailed test				
	0.05	0.025	0.01	0.005	0.0005
	Level of significance for a two-tailed test				
	0.10	0.005	0.02	0.01	0.001
N					
5	0	—	—	—	—
6	0	0	—	—	—
7	0	0	0	—	—
8	1	0	0	0	—
9	1	1	0	0	—
10	1	1	0	0	—
11	2	1	1	0	0
12	2	2	1	1	0
13	3	2	1	1	0
14	3	2	2	1	0
15	3	3	2	2	1
16	4	3	2	2	1
17	4	4	3	2	1
18	5	4	3	3	1
19	5	4	4	3	2
20	5	5	4	3	2
25	7	7	6	5	4
30	10	9	8	7	5
35	12	11	10	9	7

Calculated S most be EQUAL TO or LESS THAN the table (critical) value for significance at the level shown.
SOURCE: F. Clegg, Simple Statistics, Cambridge University Press, 1982. With the kind permission of the author and publishers.

Table 4 Critical values of χ^2

	Level of significance for a one-tailed test					
	0.10	0.05	0.025	0.01	0.005	0.005
	Level of significance for a two-tailed test					
	0.20	0.10	0.05	0.02	0.01	0.001
df						
1	1.64	2.71	3.84	5.41	6.64	10.83
2	3.22	4.60	5.99	7.82	9.21	13.82
3	4.64	6.25	7.82	9.84	11.34	16.27
4	5.99	7.78	9.49	11.67	13.28	18.46
5	7.29	9.24	11.07	13.39	15.09	20.52
6	8.56	10.64	12.59	15.03	16.81	22.46
7	9.80	12.02	14.07	16.62	18.48	24.32
8	11.03	13.36	15.51	18.17	20.09	26.12
9	12.24	14.68	16.92	19.68	21.67	27.88
10	13.44	15.99	18.31	21.16	23.21	29.59
11	14.63	17.28	19.68	22.62	24.72	31.26
12	15.81	18.55	21.03	24.05	26.22	32.91
13	16.98	19.81	22.36	25.47	27.69	34.53
14	18.15	21.06	23.68	26.87	29.14	36.12
15	19.31	22.31	25.00	28.26	30.58	37.70
16	20.46	23.54	26.30	29.63	32.00	39.29
17	21.62	24.77	27.59	31.00	33.41	40.75
18	22.76	25.99	28.87	32.35	34.80	42.31
19	23.90	27.20	30.14	33.69	36.19	43.82
20	25.04	28.41	31.41	35.02	37.57	45.32
21	26.17	29.62	32.67	36.34	38.93	46.80
22	27.30	30.81	33.92	37.66	40.29	48.27
23	28.43	32.01	35.17	38.97	41.64	49.73
24	29.55	33.20	36.42	40.27	42.98	51.18
25	30.68	34.38	37.65	41.57	44.31	52.62
26	31.80	35.56	38.88	42.86	45.64	54.05
27	32.91	36.74	40.11	44.14	46.96	55.48
28	34.03	37.92	41.34	45.42	48.28	56.89
29	35.14	39.09	42.69	49.69	49.59	58.30
30	36.25	40.26	43.77	47.96	50.89	59.70
32	38.47	42.59	46.19	50.49	53.49	62.49
34	40.68	44.90	48.60	53.00	56.06	65.25
36	42.88	47.21	51.00	55.49	58.62	67.99
38	45.08	49.51	53.38	57.97	61.16	70.70
40	47.27	51.81	55.76	60.44	63.69	73.40
44	51.64	56.37	60.48	65.34	68.71	78.75
48	55.99	60.91	65.17	70.20	73.68	84.04
52	60.33	65.42	69.83	75.02	78.62	89.27
56	64.66	69.92	74.47	79.82	83.51	94.46
60	68.97	74.40	79.08	84.58	88.38	99.61

Calculated value of x² must be EQUAL or EXCEED the table (critical) values for significance at the level shown.
Abridged from R.A. Fisher and F. Yates, Statistical Tables for Biological, Agricultural and Medical Research, *(6th ed.)*
Longman Group UK Ltd (1974).

Table 5 Critical values of U for a one-tailed test at 0.005; two-tailed test at 0.01* (Mann-Whitney)

n_2 \ n_1	1	2	3	4	5	6	7	8	9	10	11	12	13	14	15	16	17	18	19	20
1	—	—	—	—	—	—	—	—	—	—	—	—	—	—	—	—	—	—	—	—
2	—	—	—	—	—	—	—	—	—	—	—	—	—	—	—	—	—	—	0	0
3	—	—	—	—	—	—	—	—	0	0	0	1	1	1	2	2	2	2	3	3
4	—	—	—	—	—	0	0	1	1	2	2	3	3	4	5	5	6	6	7	8
5	—	—	—	—	0	1	1	2	3	4	5	6	7	7	8	9	10	11	12	13
6	—	—	—	0	1	2	3	4	5	6	7	9	10	11	12	13	15	16	17	18
7	—	—	—	0	1	3	4	6	7	9	10	12	13	15	16	18	19	21	22	24
8	—	—	—	1	2	4	6	7	9	11	13	15	17	18	20	22	24	26	28	30
9	—	—	0	1	3	5	7	9	11	13	16	18	20	22	24	27	29	31	33	36
10	—	—	0	2	4	6	9	11	13	16	18	21	24	26	29	31	34	37	39	42
11	—	—	0	2	5	7	10	13	16	18	21	24	27	30	33	36	39	42	45	48
12	—	—	1	3	6	9	12	15	18	21	24	27	31	34	37	41	44	47	51	54
13	—	—	1	3	7	10	13	17	20	24	27	31	34	38	42	45	49	53	56	60
14	—	—	1	4	7	11	15	18	22	26	30	34	38	42	46	50	54	58	63	67
15	—	—	2	5	8	12	16	20	24	29	33	37	42	46	51	55	60	64	69	73
16	—	—	2	5	9	13	18	22	27	31	36	41	45	50	55	60	65	70	74	79
17	—	—	2	6	10	15	19	24	29	34	39	44	49	54	60	65	70	75	81	86
18	—	—	2	6	11	16	21	26	31	37	42	47	53	58	64	70	75	81	87	92
19	—	0	3	7	12	17	22	28	33	39	45	51	56	63	69	74	81	87	93	99
20	—	0	3	8	13	18	24	30	36	42	48	54	60	67	73	79	86	92	99	105

Dashes in the body of the table indicate that no decision is possible at the stated level of significance.

For any n_1 and n_2 the observed value of U is significant at a given level of significance if it is equal to or less than the critical values shown.

SOURCE: R. Runyon and A. Haber (1976) Fundamentals of Behavioural Statistics (3rd ed.) Reading, Mass.: McGraw Hill, Inc. with kind permission of the publisher.

Table 5b Critical values of U for a one-tailed test at 0.01; two-tailed test at 0.02* (Mann–Whitney)

n_2 \ n_1	1	2	3	4	5	6	7	8	9	10	11	12	13	14	15	16	17	18	19	20
1	—	—	—	—	—	—	—	—	—	—	—	—	—	—	—	—	—	—	—	—
2	—	—	—	—	—	—	—	—	—	—	—	—	0	0	0	0	0	0	1	1
3	—	—	—	—	—	—	0	0	1	1	1	2	2	2	3	3	4	4	4	5
4	—	—	—	—	0	1	1	2	3	3	4	5	5	6	7	7	8	9	9	10
5	—	—	—	0	1	2	3	4	5	6	7	8	9	10	11	12	13	14	15	16
6	—	—	—	1	2	3	4	6	7	8	9	11	12	13	15	16	18	19	20	22
7	—	—	0	1	3	4	6	7	9	11	12	14	16	17	19	21	23	24	26	28
8	—	—	0	2	4	6	7	9	11	13	15	17	20	22	24	26	28	30	32	34
9	—	—	1	3	5	7	9	11	14	16	18	21	23	26	28	31	33	36	38	40
10	—	—	1	3	6	8	11	13	16	19	22	24	27	30	33	36	38	41	44	47
11	—	—	1	4	7	9	12	15	18	22	25	28	31	34	37	41	44	47	50	53
12	—	—	2	5	8	11	14	17	21	24	28	31	35	38	42	46	49	53	56	60
13	—	0	2	5	9	12	16	20	23	27	31	35	39	43	47	51	55	59	63	67
14	—	0	2	6	10	13	17	22	26	30	34	38	43	47	51	56	60	65	69	73
15	—	0	3	7	11	15	19	24	28	33	37	42	47	51	56	61	66	70	75	80
16	—	0	3	7	12	16	21	26	31	36	41	46	51	56	61	66	71	76	82	87
17	—	0	4	8	13	18	23	28	33	38	44	49	55	60	66	71	77	82	88	93
18	—	0	4	9	14	19	24	30	36	41	47	53	59	65	70	76	82	88	94	100
19	—	1	4	9	15	20	26	32	38	44	50	56	63	69	75	82	88	94	101	107
20	—	1	5	10	16	22	28	34	40	47	53	60	67	73	80	87	93	100	107	114

* Dashes in the body of the table indicate that no decision is possible at the stated level of significance.
For any n_1 and n_2 the observed value of U is significant at a given level of significance if it is equal to or less than the critical values shown.
SOURCE: R. Runyon and A. Haber (1976) Fundamentals of Behavioural Statistics (3rd ed.) Reading, Mass.: McGraw Hill, Inc. with kind permission of the publisher.

Table 5c Critical values of U for a one-tailed test at 0.025; two-tailed test at 0.05* (Mann-Whitney)

n_2										n_1										
	1	2	3	4	5	6	7	8	9	10	11	12	13	14	15	16	17	18	19	20
1	—	—	—	—	—	—	—	—	—	—	—	—	—	—	—	—	—	—	—	—
2	—	—	—	—	—	—	—	0	0	0	0	1	1	1	1	1	2	2	2	2
3	—	—	—	—	0	1	1	2	2	3	3	4	4	5	5	6	6	7	7	8
4	—	—	—	0	1	2	3	4	4	5	6	7	8	9	10	11	11	12	13	13
5	—	—	0	1	2	3	5	6	7	8	9	11	12	13	14	15	17	18	19	20
6	—	—	1	2	3	5	6	8	10	11	13	14	16	17	19	21	22	24	25	27
7	—	—	1	3	5	6	8	10	12	14	16	18	20	22	24	26	28	30	32	34
8	—	0	2	4	6	8	10	13	15	17	19	22	24	26	29	31	34	36	38	41
9	—	0	2	4	7	10	12	15	17	20	23	26	28	31	34	37	39	42	45	48
10	—	0	3	5	8	11	14	17	20	23	26	29	33	36	39	42	45	48	52	55
11	—	0	3	6	9	13	16	19	23	26	30	33	37	40	44	47	51	55	58	62
12	—	1	4	7	11	14	18	22	26	29	33	37	41	45	49	53	57	61	65	69
13	—	1	4	8	12	16	20	24	28	33	37	41	45	50	54	59	63	67	72	76
14	—	1	5	9	13	17	22	26	31	36	40	45	50	55	59	64	67	74	78	83
15	—	1	5	10	14	19	24	29	34	39	44	49	54	59	64	70	75	80	85	90
16	—	1	6	11	15	21	26	31	37	42	47	53	59	64	70	75	81	86	92	98
17	—	2	6	11	17	22	28	34	39	45	51	57	63	67	75	81	87	93	99	105
18	—	2	7	12	18	24	30	36	42	48	55	61	67	74	80	86	93	99	106	112
19	—	2	7	13	19	25	32	38	45	52	58	65	72	78	85	92	99	106	113	119
20	—	2	8	13	20	27	34	41	48	55	62	69	76	83	90	98	105	112	119	127

* *Dashes in the body of the table indicate that no decision is possible at the stated level of significance.*

For any n_1 and n_2 the observed value of U is significant at a given level of significance if it is equal to or less than the critical values shown.

SOURCE: *R. Runyon and A. Haber (1976) Fundamentals of Behavioural Statistics (3rd ed.) Reading, Mass.: McGraw Hill, Inc. with kind permission of the publisher.*

Table 5d Critical values of U for a one-tailed test at 0.05; two-tailed test at 0.10* (Mann-Whitney)

n_2	n_1 1	2	3	4	5	6	7	8	9	10	11	12	13	14	15	16	17	18	19	20
1	—	—	—	—	—	—	—	—	—	—	—	—	—	—	—	—	—	—	0	0
2	—	—	—	—	0	0	0	1	1	1	1	2	2	2	3	3	3	4	4	4
3	—	—	0	0	1	2	2	3	3	4	5	5	6	7	7	8	9	9	10	11
4	—	—	0	1	2	3	4	5	6	7	8	9	10	11	12	14	15	16	17	18
5	—	0	1	2	4	5	6	8	9	11	12	13	15	16	18	19	20	22	23	25
6	—	0	2	3	5	7	8	10	12	14	16	17	19	21	23	25	26	28	30	32
7	—	0	2	4	6	8	11	13	15	17	19	21	24	26	28	30	33	35	37	39
8	—	1	3	5	8	10	13	15	18	20	23	26	28	31	33	36	39	41	44	47
9	—	1	3	6	9	12	15	18	21	24	27	30	33	36	39	42	45	48	51	54
10	—	1	4	7	11	14	17	20	24	27	31	34	37	41	44	48	51	55	58	62
11	—	1	5	8	12	16	19	23	27	31	34	38	42	46	50	54	57	61	65	69
12	—	2	5	9	13	17	21	26	30	34	38	42	47	51	55	60	64	68	72	77
13	—	2	6	10	15	19	24	28	33	37	42	47	51	56	61	65	70	75	80	84
14	—	2	7	11	16	21	26	31	36	41	46	51	56	61	66	71	77	82	87	92
15	—	3	7	12	18	23	28	33	39	44	50	55	61	66	72	77	83	88	94	100
16	—	3	8	14	19	25	30	36	42	48	54	60	65	71	77	83	89	95	101	107
17	—	3	9	15	20	26	33	39	45	51	57	64	70	77	83	89	96	102	109	115
18	—	4	9	16	22	28	35	41	48	55	61	68	75	82	88	95	102	109	116	123
19	0	4	10	17	23	30	37	44	51	58	65	72	80	87	94	101	109	116	123	130
20	0	4	11	18	25	32	39	47	54	62	69	77	84	92	100	107	115	123	130	138

* Dashes in the body of the table indicate that no decision is possible at the stated level of significance.
For any n_1 and n_2 the observed value of U is significant at a given level of significance if it is equal to or less than the critical values shown.
SOURCE: R. Runyon and A. Haber (1976) Fundamentals of Behavioural Statistics (3rd ed.) Reading, Mass.: McGraw Hill, Inc. with kind permission of the publisher.

Table 6 Critical values of *T* in the Wilcoxon Rank Sum test

Number of scores in the larger sample (n_1)	Level of significance One-tailed	Two-tailed	\(\) Number of scores in the smaller sample (n_2) 1	2	3	4	5	6	7	8	9	10	11	12	13	14	15	16	17	18	19	20
3	0.10	0.20		3	7																	
	0.05	0.10			6																	
	0.025	0.05																				
	0.005	0.01				(4)																
4	0.10	0.20		3	7	13																
	0.05	0.10			6	11																
	0.025	0.05				10																
	0.005	0.01					(5)															
5	0.10	0.20		4	8	14	20															
	0.05	0.10		3	7	12	19															
	0.025	0.05			6	11	17															
	0.005	0.01					15	(6)														
6	0.10	0.20		4	9	15	22	30														
	0.05	0.10		3	8	13	20	28														
	0.025	0.05			7	12	18	26														
	0.005	0.01				10	16	23	(7)													
7	0.10	0.20		4	10	16	23	32	41													
	0.05	0.10		3	8	14	21	29	39													
	0.025	0.05			7	13	20	27	36													
	0.005	0.01				10	16	24	32	(8)												
8	0.10	0.20		5	11	17	25	34	44	55												
	0.05	0.10		4	9	15	23	31	41	51												
	0.025	0.05		3	8	14	21	29	38	49												
	0.005	0.01				11	17	25	34	43												

Table 6 Critical values of T in the Wilcoxon Rank Sum test (continued)

Number of scores in the larger sample (n_1)	Level of significance — One-tailed	Two-tailed	Number of scores in the smaller sample (n_2) 1	2	3	4	5	6	7	8	9	10	11	12	13	14	15	16	17	18	19	20
9	0.10	0.20	1	5	11	19	27	36	46	58	70											
	0.05	0.10		4	9	16	24	33	43	54	66											
	0.025	0.05		3	8	14	22	31	40	51	62											
	0.005	0.01			6	11	18	26	35	45	56	(10)										
10	0.10	0.20	1	6	12	20	28	38	49	60	73	87										
	0.05	0.10		4	10	17	26	35	45	56	69	82										
	0.025	0.05		3	9	15	23	32	42	53	65	78										
	0.005	0.01			6	12	19	27	37	47	58	71	(11)									
11	0.10	0.20	1	6	13	21	30	40	51	63	76	91	106									
	0.05	0.10		4	11	18	27	37	47	59	72	86	100									
	0.025	0.05		3	9	16	24	34	44	55	68	81	96									
	0.005	0.01			6	12	20	28	38	49	61	73	87	(12)								
12	0.10	0.20	1	7	14	22	32	42	54	66	80	94	110	127								
	0.05	0.10		5	11	19	28	38	49	62	75	89	104	120								
	0.025	0.05		4	10	17	26	35	46	58	71	84	99	115								
	0.005	0.01			7	13	21	30	40	51	63	76	90	105	(13)							
13	0.10	0.20	1	7	15	23	33	44	56	69	83	98	114	131	149							
	0.05	0.10		5	12	20	30	40	52	64	78	92	108	125	142							
	0.025	0.05		4	10	18	27	37	48	60	73	88	103	119	136							
	0.005	0.01			7	14	22	31	41	53	65	79	93	109	125	(14)						
14	0.10	0.20	1	7	16	25	35	46	59	72	86	102	118	136	154	174						
	0.05	0.10		5	13	21	31	42	54	67	81	96	112	129	147	166						
	0.025	0.05		4	11	19	28	38	50	62	76	91	106	123	141	160						
	0.005	0.01			7	14	22	32	43	54	67	81	96	112	129	147	(15)					
15	0.10	0.20	1	8	16	26	37	48	61	75	90	106	123	141	159	179	200					
	0.05	0.10		6	13	22	33	44	56	69	84	99	116	133	152	171	192					
	0.025	0.05		4	11	20	29	40	52	65	79	94	110	127	145	164	184					
	0.005	0.01			8	15	23	33	44	56	69	84	99	115	113	151	171					

Number of scores in the larger sample (n_1)

Critical values of T (Wilcoxon rank-sum / Mann–Whitney). The two significance columns give the two-tailed (0.20, 0.10, 0.05, 0.01) and one-tailed (0.10, 0.05, 0.025, 0.005) levels. Parenthetical column markers (16)–(20) indicate the column where $n_2 = n_1$. The smaller sample size (n_2) runs across the columns.

n_1	(2-tail)	(1-tail)	1	2	3	4	5	6	7	8	9	10	11	12	13	14	15	16	17	18	19	20
16	0.20	0.10	1	8	17	27	38	50	64	78	93	109	127	145	165	185	206	229				
	0.10	0.05		6	14	24	34	46	58	72	87	103	120	138	156	176	197	219				
	0.05	0.025		4	12	21	30	42	54	67	82	97	113	131	150	169	190	211				
	0.01	0.005			8	15	24	34	46	58	72	86	102	119	136	155	175	196				
17	0.20	0.10	1	9	18	28	40	52	66	81	97	113	131	150	170	190	212	235	259			
	0.10	0.05		6	15	25	35	47	61	75	90	106	123	142	161	182	203	225	249			
	0.05	0.025		5	12	21	32	43	56	70	84	100	117	135	154	174	195	217	240			
	0.01	0.005			8	16	25	36	47	60	74	89	105	122	140	159	180	201	223			
18	0.20	0.10	1	9	19	30	42	55	69	84	100	117	135	155	175	196	218	242	266	291		
	0.10	0.05		7	15	26	37	49	63	77	93	110	127	146	166	187	208	231	255	280		
	0.05	0.025		5	13	22	33	45	58	72	87	103	121	139	158	179	200	222	246	270		
	0.01	0.005			8	16	26	37	49	62	76	92	108	125	144	163	184	206	228	252		
19	0.20	0.10	2	10	20	31	43	57	71	87	103	121	139	159	180	202	224	248	273	299	325	
	0.10	0.05	1	7	16	27	38	51	65	80	96	113	131	150	171	192	214	237	262	287	313	
	0.05	0.025		5	13	23	34	46	60	74	90	107	124	143	163	182	205	228	252	277	303	
	0.01	0.005		3	9	17	27	38	50	64	78	94	111	129	147	168	189	210	234	258	283	
20	0.20	0.10	2	10	21	32	45	59	74	90	107	125	144	164	185	207	230	255	280	306	333	361
	0.10	0.05	1	7	17	28	40	53	67	83	99	117	135	155	175	197	220	243	268	294	320	348
	0.05	0.025		5	14	24	35	48	62	77	93	110	128	147	167	188	210	234	258	283	309	337
	0.01	0.005		3	9	18	28	39	52	66	81	97	114	132	151	172	193	215	239	263	289	315

Calculated T must be EQUAL TO or LESS THAN the table (critical) value for significance at the level shown.

SOURCE: Tate and Clelland, Non-parametric and short-cut statistics, Interstate Printers and Publishers Inc., Danville, Illinois (1957) by kind permission of the authors.

Table 7 Critical values of *T* in the Wilcoxon Signed Ranks test

	Levels of significance for a one-tailed test			
	0.05	0.025	0.01	0.001

	Levels of significance for a two-tailed test			
	0.1	0.05	0.02	0.002

Sample size				
$N = 5$	$T \leq 0$			
6	2	0		
7	3	2	0	
8	5	3	1	
9	8	5	3	
10	11	8	5	0
11	13	10	7	1
12	17	13	9	2
13	21	17	12	4
14	25	21	15	6
15	30	25	19	8
16	35	29	23	11
17	41	34	27	14
18	47	40	32	18
19	53	46	37	21
20	60	52	43	26
21	67	58	49	30
22	75	65	55	35
23	83	73	62	40
24	91	81	69	45
25	100	89	76	51
26	110	98	84	58
27	119	107	92	64
28	130	116	101	71
30	151	137	120	86
31	163	147	130	94
32	175	159	140	103
33	187	170	151	112

Calculated T *must be* EQUAL TO *or* LESS THAN *the table (critical) value for significance at the level shown.*
SOURCE: *Adapted from R. Meddis,* Statistical Handbook for Non-Statisticians, *McGraw-Hill, London (1975),*
with the kind permission of the author and publishers.

Table 8 Critical values of *t*

	Level of significance for a one-tailed test			
	0.05	0.025	0.01	0.005
	Level of significance for a two-tailed test			
	0.10	0.05	0.02	0.01
Degrees of freedom				
1	6.314	12.706	31.821	63.657
2	2.920	4.303	6.965	9.925
3	2.353	3.182	4.541	5.841
4	2.132	2.776	3.747	4.604
5	2.015	2.571	3.365	4.032
6	1.943	2.447	3.143	3.707
7	1.895	2.365	2.998	3.499
8	1.860	2.306	2.896	3.355
9	1.833	2.262	2.821	3.250
10	1.812	2.228	2.764	3.169
11	1.796	2.201	2.718	3.106
12	1.782	2.179	2.681	3.055
13	1.771	2.160	2.650	3.012
14	1.761	2.145	2.624	2.977
15	1.753	2.131	2.602	2.947
16	1.746	2.120	2.583	2.921
17	1.740	2.110	2.567	2.898
18	1.734	2.101	2.552	2.878
19	1.729	2.093	2.539	2.861
20	1.725	2.086	2.528	2.845
21	1.721	2.080	2.518	2.831
22	1.717	2.074	2.508	2.819
23	1.714	2.069	2.500	2.807
24	1.711	2.064	2.492	2.797
25	1.708	2.060	2.485	2.787
26	1.706	2.056	2.479	2.779
27	1.703	2.052	2.473	2.771
28	1.701	2.048	2.467	2.763
29	1.699	2.045	2.462	2.756
30	1.697	2.042	2.457	2.750
40	1.684	2.021	2.423	2.704
60	1.671	2.000	2.390	2.660
120	1.658	1.980	2.358	2.617
∞	1.645	1.960	2.326	2.576

Calculated t must EQUAL or EXCEED the table (critical) value for significance at the level shown.
SOURCE: *Abridged from R. A. Fisher and F. Yates,* Statistical Tables for Biological, Agricultural and Medical Research, *(6th ed.) Longman Group UK Ltd (1974).*

Table 9 Critical values of Spearman's r_s

	Level of significance for a one-tailed test			
	0.05	0.025	0.01	0.005
	Level of significance for a two-tailed test			
	0.10	0.05	0.02	0.01
N = 4	1.000			
5	0.900	1.000	1.000	
6	0.829	0.886	0.943	1.000
7	0.714	0.786	0.893	0.929
8	0.643	0.738	0.833	0.881
9	0.600	0.700	0.783	0.833
10	0.564	0.648	0.745	0.794
11	0.536	0.618	0.709	0.755
12	0.503	0.587	0.671	0.727
13	0.484	0.560	0.648	0.703
14	0.464	0.538	0.622	0.675
15	0.443	0.521	0.604	0.654
16	0.429	0.503	0.582	0.635
17	0.414	0.485	0.566	0.615
18	0.401	0.472	0.550	0.600
19	0.391	0.460	0.535	0.584
20	0.380	0.447	0.520	0.570
21	0.370	0.435	0.508	0.556
22	0.361	0.425	0.496	0.544
23	0.353	0.415	0.486	0.532
24	0.344	0.406	0.476	0.521
25	0.337	0.398	0.466	0.511
26	0.331	0.390	0.457	0.501
27	0.324	0.382	0.448	0.491
28	0.317	0.375	0.440	0.483
29	0.312	0.368	0.433	0.475
30	0.306	0.362	0.425	0.467

For n > 30, the significance of r_s can be tested by using the formula:

$$t = r_s \sqrt{\frac{n-2}{1-r_s^2}} \qquad df = n - 2$$

and checking the value of t in Table 8.

Calculated r_s must EQUAL or EXCEED the table (critical) value for significance at the level shown.
SOURCE: J. H. Zhar, Significance testing of the Spearman Rank Correlation Coefficient, Journal of the American Statistical Association, 67, 578–80. With the kind permission of the publishers.

Table 10 Critical values of Pearson's r

df (N − 2)	Level of significance for a one-tailed test			
	0.05	0.025	0.005	0.0005
	Level of significance for a two-tailed test			
	0.10	0.05	0.01	0.001
2	0.9000	0.9500	0.9900	0.9999
3	0.805	0.878	0.9587	0.9911
4	0.729	0.811	0.9172	0.9741
5	0.669	0.754	0.875	0.9509
6	0.621	0.707	0.834	0.9241
7	0.582	0.666	0.798	0.898
8	0.549	0.632	0.765	0.872
9	0.521	0.602	0.735	0.847
10	0.497	0.576	0.708	0.823
11	0.476	0.553	0.684	0.801
12	0.475	0.532	0.661	0.780
13	0.441	0.514	0.641	0.760
14	0.426	0.497	0.623	0.742
15	0.412	0.482	0.606	0.725
16	0.400	0.468	0.590	0.708
17	0.389	0.456	0.575	0.693
18	0.378	0.444	0.561	0.679
19	0.369	0.433	0.549	0.665
20	0.360	0.423	0.537	0.652
25	0.323	0.381	0.487	0.597
30	0.296	0.349	0.449	0.554
35	0.275	0.325	0.418	0.519
40	0.257	0.304	0.393	0.490
45	0.243	0.288	0.372	0.465
50	0.231	0.273	0.354	0.443
60	0.211	0.250	0.325	0.408
70	0.195	0.232	0.302	0.380
80	0.183	0.217	0.283	0.357
90	0.173	0.205	0.267	0.338
100	0.164	0.195	0.254	0.321

Calculated r *must EQUAL or EXCEED the table (critical) value for significance at the level shown.*
SOURCE: *F. C. Powell,* Cambridge Mathematical and Statistical Tables, *Cambridge University Press (1976). With kind permission of the author and publishers.*

Table 11 Critical values of F at the 5% level of significance

	Degrees of freedom for the numerator																		
	1	2	3	4	5	6	7	8	9	10	12	15	20	24	30	40	60	120	∞
1	161.4	199.5	215.7	224.6	230.2	234.0	236.8	238.9	240.5	241.9	243.9	245.9	248.0	249.1	250.1	251.1	252.2	253.3	254.3
2	18.51	19.00	19.16	19.25	19.30	19.33	19.35	19.37	19.38	19.40	19.41	19.43	19.45	19.45	19.46	19.47	19.48	19.49	19.50
3	10.13	9.55	9.28	9.12	9.01	8.94	8.89	8.85	8.81	8.79	8.74	8.70	8.66	8.64	8.62	8.59	8.57	8.55	8.53
4	7.71	6.94	6.59	6.39	6.26	6.16	6.09	6.04	6.00	5.96	5.91	5.86	5.80	5.77	5.75	5.72	5.69	5.66	5.63
5	6.61	5.79	5.41	5.19	5.05	4.95	4.88	4.82	4.77	4.74	4.68	4.62	4.56	4.53	4.50	4.46	4.43	4.40	4.36
6	5.99	5.14	4.76	4.53	4.39	4.28	4.21	4.15	4.10	4.06	4.00	3.94	3.87	3.84	3.81	3.77	3.74	3.70	3.67
7	5.59	4.74	4.35	4.12	3.97	3.87	3.79	3.73	3.68	3.64	3.57	3.51	3.44	3.41	3.38	3.34	3.30	3.27	3.23
8	5.32	4.46	4.07	3.84	3.69	3.58	3.50	3.44	3.39	3.35	3.28	3.22	3.15	3.12	3.08	3.04	3.01	2.97	2.93
9	5.12	4.26	3.86	3.63	3.48	3.37	3.29	3.23	3.18	3.14	3.07	3.01	2.94	2.90	2.86	2.83	2.79	2.75	2.71
10	4.96	4.10	3.71	3.48	3.33	3.22	3.14	3.07	3.02	2.98	2.91	2.85	2.77	2.74	2.70	2.66	2.62	2.58	2.54
11	4.84	3.98	3.59	3.36	3.20	3.09	3.01	2.95	2.90	2.85	2.79	2.72	2.65	2.61	2.57	2.53	2.49	2.45	2.40
12	4.75	3.89	3.49	3.26	3.11	3.00	2.91	2.85	2.80	2.75	2.69	2.62	2.54	2.51	2.47	2.43	2.38	2.34	2.30
13	4.67	3.81	3.41	3.18	3.03	2.92	2.83	2.77	2.71	2.67	2.60	2.53	2.46	2.42	2.38	2.34	2.30	2.25	2.21
14	4.60	3.74	3.34	3.11	2.96	2.85	2.76	2.70	2.65	2.60	2.53	2.46	2.39	2.35	2.31	2.27	2.22	2.18	2.13
15	4.54	3.68	3.29	3.06	2.90	2.79	2.71	2.64	2.59	2.54	2.48	2.40	2.33	2.29	2.25	2.20	2.16	2.11	2.07
16	4.49	3.63	3.24	3.01	2.85	2.74	2.66	2.59	2.54	2.49	2.42	2.35	2.28	2.24	2.19	2.15	2.11	2.06	2.01
17	4.45	3.59	3.20	2.96	2.81	2.70	2.61	2.55	2.49	2.45	2.38	2.31	2.23	2.19	2.15	2.10	2.06	2.01	1.96
18	4.41	3.55	3.16	2.93	2.77	2.66	2.58	2.51	2.46	2.41	2.34	2.27	2.19	2.15	2.11	2.06	2.02	1.97	1.92
19	4.38	3.52	3.13	2.90	2.74	2.63	2.54	2.48	2.42	2.38	2.31	2.23	2.16	2.11	2.07	2.03	1.98	1.93	1.88
20	4.35	3.49	3.10	2.87	2.71	2.60	2.51	2.45	2.39	2.35	2.28	2.20	2.12	2.08	2.04	1.99	1.95	1.90	1.84
21	4.32	3.47	3.07	2.84	2.68	2.57	2.49	2.42	2.37	2.32	2.25	2.18	2.10	2.05	2.01	1.96	1.92	1.87	1.81
22	4.30	3.44	3.05	2.82	2.66	2.55	2.46	2.40	2.34	2.30	2.23	2.15	2.07	2.03	1.98	1.94	1.89	1.84	1.78
23	4.28	3.42	3.03	2.80	2.64	2.53	2.44	2.37	2.32	2.27	2.20	2.13	2.05	2.01	1.96	1.91	1.86	1.81	1.76
24	4.26	3.40	3.01	2.78	2.62	2.51	2.42	2.36	2.30	2.25	2.18	2.11	2.03	1.98	1.94	1.89	1.84	1.79	1.73
25	4.24	3.39	2.99	2.76	2.60	2.49	2.40	2.34	2.28	2.24	2.16	2.09	2.01	1.96	1.92	1.87	1.82	1.77	1.71
26	4.23	3.37	2.98	2.74	2.59	2.47	2.39	2.32	2.27	2.22	2.15	2.07	1.99	1.95	1.90	1.85	1.80	1.75	1.69
27	4.21	3.35	2.96	2.73	2.57	2.46	2.37	2.31	2.25	2.20	2.13	2.06	1.97	1.93	1.88	1.84	1.79	1.73	1.67
28	4.20	3.34	2.95	2.71	2.56	2.45	2.36	2.29	2.24	2.19	2.12	2.04	1.96	1.91	1.87	1.82	1.77	1.71	1.65
29	4.18	3.33	2.93	2.70	2.55	2.43	2.35	2.28	2.22	2.18	2.10	2.03	1.94	1.90	1.85	1.81	1.75	1.70	1.64
30	4.17	3.32	2.92	2.69	2.53	2.42	2.33	2.27	2.21	2.16	2.09	2.01	1.93	1.89	1.84	1.79	1.74	1.68	1.62
40	4.08	3.23	2.84	2.61	2.45	2.34	2.25	2.18	2.12	2.08	2.00	1.92	1.84	1.79	1.74	1.69	1.64	1.58	1.51
60	4.00	3.15	2.76	2.53	2.37	2.25	2.17	2.10	2.04	1.99	1.92	1.84	1.75	1.70	1.65	1.53	1.53	1.47	1.39
120	3.92	3.07	2.68	2.45	2.29	2.17	2.09	2.02	1.96	1.91	1.83	1.75	1.66	1.61	1.55	1.50	1.43	1.35	1.25
∞	3.84	3.00	2.60	2.37	2.21	2.10	2.01	1.94	1.88	1.83	1.75	1.67	1.57	1.52	1.46	1.39	1.32	1.22	1.00

Degrees of freedom for the denominator

Values of F that equal or exceed the tabled value are significant at or beyond the 5% level.
SOURCE: J. Radford & E. Govier Textbook of Psychology (2nd ed.) Routledge (Abridged from Table 18 of The Biometrika Tables for Statisticians, Vol. 1, edited by Pearson, E. S. and Hartley, H. O. with the permission of E. S. Pearson and the trustees of Biometrika.)

Table 12 Critical values of *F* at the 1% level of significance

	Degrees of freedom for the numerator																		
	1	2	3	4	5	6	7	8	9	10	12	15	20	24	30	40	60	120	∞
1	4052	4999.5	5403	5625	5764	5859	5928	5982	6022	6056	6106	6157	6209	6235	6261	6287	6313	6339	6366
2	98.50	99.00	99.17	99.25	99.30	99.33	99.36	99.37	99.39	99.40	99.42	99.43	99.45	99.46	99.47	99.47	99.48	99.49	99.50
3	34.12	30.82	29.46	28.71	28.24	27.91	27.67	27.49	27.35	27.23	27.05	26.87	26.69	26.60	26.50	26.41	26.32	26.22	26.13
4	21.20	18.00	16.69	15.98	15.52	15.21	14.98	14.80	14.66	14.55	14.37	14.20	14.02	13.93	13.84	13.75	13.65	13.56	13.46
5	16.26	13.27	12.06	11.39	10.97	10.67	10.46	10.29	10.16	10.05	9.89	9.72	9.55	9.47	9.38	9.29	9.20	9.11	9.02
6	13.75	10.92	9.78	9.15	8.75	8.47	8.26	8.10	7.98	7.87	7.72	7.56	7.40	7.31	7.23	7.14	7.06	6.97	6.88
7	12.25	9.55	8.45	7.85	7.46	7.19	6.99	6.84	6.72	6.62	6.47	6.31	6.16	6.07	5.99	5.91	5.82	5.74	5.65
8	11.26	8.65	7.59	7.01	6.63	6.37	6.18	6.03	5.91	5.81	5.67	5.52	5.36	5.28	5.20	5.12	5.03	4.95	4.86
9	10.56	8.02	6.99	6.42	6.06	5.80	5.61	5.47	5.35	5.26	5.11	4.96	4.81	4.73	4.65	4.57	4.48	4.40	4.31
10	10.04	7.56	6.55	5.99	5.64	5.39	5.20	5.06	4.94	4.85	4.71	4.56	4.41	4.33	4.25	4.17	4.08	4.00	3.91
11	9.65	7.21	6.22	5.67	5.32	5.07	4.89	4.74	4.63	4.54	4.40	4.25	4.10	4.02	3.94	3.86	3.78	3.69	3.60
12	9.33	6.93	5.95	5.41	5.06	4.82	4.64	4.50	4.39	4.30	4.16	4.01	3.86	3.78	3.70	3.62	3.54	3.45	3.36
13	9.07	6.70	5.74	5.21	4.86	4.62	4.44	4.30	4.19	4.10	3.96	3.82	3.66	3.59	3.51	3.43	3.34	3.25	3.17
14	8.86	6.51	5.56	5.04	4.69	4.46	4.28	4.14	4.03	3.94	3.80	3.66	3.51	3.43	3.35	3.27	3.18	3.09	3.00
15	8.68	6.36	5.42	4.89	4.56	4.32	4.14	4.00	3.89	3.80	3.67	3.52	3.37	3.29	3.21	3.13	3.05	2.96	2.87
16	8.53	6.23	5.29	4.77	4.44	4.20	4.03	3.89	3.78	3.69	3.55	3.41	3.26	3.18	3.10	3.02	2.93	2.84	2.75
17	8.40	6.11	5.18	4.67	4.34	4.10	3.93	3.79	3.68	3.59	3.46	3.31	3.16	3.08	3.00	2.92	2.83	2.75	2.65
18	8.29	6.01	5.09	4.58	4.25	4.01	3.84	3.71	3.60	3.51	3.37	3.23	3.08	3.00	2.92	2.84	2.75	2.66	2.57
19	8.18	5.93	5.01	4.50	4.17	3.94	3.77	3.63	3.52	3.43	3.30	3.15	3.00	2.92	2.84	2.76	2.67	2.58	2.49
20	8.10	5.85	4.94	4.43	4.10	3.87	3.70	3.56	3.46	3.37	3.23	3.09	2.94	2.86	2.78	2.69	2.61	2.52	2.42
21	8.02	5.78	4.87	4.37	4.04	3.81	3.64	3.51	3.40	3.31	3.17	3.03	2.88	2.80	2.72	2.64	2.55	2.46	2.36
22	7.95	5.72	4.82	4.31	3.99	3.76	3.59	3.45	3.35	3.26	3.12	2.98	2.83	2.75	2.67	2.58	2.50	2.40	2.31
23	7.88	5.66	4.76	4.26	3.94	3.71	3.54	3.41	3.30	3.21	3.07	2.93	2.78	2.70	2.62	2.54	2.45	2.35	2.26
24	7.82	5.61	4.72	4.22	3.90	3.67	3.50	3.36	3.26	3.17	3.03	2.89	2.74	2.66	2.58	2.49	2.40	2.31	2.21
25	7.77	5.57	4.68	4.18	3.85	3.63	3.46	3.32	3.22	3.13	2.99	2.85	2.70	2.62	2.54	2.45	2.36	2.27	2.17
26	7.72	5.53	4.64	4.14	3.82	3.59	3.42	3.29	3.18	3.09	2.96	2.81	2.66	2.58	2.50	2.42	2.33	2.23	2.13
27	7.68	5.49	4.60	4.11	3.78	3.56	3.39	3.26	3.15	3.06	2.93	2.78	2.63	2.55	2.47	2.38	2.29	2.20	2.10
28	7.64	5.45	4.57	4.07	3.75	3.53	3.36	3.23	3.12	3.03	2.90	2.75	2.60	2.52	2.44	2.35	2.26	2.17	2.06
29	7.60	5.42	4.54	4.04	3.73	3.50	3.33	3.20	3.09	3.00	2.87	2.73	2.57	2.49	2.41	2.33	2.23	2.14	2.03
30	7.56	5.39	4.51	4.02	3.70	3.47	3.30	3.17	3.07	2.98	2.84	2.70	2.55	2.47	2.39	2.30	2.21	2.11	2.01
40	7.31	5.18	4.31	3.83	3.51	3.29	3.12	2.99	2.89	2.80	2.66	2.52	2.37	2.20	2.20	2.11	2.02	1.92	1.80
60	7.08	4.98	4.13	3.65	3.34	3.12	2.95	2.82	2.72	2.63	2.50	2.35	2.20	2.12	2.03	1.94	1.84	1.73	1.60
120	6.85	4.79	3.95	3.48	3.17	2.96	2.79	2.66	2.56	2.47	2.34	2.19	2.03	1.95	1.86	1.76	1.66	1.53	1.33
∞	6.63	4.61	3.78	3.32	3.02	2.80	2.64	2.51	2.41	2.32	2.18	2.04	1.88	1.79	1.70	1.59	1.47	1.32	1.00

Degrees of freedom for the denominator

Values of F that equal or exceed the tabled value are significant at or beyond the 1% level.

Table 13 Critical values of *P* in Jonckheere's Trend test

Number in each sample (*n*)	Level of significance	3 (K) 0.05	0.01	4 (K) 0.05	0.01	5 (K) 0.05	0.01	6 (K) 0.05	0.01
2		10	–	14	20	20	26	26	34
3		17	23	26	34	34	48	44	62
4		24	32	38	50	51	72	67	94
5		33	45	51	71	71	99	93	130
6		42	59	66	92	92	129	121	170
7		53	74	82	115	115	162	151	213
8		64	90	100	140	140	197	184	260
9		76	106	118	167	166	234	219	309
10		88	124	138	195	194	274	256	361

Values of P that equal or exceed the tabled value are significant at, or beyond, the level indicated.
For values of k and n beyond these tabled above, and/or where sample sizes differ, the significance of P can be tested using the formular in the text, see p. 323.
Taken from Jonckheere, A. R., 'A distribution-free k-sample test against ordered alternatives'. Biometrika, Vol. 41, pp. 133–145. With the permission of the trustees of Biometrika.

Table 14 Critical values of *L* in Page's Trend test

Number in each sample (*n*)	Level of significance	3 (K) 0.05	0.01	4 (K) 0.05	0.01	5 (K) 0.05	0.01	6 (K) 0.05	0.01
2		28	–	58	60	103	106	166	173
3		41	42	84	87	150	155	244	252
4		54	55	111	114	197	204	321	331
5		66	68	137	141	244	251	397	409
6		79	81	163	167	291	299	474	486
7		91	93	189	193	338	346	550	563
8		104	106	214	220	384	393	625	640
9		116	119	240	246	431	441	701	717
10		128	131	266	272	477	487	777	793

Values of L that equal or exceed the tabled value are significant at, or beyond, the level indicated.
For values of k and n beyond these tabled above, and/or where sample sizes differ, the significance of P can be tested using the formular in the text, see p. 325.
Taken from Page, E. B. 'Ordered hypotheses for multiple trements: a significance test for linear rank.'
Journal of the American Statistical Association, Vol. 58, pp. 216–230. With permission of the publishers.

References

The numbers in **bold** following each reference give the text pages on which the article or book is cited.

Agar, M. (1986) *Speaking of Ethnography*. Qualitative Research Methods Series, No. 2 London: Sage. **467**

Ainsworth, M.D.S., Beli, S.M. & Stayton, D.J. (1971) Individual differences in strange situation behaviour of one-year-olds. In Schaffer, H.R. (ed.) (1971) *The Origins of Human Social Relations*. London: Academic Press. **103, 114**

Alexander, L. & Guenther, R.K. (1986) The effect of mood and demand on memory, *British Journal of Psychology*, 77(3), 342–51. **410**

Allport, G.W. (1947) *The Use of Personal Documents in Psychological Science*. London: Holt, Rinehart and Winston. **3**

American Psychological Association (1992) *Ethical Principles of Psychologists and Code of Conduct*. Washington: American Psychological Association. **474**

Aronson, E. & Carlsmith, J.M. (1968) Experimentation in social psychology. In Lindzey, G. & Aronson, E. (eds.) (1968) *Handbook of Social Psychology*, 2: Reading, Mass.: Addison-Wesley. **76, 481**

Asch, S.E. (1956) Studies of independence and submission to group pressure, 1. A minority of one against a unanimous majority. In *Psychological Monographs*, 70 (9) (Whole No. 416). **100**

Baddeley, A. (1992) Is memory all talk? *The Psychologist*, 5, 10 (October). **209**

Bakeman, R. and Gottman, J.M. (1986) *Observing Interaction: An introduction to sequential analysis*. Cambridge: Cambridge University Press. **112**

Bandura, A. (1965) Influence of models' reinforcement contingencies on the acquisition of imitative responses. *Journal of Personality and Social Psychology*, 1, 589–95. **100, 110**

Bandura, A. (1977) *Social Learning Theory*. Englewood Cliffs, NJ: Prentice-Hall.

Barber, T.X. (1976) *Pitfalls in Human Research*. Oxford: Pergamon. **74**

Becker, H.S. (1958) Inference and proof in participant observation. *American Sociological Review*, 23, 652–60. **123**

Beltramini, R.F. (1992) Explaining the effectiveness of business gifts: a controlled field experiment. *Journal of the Academy of Marketing Science*, 20(1), 87–91. **57**

Bem, S. & Looren de Jong, H. (1997) *Theoretical Issues in Psychology*. London: Sage. **10, 12, 41, 45**

Ben-Porath, Y.S., Almagor, A., Hoffman-Chemi, A. & Tellegen, A. (1995) A cross-cultural study of personality with the Multi-dimensional Personality Questionnaire. *Journal of Cross-Cultural Psychology*, 26, 360–73. **175**

Benedict, R. (1934) *Patterns of Culture*. Boston: Houghton Mifflin. **187**

Berry, J.W. (1989) Imposed etics-emics-derived etics: The operationalization of a compelling idea. *International Journal of Psychology*, *24*, 721–35. **188**

Berry, J.W., Poortinga, Y.H., Segall, M.H. & Dasen, P.R. (1992) *Cross-cultural Psychology: Research and Applications*. Cambridge: CUP. **190**

Billig, M. (1979) *Psychology, Racism and Fascism*. Birmingham: A.F. and R. Publications. **477**

Block, N.J. & Dworkin, G. (1974) IQ – heritability and inequality. *Philosophy and Public Affairs*, 3, 331–407. **169**

Bogardus, E.S. (1925) Measuring social distance. *Journal of Applied Sociology*, 9, 299–308. **159**

Born, M.P. (1987) Cross-cultural comparison of sex-related differences on intelligence tests: a meta-analysis. *Journal of Cross Cultural Psychology*, 18(3), 283–314. **106**

Bouchard, T.J., Lykken, D.T., McGue, M., Segal, N.L. & Tellegen, A. (1990) Sources of human psychological differences: the Minnesota study of twins reared apart. *Science*, *250*, 223–8. **476**

Bowlby, J. (1953) *Child Care and the Growth of Love*. Harmondsworth: Penguin. **103**

Bracht, G.H. & Glass, G.V. (1968) The external validity of experiments. *American Educational Research Journal*, 5, 437–74. **99**

Bramel, D.A. (1962) A dissonance theory approach to defensives projection. *Journal of Abnormal and Social Psychology*, 64, 121–9. **479**

Breakwell, G.M. & Fife-Schaw, C.R. (1992) Sexual activities and preferences in a UK sample of 16–20 year olds. *Archives of Sexual Behaviour*, 21, 271–93. **183**

Brender, W.J. & Kramer, E. (1967) A comparative need analysis of immediately recalled dreams and TAT responses. In S. Fisher and R.P. Greenberg (1978) *The Scientific Evaluation of Freud's Theories and Therapy*. New York: Basic Books. **166**

Brislin, R. (1993) *Understanding Culture's Influence on Behavior*. Orlando, Fla.: Harcourt Brace Jovanovich. **192**

British Psychology Society (1998) *Code of Conduct, Ethical Principles and Guidelines*. Leicester: British Psychology Society. **474, 487**

Brody, G.H., Stoneman, Z. & Wheatley, P. (1984) Peer interaction in the presence and absence of observers. *Child Development*, 55, 1425–28. **115**

Bromley, D.B. (1986) *The Case Study Method in Psychology and Related Disciplines*. Chichester: Wiley. **126**

Brown, R., Fraser, C. & Bellugi, U. (1964) *The Aquisition of Language*. Monographs of the Society for Research in Child Development 29. 92. **116**

Bruner, E.M. & Kelso, J.P. (1980) Gender differences in graffiti: a semiotic perspective. In *Women's Studies International Quarterly*, 3, 239–52. **455**

Brunswik, E. (1947) *Systematic and Unrepresentative Design of Psychological Experiments with Results in Physical and Social Perception*. Berkeley: University of California Press. **99**

Bryant, B. Harris, M. & Newton, D. (1980) *Children and Minders*. London: Grant McIntyre. **147**

Bryman, A. (1988) *Quantity and Quality in Social Research*. London: Unwin Hyman. **463, 466, 468, 470**

Bryman, A. & Burgess, R.G. (eds.) (1994) *Analyzing Qualitative Data*. London: Routledge. **472**

Burgess, R.G. (1984) *In the Field: an introduction to Field Research*. Allen & Unwin: Hemel Hempstead. **472**

Camilli, G. & Hopkins, D. (1978) Applicability of chi-square to 2×2 contingency tables with small expected cell frequencies. *Psychological Bulletin*, 85, 1, 163–7. **311**

Campbell, D.T. & Stanley, J.C. (1966) *Experimental and Quasi-experimental Designs for Research*. Chicago: Rand McNally. **72**

Campbell, D.T. (1970) Natural selection as an epistemological model. In R. Naroll & R. Cohen (eds.) *A Handbook of Method in Cultural Anthropology* 51–85. New York: Natural History Press. **187**

Carlsmith, J., Ellsworth, P. & Aronson, E. (1976) *Methods of Research in Social Psychology*. Reading, Mass.: Addison-Wesley. **102**

Charlesworth, R. & Hartup, W.W. (1967) Positive social reinforcement in the nursery school peer group. *Child Development*, 38, 993–1002. **115**

Charmaz, K. (1995) Grounded theory. In J.A. Smith, R. Harré, & L. Van Langenhove (eds.) *Rethinking Psychology*. London: Sage. **462**

Cialdini, R.B., Reno, R.R. & Kallgren, C.A. (1990) A focus theory of normative conduct: Recycling the concept of norms to reduce litter in public places. *Journal of Personality and Social Psychology*, 58, 1015–20. **15**, **51**, **309**

Cochran, W.G. (1954) Some methods for strengthening the common x^2 tests. *Biometrics*, 10, 417–51. **311**

Cohen, L. & Holliday, M. (1982) *Statistics for Social Scientists*. London: Harper & Row.

Colby, A., Kohlberg, L., Gibbs, J. & Lieberman, M. (1983) A longitudinal study of moral development. *Monographs of the Society for Research in Child Development*, 48, (1-2 Serial No. 200). **182**

Connolly, J. (1994) 'Of Race and Right' *Irish Times*, 6 December. **477**

Cook, T.D. & Campbell, D.T. (1979) *Quasi-experimentation: Design and Analysis Issues for Field Settings*. Chicago: Rand McNally. **72**, **79**, **96**

Corcoran, S.A. (1986) Task complexity and nursing expertise as factors in decision making. *Nursing Research*, 35(2), 107–12. **130**

Craik, F. & Tulving, E. (1975) Depth of processing and the retention of words in episodic memory. *Journal of Experimental Psychology*, General, Vol 104. **423**

Crano, W.D. & Brewer, M.B. (1973) *Principles of Research in Social Psychology*. New York: McGraw-Hill. **455**

Cronbach, L.J. (1960) *Essentials of Psychological Testing*. New York: Harper & Row. **167**

Csapo, B. (1997) The development of inductive reasoning: Cross-sectional assessments in an educational context. *International Journal of Behavioral Development*, *20*, 4, 609–26. **181**

Cumberbatch, G., Woods, S. Evans, O., Irvine, N. & Lee, M. (1990) *Television Advertising and Sex Role Stereotyping: A Content Analysis* (working paper IV for the Broadcasting Standards Council), Communications Research Group, Aston University. **455**

Darwin, C. (1877) A biographical sketch of an infant. *Mind*, 2, 285–94. **120**

David, S.S.J., Chapman, A.J., Foot, H.C. & Sheehy, N.P (1986) Peripheral vision and child pedestrian accidents. *British Journal of Psychology*, vol 77, 4. **246**, **410**

Davie, R., Butler, N. & Goldstein, H. (1972) *From Birth to Seven*. London: Longman. **148**, **182**

Davis, J.H., Kerr, H.L., Atkin, R.H. & Meek, D. (1975) The decision processes of 6 and 12 person mock injuries assigned unanimous and two thirds majority rules. *Journal of Personality and Social Psychology*, 32, 1–14. **118**

De Waele, J.-P. & Harré, R. (1979) Autobiography as a psychological method. In Ginsburg, G.P. (1979) (ed.) *Emerging Strategies in Social Psychological Research*. Chichester: Wiley. **134, 201**

Denzin, N.K. & Lincoln, Y.S. (1994) *Handbook of Qualitative Research*. London: Sage. **472**

Diesing, P. (1972) *Patterns of Discovery in the Social Sciences*. London: Routledge and Kegan Paul. **117**

Dilthey, W. (1894) *Descriptive Psychology and Historical Understanding*. The Hague: Martinus Nijhoff. (English translation, 1977.) **197**

Doob, A.N. & Gross, A.E. (1968) Status of frustration as an inhibitor of horn-honking responses. *Journal of Social Psychology*, 76, 213–8. **484**

Douglas, J.D. (1972) *Research on Deviance*. New York: Random House. **121**

Eden, D. (1990) Pygmalion without interpersonal contrast effects: Whole groups gain from raising manager expectations, *Journal of Applied Psychology*, 75(4), 394–8. **75**

Edwards, D. & Potter, J. (1992) *Discursive Psychology*. London: Sage. **472**

Enriquez, V. (ed.) (1990) *Indigenous Psychologies*. Quezon City: Psychology Research and Training House. **190**

Ericsson, K.A. & Simon, H.A. (1984) *Protocol Analysis: Verbal Reports as Data*. Cambridge, Mass.: MIT Press. **129**

Erlichman, H. & Halpern, J.N. (1988) Affect and memory: Effects of pleasant and unpleasant odours on retrieval of happy and unhappy memories. *Journal of Personality and Social Psychology*, Vol 55(5), 769–779. **71**

Eron, L.D., Huesmann, L.R., Lefkowitz, M.M. & Walder, L.D. (1972) Does television violence cause aggression? *American Psychologists*, 27, 253–63. **182**

Eysenck, H.J. & Eysenck, S.B.G. (1975) *Manual of the Eysenck Personality Questionnaire*. London: Hodder and Stoughton. **135, 164**

Eysenck, H.J. (1970) *The Structure of Human Personality*. London: Methuen. **174, 175**

Eysenck, M.W. & Keane, M.T. (1995) *Cognitive Psychology: A students' handbook*. Hove: LEA. **120**

Fantz, R.L. (1961) The origin of form perception. *Scientific American*, 204(5), 66–72. **73**

Ferguson, G.A. & Takane, Y. (1989) *Statistical Analysis in Psychology and Education*. New York: McGraw-Hill. **292**

Festinger, L., Riecken, H.W. & Schachter, S. (1956) *When Prophecy Fails*. Minneapolis: University of Minnesota Press. **122**

Fielding, N.G. (ed.) (1988) *Actions and Structure*, London: Sage. **462**

Fielding, N.G. & Fielding, J.L. (1986) *Linking Data*. Qualitative Research Methods Series, No. 4. London: Sage. **462, 466**

Fife-Schaw, C.R. (1995) Surveys and sampling issues. In G.M. Breakwell, S. Hammond & C.R. Fife-Schaw (eds.) *Research Methods in Psychology*. London: Sage. **183**

Finch, J. (1984) 'It's great to have someone to talk to': the ethics and politics of interviewing women. In Bell, C. & Roberts, H. (eds.) (1984) *Social Researching: Policies, Problems and Practice*. London: Routledge and Kegan Paul. **137**

Fischer, C.S., Hout, M., Jankowski, M.S., Lucas, S.R., Swidler, A. & Voss, K. (1996) *Cracking the Bell Curve Myth*. Princeton, N.J.: Princeton University Press. **192**

References

Fisk, J .E. & Pidgeon, N. (1997) The conjunction fallacy: The case for the existence of competing heuristic strategies. *British Journal of Psychology*, 88, 1, 1–27. **15**, **500**

Flick, U. (1998) *An Introduction to Qualitative Research*. London: Sage. **206**

Fraser, S. (ed.) (1995) *The Bell Curve Wars: Race, Intelligence, and the Future of America*. New York: Basic Books. **192**

Friedman, N. (1967) *The Social Nature of Psychological Research*. New York: Basic Books. **74**

Friedrich, L.K. & Stein, A.H. (1973) Aggressive and prosocial television programs and the natural behaviour of pre-school children. *Monographs of the Society for Research in Child Development*. 38(4, serial No. 51). **104**, **110**

Ganster, D.C., Mayes, B.T., Sime, W.E. & Tharp, G.D. (1982) Managing organisational stress: a field experiment. *Journal of Applied Psychology*, 67(5), 533–42. **104**

Ginsberg, G.P. (1979) (ed.) *Emerging Strategies in Social Psychological Research*. Chichester: Wiley. **119**

Glaser, B.G. & Strauss, A.L. (1967) *The Discovery of Grounded Theory: Strategies for Qualitative Research*. Chicago: Aldine. **453**

Godden, D. & Baddeley, A.D. (1975) Context-dependent memory in two natural environments: on land and under water. *British Journal of Psychology*, 66, 325–31. **409**

Gordon, R., Bindrim, T., McNicholas, M. & Walden, T. (1988) Perceptions of blue-collar and white-collar crime: The effect of defendant race on simulated juror decisions, *Journal of Social Psychology*, 128 (2), 191–7. **413**

Gould, S.J. (1997) *The Mismeasure of Man*. London: Penguin. **186**

Grbich, C. (1999) *Qualitative Research in Health*. St Leonards, NSW, Aus: Sage. **464**

Gregor, A.J. & McPherson, D.A. (1965) A study of susceptibility to geometric illusion among cultural sub-groups of Australian Aborigines. *Psychologia Africana*, *11*, 1–13. **187**

Gregory, R.L. & Wallace, J.G. (1963) *Recovery from Early Blindness*. Cambridge: Heffer. **126**

Gross, R.D. (1992) *Psychology: the Science of Mind and Behaviour* (2nd ed.).: London: Hodder and Stoughton Educational. **12**

Gross, R.D. (1994) *Key Studies in Psychology* (2nd ed.). London: Hodder and Stoughton Educational. **128**

Gross, R.D. (1996) *Psychology: The Science of Mind and Behaviour* (3rd ed.) London: Hodder and Stoughton Educational. **2**, **10**, **15**, **45**, **167**, **169**, **478**

Gulian, E. & Thomas, J.R. (1986) The effects of noise, cognitive set and gender on mental arithmetic and performance. *British Journal of Psychology*, Vol 77, 4. **410**

Guttman, L. (1950) The third component of scalable attitudes. *International Journal of Opinion and Attitude Research*, 4, 285–7. **159**

Hall, B.L. (1975) Participatory research: an approach for change. *Convergence, an International Journal of Adult Education*, 8(2), 24–32. **201**

Halliday, S. & Leslie, J.C. (1986) A longitudinal semi-cross-sectional study of the development of mother–child interaction. *British Journal of Developmental Psychology*, 4(3), 221–32. **113**, **182**

Hammersley, M. & Atkinson, P. (1983) *Ethnography: Principles in Practice*. London: Routledge. **99**, **123**, **201**, **202**

Hammond, K.R. (1948) Measuring attitudes by error-choice: an indirect method. *Journal of Abnormal Social Psychology*, 43, 38–48. **135**

Hampden-Turner, C. (1971) *Radical Man*. London: Duckworth. **200**

Harcum, E.R. (1990) Guidance from the literature for accepting a null hypothesis when its truth is expected. *Journal of General Psychology*, 117(3), 325–44. **289**

Harré, R. (1981) The positivist–empiricist approach and its alternative. In Reason, R. & Rowan, J. (1981) *Human Inquiry: A Sourcebook of New Paradigm Research*. Chichester: Wiley. **199**

Hatfield, E. & Walster, G.W. (1981) *A New Look at Love*. Reading, Mass.: Addison–Wesley. **148**

Hayes, N. (1997) *Doing Qualitative Analysis in Psychology*. Hove: Psychology Press. **128, 453**

Hayes, N.J. (1991) Social identity, social representations and organisational cultures. PhD thesis, CNAA/Huddersfield. **453, 460**

Hays, W.L. (1973) *Statistics for the Social Sciences*. London: Holt Rinehart Winston. **318**

Heather, N. (1976) *Radical Perspectives in Psychology*. London: Methuen. **101, 200**

Henwood, K. & Pidgeon, N. (1995) Grounded theory and psychological research, *The Psychologist*, 8(3), 115–18. **199, 452**

Henwood, K.I. & Pidgeon, N.F. (1992) Qualitative research and psychological theorizing. *British Journal of Psychology*, 83, 97–111. **452**

Herrnstein, R.J. & Murray, C. (1994) *The Bell Curve: Intelligence and class structure in American life*. New York: Free Press. **476**

Hess, R., Azuma, H., Kashiwagi, K., Dickson, W.P., Nagano, S., Holloway, S., Miyake, K., Price, G., Hatano, G. & Mcdevitt, T. (1986) Family influences on school readiness and achievement in Japan and the United States: An overview of a longitudinal study. In H. Stevenson, H. Azuma & K. Hakuta (eds.) *Child Development and Education in Japan*. New York: Freeman. **188**

Hinckley, E.D. (1932) The influence of individual opinion on construction of an attitude scale. *Journal of Social Psychology*, 3, 283–96. **158**

Hitch, G.J. (1992) Why isn't discourse analysis more popular in the study of memory? *The Psychologist*, 5, 10 (October). **209**

Ho, D.Y.F. (1998) Indigenous Psychologies. *Journal of Cross-Cultural Psychology*, *29,1*, 88–103. **190**

Hofling, C.K., Brotzman, E, Dalrymple, S., Graves, N. & Pierce, C.M. (1966) An experimental study in nurse-physician relationships. *Journal of Nervous and Mental Disease*, 143, 171–80. **99**

Hollway, W. (1991) *Work Psychology and Organizational behaviour*. London: Sage. **140**

Horowitz, I.A. & Rothschild, B.H. (1970) Conformity as a function of deception and role-playing. *Journal of Personality and Social Psychology*, 14, 224–6. **481**

Hovey, H.B. (1928) Effects of general distraction on the higher thought processes. *American Journal of Psychology*, 40, 585–91. **72**

Howell, D.C. (1992) *Statistical Methods for Psychology*. Boston: PWS-Kent. **340, 342, 368**

Howitt, D. & Owusu-Bempah, J. (1994) *The Racism of Psychology*. Hemel Hempstead: Harvester Wheatsheaf. **193**

Humphreys, G.W. & Riddock, M.J. (1993) Interactions between object and space systems revealed through neuropsychology. In D.E. Myer & S.M. Kornblum (eds.) *Attention and Performance (Vol XIV)*. London: MIT Press. **64**

Humphreys, L. (1970) *Tearoom Trade*. Chicago: Aldine. **484**

Jacob, T., Tennenbaum, D., Seilhamer, R., & Bargiel, Kay. (1994) Reactivity effects during naturalistic observation of distressed and non-distressed families. *Journal of Family Psychology*, 8, 3, 354–63. **115**

Jacoby, R. & Glauberman, N. (eds.) *The Bell Curve Debate*. New York: Times Books. **192**

Jahoda-Lazarsfeld, M. & Zeisl, H. (1932) *Die Arbeitslosen von Marienthal*. Leipzig: Hirzel. **43**

Jefferson, G. (1985) An exercise in the transcription and analysis of laughter. In T. van Dijk (ed.) *Handbook of Discourse Analysis*, Vol 3. London: Academic Press. **460**

Johnston, W.M. & Davey, G.C.L. (1997) The psychological impact of negative TV news bulletins: The catastophizing of personal worries. *British Journal of Psychology*, 88, 85–91. **14**, **51**, **55**, **57**, **69**, **479**

Jones, E.E. & Sigall, H. (1971) The bogus pipeline: a new paradigm for measuring affect and attitude. *Psychological Bulletin*, 76, 349–64. **136**

Jones, F. & Fletcher, C.B. (1992) Transmission of occupational stress: a study of daily fluctuations in work stressors and strains and their impact on marital partners. *VIth European Health Psychology Society Conference* (presented as poster) University of Leipzig (August). **120**

Jones, J.S. (1981) How different are human races? *Nature*, 293, 188–90. **186**

Joravsky, D. (1989) *Soviet Psychology*. Oxford: Blackwell. **30**

Jowell, R. & Topf, R. (1988) *British Social Attitudes*. London: Gower. **147**

Jung, C.G. (1921) *Collected Works of C.G. Jung*. Princeton: Princeton University Press. **185**

Jung, C.G. (1930) Your Negroid and Indian behaviour. *Forum*, 83, 4, 193–99. **185**

Kagan, J., Kearsley, R.B. & Zelazo, P.R. (1980) *Infancy – Its Place in Human Development*. Cambridge, Mass.: Harvard University Press. **182**

Kalton, G. (1983) *Introduction to Survey Sampling*. Newbury Park, Ca.: Sage. **33**

Kamin, L. (1977) *The Science and Politics of IQ*. Harmondsworth: Penguin. **16**, **74**, **175**, **370**, **478**

Kamin, L. (1981) *Intelligence: The Battle for the Mind: Eysenck vs Kamin*. London: Pan. **16**

Kamin, L.J. (1995) Lies, damned lies and statistics. In R. Jacoby and N. Glauberman (eds.) *The Bell Curve Debate*. New York: Times Books. **16**, **74**, **185**

Keller, E.F. (1986) *Reflections on Gender and Science*. New Haven, Conn: Yale University Press. **207**

Kerlinger, F.N. (1973) *Foundations of Behavioural Research*. London: Holt, Rinehart and Winston. **274**

Kerwin, C.K., Ponterotto, J.G., Jackson, B.L. & Harris, A. (1993) Racial identity in bira-cial children: A qualitative investigation. *Journal of Counselling Psychology*, 40, 2, 221–31. **38**, **452**

Kidder, L.H. (1981a) *Selltiz Wrightsman and Cook's Research Methods in Social Relations*, 4th ed. New York: Holt, Rinehart and Winston. **124**

Kidder, L.H. (1981b) Qualitative research and quasi-experimental frameworks. In M.B. Brewer & B.E. Collins (eds.) *Scientific Enquiry and the Social Sciences*. San Francisco: Jossey-Bass. **124**, **469**

Kinsey, A.C., Pomeroy, W.B. & Martin, C.E. (1948) *Sexual Behaviour in the Human Male*. Philadelphia: Saunders. **147**

Kinsey, A.C., Pomeroy, W.B., Martin, C.E. & Gebhard, P.H. (1953) *Sexual Behaviour in the Human Female*. Philadelphia: Saunders. **147**

Kline, P. (1993) *The Handbook of Psychological Testing*. London: Routledge. **160, 170, 173**

Kohlberg, L. (1981) *Essays on Moral Development*. New York: Harper and Row. **181**

Kohler, W. (1925) *The Mentality of Apes*. New York: Harcourt Brace Jovanovich. **486**

Koluchová, J. (1976) Severe deprivation in twins: A case study. In A.M. Clarke & A.D.B. Clark, (1976) *Early Experience: Myth and Evidence*. London: Open Books. **126, 127**

Kraut, R. Patterson, M., Lundmark, V., Kiesler, S, Mukophadhyay, T. & Scherlis, W. (1998). Internet paradox: A social technology that reduces social involvement and psychological well-being? *American Psychologist*, *53*, 9, 1017–31. **55, 104**

Kuhn, T. (1962) *The Structure of Scientific Revolutions*. Chicago, III.: University of Chicago. **201**

Latané, B. & Darley, J.M. (1976) *Help in a Crisis: Bystander Response to an Emergency*. Morristown, NJ: General Learning Press. **479**

Latour, B. (1987) *Science in Action*. Milton Keynes: Open University Press. **206**

Latour, B. (1988) The politics of explanation: An alternative. In S. Woolgar (ed.) *Knowledge and Reflexivity: New Frontiers in the Sociology of Knowledge*, London: Sage. **210**

Leary, M.R. (1995) *Introduction to Behavioural Research Methods* (2nd ed.). Pacific Grove, Ca: Brooks/Cole. **85, 102, 470**

Levin, R.B. (1978) An empirical test of the female castration complex. In Fisher, S. & Greenberg, R.P. (1978) *The Scientific Evaluation of Freud's Theories and Therapy*. New York: Basic Books. **135**

Lewis, G., Croft-Jeffreys, C. & David, A. (1990) Are British psychiatrists racist? *British Journal of Psychiatry*, 157, 410–15. **62**

Leyens, J., Camino, L., Parke, R.D. & Berkowitz, L. (1975) Effects of movie violence on aggression in a field setting as a function of group dominance and cohesion. *Journal of Personality and Social Psychology*, 32, 346–60. **484**

Liem, R. (1997) Shame and guilt among first-and-second-generation Asian Americans and European Americans. *Journal of Cross-Cultural Psychology*, 28(4), 365–92. **453, 530**

Likert, R.A. (1932) A technique for the measurement of attitudes. *Archives of Psychology*, 140, 55. **158**

Lincoln, Y.S. & Guba, E.G. (1985) *Naturalistic Enquiry*. London: Sage. **468**

Lindsay, D.S. (1990) Misleading suggestions can impair eyewitnesses' ability to remember event details. *Journal of Experimental Psychology: Learning, Memory and Cognition*, 16, 1077–83. **71**

Linton, M. (1975) Memory for real world events. In D.A. Norman and D.E. Rumelhart (eds.) *Explorations in Cognition* (Chapter 14). San Francisco: Freeman. **120**

Lippmann, W. (1922) The abuse of the test. In N.J. Block & G. Dworkin (eds.) *The IQ Controversy*. New York: Pantheon, 1976. **41**

Loftus, E.F. & Palmer, J.C. (1974) Reconstruction of automobile destruction: An example of the interaction between language and memory. *Journal of Verbal Learning and Verbal Behaviour*, 13, 585–9. **71**

Lonner, W.J. & Berry, J.W. (1986) *Field Methods in Cross-Cultural Research*. **117, 187**

Luria, A.R. (1969) *The Mind of a Mnemonist*. London: Jonathan Cape. **126**

Lynn, R. (1991a) Race Differences in Intelligence: a global perspective. *Mankind Quarterly*, *31*, 254–96. **99**, **185**

Lynn, R. (1991b) The Evolution of Racial Differences in Intelligence. *Mankind Quarterly*, *32*, 99–121. **477**

MacRae, A.W. (1995) Statistics in A level psychology: a suitable case for treatment? *The Psychologist*, 8(8), 363–6. **292**

Madge, J. (1953) *The Tools of Social Science*. London: Longman. **204**

Malinowski, B. (1929) *The Sexual Life of Savages*. New York: Harcourt Brace and World. **123**

Manstead, A.S.R. & McCulloch, C. (1981) Sex-role stereotyping in British television advertisements. *British Journal of Social Psychology*, 20, 171–80. **455**

Markus, H. & Kitayama, S. (1991) Culture and the self: Implications for cognition, emotion and motivation. *Psychological Review*, 98, 224–53. **532**

Marshall, C. & Rossman, G. (1989) *Designing Qualitative Research*. London: Sage. **467**

Martin, S. L. & Klimowski, R.J. (1990) Use of verbal protocols to trace cognitions associated with self- and supervisor evaluations of performance. *Organizational Behaviour and Human Decision Processes*, 46(1), 135–54. **130**

Masling, J. (1966) Role-related behaviour of the subject and psychologist and its effect upon psychological data. In Levine, D. (ed.) (1966) *Nebraska Symposium on Motivation*. Lincoln: University of Nebraska Press. **76**

Mason, J. (1996) *Qualitative Researching*. London: Sage. **463**

McCrae, R.R., Costa, P.T., del Pilar, G.H., Rolland, J.-P. & Parker, W.D. (1998) Cross-cultural assesment of the five factor model: The revised NEO Personality Inventory. *Journal of Cross-Cultural Psychology*, *29*, 1, 171–88. **13**

Medawar, P.B. (1963) Is the scientific paper a fraud? *The Listener*, 10, 377–8. **6**, **202**

Meddis, R. (1984) *Statistics Using Ranks: A unified approach*. Oxford: Blackwell. **442**

Menges, R.J. (1973) Openness and honesty versus coercion and deception in psychological research. *American Psychologist*, 28, 1030–34. **479**

Middleton, D. & Edwards, D. (1990) *Collective Remembering*. London: Sage. **208**

Middleton, D., Buchanan, K. & Suurmond, J. (1993) Communities of memory: issues of 'remembering' and belonging in reminiscence work with the elderly. Mimeo, Loughborough University. **209**

Miles, M.B. & Huberman, A.M. (1994) *Qualitative Data Analysis*. London: Sage. **472**

Milgram, S. (1961) Nationality and conformity. *Scientific American*, 205– 45–51. **100**

Milgram, S. (1963) Behavioural study of obedience. *Journal of Abnormal and Social Psychology*, 67, 371–8. **43**, **110**

Milgram, S. (1974) *Obedience to Authority*. New York: Harper and Row. **478**

Miller, J.G., Bersoff, D.M. & Harwood, R.L. (1990) Perceptions of social responsibilities in India and the United States: moral imperatives or personal decisions? *Journal of Personality and Social Psychology*, 58, 33–47. **188**

Miller, S. (1997) Self-knowledge as an outcome of application journal keeping in social psychology. *Teaching of Psychology*, 24(2) 124–125. **456**

Mitroff, I.I. (1974) Studying the lunar rock scientist. *Saturday Review World*, 2 Nov. 64–5. **12**

Mixon, D. (1974) If you won't deceive what can you do? In Armistead, N. (ed.) (1974) *Reconstructing Social Psychology*. London: Penguin Education. **480**

Mixon, D. (1979) Understanding shocking and puzzling conduct. In Ginsburg, G.P. (ed.) (1979) *Emerging Strategies in Social Psychological Research*. Chichester: Wiley. **118**

Montagu, A. (1975) *Race and IQ*. Oxford: OUP. **186**

Neisser, U. (1978) Memory: What are the important questions? In M.M. Gruneberg, P.E. Morris, & R.N. Sykes (eds.) *Practical Aspects of Memory*. London: Academic Press. **101**

Niles, S. (1998) Achievement Goals and Means: A cultural comparison. *Journal of Cross-Cultural Psychology, 29*, 5, 656–67. **155, 169, 187**

Nisbet, R. (1971) Ethnocentrism and the comparative method. In A. Desai (ed.) *Essays on modernisation of underdeveloped societies* (Vol 1, 95–114), Bombay: Thacker. **188**

Ogilvie, D.M., Stone, D.J. & Shniedman, E.S. (1966) Some characteristics of genuine versus simulated suicide notes. In Stone, P.J., Dunphy, C., Smith, M.S. & Ogilvie, D.M. (eds.) (1966) *The General Enquirer: A Computer Approach to Content Analysis in the Behavioural Sciences*. Cambridge: MIT Press. **455**

Ora, J.P. (1965) Characteristics of the volunteer for psychological investigations. Office of Naval Research Contract 2149(03), Technical Report 27. **32**

Orne, M.T. (1962) On the social psychology of the psychological experiment: with particular reference to demand characteristics and their implications. *American Psychologist, 17*, 776–83. **76**

Orne, M.T. & Scheibe, K.E. (1964) The contribution of non-deprivation factors in the production of sensory deprivation effects: The psychology of the 'panic button'. *Journal of Abnormal and Social Psychology, 68*, 3–12. **76**

Osgood, C.E., Suci, G.J. & Tannenbaum, P.H. (1957) *The Measurement of Meaning*. Urbana: University of Illinois. **160**

Paludi, M.A. (1992) *The Psychology of Women*, DubuQue, Iowa: Wm. C. Brown Communications. **207**

Patton, M.Q. (1980) *Qualitative Evaluation Methods*. London: Sage. **121, 206, 453**

Paunonen, S.V. & Ashton, M.C. (1998) The structured assessment of personality across cultures. *Journal of Cross-Cultural Psychology*, 29(1), 150–70. **175**

Peronne, V., Patton, M.Q. & French, B. (1976) *Does Accountability Count without Teacher Support?* Minneapolis: Centre for Social Research, University of Minnesota. **134, 135**

Petty, R.E. & Cacioppo, J.T. (1984) The effects of involvement on responses to argument quantity and quality: central and peripheral routes to persuasion. *Journal of Personality and Social Psychology*, Vol 46. **413**

Pidgeon, N. & Henwood, K. (1997) Using grounded theory in psychological research. In N. Hayes (ed.) *Doing Qualitative Analysis in Psychology*, Hove: Psychology Press. **147, 458, 467, 469, 470**

Pike, K.L. (1967) *Language in relation to a unified theory of the structure of human behavior*. The Hague: Mouton. **188**

Piliavin, I.M., Rodin, J. & Piliavin, J.A. (1969) Good samaritanism: an underground phenomenon? *Journal of Personality and Social Psychology*, 13, 289–99. **484**

Popper, K.R. (1959) *The Logic of Scientific Discovery*. London: Hutchinson. **8**

Potter, J. (1996) *Representing Reality*: *Discourse Rhetoric and Social Construction*. London: Sage. **147, 459, 469**

Potter, J. & Wetherell, M. (1987) *Discourse and Social Psychology: Beyond Attitudes and Behaviour*. London: Sage. **138, 208**

Potter, J. & Wetherell, M. (1993) Analyzing discourse. In A. Bryman & R.G. Burgess (eds.) (1993) *Analysing qualitative data*. London: Routledge. **459**

Presby, S. (1978) Overly broad categories obscure important differences between therapies. *American Psychologist*, 33, 514–15. **107**

Rachel, J. (1996) Ethnography: practical implementation. In J.T.E. Richardson (ed.) *Handbook of Qualitative Research Methods for Psychology and the Social Sciences*. Leicester: BPS Books. **123**

Rafetto, A.M. (1967) Experimenter effect on subjects' reported hallucinatory experiences under visual and auditory deprivation. Master's thesis, San Francisco State College. **75**

Rank, S. & Jacobson, C. (1977) Hospital nurses' compliance with medication overdose orders: a failure to replicate. *Journal of Health and Social Behaviour*, 18, 188–93. **100**

Reason, P. & Rowan, J. (1981) (eds.) *Human Enquiry: A sourcebook in New Paradigm Research*. Chichester: Wiley. **42, 451, 480, 488**

Reason, P. & Heron, J. (1995) Co-operative enquiry. In J.A. Smith, R. Harré, & L.Van Langenhove (eds.) (1995) *Rethinking Methods in Psychology*. London: Sage. **470**

Reicher, S. & Emmler, N. (1986) Managing reputations in adolescence: the pursuit of delinquent and non-delinquent identities. In H. Beloff (ed.) *Getting into life*. London: Methuen. **43**

Reinharz, S. (1983) Experiential analysis: a contribution to feminist research. In G. Bowles & R. Dueli Klein (eds.) *Theories of Women's Studies*. London: Routledge and Kegan Paul. **210**

Rice, A.K. (1958) *Productivity and Social Organisations: The Ahmedabad Experiment*. London: Tavistock Publications. **205**

Richards, G. (1997) *"Race", Racism and Psychology*. London: Routledge. **186, 192, 477**

Richardson, J.T.E. (ed.) (1996) *Handbook of Qualitative Research Methods for Psychology and the Social Sciences*. Leicester: BPS Books. **211**

Ring, K., Wallston, K. & Corey, M. (1970) Mode of debriefing as a factor affecting subjective reaction to a Milgram-type obedience experiment: an ethical inquiry. *Representative Research in Social Psychology*, 1, 67–88. **480**

Robson, C. (1993) *Real World Research*. Oxford: Blackwell. **84, 128, 469**

Roethlisberger, F.J. & Dickson, W.J. (1970) *Management and the Worker*, Cambridge, Mass.: Harvard University Press. **75, 135, 140**

Rogers, C.R. (1961) *On Becoming a Person: a Therapist's View of Psycotherapy*. London: Constable. **21**

Rokeach, M. (1960) *The Open and Closed Mind*. New York: Basic Books. **174**

Rosenhan, D.L. (1973) On being sane in insane places. *Science*, 179, 250–8. **122**

Rosenthal, R. (1966) Covert communication in the psychological experiment. *Psychological Bulletin*, 67, 356–67. **74**

Rosenthal, R. & Jacobson, L. (1968) *Pygmalion in the Classroom*. New York: Holt. **81**

Rosenthal, R. & Fode, K. (1963) The effects of experimenter bias on the performance of the albino rat. *Behavioral Science*, 8, 183–9. **75**

Rosnow, R.L. & Rosenthal, R. (1997) *People Studying People: Artifacts and ethics in behavioral research*. New York: W.H. Freeman. **72, 74, 75**

Ross, H.L., Campbell, D.T. & Glass, G.V. (1973) Determining the social effects of a legal reform: The British 'breathalyser' crackdown of 1967. *American Behavioural Scientist*, 1970, 13, 493–509. **81, 248**

Rubin, D.C., Wetzler, S.E. & Nebes, R.D. (1986) Autobiographical memory across the life-span. In D.C. Rubin (ed.) *Autobiographical Memory*. Cambridge: Cambridge University Press. **13**

Rust, J. & Golombok, S. (1989) *Modern Psychometrics: The Science of Psychologial Assessment*. London: Routledge. **171**

Sacks, H. (1992) *Lectures on Conversation*. Oxford: Blackwell. **208**

Samuel, J. & Bryant, P. (1984) Asking only one question in the conversation experiment. *Journal of Child Psychology and Psychiatry*, Vol 25, 2. **410**

Schuman, H. & Reiger, C. (1992) Collective memory and collective memories. In M.A. Conway, D.C. Rubin, H. Spinnler & W. Wagenaar (eds.) *Theoretical Perspectives on Autobiographical Memory*. Dirdrecht: Kluwer Academic Publishers. **13**

Sears, D. (1986) College Sophomores in the laboratory: influences of a narrow database on social psychology's view of human nature. *Journal of Personality and Social Psychology*, 51, 515–30. **32**

Sears, R.R., Maccoby, E. & Levin, H. (1957) *Patterns of Child Rearing*. Evanston, Ill.: Row, Petersen & Co. **148**

Seaver, W.B. (1973) The effects of naturally induced teacher expectancies. *Journal of Persoanltiy and Social Psychology*, 28, 333–42. **81**

Segall, M.H., Campbell, D.T. & Herskovits, M.J. (1966) *The Influence of Culture on Visual Perception*. Indianapolis, Ind.: Bobbs-Nerrill. **187**

Seligman, M. (1972) *Biological Boundaries of Learning*. New York: Appleton-Century-Crofts. **486**

Shaffer, D.R. (1985) *Developmental Psychology: Theory, Research and Applications*. Pacific Grove, Ca.: Brooks/Cole. **115**

Shikanai, K. (1978) Effects of self-esteem on attribution of success-failure. *Japanese Journal of Experimental Social Psychology*, 18, 47–55. **188**

Shneidman, E.S. (1963) Plan 11. The logic of politics. In Arons, L. & May, M.A. (eds.) (1963) *Television and Human Behaviour*. New York: Appleton-Century-Crofts. **455**

Shotland, R.L. & Yankowski, L.D. (1982) The random response method: a valid and ethical indicator of the 'truth' in reactive situations. *Personality and Social Psychology Bulletin*, 8(1), 174–9. **137**

Silverman, D. (1993) *Interpreting Qualitative Data*. London: Sage. **209, 451, 465, 468, 470**

Sims, D. (1981) From ethogeny to endogeny: how participants in research projects can end up doing action research on their own awareness. In Reason, P. & Rowan, J. (1981) (eds.) *Human Enquiry: A Sourcebook in New Paradigm Research*. Chichester: Wiley. **206**

Singh, R. (1997) The warm-cold variable in impression formation: evidence for the positive-negative assymetry. *British Journal of Social Psychology*, 36, 4, 457–77. **15**

Sinha, D. (1986) *Psychology in a Third World Country: The Indian Experience*. New Delhi: Sage. **190**

Sinha, D. (1997) Indigenizing Psychology. In J.W. Berry, Y.H. Poortinga & J. Pandey (eds.) *Handbook of Cross-cultural Psychology: Vol. 1 Theory and method*. (2nd edition) Boston: Allyn and Bacon. **190**

Skinner, B.F. (1953) *Science and Human Behaviour*. New York: Macmillan. **41**

Smith, G. (1975) Reception class: The individual language follow-up programme. In G. Smith (ed.) *Education Priority, Vol 4, The West Riding Project*. London: HMSO. **182**

Smith, J.A. (1995a) Evolving issues for qualitative psychology. In J.T.E. Richardson (ed.) *Handbook of Qualitative Research Methods for Psychology and the Social Sciences*. Leicester: BPS Books. **140, 198, 466**

Smith, J.A., Harré, R. & Van Langenhove, L. (eds.) (1995a) *Rethinking Methods in Psychology*. London: Sage. **472**

Smith, J.A., Harré, R. & Van Langenhove, L. (eds.) (1995b) *Rethinking Psychology*. London: Sage. **472**

Smith, M.L. & Glass, G.V. (1977) Meta-analysis of psychotherapeutic outcome studies. *American Psychologist*, 32, 752–60. **106**

Smith, P.B. & Bond, M.H. (1993) *Social Psychology Across Cultures: Analysis and Perspectives*. London: Harvester Wheatsheaf. **193**

Solso, R.L. & Johnson, H.H. (1994) *Experimental Psychology: A case approach* (5th ed). New York: Harper Collins. **83**

Spelke, E.S., Hirst, W.C. & Neisser, U. (1976) Skills and divided attention. *Cognition*, 4, 215–30. **64**

Spradley, J.P. (1989) *The Ethnographic Interview*. New York: Holt Rinehart and Winston. **468**

Stanovich, K.E. (1992) *How to think straight about psychology*. Chicago: Scott, Foresman. **102**

Stipek, D. (1998) Differences between American and Chinese in the circumstances evoking pride, shame and guilt. *Journal of Cross-Cultural Psychology*, 29, 5, 616–29. **188**

Storms, M.D. (1973) Videotape and the attribution process: revising actors' and observers' points of view. *Journal of Personality and Social Psychology*, 27, 165–75. **119**

Sussman, S., Hahn, G., Dent, C. & Stacy, A.W. (1993) Naturalistic observation of adolescent tobacco use. *International Journal of the Addictions*, *28*, 9, 803–11. **116**

Tandon, R. (1981) Dialogue as inquiry and intervention. In Reason, P. & Rowan, J. (1981) *Human Inquiry: A Sourcebook in New Paradigm Research*. Chichester: Wiley. **120**

Tavris, C. (1993) The mismeasure of woman. *Feminism and Psychology*, *3(2)*, 149–68. **43**

Tesch, R. (1990) *Qualitative Research: Analysis Types and Software Tools*. Basingstoke: Falmer. **203**

Thigpen, C.H. & Cleckley, H. (1984) A case of multiple peronsality. *Journal of Abnormal and Social Psychology*, *49*, 175–81. **126**

Thurstone, L.L. (1931) The measurement of social attitudes. *Journal of Abnormal and Social Psychology*, 26, 249–69. **157**

Torbert, W.R. (1981) Why educational research has been so uneducational: the case for a new model of social science based on collaborative enquiry. In Reason, P. & Rowan, J. (1981) *Human Inquiry*. Chichester: Wiley. **483**

Trist, E.L. & Bamforth, K.W. (1951) Some social and psychological consequences of the longwall method of coal-cutting. *Human Relations*, 4(1), 3–38. **205**

Tucker, W.H. (1994) *The Science and Politics of Racial Research*. Chicago: University of Illinois Press. **74, 477**

Tukey, J.W. (1977) *Exploratory Data Analysis*. Reading, Mass.: Addison-Wesley. **247**

Ussher, J.M. (1991) *Women and Madness: Misogyny or mental Illness?* London: Harvester/Wheatsheaf. **43**

Ussher, J.M. (1992) Science sexing psychology: positivistic science and sender bias in clinical psychology. In Jane Ussher and Paula Nicholoson (Eds) *Gender Issues in Clinical Psychology*, London: Routledge. **43**

Valentine, E.R. (1992) *Conceptual Issues in Psychology* (2nd ed.). London: Routledge. **10, 12, 32, 45**

Vidich, A.J. & Bensman, J. (1958) *Small Town in Mass Society*. Princeton, NJ: Princeton University Press. **144**

Wagenaar, W.A. (1986) My memory: A study of autobiographical memory over six years. *Cognitive Psychology*, 18, 225–52. **101, 120**

Watson, J.B. & Rayner, R. (1920) Conditioned emotional reactions. *Journal of Experimental Psychology*, 3, 1–14. **128, 482**

Weber, S.J. & Cook, T.D. (1972) Subject effects in laboratory research: an examination of subject roles, demand characteristics and valid inference. *Psychological Bulletin*, 77, 273–95. **76**

Whyte, W.F. (1943) *Street Corner Society: the Social Structure of an Italian Slum*. Chicago: The University of Chicago Press. **122**

Wilkinson, S. (1986) *Feminist Social Psychology*. Milton Keynes: Open University Press. **207**

Williams, J.E., Bennett, S.M. & Best, D.L. (1975) Awareness and expression of sex stereotypes in young children. *Developmental Psychology*, 11, 635–42. **181**

Woolgar, S. (1988) *Science: The Very Idea*. London: Tavistock. **210**

Woolgar, S. (1996) Psychology, qualitative methods and the ideas of science. In J.T.E. Richardson (ed.) (1996) *Handbook of Qualitative Research Methods for Psychology and the Social Sciences*. Leicester: BPS Books. **197**

Word, C.H., Zanna, M.P. & Cooper, J. (1974) The non-verbal mediation of self-fulfilling prophecies in interracial interaction. *Journal of Experimental Social Psychology*, 10, 109–20. **137**

Wright, R.L.D. (1976) *Understanding Statistics*. New York: Harcourt Brace Jovanovich. **223**

Yin, R. (1994) *Case Study Research: Design and Methods* (2nd edition). Thousand Oaks, Ca.: Sage. **127**

Yin, R.K. (1989) *Case Study Research: Design and Methods*. London: Sage. **468**

Zegoib, L.E., Arnold, S. & Forehand, R. (1975) An examination of observer effects in parent-child interactions. *Child Development*, 46, 509–12. **115**

Zimbardo, P.G. (1972) Pathology of imprisonment. *Society*, April 1972. **119, 481**

Index

Note: **Bold** *page numbers refer to glossaries at the end of chapters*